Human Resource Management

Human Resource Management

Lloyd L. Byars, Ph.D.

Professor of Management
DuPree College of Management
Georgia Institute of Technology

Leslie Rue, Ph.D.

Professor Emeritus of Management
Robinson College of Business
Georgia State University

Sixth Edition

Irwin
McGraw-Hill

Boston   Burr Ridge, IL   Dubuque, IA   Madison, WI   New York   San Francisco   St. Louis
Bangkok   Bogotá   Caracas   Lisbon   London   Madrid
Mexico City   Milan   New Delhi   Seoul   Singapore   Sydney   Taipei   Toronto

McGraw-Hill Higher Education

A Division of The McGraw-Hill Companies

domestic   3 4 5 6 7 8 9 0 VNH/VNH 9 0 9 8 7 6 5 4 3 2 1 0
international   2 3 4 5 6 7 8 9 0 VNH/VNH 9 0 9 8 7 6 5 4 3 2 1 0

ISBN 0-07-229593-7

Vice president/Editor-in-Chief: *Michael W. Junior*
Publisher: *Craig S. Beytien*
Senior sponsoring editor: *John E. Biernat*
Editorial coordinator: *Erin Riley*
Marketing manager: *Ellen Cleary*
Project manager: *Alisa Watson*
Production supervisor: *Kari Geltemeyer*
Coordinator freelance design: *Mary L. Christianson*
Senior supplement coordinator: *Cathy L. Tepper*
Compositor: ElectraGraphics, Inc.
Typeface: 10/12 New Baskerville
Printer: Von Hoffmann Press, Inc.

Library of Congress Cataloging-in-Publication Data

Byars, Lloyd L.
   Human resource management / Lloyd L. Byars, Leslie W. Rue. — 6th
ed.
    p. cm.
   Includes bibliographical references and index.
   ISBN 0-07-229593-7
   1. Personnel management. I. Rue, Leslie W. II. Title.
HF5549.B937 2000
658.3—dc21   99-15561

http://www.mhhe.com

Preface

As companies begin to compete in the challenging business environment of the new millennium, an ever-increasing reason for success lies in the function of effective human resource management (HRM). A company's competitive advantage is often found in its most valuable resource—its people. The most effective and successful companies today find ways to motivate, train, compensate, and challenge their employees. This is true for all companies, whether they are manufacturing or service companies, large or small.

Since the publication of the fifth edition of *Human Resource Management*, the role of management has changed. Organizations have fewer layers, and a broader set of skills is expected of all managers, including human resource management skills. This "general managers perspective" of HRM has become quite popular and quite essential, and the sixth edition emphasizes general management applications even more so than the fifth edition. In addition, other significant changes continue to occur in the HRM area. Changing government and legal requirements, new information systems, downsizing, demands for a more skilled work force, increasing attention to diversity in the work force, and intensifying global competition are just a few of the factors that have contributed to the complexity of HRM issues for today's companies.

Features of the Book

- The sixth edition of *Human Resource Management* continues to present both the *theoretical* and *practical* aspects of HRM. The **theoretical** material is presented throughout the text and highlighted via a marginal glossary. Students are assisted in learning complex HRM terminology through these concise definitions placed in the margins. They provide a valuable study tool for students. The **practical** aspects of HRM are presented through lively and pedagogically effective examples woven throughout the text and end-of-chapter materials.

- Multiple **"HRM in Action"** boxes are included in each chapter and provide current examples that illustrate how actual organizations apply concepts presented in the chapters.

- A key feature entitled **"On the Job"** appears after several chapters and offers practical examples in areas such as résumés and job descriptions.

- New to this edition are the up-to-date URLs for companies and HRM concepts that are displayed along the margins within each chapter and also within the HRM in Action boxes.

- Video cases appear at the end of each section and focus on real companies such as Southwest Airlines, Saturn, and Budget Rent-A-Car.

- End of chapter materials include:

  - **"Summary of Learning Objectives"**—provides a synopsis and review of the key learning objectives within each chapter.

  - **"Review Questions"**—provide an opportunity to review chapter concepts through questions developed to test students' memory of key issues and concepts within the chapter.

  - **"Discussion Questions"**—provide an opportunity for students to apply critical thinking skills to in-depth questions.

- Two **"Incidents"** per chapter act as minicases students can use to analyze and dissect chapter concepts and applications via real-life scenarios.
- **"Exercises" (Experiential)** can be done in class or as homework and are designed to illustrate major points made in the chapter.

The Teaching Package

Each component of the teaching package has been carefully developed to assist both faculty and students in learning the important concepts and applications of HRM:

- The *Instructor's Manual* offers opportunities for classroom instruction, student participation, and assignments or research. Each chapter includes a chapter outline, presentation suggestions, "HRM in Action" questions, and answers for the "Discussion Questions" and "Incident Solutions" that are included within the text.
- The "Test Bank" includes over 600 questions and consists of true/false, multiple choice, and short answer questions.
- Brownstone Testing Software, available for Windows or Mac users, provides instructors with simple ways to write tests that can be administered on paper, over a campus network, or over the Internet.
- Videos are available for each section and provide an appropriate overview of the learned material.
- PP Presentation Software contains tables and figures from the text plus additional graphic material.

Organization of the Sixth Edition

The book's content is arranged in five major sections. Section 1, "Introduction and Equal Employment Opportunity," is designed to provide the student with the foundation necessary to embark on a study of the work of human resource management. This section also explores information technology for human resources and how the legal environment and the implementation of equal employment opportunity influence all areas of human resource management. Section 2, "Staffing the Organization," discusses the topics of job analysis and design, human resource planning, recruitment, and selection. Section 3, "Training and Developing Employees," describes orientation and employee training, management and organizational development, performance appraisal systems, and career planning. Section 4, "Compensating Employees," presents an introductory chapter on organizational reward systems and has separate chapters describing base wage and salary systems, incentive pay systems, and employee benefits. Section 5, "Understanding Unions," explores the legal environment and structure of unions, the collective bargaining process, employee relations, and employee health and safety.

The following individuals provided valuable assistance through their insightful reviews:

Fifth Edition Reviewers	*Previous Reviewers*
Herschel L. Apfelberg	Paul James Londrigan
California State Polytechnic University	Mott Community College
Bruce Cudney	James G. Pesek
St. Anselm College	Clarion University of Pennsylvania

Fred Maidment
Park College

Glen E. Rouze
Florida Southern College

Cynthia A. M. Simerly
Lakeland Community College

James L. Sturrock
East Texas Baptist University

We would also like to thank Charmelle Todd for her assistance in editing and typing the manuscript.

Lloyd L. Byars
Leslie W. Rue

Contents in Brief

Contents

8 Selecting Employees   175

PART III TRAINING AND DEVELOPING EMPLOYEES   203

9 Orientation and Employee Training   204

10 Management and Organizational Development   223

Introduction and Equal Employment Opportunity

1

Human Resource Management: Present and Future

Learning Objectives

After studying this chapter, you should be able to:

1. Define human resource management.
2. Describe the functions of human resource management.
3. Summarize the types of assistance provided by the human resource department.
4. Explain the desired relationship between human resource managers and operating managers.
5. Identify several challenges currently facing today's human resource managers.
6. Outline several potential challenges and contributions presented by an increasingly diverse work force.
7. Discuss the role of human resource managers in the future.
8. Summarize several guidelines to follow when communicating human resource programs.
9. Explain, in general terms, how human resource managers can affect organizational performance.

Human Resource Management Activities designed to provide for and coordinate the human resources of an organization.

Human resource management (HRM) encompasses those activities designed to provide for and coordinate the human resources of an organization. The human resources (HR) of an organization represent one of its largest investments. In fact, government reports show that approximately 72 percent of national income is used to compensate employees.[1] The value of an organization's human resources frequently becomes evident when the organization is sold. Often the purchase price is greater than the total value of the physical and financial assets. This difference, sometimes called goodwill, partially reflects the value of an organization's human resources. In addition to wages and salaries, organizations often make other sizable investments in their human resources. Recruiting, hiring, and training represent some of the more obvious examples.

Human resource management is a modern term for what has traditionally been referred to as *personnel administration* or *personnel management*. However, some experts believe human resource management differs somewhat from traditional personnel management. They see personnel management as being much narrower and more clerically oriented than human resource management. For the purposes of this book, we will use only the term *human resource management*.

Human Resource Functions

Human Resource Functions Tasks and duties human resource managers perform (e.g., determining the organization's human

Human resource functions refer to those tasks and duties performed in both large and small organizations to provide for and coordinate human resources. Human resource functions encompass a variety of activities that significantly influence all areas of an organization. The Society for Human Resource Management (SHRM) has identified six major functions of human resource management:

resource needs; recruiting, selecting, developing, counseling, and rewarding employees; acting as liaison with unions and government organizations; and handling other matters of employee well-being).

1. Human resource planning, recruitment, and selection.
2. Human resource development.
3. Compensation and benefits.
4. Safety and health.
5. Employee and labor relations.
6. Human resource research.

Table 1–1 identifies many of the activities that comprise each major human resource function. Ensuring that the organization fulfills all of its equal employment opportunity and other government obligations is an activity that overlays all six of the major human resource functions.

Figure 1–1 presents a slightly different breakdown of the human resource functions. This breakdown, called the Human Resource Wheel, was developed by the American Society for Training and Development as part of an effort to define the field of human resource management.

In an attempt to cover each of the major areas of human resource management,

---

T A B L E 1 – 1   **ACTIVITIES OF THE MAJOR HUMAN RESOURCE FUNCTIONS**

Human Resource Planning, Recruitment, and Selection

- Conducting job analyses to establish the specific requirements of individual jobs within the organization.
- Forecasting the human resource requirements the organization needs to achieve its objectives.
- Developing and implementing a plan to meet these requirements.
- Recruiting the human resources the organization requires to achieve its objectives.
- Selecting and hiring human resources to fill specific jobs within the organization.

Human Resource Development

- Orienting and training employees.
- Designing and implementing management and organizational development programs.
- Building effective teams within the organization structure.
- Designing systems for appraising the performance of individual employees.
- Assisting employees in developing career plans.

Compensation and Benefits

- Designing and implementing compensation and benefit systems for all employees.
- Ensuring that compensation and benefits are fair and consistent.

Employee and Labor Relations

- Serving as an intermediary between the organization and its union(s).
- Designing discipline and grievance handling systems.

Safety and Health

- Designing and implementing programs to ensure employee health and safety.
- Providing assistance to employees with personal problems that influence their work performance.

Human Resource Research

- Providing a human resource information base.
- Designing and implementing employee communication systems.

FIGURE 1-1   HUMAN RESOURCE WHEEL

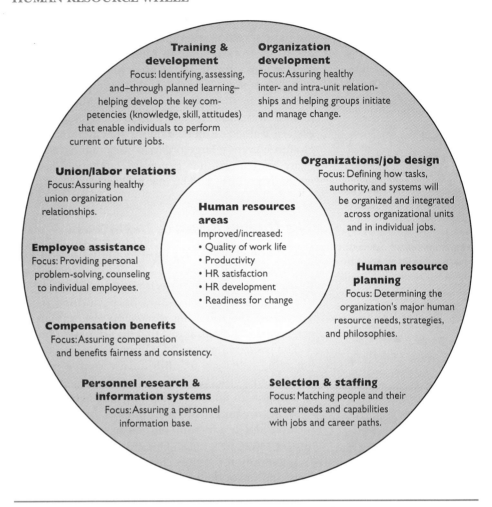

this book contains five major sections. Section 1 serves as an introduction and presents material that applies to all major human resource functions. It contains an introductory chapter, two chapters on equal employment opportunity, and one chapter on information technology for human resources. Section 2 explores those human resource functions specifically concerned with staffing the organization: job analysis and design and human resource planning, recruiting, and selecting. Section 3 concentrates on those functions related to training and developing employees, such as orientation and employee training, management and organization development, performance appraisal, and career planning. Section 4 covers all aspects of employee compensation: the organizational reward system, base wage and salary systems, incentive pay systems, and employee benefits. Section 5 deals with unions, the collective bargaining process, employee relations, and employee safety and health.

Who Performs the Human Resource Functions?

Most managers are periodically involved to some extent in each of the major human resource functions. For example, at one time or another, almost all managers are involved in some aspect of employee recruiting, selecting, training, developing, compensation, team building, and evaluation. In small organizations, most

Operating Manager Person who manages people directly involved with the production of an organization's products or services (e.g., production manager in a manufacturing plant, loan manager in a bank).

Human Resource Generalist Person who devotes a majority of working time to human resource issues, but does not specialize in any specific areas.

Human Resource Specialist Person specially trained in one or more areas of human resource management (e.g., labor relations specialist, wage and salary specialist).

human resource functions are performed by the owner or by **operating managers.** These managers perform the human resource functions in addition to their normal managerial activities. Many medium-size and even some large organizations use human resource generalists. A **human resource generalist** devotes a majority of his or her working time to human resource issues, but does not specialize in any specific areas of human resource management. Large organizations usually have a human resource department that is responsible for directing the human resource functions. In addition to one or more human resource generalists, such a department is normally staffed by one or more **human resource specialists.** These specialists are trained in one or more specific areas of human resource management. However, even in large organizations that have a human resource department with many human resource generalists and specialists, most operating managers must regularly perform and be involved with many of the human resource functions.

The Human Resource Department

As mentioned previously, most medium-size and some large organizations use human resource generalists and do not have a human resource department. In these situations, the functions performed by human resource generalists are essentially the same as those that would be performed by a human resource department. Therefore, the following discussion also applies to the role of human resource generalists in organizations that do not have a human resource department.

The primary function of a human resource department is to provide support to operating managers on all human resource matters. Thus, most human resource departments fulfill a traditional staff role and act primarily in an advisory capacity. In addition to advising operating managers, a human resource department customarily organizes and coordinates hiring and training; maintains personnel records; acts as a liaison between management, labor, and government; and coordinates safety programs. Therefore, accomplishing the human resource goals of an organization requires close coordination between the human resource department and the operating managers.

Precisely how all of the functions related to human resources are split between operating managers and the human resource department varies from organization to organization. For example, the human resource department in one company may do all of the hiring below a certain level. In another company, all the hiring decisions may be made by operating managers, with the human resource department acting only in an advisory capacity.

It is helpful to view the human resource department as providing three types of assistance: (1) specific services, (2) advice, and (3) coordination. Table 1–2 presents some typical examples of each of these types of assistance. Figure 1–2 illustrates the different roles a human resource department or a human resource generalist might fill.

As stated earlier, a human resource department normally acts in an advisory capacity and does not have authority over operating managers. As a result, conflict can occur when operating managers appear to ignore the suggestions and

TABLE 1–2

EXAMPLES OF THE TYPES OF ASSISTANCE PROVIDED BY A HUMAN RESOURCE DEPARTMENT

Specific Services	Advice	Coordination
Maintaining employee records	Disciplinary matters	Performance appraisals
Handling initial phases of employee orientation	Equal employment opportunity matters	Compensation matters

F I G U R E 2 - 2   **THREE TYPES OF ASSISTANCE PROVIDED BY A HUMAN RESOURCE DEPARTMENT**

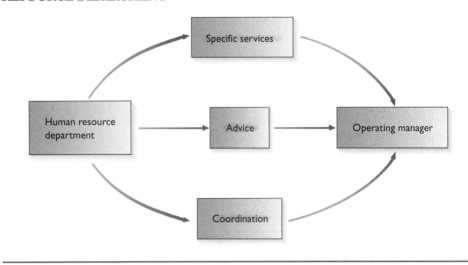

recommendations of the human resource department. If the human resource department is to be effective, it must continually cultivate good relations with operating managers. Likewise, operating managers must understand the human resource functions to effectively utilize the human resource department.

Challenges for Human Resource Managers

Human resource management has expanded and moved beyond mere administration of the traditional activities of employment, labor relations, compensation, and benefits. Today HRM is much more integrated into both the management and the strategic planning process of the organization.[2]

One reason for this expanded role is that the organizational environment has become much more diverse and complex. Compared to a work force historically dominated by white males, today's work force is very diverse and projected to become more so.[3] Diversity in the work force encompasses many different dimensions, including sex, race, national origin, religion, age, and disability. Diversity in the workplace presents new and different challenges for all managers. Other challenges are the result of changes in government requirements, organization structures, technology, and management approaches. Each of these issues is discussed next.

Diversity in the Work Force

Recent forecasts by the U.S. Bureau of Labor Statistics project that the total U.S. labor force will consist of only 38 percent white, non-Hispanic males by the year 2006.[4] Table 1–3 shows the projected numbers of entrants and leavers in the total work force of the groups shown for the years 1996–2006. As the table indicates, almost half of the new entrants during that time span will be women. This one dimension of diversity has many ramifications for organizations in the areas of child care, spouse relocation assistance programs, pregnancy leave programs, flexible hours, and stay-at-home jobs.

These same projections also predict that white, non-Hispanic males will comprise fewer than one-third of new labor force entrants for the years 1996–2006.[5] In addition to the possibility of having differing educational backgrounds, immigrant employees are likely to have language and cultural differences. Organizations must begin now to successfully integrate these people into their work forces.

TABLE 1–3

**CIVILIAN LABOR FORCE, 1996 AND PROJECTED TO 2006,
AND PROJECTED ENTRANTS, STAYERS AND LEAVERS, 1996–2006**

Group	1996	1996–2006			2006
		Entrants	**Leavers**	**Stayers**	
Total	100.0%	100.0%	100.0%	100.0%	100.0%
Men	53.8	50.4	55.9	53.4	52.6
Women	46.2	49.6	44.1	46.6	47.4
White, non-Hispanic	75.3	61.0	68.5	76.9	72.7
Men	40.7	30.6	39.3	41.0	38.2
Women	34.7	30.5	29.2	35.9	34.5
Black, non-Hispanic	11.0	15.6	20.2	9.0	10.7
Men	5.3	7.1	10.3	4.2	4.9
Women	5.8	8.5	9.9	4.8	5.8
Hispanic origin	9.5	14.9	5.2	10.5	11.7
Men	5.7	8.5	3.1	6.3	6.9
Women	3.8	6.4	2.1	4.2	4.8
Asian and other, non-Hispanic	4.1	8.4	6.1	3.6	4.9
Men	2.2	4.2	3.2	1.9	2.5
Women	1.9	4.2	2.9	1.7	2.4

Source: "Labor Force 2006: Slowing Down and Changing Composition," *Monthly Labor Review,* November 1997, p. 34.

Almost everyone has heard the phrase "the graying of America." By the year 2006, the average age of employees will climb to 40.5 from 38.2 in 1996.[6] This will be accompanied by a significant drop in the number of employees from 25 to 39 years old. In 1996, 45 percent of the labor force was age 40 or older; by 2006, almost 52 percent of the labor force will be in this age category. This age increase and drop in the younger labor pool will have a mixed effect. The older work force will likely be more experienced, reliable, and stable, but possibly less adaptable to change and retraining. One direct result of this trend is that the retirement age is already increasing.

Another dimension of diversity is related to the increasing globalization of many companies. As companies become more global, diversity must be defined in global and not just Western terms.[7] Defining diversity in global terms means looking at all people and everything that makes them different from one another, as well as the things that make them similar. Differentiating factors often go beyond race and language and may include such things as values and customs.

Challenges and Contributions of Diversity

What challenges and contributions does the increasingly diverse work force present? From an overall viewpoint, organizations must get away from the tradition of fitting employees into a single corporate mold.[8] Everyone will not look and act the same. Organizations must create new human resource policies to explicitly recognize and respond to the unique needs of individual employees.

Greater diversity will create certain specific challenges but also make some important contributions. Communication problems are certain to occur, including misunderstandings among employees and managers as well as the need to translate verbal and written materials into several languages. Solutions to these problems will necessitate additional training involving work in basic skills such as writing and problem-solving. An increase in organizational factionalism will require that increasing amounts of time be dedicated to dealing with special interest and advocacy groups.

In addition to creating the above challenges, greater diversity presents new opportunities. Diversity contributes to creating an organization culture that is more tolerant of different behavioral styles and wider views. This often leads to better business decisions. Another potential payoff is a greater responsiveness to diverse groups of customers.

The increasing diversification of the work force is fact. Learning to effectively manage a diverse work force should be viewed as an investment in the future. HRM in Action 1.1 describes the comprehensive diversity awareness strategy implemented by the Seattle Times Company.

Regulatory Changes

The deluge of government regulations and laws has placed a tremendous burden on human resource managers. Organizations face new regulations routinely issued in the areas of safety and health, equal employment opportunity, pension reform, environment, and quality of work life. Often new regulations require significant paperwork, and this burden usually falls on human resource managers. Every year thousands of cases relating to the interpretation of human resource issues are brought before the courts. Once a case has been decided, human resource managers must implement the outcome.

Structural Changes to Organizations

Downsizing Laying off of large numbers of managerial and other employees.

Today's organizations are undergoing many structural changes that present challenges for human resource managers. Some of these structural changes are caused by downsizing, outsourcing, rightsizing, and reengineering. **Downsizing** is the laying off of large numbers of managerial and other employees. As a result of

---

HRM IN ACTION

Seattle Times Company Deals with Diversity

1.1

www.seattletimes.com

In a 1992 statement to the employees of the Seattle Times Company, publisher and CEO Frank A. Blethen acknowledged that the company was aware of the changing demographics of its readership. Consequently, the Seattle Times Company developed and implemented a comprehensive diversity awareness strategy that included such initiatives as diversity training, a companywide diversity newsletter, and a diversity council. These initiatives have ingrained pluralism into the company culture. In addition, specific newsroom activities, such as minority intern programs, the creation of a diversity reporter and coach, and a newsroom diversity council, ensure that not only the company but also its products represent the community the organization serves.

The Seattle Times Company's commitment to this philosophy shows up in a work force currently composed of 21 percent people of color and 33 percent women. The newsroom has a similar makeup, with 21 percent of the reporters and editors being people of color and 44 percent being women. These figures place the *Seattle Times* in the nation's top 20 large newspapers in terms of minority representation.

The Seattle Times Company is recognized as an industry leader in this area. In 1994, as a result of his efforts, Frank Blethen received the Distinguished Diversity Award for Lifetime Achievement from the National Association of Minority Media Executives.

Source: Dawn Anfuso, "Diversity Keeps Newspaper Up with the Times," *Personnel Journal,* July 1995, pp. 30–41.

Outsourcing
Subcontracting work to an outside company that specializes in that particular type of work.

Rightsizing Continuous and proactive assessment of mission-critical work and its staffing requirements.

Reengineering Fundamental rethinking and radical redesign of business processes to achieve dramatic improvements in cost, quality, service, and speed.

downsizing, many companies are outsourcing services that the human resource department previously provided. **Outsourcing** refers to subcontracting work to an outside company that specializes in that particular type of work. Some examples of services being outsourced include 401(K) plan administration and management development programs. **Rightsizing** is the continuous and proactive assessment of mission-critical work and its staffing requirements.[9] Rightsizing differs from downsizing in that it is an ongoing planning process to determine the optimal number of employees in every area of the organization. Other companies are implementing reengineering programs. **Reengineering** refers to a fundamental rethinking and radical redesign of business processes to achieve dramatic improvements in cost, quality, service, and speed.[10] In essence, reengineering usually results in sweeping changes in management and organization structures.

Technological and Managerial Changes within Organizations

New technologies and management approaches have added to the challenges facing human resource managers. While the technological changes affecting human resource managers are widespread, none are more dramatic than those related to information systems. In addition to their uses in performing the traditional functions of accounting and payroll calculations, computerized information systems are now being used to maintain easily accessible employee data that are valuable in job placement and labor utilization. Information systems are also being used in employee training, succession planning, and compensation management, and to track and report affirmative action activity. Cyberspace and the Internet are changing the way many human resource managers operate. Today many human resource managers are going online to recruit personnel, conduct research using electronic databases, send E-mail, and engage in valuable networking and discussions.[11] Chapter 2 discusses in some depth just how human resource managers are using information systems.

Empowerment Form of decentralization that involves giving subordinates substantial authority to make decisions.

Self-managed work teams Groups of peers are responsible for a particular area or task.

Empowerment of employees and self-managed work teams are two specific management approaches that are having a significant impact on today's human resource managers. **Empowerment** is a form of decentralization that involves giving subordinates substantial authority to make decisions. Under empowerment, managers express confidence in the ability of employees to perform at high levels. Employees are also encouraged to accept personal responsibility for their work. In organizations using **self-managed work teams,** groups of employees do not report to a single manager; rather, groups of peers are responsible for a particular area or task. Eastman Kodak, Federal Express, General Motors, Rubbermaid, and Weyerhauser are some U.S. firms that have successfully implemented self-managed work teams. HRM in Action 1.2 describes the results some companies have experienced as a result of self-managed work teams.

The breadth of the changes in so many areas—work force diversity, the regulatory environment, organizational structure, new technologies, management approaches—will have a powerful impact on today's human resource managers.

Human Resource Management Tomorrow

To meet the challenges of the future, tomorrow's human resource departments must be much more sophisticated than their predecessors. Given the expanding role human resource departments must fill, it is essential that human resource managers be integrally involved in the organization's strategic and policymaking activities. Fortunately, there are signs that this is happening in many organizations. For example, in the majority of the Fortune 500 companies, the head of the human resource department is an officer (usually a vice president) who answers to the chief executive officer (CEO). In many companies, the head of the human

Benefits of Self-Managed Teams

1.2

www.ti.com
www.fedex.com
www.generalmills.com
www.3m.com

Texas Instruments has used self-managed work teams to increase productivity. Within just six months of implementing self-managed teams, TI realized a 50 percent reduction in cycle time, a 60 percent reduction in scrap, and a 30 percent improvement in productivity.

At a weekly meeting, a self-managed team at Federal Express spotted and eventually solved a billing problem that was costing the company $2.1 million a year.

At a General Mills cereal plant in Lodi, California, self-managed teams schedule, operate, and maintain machinery so effectively that the plant runs without managers during the night shift.

3M turned around one division by creating cross-functional self-managed teams that tripled the number of new products.

Source: Dean Elmuti, "Sustaining High Performance through Self-Managed Work Teams," *Industrial Management,* March/April 1996, pp. 4–9.

resource department sits on the board of directors, the planning committee, or both. A 1992 survey of top human resource executives at 151 Fortune 500 companies found that a majority of these executives have significant input in corporate policy decision making.[12] Seventy-one percent of these same executives reported that their human resource functions currently were more involved in implementing business strategy than in past years.

If tomorrow's human resource managers are to earn the respect of their colleagues and of top management, they must work to overcome certain negative impressions and biases sometimes associated with human resource management. This can be accomplished in several ways. First, human resource managers should become well-rounded businesspeople. In addition to being well grounded in the basic disciplines of the profession, human resource professionals need to understand the business complexities of the company.[13] The following suggestions are offered to help human resource managers become more familiar with their businesses:

- Know the company strategy and business plan.
- Know the industry.
- Support business needs.
- Spend more time with the line people.
- Keep your hand on the pulse of the organization.
- Learn to calculate costs and solutions in hard numbers.[14]

Thoroughly understanding the business will help to overcome the common feeling that human resource people do not understand the operating problems and issues facing the organization.

Second, human resource managers should become fully knowledgeable about present and future trends and issues. This will help them guard against becoming enamored with passing fads or ineffective techniques.

Third, human resource managers should promote effective human resource utilization within the organization. Rather than taking a moralistic approach when dealing with operating managers, human resource managers should stress the importance of increasing profits through effectively using the organization's human resources. In this light, human resource managers should learn to be proactive and seize opportunities to demonstrate how they can positively affect the bottom line.

Company Profits and the Human Resource Manager

There is no doubt that human resource managers spend considerable time working on problems and concerns related to the human side of the organization. Because of this, many people perceive human resource managers as being concerned *only* with matters that relate directly to the human side of the organization. Contrary to this view, human resource managers can have a direct impact on company profits in a number of specific ways.

1. Reduce unnecessary overtime expenses by increasing productivity during a normal day.
2. Stay on top of absenteeism and institute programs designed to reduce money spent for time not worked.
3. Eliminate wasted time by employees through sound job design.
4. Minimize employee turnover and unemployment benefit costs by practicing sound human relations and creating a work atmosphere that promotes job satisfaction.
5. Install and monitor effective safety and health programs to reduce lost-time accidents and keep medical and workers' compensation costs low.
6. Properly train and develop all employees so they can improve their value to the company and do a better job of producing and selling high-quality products and services at the lowest possible cost.
7. Decrease costly material waste by eliminating bad work habits and attitudes and poor working conditions that lead to carelessness and mistakes.
8. Hire the best people available at every level and avoid overstaffing.
9. Maintain competitive pay practices and benefit programs to foster a motivational climate for employees.
10. Encourage employees, who probably know more about the nuts and bolts of their jobs than anyone else, to submit ideas for increasing productivity and reducing costs.
11. Install human resource information systems to streamline and automate many human resource functions.[15]

From an overall standpoint, several recent large-sample, cross-industry studies have reported that firms using innovative human resource practices outperform firms that do not use such practices.[16] One study found that human resource strategy drives 15 percent of profit performance for the average company.[17] As a direct result of increasingly available information systems, numerous strategies can be used to help the human resource department contribute to the bottom line.[18] The basic idea behind these strategies is to translate knowledge of human resources into terms that have tangible and recognizable economic benefits, especially to operating managers. Examples include analysis of the cost per hire, length of time to fill a position, and new-hire performance by recruiting strategy, with the intent of identifying the most effective strategy. HRM in Action 1.3 describes how the efforts of one company's HR department significantly increased the revenues of the company.

Communicating Human Resource Programs

Communicating human resource programs has been compared to the marketing of a new product.[19] Consider the fact that approximately 90 percent of all new consumer products fail. In some cases, the failure is due to a poor product that does not fill a current need. In other cases, however, the product fails because of a

---

HRM IN ACTION

HR Program Increases Revenues **1.3** **www.stentor.com**	Stentor Resource Centre, Inc., based in Ottawa, Canada, is a subsidiary of Stentor Allian, the world's largest telecommunications company. Thanks to Stentor Resource Centre's HR department, the company enjoyed a $72 million boost in revenues in 1997. Stentor began, like most established telecommunications firms, as a regulated monopoly. As the environment changed, and became more competitive, Stentor's revenues and market share declined and employee turnover increased, primarily because the company was not an organization of leaders. In early 1997, Connie Simington, a former business development manager who took over Stentor's training and development functions in late 1996, decided to launch a program to build leaders internally. Connie's HR team used a survey to assess its current position. From there, the HR team began to plot where the organization needed to go with its training. The team initiated the Stentor Training Forum, which developed a model based on shared-learning teams of seven members each. As a result of projects tackled in the pilot learning program alone, Stentor's total revenues from the Learning Forum amounted to $72 million. In addition to the substantial increase in revenues, Simington believes the company made a quantum leap in creating leadership for the organization. *Source:* Mary Berry, "Learning 'Next Practices' Generates Revenue," *HR Magazine,* June 1998, pp. 146–52.

Web site: International
Personnel Management
Association

www.ipma-hr.org

breakdown in the marketing system. The product may have been inadequately researched, the salespeople may not have been properly trained, the distribution system may have been poor, or the overall marketing strategy may have been misguided. Unfortunately, many well-designed human resource programs also fail because they are not properly "marketed." In the case of human resource programs, the customers are the employees and the price is often employee commitment, motivation, and cooperation.

Communication is much more than talking, speaking, and reading. True communication takes place when an understanding has been transferred from one party or source to another. Therefore, **communication** can be defined as the transfer of information that is meaningful to those involved.

Communication Transfer of information that is meaningful to those involved.

In this light, each and every one of the human resource functions discussed in this book requires some degree of effective communication to succeed. For example, think of the important role communication plays in career planning, recruiting, and performance appraisal. In all too many instances, human resource managers spend tremendous amounts of time developing very good programs, only to subsequently do a poor job of communicating them. The end result is often great programs that go largely unused.

A human resource manager's first step in becoming an effective communicator is to develop an appreciation for the importance of communication. The problem is not that human resource managers tend to belittle the importance of communication; rather, they often fail to think consciously about it.

Guidelines for Communicating Human Resource Programs

As just discussed, it is helpful for human resource managers to develop a marketing approach when implementing their programs. Even when this is successfully done, there are numerous other communication-related guidelines to follow. Some of these are discussed in the following paragraphs.[20]

Avoid communicating in peer group or "privileged-class" language. The level of a communication should be determined by the receiving audience and not by the instigator of the communication. Take the common procedure for developing employee benefit information. Often a highly educated writer makes a first draft and gives it to the department head. The department head, being a specialist, then adds a few "clarifying" remarks. The company lawyer and perhaps an actuary or an insurance person then add more explanations to guard against liability and to be legally correct. Thus, the final document may be accurate and legal, but also barely understood by the employees for whom it is intended! The key is to consciously remember for whom the communication is intended.

Don't ignore the cultural aspects of communication. Be careful with words, symbols, and expressions. Today's work force is much more culturally sensitive than it was one or two decades ago. Expressions like "they wear the black hats" or "you act like an old lady" can easily be taken out of meaning and offend someone in the audience.

Back up communications with management action. The old saying "People watch what you do and not what you say" is certainly true with regard to employee communications. Promises made either orally or in writing must be backed up by actions if they are to succeed.

Periodically reinforce employee communications. Most communications tend to be forgotten unless they are periodically reinforced. This is especially true with many personnel-related communications. It is a good idea, for example, to periodically remind employees of the value of the benefits they receive.

Transmit information and not just data. **Data** has been defined as "the raw material from which information is developed; it is composed of acts that describe people, places, things, or events that have not been interpreted.[21] Data that have been interpreted and that meet a need of one or more managers are called **information**.[22] Employees receive piles of data from numerous sources, but until the data have been interpreted, they are of little value. Human resource managers need to guard against transmitting numbers, statistics, and other data that have little meaning without an accompanying interpretation.

Don't ignore the perceptual and behavioral aspects of communication. Try to anticipate employee reactions to communications and act accordingly. For example, it might be a good strategy to informally separate older employees from younger employees when introducing a new pension program through employee meetings. It would only be natural for these different groups to have different questions and levels of interest.

The preceding suggestions largely involve good common sense. It is not that human resource managers are not practical; rather, they often do not take the time to think through a communication. One good approach is to ask, "How could this message be misinterpreted?" The answer to this question should then be taken into account when structuring the communication.

Human Resource Management and Organizational Performance

The primary goal of human resource management in any organization is to facilitate organizational performance. One of the most effective ways to enhance organizational performance is to increase productivity. The American Productivity Center defines productivity as the efficiency with which an organization uses its labor, capital, material, and energy resources to produce its output. Human resource managers are somewhat limited in the impact they can have on the capital, materials, and energy aspects of productivity. However, they can have a great deal of impact on the labor component. Specifically, they can affect the commitment of

Data Raw material from which information is developed; composed of facts that describe people, places, things, or events and that have not been interpreted.

Information Data that have been interpreted and that meet a need of one or more managers.

employees and the management philosophy of the individual managers. Because of this, human resource managers have a unique opportunity to improve productivity and hence organizational performance.

SUMMARY OF LEARNING OBJECTIVES

1. **Define human resource management.**

   Human resource management encompasses those activities designed to provide for and coordinate the human resources of an organization. Human resource management is also a modern term for what has traditionally been referred to as personnel administration or personnel management.

2. **Describe the functions of human resource management.**

   Human resource functions are those tasks and duties performed in large and small organizations to provide for and coordinate human resources. Human resource functions include the following:
   a. Human resource planning, recruitment, and selection.
   b. Human resource development.
   c. Compensation and benefits.
   d. Safety and health.
   e. Employee relations.
   f. Human resource research.

3. **Summarize the types of assistance provided by the human resource department.**

   The primary function of the human resource department is to provide support to operating managers of all human resource matters. In general terms, the human resource department provides three types of assistance: (1) specific services, (2) advice, and (3) coordination.

4. **Explain the desired relationship between human resource managers and operating managers.**

   The human resource department normally acts in an advisory capacity and does not have authority over operating managers. To be effective, human resource managers must continually cultivate good relations with operating managers. Likewise, operating managers must understand the human resource functions to effectively utilize the human resource department.

5. **Identify several challenges currently facing today's human resource managers.**

   Today's human resource managers currently face several challenges. Some of the more significant issues include an increasingly diverse work force and changes in government regulations, organization structures, technology, and managerial approaches.

6. **Outline several potential challenges and contributions presented by an increasingly diverse work force.**

   An increasingly diverse work force will create specific challenges in the areas of communication, more training, and potentially higher factionalism. On the positive side, increased diversity will contribute to an organizational culture that is more tolerant of different views, which may lead to better decisions. Another potential payoff is greater organizational responsiveness to diverse groups of customers.

7. **Discuss the role of human resource managers in the future.**

   Human resource managers are predicted to play an increasingly important role in the management of organizations. In fulfilling this role, human resource managers should become thoroughly familiar with the business, be knowledgeable about present and future trends, and learn to emphasize the impact human resources can have on profit.

8. **Summarize several guidelines to follow when communicating human resource programs.**

   Overall, it is helpful for human resource managers to develop a marketing approach when implementing and communicating their programs. In addition, there are several specific guidelines to follow: avoid communicating in peer group or privileged-class language, don't ignore the cultural aspects of communication, back up communications with management action, periodically reinforce employee communications, transmit information and not just data, and don't ignore the perceptual and behavioral aspects of communication.

9. **Explain, in general terms, how human resource managers can affect organizational performance.**

   One of the most effective ways to enhance organizational performance is to positively influence the labor component of productivity. Human resource managers can have a significant impact on the commitment of employees and the management philosophy of individual managers.

REVIEW QUESTIONS

1. What is human resource management? Distinguish between a human resource generalist and a human resource specialist.
2. What functions does a human resource department normally perform? Why are these functions important in today's organizations?
3. List several challenges facing today's human resource managers.
4. What is meant by an "increasingly diverse work force"?
5. Differentiate among downsizing, outsourcing, rightsizing, and reengineering.
6. Name several specific ways human resource managers can positively affect an organization's profits.
7. List several guidelines to follow when communicating human resource programs.

DISCUSSION QUESTIONS

1. Some people believe human resource management is an area reserved for those "who can't do anything else." Why do you think this belief has emerged? Is there any factual basis for it?
2. Describe some current trends that you believe will have an impact on human resource management in the next 10 years.
3. Many human resource managers claim to love their work because they like to work with people. Do you think liking people is the most important ingredient in becoming a successful human resource manager?
4. As a human resource manager, how might you go about convincing top management that you should be heavily involved in the company's strategic planning process?

INCIDENT 1–1

Human Resource Management and Professionals

You are a senior member of a national law firm in New York City. The managing partner of the firm has asked you to head up the southern branch in Raleigh, North Carolina. This branch is 1 of 10 under the main office. On the whole, the

Web site: Society of Human
Resource Management

www.shrm.org

firm has been successful since its establishment in the mid-1920s, but in the last five years, many of the younger staff have elected to leave the organization. The managing partner is convinced the problem is not salary, because a recent survey indicated that the firm's salary structure is competitive with that of other major firms. However, he requests that you study this matter firsthand in your new assignment.

After getting settled in Raleigh, one of your first projects is to meet with the four senior managers to determine why the branch has had such a high attrition rate among the younger staff. Harding Smith, age 45, states that the younger staff lacks dedication and fails to appreciate the career opportunities provided by the firm. Wilma Thompson, age 50, says the younger staff members are always complaining about the lack of meaningful feedback on their performance, and many have mentioned that they would like to have a sponsor in the organization to assist with their development. Thompson further explains that the firm does provide performance ratings to staff and the previous manager had always maintained an open-door policy. Brian Scott, age 40, says he has received complaints that training is not relevant and is generally dull. He explains that various persons in the firm who worked with training from time to time acted mainly on guidance from New York. Denise Rutherford, age 38, says she believes the root of the problem is the lack of a human resource department. However, she says that when the idea was mentioned to the managing partner in New York, it was totally rejected.

Questions

1. What do you think about the idea of a human resource department in a professional office?

2. How would you sell the idea of a human resource department to the managing partner?

3. What type of organizational structure would you propose?

INCIDENT 1–2

Choosing a Major

Tom Russell is a junior in the school of business administration at a large midwestern university. Tom, who is an honor student, hasn't fully decided what his major should be. He has considered majoring in management, but just can't get excited about the field; it seems to be too general.

Tom's first course in management did appeal to him; however, this was largely because of the professor. Tom decided to talk to this professor about his dilemma. The following conversation occurred:

Tom: Professor, I would like your advice on selecting a major field of study. Right now, I just don't know what to do.

Professor: Tom, just let me say that you are making an important decision, and your concern is justified. How many courses have you taken in the School of Business Administration?

Tom: Only your introductory course in management, a basic course in marketing, and a statistics course. I do know that I don't want to major in statistics!

Professor: How about majoring in human resource management?

Tom: I don't think so. That is basically a staff job that can't really lead anywhere.

Professor: Hold on, Tom, I think I'd better tell you a little more about human resource management.

Questions

1. If you were the professor, what would you tell Tom?
2. Specifically, what future trends do you see that might help persuade Tom to major in human resource management?

EXERCISE 1–1

Justifying the Human Resource Department

Assume you work in the human resource department of a medium-size manufacturing company (annual sales of $50 million). The company has been unionized for many years but has never had a strike. The president of the company has just requested that all departments develop a budget for the coming fiscal year and be prepared to justify their budget requests. As part of this justification, your boss, the director of human resources, has just asked you to prepare a list of at least 10 reasons why the human resource department and its performance are important to the success of the entire company. Be prepared to present your list to the class.

EXERCISE 1–2

Are You Poised for Success?*

As discussed in this chapter, a successful career in HR demands a broader range of skills and experiences than ever before. While designed for people currently employed in HR positions, the following exam provides good insights into what is necessary to succeed in HR today. If you are currently employed in HR, take the exam and see how well you are doing. If you are not currently in HR, go over the exam questions to learn how you might prepare yourself for a career in HR.

I. Starting Points   **(10 points)**

(10 points if you have a managerial, directorial, or VP title)   _____

II. Knowledge of General Business and Finance   **(10 points)**

During the past six months, have you initiated conversations
   with the CFO or other finance executive to discuss the
   financial implications of HR programs? If yes, add 2 points   _____
Have you completed some general business courses at the
   college level? If yes, add 2 points   _____
Do you have an MBA? If yes, add 2 points   _____
Do you develop the first draft of the company's annual HR
   budget and then advocate for it during the corporate
   budget-setting sessions? If yes, add 2 points   _____
Did you meet HR budget goals (+ or –5%) during the most
   recent fiscal year? If yes, add 2 points   _____

III. Mastery of HR Disciplines   **(10 points)**

Have you initiated, developed, and implemented a specific HR
   program within a specific HR niche (e.g., training or
   compensation)? If yes, add 1 point for each program, to a
   maximum of 4 points   _____
Before assuming your present position, did you hold a title of
   manager or director of a specific HR function, such as benefits
   or staffing? If yes, add 2 points for each title, to a maximum of
   4 points   _____
Have you mentored someone else in HR who was designing a
   program within a specific HR niche? If yes, add 2 points   _____

IV. Knowledge of Your Organization   (10 points)

Can you state your company's earnings for the most recent fiscal
  year? If yes, add 1 point   _____

Can you state your company's profit (or loss) for the most
  recent fiscal year? If yes, add 1 point   _____

Can you identify your organization's primary product or service
  lines and the relative revenue generated by each? If yes, add
  1 point   _____

Can you identify your chief competitors and state your
  competitive position relative to them? If yes, add 2 points   _____

Do you report directly to the CEO? If yes, add 2 points   _____

During the past year, have you initiated a meeting or meetings
  with a line manager or other colleague at the management
  level for the express purpose of learning about their
  business needs or objectives? If yes, add 3 points   _____

V. Cross-Functional Experience   (10 points)

Have you ever "shadowed" another executive or accepted a
  temporary assignment to gain a better understanding of
  another business function? If yes, add 2 points   _____

Have you ever held a position in an industry outside the one in
  which you're presently working? If yes, add 4 points   _____

Have you ever held a position in a discipline outside HR (e.g.,
  marketing, communication, or finance)? If yes, add 4 points   _____

VI. International/Cross-Cultural Experience   (10 points)

Have you ever participated in a cross-cultural training program?
  If yes, add 1 point   _____

Have you ever served as a member of a task force addressing a
  global business issue? If yes, add 1 point   _____

Have you ever traveled abroad? If yes, add 1 point for each
  country you've visited, to a maximum of 3 points   _____

Have you ever held an overseas assignment of six months or
  longer? If yes, add 5 points   _____

VII. Mentors   (10 points)

Have you had one or more mentors during your career? If yes,
  add 4 points   _____

Have any of your mentors been:
  (a) the opposite gender?
  (b) another race or ethnic group?
  (c) in a discipline other than HR?
Add 2 points for each yes answer   _____

VIII. Career Decisions   (10 points)

Have you developed a specific career goal for yourself? If yes,
  add 4 points   _____

Have you initiated activities intended to give you the skills/
  responsibility needed to progress toward your career goal? If
  yes, add 3 points   _____

Have you sought or accepted a lateral transfer for the purpose
  of expanding your career opportunities? If yes, add 3 points   _____

IX. Technology   (10 points)

Have you directed a project in which the application of
  technology (computers, voice-response systems, etc.) improved
  HR's value or productivity? If yes, add 5 points   _____

Have you been a member of a group or task force responsible
  for applying technology to solve an HR-related issue? If yes,
  add 3 points   _____

Do you use a computer yourself in the course of doing your job?
  If yes, add 1 point   _____

Do you consider yourself conversant in the current
  technological lingo (e.g., client/server, open architecture)?
  If yes, add 1 point   _____

X. Continual Learning   **(10 points)**

Do you subscribe to and read at least two business/professional
publications? If yes, add 2 points   _____

Do you keep current on general issues that have implications
for HR (e.g., health care reform)? If yes, add 2 points   _____

Do you periodically take classes or attend seminars in areas not
directly related to HR, such as creativity or statistics? If yes,
add 2 points   _____

Do you participate in professional organizations or attend
conferences specifically directed to HR executives? If yes, add
2 points   _____

Do you regularly engage in right-brain activities, such as reading
for pleasure, going to museums, or attending performing-arts
events? If yes, add 2 points   _____

HOW DID YOU DO?

To calculate your score, add all the numbers you entered on the
spaces provided.

Enter Subtotal Here   _____

Review the score sheet. For each section in which you
gave yourself no points (for example, you earned
no points under Career Decisions or Technology),
deduct 10 points from the subtotal above.

Enter the Total Points Deducted Here   _____

Subtract the deductions (if any) from the subtotal.

Enter the Grand Total Here   _____

85–100	Congratulations! You're clearly a leader in HR.
70–84	The foundation you've built for your career is solid. You're on the way to the top.
55–69	You've got a good start; additional experience in one or two key areas should help you get to the top. Set specific goals.
40–54	You have valuable experience in some key areas, but to get to the top you need additional experience. Start now.
0–39	Getting to the top in HR will be very difficult.

Source: "Are You Poised for Success in the 90's? Take the Quiz and Find Out," *Personnel Journal,* June
1994, pp. 72–73.

E X E R C I S E 1 – 3

Test Your Knowledge of HR History[**]

Web site: Workforce Online

www.workforceonline.com

Each of these events happened in the 20th century. See if you can put them in the
correct chronological order. For a greater challenge, name the year that the event
occurred. Search for clues on the "HR Timeline" at WORKFORCE ONLINE.
(www.workforceonline.com/workforce/timeline/index.html).

a. President Kennedy sets the U.S. minimum wage at $1.25 an hour.

b. The U.S. Supreme Court upheld the use of affirmative action to remedy job
   discrimination.

c. President Clinton signs the Family and Medical Leave Act (FMLA).

d. Congress passes the Railway Labor Act, requiring employers to bargain with
   unions.

e. Congress passes the Fair Labor Standards Act (FLSA) banning child labor and
   establishing the 40-hour workweek and the minimum wage.

f. Congress passes the Occupational Safety and Health Act.

   g. President Truman seizes the steel industry when steel companies reject recommendations made by the Wage Stabilization Board.

   h. Unemployment drops dramatically as men go to war and women "fill in" at work.

   i. Congress passes the Employment Retirement Income Security Act regulating all private pension plans.

   j. The North American Free Trade Agreement is passed.

   k. Congress passes the Equal Pay Act prohibiting wage differentials based on gender for workers covered by the FLSA.

   l. President Reagan signs a welfare reform bill requiring single parents with children over three years old to get regular jobs.

   m. United States enters World War II.

   n. Frances Perkins becomes secretary of labor and the first woman named to a presidential cabinet.

**Source: Workforce, Workforce Extra Supplement, October 1998, p. 7.

NOTES AND ADDITIONAL READINGS

1. U.S. Department of Commerce, *Statistical Abstract of the United States 1997,* 114th ed. (Washington, D.C.: U.S. Government Printing Office, 1997), p. 453.
2. Peg Anthony and Lincoln Akin Norton, "Link HR to Corporate Strategy," *Personnel Journal,* April 1991, pp. 75–86; Shari Caudros, "HR Leaders Brainstorm the Profession's Future," *Personnel Journal,* August 1994, pp. 54–61.
3. Charles Bowman, "BLS Projections to 2006—A Summary," *Monthly Labor Review,* November 1997, pp. 3–5.
4. Howard N. Fullerton, Jr., "Labor Force 2006: Slowing Down and Changing Composition," *Monthly Labor Review,* November 1997, pp. 23–38.
5. Ibid.
6. Ibid., p. 36.
7. Charlene Marmer Solomon, "Global Operations Demand that HR Rethink Diversity," *Personnel Journal,* July 1994, p. 40.
8. Much of this section is drawn from Benson Rosen and Kay Lovelace, "Piecing Together the Diversity Puzzle," *HR Magazine,* June 1991, pp. 78–84; and Roger D. Wheeler, "Managing Workforce Diversity," *Tax Executive,* November/December 1997, pp. 493–95.
9. Duncan Davidson, Duane Dickson, and Jane Trice, "Rightsizing for Success," *Business Forum,* Winter–Spring 1993, pp. 10–12.
10. M. Hammer and J. Champy, *Reengineering the Corporation* (New York: Harper Collins, 1993).
11. Samuel Greengard, "Catch the Wave as HR Goes Online," *Personnel Journal,* July 1995, p. 59.
12. Stan Caudron, "HR Professionals Become Strategic Business Partners," *Personnel Journal,* August 1994, p. 58.
13. Charlene Marmer Solomon, "Managing the HR Career of the '90s," *Personnel Journal,* June 1994, p. 66.
14. Phil Farish, "Broader View Needed," *Personnel Administrator,* February 1987, p. 27; and Donald M. Burrows, "Increase HR's Contribution to Profits," *HR Magazine,* September 1996, pp. 103–10.
15. Jack F. Gow, "Human Resources Managers Must Remember the Bottom Line," *Personnel Journal,* April 1985, p. 32; and Samuel Greengard, "Increase the Value of Your Intranet," *Workforce,* March 1997, pp. 80–90.
16. "Research Reports: Evidence from Cross-Industry Studies," *Training & Development Journal,* June 1995, p. 35.

17. Keith Roberts, "The Proof of HR Is in the Profits," *People Management,* February 9, 1995, pp. 42–43.

18. Melanie J. Rhodeback, "Embrace the Bottom Line," *Personnel Journal,* May 1991, pp. 53–59; and Greengard, "Catch the Wave," *Personnel Journal,* July 1995, p. 59.

19. Joseph A. Banik, "The Marketing Approach to Communicating with Employees," *Personnel Journal,* October 1985; Joe Pasqueletto, "An HRS Marketing Strategy," *Personnel Journal,* June 1989, pp. 62–71.

20. Much of this section is drawn from Banik, "The Marketing Approach," pp. 62–68.

21. David Lynch, "MIS: Conceptual Framework, Criticisms, and Major Requirements for Success," *Journal of Business Communications,* Winter 1984, p. 20.

22. Ibid.

Information Technology for Human Resources

Learning Objectives

After studying this chapter, you should be able to:

1. Recount the general evolution of computers since the early 1960s.
2. Describe the Internet and identify the two functional categories of information available on the Internet that are most useful to human resource managers.
3. Describe an intranet.
4. Describe a client/server network.
5. Define a human resource information system (HRIS).
6. List numerous potential applications or uses of an HRIS.
7. Name the three major functional components of an HRIS.
8. Reiterate the specific procedures involved in developing and implementing an HRIS.
9. List several things human resources can do to foster data security throughout the organization.

t**The advent of the "computer age" has greatly altered, not only the availability of information, but also the manner in which it is identified and acquired. Information technology deals with how information is accessed, gathered, analyzed, and communicated. Because information technology is used today in almost all phases of human resource work, it is discussed early in this book. This chapter introduces and gives an overview of information technology that is especially useful to human resource managers. Specific applications and uses of computers and information technology to particular human resource functions are discussed in the chapter relevant to the specific application.**

The Computer Evolution

The first electronic computer, the ENIAC, was developed by the University of Pennsylvania in conjunction with the U.S. Army Ordnance Corps. The ENIAC was 8 feet high by 8 feet long, weighed 30 tons, and required about 174,000 watts of power to run.[1] On the average, it took about two days to set up ENIAC to carry out a program. It had constant maintenance problems because of its reliance on vacuum tubes and complicated wiring.

In the 1960s, large and very costly **mainframe computers** were in use by only the very largest companies and government organizations. Not only was the hardware for these systems expensive, but they also required highly paid operators, service personnel, programmers, and systems specialists. Because of the physical size and costs of these systems, they were almost always highly centralized and, more often than not, considered an extension of the accounting function.

The large computers were followed by the **minicomputers** of the 1970s. The minicomputers were much smaller in size and cost, and they were often programmed to perform specific functions for a particular business activity. Minicomputers ushered in the concept of distributed data processing, in which each operational area of an organization has control of its own computer to better respond to the needs of the area.

The decentralization first made possible by minicomputers has been taken even further by the **microcomputer** or personal computer (PC). The first commercially available personal computer was offered by Apple in 1976. Forty-four percent of all U.S. households owned a personal computer in 1997.[2] For just a few hundred dollars, a manager today can buy a microcomputer that is capable of processing mammoth amounts of data, yet occupies no more space than a typewriter!

The phenomenal improvements in computer hardware have been accompanied by improvements in software and user compatibility. Modern computers are much more **user-friendly** than those of the past. Human resource managers today do not need to know sophisticated programming languages and computer jargon to use computers. In fact, the highly competitive software environment has produced many companies that are eager to build software that is highly customized for specific functional business needs. By maintaining close contact with software suppliers, the human resource manager is the beneficiary of highly sophisticated computer specialists' knowledge and skills.

Minicomputer   Small (desk size) electronic, digital, stored-program, general-purpose computer.

Microcomputer   Very small computer, ranging in size from a "computer on a chip" to a typewriter-size unit. Also called a *personal computer*.

User-Friendly Computer
Computer that requires very little technical knowledge to use.

HR and the Internet

The internet is an excellent source for finding many types of information related to human resource management and for keeping up with new developments in the field. Today a growing number of HR managers are using the Internet to recruit personnel, conduct research, access electronic databases, send E-mail, conduct training, and network with colleagues. The Internet is a global collection of independently operating, but interconnected, computers.[3] Frequently referred to as the "information superhighway," the Internet is actually a network of computer networks. Think of the Internet as analogous to the Interstate Highway system; just as the interstate system connects to different cities via many different routes, the Internet connects computers around the world via a number of different electronic pathways. At the most basic level, a computer, a modem, and the right type of software can get a person onto the Internet.

The real value of the Internet to managers is the information that it makes available. Through the Internet, managers can access massive amounts of information by accessing computers around the world that are linked together through the Internet.

Types of Internet Resources

The type of information available and most useful for human resource managers on the Internet can be placed into two broad functional categories: (1) conversational resources or (2) reference resources. Conversational resources allow users to have conversations with individuals anywhere in the world. Mailing lists and newsgroups are the primary types of conversational resources. Mailing lists includes electronic mail (E-mail), whereby the user can electronically read messages to any other individual or group of individuals who have "subscribed" by having their name and electronic mail address placed on the sender's list of numbers. Newsgroups are essentially electronic bulletin boards. Anyone with Internet access can post an article to the board and anyone with Internet access can read the board.

The two types of reference-oriented resources most frequently encountered are the World Wide Web and Gopher. The World Wide Web (www or the Web) uses hypertext markup language (HTML) to transfer text, sound, graphics, and video. Hypertext is a form of text which allows the writer to link words in the text to other documents, graphic images, video, or even web pages stored anywhere in the world. Using the Web requires "browsers" to view documents and navigate through the intricate link structure. Numerous browsers are currently available, with Netscape Navigator and Microsoft Internet Explorer being the most popular.

Gopher sites are usually maintained by government agencies and education institutions. Gopher sites contain text-only documents such as regulations, policies, and reports of governmental agencies and research reports of educational institutions.

Recruiting was the first big online service used by HR personnel.[4] Many companies use the Internet's World Wide Web to post job openings and to search for potential recruits. An interested recruit can even apply for a job directly from his or her computer.

Professional forums, bulletin board systems, and discussion groups represent some other popular uses of the Internet by HR personnel. Through these formats, HR professionals share information on topics as diverse as training and development, payroll and benefits, and legal requirements. By posting a question in the proper place on the Internet, an HR person can get an answer in a matter of hours as opposed to days or weeks.

Many services are available to assist HR people on the Internet. For example, *Online Sources for Human Resources* is an interactive online guide with a monthly newsletter that offers tips and information on how to best use the Internet. Figure 2–1 outlines five web locations that are good places to begin looking for useful HR information.

Intranets

An intranet is a private computer network that uses Internet products and technologies to provide multimedia applications within organizations.[5] An intranet

---

FIGURE 2 – 1   **SUGGESTED WEB SITES FOR HR RELATED INFORMATION**

1. HR Professional's Gateway to the Internet *(http://www.teleport.com/~erwilson)*. This site offers more than 60 links to HR-related home pages. It is well organized and easy for a Web beginner to get around. Hint: You can start here to link to several of the sources listed below.

2. Society for Human Resource Management Online *(http://www.shrm.org/hrlinks)*. This location has several useful links to various topics of interest, including career planning, employee benefits, legal issues, recruitment, and training and development.

3. Association for Human Resources Management *(http://www.ahrm.org)*. This site has links to numerous human resources associations.

4. Human Resources Headquarters *(http://www.hrhq.com)*. This site is a good source for reference materials. Bulletin boards offer discussions on current HR topics and trends.

5. Employee Relations Web Picks: Human Resource Links *(http://www.webcom.com/~garnet/labor/misc.html)*. This site offers links to legal information, resources, list serves, and newsletters.

Source: Adapted from Sara L. Cox, "HR Tips as Close as Your Web Browser," *Credit Union Management,* August 1996, p. 50.

connects people to people and people to information and knowledge within the organization; it serves as an "information hub" for the entire organization. Most organizations set up intranets primarily for employees, but they can extend to business partners and even customers with appropriate security clearance.

Intranets are redefining HR and providing new ways to get work done. A study released in September of 1996 reported that 90 percent of Fortune 200 companies surveyed were using intranets.[6] A separate study found that 50 percent of manufacturing companies and almost 100 percent of hi-tech companies use intranets to store HR data.[7] In general, intranets can provide an easy tool that allows HR to streamline and automate a wide array of functions. The attraction of an intranet is that it doesn't require any large capital outlay, it's incredibly efficient, and it's simple to use. Figure 2–2 provides 12 suggested general uses of an intranet. Figure 2–3 presents a glossary of useful Internet/intranet terms. HRM in Action 2.1 describes a very advanced system used by MCI Corporation.

Client/Server Networks

Client/Server Networks
Relatively new systems that use personal computers (PCs) linked together to process information in a very efficient manner.

Client/server networks are relatively new systems that use personal computers (PCs) linked together to process information in a very efficient manner.[8] At the hub of each network is a computer that controls the traffic on the network and stores data in a relational database. This central computer, called the server, may be anything from a large mainframe to a powerful PC. The clients are desktop PCs used by individuals to enter or extract data or to do analyses.

The real benefit of a client/server system is that it allows a user to enter a

---

FIGURE 2 - 2   **POSSIBLE USES OF AN INTRANET**

Create an electronic employee directory. No more paper-based directories that are obsolete before the ink dries.

Automate job postings and applicant tracking. Give employees the inside scoop on open positions. With electronic resumes and powerful search engines, it's possible to zero in on talent from within.

Provide electronic pay stubs. Cut the phone cord by letting workers check on their pay, withholding, and taxes without the help of HR. No more paper also means big savings—typically $2.50 or more per pay stub.

Publish an electronic employee handbook. Let employees unearth the information they need fast—using hyperlinks and keyword searches.

Offer more enticing employee communications and newsletters. Use video, audio, and snazzy graphics to grab attention.

Let employees update their personal profiles and access their accounts, such as a 401(k). Don't stop at name and address changes. Employees can make changes to their benefits and take advantage of online modeling and projections.

Conduct open enrollment. A growing number of third-party providers—including Hartford, Connecticut-based Aetna, and Boston-based Blue Cross/Blue Shield of Massachusetts— allow individuals to choose plans and physicians online directly from their intranet sites.

Provide leave status information. Why should HR deal with phone calls when workers can find out on their own what they've piled up in sick days, vacation days, and maternity leave?

Conduct performance and peer reviews. Map employee performance against company needs or route an electronic form for peer view.

Manage succession planning. Locate employees with the right set of skills to fill openings.

Source: Samuel Greengard, "12 Ways to Use an Intranet," *Workforce*, March 1997, p. 94.

FIGURE 2–3   **GLOSSARY OF USEFUL INTERNET/INTRANET TERMS**

Domain: The name of a computer or service on the Internet—referred to by the character following "@" in an online address.

Download: The process of receiving a file from another computer.

Firewall: Hardware or software that protects a private network from an unsecured or public network.

FTP (File Transfer Protocol): An Internet protocol for transferring files to and from another server over a network.

Groupware: An application that enables users to collaborate over a network.

Homepage: The first page of a Web site or group of HTML documents.

HTML (Hypertext Markup Language): The language in which World Wide Web documents are formatted.

Hyperlink: The linking mechanism that allows a user to jump from one Web page, graphic, or document to another.

Internet: World's largest computer network enabling users to send E-mail, transfer files, participate in newsgroups and access the World Wide Web.

Intranet: A private network that uses Internet software and standards.

Java: An object-oriented language, developed by Sun Microsystems, that creates distributed Web applications.

Newsgroup: An electronic bulletin board on which users can post and exchange messages.

SSL (Secure Sockets Layer): Provides authentication and data encryption between a Web server and a Web browser.

Upload: The process of transmitting a file to another computer.

URL (Uniform Resource Locator): A standardized character string that identifies the location of an Internet document. Also known as a Web address.

Web Browser: Software that requests and displays HTML documents and other Internet or intranet data.

World Wide Web: The Internet's worldwide, HTML-based, hypertext-linked information system.

Source: Samuel Greengard, "Internet/Intranet Glossary of Useful Terms," *Workforce*, March 1997, p. 82.

HRM IN ACTION

A Sophisticated Intranet

2.1

www.wcom.com

MCI Corporation has 55,000 employees and is based in Washington, D.C. MCI's system respresents the future of intranets. While most companies are still trying to develop online employee directories and handbooks, MCI is taking employee self-service and collaborative work to a higher level. The company's online offering, known as The Source, provides employees with more than 1,400 pages of interactive services. At the mere click of a mouse, it is possible for employees to update, share, and exchange information in ways that would have seemed impossible only a few years ago.

Under MCI's intranet, employees can reallocate investments in their 401(k) retirement accounts, fill out electronic W-4 forms, and see their next pay stub a week before they're paid. Employees can see videos of management briefings, and even sign up for and experience distance-learning courses at their desks.

MCI is also using the intranet to successfully multicast presentations and meetings to groups of employees. Task force meetings, legal briefings, and financial updates now take place online. The company estimates that it's saving nearly $1.5 million per year just on this one use alone.

Source: Samuel Greengard, "Achieving Greater Intranet Efficiency," *Workforce*, September 1998, pp. 72–77.

request and receive only the specific data needed. Processing and manipulation of the data are performed at the workstation, allowing the entire system to operate faster.

Client/server systems are ideal for most human resource environments. Many human resource functions, such as payroll and benefits administration, depend on large and effective data management systems. Many other human resource applications rely on the ability to enter and extract specific information to meet very specific needs. Modern client/server systems can do both of these tasks.

Human Resource Information Systems (HRIS)

Human resource information system (HRIS) A database system that contains all relevant human resource information and provides facilities for maintaining and accessing these data.

Increased human resource requirements, government regulations, and expanded microcomputer capabilities have all helped justify the need and feasibility of an information system within the human resource department. Such an information system is referred to as a **human resource information system (HRIS).** An HRIS is a database system that contains all relevant human resource information and provides facilities for maintaining and accessing these data.[9]

The Evolution of the HRIS

The first computerized human resource application in business took place at General Electric in the early 1950s.[10] A 1984 survey of 1,000 *Personnel Journal* subscribers, which yielded 434 usable returns, revealed that 99.7 percent of the respondents used computers in one capacity or another in the human resource functions.[11] A similar survey conducted in 1988 found that 99.8 percent of the respondents had automated one or more human resource functions.[12] Today, the question is not so much whether computers are used by human resource managers and employees but rather the extent to which they are used.

The First-Generation HRIS

The first generation of computerized HRISs involved the conversion of manual information-keeping systems to computerized systems.[13] Often the resulting systems were run by a large, external server bureau or, in the case of very large firms, an in-house mainframe computer. Large, costly processors crunched payroll and other data, and end users had very limited access to the system. Data had moved from the file cabinet to a mysterious mainframe. Human resource data were now in the care of a computer group that was either in-house or contracted outside. Requests from human resource personnel for information had to be funneled through the computer group. This system did result in a significant decrease in the time required to produce most reports, but it also made human resource personnel feel dependent on the computer group. Many human resource managers regretted not having direct access to their own data. Some even longed for the old days of paper files.

The Second-Generation HRIS

As the 1970s advanced, the second generation of computerized HRISs was initiated with the introduction of the minicomputer. Minicomputers handle a network of simultaneous users and have multiple input and output devices. Minicomputers facilitated the transition from strictly batch processing (mainframes) to interactive processing.

The second generation of computerized HRISs was completed in the early 1980s with the arrival of the personal computer. The low-cost stand-alone PC moved data processing to the desktop. The data repository was moved to the human resource professional's desktop. Software proliferated, and before long the human resource record-keeping function was within reach for every size of organization. At the same time, mainframe and minicomputer systems were being made much more accessible and user friendly. From a functional standpoint, however, human resource managers were doing their jobs in the same basic manner they always had. The one major difference was that computerization allowed them to do more and do it more rapidly.

The Third-Generation HRIS

Moving the data repository from some mainframe or computer group to the desktop caused a great deal of excitement in the human resource field. Human resource professionals began to see the possibility of new applications for the computer. Rather than merely computerizing what had been done manually, they visualized ways to use the computer to fundamentally change the way they performed their jobs. The basic idea was to integrate many of the different human resource functions.

Software vendors observed the desires of human resource professionals and began to develop systems to integrate the various areas within their applications. The result was the third generation of the computerized HRIS, a feature-rich, broad-based, self-contained HRIS. The third generation took systems far beyond being mere data repositories and created tools with which human resource professionals could do much more. The extent to which organizations have developed their HRISs varies from organization to organization.

Uses of an HRIS

A major advantage of an HRIS is its potential for producing more accurate and more timely information for operating, controlling, and planning purposes than manual or payroll-based systems can produce. The speed and accuracy produced by an HRIS simply cannot be matched by manual systems. An HRIS also gets rid of many of the paper files maintained by human resource people and by other areas of the organization.

Historically the major disadvantage of an HRIS was its financial cost and the labor requirements for implementing the system. Fortunately, these problems have greatly diminished as a result of the software currently available. Today numerous off-the-shelf HRIS software packages are readily available at much lower prices than just a few years ago. The currently available software packages also are much more user friendly and, thus, require less training and time to implement.

The following areas represent some specific potential applications for an HRIS. When evaluating the feasibility of an HRIS, always remember that the overriding purpose of any HRIS should be to assist human resource managers and other top managers in making sound decisions.

1. *Clerical applications.* Automating certain routine clerical tasks will avoid the use of additional staff, overtime, and temporary help.

2. *Applicant search expenditures.* An HRIS can easily store a summary of applicant qualifications and subsequently perform searches for candidates for certain positions. This can help the company avoid the need for an employment agency.

3. *Risk management.* Today it is critical in many industries that people in certain jobs have licenses, safety training, and even physical examinations. An HRIS can be used to monitor these requirements and report any discrepancies by jobholders.

4. *Training management.* An HRIS can compare job training requirements with the actual training experiences of individual jobholders. This system can then be used to determine both individual and organizational training needs.

5. *Training experiences.* An HRIS can provide organizationwide training development and delivery, especially for jobs using computers.

6. *Financial planning.* By using an HRIS, human resource managers can simulate

the financial impact of salary and benefit changes. It is then possible for the human resource department to recommend changes in strategy that stay within an overall budget goal.

7. *Turnover analysis.* Turnover can be closely monitored with an HRIS. Turnover characteristics can be identified and analyzed for probable causes.

8. *Succession planning.* A logical progression path and the steps required for advancement can be identified by an HRIS. Individual progress can then be monitored.

9. *Flexible-benefits administration.* An HRIS can be used to administer a flexible-benefits program. Without an HRIS, such programs can be expensive to implement and administer.

10. *Compliance with government regulations.* An HRIS can be used to keep up with current EEO and related government-required regulations. An HRIS can also help keep companies in compliance by more thoroughly scanning job applicants who meet specific requirements and keeping management informed of the situation.

11. *Attendance reporting and analysis.* The documentation of sick days, vacation time, personal time, and tardiness can be a significant expense if done manually. An HRIS can easily track this information.

12. *Human resource planning.* Human resource planning can be greatly assisted by an information system that is capable of making projections based on the current work force.

13. *Accident reporting and prevention.* An HRIS can be used to record accident details and subsequently provide analyses that can help prevent future accidents.

14. *Strategic planning.* Today's client/server systems are transforming human resource people from simple administrators to strategic planners who can influence CEO decisions.[14]

In addition to being used for the above general applications, an HRIS can provide many specific performance calculations that can be of great use to managers throughout the organization. Figure 2–4 lists and describes several of these.

Necessary Capabilities of an HRIS

What should be the minimum capabilities of an HRIS?[15] When answering this question, one should always keep in mind that the critical requirement of any HRIS system is the data: if you have the data necessary to support the various human resource functions, you can easily put those data on a computer. Any HRIS system has three major functional components: inputs, data maintenance, and outputs. Each of these is discussed below as to its role in the overall system.

Input Function

Input Function Provides the capabilities needed to get human resource information into the HRIS.

The input function provides the capabilities needed to get human resource data into the HRIS. Some of the first things that must be established are the procedures and processes required to gather the necessary data. In other words, where, when, and how will the data be collected? Once collected, they must be entered into the system. Some information may require coding before entering (e.g., raw salary information may be converted to a coded salary grade).

Once the data have been input, they must be validated to ensure that they are correct. Edit/validation tables can be used to determine if the data are acceptable. These tables contain approved values against which the data are automatically checked. The system should have the capability to easily update and change the validation tables.

F I G U R E   2 - 4   **PERFORMANCE CALCULATIONS FROM AN HRIS**

10. *Healthcare Cost per Employee.* As the work force ages and healthcare costs continue to increase, this cost should be monitored.
(Employee's total cost to provide healthcare benefits/Total employees)

9. *Pay and Benefits as a Percentage of Operating Expenses.* Downsizing, outsourcing, rightsizing, and reengineering are often aimed at reducing the organization's operating expenses. This calculation will indicate if payroll cost is dropping at the same rate as other expenses.
(Pay and benefits/Operating expenses)

8. *Cost per Hire.* While hiring costs are not as important as the quality of the hire, they are important, especially since quality is very difficult to measure.
(Advertising + Agency fees + Employee referrals + Travel cost of applicant and staff + Relocation costs + Recruiter costs + Recruiter Pay and Benefits + 10 percent to cover all other costs)

7. *Return on Training.* Sometimes difficult to calculate but usually can be accurately estimated.
(Measure depends on specific case.)

6. *Volunteer Turnover Rate.* Retention of key employees is critical to any organization's success. Is this figure going up or down?
(Total voluntary separations/Total employees)

5. *Turnover Cost.* There are four basic components of turnover cost: cost to terminate, cost to hire, vacancy cost, and learning curve loss. For the typical hourly employee, turnover costs equal about six months of pay and benefits. In some sales jobs, turnover costs can be as much as three years' pay and benefit costs.
(Cost to terminate + Cost per hire + Vacancy cost + Learning curve loss)

4. *Time to Fill Jobs.* Filling jobs quickly with qualified people is critical, especially to human resource managers.
(Total calendar days from receipt of requisition until offer is accepted.)

3. *Return on Human Capital Invested.* While employee value is a philosophical question, the ratio of profit for each dollar spent on employee pay and benefits can be calculated.
(Revenue − {Operating Expense − Pay and Benefits})/Pay and benefits

2. *Human Value Added.* Shows the number of profit dollars per employee.
(Revenue − {Operating expense − Pay and benefits})/Number of full-time employees

1. *That Which Impresses Top Management the Most.* Find out what top management thinks is important and see if it can be produced.

Source: Jac Fitz-Eng, "Top 10 Calculations for Your HRIS," *HR Focus*, April 1998, p. 53.

Data Maintenance Function

The data maintenance function is responsible for the actual updating of the data stored in the various storage devices. As changes (such as a pay increase) occur in human resource information, this information should be incorporated into the system. As new data are brought into the system, it is often desirable to maintain the old data in the form of historical information.

Output Function

The output function of an HRIS is the most visible and familiar one. The reason is that the majority of HRIS users are not involved with collating, editing/validating, and updating human resource data; rather, they are concerned with the information and reports produced by the system.

Most human resource reporting consists of the following:

1. Selecting a segment of the total population for further evaluation; the selection is usually based on the values of such items as salary grades/classifications, age, sex, departments, continuous service, and so on.

2. Performing some type of calculations using the population previously selected in item 1, such as calculating average salaries, average merit increases, and so forth.

3. Providing a report containing specific information regarding the selected population and/or the calculation results.[16]

The demands of the output function are the major factors determining the particular type of software to be used.

In addition to being able to produce a specific report on request, the output function should have the capability to provide and update a reports library. A **reports library** basically stores the program and historical data necessary to generate reports that are periodically requested. This feature saves substantial time by automatically updating the data needed to produce the reports in the library.

Another desirable capability is the ability to generate turnaround documents. **Turnaround documents** basically are simple reports that show the current data values and provide a place to indicate any changes. They are used to help solicit updates to the data.

Naturally, the specific inputs, frequency of updates, and reports required for an organization's HRIS will differ somewhat with each situation. However, the basic components and capabilities just discussed should apply in almost all situations, regardless of size and complexity.

Reports Library   A type of computer software program that stores the program and historical data necessary to generate reports that are periodically requested.

Turnaround Documents
Simple reports that show the current data values of an HRIS and provide a place to indicate any changes.

Implementing an HRIS

As with any major change, proper planning and communication are absolute necessities for successful implementation or major upgrade of an HRIS. All too many human resource managers have run into serious problems when attempting to implement or upgrade an HRIS.

The steps outlined below describe the specific procedures involved in successfully selecting and implementing an HRIS.[17]

Step 1: Inception of idea. The idea for having an HRIS must originate somewhere. The originator of the idea should prepare a preliminary report showing the need for an HRIS and what it can do for the organization. This preliminary report should be designed to get management's attention. The most critical part of this step is to clearly illustrate how an HRIS can assist management in making certain decisions.

Step 2: Feasibility study. The feasibility study evaluates the present system and details the benefits of an HRIS. It evaluates the costs and benefits of an HRIS by showing the labor and material savings compared to the cost of the system. It also evaluates the intangible savings, such as increased accuracy and fewer errors. Of course, it is possible that the feasibility study would recommend against an HRIS.

Step 3: Top management support. Once the feasibility study recommends going ahead with an HRIS, it is essential to obtain the support of top management. Once the support of top management has been secured, keep them informed. Send top management timely reports on the project status.

Step 4: Selecting a project team. Once the feasibility study has been accepted, top management support secured, and the resources allocated, a project team should be selected. The project team should normally consist of a human resource representative who is knowledgeable about the organization's human resource functions and activities and about the organization itself, a payroll representative (if payroll will be part of the project), and a technical person.

Depending on the size of the project, these project team members may be assigned on a part-time or full-time basis. One person may function in two or more of the necessary roles or more than one person may function in each of these roles.

Step 5: Defining the requirements. A statement of requirements specifies in detail exactly what the HRIS will do. A large part of the statement of requirements normally deals with the details of the reports that will be produced. Naturally, the statement also describes other specific requirements. This typically includes written descriptions of how users collect and prepare data, obtain approvals, complete forms, retrieve data, and perform other nontechnical tasks associated with HRIS use.[18] The key here is to make sure the mission of the HRIS truly matches management's needs for an HRIS.[19]

Step 6: Software/hardware selection. Scores of HRIS packages are now on the market. A $3,000 HRIS package today may easily surpass the functionality and ease of use found in many $20,000 systems of just a few years ago.[20] Many systems may operate on the hardware already in use for payroll or other purposes. When evaluating available systems, use the same cost-benefit analysis that would be used for any significant purchase. Depending on your needs and your internal resources, you may consider designing your own HRIS. If an outside vendor is chosen to provide and implement the system, be sure and agree on who will do what.

Step 7: Training. Training usually begins as soon as possible after the system has been selected. First, members of the project team are trained to use the HRIS. Toward the end of the implementation, the human resource representative will train managers from other departments in how to submit information to the HRIS and how to request information from it.

Step 8: Tailoring the system. This step involves making changes to the system to best fit the specific needs of the organization. A general rule of thumb is not to modify an off-the-shelf package, because modifications frequently cause problems. An alternative approach is to develop programs that augment the purchased program rather than altering it.

Step 9: Collecting the data. Prior to start-up of the system, data must be collected and entered into the system.

Step 10: Testing the system. Once the system has been tailored to the organization's needs and the data entered, a period of testing follows. The purpose of the testing phase is to verify the output of the HRIS and to make sure it is doing what it is supposed to do. All reports should be critically analyzed for accuracy.

Step 11: Starting up. Start-up begins when all data and current actions are put into the system and reports are produced. It is wise to attempt start-up during a lull period so that as much time as possible can be devoted to the HRIS. Even though the system has been tested, some additional errors often surface during start-up.

Step 12: Running in parallel. Even after the new HRIS has been tested, it is desirable to run the new system in parallel with the old system for a period of time. This allows for the outputs of both systems to be compared and examined for any inaccuracies.

Step 13: Maintenance. It normally takes several weeks or even months for the human resource people to feel comfortable with the new system. During this stabilization period, any remaining errors and adjustments should be handled.

Step 14: Evaluation. After the HRIS has been in place for a reasonable length of time, the system should be evaluated. Is the HRIS right for the organization, and is it being properly used? Because of the importance of this step, it is covered in more detail in the next section of this chapter.

Should an organization want or need help in selecting and implementing an HRIS, there are numerous computer consulting firms that specialize in HRIS.

Evaluating an HRIS

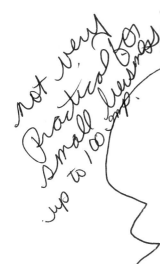

The evaluation should determine whether or not the HRIS has performed up to its expectations and if the HRIS is being used to its full advantage. Some basic performance issues can be addressed to help evaluate an HRIS.

- Compare the time spent on data entry to the value of the reports generated. Is the time well spent?
- Compare the system's response time for data entry and inquiry. Does the screen come up immediately, or is there a considerable delay?
- Does the system have real-time, online, and immediate update capability? If not, the system is antiquated by today's standards.
- Is the HRIS interfaced or integrated with the payroll system? If the HRIS is a stand-alone system that has data entry elements that are duplicated and entered on the payroll system, the answer to this question is no.
- Does the system have the capability to produce reports that provide answers to specific functional questions? For example, can an individual quickly receive information concerning the turnover rate in the finance department?
- Does the system use inquiry rather than pulling employees' files to answer questions? If files must be pulled, the system's inquiry capabilities have not been properly designed.
- Does the system generate the proper type of information? A good HRIS should generate more ad hoc, on-request reports than regular, monthly detailed reports.
- Analyze the costs to implement and maintain the current system. This includes such things as machine and software costs, maintenance agreements, supplies, and hourly salaries of data entry operators and programmers. How do these costs rate against the time saved by the system?[21]

Addressing the preceding questions should indicate whether the organization has a useful HRIS and if the HRIS is being used to its full advantage. Such an evaluation may also reveal a need to show end users how to better utilize the system.

As we emphasized earlier in this chapter, the overriding purpose of any HRIS is to assist human resource managers and other top managers in making sound decisions. If this is to be accomplished, the HRIS must produce information that is useful to the organization. Unfortunately, many human resource information systems are disappointments to managers simply because they do not produce the types of information management values. The problem is often that the managers designing the HRIS do not have a thorough understanding of what constitutes quality information to the users of the information.

If the information provided by an HRIS is to be valued by its users, it must meet five critical standards: (1) accuracy, (2) significance and relevance, (3) comprehensiveness, (4) readability and visual impact, and (5) consistency of format.[22] Accuracy should be defined by the user and does not necessarily have to be 100 percent error free. However, it should meet the expectations of the user. For example, if the user is interested primarily in a "big picture" view, there should be more tolerance for data inaccuracy than when the user is interested primarily in specific values and details. Significance and relevance mean making sure the users get the information they need and don't get information they don't need. Comprehensiveness means the information answers not only the immediate question but also probable follow-up questions. Information that is comprehensive provides insight that may not be obvious strictly from the data. Readability and visual impact should ensure that the information can be easily interpreted by the user. Graphs and tables should be used where appropriate, and information should be presented in an easy-to-read manner. Consistency of format simply means that once the right format has been developed and used, it should not be changed without good reason.

Producing information that is of quality to the user obviously requires an investment in time, effort, and communication on the part of HRIS managers. However, this investment can result in an information system that wins the respect of top management and one they can depend on. HRM in Action 2.2 describes a new HRIS software package that is very cost effective.

Data Security

According to the Computer Security Institute of San Francisco, 75 percent of companies have suffered financial losses—such as financial fraud, theft of proprietary information, and sabotage—from breaches of their computer systems.[23] This same institute has found that the biggest security threat usually comes from inside an organization. Obvious risks to HR are protecting intranet data and its HRIS. Additionally, HR is often involved in developing and implementing security-related policies that affect other parts of the organization.

Experts in the field of data security believe that successful protection involves sophisticated hardware/software protection and a work force educated to follow certain procedures and policies. From an organizational point of view, HR can and should play a major role in establishing a climate that is sensitive and aware of data security issues. Below is a checklist of specific actions HR can take to establish such a climate.

- Take time to evaluate all HR employees concerning data security measures.
- Conduct background checks on *all* new employees—even those who don't use computers.
- Include a data security workshop as part of new-employee orientation.
- Emphasize ongoing data security education through periodic workshops, newsletters, E-mail, and ongoing intranet messages.
- Develop a code of conduct and require employees to acknowledge that they understand it and will abide by it.
- Require nondisclosure agreements for all employees handling sensitive data.
- Encrypt all confidential human resources files and limit access to employees who have a need to see the data.

HRM IN ACTION

A Low-Cost HRIS

2.2

www.bestsoftware.com

Most HR managers would like all the advantages of a full-blown HRIS without all the costs. They want employee information, all kinds of reports, employee self-service, and government compliance. Even though that's a lot to ask, Best! Imperatin HRMS, from Best Software in St. Petersburg, Florida, fills the bill for some companies. While Best! Imperatin HRMS doesn't provide all of the functions of the top-line, expensive HRIS software programs, it does provide many.

Microsoft's Internet Explorer Web browser is used to get into Best! Imperatin HRMS. An existing company client/server is used by the software to access company databases. In essence, Best! Imperatin HRMS combines client/server technology with a Web browser. One advantage is that the users need only enough power at their workstations to support the browser, thus avoiding the cost of workstation upgrades. Another advantage is that prices for the software start at $20,000, which is substantially less than many of the better known HRIS software packages.

Best! Imperatin HRMS is a complete HRIS and, being browser based, it's easy to use. Thanks to its use of a client/server, Best! Imperatin HRMS has excellent performance and low cost.

Source: Jim Meade, "A Low-Cost Alternative to the Traditional HRIS," *HR Magazine,* August 1998, pp. 37–40.

HRM IN ACTION

Intranet Security at MCI

2.3

www.worldcom.com

As discussed in HRM in Action 2.1, MCI Corporation has one of the most advanced intranets around. The same is true for MCI's intranet security. Judging by the content and popularity of MCI's intranet, known as The Source, MCI employees have confidence in the security of their transactions. Currently nearly 60 percent of MCI employees, over 30,000, use The Source every month.

MCI uses personal identification numbers (PINs) to provide the appropriate level of access to data. However, MCI doesn't rely only on strict log-on controls. Once employees click past a page on their browser, the page immediately expires. This makes it impossible for an intruder to see the data by clicking the "back" button on the browser. When an employee leaves a PC while viewing secure documents, the system automatically logs off after five minutes of inactivity.

In addition to these security measures, MCI works hard to instill a sense of personal responsibility in users of the system. One aspect of this is to clearly communicate procedures and policies.

Source: Samuel Greengard, "MCI's Intranet Security System Uses PINs," *Workforce,* September 1998, p. 81.

- Adopt a team-oriented security approach that includes representatives of major departments (HR, security, legal, and information technology departments at a minimum).
- Use low-tech security devices such as locks, signatures, and paper shredders.
- Work with security or the compliance department to establish spot checks and audits.[24]

As more and more data go electronic, the risks and threats to data security grow. It is the responsibility of HR to protect not only its own data but to establish a climate attuned to data security issues throughout the organization. HRM in Action 2.3 describes some of the measures MCI uses to insure the security of its intranet.

Privacy and Legal Concerns

As technology has made it easier and cheaper for HR managers to gather and maintain large amounts of data about present and prospective employees, privacy and legal issues have become major concerns. Privacy concerns include determining (1) what types of employee information should be stored, (2) who has access to computer hardware and data, and (3) who can access and modify databases.[25] It is recommended that organizations have a good solid business purpose for any information collected.[26] Not only does this approach provide a sound legal defense but it builds credibility with employees. Laws regarding access to personnel records vary from state to state; many states have passed laws allowing employees to inspect files about themselves. Most laws allow employees to challenge information that they believe is inaccurate. Because organizations can be held accountable and liable, procedures and practices should be adopted to ensure that the collection, maintenance, use, and dissemination of personal information is necessary, lawful, current, and accurate.[27]

SUMMARY OF LEARNING OBJECTIVES

1. **Recount the general evolution of computers since the early 1960s.**

   In the 1960s, large and costly mainframe computers were used almost exclusively by very large companies and governments. In the 1970s, the large computers were followed by minicomputers that were much smaller in size and cost. Minicomputers ushered in the concept of distributed data processing. Minicomputers were followed by microcomputers, or personal computers. Microcomputers are relatively inexpensive, take up very little space, and can process large amounts of data.

2. **Describe the Internet and identify the two functional categories of information available on the Internet that are most useful to managers.**

   The Internet is a global collection of independently operating, but interconnected, computers. The two broad categories of information available on the Internet that are most useful to managers are (1) conversational resources and (2) reference resources.

3. **Describe an intranet.**

   An intranet is a private computer network that uses Internet products and technologies to provide multimedia applications within organizations.

4. **Describe a client/server network.**

   Client/server networks use personal computers linked together to produce information in a very efficient manner.

5. **Define a human resource information system (HRIS).**

   Information systems developed and used exclusively for human resource applications are referred to as human resource information systems (HRIS).

6. **List numerous potential applications or uses of an HRIS.**

   Potential uses of an HRIS include clerical applications, applicant searches, risk management, training management and experiences, financial planning, turnover analysis, succession planning, flexible benefits administration, compliance with government regulations, attendance reporting and analysis, human resource planning, accident reporting and prevention, and strategic planning.

7. **Name the three major functional components of an HRIS.**

   The three major functional components of an HRIS are inputs, data maintenance, and outputs. The input function of an HRIS should provide the capability to edit and validate data after input. The data maintenance function should provide the capability for updating the data stored on the various storage devices. The output function is the most visible function of an HRIS, responsible for producing reports.

8. **Reiterate the specific procedures involved in developing and implementing an HRIS.**

   Successfully developing and implementing an HRIS involves 14 steps: These include: (1) developing the idea, (2) conducting a feasibility study, (3) obtaining the support of top management, (4) selecting a project team, (5) defining the requirements of the system, (6) selecting the hardware and software, (7) training people to use the system, (8) tailoring the system to the needs of the users, (9) collecting the data, (10) testing the system, (11) starting up the system, (12) running the new HRIS and the old system in parallel, (13) maintaining the system, and (14) evaluating the system.

9. **List several actions human resources can take to foster data security throughout the organization.**

   Some of the actions that human resources can take to foster data security include: educate all HR employees concerning data security, conduct background checks on all new employees, include a data security workshop as part of new-employee orientation, periodically emphasize data security education, develop a code of conduct for data security, require nondisclosure agreements for all employees handling sensitive data, encrypt all confidential HR files and limit access, use a team-oriented approach to data security, use available low-tech devices, and work with security or compliance people to establish spot checks and audits.

REVIEW QUESTIONS

1. What is meant by the term *user-friendly*?
2. Distinguish between the Internet and an intranet.
3. Distinguish between conversational resources and reference resources.
4. What is a client/server network?
5. What is an HRIS?
6. Recount the different generations of HRIS.
7. List several potential uses of an HRIS.
8. What are the three major functional components of an HRIS?
9. Name the steps that should be followed when developing and implementing an HRIS.
10. Reiterate several basic performance issues that can be addressed to help evaluate an HRIS.
11. What are the five critical standards that must be met if information provided by an HRIS is to be viewed by the users as quality information?
12. List several specific actions HR can initiate to foster data security throughout the organization.
13. What are the three major concerns relating to the privacy of employee data?

DISCUSSION QUESTIONS

1. Discuss ways that information technology can help line managers fulfill their HR responsibilities.
2. Respond to the following statement: "Learning about information technology should be reserved for computer specialists."
3. Why do you think that many human resource managers are reluctant to use information technology such as the Internet or an HRIS?
4. Do you think that today's employees are overly sensitive about the privacy of their personal information? Why or why not?

INCIDENT 2–1

Getting Up to Speed

Jake Alvarez is in his mid-forties and has worked for Bates, Ltd., for almost 18 years, all in the HR department. Jake has seen Bates grow from just over 50 employees when he came to work to over 380 today. Even though Jake has progressed over the years and his responsibilities have increased, he has recently become worried about his future at Bates. Specifically, Jake has never been comfortable using computers. For the first several years at Bates, Jake's fear of computers wasn't a concern since they weren't used in any HR applications. However, over the past five years computers seem to have crept into every aspect of HR work. Furthermore, company memos are a thing of the past; everything is now done on E-mail. Almost every manager in the entire company now has a PC, everyone is Internet active, and the HR department installed a full-blown HRIS just six months ago.

It's not that Jake is incapable of learning or that he doesn't want to learn about new technology. The problem is that every time Jake tries to use his PC, something unexpected happens. Because Jake is so far behind his colleagues when it comes to computers, he is embarrassed to ask for help. Just last week the head of the HR department told Jake that he must get up to speed regarding the new HRIS.

Questions:

1. What do you suggest that Jake do to overcome his fears of the computer?

2. Do you think Jake's boss is asking too much to expect Jake to get up to speed on the HRIS?

INCIDENT 2–2

Amori Manufacturing Company

Amori Manufacturing Company, a producer of specialty industrial chemicals, employs 750 people at three locations. The company has experienced very rapid growth in the last few years and is expected to continue to grow very rapidly for at least the next three years. The number of employees is expected to increase by 20 percent within the next 18 months.

In order to meet the increased requirements for employees and managers, the company is actively involved in recruiting new employees and training existing employees. The company feels it is in a strong position to recruit well-qualified new employees because of its elaborate stock bonus plan, which is available to all employees with three years' tenure with the company.

All company records are maintained manually. Recently, a new director of human resource management was hired. The first thing she suggested was that the company invest in a computerized human resource information system.

Questions:

1. In what ways might Amori Manufacturing Company use a computerized HRIS?

2. Discuss the steps the company should take in planning and developing an HRIS. Include in your answer a discussion of who should be involved during each step and what information would be needed.

EXERCISE: HR AND THE WEB

This exercise is designed to introduce you to some of the HR resources available on the Web.

1. Begin this exercise by entering your Web browser. If you do not personally have a computer with a Web browser, one should be available at your school.

2. In the address field, enter the first of the addresses shown in Figure 2–1 *(http://www.teleport.com/~erwilson)*. After you have keyed in this address exactly as shown, hit the enter key and wait for the information to come up on your screen. You may have to wait a few seconds for the information to be downloaded from a remote location to your computer.

3. The first screen to come up should have the title "The Human Resource Professional's Gateway to the Internet." This page will have some general instructions followed by choices of where you would like to go next. Try out several of the options and look around just to see what is available. After you have explored this Web site, go back to your browser, change the address to the second entry in Figure 2–1 *(http://www.shrm.org/hrlinks),* and then explore this Web site. After you have explored the second Web site, repeat the experience for each of the other three Web sites listed in Figure 2–1. Notice how you can get to the same place and get the same information in several different ways. Having visited the five Web sites listed in Figure 2–1, you should now have a feel for the huge amount of information that is available through the Internet.

NOTES AND ADDITIONAL READINGS

1. Stan Augarten, *Bit by Bit: An Illustrated History of Computers* (New York: Ticknor & Fields, 1984), pp. 124–25, 128.
2. Edward E. Furash, "Internet Mania," *Journal of Lending & Credit Risk Management,* September 1998, pp. 88–91.
3. Byron J. Finch, *The Management Guide to Internet Resources* (New York: McGraw-Hill, 1997), p. 2. Much of this section is drawn from this source.
4. Samuel Greengard, "Leverage the Power of the Internet," *Workforce,* March 1997, p. 76.
5. Paul Barker, "The Evolving Corporate Intranet," *Telecommunications,* December 1997, pp. 67–70.
6. Samuel Greengard, "Increase the Value of Your Intranet," *Workforce,* March 1997, pp. 88–90.
7. Ibid.
8. Samuel Greengard, "The Next Generation," *Personnel Journal,* March 1994, pp. 40–46.
9. Gerson Safran, "Human Resource Information System," *Canadian Manager,* September 1994, p. 13.
10. Albert L. Lederer, "Information Technology: 1. Planning and Developing a Human Resource Information System," *Personnel,* May–June 1984, pp. 14–15.
11. Margaret Magnus and Morton E. Grossman, "Computers and the Personnel Department," *Personnel Journal,* April 1985, p. 42.
12. Morton E. Grossman and Margaret Magnus, "The Growing Dependence on HRIS," *Personnel Journal,* September 1988, p. 55.
13. Much of this and the next two sections are drawn from Bill Leonard, "The Myth of the Integrated HRIS," *Personnel Journal,* September 1991, pp. 113–15; and Terry L. Hunter, "How Client/Server Is Reshaping the HRIS," *Personnel Journal,* July 1992, pp. 38–46.
14. William I. Travis, "How to Justify a Human Resources Information System," *Personnel Journal,* February 1988, pp. 83–86; Greengard, "The Next Generation," March 1997, pp. 88–90.
15. Much of this section is adapted from Sidney H. Simon, "The HRIS: What Capabilities Must It Have?" *Personnel,* September–October 1983, pp. 36–49.
16. Ibid., p. 46.
17. These steps are adapted from Lederer, "Information Technology," pp. 19–26; Cynthia D. Diers, "Common Mistakes in Implementing an HRIS," *Employee Relations Today,* Autumn 1992, pp. 265–71; and Bill Roberts, "The New HRIS: Good Deal or $6 Million Paperweight?" *HR Magazine,* February 1998, pp. 40–48.
18. Maureen MacAdam, "HRIS Document What You're Doing," *Personnel Journal,* February 1990, pp. 56–63.
19. Joe Pasqualetto, "Evaluating the Future of HRIS," *Personnel Journal,* August 1988, p. 82.
20. Bob Lenburg, "Is an HRIS in Your Future?" *Credit Union Management,* March 1996, pp. 37–38.
21. Cynthia D. Diers, "Personnel Computing: Make the HRIS More Effective," *Personnel Journal,* May 1990, pp. 92–94; and Marc S. Miller, "Great Expectations: Is Your HRIS Meeting Them?" *HR Focus,* April 1998, pp. 51–52.
22. Kirk J. Anderson, "Putting an I in HRIS," *Personnel,* September 1988, pp. 12–20.
23. Much of this section is drawn from Samuel Greengard, "How Secure Is Your Data?" *Workforce,* May 1998, pp. 53–60; percentage data from p. 53.
24. Ibid., p. 56.
25. Raymond A. Noe, John R. Hollenbeck, Barry Gerhart, and Patrick M. Wright, *Human Resource Management: Gaining a Competitive Advantage* (Burr Ridge, Il: Richard D. Irwin, 1994).

26. Joan C. Hubbard, Karen A. Forcht, and Daphyne S. Thomas, "Human Resource Information Systems: An Overview of Current Ethical and Legal Issues," *Journal of Business Ethics,* September 1998, pp. 1319–23.
27. Ibid.

Equal Employment Opportunity: The Legal Environment

Learning Objectives

After studying this chapter, you should be able to:

1. Define equal employment opportunity.
2. Describe the intent of the Equal Pay Act of 1963.
3. Describe the intent of Title VII of the Civil Rights Act of 1964.
4. Define disparate treatment and disparate impact.
5. Discuss the purpose of the Age Discrimination in Employment Act of 1967.
6. Discuss the purpose of the Rehabilitation Act of 1973.
7. Describe the intent of the Vietnam-Era Veterans Readjustment Assistance Act of 1974.
8. Discuss the purpose of the Pregnancy Discrimination Act of 1978.
9. Describe the intent of the Immigration Reform and Control Act of 1986.
10. Describe the purpose of the Americans with Disabilities Act of 1990.
11. Explain the purpose of the Older Workers Benefit Protection Act of 1990.
12. Discuss the intent of the Civil Rights Act of 1991.
13. Explain the intent of the Family and Medical Leave Act of 1993.
14. Discuss the purposes of Executive Orders 11246, 11375, and 11478.
15. Describe the significance of the following Supreme Court decisions: *Griggs* v. *Duke Power, McDonnell Douglas* v. *Green, Albemarle Paper* v. *Moody, University of California Regents* v. *Bakke, United Steelworkers of America* v. *Weber, Connecticut* v. *Teal, Memphis Firefighters, Local 1784* v. *Stotts, City of Richmond* v. *J. A. Crosan Company, Wards Cove* v. *Atonio, Martin* v. *Wilks,* and *Adarand Contractors* v. *Peña, University of Texas—School of Law.*

t**wo of the most important external influences on human resource management are government legislation and regulations and court interpretations of the legislation and regulations. Numerous laws influence recruitment and selection of personnel, compensation, working conditions and hours, discharges, and labor relations. Whenever appropriate, this text describes government legislation and its court interpretations as they relate to the specific area of human resource management being discussed.**

However, because equal employment opportunity is so important and covers so many areas of human resource management, two separate chap-

ters are devoted to the topic. This chapter describes the legal framework of equal employment opportunity. Chapter 4 describes specific organizational requirements for implementing equal employment opportunity.

Equal Employment Opportunity Laws

In 1865, the Thirteenth Amendment to the U.S. Constitution abolished slavery. In addition, Congress passed the Civil Rights Act of 1866, the Fourteenth Amendment to the U.S. Constitution in 1868, and the Civil Rights Act of 1871. Yet Americans continued to live and work in a dual society, one black and one white. Businesses often refused to hire black workers or placed them in low-paying and low-skilled jobs.

Discrimination against women was based on the view that men should work to support their families and women should care for their families at home. Furthermore, it was a rather commonly held belief that women were not equipped to do certain jobs.

Discrimination in society and in the workplace gave impetus to the civil rights movement, which in turn pressured the U.S. Congress to pass laws designed to eliminate discrimination. As a result, Congress has passed numerous laws to ensure equal employment opportunity. Unfortunately, a common misconception is that equal employment opportunity means that an employer must give preference to women and minorities in the workplace. However, **equal employment opportunity** refers to the right of all people to work and to advance on the basis of merit, ability, and potential. HRM in Action 3–1 shows some of the benefits to having a diverse workforce.

As is true with most laws, however, ambiguities in language leave much room for interpretation by the federal agencies that enforce the laws. Furthermore, court decisions regarding the laws often raise additional questions of interpretation. For these reasons and others, equal employment opportunity is one of the most challenging and complex aspects of human resource management. Nevertheless, a good beginning point for understanding equal employment opportunity is to know the basic legislation covering the area.

margin: **Equal Employment Opportunity** The right of all persons to work and to advance on the basis of merit, ability, and potential.

Equal Pay Act (1963)

margin: **Equal Pay Act** Prohibits sex-based discrimination in rates of pay paid to men and women working on the same or similar jobs.

The **Equal Pay Act of 1963** prohibits sex-based discrimination in rates of pay paid to men and women working on the same or similar jobs. Specifically, the act states:

> *No employer having employees subject to [the minimum wage provisions of the Fair Labor Standards Act] shall discriminate, within any establishment. . . , between employees on the basis of sex by paying wages to employees in such establishment at a rate less than the rate at which he pays wages to employees of the opposite sex in such establishment for equal work on jobs the performance of which requires equal skill, effort, and responsibility, and which are performed under similar working conditions.*

The act permits differences in wages if the payment is based on seniority, merit, quantity and quality of production, or a differential due to any factor other than sex. The act also prohibits an employer from attaining compliance with the act by reducing the wage rate of any employee.

The Equal Pay Act is actually part of the minimum wage section of the Fair Labor Standards Act (FLSA), described in more detail in Chapter 12. Thus, coverage of the Equal Pay Act is coextensive (covers the same groups) with the coverage of the minimum wage provisions of the FLSA. Generally, the act covers employers engaged in commerce or in the production of goods for commerce, employers that have two or more employees, and labor organizations. Responsibility for enforcing the Equal Pay Act was originally assigned to the secretary of labor but was

4

true

4

true

HRM IN ACTION

Diversity in a Toyota Dealership

3.1

www.toyota.com

You name the language—Spanish, Korean, Arabic, Vietnamese, Hebrew, Mandarin, or Tagalog—and someone at Longo Toyota in El Monte, California, can speak it. With a 60-person sales staff that speaks more than 20 different languages, Longo has catered to its increasingly diverse customer base and become one of the top grossing dealerships in the United States. The dealership has assembled such a diverse sales staff without any formal affirmative action program. Simply by hiring and recruiting the best available talent, the staff at Longo has naturally evolved into an extremely diverse and effective group of salespeople. They've contributed to making Longo the top-grossing car dealership in California. Compared to other dealerships where half of the salespeople turn over every year, Longo retains a high 90 percent of its diverse sales staff. More than two-thirds of the managers at Longo are minorities. Ken Rankin, human resource manager at Longo, says: "If you're not recruiting on a diverse basis, you are missing a lot of talent. When you try to solve problems at any organization, you look for diverse perspectives, and that's certainly a great strength of ours."

Source: Adopted from Kevin Wallsten, *Workforce*, September 1998, pp. 91–92.

transferred to the Equal Employment Opportunity Commission (EEOC) on July 1, 1979.

Title VII, Civil Rights Act (1964)

Title VII of the Civil Rights Act of 1964 Keystone federal legislation that covers disparate treatment and disparate impact discrimination; created the Equal Employment Opportunity Commission.

Title VII of the Civil Rights Act of 1964 is the keystone federal legislation in equal employment opportunity. Several important provisions of Section 703 of the act state the following:

Sec. 703.
(a) It shall be an unlawful employment practice for an employer—
  (1) to fail or refuse to hire or to discharge any individual, or otherwise to discriminate against any individual with respect to his compensation, terms, conditions, or privileges of employment, because of such individual's race, color, religion, sex, or national origin; or
  (2) to limit, segregate, or classify his employees or applicants for employment in any way which would deprive or tend to deprive any individual, of employment opportunities or otherwise adversely affect his status as an employee, because of such individual's race, color, religion, sex, or national origin.
(b) It shall be an unlawful employment practice for an employment agency to fail or refuse to refer for employment, or otherwise to discriminate against, any individual because of his race, color, religion, sex, or national origin, or to classify or refer for employment any individual on the basis of his race, color, religion, sex, or national origin.
(c) It shall be an unlawful employment practice for a labor organization—
  (1) to exclude or to expel from its membership, or otherwise to discriminate against any individual because of his race, color, religion, sex, or national origin;
  (2) to limit, segregate, or classify its membership or applicants for membership or to classify or fail or refuse to refer for employment any individual, in any way which would deprive or tend to deprive any individual of employment opportunities, or would limit such employment opportunities or otherwise adversely affect his status as an employee or as an applicant for employment, because of such individual's race, color, religion, sex, or national origin; or

CHAPTER 3 Equal Employment Opportunity: The Legal Environment **47**

(3) to cause or attempt to cause an employer to discriminate against an individual in violation of this section.

(d) It shall be an unlawful employment practice for any employer, labor organization, or joint labor-management committee controlling apprenticeship or other training or retraining, including on-the-job training programs, to discriminate against any individual because of his race, color, religion, sex, or national origin in admission to, or employment in, any program established to provide apprenticeship or other training.

Disparate Treatment
Intentional discrimination and treating one class of employees differently from other employees.

Disparate Impact
Unintentional discrimination involving employment practices that appear to be neutral but adversely affect a protected class of people.

Section 703 covers two basic areas of discrimination: disparate treatment and disparate impact. **Disparate treatment,** Section 703(a)(1), refers to intentional discrimination and involves treating one class of employees differently from other employees. **Disparate impact,** Section 703(a)(2), refers to unintentional discrimination and involves employment practices that appear to be neutral but adversely affect a protected class of people.

Title VII, the name most frequently used to describe the Civil Rights Act, was amended by the Equal Employment Opportunity Act of 1972. Organizations presently covered by the provisions of Title VII include the following:

- All private employers of 15 or more people who are employed 20 or more weeks per year.
- All public and private educational institutions.
- State and local governments.
- Public and private employment agencies.
- Labor unions that maintain and operate a hiring hall or hiring office or have 15 or more members.
- Joint labor-management committees for apprenticeships and training.

Title VII also created the Equal Employment Opportunity Commission (EEOC) to administer the act and to prohibit covered organizations from engaging in any unlawful employment practices. The composition and powers of the EEOC are described later in this chapter. HRM in Action 3.2 shows what Shoney's and Denny's have done to overcome discrimination in their organizations.

Age Discrimination in Employment Act (1967)

Age Discrimination in Employment Act (ADEA)
Prohibits discrimination against employees over 40 years of age by all companies employing 20 or more people in the private sector.

The **Age Discrimination in Employment Act (ADEA),** passed in 1967, prohibits discrimination in employment against individuals aged 40 through 69. An amendment to the ADEA that took effect on January 1, 1987, eliminates mandatory retirement at age 70 for employees of companies with 20 or more employees. The prohibited employment practices of ADEA include failure to hire, discharge, denial of employment, and discrimination with respect to terms or conditions of employment because of an individual's age within the protected age group. Organizations covered by the ADEA include:

- Private employers of 20 or more employees for each working day in each of 20 or more calendar weeks in the current or preceding calendar year.
- Labor organizations.[1]
- Employment agencies.
- State and local governments.
- Federal government agencies, with certain differences; for example, federal employees cannot be forced to retire at any age.

One exception specified in the law concerns employees in bona fide executive or high policy-making positions. The act permits mandatory retirement at age 65 for high-level executives whose pensions exceed $44,000 a year.

Section 4(f) of the ADEA sets forth several conditions under which the act does not apply. The act does not apply where age is a bona fide occupational

---

HRM IN ACTION

Shoney's and Denny's

3.2

www.dennysrestaurants.com
www.shoneysrestaurants.com

Not so long ago, both Shoney's and Denny's were synonymous with racism. In 1992, Shoney's paid $132.8 million to settle a class-action discrimination suit brought by 20,000 employees and rejected job applicants. In 1996, Denny's paid $54.4 million to settle two class-action suits brought by black customers who claimed some restaurants refused to seat or serve them. However, in 1998 both companies appeared on the first *Fortune* magazine list of the 50 best companies for Asians, blacks, and Hispanics. Advantica, Denny's $2.6 billion-a-year parent, ranked Number 2; Shoney's, with $1.2 billion in revenues, ranked 13th. Advantica made the list because nearly one in three of its officers and managers are minorities. At Shoney's, 23.4 percent of its officials and managers and 41.4 percent of its work force are minorities. Advantica had zero contracts with minority-owned vendors and suppliers in 1992; in 1997 it had $125 million worth, 14 percent of its overall spending. At Denny's minorities now own 35 percent of the company's 737 franchised restaurants.

Source: Adapted from Anne Faircloth, *Fortune,* August 3, 1998, pp. 108–10.

---

qualification, that is, reasonably necessary to the normal operation of the particular business. For example, pilots and copilots face mandatory retirement at age 60. In addition, a bus company's refusal to consider applications of individuals between ages 40 and 65 for initial employment as intercity bus drivers was ruled legal.[2] Furthermore, it is not illegal for an employer to discipline or discharge an individual within the protected age group for good cause, such as unsatisfactory job performance.

Originally, the secretary of labor was responsible for enforcing the ADEA. On July 1, 1979, the EEOC assumed that responsibility.

Rehabilitation Act (1973)

Rehabilitation Act of 1973
Prohibits discrimination against handicapped individuals.

The **Rehabilitation Act of 1973,** as amended, contains the following general provisions:

- Prohibits discrimination against handicapped individuals by employers with federal contracts and subcontracts in excess of $2,500.
- Requires written affirmative action plans (AAPs) from employers of 50 or more employees and federal contracts of $50,000 or more.
- Prohibits discrimination against handicapped individuals by federal agencies.
- Requires affirmative action by federal agencies to provide employment opportunities for handicapped persons.
- Requires federal buildings to be accessible to handicapped persons.
- Prohibits discrimination against handicapped individuals by recipients of federal financial assistance.

Handicapped Individual
Person who has a physical or mental impairment that substantially limits one or more of major life activities, has a record of such impairment, or is regarded as having such an impairment.

Section 7(7)(B) of the Rehabilitation Act defines a **handicapped individual** as:

any person who:
(i)   has a physical or mental impairment which substantially limits one or more of such person's major life activities,
(ii) has a record of such an impairment, or
(iii) is regarded as having such an impairment. . . . Such term does not include any individual who is an alcoholic or drug abuser whose current use of alcohol or drugs prevents such individual from performing the duties of the job in question or whose employment, by reason of such current alcohol or drug abuse, would constitute a direct threat to property or the safety of others.

The primary responsibility for enforcing this act lies with the Office of Federal Contract Compliance Programs (OFCCP) of the Department of Labor. OFCCP will be described in more depth later in this chapter.

Vietnam-Era Veterans Readjustment Assistance Act (1974)

Vietnam-Era Veterans Readjustment Assistance Act of 1974   Prohibits federal government contractors and subcontractors with federal government contracts of $10,000 or more from discriminating in hiring and promoting Vietnam and disabled veterans.

The **Vietnam-Era Veterans Readjustment Assistance Act of 1974** prohibits federal government contractors and subcontractors with federal government contracts of $10,000 or more from discriminating in hiring and promoting Vietnam and disabled veterans. Furthermore, the act requires employers with 50 or more employees and contracts that exceed $50,000 to have written affirmative action programs with regard to the people protected by this act. The protected class consists of disabled veterans with a 30 percent or more disability rating or veterans discharged or released for a service-connected disability and veterans on active duty for any part of the time period between August 5, 1964, and May 7, 1975. Covered contractors and subcontractors must also list job openings with the state employment service. The OFCCP enforces this act.

Pregnancy Discrimination Act (1978)

The Supreme Court, in *General Electric Co. v. Gilbert,* made a decision that had a significant impact on the passage of the Pregnancy Discrimination Act.[3] In that case, General Electric (GE) provided nonoccupational sickness and accident benefits to all employees under its sickness and accident insurance plan in an amount equal to 60 percent of an employee's normal straight-time weekly earnings. Several female employees at GE's Salem, Virginia, plant who were pregnant presented a claim for disability benefits under the plan to cover the period they were absent from work as a result of their pregnancies. The company denied these claims on the grounds that the plan did not provide disability benefit payments for such absences. The employees filed suit alleging a violation of Title VII, which prohibits sex discrimination. The Supreme Court ruled that the exclusion of pregnancy-related absences from the plan did not constitute sex discrimination.

Pregnancy Discrimination Act (PDA)   Requires employers to treat pregnancy just like any other medical condition with regard to fringe benefits and leave policies.

As a result of this decision, in an effort to protect the rights of pregnant workers, Congress passed the **Pregnancy Discrimination Act (PDA)** as an amendment to the Civil Rights Act in 1978. The PDA, formally referenced as Section 701(K) of Title VII, states:

> *Women affected by pregnancy, childbirth, or related medical conditions shall be treated the same for all employment-related purposes, including receipt of benefits under fringe benefit programs, as other persons not so affected but similar in their ability or inability to work.*

Under the PDA, employers must treat pregnancy just like any other medical condition with regard to fringe benefits and leave policies. The EEOC, which is responsible for administering the act, has taken the view that an employer may not deny its unmarried employees pregnancy benefits and that if pregnancy benefits are given to female employees, they must also be extended to the spouses of male employees.

Immigration Reform and Control Act (1986)

Immigration Reform and Control Act   1986 act making it illegal to hire, recruit, or refer for U.S. employment anyone known to be an unauthorized alien.

Recent years have seen an increasing influx of illegal aliens into the United States. These people are often unskilled, and many do not speak English. Unfortunately, their status often leads to abuses in their employment. Thus, in 1986, the **Immigration Reform and Control Act** was passed, making it illegal for anyone to hire, recruit, or refer for employment in the United States a person known to be an unauthorized alien. To meet the requirements of the law, a company must attest, under penalty of perjury, that it has verified that the individual is not an unauthorized alien by one of the following measures:

1. Examining the individual's U.S. passport; certificate of U.S. citizenship; certificate of naturalization; unexpired foreign passport, if the passport has an appropriate, unexpired endorsement of the attorney general authorizing the individual's employment in the United States; or resident alien card.

2. Receiving verification from documents demonstrating employment authorization (social security card, birth certificate, or other documentation that the attorney general deems acceptable as proof).

3. Receiving documentation establishing identification (e.g., state driver's license with a photograph or other documentation that the attorney general deems acceptable as proof).

Americans with Disabilities Act (1990)

Americans with Disabilities Act (ADA) Gives disabled persons sharply increased access to services and jobs.

In May 1990, Congress approved the Americans with Disabilities Act (ADA), which gives disabled persons sharply increased access to services and jobs. Under this law, employers may not:

- Discriminate, in hiring and firing, against disabled persons who are qualified for a job.
- Inquire whether an applicant has a disability, but may ask about his or her ability to perform a job.
- Limit advancement opportunity for disabled employees.
- Use tests or job requirements that tend to screen out disabled applicants.
- Participate in contractual arrangements that discriminate against disabled persons.

Employers must also provide "reasonable accommodations" for disabled employees, such as making existing facilities accessible, providing special equipment and training, arranging part-time or modified work schedules, and providing readers for blind employees. Employers do not have to provide accommodations that impose an undue hardship on business operations. Table 3–1 summarizes suggestions proposed in the ADA for making the workplace accessible to disabled individuals. The bill covers all employers with 15 or more employees.

In 1997, the Equal Employment Opportunity Commission, which enforces the ADA and will be discussed in more detail later in this chapter, issued guidelines which specified that qualified individuals with psychiatric disabilities are protected from discrimination and are entitled to reasonable accommodations on the job. Mental disability is defined broadly as a mental impairment that substantially limits one or more of the major life activities of an individual, or a record of such impairment or being regarded as having such an impairment. Under this definition, the fact that an individual is regarded as having a mental disability or has a record of such disability is grounds for that person to claim that they have a mental disability. Obviously, these guidelines will raise many issues for human resource managers.

Older Workers Benefit Protection Act (1990)

Older Workers Benefit Protection Act of 1990 Provides protection for employees over 40 years of age in regard to fringe benefits and gives employees time to consider an early retirement offer.

The Older Workers Benefit Protection Act of 1990 resulted from a 1989 decision of the U.S. Supreme Court. In that decision, an Ohio county agency denied disability benefits to an employee who had been laid off at age 61 because its disability plan cut off at age 60. The Court ruled that the agency had not violated the Age Discrimination in Employment Act because, it said, the law did not cover benefits, just hirings, firings, and promotions.

Under the Older Workers Benefit Protection Act, employers may integrate disability and pension pay by paying the retiree the higher of the two; integrate

TABLE 3-1	SUGGESTIONS FOR MAKING THE WORKPLACE ACCESSIBLE TO DISABLED WORKERS

- Install wheelchair ramps.
- Make curb cuts in sidewalks and entrances.
- Reposition shelves so those with disabilities can reach materials.
- Rearrange tables, chairs, vending machines, display racks, and other furniture.
- Reposition telephones and water fountains.
- Add raised markings on elevator control buttons.
- Install flashing alarm lights.
- Widen doors.
- Install offset hinges to widen doorways.
- Eliminate turnstiles or revolving doors or provide an alternative accessible path.
- Install accessible door hardware (such as levers) instead of, or in addition to, doorknobs.
- Install grab bars in toilet stalls.
- Rearrange toilet partitions to increase maneuvering space.
- Move lavatory pipes underneath sinks to prevent burns.
- Add raised toilet seats.
- Add a full-length bathroom mirror.
- Reposition paper towel dispensers.
- Create designated accessible parking spaces.
- Add a paper cup dispenser at existing accessible water fountains.
- Remove high-pile, low-density carpeting.
- Install vehicle hand controls.

retiree health insurance and severance pay by deducting the former from the latter; and, in cases of plant closings or mass layoffs, integrate pension and severance pay by deducting from severance pay the amount added to the pension.

The act also gives employees time to consider a company's early retirement package—21 days for an individual or 45 days if a group is involved. Employees also have seven days to change their minds if they have signed a waiver of their right to sue. Coverage of this law is the same as that under the Age Discrimination in Employment Act.

Civil Rights Act (1991)

Civil Rights Act (1991) Permits women, persons with disabilities, and persons who are religious minorities to have a jury trial and sue for punitive damages if they can prove intentional hiring and workplace discrimination. Also requires companies to provide evidence that the business practice that led to the discrimination was not

The **Civil Rights Act of 1991** permits women, persons with disabilities, and persons who are religious minorities to have a jury trial and sue for punitive damages of up to $300,000 if they can prove they are victims of intentional hiring or workplace discrimination. The law covers all employers with 15 or more employees. Prior to the passage of this law, jury trials and punitive damages were not permitted except in intentional discrimination lawsuits involving racial discrimination. The law places a cap on the amount of damages a victim of nonracial, intentional discrimination can collect. The cap is based on the size of the employer: $50,000 for companies with 15 to 100 employees; $100,000 for companies with 101 to 200 employees; $200,000 for companies with 201 to 500 employees, and $300,000 for companies with more than 500 employees.

A second aspect of this act concerns the burden of proof for companies with regard to intentional discrimination lawsuits. In a series of Supreme Court decisions

discriminatory but was job related for the position in question and consistent with business necessity.

beginning in 1989, the Court began to ease the burden-of-proof requirements on companies. Several of these decisions are described later in this chapter. This act, however, requires that companies must provide evidence that the business practice that led to the discrimination was not discriminatory but was job related for the position in question and consistent with business necessity.

Family and Medical Leave Act (1993)

Family and Medical Leave Act (FMLA)   Enables qualified employees to take prolonged unpaid leave for family and health-related reasons without fear of losing their jobs.

The **Family and Medical Leave Act (FMLA)** was enacted on February 5, 1993, to enable qualified employees to take prolonged unpaid leave for family- and health-related reasons without fear of losing their jobs. Under the law, employees can use this leave if they are seriously ill, if an immediate family member is ill, or in the event of the birth, adoption, or placement for foster care of a child. To qualify for the leave, employees must have been employed for at least a year and must have worked for no less than 1,250 hours within the previous 12-month period. FMLA took effect in August 1993 for companies without collective bargaining agreements. For companies with collective bargaining agreements, the law took effect on termination of the labor contract or on February 5, 1994, whichever came first.

Executive Orders 11246, 11375, and 11478

Executive Orders   Orders issued by the president of the United States for managing and operating federal government agencies.

Executive orders are issued by the president of the United States to give direction to governmental agencies. Executive Order 11246, issued in 1965, requires every nonexempt federal contractor and subcontractor not to discriminate against employees and applicants because of race, sex, color, religion, or national origin. The primary exemption from the order is for contracts and subcontracts that do not exceed $10,000. The OFCCP within the Department of Labor is responsible for administering this executive order. The equal opportunity clause specified by Executive Order 11246 requires the contractor or subcontractor to agree to:

1. Comply with the provisions of the executive order.
2. Comply with those rules, regulations, and orders of the secretary of labor that are issued under the order.
3. Permit access to its books and records for purposes of investigation by the secretary of labor.
4. Include the equal employment clause in every subcontract or purchase order so that such provisions will be binding on each subcontractor or vendor.
5. In the event of noncompliance with the executive order, the contract may be canceled, terminated, or suspended.
6. After a hearing on the noncompliance, the contractor may be declared ineligible for future government contracts.

Utilization Evaluation   That part of the affirmative action plan that analyzes minority group representation in all job categories; past and present hiring practices; and upgrades, promotions, and transfers.

Executive Order 11246 also requires employers with 50 or more employees and contracts and subcontracts that exceed $50,000 to have a written affirmative action program (AAP). The AAP must include an identification and analysis of minority employment problem areas within the employer's work force, and where deficiencies exist, employers must establish goals and timetables for the prompt achievement of equal employment opportunity. Part of the AAP is called the **utilization evaluation,** which contains analyses of minority group representation in all job categories, present and past hiring practices, and upgrading, promotions, and transfers. Chapter 4 describes AAP in more detail.

Executive Order 11246 also gave the U.S. Office of Personnel Management (OPM) authority to issue regulations dealing with discrimination within federal agencies. In 1966, the OPM (then called the Civil Service Commission) issued regulations that required agencies to correct discriminatory practices and develop affirmative action programs.

In 1967, Executive Order 11375 amended Executive Order 11246 and prohibited sex-based wage discrimination for government contractors. Finally, Executive Order 11478, which in part suspended Executive Order 11246, was issued in 1969 along with revised regulations by the OPM. The new regulations merely modified a number of the procedures under the previous orders and regulations.

State and Local Government Equal Employment Laws

Many state and local governments have passed equal employment opportunity laws. For example, almost all states have some form of protection against employment discrimination on the basis of disability. However, at this point it is important to note the Supremacy Clause of the U.S. Constitution,[4] which states:

> The laws of the United States dealing with matters within its jurisdiction are supreme, and the judges in every state shall be bound thereby, anything in the Constitution or Laws of any State to the contrary notwithstanding.

As a result of this clause, as would be expected, many state and local laws became invalid after the passage of the Civil Rights Act and other equal employment legislation. For example, the California Supreme Court invalidated a state statute prohibiting females from tending bar.

No federal laws prohibit states from passing laws prohibiting discrimination in areas not covered by the federal law as long as the law does not require or permit an act that is unlawful under federal legislation.

One significant development at the state level on affirmative action occurred in California. Over the years an array of programs based on race had been adopted throughout California. One particular concern was a set of affirmative action programs that had been applied to the University of California. The California Civil Rights Initiative (CCRI), known as Proposition 209, was placed on the November 1996 election ballot and was adopted by a 54 to 46 percent margin. Proposition 209 calls for the state not to discriminate for or against any group in state employment and benefits. Proposition 209 will abolish any state and local preference programs in employment and education.

Table 3–2 summarizes the significant points of all of the equal employment opportunity laws discussed in this section.

Enforcement Agencies

Two federal agencies have the primary responsibility for enforcing equal employment opportunity legislation. These agencies are the Equal Employment Opportunity Commission and the Office of Federal Contract Compliance Programs.

Equal Employment Opportunity Commission

Equal Employment Opportunity Commission (EEOC) Federal agency created under the Civil Rights Act of 1964 to administer Title VII of the act and to ensure equal employment opportunity; its powers were expanded in 1979.

The **Equal Employment Opportunity Commission (EEOC)** was created by the Civil Rights Act to administer Title VII of the act. The commission is composed of five members, not more than three of whom may be members of the same political party. Members of the commission are appointed by the president of the United States, by and with the advice and consent of the Senate, for a term of five years. The president designates one member to serve as chairperson of the commission and one member to serve as vice chairperson. The chairperson is responsible on behalf of the commission for its administrative operations.

There is also a general counsel of the commission, appointed by the president with the advice of the Senate for a term of four years. The general counsel is responsible for conducting litigation under the provisions of Title VII.

TABLE 3-2   **SUMMARY OF EQUAL EMPLOYMENT OPPORTUNITY LAWS AND EXECUTIVE ORDERS**

Law/Executive Order	Year	Purpose or Intent	Coverage
Equal Pay Act	1963	Prohibits sex-based discrimination in rates of pay for men and women working in the same or similar jobs.	Private employers engaged in commerce or in the production of goods for commerce and with two or more employees; labor organizations.
Title VII, Civil Rights Act (as amended in 1972)	1964	Prohibits discrimination based on race, sex, color, religion, or national origin.	Private employers with 15 or more employees for 20 or more weeks per year, institutions, state and local governments, employment agencies, labor unions, and joint labor-management committees.
Executive Order 11246	1965	Prohibits discrimination on the basis of race, sex, color, religion, or national origin; requires affirmative action with regard to these factors.	Federal contractors and subcontractors with contracts in excess of $10,000; employers with 50 or more employees and contracts in excess of $50,000.
Executive Order 11375	1967	Prohibits sex-based wage discrimination.	Government contractors and subcontractors.
Executive Order 11478	1967	Supersedes Executive Order 11246 and modifies some of the procedures under the previous orders and regulations.	Same as Executive Order 11246.
Age Discrimination in Employment Act (ADEA)	1967	Prohibits discrimination against individuals who are at least 40 years of age but less than 70. An amendment eliminates mandatory retirement at age 70 for employees of companies with 20 or more employees.	Private employers with 20 or more employees for 20 or more weeks per year, labor organizations, employment agencies, state and local governments, and federal agencies, with some exceptions.
Rehabilitation Act, as amended	1973	Prohibits discrimination against handicapped persons and requires affirmative action to provide employment opportunity for handicapped persons.	Federal contractors and subcontractors with contracts in excess of $2,500, organizations receiving federal financial assistance, and federal agencies.
Vietnam-Era Veterans Readjustment Assistance Act	1974	Prohibits discrimination in hiring disabled veterans with 30 percent or more disability rating, veterans discharged or released for a service-connected disability, and veterans on active duty between August 5, 1964, and May 7, 1975. Also requires written AAPs for certain employers.	Federal contractors and subcontractors with contracts in excess of $10,000; employers with 50 or more employees and contracts in excess of $50,000.
Pregnancy Discrimination Act (PDA)	1978	Requires employers to treat pregnancy just like any other medical condition with regard to fringe benefits and leave policies.	Same as Title VII, Civil Rights Act.
Immigration Reform and Control Act	1986	Prohibits hiring of illegal aliens.	Any individual or company.
Americans with Disabilities Act	1990	Increases access to services and jobs for disabled workers.	Private employers with 15 or more employees.
Older Workers Benefit Protection Act	1990	Provides protection for employees over 40 years of age in regard to fringe benefits and gives employees time to consider an early retirement offer.	Same as ADEA.

TABLE 3-1

SUMMARY OF EQUAL EMPLOYMENT OPPORTUNITY LAWS AND EXECUTIVE ORDERS (CONTINUED)

Law/Executive Order	Year	Purpose or Intent	Coverage
Civil Rights Act	1991	Permits women, persons with disabilities, and persons who are religious minorities to have a jury trial and sue for punitive damages if they can prove intentional hiring and workplace discrimination. Also requires companies to provide evidence that the business practice that led to the discrimination was not discriminatory but was job related for the position in question and consistent with business necessity.	Private employers with 15 or more employees.
Family and Medical Leave Act (FMLA)	1993	Enables qualified employees to take prolonged unpaid leave for family- and health-related reasons without fear of losing their jobs.	Private employers with 15 or more employees.

Web site: United States Equal Employment Opportunity Commission

www.eeoc.gov

Originally, the EEOC was responsible for investigating discrimination based on race, color, religion, sex, or national origin. Now it is also responsible for investigating equal pay violations, age discrimination, and discrimination against disabled persons. The EEOC not only has the authority to investigate charges and complaints in these areas but also to intervene through the general counsel in a civil action on the behalf of an aggrieved party. The EEOC also develops and issues guidelines to enforce nondiscriminatory practices in all of these areas. Several of these guidelines are discussed in this and the next chapter.

Office of Federal Contract Compliance Programs

Office of Federal Contract Compliance Programs (OFCCP) Office within the U.S. Department of Labor that is responsible for ensuring equal employment opportunity by federal contractors and subcontractors.

Unlike the EEOC, which is an independent agency within the federal government, the **Office of Federal Contract Compliance Programs (OFCCP)** is within the U.S. Department of Labor. It was established by Executive Order 11246 to ensure that federal contractors and subcontractors follow nondiscriminatory employment practices. Prior to 1978, 11 different government agencies had contract compliance sections responsible for administering and enforcing Executive Order 11246. The OFCCP generally supervised and coordinated their activities. In 1978, Executive Order 12086 consolidated the administration and enforcement functions within the OFCCP.

Landmark Court Cases

Laws passed by Congress are usually broad in nature and are refined when applied to specific situations. Furthermore, the general nature of the equal employment laws allowed and caused enforcement agencies such as the EEOC to develop guidelines and enforce the acts as they interpreted them. Unfortunately, confusion often resulted among employers about the guidelines and enforcement of equal employment laws by the EEOC and OFCCP. The confusion and anger that resulted have led to many lawsuits concerning the interpretation of equal opportunity laws and guidelines. Again unfortunately, many court decisions have been not only confusing but, in some instances, apparently conflicting.

Nevertheless, several Supreme Court decisions have provided guidance in the interpretation of equal employment opportunity laws. Some of the more important decisions are described in the following sections.

Griggs v. *Duke Power Company*[5]

Web site: National
Employment Lawyers
Association

www.nela.org

The *Griggs* case concerned the promotion and transfer policies of the Duke Power company at its Dan River Steam Station. Duke permitted incumbent employees who lacked a high school education to transfer from an "outside" job to an "inside" job by passing two tests: the Wonderlic Personnel Test, which purports to measure general verbal facility, and the Bennett Mechanical Aptitude Test. The passing scores approximated the national median for high school graduates.

In a class action suit, African-American employees argued that these practices violated Title VII, since neither having a high school education nor passing the tests was necessary for successful performance on the jobs in question. The suit also argued that the practices were illegal because a much higher percentage of African-Americans did not have high school educations. The company argued that the requirements were based on the company's judgment that they would generally improve the overall quality of the work force and that the company had no discriminatory intent in instituting the requirements. The company argued that its lack of discriminatory intent was demonstrated by its efforts to help undereducated employees through company financing of two thirds of the cost of tuition for high school education.

In 1971, the Supreme Court ruled in favor of the African-American employees. The decision established several significant points concerning equal employment opportunity: (1) The consequences of employment practices, not simply the intent or motivation of the employer, are the thrust of Title VII in that practices that discriminate against one group more than another or continue past patterns of discrimination are illegal regardless of the nondiscriminatory intent of the employer; (2) The **disparate impact doctrine** provides that when the plaintiff shows that an employment practice disproportionately excludes groups protected by Title VII, the burden of proof shifts to the defendant to prove that the standard reasonably relates to job performance; and (3) the EEOC's guidelines that permitted the use of only job-related tests were supported.

Disparate Impact Doctrine
States that when the plaintiff shows that an employment practice disproportionately excludes groups protected by Title VII, the burden of proof shifts to the defendant to prove that the standard reasonably relates to job performance.

McDonnell Douglas v. *Green*[6]

Percy Green, an African-American man who had been employed by McDonnell Douglas, was laid off as a result of a reduction in McDonnell's work force. After the layoff, Green participated in a protest against alleged racial discrimination by McDonnell in its employment practices. The protest included a "stall-in," whereby Green and others stopped their cars along roads leading to the plant to block access during the morning rush hour. At a later date, McDonnell advertised for mechanics. Green applied for reemployment and was rejected by the company on the grounds of his participation in the stall-in, which the company argued was unlawful conduct.

On technical grounds, the Supreme Court remanded the case back to the district court, but at the same time its ruling set forth standards for the burden of proof in discrimination cases. These standards were as follows:

1. The complainant in a Title VII case carries the initial burden of proof in establishing a *prima facie* case of discrimination. This can be done by showing:
   (a) that he or she belongs to a racial minority; (b) that he or she applied and was qualified for a job for which the employer was seeking applicants; (c) that,

despite his or her qualifications, the applicant was rejected; and (d) that, after the rejection, the position remained open and the employer continued to seek applicants from persons of the complainant's qualifications.

2. If the complainant establishes a *prima facie* case, the burden shifts to the employer to provide some legitimate, nondiscriminatory reason for the employer's rejection.

3. The burden then shifts to the employee to prove that the employer's allegedly legitimate reason was pretextual (i.e., that the offered reason was not the true reason for the employer's action).

In its ruling, the Court stated that Green had established a *prima facie* case and that McDonnell had shown a nondiscriminatory reason for not hiring Green because of his participation in the stall-in.

Albemarle Paper v. *Moody*[7]

In the *Albemarle Paper* v. *Moody* case, the company required applicants for hire into various skilled lines of progression to take the Beta examination, which purportedly measures nonverbal intelligence, and the Wonderlic test, which purportedly measures general verbal facility. The company made no attempt to determine the job relatedness of the tests and simply adopted the national norm score as a cutoff for new job applicants.

The company allowed African-American workers to transfer to the skilled lines if they could pass the Beta and Wonderlic tests, but few succeeded. Incumbents in the skilled lines, some of whom had been hired before the adoption of the tests, were not required to pass them to retain their jobs or their promotion rights.

Four months before the case went to trial, Albemarle engaged an expert in industrial psychology to validate the relatedness of its testing program. He spent half a day at the plant and devised a study, which was conducted by plant officials without his supervision. This study showed the tests to be job related.

However, in June 1975, the Supreme Court found Albemarle's validation study to be materially defective. The Court's decision was based on the fact that Albemarle's study failed to comply with EEOC guidelines for validating employment tests. Thus, this decision reaffirmed that tests used in employment decisions must be job related, and it reaffirmed the use of EEOC guidelines in validating tests. The Court also held that if an employer establishes that a test is job related, it is the plaintiff's burden to demonstrate the existence of other tests that could comparably serve the employer's legitimate interests with a lesser impact on a protected group.

University of California Regents v. *Bakke*[8]

The medical school of the University of California at Davis opened in 1968 with an entering class of 50 students. No African-American, Hispanic, or Native American students were in this class. Over the next two years, the faculty developed a special admissions program to increase the participation of minority students. In 1971, the size of the entering class doubled, and 16 of the 100 positions were to be filled by "disadvantaged" applicants chosen by a special admissions committee. In actual practice, disadvantaged meant a minority applicant.

Allan Bakke, a white male, was denied admission to the medical school in 1973 and 1974. Contending that minority students with lower grade averages and test scores were admitted under the special program, Bakke brought suit. He argued that he had been discriminated against because of his race when he was prevented from competing for the 16 reserved positions, and he alleged that the medical

Reverse Discrimination
Condition under which
there is alleged preferential
treatment of one group
(minority or women) over
another group rather than
equal opportunity.

school's special two-track admissions system violated the Civil Rights Act of 1964. Thus, the Bakke case raised the issue of **reverse discrimination,** alleged preferential treatment of one group (minority or female) over another group rather than equal opportunity.

On June 28, 1978, the Supreme Court ruled in a 5 to 4 decision that Allan Bakke should be admitted to the medical school of the University of California at Davis and found the school's two-track admissions system to be illegal. However, by another 5 to 4 vote, the Court held that at least some forms of race-conscious admissions procedures are constitutional. The Court stated that race or ethnic background may be deemed a plus in a particular applicant's file, but it does not insulate the individual from comparison with all other candidates for the available positions. As could be expected, the somewhat nebulous decisions in the Bakke case provided an environment for further court tests of the legal status of reverse discrimination.

United Steelworkers of America **v.** *Weber*[9]

Web site: United States
National Labor Relations
Board

www.nlrb.gov

In 1974, the Kaiser Aluminum and Chemical Corporation and the United Steelworkers of America signed a collective bargaining agreement that contained an affirmative action plan designed to reduce racial imbalances in Kaiser's then almost exclusively white work force. That plan set hiring goals and established on-the-job training programs to teach craft skills to unskilled workers. The plan reserved 50 percent of the openings in the training programs for African-Americans.

At Kaiser's Gramercy, Louisiana, plant, Brian F. Weber, a white male, filed a class action suit against the company because African-American employees were accepted into the company's in-plant craft-training program before white employees with more seniority. Lower-level courts supported Weber's suit. However, in its 1979 decision on this case, the Supreme Court ruled that the voluntarily agreed-on plan between Kaiser and the steelworkers was permissible. The Court stated that the Title VII prohibition against racial discrimination did not condemn all private, voluntary, race-conscious affirmative action programs. The Court ruled that Kaiser's affirmative action plan was permissible because it (1) was designed to break down old patterns of segregation, (2) did not involve the discharge of innocent third parties, (3) did not have any barriers to the advancement of white employees, and (4) was a temporary measure to eliminate discrimination. Thus, this decision provided important guidelines for determining the legality of an affirmative action plan.

Connecticut **v.** *Teal*[10]

A Connecticut agency promoted several African-American employees to supervisory positions contingent on their passing a written examination. When they later failed the exam, the agency refused to consider them as permanent candidates for the positions. These employees alleged that Connecticut violated Title VII by requiring as an absolute condition for consideration for promotion that applicants pass a written test that disproportionately excluded African-Americans and was not job related. The passing rate on the test for African-Americans was only 68 percent of the passing rate for whites.

Bottom Line Concept
When the overall selection
process does not have an
adverse impact, the
government will usually not
examine the individual
components of that process
for adverse impact or
evidence of validity.

The agency gave promotions from the eligibility list generated by the written examination. As it turned out, however, the overall result was that 22.9 percent of the African-American candidates and 13.5 percent of the white candidates were promoted. The district court ruled that the bottom line percentages, which were more favorable to African-Americans than whites, precluded a Title VII violation. The **bottom line concept** is based on the view that the government should generally not concern itself with individual components of the selection process if the overall effect of that process is nondiscriminatory. However, the Supreme Court, on June 21, 1982, held that the nondiscriminatory bottom line results of the employer's selection process did not preclude the employees from establishing a *prima facie* case of discrimination and did not provide the employer with a defense in such a case. Thus, the conclusion reached from this case is that bottom line percentages are not determinative. Rather, the EEOC or a court will look at each test to determine whether it by itself has a disparate impact on a protected group.

Memphis Firefighters, Local 1784 v. *Stotts*[11]

The *Stotts* case concerned a conflict between a seniority system and certain affirmative action measures taken by the city of Memphis. In 1980, the Memphis Fire Department entered into a consent decree under which the department would attempt to ensure that 20 percent of the promotions in each job classification would be granted to African-Americans. The decree was silent on the issues of layoffs, demotions, or seniority.

In May 1981, budget deficits made layoffs of personnel in the fire department necessary. The layoffs were to be based on seniority. The district court issued an injunction ordering the city to refrain from applying the seniority system because it would decrease the percentage of African-American employees in certain jobs.

The city then used a modified plan to protect African-American employees. The modified plan laid off 24 employees, three of whom were African-American. If the traditional seniority system had been used, six African-American employees would have been laid off.

The Memphis Firefighters Local 1784 filed a lawsuit objecting to this modified plan. In 1984, the Supreme Court ruled that the district court had exceeded its powers in issuing the injunction requiring white employees to be laid off when the normal seniority system could have required laying off African-American employees with less seniority. This decision did not ban the use of affirmative action programs, but does indicate that a seniority system may limit the use of certain affirmative action measures.[12]

City of Richmond v. *J. A. Crosan Company*[13]

In 1983, the Richmond city council adopted, in an ordinance, a minority business utilization "set-aside" plan, which required nonminority-owned prime contractors awarded city construction contracts to subcontract at least 30 percent of the dollar amount of the contract to one or more minority business enterprises.

After the adoption of the ordinance, the city issued an invitation to bid on a project for the provision and installation of plumbing fixtures at the city jail. The only bidder, the J. A. Crosan Company, submitted a proposal that did not include minority subcontracting sufficient to satisfy the ordinance. The company asked for a waiver of the set-aside requirement, but the request was denied and the company was informed that the project was to be rebid. The company filed suit claiming that the ordinance was unconstitutional under the equal protection clause of the Fourteenth Amendment to the U.S. Constitution.

In January 1989, the Supreme Court ruled that the city of Richmond's plan was unconstitutional. The Court stated that state and local governments must avoid racial quotas and must take affirmative action steps only to correct well-documented examples of past discrimination. The Court went on to say that the Fourteenth Amendment to the U.S. Constitution, which guarantees equal protection of the laws, requires that government affirmative action programs that put whites at a disadvantage should be viewed with the same legal skepticism that has been applied to many state and local laws discriminating against minorities. The impact this decision will have on affirmative action plans for private companies is yet to be determined, but its implications may be wide-ranging.

Wards Cove v. *Atonio* [14]

In June 1989, the Supreme Court, in a close decision (5 to 4), made it easier for employers to rebut claims of racial bias based on statistical evidence. The case developed from discrimination charges against Wards Cove Packaging Company, Inc., of Seattle and Castle & Cooke, Inc., of Astoria, Oregon. The companies operate salmon canneries in remote areas of Alaska during the summer salmon run.

Minorities (in this particular case, the minorities were largely Filipinos, Alaskan natives, and Asians) alleged that while they held nearly half the jobs at the canneries, the jobs were racially stratified, with whites dominating higher-paying jobs such as machinists, carpenters, and administrators. The company argued that statistics showing that minorities held most of the lower-paying seasonal jobs and fewer better positions did not prove discrimination by the company.

The Supreme Court's decision said that when minorities allege that statistics show they are victims of discrimination, employers only have the burden of producing evidence that there is a legitimate reason for its business practices. The Court further stated that the plaintiff bears the burden of disproving an employer's assertion that the adverse employment practice is based solely on a legitimate neutral consideration. The Court also limited the statistical evidence that minorities can use to prove discrimination. It ruled that an absence of minorities in skilled jobs is not evidence of discrimination if the absence reflects a dearth of qualified minority applicants for reasons that are not the employer's fault. The Civil Rights Act of 1991 in effect reversed this Supreme Court decision.

Martin v. *Wilks* [15]

A group of white firefighters sued the city of Birmingham, Alabama, and the Jefferson County Personnel Board, alleging they were being denied promotions in favor of less qualified African-American firefighters. Prior to the filing of the suit, the city had entered into two consent decrees that included goals for hiring and promoting African-American firefighters. In filing their suit, the white firefighters claimed that the city was making promotion decisions on the basis of race in reliance on the consent decrees and that these decisions constituted racial discrimination in violation of the Constitution and federal statutes. The district court held that the white firefighters were precluded from challenging employment decisions taken pursuant to the decrees. However, on June 12, 1989, the Supreme Court ruled that the white firefighters could challenge the promotion decisions made pursuant to the consent decrees. Thus, the Court ruled that white firefighters could bring reverse discrimination claims against court-approved affirmative action plans.

Adarand Constructors v. *Peña* [16]

Adarand Constructors, a guardrail contracting firm, sued the U.S. government for allegedly applying race-based standards in granting public works contracts in Colorado. The lawsuit stemmed from a subcontract for guardrail work that Adarand lost in 1990 despite submitting the lowest bid. The subcontract was given to Gonzales Construction, a minority-owned business, by the main contractor, Mountain Gravel & Construction Company, because the Central Federal Lands Highway Division gave cash bonuses to prime contractors that hired minority-owned businesses. In a 5 to 4 decision, the Supreme Court questioned the constitutionality of government measures designed to help minorities obtain contracts, jobs, or education.

The decision did not scrap outright the federal programs that for decades have given some minority-owned businesses a competitive edge over majority-owned businesses. The decision does require lower courts to apply "strict scrutiny" to those programs, meaning the government may have to prove that each program helps only those individuals who can show they were victims of past discrimination, as opposed to simply trying to help all minorities.

University of Texas—School of Law

On March 18, 1996, the U.S. District Court of Appeals, 5th Circuit, rendered a decision concerning the affirmative action program at the School of Law of the University of Texas. This affirmative action program gave preferences to African-Americans and Mexican-Americans in the admissions program to the School of Law. This program was initiated in response to a history of discrimination against African-Americans and Mexican-Americans in the state of Texas. The District Court decision found no compelling justification to allow the School of Law to continue to elevate some races over others, even for the purpose of correcting perceived racial imbalance in the student body. The court concluded that the law school may not use race as a factor in law school admissions. The impact of this decision on affirmative action programs throughout the United States could be profound.

SUMMARY OF LEARNING OBJECTIVES

1. **Define equal employment opportunity.**
   Equal employment opportunity refers to the right of all people to work and to advance on the basis of merit, ability, and potential.

2. **Describe the intent of the Equal Pay Act of 1963.**
   This act prohibits sex-based discrimination in rates of pay for men and women working in the same or similar jobs.

3. **Describe the intent of Title VII of the Civil Rights Act of 1964.**
   Title VII of the Civil Rights Act of 1964 prohibits discrimination based on race, sex, color, religion, or national origin.

4. **Define disparate treatment and disparate impact.**
   Disparate treatment refers to intentional discrimination and involves treating one class of employees differently than other employees. Disparate impact refers to unintentional discrimination and involves employment practices that appear to be neutral but adversely affect a protected class of people.

5. **Discuss the purpose of the Age Discrimination in Employment Act of 1967.**
   This act prohibits discrimination against employees who are between the ages of 40 and 69.

6. **Discuss the purpose of the Rehabilitation Act of 1973.**
   This act prohibits discrimination against handicapped individuals and requires affirmative action to provide employment opportunities for such persons.

7. **Describe the intent of the Vietnam-Era Veterans Readjustment Assistance Act of 1974.**
   This act prohibits discrimination in hiring disabled veterans with a 30 percent or more disability rating, veterans discharged or released for a service-related disability, and veterans on active duty between August 5, 1964, and May 7, 1975. It also requires that employers with 50 or more employees and contracts in excess of $50,000 have a written AAP for the people protected under this act.

8. **Discuss the purpose of the Pregnancy Discrimination Act of 1978.**
   This act requires employers to treat pregnancy like any other medical condition with regard to fringe benefits and leave policies.

9. **Describe the intent of the Immigration Reform and Control Act of 1986.**
   This act prohibits the hiring of illegal aliens.

10. **Describe the purpose of the Americans with Disabilities Act of 1990.**
    This act increased access to services and jobs for disabled individuals with private employers having 15 or more employees.

11. **Explain the purpose of the Older Workers Benefit Protection Act of 1990.**
    This act protects employees over 40 years of age with respect to fringe benefits and gives employees time to consider an early retirement offer.

12. **Discuss the intent of the Civil Rights Act of 1991.**
    This act permits women, persons with disabilities, and persons who are religious minorities to have a jury trial and sue for punitive damages if they can prove intentional hiring and workplace discrimination. It also requires companies to provide evidence that the business practice that led to the discrimination was not discriminatory but was job related for the position in question and consistent with business necessity.

13. **Explain the content of the Family and Medical Leave Act of 1993.**
    The FMLA enables qualified employees to take prolonged unpaid leave for family- and health-related reasons without fear of losing their jobs.

14. **Discuss the purposes of Executive Orders 11246, 11375, and 11478.**
    Executive Order 11246 prohibits discrimination by federal contractors and subcontractors with contracts in excess of $10,000 on the basis of race, sex, color, religion, or national origin. Also, it requires contractors and subcontractors with 50 or more employees and contracts in excess of $50,000 to have a written AAP with regard to the protected classes. Executive Order 11375 prohibits sex-based wage discrimination. Executive Order 11478 supersedes Executive Order 11246 and modifies some of the procedures under the previous orders and regulations.

15. **Describe the significance of the following Supreme Court decisions:**
    Griggs v. *Duke Power*—Established that the consequences of employment practices, not simply the intent of the employer, are the thrust of Title VII.
    McDonnell Douglas v. *Green*—Set forth standards for the burden of proof in disparate treatment discrimination cases.
    Albemarle Paper v. *Moody*—Affirmed that tests used in employment decisions must be job related and affirmed the use of EEOC guidelines on validating tests.
    University of California Regents v. *Bakke*—Raised the issue of reverse discrimination. Stated that race or ethnic background may be deemed a plus in a particular applicant's file, but it does not insulate the individual from comparison with all other candidates for the available position.
    United Steelworkers of America v. *Weber*—Provided important guidelines for determining the legality of affirmative action programs.
    Connecticut v. *Teal*—Ruled that the bottom line results of an employer's selection process do not preclude employees from establishing a *prima facie* case of discrimination and do not provide the employer with a defense in such a case.
    Memphis Firefighters, Local 1784 v. *Stotts*—Provided that a seniority system may limit the use of certain affirmative action measures.
    City of Richmond v. *J. A. Crosan Company*—Stated that the Fourteenth Amendment requires government affirmative action programs that put whites at a disadvantage to be viewed with the same legal skepticism as laws that discriminate against minorities.
    Wards Cove v. *Atonio*—Changed the requirements in job discrimination suits. Now employees have to prove there was no legitimate business reason for a firm's alleged discriminatory acts.
    Martin v. *Wilks*—Ruled that whites may bring reverse discrimination claims against court-approved affirmative action plans.

Adarand Contractors v. *Peña*—Required the lower courts to apply strict scrutiny to minority set-aside programs, meaning the government may have to prove that each program helps only those individuals who can show they were victims of past discrimination, as opposed to simply trying to help all minorities.

University of Texas—School of Law—Concluded that the law school may not use race as a factor in law school admissions.

REVIEW QUESTIONS

1. What is equal employment opportunity?
2. Outline the intent and coverage of each of the following laws:
   a. Equal Pay Act.
   b. Title VII, Civil Rights Act.
   c. Age Discrimination in Employment Act.
   d. Rehabilitation Act.
   e. Vietnam-Era Veterans Readjustment Assistance Act.
   f. Pregnancy Discrimination Act.
   g. Immigration Reform and Control Act.
   h. Americans with Disabilities Act.
   i. Older Workers Benefit Protection Act.
   j. Civil Rights Act of 1991.
   k. Executive Order 11246.
   l. Executive Order 11375.
   m. Executive Order 11478.
3. Define disparate treatment and disparate impact.
4. What two federal agencies have primary responsibility for enforcing equal employment opportunity legislation?
5. Describe the impact of the following Supreme Court decisions:
   a. Griggs v. *Duke Power.*
   b. McDonnell Douglas v. *Green.*
   c. Albemarle Paper v. *Moody.*
   d. University of California Regents v. *Bakke.*
   e. United Steelworkers of America v. *Weber.*
   f. Connecticut v. *Teal.*
   g. Memphis Firefighters, Local 1784 v. *Stotts.*
   h. City of Richmond v. *J. A. Crosan Company.*
   i. Wards Cove v. *Atonio.*
   j. Martin v. *Wilks.*
   k. Adarand Contractors v. *Peña*
   l. University of Texas—School of Law
6. Discuss the bottom line concept.

DISCUSSION QUESTIONS

1. What area of human resource management is most affected by equal employment opportunity legislation? Discuss.
2. Do you believe most organizations meet the requirements of equal employment opportunity? Why or why not?
3. What problems do you believe have resulted from equal employment opportunity legislation?
4. Do you think misconceptions exist about equal employment opportunity? Discuss.

I N C I D E N T   3 – 1

Accept Things as They Are

Jane Harris came to work at the S&J department store two years ago. In Jane's initial assignment in the finance department, she proved to be a good and hard worker. It soon became obvious to both Jane and her department head, Rich Jackson, that she could handle a much more responsible job than the one she held. Jane discussed this matter with Rich. It was obvious to him that if a better position could not be found for Jane, S&J would lose a good employee. As there were no higher openings in the finance department, Rich recommended her for a job in the accounting department, which she received.

Jane joined the accounting department as payroll administrator and quickly mastered her position. She became knowledgeable in all aspects of the job and maintained a good rapport with her two employees. A short time later, Jane was promoted to assistant manager of the accounting department. In this job, Jane continued her outstanding performance.

Two months ago, Bob Thomas was hired in the accounting department. Ralph Simpson, vice president of administration for S&J, explained to Jane and Steve Smith, head of the accounting department, that Bob was a trainee. After Bob had learned all areas of the department, he would be used to take some of the load off both Jane and Steve and also undertake special projects for the department. Several days after Bob's arrival, Jane learned that Bob was the son of a politician who was a close friend of the president of S&J. Bob had worked in his father's successful election campaign until shortly before joining S&J.

Last week, Steve asked Jane to help him prepare the accounting department's budget for next year. While working on the budget, Jane got a big surprise: She found that Bob had been hired at a salary of $3,200 per month. At the time of Bob's hiring, Jane, as assistant manager of the accounting department, was making only $3,000 per month.

After considering her situation for several days, Jane went to see Ralph Simpson, the division head, about the problem. She told Ralph that she had learned of the difference in salary while assisting Steve with the budget and stated that it was not right to pay a trainee more than a manager. She reminded Ralph of what he had said several times—that Jane's position should pay $40,000 per year considering her responsibility—but S&J just could not afford to pay her that much. Jane told Ralph that things could not remain as they were at present, and she wanted to give S&J a chance to correct the situation. Ralph told Jane he would get back to her in several days.

About a week later, Ralph gave Jane a reply. He stated that while the situation was wrong and unfair, he did not feel that S&J could do anything about it. He told her that sometimes one has to accept things as they are, even if they are wrong. He further stated that he hoped this would not cause S&J to lose a good employee.

Questions

1. What options does Jane have?

2. What influence, if any, would the federal government have in this case?

I N C I D E N T   3 – 2

Seeing the Person, Not the Disability, in Japan*

Omron Kyoto Taiyo Electronics Company, Ltd., designed and built a factory in 1986 in Kyoto, Japan, specifically to accommodate employees with disabilities. The

*Source: Adapted from Michael A. Verespej, "Time to Focus on the Abilities," *Industry Week*, April 6, 1992, p. 18.

plant, which makes power relays and photoelectric sensors, has 191 employees, 151 of whom are disabled. Some of the tasks of employees with disabilities include the following:

- One employee who has the use of only his left arm uses a lever to take parts from stock and assemble them.

- A female employee with polio uses tweezers for a sensitive processing operation.

- A blind employee monitors product quality by sitting in a soundproof chamber to listen for abnormal sounds.

- An employee with cerebral palsy uses one of his disabled arms to air-clean a casing where a relay will be inserted.

Questions

1. Do you think most companies see the disability and not the person? Why or why not?

2. Describe a job you have seen or performed that could have been performed by a person with a disability.

3. What changes would have been required for a disabled person to perform the job described in question 2?

Web site: Federal Legal Information through Electronics

www.fedworld.gov/supcourt

EXERCISE 3–1

Legal Issues in Equal Employment Opportunity

Go to the library and review the relevant literature on recent legal cases involving equal employment opportunity. Prepare a report for presentation in class concerning the facts, issues, and current status of the case. Each team should make a 5- to 10-minute presentation in its findings.

NOTES AND ADDITIONAL READINGS

1. The definition of a covered labor union is identical to Title VII's except that where a union is not a referral union, it is not covered by ADEA unless there are 25 or more members, compared to the 15 or more under Title VII.
2. *Usery* v. *Tamiami Trail Tours, Inc.*, 531 F. 2d 224, 12FEP1233 (5th Cir. 1976).
3. *General Electric Co.* v. *Gilbert*, 429 U.S. 125 (1976).
4. Art. VI, cl. 2.
5. *Griggs* v. *Duke Power Company*, 401 U.S. 424, FEP 175 (1971).
6. *McDonnell Douglas* v. *Green*, 411 U.S. 792 (1973).
7. *Albemarle Paper* v. *Moody*, 422 U.S. 405, 95 S.CT. 2362 (1975).
8. *University of California Regents* v. *Bakke*, 483 U.S. 265 (1978).
9. *United Steelworkers of America* v. *Weber*, 99 S.CT. 2721 (1979).
10. *Connecticut* v. *Teal*, 457 U.S. 440 (1982).
11. *Memphis Firefighters, Local 1784* v. *Stotts*, 104 S.CT. 2576 (1984).
12. Theresa Johnson, "The Future of Affirmative Action: An Analysis of the Stotts Case," *Labor Law Journal*, October 1985, p. 788.
13. *City of Richmond* v. *J. A. Crosan Company*, 102 L Ed. 2d. 854.
14. *Wards Cove* v. *Atonio*, 104 L Ed. 2d. 733.
15. *Martin* v. *Wilks*, 104 L Ed. 2d. 835.
16. *Adarand* v. *Peña*, 115 S.CT. 2097 (1995).

Implementing Equal Employment Opportunity

4

Learning Objectives

After studying this chapter, you should be able to:

1. Explain the role of the Employer Information Report, EEO–1.
2. Define employment parity, occupational parity, systemic discrimination, underutilization, and concentration.
3. Describe an affirmative action plan.
4. Define bona fide occupational qualification (BFOQ).
5. Explain what is meant by business necessity.
6. Define sexual harassment.
7. Describe the comparable worth theory.

As the previous chapter indicated, the legal requirements of equal employment opportunity are quite complex. Nevertheless, each organization must develop its own approach to equal employment within the legal guidelines. Thus, this chapter provides specific information and guidelines for implementing equal employment opportunity.

Web site: United States Equal Employment Opportunity Commission

www.eeoc.gov

EEOC Compliance

The Equal Employment Opportunity Commission (EEOC) and the Office of Federal Contract Compliance Programs (OFCCP), both described in the previous chapter, are the two primary enforcement agencies for equal employment opportunity. All organizations with 20 or more employees must keep records that can be requested by either the EEOC or OFCCP.

Web site: National Employment Lawyers Association

www.nela.org

Legal Powers of the EEOC

Section 713 of Title VII (Civil Rights Act of 1964), the Age Discrimination in Employment Act (ADEA), the Equal Pay Act, the Americans with Disabilities Act (ADA) of 1990, and the Civil Rights Act of 1991 authorize the EEOC to develop and publish procedural regulations regarding the enforcement of these acts. As a result, the EEOC has issued substantive regulations (or guidelines, as they are more frequently called) interpreting Title VII, the ADEA, the Equal Pay Act, the ADA, and the Civil Rights Act of 1991. Since 1972, the EEOC has also had enforcement authority to initiate litigation and to intervene in private litigation.

EEOC Posting Requirements

Title VII requires employers, employment agencies, and labor organizations covered by the act to post EEOC-prepared notices summarizing the requirements of Title VII, the ADEA, the Equal Pay Act, the ADA, and the Civil Rights Act of 1991. The EEOC has prepared such a poster, and a willful failure to display it is punishable by a fine of not more than $100 for each offense. Organizations subject to notice requirements by Executive Order 11246 and Title VII can display a poster meeting the requirements of both the EEOC and the OFCCP.

Records and Reports

Employer Information Report (Standard Form 100) Form that all employers with 100 or more employees are required to file with the EEOC; requires a breakdown of the employer's work force in specified job categories by race, sex, and national origin.

Website: United States National Labor Relations Board

www.nlrb.gov

Employers with 100 or more employees must annually file Standard Form 100, known as the **Employer Information Report,** EEO–1. Figure 4–1 shows the form. The EEO–1 report requires a breakdown of the employer's work force in specified job categories by race, sex, and national origin. Other, similar types of forms are required of unions, political jurisdictions, educational institutions, school districts, and joint labor-management committees that control apprenticeship programs. Persons willfully making false statements on EEOC reports may be punished by fine or imprisonment.

In addition to EEO-1, Title VII requires the covered organizations to make and keep certain records that may be used to determine whether unlawful employment practices have been or are being committed. Thus, it is a good practice for covered organizations to maintain records relating to job applicants, payroll records, transfers, recalls, and discharges. The length of time required for the retention of these records varies, but a good time frame for retaining such records is three years.

Since the EEOC and OFCCP are interested in the recruitment and selection of protected groups and because the collection of certain data about the protected groups is not permitted on an organization's application form, the EEOC allows organizations to use a separate form, often called an *applicant diversity chart,* for collecting certain data. An example of such a form is shown in Figure 4–2. The data on this form must be maintained separately from all employment information.

Compliance Process

Employment Parity Situation in which the proportion of minorities and women employed by an organization equals the proportion in the organization's relevant labor market.

An individual may file a discrimination charge at any EEOC office or with any representative of the EEOC. If the charging party and respondent are in different geographic areas, the office where the charging party resides forwards the charge to the office where the respondent is located. Class action charges or charges requiring extensive investigations are processed in the EEOC's Office of Systemic Programs.

The EEOC uses two methods to determine whether discrimination against groups protected by the law has occurred: employment parity and occupational parity. When **employment parity** exists, the proportion of minorities and women employed by the organization equals the proportion in the organization's relevant labor market. **Occupational parity** exists when the proportion of minorities and women employed in various occupations within the organization is equal to their proportion in the organization's relevant labor market. Large differences in either occupational or employment parity are called **systemic discrimination.**

Relevant labor market generally refers to the geographical area in which a

F I G U R E   4 – 1   **STANDARD FORM 100**

Standard Form 100
(Rev. 12/78)
O.M.B. No. 3046-0007
100-210

EQUAL EMPLOYMENT OPPORTUNITY
EMPLOYER INFORMATION REPORT EEO-1

Joint Reporting
Committee

- Equal Employment Opportunity Commission
- Office of Federal Contract Compliance Programs

Section A - TYPE OF REPORT
Refer to instructions for number and types of reports to be filed.

1. Indicate by marking in the appropriate box the type of reporting unit for which this copy of the form is submitted (MARK ONLY ONE BOX).

(1) ☐ Single-establishment Employer Report

Multi-establishment Employer:
(2) ☐ Consolidated Report
(3) ☐ Headquarters Unit Report
(4) ☐ Individual Establishment Report (submit one for each establishment with 25 or more employees)
(5) ☐ Special Report

2. Total number of reports being filed by this Company (Answer on Consolidated Report only) _____

Section B - COMPANY IDENTIFICATION *(To be answered by all employers)*

OFFICE USE ONLY

1. Parent Company
   a. Name of parent company (owns or controls establishment in item 2) omit if same as label

Name of receiving office | Address (Number and street)

City or town | County | State | ZIP code | b. Employer Identification No.

2. Establishment for which this report is filed. (Omit if same as label)
   a. Name of establishment

Address (Number and street) | City or town | County | State | ZIP code

b. Employer Identification No. | (If same as label, skip.)

3. Parent company affiliation (Multi-establishment Employers Answer on Consolidated Report only)
   a. Name of parent-affiliated company | b. Employer Identification No.

Address (Number and street) | City or town | County | State | ZIP code

Section C - EMPLOYERS WHO ARE REQUIRED TO FILE *(To be answered by all employers)*

☐ Yes ☐ No 1. Does the entire company have at least 100 employees in the payroll period for which you are reporting?

☐ Yes ☐ No 2. Is your company affiliated through common ownership and/or centralized management with other entities in an enterprise with a total employment of 100 or more?

☐ Yes ☐ No 3. Does the company or any of its establishments (a) have 50 or more employees AND (b) is not exempt as provided by 41 CFR 60-1.5, AND either (1) is a prime government contractor or first-tier subcontractor, and has a contract, subcontract, or purchase order amounting to $50,000 or more, or (2) serves as a depository of Government funds in any amount or is a financial institution which is an issuing and paying agent for U.S. Savings Bonds and Savings Notes?

NOTE: If the answer is yes to ANY of these questions, complete the entire form, otherwise skip to Section G.

F I G U R E 4 – 1   *Concluded*

Section D - EMPLOYMENT DATA

Employment at this establishment--Report all permanent, temporary, or part-time employees including apprentices and on-the-job trainees unless specifically excluded as set forth in the instructions. Enter the appropriate figures on all lines and in all columns. Blank spaces will be considered as zeros.

JOB CATEGORIES	OVERALL TOTALS (SUM OF COL. B THRU K)	MALE					FEMALE				
		WHITE (NOT OF HISPANIC ORIGIN)	BLACK (NOT OF HISPANIC ORIGIN)	HISPANIC	ASIAN OR PACIFIC ISLANDER	AMERICAN INDIAN OR ALASKAN NATIVE	WHITE (NOT OF HISPANIC ORIGIN)	BLACK (NOT OF HISPANIC ORIGIN)	HISPANIC	ASIAN OR PACIFIC ISLANDER	AMERICAN INDIAN OR ALASKAN NATIVE
	A	B	C	D	E	F	G	H	I	J	K
Officials and Managers											
Professionals											
Technicians											
Sales Workers											
Office and Clerical											
Craft Workers (Skilled)											
Operatives (Semi-Skilled)											
Laborers (Unskilled)											
Service Workers											
TOTAL											
Total employment reported in previous EEO-1 report											

(The trainees below should also be included in the figures for the appropriate occupational categories above)

Formal On-the-job trainees	White collar										
	Production										

1. NOTE: On consolidated report, skip questions 2-5 and Section E
2. How was information as to race or ethnic group in Section D obtained?
   1 ☐ Visual Survey   3 ☐ Other—Specify ....
   2 ☐ Employment Record   ....
3. Dates of payroll period used -

4. Pay period of last report submitted for this establishment

5. Does this establishment employ apprentices?
   This year? 1 ☐ Yes 2 ☐ No
   Last year? 1 ☐ Yes 2 ☐ No

Section E - ESTABLISHMENT INFORMATION

1. Is the location of the establishment the same as that reported last year?
   1 ☐ Yes 2 ☐ No 3. ☐ Did not report last year. 4. ☐ Reported on combined basis.

2. Is the major business activity at this establishment the same as that reported last year?
   1 ☐ Yes 2 ☐ No 3. ☐ No report last year 4. ☐ Reported on combined basis.

OFFICE USE ONLY

3. What is the major activity of this establishment? (Be specific, i.e., manufacturing steel castings, retail grocer, wholesale plumbing supplies, title insurance, etc. Include the specific type of product or type of service provided, as well as the principal business or industrial activity.

Section F - REMARKS

Use this item to give any identification data appearing on last report which differs from that given above, explain major changes in composition or reporting units and other pertinent information.

Section G - CERTIFICATION (See Instructions G)

Check one
1 ☐ All reports are accurate and were prepared in accordance with the instructions (check on consolidated only)
2 ☐ This report is accurate and was prepared in accordance with the instructions.

Name of Certifying Official	Title	Signature		Date
Name of person to contact regarding this report (Type or print)	Address (Number and street)			
Title	City and State	ZIP code	Telephone Area Code	Number	Extension

All reports and information obtained from individual reports will be kept confidential as required by Section 709 (e) of Title VII.
WILLFULLY FALSE STATEMENTS ON THIS REPORT ARE PUNISHABLE BY LAW, U.S. CODE, TITLE 18, SECTION 1001

FIGURE 4-2   **APPLICANT DIVERSITY CHART**

NAME OF APPLICANT	DEGREE/ EDUCATION	DATE APPLIED	POSITION APPLIED FOR	EEO JOB CATEGORY	E.I.	SEX	AGE	HANDICAP	VETERAN	DISPOSITION

Location ____ QTR. Beginning   QTR. Ending   Group Code ____ (For EEO office use only) 1-2

CODES:

EEO JOB CATEGORY

01—Officials/Managers
02—Professionals
03—Technicians
04—Sales Workers
05—Office and Clerical
06—Craft Workers
07—Operatives
08—Laborers
09—Service Workers

ETHNIC IDENTIFICATION (E.I.)

W—White
B—Black
H—Hispanic
A—Asian or Pacific Islanders
N—American Indian or Alaskan Native

SEX

M—Male
F—Female

AGE

A—Below 40
B—40-45
C—46-50
D—51-55
F—56-60
G—61-65
H—66 & over

HANDICAP

Y—Yes
N—No

VETERAN

Y—Yes
N—No

DISPOSITION

1—Hired
2—Offer Outstanding
3—Offer Rejected
4—Applicant Regjected
5—No offer-No Opening

This Report Should Be Submitted to the Human Resource Department at the End of Every 90-Day Period

* THE NUMBERS ABOVE COLUMNS ARE FOR DATA INPUT INFORMATION ONLY.

Occupational Parity
Situation in which the proportion of minorities and women employed in various occupations within an organization is equal to their proportion in the organization's relevant labor market.

Systemic Discrimination
Occurs when there are large differences in either occupational or employment parity.

Relevant Labor Market
The geographical area in which a company recruits its employees.

Underutilization Practice of having fewer minorities or females in a particular job category than would reasonably be expected when compared to their presence in the relevant labor market.

company recruits its employees. For example, a small company may recruit its employees only within the standard metropolitan statistical area (SMSA) within which it falls; thus, its relevant labor market would be the SMSA. On the other hand, a large company that recruits nationally may have the whole nation as its relevant labor market. Furthermore, companies can have different relevant labor markets for different occupations. For example, the relevant labor market for a company's clerical employees might be the SMSA, while the relevant labor market for its engineers might be nationwide.

The EEOC can also examine the underutilization or concentration of minorities and/or females in certain jobs. **Underutilization** refers to the practice of having fewer minorities or females in a particular job category than would reasonably be expected when compared to their presence in the relevant labor market. **Concentration** refers to the practice of having more minorities or women in a job category than would reasonably be expected when compared to their presence in the relevant labor market.

Table 4–1 summarizes the steps involved in processing a discrimination charge. These are general in nature, and many variations are possible. For example, Section 706 of Title VII requires that before a charge can be filed with the EEOC, it must first be filed for 60 days with the state or local fair employment practices agency, if one exists, where the alleged discrimination occurred. The EEOC gives substantial weight to the final findings and orders of such agencies when its decision is rendered.

If the EEOC does not decide to file a lawsuit on behalf of the charging party, the individual still has the right to bring suit against the respondent. In this situation, the EEOC issues the charging party the statutory notice of a **right-to-sue letter.** The charging party must then file a civil action suit in the appropriate court within 90 days of receipt of the statutory notice of right to sue. HRM in Action 4.1 describes one EEOC lawsuit.

TABLE 4–1	STEPS IN PROCESSING A DISCRIMINATION CHARGE

Step Number	Procedure
1.	Charge is filed with the EEOC.
2.	The EEOC evaluates charge and determines whether or not to proceed with it.
3.	If it decides to proceed with the charge, the EEOC serves respondents with a copy of the actual charge within 10 days.
4.	A face-to-face, fact-finding conference is held between the charging party and the respondent. The conference is conducted by a staff member of the EEOC. The charging party is allowed ample time to explain and support each allegation, and the respondent is allowed to present and defend its position.
5.	If the charge is not resolved in step 4, the EEOC conducts an investigation of the charges.
6.	In cases where the EEOC finds reasonable cause that discrimination has occurred, a proposed conciliation agreement is sent to the respondents. The proposal normally includes a suggested remedy to eliminate the unlawful practices and to take appropriate corrective and affirmative action.
7.	If the respondents do not agree to the conciliation agreement, the EEOC makes a determination on whether the charge is "litigation worthy." As a practical matter, litigation worthy means that the evidence gathered during the investigation will support a lawsuit.
8.	If the charge is deemed litigation worthy, the EEOC then files a lawsuit in the appropriate state or federal court. Of course, decisions of these lower courts are often appealed to the Supreme Court.

Concentration   Practice of having more minorities or women in a job category than would reasonably be expected when compared to their presence in the relevant labor market.

Right-to-Sue Letter
Statutory notice by the EEOC to the charging party if the EEOC does not decide to file a lawsuit on behalf of the charging party.

Affirmative Action Plan
Written document outlining specific goals and timetables for remedying past discriminatory actions.

Preemployment Inquiry Guide

The On the Job example at the end of this chapter provides a guide to what can and cannot be asked of a job applicant in order to comply with equal employment opportunity legislation and court interpretations of that legislation. It is illustrative and attempts to answer the questions most frequently asked about equal employment opportunity law.

Affirmative Action Plans

An **affirmative action plan** is a written document outlining specific goals and timetables for remedying past discriminatory actions. All federal contractors and subcontractors with contracts over $50,000 and 50 or more employees are required to develop and implement written affirmative action plans, which are monitored by the OFCCP. In addition, all U.S. government agencies must prepare affirmative action plans. While Title VII and the EEOC do not require any specific type of written affirmative action plan, court rulings have often required affirmative action when discrimination is found.

A number of basic steps are involved in the development of an effective affirmative action plan. The EEOC has suggested the following eight steps.[1]

1. The chief executive officer of the organization should issue a written statement describing his or her personal commitment to the plan, legal obligations, and the importance of equal employment opportunity as an organizational goal.

2. A top official of the organization should be given the authority and responsibility for directing and implementing the program. In addition, all managers and supervisors within the organization should clearly understand their own responsibilities for carrying out equal employment opportunity.

3. The organization's policy and commitment to that policy should be publicized both internally and externally.

4. Present employment should be surveyed to identify areas of concentration and underutilization and determine the extent of underutilization.

HRM IN ACTION

Joe's Stone Crab House in Miami Beach

4.1

Joe's Stone Crab House, a Miami Beach Landmark restaurant which has been in existence since 1921, must for the next three years undergo court-approved hiring. As a result of a seven-year discrimination lawsuit filed against Joe's and a subsequent trial held in 1998, Judge T. K. Hurley of the U.S. District Court for the Southern District of Florida ruled that a court-appointed monitor must approve who gets hired at Joe's. In addition, the court has final approval over all help wanted ads and also determines the selection criteria for hiring. Joe's will also be required to adopt a corporate resolution indicating that it is an equal opportunity employer. Hurley's ruling stems from a suit filed by the Equal Employment Opportunity Commission against Joe's, claiming that during the period from 1986 until 1991, Joe's hired 108 men and no women as servers.

A serving position at Joe's is one of the most coveted in South Florida. Although stone crab season runs only from October through May, those selected as servers often make enough money to carry them through the remainder of the year without finding another position. Four of the five women who originally filed the suit will split roughly $155,000 in back wages and benefits. The suit has cost Joe's owner, Jo Ann Bass, more than $1 million in legal fees.

Source: Adapted from Robin Lee Allen, *Nation's Restaurant News,* September 7, 1998, p. 27.

5. Goals and timetables for achieving the goals should be developed to improve utilization of minorities and females in each area where underutilization has been identified.

6. The entire employment system should be reviewed to identify and eliminate barriers to equal employment. Areas for review include recruitment, selection, promotion systems, training programs, wage and salary structure, benefits and conditions of employment, layoffs, discharges, disciplinary actions, and union contract provisions affecting these areas.

7. An internal audit and reporting system should be established to monitor and evaluate progress in all aspects of the program.

8. Company and community programs supportive of equal opportunity should be developed. Programs might include training of supervisors in their legal responsibilities and the organization's commitment to equal employment, and job and career counseling programs.

Several Supreme Court decisions discussed in Chapter 3 (*City of Richmond* v. *J. A. Crosan Company*, and *Adarand Contractors* v. *Peña*) have removed the pressure for such plans except in cases of specific and probable acts of discrimination. The University of Texas—School of Law decision and proposition 209, which were also discussed in Chapter 3, may also have a significant impact on affirmative action programs. In addition, much discussion has been generated in both the House of Representatives and the Senate about eliminating all federal affirmative action programs. As of the writing of this text, no specific federal laws have been approved for the elimination of affirmative action programs.

Bona Fide Occupational Qualification (BFOQ)

Bona Fide Occupational Qualification (BFOQ) Permits employer to use religion, age, sex, or national origin as a factor in its employment practices when reasonably necessary to the normal operation of that particular business.

The **bona fide occupational qualification (BFOQ)** permits employers to use religion, age, sex, or national origin as a factor in their employment practices when it is reasonably necessary to the normal operation of that particular business. Section 703(e) of Title VII provides:

Notwithstanding any other provision of this [title], (1) it shall not be an unlawful employment practice for an employer to hire and employ employees, for an employment agency to classify or refer for employment any individual, or for an employer, labor organization, or joint labor management committee controlling apprenticeship or other training programs to admit or employ any individual in any such program, on the basis of his religion, sex, or national origin in those certain instances where religion, sex, or national origin is a bona fide occupational qualification reasonably necessary to the normal operation of that particular business or enterprise.

For example, to be able to use sex as a BFOQ in a job that requires lifting 100 pounds, the employer would be required to show that all or substantially all women cannot lift 100 pounds.

In fact, most employers most frequently raise the BFOQ exception because of sex. Section 1604.2(a) of the EEOC's *Guidelines on Discrimination because of Sex* states:

The Commission believes that the bona fide occupational qualification exception as to sex should be interpreted narrowly. Labels—"men's jobs" and "women's jobs"—tend to deny employment opportunities unnecessarily to one sex or the other.
(1) The Commission will find that the following situations do not warrant the application of the bona fide occupational qualification exception:
(i)   The refusal to hire a woman because of her sex based on assumptions of the comparative employment characteristics of women in general. For example, the assumption that the turnover rate among women is higher than among men.
(ii)   The refusal to hire an individual based on stereotyped characterizations of

the sexes. Such stereotypes include, for example, that men are less capable of assembling intricate equipment: that women are less capable of aggressive salesmanship. The principle of non-discrimination requires that individuals be considered on the basis of individual capacities and not on the basis of any characteristics generally attributed to the group.

(iii) The refusal to hire an individual because of the preferences of coworkers, the employer, clients or customers except as covered specifically in subparagraph (2) of this paragraph.

(2) Where it is necessary for the purpose of authenticity or genuineness, the Commission will consider sex to be a bona fide occupational qualification, e.g., an actor or actress.

The situations in which employers raise the BFOQ exception normally fall within three general categories:

1. Ability to perform (e.g., physical ability to perform jobs that involve strenuous manual labor).
2. Same-sex BFOQ that relates to accommodating the personal privacy of clients and customers.
3. Customer preference BFOQ where the customer states a desire to be served only by a person of a given sex.

However, the courts have very narrowly interpreted the sex discrimination defenses based on the BFOQ exception. For example, the courts permitted a same-sex BFOQ in a job that involved a potential invasion of another person's privacy in *City of Philadelphia* v. *Pennsylvania Human Relations Commission.*[2] The city, in operating youth study centers, restricted the employment of youth supervisors to persons of the same sex as those being supervised. On the other hand, in *Ludtke* v. *Kulm,*[3] the courts ruled that female reporters could not be excluded from a baseball team's postgame locker room since an interview area could be set up providing equal access for all reporters while protecting the privacy interests of the male ballplayers.

In the area of ability to perform the job, the courts have generally rejected the BFOQ defense and have usually held that each individual job applicant should be permitted an opportunity to demonstrate the ability to perform. The courts have also generally rejected customer preference as a BFOQ defense.

Age may be used as a BFOQ in certain limited situations. For example, age may be a BFOQ when public safety is involved, such as with airline pilots or interstate bus drivers.

Business Necessity

Business Necessity
Condition that comes into play when an employer has a job criterion that is neutral but excludes members of one sex at a higher rate than members of the opposite sex. The focus in business necessity is on the validity of stated job qualifications and their relationship to the work performed.

Business necessity comes into play when an employer has a job specification that is neutral but excludes members of one sex at a higher rate than members of the other. The focus in business necessity is on the validity of various stated job specifications and their relationship to the work performed. For example, in using a business necessity defense, an employer would be required to prove that the ability to lift 100 pounds is necessary in performing a warehouse job.

When a BFOQ is established, an employer can refuse to consider all persons of the protected group. When business necessity is established, an employer can exclude all persons who do not meet specifications regardless of whether the specifications have an adverse impact on a protected group.

Sexual Harassment

Sexual Harassment
Unwelcome sexual conduct that has the purpose or

One of the more current issues in equal employment opportunity is **sexual harassment.** The EEOC *Guidelines on Discrimination Because of Sex* define as unlawful

effect of unreasonably interfering with an individual's work performance or creating an intimidating, hostile, or offensive work environment.

any unwelcome sexual conduct that "has the purpose or effect of unreasonably interfering with an individual's work performance or creating an intimidating, hostile, or offensive work environment. Section 1604.11 of the *Guidelines* is reproduced in Table 4–2.

The very nature of sexual harassment sometimes makes it difficult to prove. The fact that such conduct normally occurs secretly and outside the employer's wishes and can grow out of or be alleged to grow out of consensual relationships makes the investigation of complaints most difficult. However, when deciding to impose liability on an employer for a supervisor's sexual harassment, the courts have considered an employer's failure to investigate complaints of sexual harassment as significant.[4]

Furthermore, the difficulty employees face in proving that an adverse decision was due to their sex and their failure to submit to sexual advances has been relaxed

T A B L E 4 – 2	**EEOC'S SEX DISCRIMINATION GUIDELINES**

(a) Harassment on the basis of sex is a violation of Sec. 703 of Title VII. Unwelcome sexual advances, requests for sexual favors, and other verbal or physical conduct of a sexual nature constitute sexual harassment when (1) submission to such conduct is made either explicitly or implicitly a term or condition of an individual's employment, (2) submission to or rejection of such conduct by an individual is used as the basis for employment decisions affecting such individual, or (3) such conduct has the purpose or effect of unreasonably interfering with an individual's work performance or creating an intimidating, hostile, or offensive working environment.

(b) In determining whether alleged conduct constitutes sexual harassment, the commission will look at the record as a whole and at the totality of the circumstances, such as the nature of the sexual advances and the context in which the alleged incidents occurred. The determination of the legality of a particular action will be made from the facts, on a case by case basis.

(c) Applying general Title VII principles, an employer, employment agency, joint apprenticeship committee or labor organization (hereinafter collectively referred to as "employer") is responsible for its acts and those of its agents and supervisory employees with respect to sexual harassment regardless of whether the specific acts complained of were authorized or even forbidden by the employer and regardless of whether the employer knew or should have known of their occurrence. The Commission will examine the circumstances of the particular employment relationship and the job functions performed by the individual in determining whether an individual acts in either a supervisory or agency capacity.

(d) With respect to conduct between fellow employees, an employer is responsible for acts of sexual harassment in the workplace where the employer (or its agents or supervisory employees) knows or should have known of the conduct, unless it can show that it took immediate and appropriate corrective action.

(e) An employer may also be responsible for the acts of non-employees, with respect to sexual harassment of employees in the workplace, where the employer (or its agents or supervisory employees) knows or should have known of the conduct and fails to take immediate and appropriate corrective action. In reviewing these cases the Commission will consider the extent of the employer's control and any other legal responsibility which the employer may have with respect to the conduct of such non-employees.

(f) Prevention is the best tool for the elimination of sexual harassment. An employer should take all steps necessary to prevent sexual harassment from occurring, such as affirmatively raising the subject, expressing strong disapproval, developing appropriate sanctions, informing employees of their right to raise and how to raise the issue of harassment under Title VII, and developing methods to sensitize all concerned.

(g) Other related practices: Where employment opportunities or benefits are granted because of an individual's submission to the employer's sexual advances or requests for sexual favors, the employer may be held liable for unlawful sex discrimination against other persons who were qualified for but denied that employment opportunity or benefit.

somewhat in favor of plaintiffs. In *Bundy* v. *Jackson*,[5] the District of Columbia Circuit Court established the allocation of the burden of proof in a sexual harassment case:

1. First, the employee must establish a *prima facie* case by proving he or she was *(a)* subjected to sexual harassment and *(b)* denied a benefit for which he or she was eligible and of which he or she had a reasonable expectation.

2. The burden then shifts to the employer to prove, by clear and convincing evidence, that its decision was based on legitimate, nondiscriminatory grounds.

3. If the employer succeeds in meeting that stringent burden, the employee may then attempt to prove that the employer's stated reasons are pretextual.

Many employers have implemented measures designed to avoid sexual harassment. Developing policies prohibiting sexual harassment and promptly investigating and responding to complaints of sexual harassment are essential to its prohibition. At a minimum, an organization's policy on sexual harassment should (1) define and prohibit sexual harassment and (2) encourage any employee who believes that he or she has been a victim of sexual harassment to come forward to express those complaints to management. HRM in Action 4.2 provides a true-false test to determine how much an individual knows about sexual harassment. It is

---

HRM IN ACTION

How Much Do You Know about Sexual Harassment?

4.2

A True or False Test for Employees   T   F

1. If I just ignore unwanted sexual attention, it will usually stop.   ☐   ☐

2. If I don't mean to sexually harass another employee, there's no way my behavior can be perceived by him or her as sexually harassing.   ☐   ☐

3. Some employees don't complain about unwanted sexual attention from another worker because they don't want to get that person in trouble.   ☐   ☐

4. If I make sexual comments to someone and that person doesn't ask me to stop, then I guess my behavior is welcome.   ☐   ☐

5. To avoid sexually harassing a woman who comes to work in a traditionally male workplace, the men simply should not haze her.   ☐   ☐

6. A sexual harasser may be told by a court to pay part of a judgment to the employee he or she harassed.   ☐   ☐

7. A sexually harassed man does not have the same legal rights as a woman who is sexually harassed.   ☐   ☐

8. About 90 percent of all sexual harassment in today's workplace is done by males to females.   ☐   ☐

9. Sexually suggestive pictures or objects in a workplace don't create a liability unless someone complains.   ☐   ☐

10. Telling someone to stop his or her unwanted sexual behavior usually doesn't do any good.   ☐   ☐

Answers: (1) False. (2) False. (3) True. (4) False. (5) False. (6) True. (7) False. (8) True. (9) False. (10) False.

A Test for Management Personnel

1. An employer is not liable for the sexual harassment of one of its employees unless that employee loses specific job benefits or is fired.   ☐   ☐

2. A court can require a sexual harasser to pay part of the judgment to the employee he or she has sexually harassed.   ☐   ☐

3. A supervisor can be liable for sexual harassment committed by one of his or her employees against another.   ☐   ☐

(Continues)

HRM IN ACTION

How Much Do You Know about Sexual Harassment?

A Test for Management Personnel

**4.2
(Continued)**

4. An employer can be liable for the sexually harassing behavior of management personnel even if it is unaware of that behavior and has a policy forbidding it.   □ □

5. It is appropriate for a supervisor, when initially receiving a sexual-harassment complaint, to determine if the alleged recipient overreacted or misunderstood the alleged harasser.   □ □

6. When a supervisor is talking with an employee about an allegation of sexual harassment against him or her, it is best to ease into the allegation instead of being direct.   □ □

7. Sexually suggestive visuals or objects in a workplace don't create a liability unless an employee complains about them and management allows them to remain.   □ □

8. The lack of sexual-harassment complaints is a good indication that sexual harassment is not occurring.   □ □

9. It is appropriate for a supervisor to tell an employee to handle unwelcome sexual behavior if he or she thinks that the employee is misunderstanding the behavior.   □ □

10. The intent behind employee A's sexual behavior is more important than the impact of that behavior on employee B when determining if sexual harassment has occurred.   □ □

Answers: (1) False. (2) True. (3) True. (4) True. (5) False. (6) False. (7) False. (8) False. (9) False. (10) False.

Source: Adopted from Brian S. Moskal, "Sexual Harassment: An Update," *Industry Week,* November 18, 1991, p. 40.

important to note that acts of sexual harassment can be committed, not only by men against women, but also by men against men, by women against women, and by women against men.

Comparable Worth and Equal Pay Issues

Comparable Worth Theory
The idea that every job has a worth to the employer and society that can be measured and assigned a value.

A controversial issue in equal employment opportunity is the **comparable worth theory.** This theory holds that every job by its very nature has a worth to the employer and society that can be measured and assigned a value. Each job should be compensated on the basis of its value and paid the same as other jobs with the same value. Under this theory, market factors such as availability of qualified workers and wage rates paid by other employers would be disregarded. This theory further holds that entire classes of jobs are traditionally undervalued and underpaid because they are held by women and that this inequality amounts to sex discrimination in violation of Title VII of the Civil Rights Act.

Proponents of this theory argue that the Equal Pay Act offers little protection to female workers because the act applies only to those job classifications in which men and women are employed. Further, the most serious form of wage discrimination occurs when women arrive at the workplace with education, training, and ability equivalent to that of men and are assigned lower-paying jobs that are held primarily by women.

In the 1981 case *County of Washington* v. *Gunther,*[6] the Supreme Court considered a claim of sex-based wage discrimination between prison matrons and prison guards. Prison matrons were being paid approximately 70 percent of what the guards were being paid. In its decision, the Court ruled that sex-based wage discrimination violates Title VII of the Civil Rights Act and that the plaintiffs could file suit under the law, even if the jobs were not equal. However, the Court's decision specifically stated that it was not ruling on the comparable worth issue.

In early 1985, the EEOC issued its first policy statement on comparable worth, stating that unequal pay for work of a similar value wasn't by itself proof of discrimination. The agency stated that it would not pursue "pure" comparable worth cases but would act in cases where it could be shown that employers intentionally paid different wages to women and men in comparable jobs. The exact meaning of this policy statement can, of course, be determined by the types of cases subsequently pursued by the EEOC.

In *AFSCME* v. *State of Washington*,[7] the employer had conducted a comparison of jobs but had not adjusted the wage rates in the female-dominated jobs to eliminate the wage differential between males and females. A district court had ordered the employer to make the adjustment partially on the basis of the comparable worth theory. However, this decision was overturned by the Ninth Circuit Court of Appeals.[8] The circuit court ruled that the value of a particular job to an employer is but one factor influencing the rate of compensation for that job. Other considerations may include the availability of workers willing to do the job and the effectiveness of collective bargaining in a particular industry. The court went further and said that a state could enact a comparable worth plan if it so chooses.

The parties to the *AFSCME* v. *State of Washington* suit reached an agreement in 1986 that settled the dispute. Under the agreement, 35,000 employees in female-dominated jobs reached pay equity with males in 1992. The estimated cost of the settlement to the state was $482 million.

Regardless of the court and EEOC decisions, however, organizations can take certain preventive steps to guard against pay inequities:

1. Employers should attempt to avoid overconcentrations of men or women (or members of various minority groups) in particular jobs.

2. Employers should evaluate whether there is any direct evidence of bias in setting wage rates, such as discriminatory statements or admission. If so and if there are also overconcentrations of females in particular jobs, the employer should formulate a new compensation plan to correct the disparity in the future. The outline of any plan, of course, will depend on each employer's particular situation.

3. Employers should resist, as much as possible, the temptation to deviate from an internal job evaluation survey or a market survey because of difficulties encountered in hiring or retaining employees at the rates established by such surveys.

4. An employer that utilizes a certain type of job evaluation system companywide and then deviates from it obviously runs a severe risk. Job evaluation is a procedure used to determine the relative worth of different jobs, and is discussed in depth in Chapter 14.

5. If an employer uses a job evaluation system or systems, it should constantly monitor the system to determine the average wages being paid to men and women for comparable jobs. Any disparities should be examined to see if they are defensible. If not, corrections should be made.

Other Areas of Employment Discrimination

Numerous other issues have arisen in the areas of employment discrimination. This section briefly covers some of these additional issues. HRM in Action 4.3 describes a recent jury award concerning obesity.

HRM IN ACTION

Obesity Discrimination

4.3

A San Francisco jury awarded $1 million to John Rossi, who said he was fired by an auto parts store because of his 400-pound girth. The 35-year-old former high school football star had accused Kragen Auto Parts of concocting a poor performance review to cover the real reason for his dismissal. The company maintained Rossi was fired for poor job performance. The jury agreed with Rossi that his obesity was a physical disability rather than a matter of overindulgence and that he was protected under a California law similar to the federal Americans with Disabilities Act.

Source: Adapted from *The Atlanta Journal/The Atlanta Constitution*, September 8, 1995, p. B8.

Religion

Title VII, as originally enacted, prohibited discrimination based on religion but did not define the term. The 1972 amendments to Title VII added 701(j):

> *The term* religion *includes all aspects of religious observance and practice, as well as belief, unless an employer demonstrates that he is unable to reasonably accommodate an employee's or prospective employee's religious observance or practice without undue hardship on the conduct of the employer's business.*

The most frequent accommodation issue under Title VII's religious discrimination provisions arises from the conflict between religious practices and work schedules. The conflict normally occurs for people who observe their Sabbath from sundown on Friday to sundown on Saturday. The EEOC's 1980 *Guidelines on Religious Discrimination* proposes the following:

1. Arranging the voluntary substitutes with similar qualifications; promoting an atmosphere where such swaps are regarded favorably; and providing a central file, bulletin board, or other means of facilitating the matching of voluntary substitutes.

2. Flexible scheduling of arrival and departure times; floating or optional holidays; flexible work breaks; and using lunch time and other time to make up hours lost due to the observation of religious practices.

3. Lateral transfers or changes in job assignments.

One significant case concerning religious discrimination is *TWA* v. *Hardison.*[9] Larry G. Hardison, a TWA employee whose religion required him to observe his Sabbath on Saturday, was discharged when he refused to work on Saturdays. Hardison had previously held a job with TWA that allowed him to avoid Saturday work because of his seniority. However, he voluntarily transferred to another job in which he was near the bottom of the seniority list. Due to his low seniority, he was required to work on Saturdays. TWA refused to violate the seniority provisions of the union contract and also refused to allow him to work a four-day workweek. TWA did agree, however, to permit the union to seek a change of work assignments for Hardison, but the union also refused to violate the seniority provisions of the contract.

The Supreme Court upheld the discharge on the grounds that (1) the employer had made reasonable efforts to accommodate the religious needs of the employee, (2) the employer was not required to violate the seniority provisions of the contract, and (3) the alternative plans of allowing the employee to work a four-day workweek would have constituted an undue hardship for the employer.[10]

The Supreme Court's ruling in this case was that an employer must reasonably accommodate religious preferences unless it creates an undue hardship for the employer. Undue hardship was defined as more than a *de minimus* cost; that is, the employer can prove it has reasonably accommodated a religious preference if it can show that the employee's request would result in more than a small (i.e., *de minimus*) cost to the employer.

Native Americans (Indians)

Courts have found Native Americans to be protected by Title VII. In addition, Section 703(i) of Title VII benefits Native Americans by exempting them from coverage by the act, in that preferential treatment can be given to Native Americans in certain employment:

> *Nothing contained in this title shall apply to any business or enterprise on or near an Indian reservation with respect to any publicly announced employment practice of such business or enterprise under which a preferential treatment is given to any individual because he is an Indian living on or near a reservation.*

HIV-Positive

In addition, individuals who are diagnosed as HIV-positive, even if they haven't developed symptoms, are considered to be disabled and entitled to the protection of the Americans with Disabilities Act (ADA). In 1998, the U.S. Supreme Court *(Bragdon* v. *Abbott)* ruled that HIV is so immediately physically devastating that it's an impairment from the moment of infection. In this case, Sidney Abbott revealed her positive status to her dentist, Randon Bragdon, and he refused to fill her tooth cavity in his office but suggested that he do the procedure at a hospital with Abbott incurring the additional expense. Abbott refused and sued Bragdon under the ADA and state law. The Supreme Court ruled in Abbott's favor and held that HIV status is a disability under the ADA.

Sexual Orientation

The EEOC and the courts have uniformly held that Title VII does not prohibit employment discrimination against effeminate males or against homosexuals.[11] Courts have also held uniformly that adverse action against individuals who undergo or announce an intention to undergo sex-change surgery does not violate Title VII.[12] Therefore, people who fall in those groups are protected only when a local or state statute is enacted to protect them. More court cases, however, must be decided before a clear picture can be gained concerning discrimination against people in these groups.

SUMMARY OF LEARNING OBJECTIVES

1. **Explain the role of the Employer Information Report, EEO–1.**
   This report, also known as *Standard Form 100,* must be completed by employers with 100 or more employees. It requires a breakdown of the employer's work force in specific job categories by race, sex, and national origin.

2. **Define employment parity, occupational parity, systemic discrimination, underutilization, and concentration.**
   When employment parity exists, the proportion of minorities and women employed by an organization equals the proportion in the organization's relevant labor market. Occupational parity exists when the proportion of minorities and women employed in various occupations within an organization is equal to their proportion in the organization's relevant labor market. Large differences in either occupational or employment parity are called systemic discrimination. Underutilization refers to the practice of having fewer minorities or females in a particular job category than would reasonably be expected when compared to their presence in the relevant labor market. Concentration means having more

minorities and women in a job category or department than would reasonably be expected when compared to their presence in the relevant labor market.

3. **Describe an affirmative action plan.**

   An AAP is a written document outlining specific goals and timetables for remedying past discriminatory actions.

4. **Define bona fide occupational qualification (BFOQ).**

   BFOQ permits employers to use religion, age, sex, or national origin as a factor in their employment practices when doing so is reasonably necessary to the normal operation of that particular business.

5. **Explain what is meant by business necessity.**

   Business necessity comes into play when an employer has a job requirement that is neutral but excludes members of one sex at a higher rate than members of the other.

6. **Define sexual harassment.**

   Sexual harassment is any unwelcome sexual conduct that has the purpose or effect of unreasonably interfering with an individual's work performance or creating an intimidating, hostile, or offensive work environment.

7. **Describe the comparable worth theory.**

   This theory holds that every job by its very nature has a worth to the employer and society and that this worth can be measured and assigned a value.

REVIEW QUESTIONS

Web site: Federal Legal Information through Electronics

www.fedworld.gov/supcourt

1. What legal powers does the EEOC have?
2. Explain the purpose of the Employer Information Report, EEO–1.
3. What is an applicant diversity chart?
4. Outline the steps in processing a discrimination charge.
5. What is an affirmative action plan?
6. What is BFOQ?
7. Define business necessity as it relates to equal employment opportunity.
8. Outline what actions constitute sexual harassment.
9. Explain what is meant by comparable worth.
10. What steps can be taken to eliminate pay inequities?

DISCUSSION QUESTIONS

1. "Affirmative action programs should be eliminated." Discuss your views on this statement.
2. "Comparable worth is an absurd idea." Discuss your views on this statement.
3. "We protect too many classes of people. Why can't we just let employers hire the best person for the job?" Discuss your views on these statements.
4. Identify several jobs for which you feel age or sex would be a BFOQ. Be prepared to discuss these jobs and your reasons for believing that age or sex is a BFOQ.

INCIDENT 4–1

Promotions for Lovers*

In *King* v. *Palmer*, 778 F.2d 878(D.C. Cir. 1985), a female employee claimed she had been denied a promotion that had gone to another female employee who was a

*Adapted from James A. Burns, Jr., "Equal Employment Opportunity," *Employee Relations Law Journal*, Spring 1990, pp. 629–37.

lover of one of the employee's supervisors. The district court first found that the plaintiff (King) had established a *prima facie* case of sex discrimination by showing that she was female, that she had applied for and been denied a promotion for which she was qualified, and that a substantial factor in that decision was a sexual relationship between a supervisor and the successful applicant for the promotion. The court also found that the employer's reason for not promoting King—that the successful applicant was better qualified for the promotion—was pretextual because it was unsupported by credible evidence. Nevertheless, the district court dismissed the case because it said King failed to provide direct evidence that the successful applicant and the supervisor were really having an affair. The court concluded that in these types of cases, a claim must not rest on rumor, knowing winks, and prurient overtones or on inferences allowed in divorce law.

The court of appeals reversed this decision, holding that King should not have been required to present direct evidence that the supervisor and the successful applicant were lovers. The court of appeals ruled that it was enough that King had presented circumstantial evidence of a sexual relationship such as kisses, embraces, and other amorous behavior.

Questions

1. What is a *prima facie* case?
2. Do you agree or disagree with the court of appeals decision? Why?

INCIDENT 4–2

Religion and Real Estate

Gloria and Robert Sapp, who run a real estate agency, are active Seventh-Day Adventists, as are most employees of the agency.

Ruth Armon, who described herself as a lapsed Lutheran at the time of her employment at the agency, states that she was emotionally upset at being unable to "tune out" statements directed to her about impending catastrophes, devil worship by Christian religions, and the asserted inadequacies of her personal religious observances.

She states that she became a target for statements critical of her beliefs and was told by Gloria Sapp that exposure to such statements was unavoidable in that workplace.

After eight months, Ruth Armon says, she had an argument with Robert Sapp growing out of her complaints about the religious talk and left the job, believing she was fired.

Questions

1. Does Ruth Armon have legitimate grounds for filing a religious discrimination case?
2. Should employees have a right to discuss their religious beliefs on the job?

EXERCISE 4–1

Affirmative Action Debate

The class divides into teams of four to five students. Each team should prepare to debate one of the following statements:

1. The federal government should not require affirmative action programs for private enterprise organizations that are federal contractors or subcontractors.

2. Affirmative action programs have been very helpful to minorities and women. Private enterprise organizations should be required to have affirmative action programs.

After the debate, the instructor should list on the board the points made by each team and discuss the issues involved.

EXERCISE 4–2

The Layoff

Two years ago, your organization experienced a sudden increase in its volume of work. At about the same time, it was threatened with an equal employment opportunity suit that resulted in an affirmative action plan. Under this plan, the organization has recruited and hired additional women and minority members.

Presently, the top level of management in your organization is anticipating a decrease in volume of work. You have been asked to rank the clerical employees of your section in the event that a layoff is necessary.

Following are biographical data for the seven clerical people in your section. Rank the seven people according to the order in which they should be laid off; that is, the person ranked first is to be laid off first, and so forth.

- **Burt Greene:** White male, age 45. Married, four children, five years with the organization. Reputed to be an alcoholic; poor work record.
- **Nan Nushka:** White female, age 26. Married, no children; husband has a steady job; six months with the organization. Hired after the affirmative action plan went into effect; average work record to date. Saving to buy a home.
- **Johnny Jones:** Black male, age 20. Unmarried: one year with organization. High performance ratings. Reputed to be shy—a "loner"; wants to start his own business some day.
- **Joe Jefferson:** White male, age 24. Married, no children, but wife is pregnant, three years with organization. Going to college at night; erratic performance attributed to work/study conflicts.
- **Livonia Long:** Black female, age 49. Widow, three grown children; two years with the organization. Steady worker whose performance is average.
- **Ward Watt:** White male, age 30. Recently divorced, one child; three years with the organization. Good worker.
- **Rosa Sanchez:** Hispanic female, age 45. Six children, husband disabled one year ago; trying to help support her family; three months with the organization. No performance appraisal data available.

Questions

1. What criteria did you use to rank the employees?
2. What implications does your ranking have in the area of affirmative action?

NOTES AND ADDITIONAL READINGS

1. *Affirmative Action and Equal Employment,* vol. 1 (Washington, D.C.: U.S. Equal Employment Opportunity Commission, 1974), pp. 10–11.
2. 7 Pa. Commw. Ct. 500, 300 A. 2d 97, 5 FEP 649 (Commw. Ct. 1973).
3. 461 F. Supp. 86, 18 FEP 246 (S.N.D.Y. 1978)
4. *Mumford* v. *James T. Barnes & Co.,* 441 F. Supp. 459, 17 FEP 107 (E.D. Mich. 1977)

5. 641 F. wd 934, 24 FEP 1155 (D.C. Cir. 1981).

6. *County of Washington* v. *Gunther,* 101 Sup. Ct. 2242 (1981).

7. *AFSCME* v. *State of Washington,* 32 FEP (BNA) 1577, Western District of Washington, September 16, 1983.

8. *AFSCME* v. *State of Washington,* CA-9, September 4, 1985.

9. 432 U.S. 64 (1977).

10. See also James G. Frierson, "Religion in the Workplace," *Personnel Journal,* July 1988, pp. 60–67.

11. Barbara L. Schlei and Paul Grossman, *Employment Discrimination Law,* 2nd ed. (Washington, D.C.: Bureau of National Affairs, 1983), p. 436.

12. Ibid.

ON THE JOB

Preemployment Inquiry Guide*

This guide is not a complete definition of what can and cannot be asked of applicants. It is illustrative and attempts to answer the questions most frequently asked about equal employment opportunity law. It is hoped that in most cases the given rules, either directly or by analogy, will guide all personnel involved in the preemployment processes of recruiting, interviewing, and selection. This guide pertains only to inquiries, advertisements, and so on, directed to all applicants prior to employment. Information required for records such as race, sex, and number of dependents may be requested after the applicant is on the payroll, provided such information is not used for any subsequent discrimination, as in upgrading or layoff.

These laws are not intended to prohibit employers from obtaining sufficient job-related information about applicants, as long as the questions do not elicit information which could be used for discriminatory purposes. Applicants should not be encouraged to volunteer potentially prejudicial information. The laws do not restrict the rights of employers to define qualifications necessary for satisfactory job performance, but require that the same standard of qualifications used for hiring be applied to all persons considered for employment.

It is recognized that the mere routine adherence to these laws will not accomplish the results intended by the courts and Congress. Employment discrimination can be eliminated only if the laws and regulations are followed in the spirit in which they were conceived.

---

*Source: C. M. Koen, Jr., "The Pre-Employment Inquiry Guide," *Personnel Journal,* October 1980, pp. 826–28. Copyright *Personnel Journal,* reprinted with permission. All rights reserved.

Subject	Permissible Inquiries	Inquiries to Be Avoided
1. Name	"Have you worked for this company under a different name? Is any additional information relative to change of name, use of an assumed name, or nickname necessary to enable a check on your work and educational record? If yes, explain."	Inquiries about name that would indicate applicant's lineage, ancestry, national origin, or descent. Inquiry into previous name of applicant where it has been changed by court order or otherwise. Inquiries about preferred courtesy title: Miss, Mrs., Ms.
2. Marital and family status	Whether applicant can meet specified work schedules or has activities, commitments, or responsibilities that may hinder the meeting of work attendance requirements. Inquiries as to duration of stay on job or anticipated absences that are made to males and females alike.	Any inquiry indicating whether an applicant is married, single, divorced, engaged, etc. Number and age of children. Information on child-care arrangements. Any questions concerning pregnancy. Any such questions that directly or indirectly result in limitation of job opportunities.
3. Age	Requiring proof of age in the form of a work permit or a certificate of age—if a minor. Requiring proof of age by birth certificate after being hired. Inquiry as to whether or not the applicant met the minimum age requirements as set by law, and requirement that upon hire proof of age must be submitted in the form of a birth certificate or other forms of proof of age. If age is a legal requirement, "If hired, can you furnish proof of age?" or statement that hire is subject to verification of age. Inquiry as to whether or not an applicant is younger than the employer's regular retirement age.	Requirement that applicant state age or date of birth. Requirement that applicant produce proof of age in the form of a birth certificate or baptismal record. The Age Discrimination in Employment Act (ADEA) of 1967 forbids discrimination against persons who are 40 years of age but less than 70. An amendment to the ADEA that took effect in 1987 eliminated mandatory retirement at age 70 for employees of companies with 20 or more employees.
4. Handicaps	For employers subject to the provisions of the Rehabilitation Act of 1973 and the Americans with Disabilities Act of 1990, applicants may be "invited" to indicate how and to what extent they are handicapped. The employer must indicate that: (1) compliance with the invitation is voluntary; (2) the information is being sought only to remedy discrimination or provide opportunities for the handicapped; (3) the information will be kept confidential; and (4) refusing to provide the information will not result in adverse treatment. All applicants can be asked if they are able to carry out all necessary job assignments and perform them in a safe manner.	An employer must be prepared to prove that any physical and mental requirements for a job are due to "business necessity" and the safe performance of the job. Except in cases where undue hardship can be proved, employers must make "reasonable accommodations" for the physical and mental limitations of an employee or applicant. "Reasonable accommodation" includes alteration of duties, alteration of work schedule, alteration of physical setting, and provision of aids. The Rehabilitation Act of 1973 forbids employers from asking job applicants general questions about whether they are handicapped or asking them about the nature and severity of their handicaps.
5. Sex	Inquiry or restriction of employment is permissible only where a bona fide occupational qualification exists. (This BFOQ exception is interpreted very narrowly by the courts and the EEOC.) The burden of proof rests on the employer to prove that the BFOQ does exist and that *all* members of the affected class are incapable of performing the job. Sex of applicant may be requested (preferably not on the employment application) for affirmative action purposes but may not be used as an employment criterion.	Sex of applicant. Any other inquiry which would indicate sex. Sex is *not* a BFOQ because a job involves physical labor (such as heavy lifting) beyond the capacity of *some* women, and employment cannot be restricted just because the job is traditionally labeled "men's work" or "women's work." Applicant's sex cannot be used as a factor for determining whether or not an applicant will be satisfied in a particular job. Questions about an applicant's height or weight, unless demonstrably necessary as requirements for the job.

Subject	Permissible Inquiries	Inquiries to Be Avoided
6. Race or color	General distinguishing physical characteristics such as scars, etc., to be used for identification purposes. Race may be requested (preferably not on the employment application) for affirmative action purposes but may not be used as an employment criterion.	Applicant's race. Color of applicant's skin, eyes, hair, etc., or other questions directly or indirectly indicating race or color.
7. Address or duration of residence	Applicant's address Inquiry into length of stay at current and previous addresses. "How long a resident of this state or city?"	Specific inquiry into foreign address that would indicate national origin. Names and relationship of persons with whom applicant resides. Whether applicant owns or rents home.
8. Birthplace	"Can you after employment submit a birth certificate or other proof of U.S. citizenship?"	Birthplace of applicant. Birthplace of applicant's parents, spouse, or other relatives. Requirement that applicant submit a birth certificate before employment. Any other inquiry into national origin.
9. Religion	An applicant may be advised concerning normal hours and days of work required by the job to avoid possible conflict with religious or other personal conviction. However, except in cases where undue hardship can be proven, employers and unions must make "reasonable accommodation" for religious practices of an employee or prospective employee. "Reasonable accommodation" may include voluntary substitutes, flexible scheduling, lateral transfer, change of job assignments, or the use of an alternative to payment of union dues.	Applicant's religious denomination or affiliation, church, parish, pastor, or religious holidays observed. Any inquiry to indicate or identify religious denomination or customs. Applicants may not be told that any particular religious groups are required to work on their religious holidays.
10. Military record	Type of education and experience in service as it relates to a particular job.	Type of discharge.
11. Photograph	May be required for identification after hiring.	Requirement that applicant affix a photograph to the application. Request that applicant, at his or her option, submit photograph. Requirement of photograph after interview but before hiring.
12. Citizenship	"Are you a citizen of the United States?" "Do you intend to remain permanently in the U.S.?" "If not a citizen, are you prevented from becoming lawfully employed because of a visa or immigration status?" Statement that, if hired, applicant may be required to submit proof of citizenship.	"Of what country are you a citizen?" Whether applicant or parents or spouse are naturalized or native-born U.S. citizens. Date when applicant or parents or spouse acquired U.S. citizenship. Requirement that applicant produce naturalization papers. Whether applicant's parents or spouse are citizens of the United States.
13. Ancestry or national origin	Languages applicant reads, speaks, or writes fluently (if another language is necessary to perform the job).	Inquiries into applicant's lineage, ancestry, national origin, descent, birthplace, or native language.
14. Education	Applicant's academic, vocational, or professional education; school(s) attended. Inquiry into language skills such as reading, speaking, and writing foreign languages.	Any inquiry asking specifically the nationality, racial, or religious affiliation of a school. Inquiry as to how foreign language ability was acquired.

Subject	Permissible Inquiries	Inquiries to Be Avoided
15. Experience	Applicant's work experience, including names and addresses of previous employers, dates of employment, reasons for leaving, salary history. Other countries visited.	
16. Conviction, arrest, and court record	Inquiry into actual *convictions* that relate reasonably to fitness to perform a particular job. (A conviction is a court ruling where the party is found guilty as charged. An arrest is merely the apprehending or detaining of the person to answer the alleged crime.)	Any inquiry relating to arrests. Any inquiry into or request for a person's arrest, court, or conviction record if not *substantially related* to functions and responsibilities of the particular job in question.
17. Relatives	Names of applicant's relatives already employed by this company. Names and address of parents or guardian (if applicant is a minor).	Name or address of any relative of adult applicant.
18. Notify in case of emergency	Names and addresses of persons to be notified in case of accident or emergency.	Name and address of *relatives* to be notified in case of accident or emergency.
19. Organizations	Inquiry into any organizations that an applicant is a member of, providing the name or character of the organization does not reveal the race, religion, color, or ancestry of the applicant. "List all professional organizations to which you belong. What offices do you hold?"	"List all organizations, clubs, societies, and lodges to which you belong." The names of organizations to which the applicant belongs, if such information would indicate through character or name the race, religion, color, or ancestry of the applicant.
20. References	"By whom were you referred for a position here?" Names of persons willing to provide professional and/or character references for applicant.	Requiring the submission of religious reference. Requesting reference from applicant's pastor.
21. Credit rating	None.	Any questions concerning credit rating, charge accounts, etc. Ownership of car.
22. Miscellaneous	Notice to applicants that any misstatements or omissions of material facts in the application may be cause for dismissal.	Any inquiry should be avoided that, although not specifically listed among the above, is designed to elicit information concerning race, color, ancestry, age, sex, religion, handicap, or arrest and court record, unless based upon a bona fide occupational qualification.

Southwest Airlines: Competing Through People*

For some organizations, the slogan "focus on customers" is merely a slogan. At Southwest Airlines, however, it is a daily goal. For example, Southwest employees responded quickly to a customer complaint: Five students who commuted weekly to an out-of-state medical school notified Southwest that the most convenient flight got them to class 15 minutes late. To accommodate the students, Southwest moved the departure time up by a quarter of an hour.

Southwest Airlines has built its business and corporate culture around the tenets of total quality management. Focus on the customer, employee involvement and empowerment, and continuous improvement are not just buzzwords to Southwest employees or to Herb Kelleher, CEO of Southwest Airlines in Dallas. In fact, Kelleher has even enlisted passengers in the effort to strengthen the customer-driven culture. Frequent fliers are asked to assist personnel managers in interviewing and selecting prospective flight attendants. Focus groups are used to help measure passenger response to new services and to generate new ideas for improving current services. In addition, the roughly 1,000 customers who write to the company every week generally get a personal response within four weeks.

The Airline Industry

Southwest has been posting hefty profits in an industry that expected to lose $2 billion in 1992. Since the 1978 Airline Deregulation Act, constant fare wars and intense competition have contributed to a turbulent environment for the industry. Under deregulation, the government no longer dictates where a given airline will fly and which cities should have service. Rates and service are now determined through competitive forces. The impact on the industry has been tremendous. In 1991 alone, three carriers went through bankruptcy and liquidation, and in early 1992, TWA sought protection from its creditors. Very few airlines, including Southwest, American, and Delta, continued to grow during the late 1980s and early 1990s.

Both external factors, such as the price of jet fuel and the strength of the economy, and internal factors, including routing system designs, computerized reservation systems, and motivated competent employees, help to determine success. The airline industry is capital intensive, with large expenditures for planes. In addition, carriers must provide superior customer service. Delayed flights, lost baggage, overbooked flights, cancellations, and unhelpful airline employees can quickly alienate an airline's passengers.

Southwest's Corporate Strategy

Herb Kelleher has been the primary force in developing and maintaining a vision and a strategy that have enabled Southwest Airlines to grow and maintain profitability. Created in the late 1960s as a low-fare, high-frequency, short-haul,

---

*Sources: J. Castelli, "Finding the Right Fit," *HRMagazine*, September 1990, 38–41; D. K. Henderson, "Southwest Luvs Passengers, Employees, Profits," *Air Transport World*, July 1991, 32–41; J. E. Hitchcock, "Southwest Airlines Renovates Benefits System," *HRMagazine*, July 1992, 54–56; C. A. Jaffe, "Moving Fast by Standing Still," *Nation's Business*, October 1991, 57–59; J. C. Quick, "Crafting an Organizational Culture: Herb's Hand at Southwest," *Organizational Dynamics*, 21 (1992), 45–56; R. S. Teitelbaum, "Southwest Airlines: Where Service Flies Right," *Fortune*, August 24, 1992, 115–16.

point-to-point, single-class, noninterlining, fun-loving airline, it expands by "doing the same old thing at each new airport," Kelleher reports.

"Taking a different approach" is the Southwest way, which has allowed the airline to maintain a 15 percent annual growth rate even during a period of drastic change. Although reservations and ticketing are done in advance of a flight, seating occurs on a first-come, first-serve basis and is only one illustration of the company's nonconformist practices. Turnaround times are kept to an industry low of 15 minutes with the help of pilots and crew, who clean and restock the planes. Refreshments are limited to soft drinks and peanuts, except on longer flights, when cookies and crackers are added to the menu. Southwest does not exchange tickets or baggage with other carriers. Kelleher has noted that if Southwest adopted an assigned seating and computerized, interlining reservation system, ground time would increase enough to necessitate the purchase of at least seven additional airplanes. At a cost of $25 million apiece, the impact on the fares customers pay would be high. Currently Southwest charges significantly less than its competitors.

Corporate Philosophy, Culture, and HRM Practices

How does Southwest maintain its unique, cost-effective position? In an industry in which antagonistic labor-management relations are common, how does Southwest build cooperation with a work force that is 85 percent unionized? Led by Kelleher, the corporation has developed a culture that treats employees the same way it treats passengers: by paying attention to them, being responsive to them, and involving them in decisions.

According to Ann Rhoades, vice president of people (the company's top HRM person), the company keeps employees not by paying them more than other airlines (although average pay is among the highest) but by treating them as part of "the family." As Kelleher has stated, "If you don't treat your own people well, they won't treat other people well." So Southwest's focus is not only on the customer but on the employees, too.

However, a positive work environment brings high expectations for employees' initiative and performance at Southwest. The company culture is evident in the recruitment and selection process, which takes place only in the cities to which Southwest flies "because we think people have to know us to understand us," says Rhoades. "We look for extroverts, people with a sense of humor and who say 'we' rather than 'I.'" Job applications for 2,400 positions in 1993 totaled approximately 90,000. This large labor pool allows the company to hire employees who most closely fit a culture in which they are asked to use their own judgment and to go beyond "the job description."

Kelleher's philosophy of "fun in the workplace" can be seen in a number of company practices. Company parties can be triggered by many events, including the CEO's birthday, when employees dress in black. The annual company chili cook-off, Southwest's annual awards dinner, and the every-Friday "Fun Day," when employees wear casual clothes or even costumes to work, illustrate the company credo that a sense of humor is a must and that relaxed people are productive people. Kevin Krone, area manager of marketing in the Detroit office, described efforts by the Detroit area airport employees to set up get-togethers to foster both fun and the commitment to the Southwest family that supports the airline's culture.

Employee involvement in decision making is another key tenet of organizational culture at Southwest. "Everyone affected by a decision is involved in making the decision," Rhoades says. An active, informal suggestion system and all types of incentives (cash, merchandise, and travel passes) reward employees for their ideas. Both teams and individuals are expected to contribute to the development of customer service improvements and cost savings.

Corporate responses to difficult issues are consistently formulated around the company philosophy. As the cost of benefits has risen, cost-conscious Southwest redesigned the employee benefits program into a flexible plan. However, the company went a step further. The director of benefits and compensation, Libby Sartain, believed that for the effort to succeed and satisfy employees, communication was critical. After seeking the advice of more than 700 employees in seven different cities, a promotional program that parodied newspapers and morning news shows was presented. Horoscopes, advice columns, and advertisements all promoted the new program, BenefitsPlus. Employees found this format more fun and less intimidating than the traditional benefits brochure. In fact, the effort won Southwest first place in the 1990 Business Insurance Employee Benefits Communication Awards competition. More important, employees understand their benefits options and appreciate the willingness of their organization to communicate openly.

Many human resource practices have been designed to support the company culture. Compensation programs are designed to increase the connections between Southwest and its employees, who enjoy the benefits of a profit-sharing program. Southwest employees own roughly 11 percent of the company's outstanding stock. The company's union contracts have avoided overly restrictive work rules to support the efficient operation of the company. Part of the company credo is that employees need (and want) to be able to step in wherever they are needed, regardless of job title or classification. In 1990, a five-year contract with the pilots was negotiated, demonstrating the trust between the employees and the organization. Annual employee turnover, at 7 percent, is the industry's lowest.

The combined focus on customers and employees has led to an increase in the diversity of Southwest's work force. To serve passengers in the southwestern United States more effectively, the company has been recruiting Spanish-speaking employees as well as offering a Spanish Berlitz course at a discount to current employees.

The employees of Southwest are actively involved in numerous community-based service projects at Ronald McDonald house and the Junior Olympics, among others. This commitment to service is encouraged and demonstrated within the organization, too. A catastrophe fund, initiated by employees, supports individual employees during personal crises. Departments frequently show appreciation to other departments by giving awards and parties.

Kelleher claims that Southwest will not expand through the purchase of other airlines because the difficulty of merging two corporate cultures, particularly when one is so strong, would be too great. "Our people are very proud of what they've created. They look on Southwest Airlines as a crusade, and a crusade is an emotional thing. I don't think you can transfer that.

"We tell our people that we value inconsistency," Kelleher explains. "By that I mean that we're going to carry 20 million passengers this year and that I can't foresee all of the situations that will arise at the stations across our system. So what we tell our people is, 'Hey, we can't anticipate all of these things, you handle them the best way possible. You make a judgment and use your discretion; we trust you'll do the right thing. If we think you've done something erroneous, we'll let you know—without criticism, without backbiting.' "

Employees offer a large number of what they consider to be "everyday examples" of ways they provide high-quality service to their customers. When a California customer service agent was approached by a harried man who needed to catch a flight to meet his vacationing family, the man wanted to check his dog onto the flight. Because Southwest does not fly animals, this could have caused him to miss the flight and his family. The service agent involved volunteered to take the dog home, care for it, and bring the dog back to meet the man upon his return two weeks later. A torn-up back yard and a very appreciative customer were the outcomes.

Critical Thinking Questions

1. How has Southwest dealt with the competitive airline industry today? Rank in order of importance the various human resource practices and business practices (such as the low-price strategy) that Southwest Airlines has developed to successfully meet its competitive challenges.

2. How might a ground crew supervisor at Southwest describe his or her job given the corporate culture and practices of this organization?

3. Which Southwest HRM strategies directly support total quality management?

4. What aspects of work life at Southwest do you think you would most enjoy and least enjoy? Why?

5. Would the HRM practices used at Southwest Airlines work in other organizations? Why or why not?

Staffing the Organization

Job Analysis and Job Design

Learning Objectives

After studying this chapter, you should be able to:

1. Define job analysis and job design.
2. Distinguish among a position, a job, and an occupation.
3. Describe several common uses of a job analysis.
4. Define job description and job specification.
5. Describe four frequently used methods of job analysis.
6. Interpret the nine-digit code used in the *Dictionary of Occupational Titles.*
7. Define essential functions and reasonable accommodation as interpreted under the Americans with Disabilities Act.
8. Identify several problems frequently associated with job analysis.
9. Define job scope and job depth and explain their relationship to job design.
10. Explain the sociotechnical approach to job design.
11. Distinguish among the following types of alternative work schedules: flextime, telecommuting, job sharing, and condensed workweek.

Job Analysis Process of determining and reporting pertinent information relating to the nature of a specific job.

Job analysis is "the process of determining and reporting pertinent information relating to the nature of a specific job. It is the determination of the tasks which comprise the job and of the skills, knowledge, abilities, and responsibilities required of the holder for successful job performance."[1] Put another way, job analysis is the process of determining, through observation and study, the pertinent information relating to the nature of a specific job.

Job analysis serves as the cornerstone of all human resource functions. Jobs must be analyzed before many of the other human resource functions can be performed. For example, effective recruitment is not possible unless the recruiter knows and communicates the requirements of the job. Similarly, it is impossible to design basic wage systems without having clearly defined jobs.

Job Design Process of structuring work and designating the specific work activities of an individual or group of individuals to achieve certain organizational objectives.

Job design is the process of structuring work and designating the specific work activities of an individual or group of individuals to achieve certain organizational objectives. Job design addresses the basic question of how the job is to be performed, who is to perform it, and where it is to be performed.

Job analysis and job design are directly linked to each other. In practice, most job analyses are performed on existing jobs that have previously been designed. However, it is not unusual for a job to be redesigned as the result of a recent job analysis. For example, a job analysis might reveal that the current method of performing a job (the job design) is inefficient or contains unnecessary tasks. This chapter examines the methods and techniques used in analyzing and designing jobs.

Basic Terminology

Today, the word *job* has different meanings depending on how, when, or by whom it is used. It is often used interchangeably with the words *position* and *task*. This section defines terms frequently encountered in job design and job analysis and shows how these terms relate to one another.

Micromotion Simplest unit of work; involves very elementary movement, such as reaching, grasping, positioning, or releasing an object.

Element An aggregation of two or more micromotions; usually thought of as a complete entity, such as picking up or transporting an object.

Task Consists of one or more elements; one of the distinct activities that constitute logical and necessary steps in the performance of work by an employee. A task is performed whenever human effort, physical or mental, is exerted for a specific purpose.

Duties One or more tasks performed in carrying out a job responsibility.

Responsibilities Obligations to perform certain tasks and assume certain duties.

Position Collection of tasks and responsibilities constituting the total work assignment of a single employee.

Job Group of positions that are identical with respect to their major or significant tasks and responsibilities and sufficiently alike to justify their being covered by a single analysis. One or many persons may be employed in the same job.

Occupation A grouping of similar jobs or job classes.

Recruitment Process of seeking and attracting a pool of people from which qualified candidates for job vacancies can be chosen.

The simplest unit of work is the micromotion. A **micromotion** involves a very elementary movement, such as reaching, grasping, positioning, or releasing an object. An aggregation of two or more micromotions forms an element. An **element** is a complete entity, such as picking up, transporting, and positioning an item. A grouping of work elements makes up a work task. Related **tasks** comprise the **duties** of a job.

Distinguishing between tasks and duties is not always easy. It is sometimes helpful to view tasks as subsets of duties. For example, suppose one duty of a receptionist is to handle all incoming correspondence. One task, as part of this duty, would be to respond to all routine inquiries. Duties, when combined with **responsibilities** (obligations to be performed), define a **position.** A group of positions that are identical with respect to their major tasks and responsibilities form a **job.** The difference between a position and a job is that a job may be held by more than one person, whereas a position cannot. For example, an organization may have two receptionists performing the same job; however, they occupy two separate positions. A group of similar jobs form an occupation. Because the job of receptionist requires similar skills, effort, and responsibility in different organizations, being a receptionist may be viewed as an **occupation.** Figure 5–1 graphically shows the relationships among elements, tasks, duties, responsibilities, positions, jobs, and occupations.

Job Analysis

Job analysis is the process of determining and reporting pertinent information relating to the nature of a specific job. It is the determination of the tasks which comprise the job and of the skills, knowledge, abilities, and responsibilities required of the holder for successful job performance.[2] The end product of a job analysis is written description of the actual requirements of the job.

As mentioned in the chapter introduction, job analysis is the cornerstone of all human resource functions. Specifically, data obtained from job analysis form the basis for a variety of human resource activities.[3] These activities include:

Job definition. A job analysis results in a description of the duties and responsibilities of the job. Such a description is useful to the current jobholders and their supervisors as well as to prospective employees.

Job redesign. A job analysis often indicates when a job needs to be redesigned.

Recruitment. Regardless of whether a job to be filled has been in existence or is newly created, its requirements must be defined as precisely as possible for **recruitment** to be effective. A job analysis not only identifies the job requirements but also outlines the skills needed to perform the job. This information helps to identify the type of people to be recruited.

Selection and placement. **Selection** is basically a matter of properly matching an individual with a job. For the process to be successful, the job and its requirements must be clearly and precisely known. A job analysis determines the importance of different skills and abilities. Once this has been done, comparisons of various candidates can be made more objectively.

Orientation. Effective job **orientation** cannot be accomplished without a clear understanding of the job requirements. The duties and responsibilities of a job must be clearly defined before a new employee can be taught how to perform the job.

Training. Job analysis affects many aspects of **training.** Whether or not a current or potential jobholder needs additional training can be decided only after the specific requirements of the job have been determined through a job analysis. Similarly, the establishment of training objectives is dependent on a job analysis.

FIGURE 5–1   **RELATIONSHIPS AMONG DIFFERENT JOB COMPONENTS**

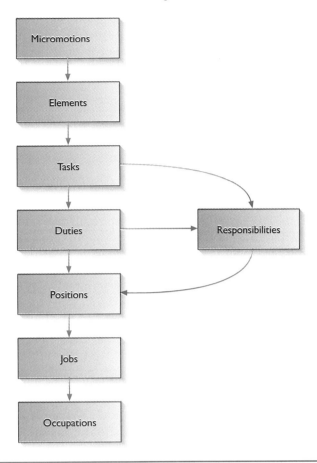

Selection Process of choosing from those available the individuals who are most likely to perform successfully in a job.

Orientation Introduction of new employees to the organization, work unit, and job.

Training Learning process that involves the acquisition of skills, concepts, rules, or attitudes to increase employee performance.

Another training-related use of job analysis is to help determine whether a problem is occurring because of a training need or because of some other reason.

Career counseling. Managers and human resource specialists are in a much better position to counsel employees about their careers when they have a complete understanding of the different jobs in the organization. Similarly, employees can better appreciate their career options when they understand the exact requirements of other jobs.

Employee safety. A thorough job analysis often uncovers unsafe practices and/or environmental conditions associated with a job. Focusing precisely on how a job is done usually uncovers any unsafe procedures.

Performance appraisal. The objective of performance appraisal is to evaluate an individual employee's performance on a job. A prerequisite is a thorough understanding of exactly what the employee is supposed to do. Then and only then can a fair evaluation be made of how an individual is performing.

Compensation. A proper job analysis helps to ensure that employees receive fair compensation for their jobs. Job analysis is the first step in determining the relative worth of a job by identifying its level of difficulty, its duties and responsibilities, and the skills and abilities required to perform the job. Once the worth of a job has been established relative to other jobs, the employer can determine an equitable wage or salary schedule.

As can be seen from the above list, most major human resource functions are dependent to some extent on a sound job analysis program.

When performing a job analysis, the job and its requirements (as opposed to the characteristics of the person currently holding the job) are studied. The analyst lists the tasks that comprise the job and determines the skills, personality characteristics, educational background, and training necessary for successfully performing the job. The initial stage of a job analysis should "report the job as it exists at the time of the analysis, not as it should exist, not as it has existed in the past, and not as it exists in similar establishments."[4] Table 5–1 outlines the general information obtained through a job analysis.

Products of Job Analysis

Job Description Written synopsis of the nature and requirements of a job.

Job analysis involves not only analyzing job content but also reporting the results of the analysis. These results are normally presented in the form of a job description and a job specification. A **job description** concentrates on describing the job as it is currently being performed. It explains, in written form, what the job is called, what is to be done, where it is to be done, and how it is to be done. While the format for job descriptions vary somewhat, most job descriptions contain sections that include the following: the job name, a brief summary description of the job, a listing of job duties and responsibilities, and an explanation of organizational relationships pertinent to the job. A **job specification** concentrates on the characteristics needed to perform the job. It describes the competency, educational, and experience qualifications the incumbent must possess to perform the job. A job specification may be prepared as a separate document or, as is more often the case, as the concluding section of a job description. Table 5–2 summarizes the information typically contained in a job description (including the job specification). The On the Job section at the end of this chapter contains a sample job description for the human resource manager of a manufacturing plant.

Job Specification Description of the competency, educational, and experience qualifications the incumbent must possess to perform the job.

A potential problem with all job descriptions is that they may become outdated. Often the job description is not periodically updated to reflect any changes that have occurred in the job. A good practice is to have the jobholder and his or her supervisor review the most current job description *annually* and determine whether the description needs updating. Ordinarily this review need not take much time; however, it seldom takes place at all unless a systematic effort is made. If it is determined that the job description needs updating, the jobholder should play a central role in revising it. Similarly, when a job description is being developed initially, the jobholder should be involved in the process.

TABLE 5–1	**INFORMATION PROVIDED BY A JOB ANALYSIS**
Area of Information	**Contents**
Job title and location	Name of job and where it is located.
Organizational relationship	A brief explanation of the number of persons supervised (if applicable) and the job title(s) of the position(s) supervised. A statement concerning supervision received.
Relation to other jobs	Describes and outlines the coordination required by the job.
Job summary	Condensed explanation of the content of the job.
Information concerning job requirements	The content of this area varies greatly from job to job and from organization to organization. Typically it includes information on such topics as machines, tools, and materials; mental complexity and attention required; physical demands and working conditions.

TABLE 5-2   CONTENTS OF A JOB DESCRIPTION

A job description should be a formal, written document, usually from one to three pages long. It should include the following:

- Date written.
- Job status (full-time or part-time; salary or wage).
- Position title.
- Job summary (a synopsis of the job responsibilities).
- Detailed list of duties and responsibilities.
- Supervision received (to whom the jobholder reports).
- Supervision exercised, if any (who reports to this employee).
- Principal contacts (in and outside the organization).
- Related meetings to be attended and reports to be filed.
- Competency or position requirements.
- Required education and experience.
- Career mobility (position[s] for which jobholder may qualify next).

Source: Adapted from Judith A. DeLapa, "Job Descriptions That Work," *Personnel Journal,* June 1989, p. 156.

Job Analysis Methods

Several methods are available for conducting a job analysis. Four of the most frequently used methods are discussed below.

Observation

Observation is a method of analyzing jobs that is relatively simple and straightforward. It can be used independently or in conjunction with other methods of job analysis. With observation, the person making the analysis observes the individual or individuals performing the job and takes pertinent notes describing the work. This information includes such things as what was done, how it was done, how long it took, what the job environment was like, and what equipment was used.

Motion Study and Time Study: Motion study and time study are both frequently used observation methods. Motion study (sometimes called *methods study*) involves determining the most efficient way to do a task or job. Basically, motion study involves determining the motions and movements necessary for performing a task or job and then designing the most efficient methods for putting those motions and movements together.

Time study is the analysis of a job or task to determine the elements of work required to perform it, the order in which these elements occur, and the times required to perform them effectively. The objective of a time study is to determine how long it should take an average person to perform the job or task in question.

One drawback to using the observation method is that the observer must be carefully trained to know what to look for and what to record. It is sometimes helpful to use a form with standard categories of information to be filled in as the job is observed to ensure that certain basic information is not omitted. A second drawback of most observation methods is that the application is somewhat limited to jobs involving short and repetitive cycles. Complicated jobs and jobs that do not have repetitive cycles require such a lengthy observation period that direct observation becomes impractical. For example, it would require a tremendous amount of time to observe the work of a traveling salesperson or a lawyer. On the other hand, the job analyst can use direct observation to get a feel for a particular job and then combine this method with another method to thoroughly analyze the

Motion Study Job analysis method that involves determining the motions and movements necessary for performing a task or job and then designing the most efficient methods for putting those motions and movements together.

Time Study Job analysis method that determines the elements of work required to perform the job, the order in which those elements occur, and the times required to perform them effectively.

job. Another possibility is to use work sampling. **Work sampling** is a type of observation method based on taking statistical samples of job actions throughout the workday, as opposed to continuous observation of all actions. By taking an adequate number of samples, inferences can be drawn about the requirements and demands of the job.

Interviews

Work Sampling   Job analysis method based on taking statistical samples of job actions throughout the workday and then drawing inferences about the requirements and demands of the job.

The *interview* method requires that the person conducting the job analysis meet with and interview the jobholder. Usually the interview is held at the job site. Interviews can be either structured or unstructured. Unstructured interviews have no definite checklist or preplanned format; the format develops as the interview unfolds. A structured interview follows a predesigned format. Structured interviews have the advantage of ensuring that all pertinent aspects of the job are covered. Also, they make it easier to compare information obtained from different people holding the same job.

The major drawback to the interview method is that it can be extremely time-consuming because of the time required to schedule, get to, and actually conduct the interview. This problem is naturally compounded when several people are interviewed for the same job.

Questionnaires

Job analysis questionnaires are typically three to five pages long and contain both objective and open-ended questions. For existing jobs, the incumbent completes the questionnaire, has it checked by the immediate manager, and returns it to the job analyst. If the job being analyzed is new, the questionnaire is normally sent to the manager who will supervise the employee in the new job. If the job being analyzed is vacant but is duplicated in another part of the organization, the questionnaire is completed by the incumbent in the duplicate job. The On the Job example at the end of this chapter contains a sample job analysis questionnaire.

The questionnaire method can obtain information from a large number of employees in a relatively short time period. Hence, questionnaires are used when a large input is needed and time and cost are limiting factors. A major disadvantage is the possibility that either the respondent or the job analyst will misinterpret the information. Also, questionnaires can be time-consuming and expensive to develop.

A popular variation of the questionnaire method is to have the incumbent write an actual description of the job, subject to the approval of the immediate supervisor. A primary advantage of this approach is that the incumbent is often the person most knowledgeable about the job. In addition, this method helps to identify any differences in perceptions about the job held by the incumbent and the manager.[5]

Position Analysis Question (PAQ):   The Position Analysis Questionnaire[6] is a highly specialized instrument for analyzing any job in terms of employee activities. It uses six major categories of employee activities (see Table 5–3). A total of 194 descriptors, called job elements, describe the six categories in detail. Using a five-point scale, one can analyze each description for the degree to which it applies to the job. Table 5–4 shows a sample page from the PAQ covering 11 elements of the information input category.

The primary advantage of the PAQ is that it can be used to analyze almost any type of job. Also, it is relatively easy to use. The major disadvantage is the sheer length of the questionnaire.

Management Position Description Questionnaire (MPDQ):   The MPDQ is a highly structured questionnaire designed specifically for analyzing managerial jobs. It contains 208 items relating to managerial responsibilities, restrictions, demands, and other miscellaneous position characteristics.[7] These 208 items are grouped under the 13 categories shown in Table 5–5. Like the PAQ, the MPDQ requires the analyst to check whether each item is appropriate to the job being analyzed.

TABLE 5-3	**EMPLOYEE ACTIVITY CATEGORIES USED IN THE PAQ**		
	Category	**Description**	**Examples**
	Information input	Where and how does the employee get the information used in performing the job?	Use of written materials. Near-visual differentiation.
	Mental processes	What reasoning, decision making, planning, and information-processing activities are involved in performing the job?	Level of reasoning in problem solving. Coding/decoding.
	Physical activities	What physical activities does the employee perform, and what tools or devices are used?	Use of keyboard devices. Assembling/disassembling.
	Relationships with other people	What relationships with other people are required in performing the job?	Instructing. Contacts with public, and/or customers.
	Job context	In what physical or social context is the work performed?	High temperature. Interpersonal conflict situations.
	Other job characteristics	What activities, conditions, or characteristics other than those described above are relevant to the job?	Specified work pace. Amount of job structure.

Functional Job Analysis

Functional job analysis (FJA) is a job analysis method developed by the U.S. Training and Employment Service (USTES) of the Department of Labor. FJA uses standardized statements and terminology to describe the content of jobs. The primary premises of FJA include the following:[8]

1. A fundamental distinction must be made between what gets done and what employees do to get things done. For example, bus drivers do not carry passengers; rather, they drive vehicles and collect fares.

2. Jobs are performed in relation to data, people, and things.

3. In relation to things, employees draw on physical resources; in relation to data, employees draw on mental resources; and in relation to people, employees draw on interpersonal resources.

4. All jobs require employees to relate data, people, and things to some degree.

5. Although the behavior of employees and their tasks can be described in numerous ways, only a few definitive functions are involved. For example, in interacting with machines, employees feed, tend, operate, and/or set up. Although each of these functions occurs over a wide range of difficulty and content, each essentially draws on a relatively narrow and specific range of similar kinds and degrees of employee characteristics and qualifications.

6. The levels of difficulty required in dealing with data, people, and things are hierarchical and can be represented by an ordinal scale.

Table 5–6 defines the levels of difficulty for various jobs with regard to data, people, and things. The lower the number associated with the function, the more difficult the function is. For example, synthesizing data (0) is more difficult than compiling data (3). After a job's difficulty has been described using this numerical scheme, the information can be combined with some general information to compare and identify jobs using the *Dictionary of Occupational Titles* (DOT). Once the closest job in the DOT has been located, the accompanying job description can be

T A B L E   5 – 4   **SAMPLE PAGE FROM THE POSITION ANALYSIS QUESTIONNAIRE (PAQ)**

Information Input

I.I Sources of Job Information

Rate each of the following items in terms of
the extent to which it is used by the worker as
a source of information in performing
the job.

Code	Extent of Use
N	Does not apply
1	Nominal/very infrequent
2	Occasional
3	Moderate
4	Considerable
5	Very substantial

I.I.I Visual Sources of Job Information

1 ___ Written materials (books, reports, office notes, articles, job instructions, signs, etc.)

2 ___ Quantitative materials (materials which deal with quantities or amounts, such as graphs, accounts, specifications, tables of numbers, etc.)

3 ___ Pictorial materials (pictures or picturelike materials used as *sources* of information, for example, drawings, blueprints, diagrams, maps, tracings, photographic films, x-ray films, TV pictures, etc.)

4 ___ Patterns/related devices (templates, stencils, patterns, etc., used as *sources* of information when *observed* during use; do *not* include here materials described in item 3 above)

5 ___ Visual displays (dials, gauges, signal lights, radarscopes, speedometers, clocks, etc.)

6 ___ Measuring devices (rules, calipers, tire pressure gauges, scales, thickness gauges, pipettes, thermometers, protractors, etc., used to obtain visual information about physical measurements; do *not* include here devices described in item 5 above)

7 ___ Mechanical devices (tools, equipment, machinery, and other mechanical devices which are *sources* of information when *observed* during use or operation)

8 ___ Materials in process (parts, materials, objects, etc., which are *sources* of information when being modified, worked on, or otherwise processed, such as bread dough being mixed, workpiece being turned in a lathe, fabric being cut, shoe being resoled, etc.)

9 ___ Materials *not* in process (parts, materials, objects, etc., not in the process of being changed or modified, which are *sources* of information when being inspected, handled, packaged, distributed, or selected, etc., such as items or materials in inventory, storage, or distribution channels, items being inspected, etc.)

10 ___ Features of nature (landscapes, fields, geological samples, vegetation, cloud formations, and other features of nature which are observed or inspected to provide information)

11 ___ "Man-made" features of environment (structures, buildings, dams, highways, bridges, docks, railroads, and other "man-made" or altered aspects of the indoor or outdoor environment which are *observed* or *inspected* to provide job information; do not consider equipment, machines, etc., that individuals use in their work, as covered by item 7)

Source: E. J. McCormick, P. R. Jeanneret, and R. C. Mecham, *Position Analysis Questionnaire.* Copyright 1969 by Purdue Research Foundation, West Lafayette, Ind. Reprinted with permission.

TABLE 5-5	MANAGEMENT POSITION DESCRIPTION QUESTIONNAIRE CATEGORIES

1. Product, marketing, and financial strategy planning.
2. Coordination of other organizational units and personnel.
3. Internal business control.
4. Products and services responsibility.
5. Public and customer relations.
6. Advanced consulting.
7. Autonomy of actions.
8. Approval of financial commitments.
9. Staff service.
10. Supervision.
11. Complexity and stress.
12. Advanced financial responsibility.
13. Broad personnel responsibility.

Source: W. B. Tornov and P. R. Pinto, "The Development of a Managerial Job Taxonomy: A System for Describing, Classifying, and Evaluating Executive Positions," *Journal of Applied Psychology* 61, no. 4 (1976), p. 414.

modified as necessary to fit the specific job being analyzed. At the very least, the DOT job description provides a very good starting point. Functional job analysis has the advantages of being relatively easy to learn and using a standardized format.

Dictionary of Occupational Titles

Compiled by the federal government, the DOT classifies and describes approximately 20,000 jobs. A nine-digit code is used to classify each job. The first digit indicates the occupational category, of which there are nine primary categories; Table 5–7 lists these categories. The second digit indicates a division within the primary occupational category. For example, occupations in administrative specialization

TABLE 5-6	LEVELS OF DIFFICULTY FOR WORKER FUNCTIONS IN FJA

Data		People		Things	
0	Synthesizing	0	Mentoring	0	Setting up
1	Coordinating	1	Negotiating	1	Precision working
2	Analyzing	2	Instructing	2	Operating-controlling
3	Compiling	3	Supervising	3	Driving-operating
4	Computing	4	Diverting	4	Manipulating
5	Copying	5	Persuading	5	Tending
6	Comparing	6	Speaking-signaling	6	Feeding-offbearing
		7	Serving	7	Handling
		8	Taking instructions-helping		

Note: The hyphenated factors—speaking-signaling, taking instructions-helping, operating-controlling, driving-operating, and feeding-offbearing—are single functions.

Source: U.S. Department of Labor, *Handbook for Analyzing Jobs* (Washington, D.C.: U.S. Government Printing Office, 1972), p. 73.

T A B L E   5 – 7   **NINE OCCUPATIONAL CATEGORIES USED BY THE DOT**

> 1. Professional, technical, and managerial
> 2. Clerical and sales
> 3. Service
> 4. Agriculture, fishing, forestry, and related
> 5. Processing
> 6. Machine trades
> 7. Bench work
> 8. Structural work
> 9. Miscellaneous

comprise a division within the primary category of professional, technical, and managerial occupations. The third digit indicates the group within the division into which the job is classified. For example, occupations in personnel administration are a group within the administrative specialization division. The fourth, fifth, and sixth digits reflect the difficulty on the job with regard to data, people, and things, respectively, using the numerical scheme shown in Table 5–6.

The last three digits differentiate, in alphabetical order, those jobs that have the same first six digits. Thus, a number of occupations may have the same first six digits, but no two can have the same nine digits. If the first six digits apply to only one occupational title, the last three digits are always 011. Figure 5–2 shows how the DOT classifies a human resources manager.

O*NET Dictionary of Occupational Titles[9]

The O*NET is a new computerized database of information on occupations. Developed by the U.S. Department of Labor, O*NET stands for "The Occupational Information Network." The O*NET, first released in early 1998, will eventually replace the DOT, which was last revised in 1991. Many of the 12,741 occupations listed in the DOT were similar, highly specialized, or employed few people. The O*NET, with 1,172 occupations (others will be added), is much smaller and hopefully more useful.

O*NET is not a book but rather a database with many details about each occupation. In addition to a narrative description, each O*NET occupation includes material on 445 data element descriptions. Access to the electronic form of the O*NET data will become readily available in the future.

The ADA and Job Analysis[10]

As discussed in Chapter 3, the Americans with Disabilities Act (ADA) prohibits discrimination against qualified individuals with disabilities in regard to all employment practices, terms, conditions, or privileges of employment. In essence, this prohibition covers the entire employment process. "Qualified individuals with disabilities" are persons who have a disability and meet the skill, education, experience, and other job-related requirements of the position held or desired and can perform the essential functions of the position with or without reasonable accommodation. The ADA also requires the identification of the essential functions of each job and a reasonable accommodation to the disabilities of qualified individuals. The job analysis process is the basic method used to identify essential job functions. An *essential job function* is one that is fundamental to successful performance of the job; in contrast, *marginal job functions* may be performed at certain times but are incidental to the main purpose of the job. A particular job function is

F I G U R E   5 – 2   HUMAN RESOURCES MANAGER AS CLASSIFIED BY THE DOT

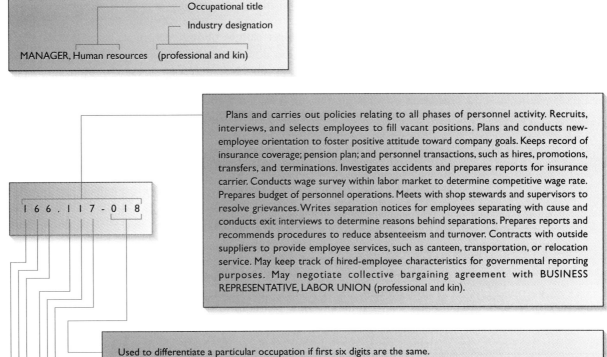

Plans and carries out policies relating to all phases of personnel activity. Recruits, interviews, and selects employees to fill vacant positions. Plans and conducts new-employee orientation to foster positive attitude toward company goals. Keeps record of insurance coverage; pension plan; and personnel transactions, such as hires, promotions, transfers, and terminations. Investigates accidents and prepares reports for insurance carrier. Conducts wage survey within labor market to determine competitive wage rate. Prepares budget of personnel operations. Meets with shop stewards and supervisors to resolve grievances. Writes separation notices for employees separating with cause and conducts exit interviews to determine reasons behind separations. Prepares reports and recommends procedures to reduce absenteeism and turnover. Contracts with outside suppliers to provide employee services, such as canteen, transportation, or relocation service. May keep track of hired-employee characteristics for governmental reporting purposes. May negotiate collective bargaining agreement with BUSINESS REPRESENTATIVE, LABOR UNION (professional and kin).

Used to differentiate a particular occupation if first six digits are the same.

Difficulty regarding things (7 indicates handling of things is required).

Difficulty regarding people (1 indicates negotiating with people is required).

Difficulty regarding data (1 indicates coordination of data is required).

Group within division of primary occupational category (166 indicates occupations in personnel administration).

Division of primary occupational category (16 indicates occupations in administrative specializations).

Primary occupational category (1 indicates professional, technical, and managerial).

Source: U.S. Department of Labor, Employment and Training Administration, *Dictionary of Occupational Titles,* 4th ed., rev. 1991 (Washington, D.C.: U.S. Government Printing Office, 1991).

considered marginal if its performance is a matter of convenience and not a necessity. Table 5–8 presents several questions that should be asked to determine whether a particular job function is essential.

Reasonable accommodation means the employer may be required to alter the conditions of a particular job so as to enable the candidate to perform all essential functions. However, an employer cannot be required to make an accommodation that causes undue hardship for the employer. Undue hardship refers to any accommodation that would be unduly costly, substantial, or descriptive or that would fundamentally alter the nature or operation of the business. HRM in Action 5.1 discusses a recent agreement between Wendy's International and the U.S. Department of Justice regarding the physical layout of some Wendy's stores.

Potential Problems with Job Analysis

In analyzing jobs, certain problems can occur. Some of these problems result from natural human behavior; others stem from the nature of the job analysis process. Some of the most frequently encountered problems associated with job analyses are the following:[11]

Top management support is missing. Top management should at least make it clear to all employees that their full and honest participation is extremely important to the process. Unfortunately, the message is often not communicated.

Only a single means and source are used for gathering data. As discussed in this chapter, there are many proven methods for gathering job data. All too often, a job analysis relies on only one of these methods when a combination of methods might provide better data.

The supervisor and the jobholder do not participate in the design of the job analysis procedure. Too many analyses are planned and implemented by one person who assumes exclusive responsibility for the project. The jobholder and his or her supervisor should be involved early in the planning of the project.

No training or motivation exists for jobholders. Job incumbents are potentially a great source of information about the job. Unfortunately, they are seldom trained

---

T A B L E 5 – 8   **QUESTIONS TO BE ADDRESSED TO DETERMINE ESSENTIAL FUNCTIONS**

1. Does the position exist to perform these functions? If the performance of a particular function is the principal purpose for hiring a person, it would be an essential function.

2. Would the removal of the function fundamentally alter the position? If the purpose of the position can be fulfilled without performing the function, it isn't essential.

3. What's the degree of expertise or skill required to perform the function? The fact that an employee is hired for his or her specialized expertise to perform a particular function is evidence that the function is essential.

4. How much of the employee's time is spent performing the function? The fact that an employee spends a substantial amount of time performing a particular function is evidence that the function is essential.

5. What are the consequences of failure to perform the function? The fact that the consequences of failure are severe is evidence that the function is essential.

6. How many other employees are available among whom the function can be distributed? The smaller the number of employees available for performing a group of functions, the greater the likelihood that any one of them will have to perform a particular function.

Source: Wayne E. Barlow and Edward Z. Hare, "A Practical Guide to the Americans with Disabilities Act," *Personnel Journal,* June 1992, p. 54.

HRM IN ACTION

ADA and Wendy's

5.1

www.wendys.com

Since the Americans with Disabilities Act (ADA) went into effect, new buildings that accommodate the public must be constructed within certain architectual guidelines. The primary focus of these guidelines has been to provide wheelchair access. For restaurants built before 1993 the law requires "reasonable physical changes." These "reasonable physical changes" have included entrance ramps with handrails and access to bathrooms.

A recent agreement between Wendy's International and the U.S. Department of Justice goes beyond just the issue of access. In the agreement, Wendy's consented to altering their serpentine queue lines (winding-customer waiting lines) to a minimum of 42 inches wide with a 48-inch turn radius or 36 inches wide with a 60-inch turning radius. Previously, many restaurant chains said they have accommodated customers in wheelchairs by having them bypass the serpentine queue and go straight to the counter. However, perple with disabilities have said that they do not want special treatment and that they don't want to be forced to wait on the side of the line until an employee notices them. Wendy's officials believe that renovation costs per store will be minimal.

Source: Amy Zuber, "Wendy's to Make Stores More Accessible to Disabled," *Nation's Restaurant News*, September 21, 1998, p. 6.

or prepared to generate quality data for a job analysis. Also, jobholders are rarely made aware of the importance of the data and almost never are rewarded for providing good data.

Employees are not allowed sufficient time to complete the analysis. Usually a job analysis is conducted as though it were a crash program, and employees are not given sufficient time to do a thorough job analysis.

Activities may be distorted. Without proper training and preparation, employees may submit distorted data, either intentionally or not. For example, employees are likely to speed up if they know they are being watched. Employee involvement from the beginning of the project is a good way to minimize this problem.

There is a failure to critique the job. Many job analyses do not go beyond the initial phase of reporting what the jobholder currently does. These data are extremely valuable, but the analysis should not stop here. The job should be critiqued to determine whether it is being done correctly or whether improvements can be made.

Job Design

As mentioned in the introduction to this chapter, job design is the process of structuring work and designating the specific work activities of an individual or group of individuals to achieve certain organizational objectives. Designing a job involves making decisions as to who, what, where, when, why, and how the job will be performed.

The job design process can generally be divided into three phases:

1. The specification of individual tasks: What different tasks must be performed?

2. The specification of the method of performing each task: Specifically, how will each task be performed?

3. The combination of individual tasks into specific jobs to be assigned to individuals: How will the different tasks be grouped to form jobs?[12]

Phases 1 and 3 determine the content of the job, while phase 2 indicates precisely how the job is to be performed. The overall goal of job design is to develop work assignments that meet the requirements of the organization and the technology; and that satisfy the personal and individual requirements of the jobholder.[13] The key to successful job design is to balance the requirements of the organization and the jobholder. For many years, the prevailing practice in designing jobs was to focus almost entirely on simplifying the tasks to be undertaken. This usually resulted in making jobs as specialized as possible. While job specialization has many advantages, as outlined in Table 5–9, it can result in boredom and even degradation of the jobholder. A classic example of specialization is the automobile assembly line. The idea is to specialize but not overdo it. HRM in Action 5.2 discusses a very early example of specialization.

Job Scope and Job Depth

Job Scope   Number and variety of tasks performed by the jobholder.

Job scope and job depth are two important dimensions of job design. **Job scope** refers to the number and variety of different tasks performed by the jobholder. In a job with narrow scope, the jobholder performs a few different tasks and repeats those tasks frequently. The negative effects of jobs limited in scope vary with the jobholder, but can result in more errors and lower quality.

Job Depth   Freedom of jobholders to plan and organize their own work, work at their own pace, and move around and communicate.

Job depth refers to the freedom of jobholders to plan and organize their own work, work at their own pace, and move around and communicate as desired. A lack of job depth can result in job dissatisfaction, which in turn can lead to tardiness, absenteeism, and even sabotage.

A job can be high in job scope and low in job depth, or vice versa. For example, newspaper delivery involves the same few tasks each time, but there is considerable freedom in organizing and pacing the work. Therefore, the job is low in scope but high in depth. Of course, many jobs are low (or high) in both job scope and job depth.

Sociotechnical Approach to Job Design

The *sociotechnical approach* to job design was first introduced as an alternative to viewing job design strictly as a matter of specializing the job as much as possible. The thrust of the sociotechnical approach is that both the technical system and the accompanying social system should be considered when designing jobs.[14] According to this concept, employers should design jobs by taking a holistic, or systems, view of the entire job situation, including its physical and social environment. The sociotechnical approach is situational because few jobs involve identical technical requirements and social surroundings. Specifically, the sociotechnical approach requires that the job designer carefully consider the role of the employees in the sociotechnical system, the nature of the tasks performed, and the autonomy of the work group. Ideally, the sociotechnical approach merges the technical

---

T A B L E   5 – 9   **ADVANTAGES OF JOB SPECIALIZATION**

1. Fewer skills required per person, which makes it easier to recruit and train employees.

2. Increased proficiency through repetition and practice of the same tasks.

3. More efficient use of skills by primarily utilizing each employee's best skills.

4. Low wages due to the ease with which labor can be substituted.

5. More conformity in the final product or service.

6. Different tasks performed concurrently.

HRM IN ACTION

Adam Smith and Specialization

5.2

Specialization was of concern to managers at least as early as 1776. In *An Inquiry into the Nature and Causes of the Wealth of Nations,* Adam Smith discussed at length the importance of specialization and used pinmaking as an example of the benefits. According to Smith, specialization in pinmaking meant that "one man draws out the wire, another straightens it, a third cuts it, a fourth points, a fifth grinds it at the top for receiving the head, and so on. In a factory of 10 men, . . . they could, when they exerted themselves, make among them about 12 pounds of pins in a day. There are in a pound upwards of 4,000 pins of middling size." Smith says, "If they had all wrought separately and independently . . . they certainly could not each have made 20, perhaps not 1 pin in a day." Smith concluded that three different circumstances led to the benefits of specialization: (1) the increased dexterity of every individual worker, (2) the saving of time lost in moving from one type of work to another, and (3) the invention of machines that enabled one worker to do the work of many.

Source: Adam Smith, *An Inquiry into the Nature and Causes of the Wealth of Nations* (Edinburgh, Scotland: Arch. Constable, 1806), pp. 7–8.

needs of the organization with the social needs of the employees involved in decision making. The following guidelines use the sociotechnical approach to designing jobs:[15]

1. A job needs to be reasonably demanding for the individual in terms other than sheer endurance, yet provide some variety (not necessarily novelty).

2. Employees need to be able to learn on the job and to continue learning.

3. Employees need some minimum area of decision making that they can call their own.

4. Employees need some minimal degree of social support and recognition in the workplace.

5. Employees need to be able to relate what they do and what they produce to their social lives.

6. Employees need to believe that the job leads to some sort of desirable future.

The sociotechnical approach to job design has been applied in many countries, often under the heading "autonomous work groups" or "individual democracy" projects.[16] Modern-day job designs based on the concepts of self-managed work teams or group productivity usually have their roots in the sociotechnical approach.

The Physical Work Environment

The physical work environment, which includes factors such as temperature, humidity, ventilation, noise, light, and color, can have an impact on the design of jobs. While studies clearly show that adverse physical conditions have a negative effect on performance, the degree of influence varies from individual to individual.

The implementation of the Occupational Safety and Health Act (OSHA) in 1970 magnified the importance of safety considerations in the design process. Designed to reduce the incidence of job-related injuries and illnesses, the act outlines very specific federal safety guidelines that all organizations in the United States must follow. Chapter 20 discusses OSHA at length.

In general, the work environment should allow for normal lighting, temperature, ventilation, and humidity. Baffles, acoustical wall materials, and sound absorbers should be used where necessary to reduce unpleasant noises. If employees must be exposed to less than ideal conditions, it is wise to limit these exposures to short periods of time to minimize the probability that the worker will suffer any permanent physical or psychological damage.

Alternative Work Schedules

Another factor that affects job design is the work schedule. In the last several years, organizations have increasingly departed from traditional work schedules in an attempt to increase productivity or decrease cost. While changes in the work schedule do not generally alter work to be done, they can affect how the work is allocated. The most common alternative work schedules are flextime, telecommuting, job sharing, and the condensed workweek.

Flextime

Flextime, or flexible working hours, allows employees to choose, within certain limits, when they start and end their workday. Usually the organization defines a core period (such as 10 A.M. to 3 P.M.) when all employees will be at work. It is then left to each employee to decide when to start and end the workday as long as the hours encompass the core period. Some flextime programs allow employees to vary the hours worked each day as long as they meet some specific total, which is usually 40 hours. Flextime has the advantage of allowing different employees to accommodate different lifestyles and schedules. Other potential advantages include avoiding rush hours and having less absenteeism and tardiness. From the employer's viewpoint, flextime can have the advantage of providing an edge in recruiting new employees and also in retaining hard-to-find qualified employees. Also, organizations with flextime schedules have reported an average increase of 1 to 5 percent in productivity.[17] On the downside, flextime can create communication and coordination problems for supervisors and managers.

Telecommuting

Telecommuting is the practice of working at home or while traveling and being able to interact with the office. Today's information technology (PCs, the Internet, cellular phones, etc.) has made telecommuting a reality for many companies. According to the American Business Association, some 30 million Americans now work at home at least part of the time, and nearly 9 million of these are corporate employees who used to work at central work places.[18] A large number of companies are now using telecommuting to recruit qualified employees, especially in tight labor markets.[19]

Advantages of telecommuting include less travel time, avoiding rush hour, avoiding distractions at the office, and being able to work flexible hours. Potential disadvantages of telecommuting are insurance concerns relating to the health and safety of employees working at home. Another drawback is that some state and local laws restrict just what work can be done at home. HRM in Action 5.3 describes a telecommuting program used by Florida Power and Light.

Job Sharing

Job sharing is a relatively new concept whereby two or more part-time individuals perform a job that would normally be held by one full-time person. Job sharing can be in the form of equally shared responsibilities or split duties, or a combination of both. Job sharing is especially attractive to people who want to work, but not full-time. A critical factor relating to job sharing is how benefits are handled. Often benefits are prorated between the part-time employees. Some organizations allow job-sharing employees to purchase full health insurance by paying the difference between their prorated benefit and the premium for a full-time employee. HRM in Action 5.4 discusses an example of job sharing at the executive level.

Telecommuting at Florida Power and Light

5.3

www.fpl.com

What started as a pilot group of 8 Florida Power and Light (FPL) employees in the Customer Relations and Sales department in January 1995 has now grown to nearly 400 employees working from home. Willie Ho, FPL's south area customer relations and sales manager thought telecommuting could help FPL cut costs while enabling sales representatives to be more productive. A team charged with evaluating the plusses and minuses of his department soon realized that sales representatives would need mobile computer equipment to gain access to customer information and energy management data as they traveled around their territories. Human resource people worked with industry consultants to provide training and support for future telecommuters.

Sales representatives at FPL now do home duties at what used to be normal work hours; this then allows them to meet with customers at the customers' convenience, including evenings and Saturdays. FPL believes that, with rush hour traffic and distractions minimized, their field reps are now more effective. Corporate costs are also reduced. In Ho's sales department alone, FPL eliminated five offices and consolidated three others, thus eliminating 10,000 square feet of office space.

Source: Brian Packs, "Telecommuting Brightens the Future for Florida Power and Light," *Employee Relations Today,* Winter 1998, pp. 65–72; and Rick Bush, "Telecommuting on the Rise," *Transmission & Distribution World,* November 1997, p. 4.

Condensed Workweek

Under the *condensed workweek,* the number of hours worked per day is increased and the number of days in the workweek is decreased. Typically, this is done by having employees work 10 hours per day for four days per week (known as 4/40). Other variations of the condensed workweek include reducing the total hours worked to 36 or 38 hours. Advantages of the condensed workweek are lower absenteeism and tardiness, less start-up time, and more time available for employees to take care of personal business. One potential disadvantage is the fatigue that often accompanies longer hours. A recent survey by Buck Consultants, Inc., reported that 52 percent of employers offer flextime, 22 percent offer condensed workweeks, and 16 percent offer telecommuting.[20]

Job Sharing at a Radisson Hotel

5.4

www.radisson.com

The Radisson Phoenix Airport Hotel is reaping rewards for implementing flextime and allowing two employees—Kelly Clark Theut and Laura Scheller—to share the position and work load of sales director. While job sharing requires constant communication and cooperation, Theut and Scheller agree that the benefits far outweigh the problems. By relieving the stresses of trying to balance home and career, both women believe that they can better concentrate on their job while at work and on their families when at home.

The general manager of the hotel, Paul Gibson, believes that the arrangement is beneficial for the hotel. "We have the benefit of capitalizing on ideas and energies from two people," Gibson said. "The fact that both are more satisfied with their professional and personal lives adds to their effectiveness on the job." Job sharing at the executive level is rare in the hospitality industry, according to Radisson Hotels Worldwide.

Source: Adapted from Marty Whitford, "Managers Juggle Schedules to Accommodate Employees," *Hotel & Motel Management,* September 7, 1998, p. 48–50.

SUMMARY OF LEARNING OBJECTIVES

1. **Define *job analysis* and *job design*.**
   Job analysis is the process of determining and reporting pertinent information relating to the nature of a specific job. It is the determination of the tasks that comprise the job and of the skills, knowledge, abilities, and responsibilities required of the holder for successful job performance. Job design is the process of structuring work and designating the specific work activities of an individual or group of individuals to achieve certain organizational objectives. Job design addresses the basic question of how the job is to be performed, who is to perform it, and where it is to be performed.

2. **Distinguish among a position, a job, and an occupation.**
   Job duties, when combined with responsibilities, define a position. A group of positions that are identical with respect to their major tasks and responsibilities form a job. A group of similar jobs form an occupation.

3. **Describe several common uses of a job analysis.**
   Several of the most common uses of a job analysis include job definition, job redesign, recruitment, selection and placement, orientation, training, career counseling, employee safety, performance appraisal, and compensation.

4. **Define *job description* and *job specification*.**
   A job description concentrates on the job. It explains what the job is and what the duties, responsibilities, and general working conditions are. A job specification concentrates on the characteristics needed to perform the job. It describes the qualifications the incumbent must possess to perform the job.

5. **Describe four frequently used methods of job analysis.**
   Four frequently used methods of job analysis are observation, interviews, questionnaires, and functional job analysis.

6. **Interpret the nine-digit code used in the *Dictionary of Occupational Titles*.**
   The first digit indicates the primary occupational category. The second digit indicates a division within the primary occupational category. The third digit indicates the group within the division into which the job is classified. The fourth, fifth, and sixth digits reflect the difficulty of the job with regard to data, people, and things, respectively. The last three digits differentiate, in alphabetical order, those jobs that have the same first six digits.

7. **Define *essential functions* and *reasonable accommodation* as interpreted under the Americans with Disabilities Act.**
   Under the Americans with Disabilities Act, an essential job function is one that is fundamental to successful performance of the job as compared to marginal job functions, which may be performed at certain times but are incidental to the main purpose of the job. Reasonable accommodation means the employer may be required to alter the conditions of a particular job to enable the candidate to perform all essential functions.

8. **Identify several problems frequently associated with job analyses.**
   Some of the most frequently encountered problems with job analyses include the following: top management support is missing; only a single means and source for gathering data are used; the supervisor and jobholder do not participate in the design of the job analysis procedure; no training or motivation is provided; employees are not allowed sufficient time to complete the analysis; jobholder activities may be distorted; there is a failure to critique the job.

9. **Define *job scope* and *job depth* and explain their relationship to job design.**
   Job scope and job depth are both dimensions of job design. *Job scope* refers to the number and variety of tasks performed by the jobholder. *Job depth* refers to the freedom of jobholders to plan and organize their own work, work at their own pace, and move around and communicate as desired.

10. **Explain the sociotechnical approach to job design.**

   The thrust of the sociotechnical approach to job design is that both the technical system and the accompanying social system should be considered in designing jobs.

11. **Distinguish among the following types of alternative work schedules: flextime, telecommuting, job sharing, and condensed workweek.**

   Flextime allows employees to choose, within certain limits, when they start and end their workday. Telecommuting is the practice of working at home or while traveling and being able to interact with the office. Job sharing is the practice whereby two or more part-time individuals perform a job that would normally be held by one full-time person. Under the condensed workweek, the number of hours worked per day is increased and the number of days in the workweek is decreased.

REVIEW QUESTIONS

1. Define *job analysis* and *job design*.
2. Differentiate among the terms *duties, position,* and *job*.
3. From a human resource manager's viewpoint, what are several potential uses of a job analysis?
4. Define *job descriptions* and *job specifications*. How do they relate to the job analysis process?
5. Briefly describe four of the most frequently used methods for analyzing jobs.
6. Define the concepts of *essential functions* and *reasonable accommodation* as interpreted under the Americans with Disabilities Act.
7. What are some potential problems associated with job analysis?
8. What is the sociotechnical approach to job design?
9. Briefly explain the following types of alternative work schedules: flextime, telecommuting, job sharing, and the condensed workweek.

DISCUSSION QUESTIONS

1. After completing school, you will probably enter the work force. What are the implications of job analysis and job design for you?
2. What method of job analysis do you think would be most applicable for jobs in a large grocery store? For jobs in a public library?
3. Comment on the following statement, which is attributed to Robert Heinlein: "A human being should be able to change a diaper, plan an invasion, butcher a hog, conn a ship, design a building, write a sonnet, balance accounts, build a wall, set a bone, comfort the dying, take orders, give orders, cooperate, act alone, solve equations, analyze new problems, pitch manure, program a computer, cook a tasty meal, fight efficiently, die gallantly. Specialization is for insects."
4. How do the requirements of the Americans with Disabilities Act affect the job analysis process?

INCIDENT 5–1

The Tax Assessor's Office

A workday begins each morning at 8 A.M. in the tax assessor's office. The staff is composed of the director, two secretaries, two clerk-typists, and three file clerks.

Until last year, the office operated smoothly, with even workloads and well-defined responsibilities.

Over the last year or so, the director has noticed more and more disagreements among the clerk-typists and file clerks. When they approached the director to discuss their disagreements, it was determined that problems had arisen from misunderstandings concerning responsibility for particular duties. There is a strong undercurrent of discontent because the clerk-typists feel the file clerks have too much free time to spend running personal errands and socializing. On the other hand, the secretaries and clerk-typists frequently have to work overtime doing work they believe could easily be picked up by the file clerks. The file clerks claim they should not have to take on any additional duties, since their paychecks would not reflect the extra responsibilities.

Each person in the office has a general job description that was written several years ago. However, the nature of most positions has changed considerably since then because of the implementation of the computer system. No attempt has been made to put these changes in writing. The director formerly held staff meetings to discuss problems that arose within the office; however, no meetings have been held in several months.

Questions

1. What actions would you recommend to the director?
2. Why do you think job descriptions are not updated in many organizations?

INCIDENT 5–2

Turnover Problems

Ms. Shivers is the manager of a computer division in the federal government. Among her various responsibilities is the central data entry office, with 10 GS–4 data entry clerks and one GS–5 supervisor.

The starting salary range for a GS–4 data entry clerk with limited skills is comparable to the starting salary in private industry. However, after about six months of on-the-job experience, most data entry clerks can get a substantial pay increase by taking a job in private industry. It has become common knowledge in industry that Ms. Shivers has a very good training program for data entry clerks and that her division represents a good source of personnel. As a result of this reputation, Ms. Shivers has experienced a heavy turnover during the last several months. In fact, the problem has recently become severe enough to create a tremendous work backlog in her division. In short, she has had to oversee so many trainees that the division's overall productivity has declined.

Within the data entry section are three notable exceptions who have worked for Ms. Shivers for several years. These three have recently been responsible for most of the work turned out in the division. The GS–5 supervisor has been running the section for five years. Just recently, she informed Ms. Shivers that she had been offered a job with another company with a small pay increase and no supervisory responsibilities.

Ms. Shivers has always felt that the data entry clerks should be upgraded to the GS–5 level and the supervisor's job to GS–6. In fact, on several occasions, Ms. Shivers has mentioned this idea to her boss, John Clayton. She believes not only that these jobs should be upgraded but also that this action would go a long way toward solving her turnover problem. Unfortunately, Clayton has never shown much interest in Ms. Shivers' idea.

Questions

1. What do you suggest Ms. Shivers do to further promote the idea of upgrading the data entry clerk and supervisory positions?

2. What can Ms. Shivers do from a job design standpoint to help with the turnover problem?

EXERCISE

Performing a Job Analysis

Your instructor may ask you to do both parts of this exercise or only part *a* or part *b.*

a. Use the job analysis questionnaire in the "On the Job" example at the end of this chapter to analyze the most recent job you have held. Your job may have been a summer, part-time, or full-time job. You need not fill in the heading information. After you have completed the questionnaire, answer the following questions:

1. Do you believe the job analysis questionnaire captured the essence of your job? If not, what was left out?

2. What improvements would you recommend in the job analysis questionnaire?

3. Do you think your boss would have answered the questionnaire basically the same way you did? Why or why not?

b. Using the same job analysis questionnaire found in the "On the Job" example at the end of this chapter, go out and interview an actual jobholder of your choice. After you have completed the job analysis questionnaire, write a complete job description for the job.

NOTES AND ADDITIONAL READINGS

1. War Manpower Commission, Division of Occupational Analysis, *Training and Reference Manual for Job Analysis* (Washington, D.C.: U.S. Government Printing Office, June 1944), p. 7.
2. Ibid.
3. This list is partially adapted from J. Markowitz, "Four Methods of Job Analysis," *Training and Development Journal,* September 1981, p. 112.
4. U.S. Department of Labor, *Handbook for Analyzing Jobs* (Washington, D.C.: U.S. Government Printing Office, 1972).
5. N. R. F. Maier, R. Hollman, J. J. Hoover, and W. H. Reed, *Superior-Subordinate Communication in Management* (New York: American Management Association, 1961).
6. The Position Analysis Questionnaire (PAQ) is copyrighted by the Purdue Research Foundation. The PAQ and related materials are available through the University Book Store, 360 West State Street, West Lafayette, IN 47906. Further information regarding the PAQ is available through PAQ Services, Inc., P.O. Box 3337, Logan, UT 84321. Computer processing of PAQ data is available through the PAQ Data Processing Division at this same address in Utah.
7. W. W. Tornov and P. R. Pinto, "The Development of a Managerial Job Taxonomy: A System for Describing, Classifying, and Evaluating Executive Positions," *Journal of Applied Psychology* 61, no. 4 (1976), p. 413.
8. D. Yoder and H. G. Henneman, Jr., eds., *ASPA Handbook of Personnel and Industrial Relations,* 1 (Washington, D.C.: Bureau of National Affairs, 1974), pp. 4–58.
9. Much of this section is drawn from *The O*NET Dictionary of Occupational Titles* (Indianapolis: JISJ Works, Inc., 1998), pp. xxv–xxvii. This book provides an introduction and several sample descriptions from the O*NET.
10. Much of this section is based on Wayne E. Barlow and Edward Z. Hare, "A Practical Guide to the Americans with Disabilities Act," *Personnel Journal,* June 1992, p. 53.

11. Parts of this list are adapted from Philip C. Grant, "What Use Is a Job Description?" *Personnel Journal,* February 1988, pp. 50–55.

12. L. E. Davis, "Job Design and Productivity: A New Approach," *Personnel,* March 1957, p. 420.

13. Richard B. Chase and Nicholas J. Aquilano, *Production and Operations Management: A Life-Cycle Approach,* 6th ed. (Homewood, Ill.: Richard D. Irwin, 1992), p. 494.

14. P. B. Vaill, "Industrial Engineering and Socio-Technical Systems," *Journal of Industrial Engineering,* September 1967, p. 535.

15. Louis E. Davis, *Job Satisfaction—A Socio-Technical View,* Report 515–69 (Los Angeles: University of California, 1969), p. 14.

16. Chase and Aquilano, *Production and Operations Management,* p. 256.

17. Brian Gill, "Flextime Benefits Employees and Employers," *American Printer,* February 1998, p. 70.

18. Mitchell Schechter, "Telecommuting May Make Dinosaurs Of Us All," *Food Management,* April 1998, pp 28–32.

19. Elaine McShulskis, "Telecommuting Becomes a Standard Benefit," *HR Magazine,* February 1998, pp. 28–29.

20. Judy Greenwald, "Employers Warming Up to Flexible Schedules," *Business Insurance,* June 15, 1998, pp. 3, 6.

Sample Job Description

Title of Position: Human Resource Manager, Plant*

Basic Purpose

To develop and maintain an employee relations climate that creates and permits a stable and productive work force. To manage and coordinate all functions of employee relations, including employment, labor relations, compensation and benefit services, work force planning, training and development, affirmative action, and security.

Duties and Responsibilities

1. Selects, trains, develops, and organizes a subordinate staff to perform and meet department responsibilities and objectives effectively.
2. Provides leadership in the establishment and maintenance of employee relations that will assist in attracting and retaining a desirable and productive labor force.
3. Manages the interpretation and application of established corporate and division personnel policies.
4. Directs the preparation and maintenance of reports necessary to carry out functions of the department. Prepares periodic reports for the plant manager; director, employee relations; manager, labor relations; and/or manager, compensation and benefits, as necessary or requested.
5. Directs and maintains various activities designed to achieve and maintain a high level of employee morale.
6. Plans, implements, and maintains a program of orientation for new employees.
7. Provides and serves as the necessary liaison between the location employees and the location plant manager.
8. Supervises the labor relations staff in administration of the labor agreements and interpretation of contract language and ensures that the supervisor, labor relations, is well informed to administer the provisions effectively and in accordance with management's philosophy and objectives.
9. Strives to establish an effective working relationship with union representatives to resolve and minimize labor problems more satisfactorily and to avoid inefficient practices and work stoppages.
10. Determines or, in questionable cases, recommends whether grievance cases appealed to the arbitration stage should be settled by concessions or arbitrated. Prepares and presents such cases or supervises subordinates in same.
11. Manages and coordinates planning for plant labor contract negotiations; ensures that labor cost aspects are defined and that major position papers are prepared. Supervises the preparation and publication of contract language

---

*Source: Reprinted by permission of publisher from, *Job Descriptions in Manufacturing Industries*, by John D. Ulery. Copyright 1981 by AMACOM, a division of American Management Association, New York. All rights reserved.

and documentation. Serves as chief spokesperson or assists in negotiations at the operating unit level.

12. Establishes procedures for ensuring timely compliance with notice, reporting, and similar obligations under agreements with labor organizations.

13. Supervises the compensation and benefits staff in the administration and/or implementation and communication of current and new compensation and benefit programs, policies, and procedures.

14. Directs the development and implementation of approved location affirmative action plans to achieve and maintain compliance in accordance with the letter and intent of equal employment opportunity laws and executive orders.

15. Plans, implements, and maintains supervisory and management development activities.

16. Provides leadership in the establishment and maintenance of a plant security force.

17. Represents the company in the community and promotes the company's goodwill interests in community activities.

Organizational Relationships

This position reports directly to the plant manager and functionally to the director, employee relations. Directly supervises supervisor, labor relations; supervisor, employment; supervisor, compensation benefits; and supervisor, security; and indirectly supervises additional nonexempt employees. Interfaces daily with management and division employee relations.

Position Specifications

Bachelor's degree, preferably in personnel management or equivalent plus six to eight years' related experience, including supervisory/managerial experience in a wide range of employee relations activities. Must possess an ability to understand human behavior and be able to lead and motivate people. Must have mature judgment and decision-making ability.

Sample Job Analysis Questionnaire*

Job Analysis Information Format

Your job title _____ Code _____ Date _____

Class title _____ Department _____

Your name _____ Facility_____

Superior's title _____ Prepared by _____

Superior's name_____ Hours worked ____ AM ____ to ____ AM ____
                                                              PM   PM

1. What is the general purpose of your job?

2. What was your last job? If it was in another organization, please name it.

3. To what job would you normally expect to be promoted?

4. If you regularly supervise others, list them by name and job title.

5. If you supervise others, please check those activities that are part of your supervisory duties:

   ☐ Hiring   ☐ Coaching   ☐ Promoting
   ☐ Orienting   ☐ Counseling   ☐ Compensating
   ☐ Training   ☐ Budgeting   ☐ Disciplining
   ☐ Scheduling   ☐ Directing   ☐ Terminating
   ☐ Developing   ☐ Measuring performance ☐ Other _____

6. How would you describe the successful completion and results of your work?

7. *Job duties*—Please briefly describe WHAT you do and, if possible, HOW you do it. Indicate those duties you consider to be most important and/or most difficult.

   (a) *Daily duties:*

   (b) *Periodic duties* (Please indicate whether weekly, monthly, quarterly, etc.):

   (c) *Duties performed at irregular intervals:*

8. *Education*—Please check the blank that indicates the education *requirements* for the job, not your *own* educational background:

   ☐ No formal education required   ☐ 4-year college degree
   ☐ Less than high school diploma   ☐ Education beyond undergraduate
   ☐ High school diploma or equivalent   degree and/or professional license
   ☐ 2-year college certificate or equivalent

   List advanced degrees or specified professional license or certificate required.

   Please indicate the education you had when you were placed on this job.

9. *Experience*—Please check the amount needed to perform your job:

   ☐ None   ☐ More than 1 year to 3 years
   ☐ Less than 1 month   ☐ More than 3 years to 5 years
   ☐ 1 month to less than 6 months ☐ More than 5 years to 10 years
   ☐ 6 months to 1 year   ☐ Over 10 years

   Please indicate the experience you had when you were placed on this job.

**Source:* Richard I. Henderson, *Compensation Management: Rewarding Performance in the Modern Organization* (1976), pp. 98–102. Reprinted by permission of Prentice Hall, Inc., Englewood Cliffs, NJ.

10. *Skills*—Please list any skills required in the performance of your job (e.g., amount of accuracy, alertness, precision in working with described tools, methods, systems).

    Please list skills you possessed when you were placed on this job.

11. *Equipment*—Does your work require the use of any equipment? Yes ____ No ____ If yes, please list the equipment and check whether you use it rarely, occasionally, or frequently:

Equipment	Rarely	Occasionally	Frequently
(1) _____	☐	☐	☐
(2) _____	☐	☐	☐
(3) _____	☐	☐	☐
(4) _____	☐	☐	☐

12. *Physical demands*—Please check all undesirable physical demands required on your job and whether you are required to do so rarely, occasionally, or frequently:

	Rarely	Occasionally	Frequently
☐ Handling heavy material	☐	☐	☐
☐ Awkward or cramped positions	☐	☐	☐
☐ Excessive working speeds	☐	☐	☐
☐ Excessive sensory requirements (seeing, hearing, touching, smelling, speaking)	☐	☐	☐
☐ Vibrating equipment	☐	☐	☐
☐ Others_____	☐	☐	☐

13. *Emotional demands*—Please check all undesirable emotional demands placed on you by your job and whether it is rarely, occasionally, or frequently:

	Rarely	Occasionally	Frequently
☐ Contact with general public	☐	☐	☐
☐ Customer contact	☐	☐	☐
☐ Close supervision	☐	☐	☐
☐ Deadlines under pressure	☐	☐	☐
☐ Irregular activity schedules	☐	☐	☐
☐ Working alone	☐	☐	☐
☐ Excessive traveling	☐	☐	☐
☐ Other	☐	☐	☐

14. *Workplace location*—Check the type of location of your job and if you consider it to be unsatisfactory or satisfactory.

	Unsatisfactory	Satisfactory
☐ Outdoor	☐	☐
☐ Indoor	☐	☐
☐ Underground	☐	☐
☐ Pit	☐	☐
☐ Scaffold	☐	☐

15. *Physical surroundings*—Please check whether you consider the following physical conditions of your job to be poor, good, or excellent.

	Poor	Good	Excellent
☐ Lighting	☐	☐	☐
☐ Ventilation	☐	☐	☐

☐ Sudden temperature change   ☐   ☐   ☐

☐ Vibration   ☐   ☐   ☐

☐ Comfort of furnishings   ☐   ☐   ☐

16. *Environmental conditions*—Please check the objectionable conditions under which you must perform your job and check whether the condition exists rarely, occasionally, or frequently:

	Rarely	**Occasionally**	**Frequently**
☐ Dust	☐	☐	☐
☐ Dirt	☐	☐	☐
☐ Heat	☐	☐	☐
☐ Cold	☐	☐	☐
☐ Fumes	☐	☐	☐
☐ Odors	☐	☐	☐
☐ Noise	☐	☐	☐
☐ Wetness	☐	☐	☐
☐ Humidity	☐	☐	☐
☐ Other _____	☐	☐	☐

17. *Health and safety*—Please check all undesirable health and safety factors under which you must perform your job and whether you are required to do so rarely, occasionally, or frequently:

	Rarely	**Occasionally**	**Frequently**
☐ Height of elevated workplace	☐	☐	☐
☐ Radiation	☐	☐	☐
☐ Mechanical hazards	☐	☐	☐
☐ Moving objects	☐	☐	☐
☐ Explosives	☐	☐	☐
☐ Electrical hazards	☐	☐	☐
☐ Fire	☐	☐	☐
☐ Other _____	☐	☐	☐

_____   _____

Signature   Date

Supervisory Review

Do the incumbent's responses to the questionnaire accurately describe the work requirements and the work performed in meeting the responsibilities of the job? Yes ____ No ____ If no, please explain and list any significant omissions or additions.

Human Resource Planning

Learning Objectives

After studying this chapter, you should be able to:

1. Define human resource planning (HRP).
2. Summarize the relationship between HRP and organizational planning.
3. Explain strategy-linked HRP.
4. Identify the steps in the HRP process.
5. Describe the different methods used for forecasting human resource needs.
6. Define the concept of benchmarking.
7. Discuss the purpose of a skills inventory.
8. Describe succession planning, commitment manpower planning, and ratio analysis.
9. List several common pitfalls in HRP.

Human Resource Planning (HRP) Process of determining the human resource needs of an organization and ensuring that the organization has the right number of qualified people in the right jobs at the right time.

Human resource planning (HRP), sometimes referred to as *work force planning* or *personnel planning*, has been defined as the process of "getting the right number of qualified people into the right job at the right time."[1] Put another way, HRP is "the system of matching the supply of people—internally (existing employees)—and externally (those to be hired or searched for)—with the openings the organization expects to have over a given time frame."[2] The Tennessee Valley Authority (TVA) defines the HRP process as "the systematic assessment of future HR needs and the determination of the actions required to meet those needs."[3] As the TVA's definition indicates, the first challenge of HRP is to translate the organization's plans and objectives into a timed schedule of employee requirements. Once the employee requirements have been determined, HRP must devise plans for securing the necessary employees. Basically, all organizations engage in human resource planning either formally or informally. Some organizations do a good job and others a poor job.

The long-term success of any organization ultimately depends on having the right people in the right jobs at the right time. Organization objectives and the strategies for achieving those objectives are meaningful only when people with the appropriate talents, skills, and desire are available to carry out those strategies.

Poor human resource planning can also cause substantial problems in the short term. Consider the following examples:

- Despite an aggressive search, a vital middle management position in a high-technology organization has gone unfilled for six months. Productivity in the section has plummeted.

- In another company, employees hired just nine months ago have been placed on indefinite layoff because of an unforeseen lag in the workload in a specific production area.

- In still another company, thanks to the spectacular efforts of a talented marketing manager, product demand has soared. However, because the rise in demand was unanticipated, the company has not been able to hire enough production employees.[4]

The need for HRP is due to the significant lead time that normally exists between the recognition of the need to fill a job and the securing of a qualified person to fill that need. In other words, it is usually not possible to go out and find an appropriate person overnight. Effective HRP can also help reduce turnover by keeping employees apprised of their career opportunities within the company.

How HRP Relates to Organizational Planning

HRP involves applying the basic planning process to the human resource needs of the organization. To be effective, any human resource plan must be derived from the long-term and operational plans of the organization. In essence, the success of HRP depends largely on how closely the human resource department can integrate effective people planning with the organization's business planning process.[5] Unfortunately, HRP is often inadequately tied to overall corporate planning.

Strategic business planning seeks to identify various factors critical to the success of the organization. It also focuses on how the organization can become better positioned and equipped to compete in its industry. To accomplish this, the planning process should provide

- A clear statement of the organization's mission.
- A commitment from staff members to the mission.
- An explicit statement of assumptions.
- A plan of action in light of available or acquirable resources, including trained and talented people.[6]

Human resource planning contributes significantly to the strategic management process by providing the means to accomplish the outcomes desired from the planning process. In essence, the human resource demands and needs are derived from the strategic and operating planning and then compared with human resource availability. Then a variety of programs such as recruiting, training, and reallocation address the resulting gaps.[7]

A common error occurs when human resource planners focus on the short-term replacement needs and fail to coordinate their plans with the long-term plans of the organization. Focusing on short-term replacement needs is a natural consequence of failing to integrate human resource planning with strategic planning. A nonintegrated approach almost always leads to surprises that force human resource planners to concentrate on short-term crises.

Strategy-Linked HRP

All managers, especially line managers, should view human resource planning as one of their most important job responsibilities. Unfortunately, this is not often the case. Far too many managers view HRP as something to do only after everything else has been done. Furthermore, managers often think HRP should be handled solely by human resource personnel. But HRP is not strictly a human resource function. The role of human resource personnel is to assist operating managers in developing their individual plans and integrating those different plans into an overall scheme. The individual managers must, however, provide the basic data on which the plan is built. The process requires a joint effort by the individual managers and human resource personnel. In general, human resource personnel provide the structure, the impetus, and assistance. However, individual managers must be actively involved.

One of the best ways to encourage genuine cooperation between human resource managers and line managers is to use what is called *strategy-linked HRP*. Strategy-linked HRP is based on a close working relationship between human resource staff and line managers.[8] Human resource managers serve as consultants to line managers concerning the people-management implications of business objectives and strategies. Line managers, in turn, have a responsibility to respond to the business implications of human resource objectives and strategies. Another important ingredient is the commitment of top management, which should be evident to other managers and employees.

Table 6–1 summarizes several actions human resource managers can take to link human resource planning to the organization's strategic plans.

Steps in the HRP Process

HRP consists of four basic steps:

1. Determining the impact of the organization's objectives on specific organizational units.
2. Defining the skills, expertise, and total number of employees (demand for human resources) required to achieve the organizational and departmental objectives.
3. Determining the additional (net) human resource requirements in light of the organization's current human resources.
4. Developing action plans to meet the anticipated human resource needs.[9]

Figure 6–1 illustrates the steps in HRP.

Determining Organizational Objectives

As emphasized earlier, human resource plans must be based on organizational strategic plans. In practice, this means the objectives of the human resource plan must be derived from organizational objectives. Specific human resource requirements in terms of numbers and characteristics of employees should be derived from the objectives of the entire organization.

TABLE 6 – 1	LINKING HRP TO THE BUSINESS STRATEGY

Be familiar with the business strategy.

Ensure that all traditional human resource programs are satisfying the needs of senior and functional management.

Identify the human resource implications of the organization's business strategy.

Identify those human resource issues that may affect business objectives, and notify the appropriate functional managers.

Convert business objectives into human resource objectives that can provide the foundation for a strategic human resource plan.

Review the strategic planning process to identify new opportunities to involve human resource personnel.

Sources: G. Christopher Wood, "Planning for People" (letters to the editor), *Harvard Business Review*, November–December 1985, p. 230; David R. Leigh, "Business Planning Is People Planning," *Personnel Journal*, May 1984, pp. 44–54.

FIGURE 6–1   STEPS IN THE HUMAN RESOURCE PLANNING PROCESS.

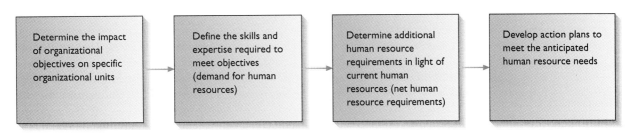

| Determine the impact of organizational objectives on specific organizational units | Define the skills and expertise required to meet objectives (demand for human resources) | Determine additional human resource requirements in light of current human resources (net human resource requirements) | Develop action plans to meet the anticipated human resource needs |

Organizational Objectives Statements of expected results that are designed to give the organization and its members direction and purpose.

Cascade Approach Objective-setting process designed to involve all levels of management in the organizational planning process.

Organizational objectives, which give the organization and its members direction and purpose, should be stated in terms of expected results. The objective-setting process begins at the top of the organization with a statement of mission, which defines the organization's current and future business. Long-range objectives and strategies are formulated based on the organization's mission statement. These can then be used to establish short-term performance objectives. Short-term performance objectives generally have a time schedule and are expressed quantitatively. Divisional and departmental objectives are then derived from the organization's short-term performance objectives. Establishing organizational, divisional, and departmental objectives in this manner has been called the cascade approach to objective setting. Figure 6–2 illustrates this approach.

The cascade approach is not a form of top-down planning, whereby objectives are passed down to lower levels of the organization. The idea is to involve all levels

FIGURE 6–2   CASCADE APPROACH TO SETTING OBJECTIVES

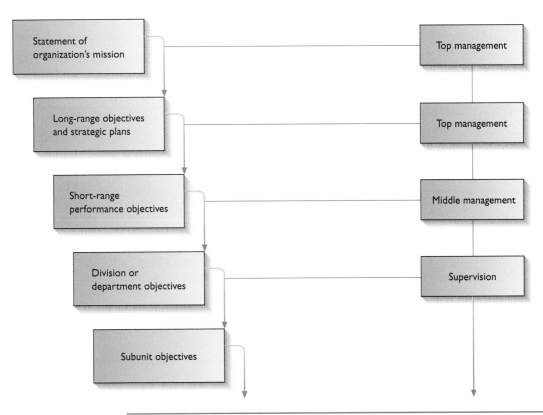

Source: Redrawn from *Managing by Objectives* by Anthony P. Raia. (Scott Foresman and Company, 1974), p. 30. Reprinted by permission of the author.

of management in the planning process. Such an approach leads to an upward and downward flow of information during planning. This also ensures that the objectives are communicated and coordinated through all levels of the organization.

When properly used, the cascade approach involves both operating managers and human resource personnel in the overall planning process. During the early stages, human resource personnel can influence objective setting by providing information about the organization's human resources. For example, if human resource personnel have identified particular strengths and weaknesses in the organization's staff, this information can significantly influence the overall direction of the organization.

Determining the Skills and Expertise Required (Demand)

After establishing organizational, divisional, and departmental objectives, operating managers should determine the skills and expertise required to meet their respective objectives. The key here is not to look at the skills and abilities of present employees but to determine the skills and abilities required to meet the objectives. For example, suppose an objective of the production department is to increase total production of a certain item by 10 percent. Once this objective has been established, the production manager must determine precisely how this translates into human resource needs. A good starting point is to review current job descriptions. Once this has been accomplished, managers are in a better position to determine the skills and expertise necessary to meet their objectives. The final step in this phase is to translate the needed skills and abilities into types and numbers of employees.

Methods of Forecasting Human Resource Needs

Managerial Estimates Judgmental method of forecasting that calls on managers to make estimates of future staffing needs.

Delphi Technique Judgmental method of forecasting that uses a panel of experts to make initially independent estimates of future demand. An intermediary then presents each expert's forecast and assumptions to the other members of the panel. Each expert is then allowed to revise his or her forecast as desired. This process continues until some consensus or composite emerges.

Scenario Analysis Using work force environmental scanning data to develop alternative work force scenarios.

The organization's future human resource needs can be forecasted using a variety of methods, some simple and some complex. Regardless of the method used, forecasts represent approximations and should not be viewed as absolutes.

Methods for forecasting human resource needs can be either judgmentally or mathematically based. Judgmental methods include managerial estimates, the Delphi technique, and scenario analysis. Under the **managerial estimates** method, managers make estimates of future staffing needs based primarily on past experience. These estimates can be made by top-level managers and passed down, by lower-level managers and passed up for further revision, or by some combination of upper- and lower-level managers. With the **Delphi technique,** each member of a panel of experts makes an independent estimate of what the future demand will be, along with any underlying assumptions. An intermediary then presents each expert's forecast and assumptions to the others and allows the experts to revise their positions if they desire. This process continues until some consensus emerges.

Scenario analysis involves using work force environmental scanning data to develop alternative work force scenarios.[10] These scenarios are developed by having brainstorming sessions with line managers and human resource managers who forecast what they think their work force will look like five or more years into the future. Once these forecasts have been crystalized, the managers then work backwards to identify key change points. The biggest advantage of scenario analysis is that it encourages open, out-of-the-box thinking.

Mathematically based methods for forecasting human resource needs include various statistical and modeling methods. Statistical methods use historical data in some manner to project future demand. Modeling methods usually provide a simplified abstraction of the human resource demands throughout the organization. Changing the input data allows the human resource ramifications for different demand scenarios to be tested. Table 6–2 summarizes four of the most frequently used statistical and/or modeling methods.

Historically, judgmental forecasts have been used more frequently than mathematically based forecasts. Judgmental methods are simpler and usually do not re-

TABLE 6-2   **STATISTICAL MODELING TECHNIQUES USED TO FORECAST HUMAN RESOURCE NEEDS**

Technique	Description
1. Time series analysis	Past staffing levels (instead of workload indicators) are used to project future human resource requirements. Past staffing levels are examined to isolate seasonal and cyclical variations, long-term trends, and random movements. Long-term trends are then extrapolated or projected using a moving average, exponential smoothing, or regression technique.
2. Personnel ratios	Past personnel data are examined to determine historical relationships among the number of employees in various jobs or job categories. Regression analysis or productivity ratios are then used to project either total or key group human resource requirements, and personnel ratios are used to allocate total requirements to various job categories or to estimate requirements for non-key groups.
3. Productivity ratios	Historical data are used to examine past levels of a productivity index, $$P = \frac{\text{Workload}}{\text{Number of people}}$$ Where constant, or systematic, relationships are found, human resource requirements can be computed by dividing predicted workloads by P.
4. Regression analysis	Past levels of various workload indicators, such as sales, production levels, and value added, are examined for statistical relationships with staffing levels. Where sufficiently strong relationships are found, a regression (or multiple regression) model is derived. Forecasted levels of the related indicator(s) are entered into the resulting model and used to calculate the associated level of human resource requirements.

Source: Lee Dyer, "Human Resource Planning," in *Personnel Management,* ed. Kendrith M. Rowland and Gerald R. Ferris (Boston: Allyn & Bacon, 1982), p. 59.

quire sophisticated analyses. However, with the increasing proliferation of user-friendly computers, mathematically based methods will probably be used more frequently.

In addition to the previously described judgmentally and mathematically based forecasting techniques, some organizations help forecast human resource needs by benchmarking what other successful organizations are doing. **Benchmarking** involves thoroughly examining internal practices and procedures and measuring them against the ways other successful organizations operate.[11] With regard to HRP, benchmarking involves learning what other successful organizations in the industry are forecasting and how they are arriving at their forecasts. Your forecasts and methods can then be compared to theirs. Consultants and professional organizations, such as industry associations can be employed to help with the benchmarking process. A major advantage of benchmarking is that it forces you to look at other ways of doing things. HRM in Action 6.1 discusses how Xerox has successfully used benchmarking within several areas of HR.

Benchmarking Thoroughly examining internal practice and procedures and measuring them against the ways other successful organizations operate.

Determining Additional (Net) Human Resource Requirements

Once a manager has determined the types and numbers of employees required, he or she analyzes these estimates in light of the current and anticipated human resources of the organization. This process involves a thorough analysis of presently employed personnel and a forecast of expected changes.

HRM IN ACTION

Benchmarking at Xerox

6.1

www.xerox.com

Benchmarking has recently become very fashionable. More than 70 percent of Fortune 500 companies, including AT&T, Eastman Kodak, Ford, IBM, Weyerhaeuser, and Xerox, use benchmarking on a regular basis. Xerox, perhaps more than any other company, has proven just how powerful benchmarking techniques can be. Within human resources, Xerox has scrutinized everything from training to work-and-family issues. Xerox's benchmarking process includes the following 10 steps: (1) identify what is to be benchmarked, (2) identify comparative companies, (3) determine data collection method and collect data, (4) determine current performance levels, (5) project future performance levels, (6) communicate benchmark finds and gain acceptance, (7) establish functional goals, (8) develop action plans, (9) implement specific actions and monitor progress, (10) recalibrate benchmarks.

Patricia Nazemetz, director of Human Resource Policies at Xerox, has summed up benchmarking, "The realization that companies can share information—particularly in HR—and that it can benefit everyone is important. It can help people do their jobs more effectively and efficiently and greatly streamline processes. Benchmarking isn't about copying other companies or importing best practices wholesale; it's about integrating bits and pieces of useful information into a company and its culture. When that happens, and when goals are aligned with the larger mission of the company, it's possible to make tremendous progress."

Source: Samuel Greengard, "Discover Best Practices through Benchmarking," *Personnel Journal,* November 1995, pp. 62–65.

Skills Inventory

Skills Inventory
Consolidated list of biographical and other information on all employees in the organization.

A **skills inventory** consolidates information about the organization's human resources. It provides basic information on all employees, including, in its simplest form, a list of the names, certain characteristics, and skills of employees. Because the information from a skills inventory is used as input into promotion and transfer decisions, it should contain information about each employee's portfolio of skills and not just those relevant to the employee's current job. Thomas H. Patten has outlined seven broad categories of information that should be included in a skills inventory:

1. Personal data: age, sex, marital status.
2. Skills: education, job experience, training.
3. Special qualifications: membership in professional groups, special achievements.
4. Salary and job history: present and past salary, dates of raises, various jobs held.
5. Company data: benefit plan data, retirement information, seniority.
6. Capacity of individual: test scores on psychological and other tests, health information.
7. Special preferences of individual: geographic location, type of job.[12]

The popularity of skills inventories has increased rapidly since the proliferation of computers. Although traditionally most of the desired information was available from individual personnel files, compiling it was time-consuming before computers became readily available. Today's intranets even have the ability to conduct comprehensive skills inventories and then slot employees into training to fit the needs of the organization.[13]

The primary advantage of a skills inventory is that it furnishes a means to quickly and accurately evaluate the skills available within the organization. In addition to helping determine promotion and transfer decisions, this information is often necessary for making other decisions, such as whether to bid on a new contract or introduce a new product. A skills inventory also aids in planning future employee training and management development programs and in recruiting and selecting new employees. Figure 6–3 presents a skills inventory form used by PPG Industries. HRM in Action 6.2 describes a sophisticated skills inventory system that has enabled AMP, Inc., to remain globally competitive.

Management Inventory

Because the type of information about management personnel that may be required sometimes differs from that for nonmanagerial employees, some organizations maintain a separate management inventory. In addition to biographical data, a **management inventory** often contains brief assessments of the manager's past performance, strengths, weaknesses, and potential for advancement. In essence, a management inventory is a specialized type of skills inventory just for management.

Anticipating Changes in Personnel

Management Inventory
Specialized expanded form of skills inventory for an organization's current management team; in addition to basic types of information, it usually includes a brief assessment of past performance and potential for advancement.

In addition to appraising present human resources through a skills inventory, managers must take future changes into account. Managers can accurately and easily estimate certain changes, but cannot so easily forecast other changes. However, information is almost always available to help make these forecasts.

Changes such as retirements can be forecasted with reasonable accuracy from information in the skills inventory. Other changes, such as transfers and promotions, can be estimated by taking into account such factors as the ages of individuals in specific jobs and the requirements of the organization. Individuals with potential for promotion can and should be identified. Other factors, such as deaths, resignations, and discharges, are much more difficult to predict. However, past experience and historical records often can provide useful information in these areas.

Planned training and development experiences should also be considered when evaluating anticipated changes. By combining the forecast for the human resources needed with the information from the skills inventory and from anticipated changes, managers can make a reasonable prediction of their net human resource requirements for a specified time period.

Developing Action Plans

Once the net human resource requirements have been determined, managers must develop action plans for achieving the desired results. If the net requirements indicate a need for additions, decisions must be made whether to make permanent hires, temporary hires, or to outsource the work. If the decision is to make permanent or temporary hires, plans must be made to recruit, select, orient, and train the specific numbers and types of personnel needed (Chapters 7, 8, and 9 deal with these topics). If the decision is to outsource, then potential clients for outsourcing must be identified and evaluated. Outsourcing has become attractive in many situations because often the work can be contracted outside at a cost savings. One reason for this is that the company providing the service may not offer its employees benefits as attractive as the parent company. Another reason to outsource is to allow the parent company to focus on its core business. There are also many environmental factors that may impact the decision to hire permanently, temporarily, or to outsource. Some of these factors include the permanency of the needs, the availability of qualified recruits, and the union contract (if applicable).

If a reduction in human resources is necessary, plans must be made to realize the necessary adjustments. If time is not of the essence, natural attrition can be used to reduce labor personnel. However, if the organization cannot afford the luxury of natural attrition, it can cut overhead either by reducing the total number of employees or by making other adjustments that do not result in employees leaving the organization.

F I G U R E   6 – 3   **SKILLS INVENTORY FORM USED BY PPG INDUSTRIES**

PPG   **PERSONAL HISTORY PROFILE**

PRINTED FOR   DATE

PPG JOB HISTORY

DATE ASSIGNED	JOB TITLE	BUSINESS/CORPORATE DEPARTMENT	ORGANIZATIONAL UNIT

PRE-PPG JOB HISTORY   FUNCTIONAL PREFERENCES

	COMPANY AND LOCATION	JOB TITLE	FROM	TO		
1.					1.	
2.					2.	
3.					3.	

EDUCATION   OTHER ACHIEVEMENTS, ACTIVITIES, TRAINING

	LEVEL	YEAR	SCHOOL	STATE	SUBJECT
1.					
2.					
3.				CREDITS	
DEGREE IN PROGRESS			EARNED	REQUIRED	

1.
2.
3.
4.
5.
6.
7.
8.
9.
10.

LANGUAGES   PPG TRAINING COURSES

	PROFICIENCY LEVEL		YEAR
1.			
2.			
3.			

1.
2.
3.
4.
5.
6.
7.
8.
9.
10.

PROFESSIONAL SOCIETIES AND ORGANIZATIONS   MEMBER STATUS   YEAR

1.			
2.			
3.			

PROFESSIONAL LICENSES AND CERTIFICATES   RELOCATION INTEREST

		ISSUING AUTHORITY	YR. RECD./EXP.
1.			
2.			
3.			

POTENTIAL INTEREST: YES ☐   NO ☐
GEOGRAPHIC PREFERENCE:

    ANY AREA ☐   U.S. ☐   CANADA ☐

LATIN AMERICA ☐   EUROPE ☐   ASIA PACIFIC ☐

WORK EXPERIENCE AND KNOWLEDGE   ┌─── ACTION

CATEGORY	DESCRIPTION	FUNCTIONAL AREA	YRS. EXP.	LAST YR.		YRS. EXP.	LAST YR.

MAILING CODE   ID   FLSA   CATG   ORIGINAL HIRE DATE   LATEST HIRE DATE   CONTINUOUS SERVICE

**Tracking Job Skills
at AMP, Inc.**

6.2

www.amp.com

AMP Inc., a manufacturer of electrical and electronic connection devices, is headquartered in Harrisburg, Pennsylvania, and employs 16,000 people. In the late 1980s, AMP realized that it could significantly reduce the time required to bring a new product from concept to market by tracking job skills. Such a system would allow the design engineers to readily identify employees proficient in operating the specific equipment needed to produce the new product. The engineers and operating personnel could then work together to adapt the machinery to fit the new product design. Thus, the time needed to roll out a new product or implement a new methodology could be shortened considerably. Based on this concept, AMP launched a mission in 1989 to create a skills inventory for its domestic operations to provide instant identification of manufacturing employees' job skills. The result was a system called the *Manufacturing Skills Inventory System (MSIS)*. The system has been in operation since March 1992 and enables the company to do the following:

1. Assess quickly and accurately whether its work force has the skills necessary to develop and manufacture new products.

2. Determine, before the hiring process begins, the precise skills each applicant must have mastered to succeed in a certain position.

3. Communicate to employees the specific skills they need for a promotion, the training needed to acquire these skills, and the schedule of available training opportunities.

4. Identify the expert employees in the work force who are capable of training colleagues in given skills areas.

5. Evaluate supervisors accurately on their success in developing subordinates.

6. Tabulate the hours of all on-the-job training activities.

Source: Dennis E. Guessford, Albert B. Boynton, Jr., Robert Laudeman, and Joseph P. Grusti, "Tracking Job Skills Improves Performance," *Personnel Journal,* June 1993, pp. 109–14.

As mentioned in Chapter 1, reducing the total number of employees is referred to as *downsizing.* There are four basic ways to downsize: (1) layoffs, (2) terminations, (3) early retirement inducements, and (4) voluntary resignation inducements.[14] A layoff, as opposed to a termination, assumes it is likely that the employee will be recalled at some later date. Most early retirement and voluntary resignation plans provide some financial inducement to retire early or to resign. HRM in Action 6.3 discusses a series of terminations at Little Caesars Pizza.

Approaches that do not result in employees leaving the organization include: (1) reclassification, (2) transfer, and (3) work sharing. Reclassification involves a demotion of an employee or the downgrading of job responsibilities, or a combination of the two. Usually reclassification is accompanied by a reduction in pay. A transfer involves moving the employee to another part of the organization. Work sharing seeks to limit layoffs and terminations through the proportional reduction of hours among employees (i.e., all employees in a department could be cut back to 35 hours per week instead of 40).

Synthesizing the HRP Process

Figure 6–4 depicts the relationship between organizational planning and human resource planning. As can be seen, organization objectives are influenced by many historical and environmental factors. Environmental factors include variables such

Terminations at Little Caesars

6.3

www.littlecaesarsps.com

In 1998, Little Caesars, the nation's third-largest pizza chain, experienced its third consecutive year of decreases in systemwide sales, market share, and unit counts. As a result of these declines, Little Caesars experienced its second corporate shake-out in the previous 14 months. The latest turmoil resulted in the dismissal of approximately 100 employees at the corporate offices in Detroit and 30 employees at its quality assurance center and Blue Line distribution facilities in Farmington, Michigan. In July of 1997 Little Caesars slashed 27 corporate management positions at its headquarters. The 1997 terminations were explained as "reorganization that was necessary to bring corporate management closer to customers, franchises and the marketplace." These firings were not based on job performance. In 1998, company spokespeople declined to comment on the firings.

Source: Amy Zuber, "Little Caesars Cuts Staff, Fires 100+ Workers," *Nation's Restaurant News*, October 5, 1998, p. 1, 171.

as the economy, interest rates, competition, labor availability, and technology. Once the organizational objectives have been established, they are translated into divisional and departmental objectives. Individual managers then determine the human resources necessary to meet their respective objectives. Human resource personnel assimilate these different requirements and determine the total human resources demand for the organization. Similarly, HR personnel determine the additional (net) human resource requirements based on the information submitted by the various organizational units in light of available resources and anticipated changes. If the net requirements are positive, the organization implements recruitment, selection, training, and development (see Chapters 7, 8, and 9). If the requirements are negative, downsizing must be realized through attrition, layoffs, terminations, early retirements, or voluntary resignations. As these changes take place, they should be reflected in the skills inventory. Human resource planning is an ongoing process that must be continuously evaluated as conditions change. HRM in Action 6.4 describes the HRP process used by the Tennessee Valley Authority.

Tools and Techniques of HRP

Succession Planning
Technique that identifies specific people to fill future openings in key positions throughout the organization.

Organization Replacement Chart   Chart that shows both incumbents and potential replacements for given positions within the organization.

Many tools are available to assist in the human resource planning process. The skills inventory discussed earlier is one of the most frequently used human resource planning tools. A second useful tool is succession planning. Succession planning identifies specific people to fill key positions throughout the organization. Succession planning almost always involves the use of a replacement chart. While many variations exist, a basic organization replacement chart shows both incumbents and potential replacements for given positions. Figure 6–5 is an example of a simple replacement chart. To be effective, replacement charts must be periodically updated to reflect changes in scenarios and potential requirements. Under an optimal succession planning system, individuals are initially identified as candidates to move up after being nominated by management. Then performance appraisal data are reviewed, potential is assessed, developmental programs are formulated, and career paths are mapped out. Sophisticated succession planning helps ensure that qualified internal candidates are not overlooked.

One problem with many succession plans, especially informal plans and those for large organizations, is the "crowned prince" syndrome.[15] This occurs when management considers for advancement only those who have managed to become

FIGURE 6 – 4   **ORGANIZATIONAL AND HUMAN RESOURCE PLANNING**

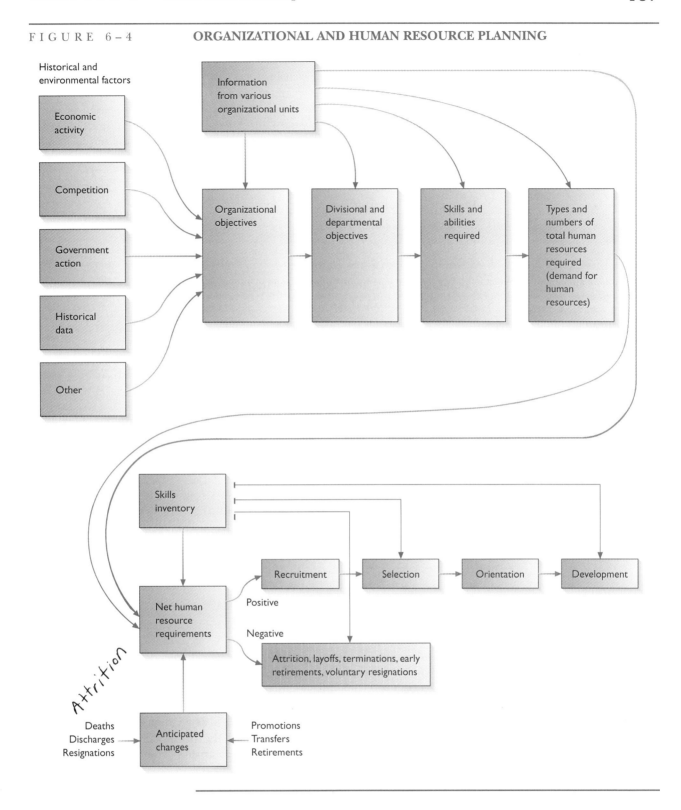

HRM IN ACTION

HRP at TVA

6.4

www.tva.com

The Tennessee Valley Authority (TVA) is a federal agency involved in power production, transmission, and distribution, with headquarters in Knoxville, Tennessee. The TVA employs over 18,000 people and has developed an eight-step methodology for human resource planning. It began this system at the business unit level in late 1991, brought it to the corporate level in late 1992, and introduced it agencywide in the spring of 1993. The steps are as follows:

1. Lay out a plan and a schedule.
2. Perform a staffing assessment.
3. Develop demand data.
4. Develop supply data.
5. Compare demand and supply data.
6. Develop the work force plan.
7. Communicate and implement the work force plan.
8. Evaluate and update the plan.

The TVA emphasizes that HRP should become a part of the organization's business plan and must be effectively communicated to employees. The TVA's HRP process was readily accepted by the entire organization because it was viewed as a vehicle to help stabilize employment. The process has also enjoyed the full support of top management.

Source: David E. Ripley, "How to Determine Future Work-Force Needs," *Personnel Journal,* January 1995, pp. 83–89.

visible to senior management. Another problem with succession planning is that so much information must be tracked that it is very difficult to do it manually. In situations such as this, the succession plan should be computerized using mostly data that are already available from human resources personnel. HRM in Action 6.5 describes such a program at the Marine Safety Agency in Great Britain. HRM in Action 6.6 discusses succession planning at General Electric.

Commitment Manpower Planning

Commitment Manpower Planning (CMP)   A systematic approach to human resource planning designed to get managers and their subordinates thinking about and involved in human resource planning.

Ratio Analysis   A tool used in human resource planning to measure the organization's human resource vitality as indicated by the presence of promotable personnel and existing backups.

Commitment manpower planning (CMP) is a relatively recent approach to human resource planning designed to get managers and their employees thinking about and involved in HRP. In addition to encouraging managers and employees to think about human resource planning, CMP provides a systematic approach to human resource planning.[16] CMP generates three reports that supply the following information: (1) the supply of employees and the promotability and placement status of each; (2) the organization's demand, arising from new positions and turnover and projected vacancies for each job title; and (3) the balance or status of supply versus demand, including the name, job, and location of all those suitable for promotions.

Ratio Analysis

Ratio analysis is another tool that can aid in human resource planning. Two basic premises underlie ratio analysis as it applies to human resource planning.[17] The first is that an organization is "vital" in terms of its human resources to the extent that it has people with high potential who are promotable, either now or in the

FIGURE 6–5   SIMPLE ORGANIZATION REPLACEMENT CHART

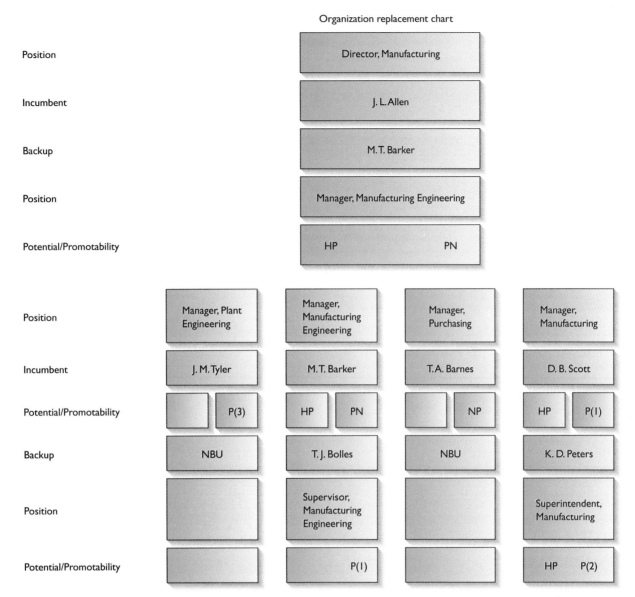

Legend definitions:

HP (high potential) = An above-average or outstanding performer with the potential to advance at least two levels above current position within five years.

PN (promotable now) = An individual who is promotable now to an identified position one level above current position.

P (years) = An individual who is promotable in "x" years to an identified position one level above current position.

NP (not promotable) = An individual who is not promotable above current positions (e.g., individual desires to remain in current position, has retirement pending, has been promoted to maximum capabilities, etc.).

NBU (no backup) = No individual identified as a backup for this position.

Source: D. L. Chicci, "Four Steps to an Organization/Human Resource Plan," *Personnel Journal,* June 1979, p. 392.

HRM IN ACTION

Computerized Succession Planning

6.5

The Marine Safety Agency is responsible for the safety of all ships sailing in United Kingdom (UK) waters. The agency employs approximately 160 marine surveyors to inspect vessels and prevent them from causing pollution.

Most of the positions are occupied by former members of the merchant marine, people who have been ships' masters, engineers, or naval architects in the past. Since these are specialized posts and the pool of qualified people is getting smaller in Britain, the agency is having to recruit on a worldwide basis.

Because most marine surveyors are in their second careers, a considerable number reach retirement age every year. From a succession planning point of view, the agency needed an information system that would help them keep track of approaching retirements and devise future recruitment campaigns. The agency also needed for their information system to be capable of maintaining a detailed skills inventory on every employee, including not only technical expertise but also language skills.

The agency purchased an information systems package from PeopleSoft. The package was up and running in one month! Alan Miller, head of human resources, believes the system will eventually relieve his office of many administrative tasks.

Source: Anat Arkin, "Network Solutions," *People Management,* January 23, 1997, pp. 43–44.

HRM IN ACTION

Top Succession at General Electric

6.6

www.ge.com

In May 1995, General Electric (GE) CEO Jack Welch had an angioplasty and 10 days later underwent elective triple-bypass surgery. *Business Week* reported that "there is no apparent successor to Welch" and asked, "What happens when the boss departs?" The *Wall Street Journal* described GE as suffering from "a case of succession jitters" that left it "scrambling to find a new leader."

The media reaction was surprising, since GE has been described as "North America's first developer of senior-management talent." The truth was that no single executive had been identified as the inheritor of Welch's job. However, an envelope existed containing the names of two or three executives who, the board and Welch had agreed, were capable of immediately taking over the top job.

What sets GE's succession system apart from those of other companies is that board members are closely involved in a continuing evolution of the company's 130 highest-ranking executives. Twice a year directors study the dossiers of approximately 15 of the top executives (15 each session, 30 per year). The dossiers are refined from extensive interviews with the executives, their bosses, former associates, and subordinates. Directors get a feel for the executives' strengths and weaknesses, contribute suggestions for their development, and debate future assignments. When the day comes, the board will be prepared to make a considered decision rather than rubber-stamping an insider's recommendation or making a rushed decision.

Source: Linda Grant, "GE: The Envelope, Please," *Fortune,* June 26, 1995, pp. 89–90.

Organizational Vitality Index (OVI) Index that results from ratio analysis; reflects the organization's human resource vitality as measured by the presence of promotable personnel and existing backups.

near future, and backups have been identified to replace them. The second premise is that an organization is "stagnant" to the extent that employees are not promotable and no backups have been identified to replace the incumbents. The end product of ratio analysis is an overall **organizational vitality index (OVI)**, which can be used as a broad measure of the organization's human resource vitality. The index is calculated based on the number of promotable personnel and the number of existing backups in the organization.

Time Frame of HRP

Because HRP is so closely tied to the organizational planning process, the time frames covered by human resource plans should correspond with those covered by the organizational plans. Organizational plans are frequently classified as short-range (zero to two years), intermediate range (two to five years), or long-range (beyond five years). Ideally, an organization prepares a plan for each of these horizons. Table 6–3 summarizes the major factors affecting long-, intermediate-, and short-range human resource planning.

HRP: An Evolving Process

An organization's human resource planning efforts should be viewed not as an all-or-nothing process but as falling at some point along a continuum. At one end of this continuum are those organizations that do no human resource planning; at the other end are those that completely integrate long-range human resource planning into their strategic business plans.

D. Quinn Mills has identified five stages, or benchmarks, along this continuum.[18] Stage 1 companies have no long-term business plans, and they do little or no human resource planning. Companies at stage 2 have a long-term business plan, but tend to be skeptical of HRP. At the same time, such companies do realize to some degree that human resource planning is important. Stage 3 companies do engage in some aspects of human resource planning, but for the most part these efforts are not integrated into the long-range business plan. Stage 4 companies do a good deal of human resource planning, and their top managers are enthusiastic

TABLE 6-3   **FACTORS AFFECTING THE TIME FRAME OF HRP**

Forecast Factor	Short Range (0–2 Years)	Intermediate Range (2–5 Years)	Long Range (Beyond 5 Years)
Demand	Authorized employment including growth, changes, and turnover	Operating needs from budgets and plans	In some organizations, the same as "intermediate"; in others, an increased awareness of changes in environment and technology—essentially judgmental.
Supply	Employee census less expected losses plus expected promotions from subordinate groups	Human resource vacancies expected from individual promotability data derived from development plans	Management expectations of changing characteristics of employees and future available human resources.
Net needs	Numbers and kinds of employees needed	Numbers, kinds, dates, and levels of needs	Management expectations of future conditions affecting immediate decisions.

Source: Adapted from J. Walker, "Forecasting Manpower Needs," in *Manpower Planning and Programming*, ed. E. H. Burack and J. W. Walker (Boston: Allyn & Bacon, 1972), p. 94.

about the process. These companies have at least one human resource component integrated into the long-range plan. Stage 5 companies treat human resource planning as an important and vital part of their long-term business plan. Naturally, companies at stage 5 are highly enthusiastic about HRP.

Specific Role of Human Resource Personnel

As mentioned earlier, each step in HRP requires a joint effort of the human resource personnel and the individual managers in the organization. The primary roles of human resource personnel are to coordinate, monitor, and synthesize the process. Human resource personnel usually provide the structure and establish the timetable to be followed by operating managers. This helps ensure a unified effort. As individual managers determine their human resource needs, they can channel this information through the human resource staff to be coordinated and synthesized. By funneling all the information through a central source, they can attain maximum efficiency in the process.

Common Pitfalls in HRP

Unfortunately, HRP is not always successful. While myriad things can go wrong, the following eight stumbling blocks are some of the most frequently encountered.[19]

The Identity Crisis: Human resource planners work in an environment characterized by ambiguous regulations, company politics, and diverse management styles. Unless human resource planners develop a strong sense of mission (direction), they often spend much of their time looking for something meaningful to do while the organization questions the reason for their existence.

Sponsorship of Top Management: For HRP to be viable in the long run, it must have the full support of at least one influential senior executive. Such high-ranking support can ensure the necessary resources, visibility, and cooperation necessary for the success of an HRP program.

Size of the Initial Effort: Many HRP programs fail because of an overcomplicated initial effort. Successful HRP programs start slowly and gradually expand as they meet with success. Developing an accurate skills inventory and a replacement chart is a good place to start.

Coordination with Other Management and Human Resource Functions: Human resource planning must be coordinated with the other management and human resource functions. Unfortunately, HRP specialists tend to become absorbed in their own function and fail to interact with others.

Integration with Organization Plans: As emphasized earlier in this chapter, human resource plans must be derived from organization plans. The key here is to develop good communication channels between the organization planners and the human resource planners.

Quantitative versus Qualitative Approaches: Some people view HRP as a numbers game designed to track the flow of people in, out, up, down, and across the different organizational units. These people take a strictly quantitative approach to HRP. Others take a strictly qualitative approach and focus on individual employee concerns such as individual promotability and career development. As is so often the case, a balanced approach usually yields the best results.

Noninvolvement of Operating Managers: HRP is not strictly a human resource department function. Successful HRP requires a coordinated effort on the parts of operating managers and human resource personnel.

The Technique Trap: As HRP has become more and more popular, new and sophisticated techniques have been developed to assist in HRP. (Several of these were discussed earlier in this chapter.) While many are useful, there is sometimes a tendency to adopt one or more of these methods not for what they can do but rather because "everyone is using them." HRP personnel should avoid becoming enamored of a technique merely because it is the "in thing."

SUMMARY OF LEARNING OBJECTIVES

1. **Define human resource planning (HRP).**
   HRP is the process of getting the right number of qualified people into the right job at the right time. Put another way, HRP is the system of matching the supply of people—internally (existing employees) and externally (those to be hired or searched for)—with the openings the organization expects to have over a given time.

2. **Summarize the relationship between HRP and organizational planning.**
   To be effective, any human resource plan must be derived from the long-range and operational plans of the organization. In essence, the success of HRP depends largely on how closely human resource personnel can integrate effective people planning with the organization's business planning process.

3. **Explain strategy-linked HRP.**
   Strategy-linked HRP is based on a close working relationship between human resource staff and line managers. Human resource managers serve as consultants to line managers concerning the people management implications of business objectives and strategies. Line managers, in turn, have a responsibility to respond to the business implications of human resource objectives and strategies. Top management must also be committed to the HRP process.

4. **Identify the steps in the HRP process.**
   HRP consists of four basic steps: (1) determining the impact of the organization's objectives on specific organizational units; (2) defining the skills, expertise, and total number of employees required to achieve the organizational and departmental objectives; (3) determining the additional human resource requirements; and (4) developing action plans to meet the anticipated human resource needs.

5. **Identify the different methods used for forecasting human resource needs.**
   Methods for forecasting human resource needs can be either judgmentally or mathematically based. Judgmental methods include managerial estimates, the Delphi technique, and scenario analysis. Mathematically based methods include various statistical and modeling methods.

6. **Define the concept of benchmarking.**
   Benchmarking involves thoroughly examining internal practices and procedures and measuring them against the ways other successful organizations operate.

7. **Discuss the purpose of a skills inventory.**
   A skills inventory consolidates information about the organization's human resources. It provides basic information on all employees, including, in its simplest form, a list of the names, certain characteristics, and skills of employees.

8. **Describe succession planning, commitment manpower planning, and ratio analysis.**
   Succession planning identifies specific people to fill key positions throughout the organization. Commitment manpower planning is a relatively recent approach to human resource planning designed to get managers and their subordinates thinking about and involved in HRP. Ratio analysis produces the organizational vitality index, a broad measure of an organization's human resource vitality. The index is calculated based on the number of promotable personnel and the number of existing backups in the organization.

9. List several common pitfalls in HRP.
Some of the most frequently encountered stumbling blocks to HRP include an "identity crisis," a lack of sponsorship by top management, an overcomplicated initial effort, a lack of coordination with other management functions, a lack of integration with the organizational plan, taking a strictly quantitative approach, noninvolvement of operating managers, and inappropriate use of certain techniques.

REVIEW QUESTIONS

1. What is human resource planning (HRP)?
2. How does human resource planning relate to organizational planning?
3. What are the four basic steps in the human resource planning process?
4. Explain the cascade approach to setting objectives.
5. Identify several tools that might be used as aids in the human resource planning process.
6. What is the role of human resource personnel in the human resource planning process?
7. List eight common pitfalls in human resource planning.

DISCUSSION QUESTIONS

1. Do you think better HRP could have prevented much of the downsizing that has gone on in many large companies? Why or why not?
2. Do you think most human resource planning is undertaken on the basis of organizational objectives or on an "as necessary" basis?
3. How is it possible to accomplish good organizational planning, and hence good human resource planning, in light of the many changing environmental factors over which the organization has no control?

INCIDENT 6–1

Human Resource Planning—What Is That?

You are a human resource consultant. You have been called by the newly appointed president of a large paper manufacturing firm:

President: I have been in this job for about one month now, and all I seem to do is interview people and listen to personnel problems.

You: Why have you been interviewing people? Don't you have a human resource department?

President: Yes, we do. However, the human resource department doesn't hire top management people. As soon as I took over, I found out that two of my vice presidents were retiring and we had no one to replace them.

You: Have you hired anyone?

President: Yes, I have, and that's part of the problem. I hired a guy from the outside. As soon as the announcement was made, one of my department heads came in and resigned. She said she had wanted that job as vice president for eight years. She was angry because we had hired someone from the outside. How was I supposed to know she wanted the job?

You: What have you done about the other vice president job?

President: Nothing, because I'm afraid someone else will quit because they weren't considered for the job. But that's only half my problem. I just found out that among our youngest professional employees—engineers and accountants—there has been an 80 percent turnover rate during the past three years. These are the people we promote around here. As you know, that's how I started out in this company. I was a mechanical engineer.

You: Has anyone asked them why they are leaving?

President: Yes, and they all give basically the same answer: They say they don't feel that they have a future here. Maybe I should call them all together and explain how I progressed in this company.

You: Have you ever considered implementing a human resource planning system?

President: Human resource planning? What's that?

Questions

1. How would you answer the president's question?
2. What would be required to establish a human resource planning system in this company?

INCIDENT 6–2

A New Boss

The grants management program of the Environmental Protection Agency (EPA) water division was formed several years ago. The program's main functions are to review grant applications, engineering design reports, and change orders and to perform operation and maintenance inspection of wastewater treatment facilities.

Paul Wagner, chief of the section, supervised four engineers, one technician, and one secretary. Three of the engineers were relatively new to the agency. The senior engineer, Waymon Burrell, had approximately three years' experience in the grants management program.

Because only Waymon Burrell had experience in grants management, Wagner assigned him the areas with the most complicated projects within the state. The other three engineers were given regions with less complex projects; they were assigned to work closely with Burrell and to learn all they could about the program.

At the beginning of the year, Wagner decided the new engineers had enough experience to undertake more difficult tasks; therefore, the division's territory could be allocated on a geographical basis. The territory was divided according to river basins, with each engineer assigned two or three areas.

This division according to geography worked fine as the section proceeded to meet all its objectives. However, three months ago, Wagner was offered a job with a consulting engineering company and decided to leave the EPA. He gave two months' notice to top management.

Time passed, but top management did not even advertise for a new section chief. People in the section speculated as to who might be chosen to fill the vacancy; most of them hoped it would be Waymon Burrell, since he knew the most about the workings of the section.

On the Monday of Wagner's last week, top executives met with him and the section members to announce they had decided to appoint a temporary section chief until a new one could be hired. The division chief announced that the temporary section chief would be Sam Kutzman, a senior engineer from another EPA division. This came as quite a surprise to Burrell and the others in the grants management program.

Sam Kutzman had no experience in the program. His background was in technical assistance. His previous job had required that he do research in certain treatment processes so that he could provide more technical performance information to other divisions within the EPA.

Questions

1. Do you think Sam Kutzman was a good choice for temporary section chief?
2. How well has human resource planning worked in this situation?

EXERCISE

Avoiding the Pitfalls of Human Resource Planning

The last section of this chapter discusses eight potential pitfalls of human resource planning. Carefully review the list, and then rank-order each item as to which ones you think would cause you the most problems if you were in charge of the human resource planning effort in an actual company. The pitfall ranked number 1 should be the one you think would be the hardest to avoid, and the one ranked 8 should be the one easiest to avoid. Make any assumptions you deem necessary, and be prepared to justify your ranking.

NOTES AND ADDITIONAL READINGS

1. C. F. Russ, Jr., "Manpower Planning Systems: Part I," *Personnel Journal,* January 1982, p. 41.
2. Ibid.
3. David E. Ripley, "How to Determine Future Work-Force Needs," *Personnel Journal,* January 1995, p. 83.
4. Craig B. Mackey, "Human Resource Planning: A Four-Phased Approach," *Management Review,* May 1981, p. 17. Copyrighted in 1981 by AMACOM, a division of American Management Association, New York. All rights reserved. Excerpted by permission of the publisher.
5. James W. Walker, "Human Resource Planning, 1990's Style," *Human Resource Planning,* December 1990, pp. 229–30; John A. Hooper, Ralph E. Catalanello, and Patrick L. Murray, "Shoring Up the Weakest Link," *Personnel Administrator,* April 1987, p. 50.
6. Ernest C. Miller, "Strategic Planning Pays Off," *Personnel Journal,* April 1989, p. 127.
7. Douglas M. Morrill, Jr., "Human Resources Planning in the 1990s," *Best's Review—Property-Casualty Insurance Edition,* July 1990, pp. 104–7.
8. Much of this section is drawn from Hooper, Catalanello, and Murray, "Shoring Up," pp. 49–55.
9. Adapted from D. L. Chicci, "Four Steps to an Organization/Human Resource Plan," *Personnel Journal,* June 1979, pp. 290–92.
10. Dan Ward, "Workforce Demand Forecasting Techniques," *Human Resource Planning* 19 (no. 1), 1996, pp. 54–55.
11. Samuel Greengard, "Discover Best Practices through Benchmarking," *Personnel Journal,* November 1995, pp. 62–65.
12. Thomas H. Patten, *Manpower Planning and the Development of Human Resources* (New York: John Wiley & Sons, 1971), p. 243.
13. Samuel Greengard, "How to Move to the Next Step," *Workforce,* September 1998, p. 74.
14. Much of this section is drawn from Richard I. Lehr and David J. Middlebrooks, "Work Force Reduction: Strategies and Options," *Personnel Journal,* October 1984, pp. 50–55.
15. James E. McElwain, "Succession Plans Designed to Manage Change," *HR Magazine,* February 1991, pp. 67–71.

16. For a more in-depth discussion of CMP, see C. F. Russ, Jr., "Manpower Planning Systems: Part II," *Personnel Journal,* February 1982, pp. 119–23.

17. Chicci, "Four Steps," p. 392.

18. D. Quinn Mills, "Planning with People in Mind," *Harvard Business Review,* July–August 1985, pp. 97–105.

19. Adapted from Mackey, "Human Resource Planning," pp. 17–20.

Recruiting Employees

Learning Objectives

After studying this chapter, you should be able to:

1. Define recruitment.
2. Discuss job analysis, human resource planning, and recruitment.
3. Explain the purpose of a personnel requisition form.
4. Describe the advantages and disadvantages of using internal methods of recruitment.
5. Discuss job posting and bidding.
6. Describe the advantages and disadvantages of using external methods of recruitment.
7. Define realistic job previews.
8. Explain organizational inducements.

Recruitment Process of seeking and attracting a pool of people from which qualified candidates for job vacancies can be chosen.

[handwritten marginal note: have the greatest chance to be successful]

Recruitment involves seeking and attracting a pool of people from which qualified candidates for job vacancies can be chosen. Most organizations have a recruitment (or, as it is sometimes called, employment) function managed by the human resource department. In an era when the focus of most organizations has been on efficiently and effectively running the organization, recruiting the right person for the job is a top priority. HRM in Action 7.1 provides some information about recruiting on the Internet.

The magnitude of an organization's recruiting effort and the methods to be used in that recruiting effort are determined from the human resource planning process and the requirements of the specific jobs to be filled. As brought out in Chapter 6, if the forecasted human resource requirements exceed the net human resource requirements, the organization usually actively recruits new employees. However, organizations do have options other than recruiting new employees to accomplish the work. Some of these options include using temporary workers, offering overtime to existing employees, subcontracting the work to another organization (this approach is often used on construction projects or projects that have a fixed time period for completion), and leasing of employees.

In addition, recruitment should include seeking and attracting qualified job candidates. Successful recruiting is difficult if the jobs to be filled are vaguely defined. Regardless of whether the job to be filled has been in existence or is newly created, its requirements must be defined as precisely as possible for recruiting to be effective. As discussed in Chapter 5, job analysis provides information about the nature and requirements of specific jobs.

Recruiting on the Internet

7.1

The use of the Internet to recruit employees is growing rapidly. Today, college graduates and professionals are just as likely to send in an electronic resume as a traditional paper-based document. For example, Silicon Graphics, a California-based manufacturer of computer workstations, collects 4,000 to 12,000 resumes each month through the Internet *(http://www.sgi.com)*. IBM's CyberBlue site *(http://www.cybrblu.ibm.com)* offers searchable job postings, job fair information for college students, benefits information, a resume builder, and a page that links to some of the most entertaining sites on the Web, including Calvin and Hobbes and The Dilbert Zone. Other companies use Internet services such as E-Span *(http://www.espan.com)*, Career Mosaic *(http://www.careermosaic.com)*, IntelliMatch *(http://www.intellimatch.com)*, JobTrak *(http://www.jobtrak.com)*, and the Monster Board *(http://www.monster.com)* to get job postings on the Web.

Source: Adapted from Samuel Greenfard, "Use the Web to Automate Recruiting," *Workforce*, March 1997, p. 78.

Job Analysis, Human Resource Planning, and Recruitment

Figure 7–1 illustrates the relationships among job analysis, human resource planning, recruitment, and the selection process. Job analysis gives the nature and requirements of specific jobs. Human resource planning determines the specific number of jobs to be filled. Recruitment concerns providing a pool of people qualified to fill these vacancies. Questions that are addressed in the recruitment process include: What are the sources of qualified personnel? How are these qualified personnel to be recruited? Who is to be involved in the recruiting process? What inducements does the organization have to attract qualified personnel? The selection process, discussed in detail in the next chapter, concerns choosing from

FIGURE 7–1   **RELATIONSHIPS AMONG JOB ANALYSIS, HUMAN RESOURCE PLANNING, RECRUITMENT, AND SELECTION**

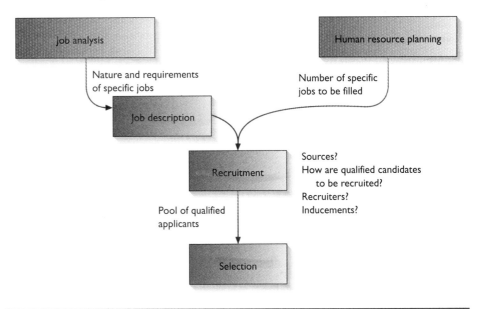

the pool of qualified candidates the individual or group of individuals most likely to succeed in a given job.

Personnel Requisition Form

Most organizations use a **personnel requisition form** to officially request that the human resource manager take action to fill a particular position. The personnel requisition form describes the reason for the need to hire a new person and the requirements of the job. Figure 7–2 shows an example of a personnel requisition form. It is a good idea to attach a job description to the personnel requisition form.

Sources of Qualified Personnel

An organization may fill a particular job either with someone already employed by the organization or with someone from outside. Each of these sources has advantages and disadvantages.

Internal Sources

If an organization has been effective in recruiting and selecting employees in the past, one of the best sources of talent is its own employees. This has several advantages. First the organization should have a good idea of the strengths and weaknesses of its employees. If the organization maintains a skills inventory, it can use this as a starting point for recruiting from within. In addition, performance evaluations of employees are available. Present and prior managers of the employee being considered can be interviewed to obtain their evaluations of the employee's potential for promotion. In general, more accurate data are available concerning current employees, thus reducing the chance of making a wrong decision.

Not only does the organization know more about its employees, but the employees know more about the organization and how it operates. Therefore, the likelihood of the employee having inaccurate expectations and/or becoming dissatisfied with the organization is reduced when recruiting is done from within.

Another advantage is that recruitment from within can have a significant, positive effect on employee motivation and morale when it creates promotion opportunities or prevents layoffs. When employees know they will be considered for openings, they have an incentive for good performance. On the other hand, if outsiders are usually given the first opportunity to fill job openings, the effect can be the opposite.

A final advantage relates to the fact that most organizations have a sizable investment in their work force. Full use of the abilities of the organization's employees improves the organization's return on its investment.

However, there are disadvantages to recruiting from within. One danger associated with promotion from within is that infighting for promotions can become overly intense and have a negative effect on the morale and performance of people who are not promoted. Another danger involves the inbreeding of ideas. When recruiting comes only from internal sources, precautions must be taken to ensure that new ideas and innovations are not stifled by such attitudes as "We've never done it before" or "We do all right without it."

Two major issues are involved if an organization promotes from within. First, the organization needs a strong employee and management development program to ensure that its people can handle larger responsibilities. The second issue concerns the desirability of using seniority as the basis for promotions. Unions generally prefer promotions based on seniority for unionized jobs. Many organiza-

FIGURE 7–2   **PERSONNEL REQUISITION FORM**

PREPARE IN DUPLICATE, SEND ORIGINAL TO PERSONNEL

PERSONNEL REQUISITION

To Requisitioner: The Civil Rights Act of 1963 prohibits discrimination in employment because of race, color, creed, religion, sex or national origin. Federal law also prohibits other types of discrimination such as age. The laws of most States also prohibit some or all of the above types of discrimination as well as some additional types such as discrimination based upon ancestry, marital status or physical or mental handicap or disability. Any expression of limitations in these areas expressed in this requisition should be warranted by a bona fide occupational qualification or legally permissible reason.

DATE _____

FROM _____   _____
                        NAME   DEPARTMENT

I. DESCRIPTION OF NEED

DATE NEEDED	NUMBER OF EMPLOYEES	JOB TITLE	JOB CLASSIFICATION NUMBER	HIRING SALARY RANGE	JOB SALARY RANGE

PERMANENT _____ TEMPORARY _____ If temporary, for how long? _____ WHICH SHIFT? _____

PART TIME _____ FULL TIME _____ If part time, what hours or days? _____

II. REASON FOR NEED

REPLACEMENT: YES__ NO__ If yes, person(s) replaced _____   ADDITION: YES__ NO__ If yes, state reasons _____

III. REQUIREMENTS

EDUCATION: GRADE SCHOOL_____ HIGH SCHOOL_____ COLLEGE_____ COMMERCIAL_____ OTHER_____

EXPERIENCE: Please indicate, clearly, what is absolutely required as a prerequisite.

REQUIRED _____

DESIRABLE _____

ANY OTHER REQUIREMENTS: _____

DATE _____   APPROVED BY _____

DO NOT WRITE BELOW THIS LINE

DATE FILLED _____ By WHOM _____

© Copyright, 1965, 1972, 1978, 1985—V.W. EIMICKE ASSOCIATES, INC., Bronxville, N.Y.   Form 116

Source: Victor W. Eimicke and Laura Klimley, *Managing Human Resources: Documenting the Personnel Function* (Oxford: Pergamon Press, 1987), p. 23.

tions, on the other hand, prefer promotions based on prior performance and potential to do the new job.

Job Posting and Bidding

Job Posting and Bidding   A method of informing employees of job vacancies by posting a notice in central locations and giving a specified period to apply for the job.

Job posting and bidding is an internal method of recruitment in which notices of available jobs are posted in central locations throughout the organization and employees are given a specified length of time to apply for the available jobs. Other methods used in publicizing jobs include memos to supervisors and listings in employee publications. Normally the job notice specifies the job title, rate of pay, and necessary qualifications. The usual procedure is for all applications to be sent to the human resource department for an initial review. The next step is an interview by the prospective manager. Then a decision is made based on qualifications, performance, length of service, and other pertinent criteria.

A successful job posting and bidding program requires the development of specific implementation policies. Some suggestions include the following:

- Both promotions and transfers should be posted.
- Openings should be posted for a specified time period before external recruitment begins.
- Eligibility rules for the job posting system need to be developed and communicated. For example, one eligibility rule might be that no employee can apply for a posted position unless the employee has been in his or her present position for six months.
- Specific standards for selection should be included in the notice.
- Job bidders should be required to list their qualifications and reasons for requesting a transfer or promotion.
- Unsuccessful bidders should be notified by the human resource department and advised as to why they were not accepted.

Naturally, the actual specifications for a job posting and bidding program must be tailored to the particular organization's needs.

In unionized organizations, job posting and bidding procedures are usually spelled out in the collective bargaining agreement. Because they are concerned about the subjective judgments of managers, unions normally insist that seniority be one of the primary determinants used in selecting people to fill available jobs.

External Sources

Organizations have at their disposal a wide range of external sources for recruiting personnel. External recruiting is needed in organizations that are growing rapidly or have a large demand for technical, skilled, or managerial employees.

One inherent advantage of recruiting from outside is that the pool of talent is much larger than that available from internal sources. Another advantage is that employees hired from outside can bring new insights and perspectives to the organization. In addition, it is often cheaper and easier to hire technical, skilled, or managerial people from the outside rather than training and developing them internally. This is especially true when the organization has an immediate demand for this type of talent.

One disadvantage of external recruitment is that attracting, contacting, and evaluating potential employees is more difficult. A second potential disadvantage is that employees hired from the outside need a longer adjustment or orientation period. This can cause problems because even jobs that do not appear to be unique to the organization require familiarity with the people, procedures, policies, and special characteristics of the organization in which they are performed. A final problem is that recruiting from outside may cause morale problems among people within the organization who feel qualified to do the jobs.

Advertising

Job Advertising   The placement of help-wanted advertisements in daily newspapers, in trade and professional publications, or on radio and television.

Web site: Career Resource Center

www.careers.org

Web site: The Computer Jobs Store

www.computerjobs.com

One of the more widely used methods of recruitment is **job advertising.** Help-wanted ads are commonly placed in daily newspapers and in trade and professional publications. Other, less frequently used media for advertising include radio, television, and billboards.

In the past, human resource managers have been encouraged to ensure that their ads accurately describe the job opening and the requirements or qualifications needed to secure the position. However, one study found that the difference was not significant between reader response to a given advertisement that contained a specific description of the candidate qualifications and one containing a nonspecific description.[1] The same study found that corporate image was a more important factor in reader response. In other words, people responded more frequently to advertisements from companies with a positive corporate image than to those companies with a lower corporate image.

In light of such studies, the widespread use of advertising is probably more a matter of convenience than proven effectiveness. If advertising is to be used as a primary source of recruitment, planning and evaluation of the advertising program should be a primary concern of human resource personnel.

Employment Agencies

Web site: America's Job Bank

www.ajb.dni.us

Web site: Global Employer's Network, Inc.

www.geni.jobnet.com

Both public and private employment agencies can be helpful in recruiting new employees. State employment agencies exist in most U.S. cities with populations of 10,000 or more. Although each state administers its respective agencies, the agencies must comply with the policies and guidelines of the Employment and Training Administration of the U.S. Department of Labor to receive federal funds. The Social Security Act requires all eligible individuals to register with the state employment agency before they can receive unemployment compensation. Thus, state employment agencies generally have an up-to-date list of unemployed persons. State employment agencies provide free service for individuals seeking employment and for business organizations seeking employees.

Two types of private employment agencies exist. The executive search firm (or headhunter) seeks candidates for positions with salaries of $50,000 or more. (The term *headhunter* apparently comes from the concept of hiring a replacement head of an organization, such as chief executive officer or chief operating officer.) Thus, customers of executive search firms are organizations seeking to fill high-level vacancies. The second type of employment agency attempts to fill positions paying less than $50,000. Customers of this type of employment agency may be job applicants seeking employment or business firms seeking employees. The fees of private employment agencies are paid by the individual or the employing organization. If the fees are paid by the employing organization, the private employment agency will likely advertise the job as a "fee paid" position.

Temporary Help Agencies and Employee Leasing Companies

Temporary Help   People working for employment agencies who are subcontracted out to businesses at an hourly rate for a period of time specified by the businesses.

Employee Leasing Companies   Provide permanent staffs at customer companies.

One of the fastest-growing areas of recruitment is **temporary help** hired through employment agencies. The agency pays the salary and benefits of the temporary help; the organization pays the employment agency an agreed-upon figure for the services of the temporary help. The use of temporary help is not dependent on economic conditions. When an organization is expanding, temporary employees are used to augment the current staff. When an organization is downsizing, temporary employees create a flexible staff that can be laid off easily and recalled when necessary. One obvious disadvantage of using temporary employees is their lack of commitment to the organization.

Unlike temporary agencies, which normally place people in short-term jobs at various companies, **employee leasing companies** provide permanent staff at customer companies, issue the workers' paychecks, take care of personnel matters, ensure compliance with workplace regulations, and provide various employee benefits.[2] In addition, highly skilled technical workers such as engineers and information technology specialists are supplied for long-term projects under contract between a company and a technical services firm.

Employee Referrals and Walk-ins/Unsolicited Applications

Many organizations involve their employees in the recruiting process. These recruiting systems may be informal and operate by word-of-mouth, or they may be structured with definite guidelines to be followed. Incentives and bonuses are sometimes given to employees who refer subsequently hired people. One drawback to the use of employee referrals is that cliques may develop within the organization because employees tend to refer only friends or relatives.

Walk-ins and unsolicited applications are also a source of qualified recruits. Corporate image has a significant impact on the number and quality of people who apply to an organization in this manner. Compensation policies, working conditions, relationships with labor, and participation in community activities are some of the many factors that can positively or negatively influence an organization's image.

Campus Recruiting

Campus Recruiting
Recruitment activities of employers on college and university campuses.

Recruiting on college and university campuses is a common practice of both private and public organizations. Campus recruiting activities are usually coordinated by the university or college placement center. Generally, organizations send one or more recruiters to the campus for initial interviews. The most promising recruits are then invited to visit the office or plant before a final employment decision is made.

If the human resource department uses campus recruiting, it should take steps to ensure that recruiters are knowledgeable concerning the organization and the jobs to be filled and that they understand and use effective interviewing skills. Recruitment interviewing is discussed later in this chapter.

College recruiters generally review an applicant's résumé before conducting the interview. The On the Job example at the end of this chapter provides guidance in résumé writing.

Another method of tapping the products of colleges, universities, technical/vocational schools, and high schools is through cooperative work programs. Through these programs, students may work part-time and go to school part-time, or they may go to school and work at different times of the year. These programs attract people because they offer an opportunity for both a formal education and work experience. As an added incentive to finish their formal education and stay with the organization, employees are often promoted when their formal education is completed.

HRM in Action 7.2 describes campus recruiting activities of EDS.

Effectiveness of Recruitment Methods

Organizational recruitment programs are designed to bring a pool of talent to the organization. From this pool, the organization hopes to select the person or persons most qualified for the job. An obvious and very important question faced by human resource departments is which method of recruitment supplies the best talent pool.

Many studies have explored this issue. One study concluded that employee referrals were the most effective recruitment source when compared to newspaper advertisements, private employment agencies, and walk-in applicants.[3] This study found that turnover rates for employees hired from employee referrals were lower than for employees hired through the other methods.

Another study examined the relationship among employee performance, absenteeism, work attitudes, and methods of recruitment.[4] This study showed that individuals recruited through a college placement office and, to a lesser extent, those recruited through newspaper advertisements were lower in performance (i.e., quality and dependability) than individuals who made contact with the company on their own initiative or through a professional journal or convention advertisement. This study concluded that campus recruiting and newspaper advertising were poorer sources of employees than were journal/convention advertisements and self-initiated contacts.

Campus Recruiting Practices of EDS

7.2

www.eds.com

EDS, a professional services firm that supplies consulting, business systems, and technology to clients worldwide recruits 2,000 to 3,000 new employees a year from colleges. The company has 50 targeted colleges that it uses to find these employees. As part of its relationship with these targeted colleges, EDS offers résumé writing and other similar services. Once a year the EDS offers a "Case Challenge." Each of the 50 schools has a team of four students—a technical major, a financial major, a marketing or sales major, and student interested in human resource management. EDS gives the teams a business scenario and expects them to come up with business applications of the work they are doing in school and then make presentations. From this group, EDS selects a series of finalists and has a competition. EDS executives are judges and select the winning school, which receives a scholarship. The series of finalists come to the EDS campus, where they are exposed to the senior managers, learn about the company, and talk with company employees, who begin the process of developing a longer-term relationship with the students.

Source: Adapted from Charlene Marmer Soloman, "Stellar Recruiting for a Tight Labor Market," *Workforce,* August 1998, pp. 66–71.

Generally, it seems safe to say that research has not identified a single best source of recruitment. Thus, each organization should take steps to identify its most effective recruitment sources. For example, a human resource department could monitor the effectiveness of recent hires in terms of turnover, absenteeism, and job performance. It might then contrast the different recruitment sources with respect to employee effectiveness and identify which of the specific recruitment sources produces the best employees.

Table 7–1 summarizes the advantages and disadvantages of the internal and external methods of recruitment.

Realistic Job Previews

Realistic Job Previews A method of providing complete information, both positive and negative, to the job applicant.

One method proposed for increasing the effectiveness of all recruiting methods is the use of realistic job previews. **Realistic job previews (RJP)** provide complete job information, both positive and negative, to the job applicant.

Traditionally, organizations have attempted to sell the organization and the job to the prospective employee by making both look good. Normally this is done to obtain a favorable selection ratio, that is, a large number of applicants in relation to the number of job openings. Then, of course, the company can select the cream of the crop. Unfortunately, these attempts sometimes set the initial job expectations of the new employees too high and can produce dissatisfaction and high turnover among employees recruited in this manner. Figure 7–3 contrasts some of the outcomes that can develop from traditional and realistic job previews.

Research on the effectiveness of RJP indicates that it seems to reduce new employee turnover.[5] However, much more research is needed to ascertain its impact on employee performance on the job.

Who Does the Recruiting, and How?

In most large and middle-size organizations, the human resource department is responsible for recruiting. These organizations normally have an employment office within the human resource department. The employment office has recruiters, in-

TABLE 7-1   **ADVANTAGES AND DISADVANTAGES OF INTERNAL AND EXTERNAL RECRUITING**

Source	Advantages	Disadvantages
Internal	• Company has a better knowledge of strengths and weaknesses of job candidate. • Job candidate has a better knowledge of company. • Morale and motivation of employees are enhanced. • The return on investment that an organization has in its present work force is increased.	• People might be promoted to the point where they cannot successfully perform the job. • Infighting for promotions can negatively affect morale. • Inbreeding can stifle new ideas and innovation.
External	• The pool of talent is much larger. • New insights and perspectives can be brought to the organization. • Frequently it is cheaper and easier to hire technical, skilled, or managerial employees from outside.	• Attracting, contacting, and evaluating potential employees is more difficult. • Adjustment or orientation time is longer. • Morale problems can develop among those employees within the organization who feel qualified to do the job.

terviewers, and clerical personnel who handle the recruitment activities both at the organization's offices and elsewhere.

The role of personnel in the employment office is crucial. Walk-ins/write-ins and respondents to advertising develop an impression of the organization through their contacts with the employment office. If the applicant is treated indifferently or rudely, he or she may develop a lasting negative impression. On the other hand, if the applicant is pleasantly greeted, provided with pertinent information about job openings, and treated with dignity and respect, she or he may develop a lasting positive impression. Having employees trained in effective communication and interpersonal skills is essential in the employment office.

When recruiting is done away from the organization's offices, the role of the recruiter is equally critical. Job applicants' impressions about the organization are significantly influenced by the knowledge and expertise of the recruiter.

In small organizations, the recruitment function, in addition to many other responsibilities, is normally handled by one person, frequently the office manager. Also, it is not unusual for line managers in small organizations to recruit and interview job applicants.

Organizational Inducements in Recruitment

Organizational Inducements
Positive features and benefits offered by an organization to attract job applicants.

The objective of recruitment is to attract a number of qualified personnel for each particular job opening. **Organizational inducements** are all the positive features and benefits the organization offers to attract job applicants. Three of the more important organizational inducements are organizational compensation systems, career opportunities, and organizational reputation.

Starting salaries, frequency of pay raises, incentives, and the nature of the organization's fringe benefits can all influence the number of people attracted through the recruitment process. For example, organizations that pay low starting

FIGURE 7–3   TYPICAL CONSEQUENCES OF JOB PREVIEW PROCEDURES

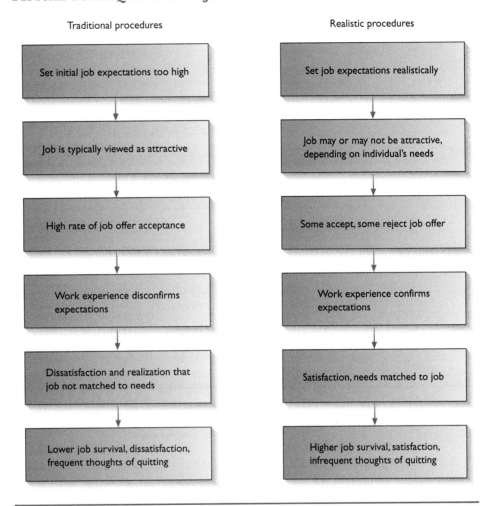

salaries have a much more difficult time finding qualified applicants than do organizations that pay higher starting salaries.

Organizations that have a reputation for providing employees with career opportunities are also more likely to attract a larger pool of qualified candidates through their recruiting activities. Employee and management development opportunities enable present employees to grow personally and professionally; they also attract good people to the organization. Assisting present employees in career planning develops feelings that the company cares. It also acts as an inducement to potential employees.

Finally, the organization's overall reputation, or image, serves as an inducement to potential employees. Factors that affect an organization's reputation include its general treatment of employees, the nature and quality of its products and services, and its participation in worthwhile social endeavors. Unfortunately, some organizations accept a poor image as "part of our industry and business." Regardless of the type of business or industry, organizations should strive for a positive image.

Equal Employment Opportunity and Recruitment

The entire subject of recruitment interviewing is made even more complex by equal employment opportunity legislation and court decisions relating to this legislation. For example, if an interviewer asks for certain information such as race, sex, age, marital status, and number of children during the interview, the company risks the chance of an employment discrimination suit. Prior to employment, interviewers should not ask for information that is potentially prejudicial unless the company is prepared to prove (in court, if necessary) that the requested information is job related.

Equal opportunity legislation has significantly influenced recruitment activities. All recruitment procedures for each job category should be analyzed and reviewed to identify and eliminate discriminatory barriers. For example, the Equal Employment Opportunity Commission (EEOC) encourages organizations to avoid recruiting primarily by employee referral and walk-ins because these practices tend to perpetuate the present composition of an organization's work force. If minorities and females are not well represented at all levels of the organization, reliance on such recruitment procedures has been ruled by the courts to be a discriminatory practice.

The EEOC also suggests that the content of help-wanted ads should not indicate any race, sex, or age preference for the job unless age or sex is a bona fide occupational qualification (BFOQ). Organizations are also encouraged to advertise in media directed toward minorities and women. Advertising should indicate that the organization is an equal opportunity employer and does not discriminate. However, one study has concluded that despite the passage of equal opportunity legislation and numerous court decisions, recruitment ads that discriminate on the basis of sex continue to be widespread.[6]

Campus recruiting visits should be scheduled at colleges and universities with large minority and female enrollment. The EEOC also recommends that employers develop and maintain contacts with minority, female, and community organizations as sources of recruits.

Employers are encouraged to contact nontraditional recruitment sources, such as organizations that place physically and mentally handicapped persons. It is likely that hiring of both females and minority groups will continue to receive attention, and increased emphasis will be placed on hiring those groups.

More than likely, recruiters will also have to pay more attention to the spouse, male or female, of the person being recruited. It may become necessary to assist in finding jobs for spouses of recruits. In hiring women, especially for managerial and professional jobs, it may be necessary to consider hiring the husband as well.

SUMMARY OF LEARNING OBJECTIVES

1. **Define recruitment.**
   Recruitment involves seeking and attracting a pool of people from which qualified candidates for job vacancies can be chosen.

2. **Discuss job analysis, human resource planning, and recruitment.**
   Job analysis gives the nature and requirements of specific jobs. Human resource planning determines the specific number of jobs to be filled. Recruitment provides a pool of qualified people to fill the vacancies.

3. **Explain the purpose of a personnel requisition form.**
   A personnel requisition form describes the reason for the need to hire a new person and the requirements of the job.

4. **Describe the advantages and disadvantages of using internal methods of recruitment.**
   The advantages are that the company has a better knowledge of the strengths and weaknesses of the job candidates; the job candidates have a better knowledge of the company; employee motivation and morale are enhanced; and the return on investment that an organization has in its work force is increased. The disadvantages are that people can be promoted to the point where they cannot successfully perform the job; infighting for promotions can negatively affect morale; and inbreeding can stifle new ideas and innovation.

5. **Discuss job posting and bidding.**
   Job posting and bidding is an internal method of recruitment in which notices of available jobs are posted in central locations throughout the organization and employees are given a specified length of time to apply for the available jobs.

6. **Describe the advantages and disadvantages of using external methods of recruitment.**
   The advantages are that the pool of talent is much larger; new insights and perspectives can be brought to the organization; and it is frequently cheaper and easier to hire technical, skilled, or managerial employees from outside. The disadvantages are that attracting, contacting, and evaluating potential employees are more difficult; adjustment or orientation time is longer; and morale problems can develop among those employees within the organization who feel qualified to do the job.

7. **Define *realistic job previews*.**
   Realistic job previews provide complete job information, both positive and negative, to the job applicant.

8. **Explain organizational inducements.**
   Organizational inducements are all the positive features and benefits offered by an organization that serve to attract job applicants.

REVIEW QUESTIONS

1. What is recruitment?
2. Describe the relationships among job analysis, personnel planning, recruitment, and selection.
3. What is a personnel requisition form?
4. Describe several advantages of recruiting from internal sources and several advantages of recruiting from external sources.
5. Name and describe at least five methods of recruiting.
6. What are realistic job previews?
7. Define and give examples of organizational inducements.
8. Outline some specific EEOC recommendations for job advertising.

DISCUSSION QUESTIONS

1. Discuss the following statement: "An individual who owns a business should be able to recruit and hire whomever he or she pleases."
2. Employees often have negative views on the policy of hiring outsiders rather than promoting from within. Naturally, employees believe they should always be given preference for promotion before outsiders are hired. Do you think this is in the best interest of the organization?
3. As a potential recruit who will probably be looking for a job upon completion of school, what general approach and method or methods of recruiting do you think would be most effective in attracting you?

INCIDENT 7–1

Inside or Outside Recruiting?

Powermat, Inc., has encountered difficulty over the last few years in filling its middle management positions. The company, which manufactures and sells complex machinery, is organized into six semiautonomous manufacturing departments. Top management believes it is necessary for the managers of these departments to make many complex and technical decisions. Therefore, the company originally recruited strictly from within. However, it soon found that employees elevated to middle management often lacked the skills necessary to discharge their new duties.

A decision was then made to recruit from outside, particularly from colleges with good industrial management programs. Through the services of a professional recruiter, the company was provided with a pool of well-qualified industrial management graduates. Several were hired and placed in lower management positions as preparation for the middle management jobs. Within two years, all these people had left the company.

Management reverted to its former policy of promoting from within and experienced basically the same results as before. Faced with the imminent retirement of employees in several key middle management positions, the company decided to call in a consultant for solutions.

Questions

1. Is recruiting the problem in this company?
2. If you were the consultant, what would you recommend?

I N C I D E N T   7 – 2

A Malpractice Suit against a Hospital

Hospital jumping is a term used by hospital personnel to describe the movement of incompetent and potentially negligent employees from hospital to hospital. One factor contributing to hospital jumping is the reluctance of hospitals to release information to other hospitals that are checking references.

Ridgeview Hospital was sued for negligence in its screening of employees. The case involved the alleged incorrect administration to an infant of a medication that nearly caused the child's death. The party bringing suit contended that the nurse who administered the drug was negligent, as was the hospital because it had failed to make a thorough investigation of the nurse's work history and background. It was learned that the nurse had been hired by Ridgeview before it had received a letter of reference from her previous employer verifying her employment history. In support of the plaintiff's case, uncontested information was presented about a similar incident of negligence in patient care by the nurse in her previous employment.

Ridgeview Hospital's personnel director, John Reeves, took the position that reference checks were a waste of time because area hospital personnel directors would not provide what they thought might be defamatory information about former employees. He further stated that in checking reference sources, these same personnel directors would request information they themselves would not give.

Reeves's lawyer concluded that the hospital would have to choose between two potentially damaging alternatives in adopting a personnel screening policy. It could continue not to verify references, thereby risking malpractice suits such as the one discussed. Alternatively, it could implement a policy of giving out all information on past employees and risk defamation suits. The lawyers recommended the second alternative because they thought the potential cost would be significantly less if the hospital were convicted of libel or slander than if it were judged guilty of negligence.

Questions

1. Which of the two alternatives would you recommend to the hospital?
2. What questions could be asked in a recruitment interview to help eliminate the problem?

EXERCISE

Writing a Résumé

Read the On the Job example at the end of this chapter. From the material you read develop your own résumé. Bring the résumé to class and have another student or your professor evaluate it.

NOTES AND ADDITIONAL READINGS

1. J. A. Belt and J. G. P. Paolillo, "The Influence of Corporate Image and Specificity of Candidate Qualifications in Response to Recruitment Advertisement," *Journal of Management,* Spring 1982, p. 110.
2. Jane Ester Bahls, "Employment for Rent," *Nation's Business,* June 1991, p. 36.
3. D. P. Schwab, "Organizational Recruiting and the Decision to Participate," in *Personnel Management: New Perspectives,* ed. K. Rowland and G. Ferris (Boston: Allyn & Bacon, 1982).
4. J. A. Breagh, "Relationship between Recruiting Sources and Employee Performance, Absenteeism, and Work Attitudes," *Academy of Management Journal,* March 1981, p. 145.
5. Paula Popovich and John P. Wanous, "The Realistic Job Preview as a Persuasive Communication," *Academy of Management Review* 7 (1982), p. 572.
6. See John P. Kohl and David B. Stephens, "Wanted: Recruitment Advertising That Doesn't Discriminate," *Personnel,* February 1989, pp. 18–26.

Writing a Résumé*

For employers, the résumé is a screening device. Big corporations get hundreds of thousands of them every year. You can pay an employment agency a hundred dollars to come up with a work of art on 30-weight paper, but it's still junk mail to the person who has to read a hundred of them a day. So you've got 10, maybe 20 seconds to show that person that your résumé is worth a second look.

It's got to look "mahvelous." Which isn't all that hard to make happen. Use high-quality 8 1/2" × 11" paper—white, off-white, light gray, or beige. Maybe a designer or entertainer could go with something flashier, but most job seekers are best served by a conservative, professional look.

Put your résumé on a word processor. (This is just one more instance where computer skills come in handy.) If you don't know word processing, any professional résumé service will be able to do it for you. Don't run it off on a cheap dot-matrix printer. Having it printed looks great, but then you're locked into one generic résumé, and that has some real disadvantages. We'll elaborate shortly. All you really need is a good original. You can have any number duplicated on high-quality paper at a copy center.

Appearance, as well as content, tells the employer a lot about you. Your résumé reflects the kind of work you're capable of producing. It should show that you're well organized, that you can communicate clearly, and that you can make a strong visual presentation. The acid test: Does it look good enough for prospective employers to send out as their own work? If it does not, it is not good enough.

Use some of the tricks that commercial artists use. When they design ads, they play up important information in the white space, those areas free from text. In poorly constructed résumés, we often see dates in those big chunks of white space known as the margin. Dates are *not* selling points. Instead, use information that is: job titles, degrees, skills, and so on.

Stay away from long paragraphs. Your résumé should not look like a page out of your American history text. Ads use a few key words, carefully chosen and strategically placed. You further focus attention by using bold print, larger type, bullets, or asterisks. Remember, you've got just 10 seconds to get their attention.

The job objective is crucial because it informs the employer if there is a match. The job objective, unlike the rest of the résumé, gets close attention on the first pass-through. Therefore, it comes immediately after your name and address at the top of the page. If you're offering what the employer is seeking, he or she will read on.

Taking a Second Look

OK, the employer looked at your résumé, and it looked good. Your career objectives match one of the positions to be filled. Now, the employer is willing to look more closely. And when this happens, there must *not* be any misspelled words, typos, or grammatical errors. So proofread it carefully. Wait a day, and proof it again. Then let a friend take a look at it. Obviously, this means you don't start working on your résumé at the last minute. But since you are a blue-chipper, you have got organizational skills. You'll have time to do it right.

Name and Address

You want them to remember your name, so you put it at the top of the page. If possible, use a larger type size than you use on the rest of your résumé. If your printer doesn't have this capability, there are several other alternatives: rub-on-type, lettering templates, or a Kroy lettering machine. Check with your campus computer lab or copy center if you need help. Include your address and a phone number

---

*Adapted from Bill Osher, Ph.D., and Sioux Henley Campbell, *The Blue-Chip Graduate* (Atlanta: Peachtree Publishers, 1987), pp. 155–79.

where you can be reached or a message can be left for you during working hours. You might want to consider buying or sharing an answering machine. Or you may be able to have messages left with a friend, neighbor, or relative. In some cases, you can have messages taken at the departmental headquarters of your academic major.

Example

MARY Q. STUDENT

Campus Box 007   Atlanta, GA 30332   (404) 894-2607

Job Objective

We've already mentioned that the job objective is the most important piece of information on the page. If employers do not see a potential match, they might not look further, no matter how outstanding your record. Ideally, the job you're looking for is identical to the one they are trying to fill (see the following job objective components chart).

The Job Objective

The following is a component sheet useful in developing a job objective. Pick the ones you feel are applicable to your situation.

- Include the exact job title if you know it. Do not guess! The job objective is used as a screening device. If you apply for a job that does not exist, your résumé will probably be eliminated before it is read thoroughly. Don't chance it.

- Make the objective meaningful. Everything else in the résumé must support and reflect what is said in the objective.

- Be specific and to the point. Broad objectives are often misinterpreted to be vague and uncertain. Avoid the use of platitudes and cliches. They say nothing and cast doubt on the rest of the résumé.

- Include the field you were trained in if this is a selling point. This is especially applicable to those in technical fields.

- Include a subdiscipline if you have specialized in one. This will help to pinpoint where in the company you might be most useful.

- Include the functional area of the company where you want to work. Examples of these company divisions are research and development, production, technical services, information systems/processing, marketing and sales, and administration and finance.

- Include skills/qualifications that are relevant to the job you are seeking. This will help promote you as a strong job candidate.

Example: seek a position in civil engineering as a Structural Engineer utilizing my skills in structures, computer programming, and construction.

- Include the type of organization if it is important to you. Keep in mind that this may limit the number of opportunities open to you.

- Note: If you have several different job objectives, you should have several different résumés.

Avoid platitudes and vagueness. All graduates want "a challenging position with opportunities for advancement." If this is your stated career objective, you have told an employer nothing.

Give any information that will tell the employer where you would fit best. For instance, identify where you want to work in the company (sales, finance, etc.); you may also want to indicate the key skills you have to offer (administrative, quantitative, etc.). Companies don't hire generic employees. They hire researchers, accountants, and human resource directors.

We also advise against listing plural job objectives unless they are closely related. You wouldn't, for instance, say you were looking for an "entry-level position in sales or research" because it makes you look as if you have no clear career goals. If you are looking at rather different positions with different companies, we strongly recommend a different résumé highlighting the appropriate skills and experience for each position. This is where having a generic résumé on a computer, whether it's yours or a professional word processor's, is invaluable. When it comes time to apply for a new job, it is easy to rearrange the material.

Use the actual job titles when you know them—catch the employer's attention right away by showing the possibility of a match. However, don't guess if you're not sure. Personnel may be doing the screening, and they might eliminate you if they don't see what they've been told to look for. If you don't know the exact title, use a standard area such as finance, sales, or research.

Everything else on the résumé complements the job objective. The education, experience, and skills all show that you can do the job you're trying to get.

Example

OBJECTIVE: Seek a position as an **Advertising Sales Representative** using my academic background, proven sales skills, and retail experience.

Education

List your educational experience in reverse chronological order. If you went to a prestigious school, highlight the fact by using boldface letters or caps. Be sure to include a high GPA and any honors or awards. List the key courses relevant to the job you are seeking. Omit insignificant schooling such as the summer course you took at the junior college back home. Don't mention your high school unless you went to a truly outstanding one or had an especially distinguished record.

Example

EDUCATION:
St. Anselm's College   GPA: 2.9/4.0
B.A. Communications   6/98

Coursework: Marketing, Advertising, Media Planning, Principles of Persuasion, Managerial Accounting & Control, Consumer Psychology, Communication Ethics & Law, Public Speaking, FORTRAN

Honors and Activities: Dean's List, earned **80%** of college expenses, Young Business Leaders Club

---

Skills

Employers want to know what skills you have. You can embed them in your work history, but sometimes it's a good idea to have a separate skills section. There you can highlight the main skills required of the position you're seeking. By doing so, you increase your chances of creating a match in the employer's mind.

Use the STAR Technique: situation, action, results. Positive results create positive reactions. And if you can quantify your results, you're talking in a language employers understand.

	Example
Marketing	• Successfully participated in three-month-long computer-based marketing game that simulated the soft drink industry.
Organizational Ability	• Actively involved in arranging campus international festival—responsibilities included arranging media events, designing pamphlets, and coordinating the various committees involved.

Work Experience

List in reverse chronological order. Play up your work if it's career related or requires skills you want to emphasize. Whenever possible, use job descriptions that are results oriented.

Example	
WORK HISTORY: MACY'S DEPARTMENT STORE	
Sales Representative	9/90–12/95
Retail Sales	Created furniture displays and performed price markdowns that led to **10% increase in departmental sales** for 1995
Communication Skills	Reinforced and **interpreted company procedures** and policies to new company employees during training periods

Some students find it helpful to have two separate work sections—career related, which is prominently displayed, and other work, which goes toward the bottom of the page. If you have paid for your own education or a good portion of it, say so. It indicates that you're hard working and self-sufficient. Even if work is not directly related to your job objective, you often learn skills that are relevant to it. For example, getting customers for a summer lawn care business demonstrates sales ability.

Additional Information

Every inch of your résumé should be used to your advantage. List only information that would be a selling point. Most employers don't really need to know that you enjoy swimming and scuba diving. A marine biologist, however, might find it helpful to include these. An engineer cited her plumbing experience when she applied for a position that required wearing a hard hat. She wanted to show that being a woman did not mean she was afraid to get her hands dirty. One candidate noted that hunting was one of his hobbies. He was applying for a position in a rural area where hunting was extremely popular. By mentioning his interest in guns, he was able to show that he could be one of the gang even though he'd gone to school in a big city. If you can't find another place to include a selling point, stick it in here. Leave it off if it is not relevant.

References

Choose them carefully. Hopefully, you may have many to choose from. Ask them if they are comfortable writing a favorable recommendation for you. Make sure they have copies of your résumé. It will help them to discuss you more knowledgeably when they are contacted by employers. Also, when they see the total package, they might be able to come up with other job leads for you. We recommend not listing your references on the résumé. It is better to use every precious inch of space to promote yourself.

Wording and Phrasing

You control the tone of your résumé by the way you write it. There should be no negatives. One student once listed a course in which he made a *D*. That made a memorable résumé, but not in a good way.

Your résumé should be crisp and have punch. Remember, it is your personal ad. Start sentences with verbs or action words, and you'll create the impression that you're a "doer," not one who sits and waits. Delete pronouns and anything superfluous.

The whole idea is to boil your marketability down to its essence. Recruiters and interviewers then will find it easy to remember you—and why they should hire you. Not every recruiter has been trained in human resources. Frequently corporations send new, inexperienced employees to handle screening interviews at college placement centers. They do not necessarily know how to compare the credentials of many different candidates. It is to your advantage to make their job easier. A sharp résumé is a first step. Make it clear why you're the one their company is looking for.

Exhibit 7–A shows a sample résumé format.

Action Words for Résumé Construction

A résumé will be the first impression an employer has of you. Make it count! Set the tone by using both action and positive words. Starting sentences with verbs can make your message stronger. Be honest, but do not diminish your abilities by using lackluster words.

E X H I B I T   7 — A

RÉSUMÉ FORMAT

Name

Address	City	State	Zip	Phone

Job Objective: Most important piece of information on résumé; used by employers as screening device or to signal job match; must grab attention and motivate employer to read further (see section on Job Objectives).

Education: List in reverse chronological order, putting the most promotable fact—school or degree—first.
Mention any outstanding honors or achievements, such as high GPA, Dean's List.
Give examples of relevant coursework and school related activities if a recent graduate.

Skills Choose skills that are most relevant to job objective.
• Give short statements to support skills.
• Make support statements results oriented.
• Position most marketable skills first.

Employment: Place stronger of the two sections, employment or education, first.
List in reverse chronological order, putting the most promotable facts—employer or job title—first.
Give functional description of job if employment history is strong and supports job objective.

Miscellaneous: • Call this section anything applicable—INTERESTS, ACTIVITIES, ACCOMPLISHMENT, or ACHIEVEMENTS.
• Give only information that an employer would be interested in knowing.
• Stay away from personal and chatty information.

References: Furnished upon request.

Remember: There are no concrete rules in résumé preparation. Modify this guide when necessary, to make the most favorable impression.

Exhibit 7–B provides a list of action words to use in constructing your résumé. Refer to it often.

Types of Résumés

Chronological

This is the most traditional type—which is its advantage. Employers are familiar with it. The disadvantage of the chronological résumé is that it plays up your work history even if it is sketchy or unrelated to your job objective. If you have followed the blue-chip Master Plan, you should have a solid work history. If your professional experience is weak, consider another type of résumé. Exhibit 7–C shows a chronological résumé.

Functional

Since work history is played down, you can emphasize the skills necessary to perform the job you are seeking. And since you are not following any prescribed order, you can position the most relevant skills—experience, for example—higher on the page. Its main disadvantage is that employers see fewer of this type, and that might bother some of them. Of course, it might also catch their eye. Exhibit 7–D shows a functional résumé.

Hybrid

We believe there is nothing sacred about résumé construction. Your ultimate goal is to create a message that effectively promotes you. We read the résumé experts, and we considered the principles of advertising. We did some research of our

---

EXHIBIT 7 – B   LIST OF ACTION WORDS

actively	chaired	directed	function	managed	primary	reviewed
accelerated	changed	diverted	generated	manufactured	principal	satisfactorily
accomplished	channeled	drafted	graduated	marketed	produced	saved
accurately	chiefly	drew up	guided	maximum	proficient	scheduled
achieved	chosen	earned	helped	measurable	programmed	schematic
adapted	clarified	economically	hired	mediation	progressed	selected
addressed	coached	edited	honored	merchandised	projected	served
adjusted	collaborated	effective	illustrated	merit	promoted	significantly
administered	commended	elected	implemented	methodically	proposed	simplified
adopted	communication	eliminated	improved	minimal	proved	sold
advised	compiled	enhanced	increased	moderated	provided	solved
analyzed	completed	enthusiastic	indexed	modified	publicized	solution
applied	conducted	erected	influenced	most	qualified	specialized
appointed	consistently	established	innovation	motivated	quoted	spoke
appraised	constructed	estimated	inspected	motorized	recommended	stabilized
approved	consulted	evaluated	installed	narrated	recorded	strategy
arbitrated	coordinated	examined	instituted	navigated	reduced (losses)	streamlined
arranged	contracted	executive	instrumental	negotiated	reinforced	structured
assembled	counseled	exhibited	integrated	obtained	renovated	successfully
assessed	created	expanded	interpreted	organized	reorganized	suggested
assisted	credited (with)	expedited	interviewed	originated	reported	summarized
attentive	debated	experienced	judged	overcame	represented	supervised
audited	decided	explained	knowledgeable	participated	researched	supplemented
authenticated	delegated	expressed	launched	perceptive	resolved	supported
budgeted	delivered	facilitated	lead	performed	responsible	surveyed
built	demonstrated	familiar (with)	lectured	persuaded	responsibilities	systematized
calculated	designed	filed	licensed	pinpointed	restored	taught
capable	determined	finalist	lobbied	planned	revamped	trained
careful	detected	finished	logical	positive	revenue	upgraded
cataloged	developed	forecasted	maintained	prepared	revised	wrote
certified	devised	founded	major	presented		

EXHIBIT 7-C   **CHRONOLOGICAL RESUME**

ANDREW FOENSTER

Campus Address: P.O. Box 64902, St. Cloud, MN 56301   612/255–9000
Permanent Address: 17 Faribault Place, Omaha, NE   402/448–6413
68178

OBJECTIVE: Position as **Medical Technologist** in clinical laboratory

EDUCATION:

ST. CLOUD STATE UNIVERSITY   12/95
   B.S. Medical Technology
LINCOLN COMMUNITY COLLEGE   6/92
   A.S. General Sciences
Significant Coursework:
   • Hematology   • Microbiology
   • Immunology   • Microscopy
   • Clinical Chemistry • Immunohematology
   • Histology   • Cell Biology

WORK EXPERIENCE:
HENNEPIN COUNTY MEDICAL CENTER
   Intern Technologist   Minneapolis, MN
                                                             1/91–present
Performed **microscopic examinations** of blood and bone marrow. Isolated and identi-
fied **microbiological cultures.** Conducted **renal function tests;** including chemical and
microscopic examinations of body fluid analysis. Performed and correlated **serologi-
cal testing.**
BHP, INC.   Redland, MN
   Operator I/Operator II   10/89–11/90
Manufactured **blood references** for Coulter counters and other specialized medical
uses. Mixed chemical solutions, washed blood, sampled materials, mixed blood solutions to specified concentrations of various cell types. **Promoted** from operator I to
operator II in three weeks.
GREATER LINCOLN BLOOD PROGRAM
   Interviewed prospective donors   Lincoln, NE
                                                             Summers
                                                             1988/89

ACTIVITIES:
Provided **100%** of college expenses; member, **Medical Technology Association;** member, St.
Cloud State Ski Club

REFERENCES AVAILABLE UPON REQUEST

own—asking recruiters and personnel directors how they appraised résumés. Our
guidelines evolved from all these sources. But they are still only guidelines.

Different students may have unique situations that require novel résumés. What
about the student who makes a dramatic shift in educational focus? How can you
get the most mileage out of a double or dual degree program? Nontraditional students also present unique problems. How do you highlight your strengths, if
you're a middle-aged homemaker returning to the work force? (Returning to the
paid work force would be more accurate.) Or suppose you are returning to school
after a substantial work history. Some résumés break the rules, but we think they
come out stronger for doing so.

Cover Letters   Cover letters should be strong enough to stand on their own and promote you even
when separated from your other credentials. In other words, no "Dear Mr. Gronk,

EXHIBIT 7-D   **FUNCTIONAL RESUME**

BENNETT TINDALL

Post Office Box 15933
Atlanta, Georgia 30332
404/892-4400

OBJECTIVE: Seek position as an **industrial designer** using strong design and project management skills

EDUCATION: **GEORGIA INSTITUTE OF TECHNOLOGY**   6/98

B.S. Industrial Design — Concentrated in product package, exhibit and graphic design; additional courses included production processes and materials, computer-aided design (CAD), ergonomics, and solid modeler experience

DUKE UNIVERSITY   6/96–9/96

Studies Abroad Program/France — Studied art history and figure drawing; traveled throughout Europe for two months

QUALIFICATIONS:

Product Design — Concept model of **mobile parapodium** retained by Atlanta's Henrietta Eggleston Hospital for further development

Computer-Aided Design — Proficient in **solid modeler** and design drafting techniques

Project Management — Served as **President** and **Board Member** for campus organization; responsibilities included revising and implementing annual budget, organizing programs and events, and proposing ideas and strategies for annual goals

WORK HISTORY: Contributed **60%** of college expenses through work and financial aid as follows:

Delivery Manager — **FUN COMPANY, INC.**   Summers 1990–91
Coordinated, scheduled, and produced employee picnics and conventions; **supervised** staffing groups of 20–60

ACTIVITIES: President and Board Member, Black Student Fellowship—3 years; **Dean's List;** staff artist for student newspaper

REFERENCES AND PORTFOLIO AVAILABLE UPON REQUEST

I'm interested in working for your organization. Enclosed, please find my résumé. Sincerely. . . ."

Use the cover letter to elaborate on any information that is briefly covered in the résumé and is a selling point. Use key phrases taken from your résumé. Advertising relies on repeated presentations, and you are advertising yourself. "Where's the beef?" is probably still familiar to you several years after the ad stopped running because you heard it so many times.

Format   The opening paragraph needs to serve as a "hook." It should motivate employers to read further. Mentioning something interesting about the company (not just something found in the yellow pages) shows that you believe their company is worth spending time on. Like the résumé, the cover letter needs to show how a candidate's skills meet the employer's needs. State specifically how you can help solve the employer's problems. Indicate why you're contacting the employer and how you found out about the job (magazine article, newspaper ad, professional contact, etc.).

You'll probably need to do some research in sources such as the *Business Periodi-*

cal Index, Reader's Guide, Moody's Index, and *Dun's Career Guide.* Say specifically why you're interested in the particular organization you're contacting.

Body of Letter   Present your case as a strong candidate. Briefly cite whichever of your academic achievements, skills, accomplishments, and work history are relevant. Give specific examples with details. Repeat some of the key phrases contained in your résumé to reinforce your selling points. Tell them "where the beef is." Mention enclosing a résumé for their convenience.

Closing Paragraph   Ask for action. Be confident and assertive about doing so. You wouldn't apply for the job if you didn't think you were the right one to do it. State that you will contact them in 10 days to two weeks. *And do it.* Exhibit 7–E gives an illustration of a cover letter.

EXHIBIT 7–E   **SAMPLE COVER LETTER**

February 2, 1999

Museum of Natural Artifacts
    and History
1748 Lincoln Square
New York, NY 10025

Attn: Mr. Carson Donnelly
        Director of Student Internship Program

Dear Mr. Donnelly:

I am interested in applying for a summer internship offered through the Museum of Natural Artifacts and History. *American Historian* magazine recently reported that the MNAH provided the "most extensive training—outside of a dig—to those students interested in archaeology and anthropology." Although you have 25 summer internships, it's obvious that you have to be selective in choosing participants. Here's why I can make a positive contribution.

First, I have prior experience working in a museum. While in high school, I was volunteer at the Vandernessen Museum of Fine Arts. There I helped the curator set up exhibits and prepare art objects for shipment. One project that I particularly enjoyed working on included over 250 Indian artifacts and featured a full-scale replica of a wigwam.

Second, my academic accomplishments include a GPA of 3.7, after one semester as an anthropology major at Bates College, and membership in the National Honor Society.

Finally, I have strong communication and leadership skills. I have proven experience in leading groups, being a team member, and working with the public, all assets that are helpful in a museum environment.

I have enclosed a résumé for your convenience. I am eager to discuss internship opportunities and will contact you in three weeks to arrange an interview.

Sincerely,

Nicholas Bennings

Nicholas Bennings
37-G Addison Hall
Bates College
Lewiston, ME 04240

Résumé Checklist

You want your résumé to be memorable to the employer—but for all the right reasons. An omission or mistake should not be noted as your résumé's most outstanding feature. Use this chart to check for any oversights. Have it double-checked by a friend just to ensure you haven't missed anything.

Did You:	Yes	No
1. Prominently display your name?		
2. Put in a complete address and zip code?		
3. List a daytime telephone number and area code?		
4. Specify your job objective?		
5. Position your strongest information first?		
6. Describe your education?		
7. Complete a work experience section?		
8. Detail your relevant skills?		
9. Include information on affiliations?		
10. Use both positive and action words?		
11. Check for accuracy of information—names, dates, and so on?		
12. Verify technical terms and descriptions?		
13. Correct any poor grammar?		
14. Shorten or tighten sentences?		
15. Eliminate repetitiveness?		
16. Leave out anything important?		

Selection, Motivation, and Performance at Nucor Steel

Managers need to understand the basic properties of selection, and the common selection methods to effectively fill the positions of tomorrow's leading organizations. Selection techniques vary within industries and companies. But whatever method is used, it's important that the method be reliable and valid.

Reliability is defined as the degree to which a measure is free from random error. If a measure is reliable, then a score a person receives based on that measure will be consistent over time and over different contexts. The more reliable the measure, the more it can be trusted as a basis for decision making.

Validity is the extent to which performance on a measure is related to performance on the job. If what is being measured isn't a criterion for the job being filled, then the test isn't valid.

HRM professionals apply standards to reliability and validity to various common selection methods, including interviews, references, biographical data, personality inventories, work samples, and physical and cognitive abilities tests.

Nucor has a very lean corporate structure which requires flexibility and multi-tasking for every job description. This unique environment keeps everyone employed and busy even during down time. Their bonus structure, based on team output of quality steel, ranges as high as 150% of base pay. As a result, Nucor employees are some of the highest paid in the industry.

When recruiting began, Nucor managers needed to find people who would be motivated by the incentive pay structure, and who could work within this flexible new environment. HRM manager Vincent Schiavoni said, "We have a pretty unique structure here. We're looking to get people who are used to working in team environments."

Tracy L. Shellabarger, Nucor's controller, commented on the company's hiring practices: "When we got started, the central feature to us was that we didn't have any job descriptions to work from. We were looking more for general types of skills and the ability for someone to be motivated by the types of things that we offered, for example, our incentive pay system. We also were looking for multitalented kinds of people because cross-training is very important in a lean environment like ours. We placed an ad in the paper and we advertised for a four hour period, 8 a.m. to noon. In that four-hour time period we accepted just a little ever 900 applications. Of those 900 people we were looking for 40 to 50 initial employees. So any department manager that was looking to fill positions would look through those applications and bring in whoever they thought was the best qualified from that group.

"Once the employee was brought in, then we would have that person interviewed by generally one or two supervisors in the work area where they would be going to work. At the same time that they did those interviews they would also allow that potential employee to take some basic tests—aptitude, personality skills—to see if they fit into the mold of the person they were looking for. Once a person had passed both the interview and the test, then we would take the best of those people and send them to psychologists for further interviews."

Nucor wasn't always so efficient with its hiring practices. Lewis Kirven, Nucor's hot mill supervisor, said, "The way we used to do it was kind of like Russian roulette. Now I guess we probably have got it to where we can hit. I'm guessing 90% good people coming on board."

Critical Thinking Questions

1. In the context of selection methods, define "reliability" and "validity." Could a selection technique be reliable but not valid? Explain.

2. Nucor has combined high-tech steel making with careful employee selection. Do you think that employee selection is more important at Nucor than at a traditional steel plant?

3. What trends over the last several decades have made employee selection critical for manufacturers?

Selecting Employees

Learning Objectives

After studying this chapter, you should be able to:

1. Outline the steps in the selection process.
2. Describe aptitude, psychomotor, job knowledge, proficiency, interest, and personality tests.
3. Explain a polygraph test.
4. Describe structured and unstructured interviews.
5. Define validity.
6. Explain predictive validity.
7. Explain concurrent validity.
8. Describe content validity.
9. Discuss construct validity.
10. Define reliability.
11. Define adverse (or disparate) impact.

Selection The process of choosing from among available applicants the individuals who are most likely to successfully perform a job.

The objective of the **selection** process is to choose the individual who can successfully perform the job from the pool of qualified candidates. Job analyses, human resource planning, and recruitment are necessary prerequisites to the selection process. A breakdown in any of these processes can make even the best selection system ineffective.

The Selection Process

Processing an applicant for a job normally entails a series of steps. Figure 8–1 illustrates the steps in a typical selection process. The size of the organization, the types of jobs to be filled, the number of people to be hired, and outside pressures from the EEOC or union all influence the exact nature of an organization's selection process. Most organizations use a multiple cutoff technique in selection. With this technique, an applicant must be judged satisfactory through a series of screening devices, such as application forms, interviews, and tests. The applicant is eliminated from consideration for the job if any of these devices is unsatisfactory. All of these screening devices must be validated if they produce adverse or disparate impact.

Application Form

Completing an application form is normally the first step in most selection procedures. The application provides basic employment information for use in later steps of the selection process and can be used to screen out unqualified appli-

FIGURE 8 - 1   STEPS IN THE SELECTION PROCESS

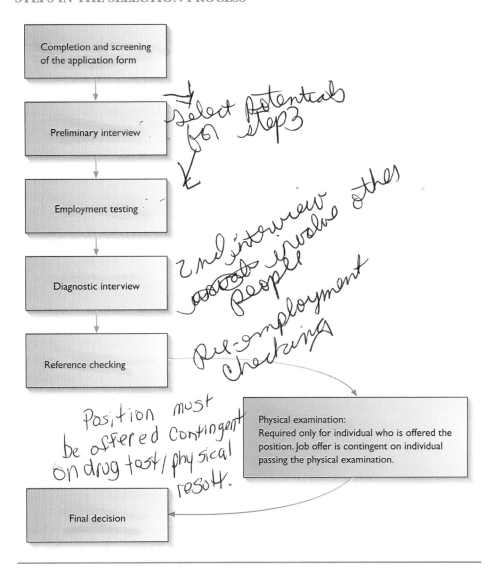

cants. For example, if the job opening requires the ability to use a word processor and the applicant indicates an inability to use a word processor, there is no need to process the application further.

EEOC Requirements

The EEOC and the courts have found that many application and interview inquiries disproportionately reject minorities and females and frequently are not job related. Many questions have therefore been explicitly prohibited. Some of the major questions that should be eliminated from preemployment inquiries (both application forms and interviews) or carefully reviewed to ensure their use is job related and nondiscriminatory include the following:

1. *Race, color, national origin, and religion.* Inquiries about race, color, national origin, or religion are not illegal per se, but asking or recording this information in employment records can invite careful scrutiny if discrimination charges are filed against the employer.

2. *Arrest and conviction records.* An individual's arrest record has been ruled by the courts to be an unlawful basis for refusal to hire unless the job relatedness for such a policy can be established.[1]

3. *Credit rating.* An applicant's poor credit rating has also been ruled by the courts to be an unlawful basis for refusal to hire unless a business necessity for such a policy can be established.[2] Inquiries about charge accounts and home or car ownership may be unlawful unless required because of business necessity.

The On the Job example at the end of Chapter 3 provides a comprehensive listing of permissible questions and questions to be avoided, not only in preemployment interviews but also on application forms. One study of 151 of the largest employers in the United States revealed that all but two employers had at least one inappropriate question on their forms. Fifty-seven of the employers need to examine and redesign their application forms.[3]

Processing

Weighted Application Forms
Application forms that
assign different weights to
different questions.

Normally a member of the human resource department reviews the information on the application form to determine the applicant's qualifications in relation to the requirements of currently available jobs. Another screening procedure is the use of **weighted application forms.** These forms assign different weights to different questions. Weights are developed by determining which item responses were given more frequently by applicants who proved to be higher performers but less frequently by applicants who proved to be poorer performers. Weighted application forms are subject to the validity requirements discussed earlier in this chapter. Studies have shown the weighted application form to be useful in the selection of salespeople, clerical workers, production workers, secretaries, and supervisors.[4]

Accuracy of Information

The accuracy of information given on application forms is open to debate. Placing full reliance on information provided on the application form may not be prudent unless some means of verification is used. Some of the information on the application form can be verified through reference checking, which is described later in this chapter.

In an attempt to ensure that accurate information is given, many employers require the applicant to sign a statement similar to the following:

I hereby certify that the answers given by me to the foregoing questions and statements made are true and correct, without reservations of any kind whatsoever, and that no attempt has been made by me to conceal pertinent information. Falsification of any information on this application can lead to immediate discharge at the time of disclosure.

Whether this statement actually increases the accuracy of information provided is not known. However, employers view falsification of an application form as a serious offense that, if detected, normally leads to discharge.

Applicant Flow Record

Applicant Flow Record A
form completed voluntarily
by a job applicant and used
by an employer to obtain
information that could be
used to illegally
discriminate.

At the time of completing the application form, the applicant is frequently asked to complete an applicant flow record. An **applicant flow record** is a form used by a company to obtain from a job applicant information that could be used to illegally discriminate. This record is completed voluntarily by the applicant. The On the Job example at the end of this chapter shows a sample combination application form and applicant flow record. Data and information from the applicant flow record can then be used to provide statistical reports to the EEOC or OFCCP or used in defense against charges of discrimination concerning the employer's recruitment and selection activities.

Preliminary Interview

The preliminary interview is used to determine whether the applicant's skills, abilities, and job preferences match any of the available jobs in the organization, to explain to the applicant the available jobs and their requirements, and to answer any questions the applicant has about the available jobs or the employer. A preliminary interview is usually conducted after the applicant has completed the application form. It is generally a brief, exploratory interview that is normally conducted by a specialist from the human resource department. The interview screens out unqualified or uninterested applicants. Interview questions must be job related and are subject to demonstrations of validity. The Preemployment Inquiry Guide at the end of Chapter 4 provides a summary of permissible inquiries and inquiries to be avoided during the preliminary interview.

Formal Testing

In *Albemarle* v. *Moody*, the Supreme Court ruled that any procedure used to make selection decisions is to be construed as a test. If a test is to be used in the selection process and if the selection process has adverse impact on legally protected groups, the EEOC requires the employer to establish validity and reliability using the procedures outlined in the "Uniform Guidelines on Employee Selection Procedures," which are described later in this chapter.

Many types of commercial tests are available to organizations for use in the selection process. Many of these tests have undergone validation and reliability studies. One useful source for review of these tests is the *Mental Measurements Yearbook*, which is published by the University of Nebraska.[5] This handbook summarizes a wide variety of commercial tests and also provides an evaluation of the tests by several experts. HRM in Action 8.1 provides a description and review of a test from this handbook.

The following sections examine five categories of tests: aptitude, psychomotor, job knowledge and proficiency, interests, and personality. In addition, the use of polygraphs, graphology, and drug and AIDS testing is discussed.

Aptitude Tests   Aptitude tests measure a person's capacity or potential ability to learn and perform a job. Some of the more frequently used tests measure verbal ability, nu-

---

HRM IN ACTION

Sales Staff Selector Test

8.1

www.waldentesting.com

The Sales Staff Selector Test is a battery of seven tests that purports to evaluate the suitability of candidates of all levels of experience for the position of sales representative. The seven tests consist of numerical skills, problem-solving ability, fluency, sales comprehension, sales motivation, interest in working with people, and emotional stability. The company that provides the test, Wolfe Personnel Testing & Training Systems, Inc., grades the test and provides a personalized report on each person.

The first test, Numerical Skills, is a five-minute timed test to evaluate ability to perform simple arithmetic. Problem-Solving Ability is another five-minute test to determine the last item in a progressive series of numbers and letters. Fluency comprises three two-minute timed tests in which respondents write all the words they can think of that begin or end with a particular syllable. Sales Comprehension is a 30-item, multiple-choice test that differentiates between salespeople and nonsalespeople. Sales Motivation consists of 75 items to distinguish between salespeople and nonsalespeople. Interest in Working with People contains 40 items to measure the introversion-extroversion dimension of personality. Emotional Stability is a 40-item measure of personal stability.

All of the reviewers of the test in the *Mental Measurements Yearbook* recommend caution in the use of the test because the company providing it did not provide validity or reliability data for the test.

Source: Adapted from Jane Close Conoley and Jack J. Kramer, eds. *The Tenth Mental Measurements Yearbook* (Lincoln, Neb.: The Buros Institute of Mental Measurements, University of Nebraska Press, 1989), pp. 707–9.

Aptitude Tests Means of measuring a person's capacity or latent ability to learn and perform a job.

merical ability, perceptual speed, spatial ability, and reasoning ability. Verbal-aptitude tests measure a person's ability to use words in thinking, planning, and communicating. Numerical tests measure ability to add, subtract, multiply, and divide. Perception speed tests measure ability to recognize similarities and differences. Spatial tests measure ability to visualize objects in space and determine their relationships. Reasoning tests measure ability to analyze oral or written facts and make correct judgments concerning these facts on the basis of logical implications.

One of the oldest and, prior to the passage of equal opportunity legislation, most frequently used aptitude tests was the general intelligence test. The EEOC views this type of test with disfavor because such tests often contain questions that are not related to successful performance on the job. Thus, employers have largely abandoned the use of intelligence tests in employee selection.

Psychomotor Tests

Psychomotor Tests Tests that measure a person's strength, dexterity, and coordination.

Psychomotor tests measure a person's strength, dexterity, and coordination. Finger dexterity, manual dexterity, wrist-finger speed, and speed of arm movement are some of the psychomotor abilities that can be tested. Abilities such as these might be tested for hiring people to fill assembly-line jobs.

Job Knowledge and Proficiency Tests

Job Knowledge Tests Tests used to measure the job-related knowledge of an applicant.

Job knowledge tests measure the job-related knowledge possessed by a job applicant. These tests can be either written or oral. The applicant must answer questions that differentiate experienced and skilled workers from less experienced and less skilled workers. **Proficiency tests** measure how well the applicant can do a sample of the work to be performed. A word processing test given to applicants for a secretarial job is an example of a proficiency test.

Interest Tests

Proficiency Tests Tests used to measure how well a job applicant can do a sample of the work to be performed in the job.

Interest tests are designed to determine how a person's interests compare with the interests of successful people in a specific job. These tests indicate the occupations or areas of work in which the person is most interested. The basic assumption in the use of interest tests is that people are more likely to be successful in jobs they like. The primary problem with using interest tests for selection purposes is that responses to the questions are not always sincere.

Personality Tests

Interest Tests Tests designed to determine how a person's interests compare with the interests of successful people in a specific job.

Personality Tests Tests that attempt to measure personality traits.

Personality tests attempt to measure personality characteristics. These tests are generally characterized by questionable validity and low reliability and presently have limited use for selection purposes. Two of the better-known personality tests are the Rorschach inkblot test and the Thematic Apperception Test (TAT). In the Rorschach test, the applicant is shown a series of cards that contain inkblots of varying sizes and shapes. The applicant is asked to tell what the inkblots look like to him or her. With the TAT, the applicant is shown pictures of real-life situations for interpretation. With both of these methods, the individual is encouraged to report whatever immediately comes to mind. Interpretation of these responses requires subjective judgment and the services of a qualified psychologist. Furthermore, responses to personality tests can also be easily fabricated. For these reasons, personality tests presently have limited application in selection decisions.

Polygraph Tests

Polygraph A device that records physical changes in a person's body as he or she answers questions (also known as a *lie detector*).

The **polygraph,** popularly known as the *lie detector,* is a device that records physical changes in the body as the test subject answers a series of questions. The polygraph records fluctuations in blood pressure, respiration, and perspiration on a moving roll of graph paper. The polygraph operator makes a judgment as to whether the subject's response was truthful or deceptive by studying the physiological measurements recorded on paper.

The use of a polygraph rests on a series of cause-and-effect assumptions: stress causes certain physiological changes in the body; fear and guilt cause stress; lying causes fear and guilt. The theory behind the use of a polygraph test assumes a direct relationship between the subject's responses to the questions and the physiological responses recorded on the polygraph. However, the polygraph machine itself does not detect lies; it detects only physiological changes. The operator must interpret the data recorded by the machine. Thus, the operator, not the machine is the real lie detector.

The Employee Polygraph Protection Act of 1988, with a few exceptions, prohibits employers from conducting polygraph examinations on all job applicants and most employees. It also prevents the use of voice stress analyzers and similar devices that attempt to measure honesty. Paper-and-pencil tests and chemical testing, such as for drugs or AIDS, are not prohibited.

The major exemptions to the law are as follows: (1) all local, state, and federal employees are exempt from coverage, although state laws may be passed to restrict the use of polygraphs; (2) industries with national defense or security contracts are permitted to use polygraphs; (3) businesses with nuclear power–related contracts with the Department of Energy may use polygraphs; and (4) businesses and consultants with access to highly classified information may use polygraphs.

Private businesses are also allowed to use polygraphs under certain conditions: when hiring private security personnel, when hiring persons with access to drugs, and during investigations of economic injury or loss by the employer.[6]

Graphology

Graphology (Handwriting Analysis)   Use of a trained analyst to examine a person's handwriting to assess the person's personality, emotional problems, and honesty.

Graphology (handwriting analysis) involves using an analyst to examine the lines, loops, hooks, strokes, curves, and flourishes in a person's handwriting to assess the person's personality, performance, emotional problems, and honesty. As with the polygraph, the use of graphology is dependent on the training and expertise of the person (called *graphologist*) doing the analysis.

Graphology has had limited acceptance by organizations in the United States. However, acceptance of graphology may very well increase, since the passage of the Employee Polygraph Protection Act does not prohibit its use.[7]

Drug and AIDS Testing

Drug testing is being increasingly used by organizations. The most common practice is to test current employees when their job performance suggests substance abuse and all new potential employees. Most companies will not hire a potential employee who tests positive for drug abuse.

Urine sampling is one of the most common forms of drug testing. In addition, a more currently used technique involves measuring drug molecules from a person's hair to identify usage levels of drugs. Some experts believe hair testing is more accurate than urine sampling. Most experts agree that testing for drug abuse alone among current employees is a less than satisfactory solution to the problem. Testing can create an adversarial relationship in which the employee tries to escape the employer's detection. Education and employee assistance provide a much more positive relationship. This approach has led to the establishment of employee assistance programs, which are described in more detail in Chapter 20.

People with AIDS and people who test positive for HIV antibodies are protected in their jobs by the Vocational Rehabilitation Act and the Americans with Disabilities Act. However, voluntary workplace testing is not only permitted but is encouraged by some major health organizations. Furthermore, these laws permit HIV-antibody testing in certain defined circumstances. AIDS testing is much more common among healthcare firms because of a high potential for employee exposure to HIV-infected patients.[8]

In some instances, AIDS in the workplace has caused fear among employers and co-workers, who often seek to be separated from those infected by the virus. In order for an HIV-testing program to be considered not to violate an employee's basic rights, an employer should be able to show that the interests to be served by testing outweigh privacy expectations.[9] HRM in Action 8.2 gives several examples of drug testing programs.

HRM IN ACTION

Drug Testing Programs

8.2

Several recent court cases and federal legislation have been directly related to drug testing. In *Vernonia School District* v. *Acton* the Supreme Court ruled that a school district in Oregon was not guilty of a Fourth Amendment violation when it conducted random drug testing on students taking part in athletic programs. The California Supreme Court's decision in *Hill* v. *National Collegiate Athletic Association* made invasion of privacy claims in drug testing harder to prove. The case also dealt with the drug testing of athletes. The court ruled that the athlete's privacy had not been invaded because a drug test was no more invasive than the common awareness of physical matters between coach and athlete, advance notice was given, and the athlete had consented to the test. Finally, all drivers required to have commercial driver's licenses are mandated to undergo drug and alcohol testing pursuant to the Omnibus Transportation Employee Testing Act of 1991. School bus drivers, teachers, and coaches who drive activity buses are covered by the act.

Sources: Barrie Tabin, "School Drug Testing Is a Victory for Cities," *Nation's Cities Weekly,* July 3, 1995, p. 5; John F. Meyers, "*Hill* v. *NCAA*: California Adopts a New Standard for Invasion of Privacy," *Employee Relations Law Journal,* Summer 1994, pp. 73–84; Jim Wright, "New Federal Law Requires Drug and Alcohol Testing of Commercial Driver's License Employees," *School and College,* March 1994, p. 13.

Second or Follow-up Interview

Most organizations use the second or follow-up interview as an important step in the selection process. Its purpose is to supplement information obtained in other steps in the selection process to determine the suitability of an applicant for a specific opening. All questions asked during an interview must be job-related. Equal employment opportunity legislation has placed limitations on the types of questions that can be asked during an interview (see the On the Job example at the end of Chapter 4).

Types of Interviews

Structured Interview An interview conducted according to a predetermined outline.

Unstructured Interview An interview conducted without a predetermined checklist of questions.

Stress Interview Interview method that puts the applicant under pressure, to determine whether he or she is highly emotional.

Board or Panel Interviews Interview method in which two or more people conduct an interview with one applicant.

Organizations use several types of interviews. The **structured interview** is conducted using a predetermined outline that is based on a thorough job analysis. Through the use of this outline, the interviewer maintains control of the interview so that all pertinent information on the applicant is covered systematically. Advantages of the structured interview are that it provides the same type of information on all interviewees and allows systematic coverage of all questions deemed necessary by the organization.

Interviewers also conduct **unstructured interviews,** which do not have a predetermined checklist of questions. They use opened-ended questions such as "Tell me about your previous job." Interviews of this type pose numerous problems, such as lack of systematic coverage of information, and are very susceptible to the personal biases of the interviewer. However, they do provide a more relaxed atmosphere.

Organizations use three other types of interviewing techniques to a limited extent. The **stress interview** is designed to place the interviewee under pressure. In the stress interview, the interviewer assumes a hostile and antagonistic attitude toward the interviewee. The purpose of this type of interview is to detect the highly emotional person. In **board or panel interviews,** two or more interviewers conduct a single interview with the applicant. **Group interviews,** in which several job applicants are questioned together in a group discussion, are also sometimes used. Panel interviews and group interviews can involve either a structured or an unstructured format.

Problems in Conducting Interviews

Group Interview Interview method in which several applicants are questioned together.

Although interviews have widespread use in selection procedures, a host of problems exist. The first and certainly one of the most significant problems is that interviews are subject to the same legal requirements of validity and reliability as other steps in the selection process. However, research has indicated that the validity and reliability of most interviews are very questionable.[10] One primary reason seems to be that it is easy for the interviewer to become either favorably or unfavorably impressed with the job applicant for the wrong reasons. First, the interviewer often draws conclusions about the applicant within the first 10 minutes of the interview. If this occurs, he or she either overlooks or ignores any additional relevant information about the applicant. Furthermore, interviewers (like all people) have personal biases that play a role in the interviewing process. For example, a qualified male applicant should not be rejected merely because the interviewer dislikes long hair on males.

Halo Effect Occurs when managers allow a single prominent characteristic of the employee to influence their judgment on several items of a performance appraisal.

Closely related is the problem of the halo effect that occurs when the interviewer allows a single prominent characteristic to dominate judgment of all other traits. For instance, it is often easy to overlook other characteristics when a person has a pleasant personality. However, merely having a pleasant personality does not necessarily ensure that the person will be a good employee.

Overgeneralizing is another common problem. An interviewee may not behave exactly the same way on the job as during the interview. For example, the interviewer must remember that the interviewee is under pressure during the interview and that some people just naturally become very nervous during an interview.

Conducting Effective Interviews

The problems associated with interviews can be partially overcome through careful planning. The following suggestions are offered to increase the effectiveness of the interviewing process.[11]

1. Give careful attention to the selection and training of interviewers. Interviewers should be outgoing and emotionally well-adjusted persons. Interviewing skills can be learned, and the persons responsible for conducting interviews should be thoroughly trained in these skills.

2. The plan for the interview should include an outline specifying the information to be obtained and the questions to be asked. The plan should include room arrangements. Privacy and some degree of comfort are important. If a private room is not available, the interview should be conducted in a place where other applicants are not within hearing distance.

3. The interviewer should attempt to put the applicant at ease. He or she should not argue with the applicant or put the applicant on the spot. A brief conversation about a general topic of interest or offering the applicant a cup of coffee can help ease the tension. The applicant should be encouraged to talk. However, the interviewer must maintain control and remember the primary goal of the interview is to gain information that will aid in the selection decision.

4. The facts obtained in the interview should be recorded in writing immediately after the interview.

5. Finally, evaluate the effectiveness of the interviewing process. One way to evaluate effectiveness is to compare the performance appraisals of hired individuals to assessments made during the interview. This cross-check can serve to evaluate the effectiveness of individual interviewers as well as of the total interviewing program.

Reference Checking

Reference checking can take place either before or after the second interview. Many organizations realize the importance of reference checking and provide space on the application form for listing references. Most prospective employers contact individuals from one or more of the three following categories: personal, school, or past employment references. For the most part, personal references have limited value because generally no applicant will list someone who will not give a positive recommendation. Contacting individuals who have taught the applicant in school, college, or university may be of limited value for similar reasons. Previous employers are clearly the most often used source and are in a position to supply the most objective information.

Reference checking is most frequently conducted by telephoning previous employers. However, many organizations will not answer questions about a previous employee unless the questions are put in writing. The amount and type of information a previous employer is willing to divulge varies from organization to organization. The least that normally can be accomplished is to verify the information given on the application form. However, most employers are hesitant to answer questions about previous employees because of the threat of defamation lawsuits.

Government legislation has significantly influenced the process of reference checking. The Privacy Act of 1974 prevents government agencies from making their employment records available to other organizations without the consent of the individual involved. The Fair Credit and Reporting Act (FCRA) of 1971 requires private organizations to give job applicants access to information obtained from a reporting service. It is also mandatory that an applicant be made aware that a check is being made on him or her. Because of these laws, most employment application forms now contain statements, which must be signed by the applicant, authorizing the employer to check references and conduct investigations. HRM in Action 8.3 describes the problems one company encountered by failing to check references adequately.

Physical Examination

The physical examination is normally required only for the individual who is offered the job, and the job offer is often contingent on the individual passing the physical examination. The exam is given to determine not only whether the applicant is physically capable of performing the job but also his or her eligibility for group life, health, and disability insurance. Because of the expense, physical exam-

---

HRM IN ACTION

Legal Liability in Preemployment Checking

8.3

In *Abbott* v. *Payne et al.* (57 So. 2d 1156 {Fla App. 4 Dist. 1984}), a customer contracted with Abbott Termite & Pest Control Company to provide regular service for her home. The customer worked full-time, so it was necessary for the pest control company to have access to the customer's home while she was away. Therefore, the company requested that the customer provide a passkey to the home.

The customer sought and obtained representations from the company that the company's employee who would service the home was reliable and trustworthy. Based on assurances from the company, the customer allowed the employee to enter her home with the passkey.

Shortly after the employee left the employment of Abbott, he used the passkey to break into the customer's home at night and physically assaulted her. The customer brought suit against the company. The court found in favor of the customer, saying that liability for an ex-employee's conduct can occur and that the employer has a duty to inquire into the background of a job applicant, including past employment and references.

Source: James W. Fenton, Jr., "Recruitment: Negligent Hiring/Retention Adds to Human Resources Woes," *Personnel Journal*, April 1990, pp. 64–65.

inations are normally one of the last steps in the selection process. The expense of physical examinations has also caused many organizations to have applicants complete a health questionnaire when they fill out their application form. If no serious medical problems are indicated on the medical questionnaire, the applicant usually is not required to have a physical examination.

The Rehabilitation Act of 1973 and the Americans with Disabilities Act of 1990 have also caused many employers to reexamine the physical requirements for many jobs. These acts do not prohibit employers from giving medical exams. However, they do encourage employers to make medical inquiries directly related to the applicant's ability to perform job-related functions and require employers to make reasonable accommodations to help handicapped people to perform the job. Furthermore, the Americans with Disabilities Act requires that a physical exam cannot be conducted until after a job offer has been extended to a job candidate.

Making the Final Selection Decision

The final step in the selection process is choosing one individual for the job. The assumption made at this point is that there will be more than one qualified person. If this is true, a value judgment based on all of the information gathered in the previous steps must be made to select the most qualified individual. If the previous steps have been performed properly, the chances of making a successful judgment improve dramatically.

The responsibility for making the final selection decision is assigned to different levels of management in different organizations. In many organizations, the human resource department handles the completion of application forms, conducts preliminary interviews, testing, and reference checking, and arranges for physical exams. The diagnostic interview and final selection decision are usually left to the manager of the department with the job opening. Such a system relieves the manager of the time-consuming responsibilities of screening out unqualified and uninterested applicants.

In other organizations, the human resource department handles all of the steps up to the final decision. Under this system, the human resource department gives the manager with a job opening a list of three to five qualified applicants. The manager then chooses the individual he or she believes will be the best employee based on all the information provided by the human resource department. Many organizations leave the final choice to the manager with the job opening, subject to the approval of those at higher levels of management.

In some organizations, the human resource department handles all of the steps in the selection process, including the final decision. In small organizations, the owner often makes the final choice.

An alternative approach is to involve peers in the final selection decision. Peer involvement has been used primarily in the selection of upper-level managers and professional employees. Peer involvement naturally facilitates the acceptance of the new employee by the work group.

In the selection of managers and supervisors, assessment centers are also sometimes used. An assessment center utilizes a formal procedure involving interviews, tests, and individual and group exercises aimed at evaluating an individual's potential as a manager/supervisor and determining his or her developmental needs. Chapter 10 describes assessment centers at length.

Validation of Selection Procedures

The selection decision requires the decision maker to know what distinguishes successful performance from unsuccessful performance in the available job and to forecast a person's future performance in that job. Therefore, job analysis is essen-

Criteria of Job Success
Ways of specifying how
successful performance of
the job is to be measured.

Criterion Predictors
Factors such as education,
previous work experience,
and scores on tests that are
used to predict successful
performance of a job.

Validity   Refers to how
accurately a predictor
actually predicts the criteria
of job success.

tial in the development of a successful selection system. As discussed in Chapter 5, both job descriptions and job specifications are developed through job analysis. A job description facilitates determining how successful performance of the job is to be measured. These measures are called criteria of job success. Possible criteria of job success include performance appraisals, production data (such as quantity of work produced), and personnel data (such as rates of absenteeism and tardiness).

A job specification facilitates identifying the factors that can be used to predict successful performance of the job. These factors are called criterion predictors. Possible criterion predictors include education, previous work experience, scores on tests, data from application blanks, previous performance appraisals or evaluations, and results of interviews.

Validity refers to how accurately a predictor actually predicts the criteria of job success. For example, a job applicant for a typist position who types 120 words per minute should be able to perform well in the job if typing speed is a valid criterion for job success. Any predictor used in a selection decision must be valid. Figure 8–2 shows the relationship between job analysis and validity.

Some criteria, such as performance appraisals, can be used as both predictors and criteria of job success. For example, if past performance appraisals are used to forecast how successfully an individual will perform a different job, the performance appraisals are predictors. Thus, how the criterion is used determines whether it is a predictor or a criterion of job success.

Validity is an extremely important concept in human resource management. Validity in selection decisions can be demonstrated using criterion-related content and construct methods. Each of these methods is discussed in the following sections.

FIGURE 8–2   **RELATIONSHIP BETWEEN JOB ANALYSIS AND VALIDITY**

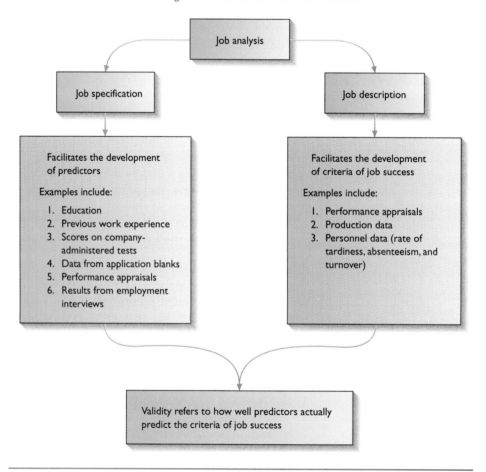

Criterion-Related Validity *Complex* *to insure* *fairness*

Criterion-related validity is established by collecting data and using correlation analysis (a statistical method used to measure the relationship between two sets of data) to determine the relationship between predictor and the criteria of job success. The degree of validity for a particular predictor is indicated by the magnitude of the coefficient of correlation (*r*), which can range from +1 to −1. Both +1 and −1 represent perfect correlation. Zero represents total lack of correlation or validity. A positive sign (+) on the coefficient of correlation means the two sets of data are moving in the same direction, whereas a negative (−) sign means the two sets of data are moving in opposite directions.

A predictor never correlates perfectly with a criterion of job success. Thus, a significant issue in validity is the degree of correlation required between the predictor and the criterion of job success in order to establish validity. The "Uniform Guidelines on Employee Selection Procedures" (more commonly referred to as "Uniform Guidelines"), which are described later in this chapter, take the position that no minimum correlation coefficient is applicable to all employment situations.[12] The American Psychological Association's Division of Organizational and Industrial Psychology has provided the following guidelines on the significance of correlation coefficients: Correlations rarely exceed 0.50; a correlation of 0.40 is ordinarily considered very good, and most personnel research workers are usually pleased with a correlation of 0.30.[13] Generally, it is safe to say that predictors having a correlation coefficient of under 0.30 would not be accepted as valid.

Two primary methods for establishing criterion-related validity are predictive validity and concurrent validity.

Predictive Validity

Predictive Validity Validity established by identifying a predictor, administering it to applicants, hiring without regard to scores, and later correlating scores with job performance

Predictive validity is established by identifying a predictor such as a test, administering the test to the entire pool of job applicants, and then hiring people to fill the available jobs without regard to their test scores. At a later date, the test scores are correlated with the criteria of job success to see whether those people with high test scores performed substantially better than those with low test scores.

For example, suppose a company wants to determine the validity of a test for predicting future performance of production workers. In this example, test scores would be the predictor. Further suppose the company maintains records on the quantity of output of individual workers and that quantity of output is to be used as the criterion of job success. In a predictive-validation study, the test would be administered to the entire pool of job applicants, but people would be hired without regard to their test scores. The new employees would be given the same basic orientation and training. Some time later (e.g., one year), the test scores would be correlated to quantity of output. If an acceptable correlation exists, the test is shown to be valid and can be used for selection of future employees. Figure 8–3 summarizes the steps in performing a predictive-validation study.

Predictive validation is used infrequently because it is costly and slow.[14] To use this method, a large number of new employees must be hired at the same time without regard to their test scores. Potentially, an organization may hire both good and bad employees. Furthermore, for criteria to be predictive, all new employees must have equivalent orientation and training.

Concurrent Validity

Concurrent Validity Validity established by identifying a predictor, administering it to current employees, and correlating

Concurrent validity is determined by identifying a predictor such as a test, administering the test to present employees, and correlating the test scores with the present employees' performance on the job. If an acceptable correlation exists, the test can be used for selection of future employees. Figure 8–4 summarizes the concurrent-validation process.

One disadvantage of concurrent validation is that in situations in which either racial or sexual discrimination has been practiced in the past, minorities and

F I G U R E   8 - 3   **PREDICTIVE VALIDATION PROCESS**

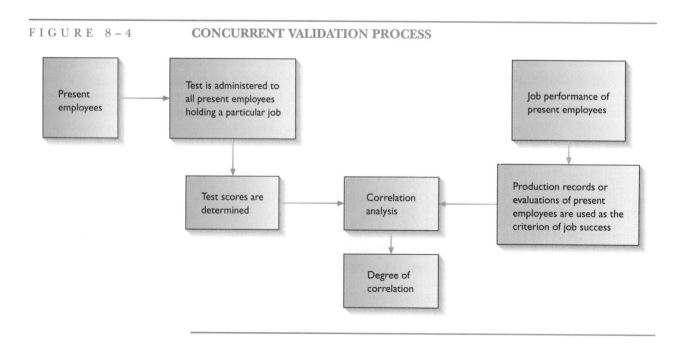

F I G U R E   8 - 4   **CONCURRENT VALIDATION PROCESS**

the test data with the current employee's job performance

women will not be adequately represented. Another potential drawback is that among present employees in a particular job, the poorer performers are more likely to have been discharged or quit and the best performers have frequently been promoted. Obviously, a correlation coefficient obtained under these conditions can be misleading.

Criterion-related validation procedures (either predictive or concurrent) are preferred by the Equal Employment Opportunity Commission (EEOC) in validation studies. However, because of the cost and difficulties associated with criterion-related validation, other methods are frequently used. These validation methods are also accepted by the EEOC.

Content and Construct Validity

Content Validity The extent to which the content of a selection procedure or instrument is representative of important aspects of job performance.

Two other methods of validation are content validity and construct validity. **Content validity** refers to whether the content of a selection procedure or selection instrument such as a test is representative of important aspects of performance on the job. Thus, a typing test is content valid for hiring secretaries, although it does not cover all of the skills required to be a good secretary. Content validity is especially useful in those situations where the number of employees is not large enough to justify the use of empirical validation methods. To use content validity, an employer must determine the exact performance requirements of a specific job and develop a selection procedure or selection instrument around an actual sample of the work that is to be performed.

Construct Validity The extent to which a selection criterion measures the degree to which job candidates have identifiable characteristics determined to be important for successful job performance.

Construct validity refers to the extent to which a selection procedure or instrument measures the degree to which job candidates have identifiable characteristics that have been determined to be important for successful job performance. Examples of job-related constructs might include verbal ability, space visualization, and perceptual speed. For example, if a job requires blueprint reading, a test of space visualization might be construct valid for use in employment decisions.

Both of the nonempirical methods of validation are dependent on judgment. However, in many validation situations, they may be the only available options.

Reliability

Reliability The reproducibility of results with a predictor.

Another important consideration for a selection system is reliability. **Reliability** refers to the reproducibility of results with a predictor. For example, a test is reliable to the extent that the same person working under the same conditions produces approximately the same test results at different time periods. A test is not reliable if a person fails it on one day but makes an *A* in taking it again a week later (assuming, of course, that no learning has taken place in the meantime).

Test-Retest One method of showing a test's reliability; involves testing a group and giving the same group the same test at a later time.

Parallel Forms A method of showing a test's reliability; involves giving two separate but similar forms of the test at the same time.

Split Halves A method of showing a test's reliability; involves dividing the test into halves to determine whether performance is similar on both halves.

Three methods can be used to demonstrate the reliability of a predictor. Suppose a given test is used. One method of showing the reliability of the test is **test-retest.** This involves testing a group and later, usually in about two weeks, giving the group the same test. The degree of similarity between the sets of scores determines the test's reliability. Obviously, the results can be influenced by whether the individual studied during the time between tests. A second method of showing reliability, **parallel forms,** involves giving two separate but similar forms of the test at the same time. The degree to which the sets of scores coincide determines reliability. The third method, **split halves,** involves dividing the test into halves to determine whether performance is similar on both halves. Again, the degree of similarity determines reliability.

A test or other predictor can be reliable without being valid. However, it cannot be valid if it is not reliable. Consequently, the reliability of a predictor plays an important role in determining its validity.

Uniform Guidelines on Employee Selection Procedures

Web site: HR Online

www.hr2000.com

The EEOC, the Office of Personnel Management, the Department of Justice, and the Department of Labor have adopted and published a document entitled "Uniform Guidelines on Employee Selection Procedures," more commonly referred to as "Uniform Guidelines."[15] The "Uniform Guidelines" are designed to provide the framework for determining the proper use of tests and other selection procedures used for any employment decision. Employment decisions include but are not limited to hiring, promotion, demotion, membership (e.g., in a labor organization), referral, retention, licensing and certification, selection for training, and transfers.

The "Uniform Guidelines on Employee Selection Procedures" also contain technical standards and documentation requirements for the validation of selection procedures. The guidelines broadly define selection procedures to include not only hiring but also promotion decisions, selection for training programs, and virtually every selection decision made by an organization. The guidelines are intended to be consistent with generally accepted professional standards for evaluating selection procedures, such as those described in the *Standards for Educational and Psychological Tests* prepared by a joint committee of the American Psychological Association, the American Educational Research Association, and the National Council of Measurement in Education.[16] These standards are more commonly called the *APA Standards*. Either the "Uniform Guidelines" or *APA Standards* can be used in validation studies. In fact, several court decisions have tended to place more reliance on the professional standard than on the guidelines. The "Uniform Guidelines" permit criterion-related, content, and construct validity studies. In conducting a validity study, employers are also encouraged to consider available alternatives with less adverse impact for achieving business purposes.

All validation studies must be thoroughly documented, and the "Uniform Guidelines" specify in detail the types of records that must be kept in any study. Since job analysis is an essential part of a validation study, specific guidelines are also provided for conducting job analyses.

χ *Adverse (or Disparate) Impact*

Adverse Impact Condition that occurs when the selection rate for minorities or women is less than 80 percent of the selection rate for the majority group in hiring, promotions, transfers, demotions, or any selection decision.

4/5ths or 80 Percent Rule A limit used to determine whether or not there are serious discrepancies in hiring decisions and other employment practices affecting women or minorities.

The fundamental principle underlying the "Uniform Guidelines" is that employment policies and practices that have an adverse impact on employment opportunities for any race, sex, religion, or national origin group are illegal unless justified by a demonstration of job relatedness. A selection procedure that has no adverse impact is generally considered to be legal. If adverse impact exists, however, it must be justified on the basis of job relatedness. Normally this means by validation that demonstrates the relationship between the selection procedure and performance on the job.

The "Uniform Guidelines" adopt a rule of thumb as a practical means of determining adverse impact. This rule is known as the **4/5ths or 80 percent rule**. This rule is not a legal definition of discrimination but a practical device for determining serious discrepancies in hiring, promoting, or other employment decisions. For example, suppose an employer is doing business in an area where the labor force is 25 percent African-Americans. Further, suppose that the employer has 1,000 employees and 100 (10 percent) of the employees are African-Americans. Adverse impact exists because 4/5ths of 25 percent equals 20 percent and African-Americans make up only 10 percent of the employer's work force. (See Figure 8–5.)

Figure 8–6 illustrates how adverse impact can be assessed in an employer's hiring decisions. Suppose 25 men have applied for a job opening and 15 of the men were hired. Suppose only 20 women applied and 5 were hired. Adverse impact exists because 4/5ths of 60 percent equals 48 percent, and a selection rate for women below 48 percent indicates adverse impact.

FIGURE 8 – 5   DETERMINING ADVERSE IMPACT IN AN EMPLOYER'S WORK FORCE

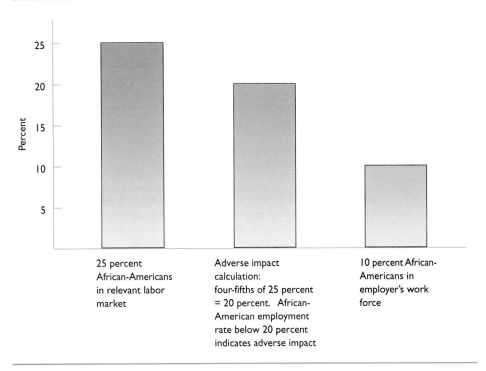

25 percent African-Americans in relevant labor market

Adverse impact calculation: four-fifths of 25 percent = 20 percent. African-American employment rate below 20 percent indicates adverse impact

10 percent African-Americans in employer's work force

FIGURE 8 – 6   DETERMINING ADVERSE IMPACT IN AN EMPLOYER'S HIRING DECISIONS

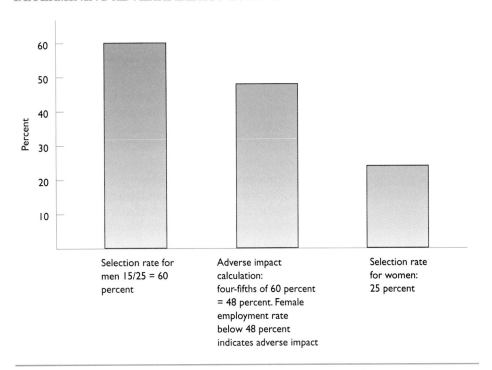

Selection rate for men 15/25 = 60 percent

Adverse impact calculation: four-fifths of 60 percent = 48 percent. Female employment rate below 48 percent indicates adverse impact

Selection rate for women: 25 percent

Where Adverse Impact Exists: The Basic Options

After it has been established that adverse impact exists, what steps do the "Uniform Guidelines" require? First, the employer has the option to modify or eliminate the procedure that produces the adverse impact. If the employer does not do so, it must justify the use of the procedure on the grounds of job relatedness. This normally means showing a clear relation between performance on the selection procedure and performance on the job. In the language of industrial psychology, the employer must validate the selection procedure.

SUMMARY OF LEARNING OBJECTIVES

1. **Outline the steps in the selection process.**
   The steps in the selection process are the application form, the preliminary interview, formal testing, the follow-up interview, reference checking, the physical examination, and making the final selection decision.

2. **Describe aptitude, psychomotor, job knowledge, proficiency, interest, and personality test.**
   Aptitude tests measure a person's capacity or potential ability to learn and perform a job. Psychomotor tests measure a person's strength, dexterity, and coordination. Job knowledge tests measure the job-related knowledge possessed by a job applicant. Proficiency tests measure how well the applicant can do a sample of the work required in the position. Interest tests are designed to determine how a person's interests compare with the interests of successful people in a specific job. Personality tests attempt to measure personality characteristics.

3. **Explain a polygraph test.**
   The polygraph records physical changes in the body as the test subject answers a series of questions. The operator makes a judgment on whether the subject's response was truthful or deceptive by studying the physiological measurements recorded as the questions were answered.

4. **Describe structured and unstructured interviews.**
   The structured interview is conducted using a predetermined outline. Unstructured interviews are conducted without a predetermined check list of questions.

5. **Define validity.**
   Validity refers to how well a predictor actually predicts the criteria of job success.

6. **Explain predictive validity.**
   Predictive validity is established by identifying a predictor such as a test, administering the test to the entire pool of job applicants, and hiring people to fill the available jobs without regard to their test scores. At a later date, the test scores are correlated with the criteria of job success to see whether those people with high test scores performed substantially better than those with low test scores.

7. **Explain concurrent validity.**
   Concurrent validity is established by identifying a predictor such as a test, administering the test to present employees, and correlating the test scores with the present employee's performances on the job.

8. **Describe content validity.**
   Content validity refers to whether the content of a selection procedure or selection instrument, such as a test, is representative of important aspects of performance on the job.

9. **Discuss construct validity.**
   Construct validity refers to the extent to which a selection procedure or instrument measures the degree to which job candidates have identifiable characteristics that have been determined to be important for successful job perfor-

mance. Job-related constructs might include verbal ability, space visualization, and perceptual speed.

10. Define reliability.

Reliability refers to the reproducibility of results with a predictor.

11. Define adverse (or disparate) impact.

Adverse impact is a condition that occurs when the selection rate for minorities or women is less than 80 percent of the selection rate for the majority group in hiring, promotions, transfers, demotions, or other employment decisions.

REVIEW QUESTIONS

1. Outline the steps in the selection process.
2. Describe some preemployment inquiries that should be eliminated or carefully reviewed to ensure their job relatedness.
3. What is a weighted application form?
4. How is an applicant flow record used?
5. Outline and briefly describe five categories of tests.
6. What is a polygraph test?
7. What is graphology?
8. What is reference checking?
9. Briefly describe some of the procedures organizations use in making the final decision.
10. Define the following terms:
    a. Criterion of job success.
    b. Predictor.
    c. Validity.
    d. Reliability.
11. Describe the following methods of validation:
    a. Predictive.
    b. Concurrent.
    c. Content.
    d. Construct.
12. What is adverse (or disparate) impact?
13. Describe the 4/5ths rule.

DISCUSSION QUESTIONS

1. "Tests often do not reflect an individual's true ability." What are your views on this statement?
2. "Organizations should be able to hire employees without government interference." Do you agree or disagree? What do you think would happen if organizations could do this?
3. "Reference checking is a waste of time." Do you agree or disagree? Why?
4. How do you feel about the establishment of minimum entrance scores on national tests for acceptance to a college or university?

INCIDENT 8–1

Promotions at OMG

Old Money Group (OMG) is a mutual fund management company based in Seattle. It operates four separate funds, each with a different goal: one each for income growth and income interest production, one for a combination or balance of growth and production, and one for dealing in short-term securities (a money market fund). OMG was formed in early 1990 as a financial management firm. By the end of 1994, OMG had almost $47 million under its management. Over this time period, the company had slightly outperformed the Standard & Poor's 500 average and done slightly better than the stock market as a whole.

The Keogh Act permits self-employed individuals to set up retirement plans. All contributions to and earnings from the plans are tax exempt until the money is withdrawn by the individual on retirement.

OMG recognized the great potential of using Keogh plans to help market shares in its mutual funds. It launched an aggressive marketing program aimed at persuading those with Keogh plans to buy into the fund. This was very successful. As a result, OMG found it necessary to establish a separate department to handle only Keogh plans. This new department was placed in the corporate account division under division vice president Ralph Simpson. The Keogh department grew rapidly and by the end of 1997 was managing approximately 3,000 separate Keogh plans. The department was responsible for all correspondence, personal contact, and problem-solving involved with these accounts.

John Baker, who had graduated from college the previous fall with a degree in history, joined OMG in February 1997. In his interview, John had impressed the human resource department as having managerial potential. The human resource department wanted to place him in an area where he could move into such a position, but at that time none were available.

A job that could be used as a stepping stone to more responsible positions opened up in the Keogh department. In April, John became assistant to the administrator of the department. He was told that if he handled this position well, he would be considered for a job as plan administrator when an opening occurred. This was communicated to John both by the human resource department and by the head of the Keogh department.

Over the next six months, it became apparent that John was not working out well. He seemed to show little interest in his work and did only what he had to do to get by; at times, his work was unsatisfactory. He appeared to be unhappy and not suited to the job. John let it be known that he had been looking for another position.

In October, Roy Johnson, head of the Keogh department, gave John his six-month review. Knowing that John was looking for another job, Roy decided to take the easy way out. Instead of giving John a bad review and facing the possibility of having to fire him, he gave John a satisfactory performance review. He hoped John would find another job so the problem would go away.

In early December, one of the plan administrators said she would be leaving OMG in late December. Roy faced the task of selecting someone to fill her position. Of those who had expressed an interest in the job, Fran Jenkins appeared the best suited for it. Fran was secretary to the head of the corporate division. She had become familiar with the plan administrators' work because she had helped them during their peak periods for the past three years. The only problem was Fran's lack of a college degree, which was stipulated as a requirement in the job description. Although she was currently taking night courses, she had completed only two and one-half years of college. After Roy discussed the problem with the head of the human resource department, this requirement was waived. Roy then announced that Fran would assume the position of plan administrator in December.

Two weeks later, John Baker informed the head of the human resource department that he had talked to his lawyer. He felt he had been discriminated against and believed he should have gotten the position of plan administrator.

Questions

1. Do you think John has a legitimate point?
2. What went wrong in this selection process?

INCIDENT 8–2

The Pole Climbers

Ringing Bell Telephone Company has implemented an affirmative action plan in compliance with the Equal Employment Opportunity Commission. Under the current plan, to eliminate discrimination based on sex, women must be placed in jobs traditionally held by men. Therefore, the human resource department has emphasized recruiting and hiring women for such positions. Women who apply for craft positions are encouraged to try for outdoor craft jobs, such as those titled installer-repairer and line worker.

All employees hired as outside technicians must first pass basic installation school, which includes a week of training for pole climbing. During this week, employees are taught to climb 30-foot telephone poles. At the end of the week, they must demonstrate the strength and skills necessary to climb the pole and perform exercises while on it, such as lifting heavy tools and using a pulley to lift a bucket. Only those who pass this first week of training are allowed to advance to the segment dealing with installation.

Records have been maintained on the rates of success or failure for employees who attend the training school. For men, the failure rate has remained fairly constant at 30 percent. However, it has averaged 70 percent for women.

The human resource department has become concerned because hiring and training employees who must resign at the end of one week is a tremendous expense. In addition, the goal of placing women in outdoor craft positions is not being reached.

As a first step in solving the problem, the human resource department has started interviewing the women who have failed the first week of training. Each employee is asked her reasons for seeking the position and encouraged to discuss probable causes for failure. Interviews over the last two months disclosed that employees were motivated to accept the job because of their wishes to work outdoors, work without close supervision, obtain challenging work, meet the public, have variety in their jobs, and obtain a type of job unusual for women. Reasons for failure were physical inability to climb the pole, fear of height while on it, an accident during training such as a fall from the pole, and a change of mind about the job after learning that strenuous work was involved.

In many instances, the women who mentioned physical reasons also stated they were not physically ready to undertake the training; many had no idea it would be so difficult. Even though they still wanted the job, they could not pass the physical strength test at the end of one week.

Some stated that they felt "influenced" by their interviewer from the human resource department to take the job; others said they had accepted it because it was the only job available with the company at the time.

Questions

1. What factors would you keep in mind in designing an effective selection process for the position of outdoor craft technician?

2. What would you recommend to help Ringing Bell reduce the failure rate among women trainees?

EXERCISE

Developing a Test

You will be given one minute to copy the letter *T* on a blank sheet of paper as many times as possible. The exercise is timed, and exactly one minute is permitted. A frequency distribution will then be developed by your instructor (or the class) to show how well the class performed.

1. What is the shape of the distribution?
2. Why is the distribution shaped in this manner?
3. Could this test be used as a selection device for certain jobs? If so, what types of jobs?
4. How would you demonstrate the validity of this test?

NOTES AND ADDITIONAL READINGS

1. *Gregory* v. *Litton,* 316 F. Supp. 401 (C.D. California 1970).
2. Commission Decision No. 72–0427, CCH Employment Practice Guide 6312 (August 31, 1971).
3. E. C. Miller, "An EEO Examination of Employment Applications," *Personnel Administrator,* March 1980, pp. 63–69.
4. D. Yoder and H. G. Henneman, Jr. *ASPA Handbook of Personnel and Industrial Relations* (Washington, D.C.: Bureau of National Affairs, 1979), pp. 4–131.
5. Jane Close Conoley and Jack J. Kramer, eds. *The Tenth Mental Measurements Handbook* (Lincoln, Neb.: The Buros Institute of Mental Measurement, University of Nebraska Press, 1989).
6. James G. Frierson, "New Polygraph Test Limits," *Personnel Journal,* December 1988, pp. 84–92.
7. Dana Bottorff, "While Not as Telling as Pinocchio's Nose, Tests that Screen for Honesty Gain Favor," *New England Business,* February 16, 1987, p. 35.
8. Eric Rolfe Greenberg, "Workplace Testing: Who's Testing Whom?" *Personnel,* 1989, pp. 39–45.
9. Jon D. Bible, "When Employers Look for Things Other than Drugs: The Legality of AIDS, Genetic, Intelligence, and Honesty Testing in the Workplace," *Labor Law Journal,* April 1990, pp. 204–5.
10. Yoder and Henneman, *ASPA Handbook,* pp. 4-146–4-148.
11. Ibid., pp. 4-152–4-154.
12. "Uniform Guidelines on Employee Selection Procedures," *Federal Register,* August 25, 1978, p. 38301.
13. *Amicus Curiae,* Brief of the Executive Committee of the Division of Industrial and Organizational Psychology, American Psychological Association, in *United States* v. *Georgia Power,* 474 F. 2d 906, 5 FEP 587 (5th Cir. 1973).
14. Yoder and Henneman, *ASPA Handbook,* pp. 4–125.
15. See "Uniform Guidelines," pp. 38290–315.
16. The most current version is *Standards for Educational and Psychological Tests* (Washington, D.C.: American Psychological Association, 1985).

ON THE JOB

Sample Application for Employment and Applicant Flow Record*

This On the Job example illustrates the types of questions normally asked on an application for employment and an applicant flow record. The application form in Exhibit 8–1 provides basic employment information to determine the applicant's qualifications in relation to the requirements of the available jobs and to screen out unqualified applicants. As can be seen, the applicant flow record is a separate document voluntarily completed by the applicant. Employers use the flow record to obtain information and data that might be viewed as discriminatory. These data can then be used to provide statistical reports to the EEOC regarding recruitment and selection of women and minorities. Duke Power Company is a public utility that services customers in the western part of North and South Carolina.

*Used with permission.

EXHIBIT A8–1

DUKE POWER COMPANY

APPLICATION FOR EMPLOYMENT

AN EQUAL OPPORTUNITY/AFFIRMATIVE ACTION EMPLOYER

DUKE POWER

Lighting up the future

EXHIBIT A8–1   **CONTINUED**

Form 08004 (1-81)   **DUKE POWER COMPANY**   Page 1
                                       APPLICATION FOR EMPLOYMENT

Please Print In Ink Or Type And Complete All Applicable Sections, Even If Resume is Included   Social

Name _____   Sec. No. _____
          Last   First   Middle

Present Mailing Address _____   ( )
                    No. & Street, P.O. Box, Rt. #   City   State   Zip Code   Telephone No.

Home Mailing Address _____   ( )
(If Different From Above) No. & Street, P.O. Box, Rt. #   City   State   Zip Code   Telephone No.

Weekday Telephone Number ( )_____

Position or Type of Work Desired _____

Salary Expected $_____ Hr., Wk., Mo., Yr. Will You Consider A Position That Pays Less Than The Expected Amount Listed? ☐ Yes ☐ No

Date Available _____ Do you Have Any Geographical Restrictions? ☐ Yes ☐ No If Yes, Where?_____

Have You Previously Applied For Employment With Duke Power Company? ☐ Yes ☐ No If Yes, When? _____

Where?_____ Have You Previously Been Employed By Duke Power Co.? ☐ Yes ☐ No

If Yes When?_____ Where?_____

In Emergency, Notify: (Name)_____ Telephone No. ( )_____

Have You Ever Been Convicted Of A Crime? (Include Military Convictions) ☐ Yes ☐ No If Yes, Explain (Use Separate Paper, If Necessary). _____

Name of School	Dates Attended	Date Graduated Or Expect To Graduate	Certificate/Diploma/Degree (If Applicable)	Major (If Applicable)
High School/Equivalent Training				
Location				
Technical or Business				
Location				
College or University				
Location				
College or University				
Location				
Graduate School				
Location				
Armed Services, Correspondence				
Location				

EDUCATION

MILITARY

Branch of Service _____   Date Inducted And Rank _____

Date Discharged and Rank _____

Primary Military Occupation _____

EXHIBIT A8–1 CONTINUED

Page 2

Beginning With The Most Recent, List Below The NAMES & ADDRESSES Of All Your Employers, Including Military If Applicable	Dates Employed				Salary At Leaving	Position or Type Of Work Performed	Department/ Supervisor	Reasons For Leaving
	From		To					
	Mo.	Year	Mo.	Year				
Company								
Address								
Company								
Address								
Company								
Address								
Company								
Address								
Company								
Address								
Company								
Address								

EMPLOYMENT

OTHER TRAINING AND SKILLS

Please Provide Any Additional Information That May Aid Us In The Consideration Of Your Application Including Special Skills, Training, Qualifications, Membership In Professional Societies, Etc.

_____

_____

_____

I UNDERSTAND THAT the completion of this application does not indicate there are open positions and does not obligate Duke Power Company in any way. If accepted, employment in the position offered will be subject to a determination of physical and mental capability by a physician approved by the Company in accordance with the provisions of the Company's Affirmative Action Plan for the Handicapped.

I FURTHER UNDERSTAND THAT this application will be retained for active consideration for sixty (60) days from date submitted; however, I may reactivate my application for additional 60-day periods upon proper notification to the Company.

I HEREBY CERTIFY THAT my answer to each of the previous questions is true.

I AUTHORIZE the procurement of all available information from past and present employers and other applicable sources and realize that any evidence of falsification of information on this application may be considered adequate cause for discharge.

If the position for which you will be considered requires a security clearance, your offer of employment will be contingent upon receipt of this clearance. Public Law 91-508 requires that we advise you that a routine inquiry may be made which will provide applicable information concerning character, general reputation, personal characteristics and mode of living. Further information on the nature and scope of such report, if made, will be made available to you upon written request.

All information required in this form is necessary to process your application properly and to enable the Company to comply with state and federal laws and regulations.

Applicant's Signature _____   **Date Submitted** _____

EXHIBIT A8–1   **CONTINUED**

Page 3

INVITATION TO APPLICANTS

I.   Handicapped

Duke Power is a government contractor subject to Section 503 of the Rehabilitation Act of 1973. In accordance with this law, it is a company goal to take affirmative action to employ and advance in employment qualified handicapped individuals. A handicapped individual is defined as a person having: (1) a physical or mental impairment which limits one or more life functions, (2) a record or history of such an impairment, or (3) is regarded as having such an impairment. If you have a handicap and would like to be considered under the Affirmative Action Program, please tell us. Submission of this information is voluntary and refusal to provide it will not subject you to discharge or disciplinary treatment. Information obtained concerning individuals shall be kept confidential, except that (i) supervisors and managers may be informed regarding restrictions on the work or duties of handicapped individuals, and regarding necessary accommodations, (ii) first aid and safety personnel may be informed, when and to the extent appropriate, if the condition might require emergency treatment, and (iii) government officials investigating compliance with the Act shall be informed.

If you are handicapped, we would like to include you under the Affirmative Action Program. It would assist us if you tell us about (1) any special methods, skills and procedures which qualify you for positions that you might not otherwise be able to do because of your handicap, so that you will be considered for any positions of that kind, and (2) the accommodations which we could make which would enable you to perform the job properly and safely, including special equipment, changes in the physical layout of the job, elimination of certain duties relating to the job, or other accommodations.

II.   Disabled Veterans and Veterans of the Vietnam Era.

Duke Power is also a government contractor subject to Section 402 of the Vietnam Era Veterans Readjustment Assistance Act of 1974 as ammended which requires government contractors to take affirmative action to employ and advance in employment qualified disabled veterans and veterans of the Vietnam Era. A disabled veteran is a person entitled to at least 30 percentum disability compensation under laws administered by the Veterans Administration or whose discharge from active duty was for disability incurred or aggravated in the line of duty. Veteran of the Vietnam Era means a person (1) who (i) served on active duty for a period of more than 180 days, any part of which occurred between August 5, 1964 and May 7, 1975, and was discharged or released therefrom with other than a dishonorable discharge, or (ii) was discharged or released from active duty for a service-connected disability if any part of such active duty was performed between August 5, 1964 and May 7, 1975. If you are a disabled veteran covered by this program and would like to be considered under the Affirmative Action Program please tell us. This information is voluntary and refusal to provide it will not subject you to discharge or disciplinary treatment. Information obtained concerning individuals shall be kept confidential, except that (i) supervisors and managers may be informed regarding restrictions on tne work or duties of disabled veterans, and regarding necessary accommodations, and (ii) first aid personnel may be informed, when and to the extent appropriate, if the condition might require emergency treatment. In order to assure proper placement of all employees, we request that you respond to the following statement:

If you have a disability which might affect your performance or create a hazard to yourself or others in connection with the job for which you are applying, please state the following: (1) the skills and procedures you use or intend to use to perform the job notwithstanding the disability and (2) the accommodations we could make which would enable you to perform the job properly and safely, including special equipment, changes in the physical layout of the job, elimination of certain duties relating to the job or other accommodations.

. . . .

NOTE: Please complete page 4 of this form if you wish to be included in the Affirmative Action Program(s) described above.

EXHIBIT A8-1   **CONCLUDED**

Page 4

NOTE: COMPLETION OF THIS PAGE IS VOLUNTARY; DO NOT COMPLETE UNTIL YOU HAVE READ <u>PAGE 3</u> THOROUGHLY.

I am ☐ handicapped   ☐ a disabled veteran   ☐ a Vietnam Era Veteran and would like to be included in your Affirmative Action Program.

My Handicap/Disability is: _____

_____

Recommendations for accommodations are indicated below.

_____

_____

_____

_____

_____

AN EQUAL OPPORTUNITY/AFFIRMATIVE ACTION EMPLOYER

(TO BE DETACHED BY AUTHORIZED COMPANY REPRESENTATIVE)

(TO BE DETACHED BY AUTHORIZED COMPANY REPRESENTATIVE)   Page 5
DUKE POWER COMPANY

Federal laws and regulations require employers to monitor and report the status of their equal employment opportunity and affirmative action programs on a continuing basis. Therefore, it is requested that you complete the information below. This information will be maintained only for the purpose of monitoring and reporting compliance in accordance with applicable laws and regulations as well as to insure compliance with Company policies and procedures and will not be used for any other purpose.

Name _____   Address _____   Social Security No. _____

☐ Male   ☐ Female   Date of Birth _____ / _____ / _____
                                              Month   Day   Year

Are you a United States Citizen or Permanent Resident of the United States or otherwise eligible for full-time permanent employment in the United States?
☐ Yes   ☐ No

ETHNIC IDENTIFICATION: ☐ White   ☐ Black   ☐ Hispanic   ☐ Asian or Pacific Islander   ☐ American Indian or Alaskan Native

Do you have any relatives currently employed by Duke Power? ☐ Yes   ☐ No

If so, give Name(s) _____   Relationship(s) _____   Department(s) _____

_____   _____   _____

_____   _____   _____

Signature _____   Date _____

Training and Developing Employees

Orientation and Employee Training

Learning Objectives

After studying this chapter, you should be able to:

1. Define orientation.
2. Describe an orientation kit.
3. Define training.
4. Describe needs assessment.
5. Outline three categories of training objectives.
6. Describe job rotation.
7. Explain apprenticeship training.
8. Outline the seven principles of learning.
9. List the four areas of training evaluation.

Web site: HR Online

www.hr2000.com

After people are hired, they must be oriented to the organization and to their jobs; they must also be trained to perform their jobs. Furthermore, employees must periodically have their skills updated and learn new skills. The orientation and training of new employees and the training of longer-term employees are major responsibilities of the human resource department.

Orientation

Orientation The introduction of new employees to the organization, work unit, and job.

Orientation is the introduction of new employees to the organization, their work units, and their jobs. Employees receive orientation from their coworkers, and from the organization. The orientation received from coworkers is usually unplanned and unofficial, and it often provides the new employee with misleading and inaccurate information. This is one of the reasons the official orientation provided by the organization is so important. An effective orientation program has an immediate and lasting impact on the new employee and can make the difference between his or her success or failure.

Job applicants get some orientation to the organization even before they are hired. The organization has a reputation as to the type of employer it is and the types of products or services it provides. During the selection process, the new employee usually also learns other general aspects of the organization and what the duties, working conditions, and pay will be.

After hiring the employee, the organization begins a formal orientation program. Regardless of the type of organization, orientation should usually be conducted at two distinct levels:

1. Organizational orientation—presents topics of relevance and interest to all employees.
2. Departmental and job orientation—describes topics that are unique to the new employee's specific department and job.

Shared Responsibility

Since there are two distinct levels of orientation, the human resource department and the new employee's immediate manager normally share responsibility for orientation. The human resource department is responsible for initiating and coordinating both levels of orientation, training line managers in procedures for conducting the departmental and job orientation, conducting the general company orientation, and following up the initial orientation with the new employee. The new employee's manager is usually responsible for conducting the departmental and job orientation. Some organizations have instituted a "buddy system" in which the job orientation is conducted by one of the new employee's coworkers. If a buddy system is to work successfully, the employee chosen for this role must be carefully selected and properly trained for such orientation responsibilities.

Organizational Orientation

Organizational Orientation General orientation that presents topics of relevance and interest to all employees.

The topics presented in the **organizational orientation** should be based on the needs of both the organization and the employee. Generally, the organization is interested in making a profit, providing good service to customers and clients, satisfying employee needs and well-being, and being socially responsible. New employees, on the other hand, are generally more interested in pay, benefits, and specific terms and conditions of employment. A good balance between the company's and the new employee's needs is essential if the orientation program is to have positive results. Figure 9–1 provides a listing of suggested topics that might be covered in an organization's orientation program.

Departmental and Job Orientation

Departmental and Job Orientation Specific orientation that describes topics unique to the new employee's specific department and job.

The content of **departmental and job orientation** depends on the specific needs of the department and the skills and experience of the new employee. Experienced employees are likely to need less job orientation. However, even experienced employees usually need some basic orientation. Both experienced and inexperienced employees should receive a thorough orientation concerning departmental matters. Figure 9–2 presents a checklist for the development of departmental and job orientation programs.

Orientation Kit

Orientation Kit A supplemental packet of written information for new employees.

It is desirable for each new employee to receive an **orientation kit,** or packet of information, to supplement the verbal orientation program. This kit, which is normally prepared by the human resource department, can provide a wide variety of

FIGURE 9–1   **POSSIBLE TOPICS FOR ORGANIZATIONAL ORIENTATION PROGRAM**

1. Overview of the company
- ☐ Welcoming speech
- ☐ Founding, growth, trends, goals, priorities, and problems
- ☐ Traditions, customs, norms, and standards
- ☐ Current specific functions of the organization
- ☐ Products/services and customers served
- ☐ Steps in getting products/services to customers
- ☐ Scope and diversity of activities
- ☐ Organization, structure, and relationship of company and its branches
- ☐ Facts on key managerial staff
- ☐ Community relations, expectations, and activities

2. Key policies and procedures review

3. Compensation
- ☐ Pay rates and ranges
- ☐ Overtime
- ☐ Holiday pay
- ☐ Shift differential
- ☐ How pay is received
- ☐ Deductions: required and optional, with specific amounts
- ☐ Option to buy damaged products and costs thereof
- ☐ Discounts
- ☐ Advances on pay
- ☐ Loans from credit union
- ☐ Reimbursement for job expenses

4. Fringe benefits
- ☐ Insurance:
  - ☐ Medical/dental
  - ☐ Life
  - ☐ Disability
  - ☐ Workers' compensation
- ☐ Holidays and vacations (e.g., patriotic, religious, birthday)
- ☐ Leave: personal illness, family illness, bereavement, maternity, military, jury duty, emergency, extended absence
- ☐ Retirement plans and options
- ☐ On-the-job training opportunities
- ☐ Counseling services
- ☐ Cafeteria
- ☐ Recreation and social activities
- ☐ Other company services to employees

5. Safety and accident prevention
- ☐ Completion of emergency data card (if not done as part of employment process)
- ☐ Health and first-aid clinics
- ☐ Exercise and recreation centers
- ☐ Safety precautions
- ☐ Reporting of hazards

- ☐ Fire prevention and control
- ☐ Accident procedures and reporting
- ☐ OSHA requirements (review of key sections)
- ☐ Physical exam requirements
- ☐ Use of alcohol and drugs on the job
- ☐ Tax shelter options

6. Employees and union relations
- ☐ Terms and conditions of employment review
- ☐ Assignment, reassignment, and promotion
- ☐ Probationary period and expected on-the-job conduct
- ☐ Reporting of sickness and tardiness to work
- ☐ Employee rights and responsibilities
- ☐ Manager and supervisor rights
- ☐ Relations with supervisors and shop stewards
- ☐ Employee organizations and options
- ☐ Union contract provisions and/or company policy
- ☐ Supervision and evaluation of performance
- ☐ Discipline and reprimands
- ☐ Grievance procedures
- ☐ Termination of employment (resignation, layoff, discharge, retirement)
- ☐ Content and examination of personnel record
- ☐ Communications: channels of communication (upward and downward), suggestion system, posting materials on bulletin board, sharing new ideas
- ☐ Sanitation and cleanliness
- ☐ Wearing of safety equipment, badges, and uniforms
- ☐ Bringing things and removing things from company grounds
- ☐ On-site political activity
- ☐ Gambling
- ☐ Handling of rumors

7. Physical facilities
- ☐ Tour of facilities
- ☐ Food services and cafeteria
- ☐ Restricted areas for eating
- ☐ Employee entrances
- ☐ Restricted areas (e.g., from cars)
- ☐ Parking
- ☐ First aid
- ☐ Rest rooms
- ☐ Supplies and equipment

8. Economic factors
- ☐ Costs of damage to select items with required sales to balance
- ☐ Profit margins
- ☐ Labor costs
- ☐ Cost of equipment
- ☐ Costs of absenteeism, tardiness, and accidents

Source: W. D. St. John, "The Complete Employee Orientation Program," *Personnel Journal,* May 1980, pp. 376–77. Reprinted with the permission of *Personnel Journal,* Costa Mesa, California; all rights reserved.

FIGURE 9–2   **POSSIBLE TOPICS FOR DEPARTMENTAL AND JOB ORIENTATION PROGRAMS**

1. **Department functions**
   - ☐ Goals and current priorities
   - ☐ Organization and structure
   - ☐ Operational activities
   - ☐ Relationship of functions to other departments
   - ☐ Relationships of jobs within the department

2. **Job duties and responsibilities**
   - ☐ Detailed explanation of job based on current job description and expected results
   - ☐ Explanation of why the job is important and how the specific job relates to others in the department and company
   - ☐ Discussion of common problems and how to avoid and overcome them
   - ☐ Performance standards and basis of performance evaluation
   - ☐ Number of daily work hours and times
   - ☐ Overtime needs and requirements
   - ☐ Extra duty assignments (e.g., changing duties to cover for an absent worker)
   - ☐ Required records and reports
   - ☐ Checkout on equipment to be used
   - ☐ Explanation of where and how to get tools, and have equipment maintained and repaired
   - ☐ Types of assistance available, when and how to ask for help
   - ☐ Relations with state and federal inspectors

3. **Policies, procedures, rules, and regulations**
   - ☐ Rules unique to the job and/or department
   - ☐ Handling emergencies
   - ☐ Safety precautions and accident prevention
   - ☐ Reporting of hazards and accidents
   - ☐ Cleanliness standards and sanitation (e.g., cleanup)
   - ☐ Security, theft problems, and costs
   - ☐ Relations with outside people (e.g., drivers)
   - ☐ Eating, smoking, and chewing gum, etc., in department area
   - ☐ Removal of things from department
   - ☐ Damage control (e.g., smoking restrictions)
   - ☐ Time clock and time sheets
   - ☐ Breaks/rest periods
   - ☐ Lunch duration and time
   - ☐ Making and receiving personal telephone calls
   - ☐ Requisitioning supplies and equipment
   - ☐ Monitoring and evaluating of employee performance
   - ☐ Job bidding and requesting reassignment
   - ☐ Going to cars during work hours

4. **Tour of department**
   - ☐ Rest rooms and showers
   - ☐ Fire-alarm box and fire extinguisher stations
   - ☐ Time clocks
   - ☐ Lockers
   - ☐ Approved entrances and exits
   - ☐ Water fountains and eye-wash systems
   - ☐ Supervisors' quarters
   - ☐ Supply room and maintenance department
   - ☐ Sanitation and security offices
   - ☐ Smoking area
   - ☐ Locations of services to employees related to department
   - ☐ First-aid kit

5. **Introduction to department employees**

Source: W. D. St. John, "The Complete Employee Orientation Program," *Personnel Journal,* May 1980, p. 377. Reprinted with the permission of *Personnel Journal,* Costa Mesa, California; all rights reserved.

materials. Care should be taken in the design not only to ensure that essential information is provided but also that too much information is not given. Some materials that might be included in an orientation kit include

Company organization chart.

Map of the company's facilities.

Copy of policy and procedures handbook.

List of holidays and fringe benefits.

Copies of performance appraisal forms, dates, and procedures.

Copies of other required forms (e.g., expense reimbursement form).

Emergency and accident prevention procedures.

Sample copy of company newsletter or magazine.

Telephone numbers and locations of key company personnel (e.g., security personnel).

Copies of insurance plans.

Many organizations require employees to sign a form indicating they have received and read the orientation kit. This is commonly required in unionized organizations to protect the company if a grievance arises and the employee alleges he or she was not aware of certain company policies and procedures. On the other hand, it is equally important that a form be signed in nonunionized organizations, particularly in light of an increase in wrongful discharge litigation. Whether signing a document actually encourages new employees to read the orientation kit is questionable.

Orientation Length and Timing

It is virtually impossible for a new employee to absorb in one long session all of the information in the company orientation program. Brief sessions, not to exceed two hours, spread over several days increase the likelihood that the new employee will understand and retain the information presented. Too many organizations conduct a perfunctory orientation program lasting for a half day or full day. Programs of this nature can result in a negative attitude on the part of new employees.

Unfortunately, many departmental and job orientation programs produce the same results. Frequently, upon arriving in a department, new employees are given a departmental procedures manual and told to read the material and ask any questions they may have. Another frequently used departmental and job orientation method is to give new employees menial tasks to perform. Both of these methods are likely to produce poor results.

Departmental orientations should also be brief and spread over several days. Job orientations should be well planned and conducted using appropriate techniques. HRM in Action 9.1 describes the orientation program at DuPont Merck Pharmaceutical Company.

Follow-up and Evaluation

Formal and systematic follow-up to the initial orientation is essential. The new employee should not be told to drop by if any problems occur. The manager should regularly check on how well the new employee is doing and answer any questions that may have arisen after the initial orientation. The human resource department should conduct a scheduled follow-up after the employee has been on the job for a month.

HRM IN ACTION

Employee Orientation at DuPont Merck Pharmaceutical Company

9.1

www.dupontmerck.com

When E. I. DuPont De Nemours & Company and Merck & Company formed DuPont Merck Pharmaceutical Company, it began operations with approximately 4,300 employees. The new organization needed all its employees to hit the ground running with a clear understanding of their responsibilities. Because 85 percent of its work force transferred over from DuPont, the new company needed to synthesize and rechannel the talents and energy of these employees, as well as those who came from Merck. To ensure complete acclimation for employees, DuPont Merck designed a three-tiered approach to new-employee orientation which it calls orienteering. Orienteering consists of a process of introducing new employees to their work units, divisions, and the company as a whole. Work-unit orienteering shapes an employee's perception of his or her role within the company. Company orienteering is designed to ensure that all employees adapt to DuPont Merck's culture. Divisional orienteering helps the employee bring the company goals and vision into focus at the divisional level.

Source: Adapted from Carol S. Klein and Jeff Taylor, "Employee Orientation Is an On-going Process at the DuPont Merck Pharmaceutical Company," *Personnel Journal,* May 1994, p. 67.

The human resource department should also conduct an annual evaluation of the total orientation program. The purpose of this evaluation is to determine whether the current orientation program is meeting the company's and new employee's needs and ascertain ways to improve the present program.

Feedback from new employees is one method of evaluating the effectiveness of an organization's orientation program. Feedback can be obtained using the following methods:

Unsigned questionnaires completed by all new employees.

In-depth interviews of randomly selected new employees.

Group discussion sessions with new employees who have settled comfortably into their jobs.

Feedback of this type enables an organization to adapt its orientation program to the specific suggestions of actual participants.

Finally, organizations should realize that new employees will receive an orientation that has an impact on their performance—either from coworkers or from the company. It is certainly in the best interest of the company to have a well-planned, well-executed orientation program.

Training Employees

Training A learning process that involves the acquisition of skills, concepts, rules, or attitudes to enhance employee performance.

Training is a learning process that involves the acquisition of skills, concepts, rules, or attitudes to enhance the performance of employees. Generally, the new employee's manager has primary responsibility for job training. Sometimes this training is delegated to a senior employee in the department. Regardless, the quality of this initial training can have a significant influence on the employee's productivity and attitude toward the job.

Economic, social, technological, and governmental changes significantly influence the objectives and strategies of all organizations. Changes in these areas can make the skills learned today obsolete in the future. Also, planned organizational changes and expansions can make it necessary for employees to update their skills or acquire new ones.

Needs Assessment

Needs Assessment A systematic analysis of the specific training activities the organization requires to achieve its objectives.

Training must be directed toward accomplishment of some organizational objective, such as more efficient production methods, improved quality of products or services, or reduced operating costs. This means an organization should commit its resources only to those training activities that can best help in achieving its objectives. Needs assessment is a systematic analysis of the specific training activities the organization requires to achieve its objectives. In general, five methods can be used to gather needs assessment information: interviews, surveys/questionnaires, observations, focus groups, and document examination.[1]

Interviews with employees can be conducted by specialists in the human resource department or by outside experts. Basic questions that should usually be asked are as follows:

1. What problems is the employee having in his or her job?
2. What additional skills and/or knowledge does the employee need to better perform the job?
3. What training does the employee believe is needed?

Of course, in conducting interviews, every organization would have several additional questions about specific issues. In addition, if interviews are to provide useful information, employees must believe their input will be valued and not be used against them.

Surveys and/or questionnaires are also frequently used in needs assessment. Normally this involves developing a list of skills required to perform particular jobs effectively and asking employees to check those skills in which they believe they need training. Figure 9–3 shows some typical areas that a needs assessment questionnaire might cover. Employee attitude surveys can also be used to uncover training needs. Usually most organizations bring in an outside party or organization to conduct and analyze employee attitude surveys. Customer surveys can also indicate problem areas that may not be obvious to employees of the organization. Responses to a customer survey may indicate areas of training for the organization as a whole or particular functional units.

To be effective, observations for determining training needs must be conducted by individuals trained in observing employee behavior and translating observed behavior into specific training needs. Specialists in the human resource department who have been trained in performing job analyses should be particularly adept at observing to identify training needs.

Focus groups are composed of employees from various departments and various levels within the organization. A specialist in the human resource department or an outside expert can conduct the focus group sessions. Focus group topics should address issues such as the following:

1. What skills/knowledge will our employees need for our organization to stay competitive over the next five years?

2. What problems does our organization have that can be solved through training?

Document examination involves examining organizational records on absenteeism, turnover, and accident rates to determine if problems exist and whether any problems identified can be addressed through training. Another useful source to examine is performance appraisal information gathered through the organization's performance appraisal system. Performance problems common to many employees are likely areas to address through training. Regardless of the method employed, a systematic and accurate needs assessment should be undertaken before any training is conducted.

Web site: North American Training and Development Resource Center

www.trainnet.com

Establishing Training Objectives

After training needs have been determined, objectives must be established for meeting those needs. Unfortunately, many organizational training programs have no objectives. "Training for training's sake" appears to be the maxim. This philosophy makes it virtually impossible to evaluate the strengths and weaknesses of a training program.

FIGURE 9–3   NEEDS ASSESSMENT QUESTIONNAIRE WITH SELECTED QUESTIONS

Instructions: Please read the list of training areas carefully before answering. Circle Yes if you believe you need training in that skill, either for use in your current job or for getting ready for promotion to a better position. Circle the question mark if uncertain. Circle No if you feel no need for training in that area.

1. How to more effectively manage my time	Yes	?	No
2. How to handle stress on the job	Yes	?	No
3. How to improve my written communication skills	Yes	?	No
4. How to improve my oral communication skills	Yes	?	No
5. How to improve my listening skills	Yes	?	No
6. How to improve my personal productivity	Yes	?	No

Effective training objectives should state what will result for the organization, department, or individual when the training is completed. The outcomes should be described in writing. Training objectives can be categorized as follows:

1. Instructional objectives.
   - What principles, facts, and concepts are to be learned in the training program?
   - Who is to be taught?
   - When are they to be taught?
2. Organizational and departmental objectives.
   - What impact will the training have on organizational and departmental outcomes such as absenteeism, turnover, reduced costs, and improved productivity?
3. Individual performance and growth objectives.
   - What impact will the training have on the behavioral and attitudinal outcomes of the individual trainee?
   - What impact will the training have on the personal growth of the individual trainee?

When clearly defined objectives are lacking, it is impossible to evaluate a program efficiently. Furthermore, there is no basis for selecting appropriate materials, content, or instructional methods.

Methods of Training

Several methods can be used to satisfy an organization's training needs and accomplish its objectives. Some of the more commonly used methods include on-the-job training, job rotation, apprenticeship training, and classroom training.

Web site: The Training Net

www.trainingnet.com

On-the-Job Training and Job Rotation

On-the-job training (OJT) is normally given by a senior employee or a manager. The employee is shown how to perform the job and allowed to do it under the trainer's supervision.

One form of on-the-job training is **job rotation,** sometimes called **cross training.** In job rotation, an individual learns several different jobs within a work unit or department and performs each job for a specified time period. One main advantage of job rotation is that it makes flexibility possible in the department. For example, when one member of a work unit is absent, another can perform that job.

The advantages of on-the-job training are that no special facilities are required and the new employee does productive work during the learning process. Its major disadvantage is that the pressures of the workplace can cause instruction of the employee to be haphazard or neglected.

In training an employee on the job, the trainer can use several steps to ensure that the training is effective. Table 9–1 summarizes the steps in the training process. Each step is explained more fully next.

Preparation of the Trainee for Learning the Job: An employee almost always desires to learn a new job. Showing an interest in the person, explaining the importance of the job, and explaining why it must be done correctly enhance the employee's desire to learn. Determining the employee's previous work experience in similar jobs enables the trainer to use that experience in explaining the present job or to eliminate unnecessary explanations.

Breakdown of Work into Components and Identification of Key Points: This breakdown consists of determining the segments that make up the total job. In each segment, something is accomplished to advance the work toward completion. Such a breakdown can be viewed as a detailed road map that guides the employee through the

On-the-Job Training (OJT) Training that shows the employee how to perform the job and allows him or her to do it under the trainer's supervision.

Job Rotation (Cross Training)   Training that requires an individual to learn several different jobs in a work unit or department and perform each job for a specified time period.

TABLE 9–1	**STEPS LEADING TO EFFECTIVE ON-THE-JOB TRAINING**

A. Determining the training objectives and preparing the training area:
   1. Decide what the trainee must be taught to do the job efficiently, safely, economically, and intelligently.
   2. Provide the right tools, equipment, supplies, and material.
   3. Have the workplace properly arranged just as the trainee will be expected to keep it.

B. Presenting the instruction:
   Step 1. Preparation of the trainee for learning the job:
      a. Put the trainee at ease.
      b. Find out what the trainee already knows about the job.
      c. Get the trainee interested in and desirous of learning the job.
   Step 2. Breakdown of work into components and identification of key points:
      a. Determine the segments that make up the total job.
      b. Determine the key points, or "tricks of the trade."
   Step 3. Presentation of the operations and knowledge:
      a. Tell, show, illustrate, and question to put over the new knowledge and operations.
      b. Instruct slowly, clearly, completely, and patiently, one point at a time.
      c. Check, question, and repeat.
      d. Make sure the trainee understands.
   Step 4. Performance tryout:
      a. Test the trainee by having him or her perform the job.
      b. Ask questions beginning with *why, how, when,* or *where.*
      c. Observe performance, correct errors, and repeat instructions if necessary.
      d. Continue until the trainee is competent in the job.
   Step 5. Follow-up:
      a. Put the trainee on his or her own.
      b. Check frequently to be sure the trainee follows instructions.
      c. Taper off extra supervision and close follow-up until the trainee is qualified to work with normal supervision.

entire work cycle in a rational, easy-to-understand manner, without injury to the person or damage to the equipment.

A key point is any directive or information that helps the employee perform a work component correctly, easily, and safely. Key points are the "tricks of the trade" and are given to the employee to help reduce learning time. Observing and mastering the key points help the employee acquire needed skills and perform the work more effectively.

Presentation of the Operations and Knowledge: Simply telling an employee how to perform the job is usually not sufficient. An employee must not only be told but also shown how to do the job. Each component of the job must be demonstrated. While each is being demonstrated, the key points for the component should be explained. Employees should be encouraged to ask questions about each component.

Performance Tryout: An employee should perform the job under the guidance of the trainer. Generally, an employee should be required to explain what he or she is going to do at each component of the job. If the explanation is correct, the employee is then allowed to perform the component. If the explanation is incorrect, the mistake should be corrected before the employee is allowed to actually perform the component. Praise and encouragement are essential in this phase.

Follow-up: When the trainer is reasonably sure an employee can do the job without monitoring, the employee should be encouraged to work at his or her own pace while developing skills in performing the job and should be left alone. The trainer should return periodically to answer any questions and see that all is going well. Employees should not be turned loose and forgotten. They will have questions and will make better progress if the trainer is around to answer questions and help with problems.

Apprenticeship Training

Apprenticeship Training
Giving instruction, both on
and off the job, in the
practical and theoretical
aspects of the work required
in a highly skilled
occupation.

Apprenticeship training provides beginning workers with comprehensive training in the practical and theoretical aspects of work required in a highly skilled occupation. Apprenticeship programs combine on-the-job and classroom training to prepare workers for more than 800 skilled occupations such as bricklayer, machinist worker, computer operator, and laboratory technician. About two-thirds of apprenticeable occupations are in the construction and manufacturing trades, but apprentices also work in such diverse fields as electronics, the service industries, public administration, and medical and health care.[2] The length of an apprenticeship varies by occupation and is determined by standards adopted by the industry. Table 9–2 gives the length of some occupational apprenticeship periods.

A skilled and experienced employee conducts on-the-job training during the apprenticeship period. The purpose of this training is to learn the practical skills of the job. Apprentices learn the theoretical side of their jobs in classes they attend. Some of the subjects that might be covered in the classroom training include mathematics, blueprint reading, and technical courses required for specific occupations.

Wages paid apprentices usually begin at half those paid fully trained employees. However, the wages are generally advanced rapidly at six-month intervals.

The U.S. Department of Labor's Bureau of Apprenticeship and Training (BAT) is responsible for providing services to existing apprenticeship programs and technical assistance to organizations that wish to establish programs. The BAT has established the following minimum standards for apprenticeship programs:

1. Nondiscrimination in all phases of apprenticeship employment and training.
2. Organized instruction designed to provide the apprentice with a knowledge in technical subjects related to the trade or skill (a minimum of 144 hours per year is normally considered necessary).
3. A schedule of work processes in which an apprentice is to receive training and experience on the job.
4. A progressively increasing schedule of wages.
5. Proper supervision of on-the-job training, with adequate facilities to train apprentices.
6. Periodic evaluation of the apprentice's progress in both job performance and related instruction.
7. Recognition for successful completions.

TABLE 9–2   **LENGTH OF SELECTED APPRENTICESHIP COURSES**

Occupation	Length of Course (years)
Airplane mechanic	3–4
Automotive mechanic	3–4
Barber	2
Brewer	2–3
Butcher	2–3
Carpenter	4
Musical instrument mechanic	3–4
Photographer	3
Radio electrician	4–5
X-ray technician	4

Source: Bureau of Apprenticeship and Training, U.S. Department of Labor.

Classroom Training

Classroom Training The most familiar training method; useful for quickly imparting information to large groups with little or no knowledge of the subject.

Classroom training is conducted off the job and is probably the most familiar training method. It is an effective means of imparting information quickly to large groups with limited or no knowledge of the subject being presented. It is useful for teaching factual material, concepts, principles, and theories. Portions of orientation programs, some aspects of apprenticeship training, and safety programs are usually presented utilizing some form of classroom instruction. More frequently, however, classroom instruction is used for technical, professional, and managerial employees. HRM in Action 9.2 describes Motorola's virtual reality training. Several specific techniques used in classroom training are discussed in Chapter 10.

Principles of Learning

Previous sections of this chapter discussed not only how training needs are determined but also how they can be met. The use of sound learning principles during the development and implementation of these programs helps to ensure that the programs will succeed. The following sections present several principles of learning.

Motivation to Achieve Personal Goals

People strive to achieve objectives they have set for themselves. The most frequently identified objectives of employees are job security, financially and intellec-

---

HRM IN ACTION

Virtual Reality Training at Motorola

9.2

www.mot.com

Motorola, which employs 60,000 manufacturing employees worldwide, makes an array of products, including pagers, cellular telephones, handheld two-way communication radios, semiconductors, and base station equipment that supports those technologies. Training courses teach employees how to run the company's assembly lines at plants around the world. Motorola University, which is responsible for educating Motorola's employees in diverse skills, is testing PC-based virtual reality (VR) technology to replicate the assembly-line setting. VR is a computer-based technology that gives students a three-dimensional learning experience. By using specialized equipment or viewing the virtual model on the computer screen, students move through the simulated world and interact with its components.

Programmers spent about six weeks creating a computer model of the 25' × 30' advanced manufacturing laboratory that replicates an actual assembly line. Measurements and photographs were taken of the actual lab space, robots, and tooling. This virtual world also contains complex elements found on the real-world assembly lines at the plants: a conveyor system, three pager-assembling robotic work cells, a machine vision inspection system to inspect products for functionality, and a laser-marking system that etches an identification number on each product.

This virtual model was programmed to replicate the actions of the laboratory machinery so that the model would react correctly. When the student turns on a power switch, the corresponding lights or equipment are powered. Of course, if the power hasn't been turned on and the student tries to start equipment, there is no response. Students hear the same whirs, clicks, and hums they would hear if they were using real equipment.

Source: Nina Adams, "Lessons from the Virtual World," *Training,* June 1995, pp. 45–48.

tually rewarding work, recognition, status, responsibility, and achievement. If a training program helps employees achieve some of these objectives, the learning process is greatly facilitated. For example, unskilled employees who are given the opportunity to learn a skilled trade may be highly motivated because they can see that more money and job security will probably result.

Knowledge of Results

Knowledge of results (feedback) influences the learning process. Keeping employees informed of their progress as measured against some standard helps in setting goals for what remains to be learned. The continuous process of analyzing progress and establishing new objectives greatly enhances learning. However, precautions should be taken to ensure that goals are not so difficult to achieve that the employee becomes discouraged.

Oral explanations and demonstrations by the trainee and written examinations are frequently used tools for providing feedback to both the trainee and the trainer. In addition, the progress of an individual or a group can be plotted on a chart to form what is commonly called a *learning curve*. The primary purpose of a learning curve is to provide feedback on the trainee's progress. It can also help in deciding when to increase or decrease training or when to change methods. Figure 9–4 illustrates two different learning curves. Although the decreasing returns curve is most frequently encountered, many other shapes of learning curves are possible.

Reinforcement

The general idea behind reinforcement is that behavior that appears to lead to a positive consequence tends to be repeated, while behavior that appears to lead to a negative consequence tends not to be repeated. A positive consequence is a reward. Praise and recognition are two typical rewards that can be used in training. For example, a trainee who is praised for good performance is likely to continue to strive to achieve additional praise.

FIGURE 9–4   **SAMPLE LEARNING CURVES**

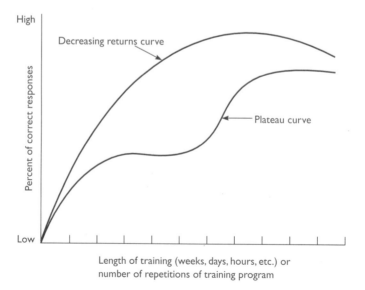

Flow of the Training Program

Each segment of training should be organized so that the individual can see not only its purpose but also how it fits in with other parts of the program. In addition, later segments should build on those presented earlier. Gaps and inconsistencies in material are not conducive to effective learning.

Practice and Repetition

The old adage "practice makes perfect" is applicable in learning. Having trainees perform a particular operation helps them concentrate on the subject. Repeating a task several times develops facility in performing it. Practice and repetition almost always enhance effective learning.

Spacing of Sessions

Managers frequently want to get an employee out of training and into a productive job as quickly as possible. However, trade-offs are involved in deciding whether the training should be given on consecutive days or at longer intervals. Generally, spacing out training over a period of time facilitates the learning process. However, the interval most conducive to learning depends on the type of training.

Whole or Part Training

Should training for a job be completed at once, or should the employee train separately for each job component? The decision should be based on the content of the specific job, the material being taught, and the needs of those being trained. One often successful method is to first give trainees a brief overview of the job as a whole and then divide it into portions for in-depth instruction.

Evaluating Training

When the results of a training program are evaluated, a number of benefits accrue. Less effective programs can be withdrawn to save time and effort. Weaknesses within established programs can be identified and remedied.

Evaluation of training can be broken down into four areas:

1. *Reaction:* How much did the trainees like the program?
2. *Learning:* What principles, facts, and concepts were learned in the training program?
3. *Behavior:* Did the job behavior of the trainees change because of the program?
4. *Results:* What were the results of the program in terms of factors such as reduced costs or reduction in turnover?[3]

Even when great care is taken in designing evaluation procedures, it is difficult to determine the exact effects of training on learning, behavior, and results. Because of this, evaluation of training is still limited and often superficial.[4]

Reaction

Reaction evaluation should consider a wide range of topics, including program content, program structure and format, instructional techniques, instructor abilities and style, the quality of the learning environment, the extent to which training objectives were achieved, and recommendations for improvement. Figure 9–5 illustrates a typical reaction evaluation questionnaire.

FIGURE 9–5   **SAMPLE REACTION EVALUATION QUESTIONNAIRE**

Name of program _____

Instructor _____

Date _____

1. How would you rate the overall program?

   ☐ Excellent   ☐ Very Good   ☐ Good   ☐ Fair   ☐ Poor

   Comments: _____

   _____

2. How were the meeting facilities, luncheon arrangements, etc.?

   ☐ Excellent   ☐ Very Good   ☐ Good   ☐ Fair   ☐ Poor

   Comments: _____

   _____

3. Would you like to attend programs of a similar nature in the future?

   ☐ Yes   ☐ No   ☐ Not sure

   Comments: _____

   _____

4. To what extent was the program relevant to your current job?

   ☐ To a large extent   ☐ To some extent   ☐ Very little

   Comments: _____

   _____

5. How would you rate the abilities and style of the instructor?

   ☐ Excellent   ☐ Very Good   ☐ Good   ☐ Fair   ☐ Poor

6. Other comments and suggestions for future programs:

   Signature (optional) _____

   _____

Reaction evaluation questionnaires are normally administered immediately following the training, but they can be administered several weeks later. The major flaw in using only reaction evaluation is that the enthusiasm of trainees cannot necessarily be taken as evidence of improved ability and performance.

Learning

Learning evaluation concerns how well the trainees understood and absorbed the principles, facts, and skills taught. In the teaching of skills, classroom demonstrations by trainees are a fairly objective way to determine how much learning is occurring. Where principles and facts are being taught, paper and pencil tests can be used. Standardized tests can be purchased to measure learning in many areas. In other areas, the trainers must develop their own tests. To obtain an accurate picture of what was learned, trainees should be tested both before and after the program.

Behavior

Behavior evaluation deals with the nature of the change in job behavior of the trainee and is much more difficult than reaction or learning evaluation. The following guidelines are offered for evaluating behavioral change.

1. A systematic appraisal should be made of on-the-job performance on a before-and-after basis.

HRM IN ACTION

Assessment of Training Programs at TVA University

9.3

www.tra.com

The Tennessee Valley Authority (TVA) University offers hundreds of courses each month via computer-based training (CBT), interactive videoconferencing, live satellite broadcasts, and classroom training to TVA employees located in seven states. TVA University has about 20 locations equipped with electronic classrooms that can receive live or taped video broadcasts. TVA University used its own optical-fiber network so only their own bandwidth and pipeline size limit the amount of programming they can send. TVA University has two full-time employees on the staff devoted to evaluation. There are automated systems for assessing, collecting, in-putting, processing, and reporting automatically. Data is used to manage the performance of instructors and vendors, validate the educational program design, make curriculum decisions, and remove courses that aren't performing well. The system can even identify a performance band for acceptable instructor and course performance. If the response for a class falls above the acceptable limits, the system automatically produces a congratulatory E-mail to the instructor.

Sources: Adapted from Janice Snow Lohmann, "Classroom without Walls: Three Companies That Took the Plunge," *Training & Development,* September 1998, pp. 38–41.

2. The appraisal of performance should be made by one or more of the following groups (the more the better):

   a. The trainee.

   b. The trainee's superior or superiors.

   c. The trainee's subordinates.

   d. The trainee's peers or other people thoroughly familiar with his or her performance.

3. A statistical analysis should be made to compare performance before and after training and to relate changes to the training program.

4. The post-training appraisal should be made several months after the training so that the trainees have an opportunity to put what they have learned into practice.

5. A control group (one not receiving the training) should be used.[5]

Results

Results evaluation attempts to measure changes in variables such as reduced turnover, reduced costs, improved efficiency, reduction in grievances, and increases in quantity and quality of production. As with behavior evaluation, pretests, posttests, and control groups are required in performing an accurate results evaluation. HRM in Action 9.3 describes the evaluation system used by TVA University.

SUMMARY OF LEARNING OBJECTIVES

1. **Define orientation.**

   Orientation is the introduction of new employees to the organization, work unit, and job.

2. **Describe an orientation kit.**

   An orientation kit is a packet of information given to the new employee to supplement the verbal orientation program.

3. **Define training.**

   Training is a learning process that involves the acquisition of skills, concepts, rules, or attitudes to enhance employee performance.

4. **Describe needs assessment.**

   Needs assessment is a systematic analysis of the specific training activities the organization requires to achieve its objectives.

5. **Outline three categories of training objectives.**

   Training objectives can be categorized as instructional objectives, organizational and departmental objectives, and individual performance and growth objectives.

6. **Describe job rotation.**

   In job rotation, an individual learns several different jobs within a work unit or department and performs each job for a specified time period.

7. **Explain apprenticeship training.**

   Apprenticeship training is a system in which an employee is given instruction and experience, both on and off the job, in all the practical and theoretical aspects of the work required in a skilled occupation, craft, or trade.

8. **Outline the seven principles of learning.**

   The seven principles of learning are motivation to achieve personal goals, knowledge and results, reinforcement, flow of the training program, practice and repetition, spacing of sessions, and whole or part training.

9. **List the four areas of training evaluation.**

   Evaluation of training consists of reaction, learning, behavior, and results evaluation.

REVIEW QUESTIONS

1. What is orientation? General company orientation? Departmental and job orientation?
2. Outline several possible topics for a general company orientation.
3. What is an orientation kit?
4. What is training?
5. Define
   a. On-the-job training.
   b. Job rotation.
6. Outline five steps that should be followed in training a new employee in how to perform a job.
7. Define apprenticeship training.
8. What learning principles should be used in all training programs?
9. List and explain the four logical areas for evaluating training.

DISCUSSION QUESTIONS

1. Why are most training programs not evaluated?
2. Which principles of learning are applied in college classrooms? Which ones are most appropriate for use in college classrooms?
3. Why are training programs one of the first areas to be eliminated when an organization's budget must be cut?
4. If you were asked to develop a training program for taxicab drivers, how would you do it? How would you evaluate the program?

INCIDENT 9–1

Starting a New Job

Jack Smythe, branch manager for a large computer manufacturer, had been told by his marketing manager, Linda Sprague, that Otis Brown had just given two weeks' notice. When Jack had interviewed Otis, he had been convinced of his tremendous potential in sales. Otis was bright and personable, an MIT honor graduate in electrical engineering who had the qualifications the company looked for in computer sales. Now he was leaving after only two months with the company. Jack called Otis into his office for an exit interview.

Jack: Come in, Otis, I really want to talk to you. I hope I can change your mind about leaving.

Otis: I don't think so.

Jack: Well, tell me why you want to go. Has some other company offered you more money?

Otis: No. In fact, I don't have another job; I'm just starting to look.

Jack: You've given us notice without having another job?

Otis: Well, I just don't think this is the place for me!

Jack: What do you mean?

Otis: Let me see if I can explain. On my first day at work, I was told that formal classroom training in computers would not begin for a month. I was given a sales manual and told to read and study it for the rest of the day.

The next day, I was told that the technical library, where all the manuals on computers are kept, was in a mess and needed to be organized. That was to be my responsibility for the next three weeks.

The day before I was to begin computer school, my boss told me that the course had been delayed for another month. He said not to worry, however, because he was going to have James Crane, the branch's leading salesperson, give me some on-the-job training. I was told to accompany James on his calls. I'm supposed to start the school in two weeks, but I've just made up my mind that this place is not for me.

Jack: Hold on a minute, Otis. That's the way it is for everyone in the first couple of months of employment in our industry. Any place you go will be the same. In fact, you had it better than I did. You should have seen what I did in my first couple of months.

Questions

1. What do you think about the philosophy of this company pertaining to a new employee's first few weeks on the job? unorganized

2. What suggestions do you have for Jack to help his company avoid similar problems of employee turnover in the future?

INCIDENT 9–2

Implementing On-the-Job Training

The first-year training program for professional staff members of a large national accounting firm consists of classroom seminars and on-the-job training. The objectives of the training are to ensure that new staff members learn fundamental auditing concepts and procedures and develop technical, analytical, and communication skills that, with further experience and training, will help them achieve their maximum potential with the organization.

Classroom training is used to introduce concepts and theories applicable to the work environment. It consists of three two-day and two three-day seminars presented at varying intervals during the staff member's first year. Although new staff members do receive this special training, actual work experience is the principal means by which they develop the many skills necessary to become good auditors.

Teams supervised by the senior member perform most of the firm's audits. This individual is responsible for conducting the review and producing the required reports. Normally teams are assembled on the basis of member availability. For this reason, a senior auditor may be assigned one or more first-year employees for a team that must undertake a complex assignment. Because senior auditors are measured on productivity, their attention is usually focused on the work being produced. Therefore, they assign routine tasks to new staff employees, with little or no thought to furthering the career development of these employees. Most senior auditors assume the next supervisor or the individuals themselves will take care of their training and development needs.

Recently the firm has lost several capable first-year people. The reason most gave for leaving was that they were not learning or advancing in their profession.

Questions

1. What, if anything, do you think the company should do to keep its young employees?
2. Do you think on-the-job training will work in a situation such as the one described?

EXERCISE

McDonald's Training Program

Your class has recently been hired by McDonald's to make recommendations for improving the orientation and training programs of employees in the company's franchise operations. The key job activities in franchise operations are food preparation, order taking and dealing with customers, and routine cleanup operations. McDonald's wants you to make your recommendations based on your observations as customers.

Your assignment is to design a comprehensive orientation and employee training program for each of the key job activities in franchise operations. Be specific by providing an outline, methods of training, and program evaluation procedures for each activity.

1. The class divides into teams of four to five students.
2. Each group is responsible for designing the program for one of the key job activities.
3. Each team is to prepare a 10- to 15-minute presentation on its recommendations.

NOTES AND ADDITIONAL READINGS

1. Allison Rossett, "Assess for Success," *Training and Development Journal,* May 1989, pp. 55–59.
2. James Van Erden, "Linking Past & Present, Students and Jobs," *Vocational Education Journal,* October 1991, p. 31.
3. See D. L. Kirkpatrick, "Evaluation of Training," in *Training and Development Handbook,* ed. R. L. Craig and L. R. Bittel (New York: McGraw-Hill, 1986), p. 18.
4. See Nancy M. Dixon, "Meeting Training's Goals without Reaction Forms," *Personnel Journal,* August 1987, pp. 108–15.
5. Kirkpatrick, "Evaluation of Training," pp. 18-16–18-17.

Management and Organizational Development

10

Learning Objectives

After studying this chapter, you should be able to:

1. Define management development.
2. Describe a management inventory.
3. Describe a management succession plan.
4. Define the in-basket technique.
5. Explain programmed or computer-assisted instruction.
6. Describe a business game.
7. Define an assessment center.
8. Describe organizational development (OD).
9. Discuss behavior modeling.
10. Describe adventure learning.

The previous chapter focused on the orientation and training of new employees and the training of longer-term employees. In addition, an organization must be concerned with developing the abilities of its management team, including supervisors, middle-level managers, and executives. The development and implementation of programs to improve management effectiveness is a major responsibility of the human resource department.

The Management Development Process

Management Development
Process concerned with developing the experience, attitudes, and skills necessary to become or remain an effective manager.

Management development is concerned with developing the experience, attitudes, and skills necessary to become or remain an effective manager. To be successful, it must have the full support of the organization's top executives. Management development should be designed, conducted, and evaluated on the basis of the objectives of the organization, the needs of the individual managers who are to be developed, and anticipated changes in the organization's management team. Figure 10–1 summarizes the total management development process; the following sections discuss each of its elements in depth. HRM in Action 10.1 shows McDonald's approach to management development.

FIGURE 10-1 **THE MANAGEMENT DEVELOPMENT PROCESS**

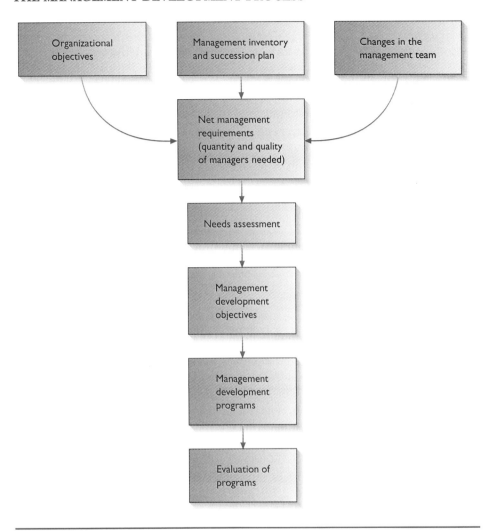

Determining the Net Management Requirements

Organizational Objectives

An organization's objectives play a significant role in determining the organization's requirements for managers. For instance, if an organization is undergoing a rapid expansion program, new managers will be needed at all levels. If, on the other hand, the organization is experiencing limited growth, few new managers may be needed, but the skills of the present management team may need to be upgraded.

Management Inventory
Specialized, expanded form of skills inventory for an organization's current management team; in addition to basic types of information, it usually includes a brief assessment of past performance and potential for advancement.

Management Inventory and Succession Plan

A **management inventory,** which is a specialized type of skills inventory, provides certain types of information about an organization's current management team. Management inventories often include information such as present position, length of service, retirement date, education, and past performance evaluations. Table 10–1 illustrates a simplified management inventory.

Hamburger University at McDonald's

10.1

www.mcdonalds.com

Hamburger University (HU) is McDonald's answer to handling the management development needs for this international organization. The first training class, which consisted of 12 students, was held in 1961 in the basement of an Elk Grove Village, Illinois, McDonald's restaurant. In 1983 HU was moved to its current 80-acre site adjacent to the company's headquarters in Oak Brook, Illinois. The facilities in Oak Brook resemble a modern college campus, including six theater-style classrooms. Since HU first began, more than 56,000 management employees have graduated from the program. HU is breaking new ground by offering its curriculum in 24 different languages. The curriculum focuses on management training, including human relations, interpersonal communications, leadership, and problem-solving. Upon graduation, each student receives a "bachelor of hamburgerology," which can be applied toward more than 30 credits of a college degree.

Source: Adapted from Amy Zuber, "Hamburger University Beefs Up Program with Global Curriculum," *Nation's Restaurant News*, October 27, 1997, pp. 112–13.

A management inventory can be used to fill vacancies that occur unexpectedly—for example, as a result of resignations or deaths. Another use is in planning the development needs of individual managers and using these plans to pinpoint development activities for the total organization.

Management Succession Plan Chart or schedule that shows potential successors for each management position within the organization.

A management inventory can also be used to develop a management succession plan, sometimes called a *replacement chart* or *schedule*. A **management succession plan** records potential successors for each manager within the organization. Usually presented in a format similar to an organization chart, this plan may simply be a list of positions and potential replacements. Other information, such as length of service, retirement data, past performance evaluations, and salary, might also be shown on the replacement chart. Figure 10–2 is an example of a replacement chart for a company's administrative division.

TABLE 10–1 **SAMPLE OF A SIMPLIFIED MANAGEMENT INVENTORY**

Name	Present Position	Length of Service	Retirement Year	Replacement Positions	Previous Training Received
James W. Burch	Industrial relations manager, Greenville plant	5 years	2007	Corporate industrial relations staff	B.B.A., University of South Carolina; middle management program, Harvard
Judy S. Chesser	Engineering trainee	9 months	2017	Plant engineering manager, corporate engineering staff	B.E.E., Georgia Tech
Thomas R. Lackey	Supervisor, receiving department, night shift	15 years	2001	Department manager, shipping and receiving	High school diploma, supervisory skills training
Brenda C. Sabo	Eastern regional marketing manager	8 years	2010	Vice president, marketing	B.B.A., UCLA; M.B.A., USC; executive development program, Stanford

FIGURE 10-2   REPLACEMENT PLAN FOR ADMINISTRATIVE DIVISION OF A TYPICAL ORGANIZATION

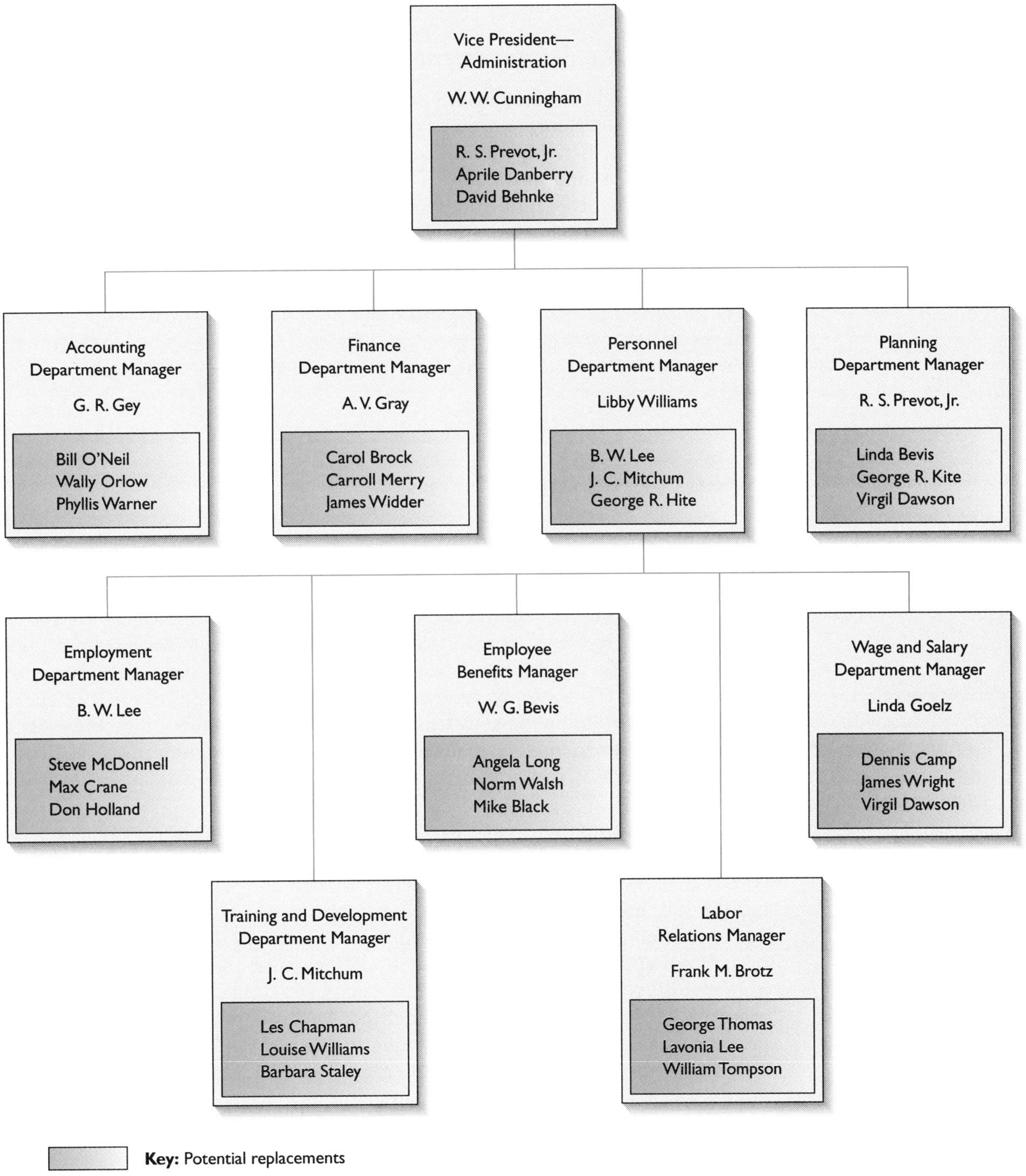

Vice President—
Administration

W. W. Cunningham

R. S. Prevot, Jr.
Aprile Danberry
David Behnke

Accounting
Department Manager

G. R. Gey

Bill O'Neil
Wally Orlow
Phyllis Warner

Finance
Department Manager

A. V. Gray

Carol Brock
Carroll Merry
James Widder

Personnel
Department Manager

Libby Williams

B. W. Lee
J. C. Mitchum
George R. Hite

Planning
Department Manager

R. S. Prevot, Jr.

Linda Bevis
George R. Kite
Virgil Dawson

Employment
Department Manager

B. W. Lee

Steve McDonnell
Max Crane
Don Holland

Employee
Benefits Manager

W. G. Bevis

Angela Long
Norm Walsh
Mike Black

Wage and Salary
Department Manager

Linda Goelz

Dennis Camp
James Wright
Virgil Dawson

Training and Development
Department Manager

J. C. Mitchum

Les Chapman
Louise Williams
Barbara Staley

Labor
Relations Manager

Frank M. Brotz

George Thomas
Lavonia Lee
William Tompson

Key: Potential replacements

Management inventories and succession plans are generally kept confidential and can be computerized. They are also maintained by the human resource department for the use of top executives of the organization.

Changes in the Management Team

Certain changes in the management team can be estimated fairly accurately and easily, while other changes are not so easily determined. Changes such as retirements can be predicted from information in the management inventory; changes such as transfers and promotions can be estimated from such factors as the planned retirements of individuals in specific jobs and the objectives of the organization. Deaths, resignations, and discharges are, of course, difficult to forecast. However, when these changes do occur, the management inventory and succession plan can be used to help fill these vacancies. Analyzing the organization's objectives, studying the management inventory and succession plan, and evaluating changes in the management team can give the human resource department a good picture of both the quantity and quality of managers the organization will need.

Needs Assessment

Every organization has physical, financial, and human resource needs. Needs relate to what the organization must have to achieve its objectives. A fundamental need of any organization is the need for an effective management team. One method of meeting this need is the use of a well-organized management development program. However, before management development activities are undertaken, the specific development needs of the managers in the organization must be determined. Thus, **needs assessment** is a systematic analysis of the specific management development activities the organization requires to achieve its objectives. The management development needs of any organization result from the overall needs of the organization and the development needs of individual managers.

Basically, four methods exist to determine management development needs: a training needs survey, competency studies, task analysis, and performance analysis. A training needs survey focuses on the knowledge and skills required in performing the job. Figure 10–3 provides an example of a needs survey instrument for managerial employees. This instrument lists 18 areas of skill/knowledge required by managerial personnel. Competency studies examine the competencies required in performing the managerial job. Task analysis is concerned with what tasks are required in performing the managerial job. Performance analysis deals with job performance requirements in performing the managerial job. Table 10–2 summarizes the general approach, advantages, and disadvantages of each of these methods of determining management development needs.

Needs Assessment A systematic analysis of the specific management development activities required by the organization to achieve its objectives.

Establishing Management Development Objectives

After the management development needs of the organization have been determined, objectives for the overall management development program and for individual programs must be established to meet those needs. Both types of objectives should be expressed in writing and should be measurable. As discussed in the previous chapter, training objectives can be categorized within three broad areas: instructional, organizational and departmental, and individual performance and growth. This categorization scheme can also be used for management development objectives.

FIGURE 10-3   **MANAGEMENT DEVELOPMENT PROGRAM NEEDS ASSESSMENT QUESTIONNAIRE**

Employee_____ Social Security No. _____

Position Title _____

Organization _____ Location _____

Supervisor (Name & Title) _____

Employee: Please review each "Supervisory/Managerial Function" to assess your need for improving related skills through appropriate developmental opportunities. Your evaluations are to be shown in the "Employee" portion of the "Developmental Requirement" section. One of the following codes should be entered in each box: O = No Need, S = Some Need, or N = Need. **Immediate Supervisor:** Please review the employee's assessments to indicate your findings in respective boxes ("Manager" portion of the "Developmental Requirement" section).

Supervisory/Managerial Function	Employee	Manager
A. Helping Workers with Problems		
1. Help employees with job adjustment problems	☐	☐
2. Help subordinates improve performance	☐	☐
3. Help employees solve personal problems	☐	☐
4. Listening skill development	☐	☐
5. Conflict resolution	☐	☐
6. Employee assistance referral techniques	☐	☐
B. Giving Information to Employees		
1. Keeping employees informed	☐	☐
2. Conducting effective meetings	☐	☐
3. Responding to employee suggestions	☐	☐
C. Receiving Information from Employees		
1. Responding to productivity concepts	☐	☐
2. Encouraging employee participation	☐	☐
3. Consulting with employee concerning work procedures and activities to improve working conditions	☐	☐
D. Labor-Management Relations		
1. Employee rights under agreement	☐	☐
2. Handling employee grievances	☐	☐
E. Leadership		
1. Participative management concepts	☐	☐
2. Encouraging employees to assume personal responsibility for work performance	☐	☐
3. Promoting employee cooperation	☐	☐
F. Safety and Health		
1. Promoting employee understanding of health services and occupational health hazards	☐	☐
2. Promoting adherence to safety regulations	☐	☐
G. Representing Company Management		
1. Defining and defending company goals and objectives	☐	☐
2. Communicating employee views to company management	☐	☐
3. Assuming responsibility for work group's problems	☐	☐
H. Employee Development		
1. Providing detailed work instruction	☐	☐
2. Introducing change	☐	☐
3. Teaching and coaching skills	☐	☐
4. Encouraging employee skill development	☐	☐

(continued)

F I G U R E   1 0 – 3   **(Concluded)**

	Developmental Requirement	
	Employee	**Manager**
I. Employee Utilization		
1. Assessing individual abilities to more effectively assign work	☐	☐
2. Matching individuals with jobs	☐	☐
3. Considering individual interests	☐	☐
4. Understanding employee feelings about their assignments	☐	☐
J. Planning, Scheduling, and Organizing		
1. Division of labor assignments	☐	☐
2. Planning strategies and policies	☐	☐
3. Time management	☐	☐
4. Setting priorities	☐	☐
5. Following up to ensure work completion	☐	☐
K. Controlling Work Progress		
1. Assessing daily developments and progress	☐	☐
2. Reviewing individual progress in carrying out orders	☐	☐
3. Correcting employee work problems	☐	☐
4. Early detection of productivity problems	☐	☐
5. Employee participation in setting goals and associated deadlines	☐	☐
L. Appraising Performance		
1. Establishing job performance standards	☐	☐
2. Effective employee discussion techniques; feedback on good or poor performance	☐	☐
3. Constructive criticism	☐	☐
M. Cooperation		
1. Ensuring that employees have required equipment and materials through obtaining cooperation from other company units	☐	☐
2. Effective coordination with other members of management to resolve problems	☐	☐
N. Resource Utilization		
1. Effective budgeting techniques	☐	☐
2. Financial management	☐	☐
O. Administration		
1. Properly prepare paperwork in a timely manner	☐	☐
2. Administrative policies and procedures	☐	☐
3. Preparation and maintenance of records	☐	☐
4. New employee interviewing techniques and selection criteria	☐	☐
P. Equal Employment Opportunity and Affirmative Action Plan Implementation		
1. Equal treatment of employees in work	☐	☐
2. Equal treatment of employees in advancement decisions	☐	☐
Q. Disciplinary Actions		
1. Verbal and written disciplinary actions	☐	☐
2. Resolving employee conduct problems	☐	☐
R. Personal		
1. Psychological concepts—understanding human behavior	☐	☐
2. Self-analysis for improving effectiveness	☐	☐
3. Coping with stress	☐	☐
4. Improving communications skills (oral and written)	☐	☐

Signature _____ Date _____

Supervisor _____ Date _____

Source: Axel R. Granholm, *Human Resource Director's Portfolio of Personnel Forms, Records, and Reports* (Englewood Cliffs, N.J.: Prentice Hall, 1988), pp. 237–39.

Instructional objectives might incorporate targets relating to the number of trainees to be taught, hours of training, cost per trainee, and time required for trainees to reach a standard level of knowledge. Furthermore, objectives are needed for the principles, facts, and concepts to be learned in the management development programs(s).

Organizational and departmental objectives concern the impact the programs will have on organizational and departmental outcomes, such as absenteeism, turnover, safety, and number of grievances. Individual and personal growth objectives concern the impact on the behavioral and attitudinal outcomes of the individual. They may also involve the impact on the personal growth of the individuals participating in the programs.

After the overall management development objectives have been established, individual program objectives specifying the skills, concepts, or attitudes that should result must be identified. After these objectives are developed, course content and method of instruction can be specified.

Methods Used in Management Development

After the company's needs have been assessed and its objectives stated, management development programs can be implemented. This section examines some of the more frequently used methods of management development. At this point, recall the list of conditions for effective learning discussed in the previous chapter. These principles of learning also apply to management development programs.

The On the Job example at the end of this chapter defines and summarizes the strengths and weaknesses of training methods used in both management development and employee training courses. As with employee training, management development can be achieved both on and off the job. Some of the most popular methods of management development are summarized in Table 10–3 and discussed next.

Understudy Assignments

Understudy Assignments
Method of on-the-job training in which one individual, designated as the heir to a job, learns the job from the present jobholder.

Generally, **understudy assignments** are used to develop an individual's capabilities to fill a specific job. An individual who will eventually be given a particular job works for the incumbent. The title of the heir to the job is usually assistant manager, administrative assistant, or assistant to a particular manager.

The advantage of understudy assignments is that the heir realizes the purpose of the training and can learn in a practical and realistic situation without being directly responsible for operating results. On the negative side, the understudy learns the bad as well as the good practices of the incumbent. In addition, understudy assignments maintained over a long period can become expensive. If an understudy assignment system is used, it should generally be supplemented with one or more of the other management development methods.

Coaching

Coaching Method of management development conducted on the job that involves experienced managers advising and guiding trainees in solving managerial problems.

Coaching, which is carried out by experienced managers, emphasizes the responsibility of all managers for developing employees. Under this method of management development, experienced managers advise and guide trainees in solving managerial problems. The idea behind coaching should be to allow the trainees to develop their own approaches to management with the counsel of a more experienced manager.

One advantage to coaching is that trainees get practical experience and see the results of their decisions. However, there is a danger that the coach will neglect

TABLE 10-2   **COMPARISON OF FOUR APPROACHES TO DETERMINING MANAGEMENT DEVELOPMENT NEEDS**

Starting Point	Training Needs Survey: What Knowledge/Skill (K/S) Is Required?	Competence Study: What Competencies Are Required?
General approach	1. Ask key people what K/S they think/feel the trainees/performers require to do their job. 2. Prioritize the K/S recommended and summarize as a topical list, a training agenda, curriculum, etc.	1. Ask key people what competencies they think/feel the trainee/performer requires to do his or her job. 2. Determine the K/S required to attain the stated competencies. 3. Prioritize the K/S recommended and summarize as a training agenda, or curriculum.
Advantages of this approach	• Fast, inexpensive. • Broad involvement. • Low risk. • Low visibility.	• Relatively fast, inexpensive. • Broad involvement. • Consensus. • In addition to training needs, articulation and agreement on a success profile for the performer. • Identify generic training needs covering a broad population (first-time supervisors, first-time managers, etc.).
Disadvantages of this approach	• Not precise or specific. • Based on opinion, albeit "expert." • Difficult to validate. • Difficult to set priorities. • Difficult to relate to output, to evaluate importance of training. • Once you ask people what training they feel is important, there is an implicit expectation that you will deliver it.	• Difficult to relate to output, to evaluate training. • Difficult to assess relative importance of competencies and therefore difficult to set priorities for K/S input. • Consensus will not necessarily identify the critical difference between exemplary and average performance. • Does not address other factors influencing performance. • Can be highly visible.

training responsibilities or pass on inappropriate management practices. The coach's expertise and experience are critical with this method.

Experience

Many organizations use development through experience. With this method, individuals are promoted into management jobs and allowed to learn on their own from their daily experiences. The primary advantage of this method is that the individual, in attempting to perform a specific job, may recognize the need for management development and look for a means of satisfying it. However, employees who are allowed to learn management only through experience can create serious problems by making mistakes. Also, it is frustrating to attempt to manage without the necessary background and knowledge. Serious difficulties can be avoided if the experience method is supplemented with other management development techniques.

Job Rotation

Job rotation is designed to give an individual broad experience through exposure to many different areas of the organization. In understudy assignments, coaching, and experience, the trainee generally receives training and development for one particular job. In job rotation, the trainee goes from one job to another within the organization, generally remaining in each from six months to a year. Large organizations frequently use this technique for training recent college graduates.

TABLE 10-2   (Concluded)

Task Analysis: What Tasks Are Required?	Performance Analysis: What Job Performance Is Required?
1. Determine what tasks are required of the trainee/performer in order for the job to be performed correctly/successfully. 2. Determine the K/S required to correctly perform the tasks identified. 3. Prioritize the tasks, and thereby the K/S, and summarize as a training design document, training agenda, or curriculum.	1. Determine what performance is required. 2. Determine the critical job outputs or "accomplishments." 3. Determine what tasks are required of the trainee/performer to produce the job outputs or "accomplishments." 4. Determine the K/S required to correctly perform the tasks identified. 5. Determine what other factors in addition to K/S influence job performance, such as job design, resources, consequences, and feedback. 6. Prioritize the K/S required based on impact on job performance and summarize as a training design document, training agenda, or curriculum. 7. Summarize recommendations to modify negative influences on performance, as identified in #4 above.
• Precise identification of tasks and required K/S • Is a form of output and can be measured. • Broad involvement. • Objective, validated by observation.	
• Takes time and skill. • Visible. • Difficult to assess relative importance of tasks and therefore difficult to set priorities for K/S input. • Does not address other factors affecting performance.	• Links K/S requirements to job performance. • Can validate, evaluate. • Addresses other factors affecting performance. • Impact of job outputs is established and therefore can prioritize K/S input. • Takes time and skill. • Visible.

Source: George S. Odiorne and Geary A. Rummler, *Training and Development:* A Guide for Professionals (Chicago: Commerce Clearing House, 1988), pp. 148–49.

TABLE 10-3   **SELECTED METHODS USED IN MANAGEMENT DEVELOPMENT**

On the Job	Off the Job
Understudy assignments	Classroom training
Coaching	Lectures
Experience	Case studies
Job rotation	Role playing
Special projects and committee assignments	In-basket technique
	Programmed instruction
	Business games
	University and professional association seminars

One advantage of job rotation is that the trainees can see how management principles can be applied in a cross section of environments. Also, the training is practical and allows the trainee to become familiar with the entire operation of the company. One serious disadvantage of this method is that the trainee is frequently given menial assignments in each job. Another disadvantage is the tendency to leave the trainee in each job longer than necessary. Both of these disadvantages can produce negative attitudes.

Special Projects and Committee Assignments

Special projects require the trainee to learn about a particular subject. For example, a trainee may be told to develop a training program on safety. This would require learning about the organization's present safety policies and problems and the safety training procedures used by other companies. The trainee must also learn to work and relate to other employees. However, it is critical that the special assignments provide a developing and learning experience for the trainee and not just busywork.

Committee assignments, which are similar to special projects, can be used if the organization has regularly constituted or ad hoc committees. In this approach, an individual works with the committee on its regularly assigned duties and responsibilities. Thus, the person develops skills in working with others and learns through the activities of the committee.

Classroom Training

In classroom training, the most familiar type of training, several methods can be used. Classroom training is used not only in management development programs but also in the orientating and training activities discussed in the previous chapter. Therefore, some of the material in this section also applies to those activities. In addition, several of the approaches used in organizational development (discussed later in this chapter) involve classroom training.

Lectures

One of the most common methods of instruction is lecturing, or teaching by the spoken word. Of course, lectures can include other media such as transparencies, slides, or videotapes. Strengths of the lecture method of instruction include the following:

1. Lectures can communicate the intrinsic interest of the subject matter. The lecturer can communicate his or her enthusiasm for the subject, which should enhance the audience's interest in learning.
2. Lectures can cover material not otherwise available.
3. Lecturers can reach many learners at one time.
4. Lecturers can serve as effective models for their audience. An effective lecturer not only conveys information but also conveys what does and does not work in different settings.
5. The lecture method lets the instructor control what will be covered, the sequence in which it will be covered, and how much time will be devoted to each topic.
6. Lectures pose a minimal threat to the learner.

Weaknesses of the lecture method include the following:

1. Lectures often do not allow for feedback from the audience.
2. Listeners are often passive.
3. The length of lecture periods often does not match listeners' interest spans.

4. Lecturing fails to allow for individual differences in ability or experience.

5. Lectures are unsuitable for certain higher forms of learning, such as analysis and diagnosis.

6. Lectures are partially dependent on the public speaking skills and abilities of the lecturer.[1]

Case Studies

Case Study   Method of classroom training in which the learner analyzes real or hypothetical situations and suggests not only what to do but also how to do it.

In the **case study** technique, popularized by the Harvard Business School, real and/or hypothetical situations are presented for the learner to analyze. Ideally, the case study should force the learner to think through problems, propose solutions, choose among them, and analyze the consequences of the decision.

Some major advantages of the case method are as follows:

1. Cases emphasize the analysis of a situation that is typical of the manager's world.

2. The case study method improves the learner's verbal and written communications skills.

3. Cases expose learners to a wide range of true-to-life management problems.

4. Cases inspire interest in otherwise theoretical and abstract training material.

Some possible weaknesses of the case study method include the following:

1. Cases often focus on past and static considerations.

2. Case analysis often lacks emotional involvement on the part of the learner and thus is unrealistic in terms of what the learner would actually do in the situation.

3. Case analysis can sometimes confuse learners who are used to definite solutions.

Incident Method   Form of case study in which learners are initially given the general outline of a situation and receive additional information from the instructor only as they request it.

Furthermore, the success of the case study method depends heavily on the skills of the instructor. Asking probing questions and keeping everyone involved in the analysis of the case are critical to the success of the method.[2]

One variation of the case study is the **incident method.** The learner is initially given only the general outline of a situation. The instructor then provides additional information as the learner requests it. Theoretically, the incident method makes students probe the situations and seek additional information, much as they would be required to do in real life.

Role Playing

In this method, participants are assigned different roles and required to act out those roles in a realistic situation. The idea is for the participants to learn from playing out the assigned roles. The success of this method depends on the ability of participants to assume the roles realistically. Videotaping allows for review and evaluation of the exercise to improve its effectiveness.

In-basket Technique

In-Basket Technique Method of classroom training in which the participant is required to simulate the handling of a specific manager's mail and telephone calls and to react accordingly.

The **in-basket technique** simulates a realistic situation by requiring each participant to answer one manager's mail and telephone calls. Important duties are interspersed with routine matters. For instance, one call may come from an important customer who is angry, while a letter from a local civic club may request a donation. Participants analyze the situations and suggest alternative actions. They are evaluated on the basis of the number and quality of decisions and on the priorities assigned to each situation. The in-basket technique has been used not only for management development but also in assessment centers, which are discussed later in this chapter.

Programmed and Computer-Assisted Instruction

Programmed instruction requires the trainee to read material on a particular subject and answer questions about the material. Correct answers allow the trainee to move on to more advanced or new material. If the trainee's answers are incorrect, he or she is required to reread the material and answer additional questions. The material in programmed instruction is presented either in text form or on com-

Programmed Instruction
Method of classroom training in which material is presented in text form or on computer video displays; participants are required to correctly answer questions

puter video displays. Regardless of the type of presentation, programmed instruction provides active practice, a gradual increase in difficulty over a series of steps, immediate feedback, and an individualized rate of learning. Programmed instruction is normally used to teach factual information. The increased availability and lower cost of small computers may increase the use of programmed instruction, not only in management development but also in employee training and orientation.

Business Games

about the subject presented before progressing to more advanced material.

Business Game   Method of classroom training that simulates an organization and its environment and requires a team of players to make operating decisions based on the situation.

Business games generally provide a setting of a company and its environment and require a team of players to make decisions involving company operations.[3] They also normally require the use of computer facilities. In a business game, several teams act as companies within a type of industry. This method forces individuals not only to work with other group members but also to function in an atmosphere of competition within the industry. Advantages of business games are that they simulate reality, decisions are made in a competitive environment, feedback is provided concerning decisions, and decisions are made using less than complete data. The main disadvantage is that many participants simply attempt to determine the key to winning.[4] When this occurs, the game is not used to its fullest potential as a learning device.

University and Professional Association Seminars

Web site: Online Courses

www.caso.com

Many colleges and universities offer both credit and noncredit courses intended to help meet the management development needs of various organizations. These offerings range from courses in principles of supervision to advanced executive management programs. Professional associations such as the American Management Association also offer a wide variety of management development programs. These programs use many of the previously discussed classroom techniques.[5] HRM in Action 10.2 describes how Disney World provides training to human resource managers.

Evaluation of Management Development Activities

Four alternatives exist for evaluating management development activities. Each alternative focuses on the following questions:

Alternative I—Are the trainees happy with the course?

Alternative II—Does the training course teach the concepts?

Alternative III—Are the concepts used on the job?

Alternative IV—Does the application of the concepts positively affect the organization?[6]

For each of the four alternatives, an organization must determine what might be measured to answer the question posed by the alternative and what sources of data can help in its measurement. Table 10–4 provides a summary of the alternatives, possible measures, and possible sources of data.

Assessment Center   Formal method used in training and/or selection and aimed at evaluating an individual's potential as a manager by exposing the individual to simulated problems that would be faced in a real-life managerial situation.

Assessment Centers

An **assessment center** is a method in which various personality traits of assessees are evaluated by trained observers based on the assessees' performance in specially chosen exercises. Assessment centers are used for making decisions on promoting, evaluation, and training managerial personnel.[7]

Developing the list of personality characteristics to be assessed is a critical element in any assessment center. The personality characteristics should be di-

I'm Going to Disney World

10.2

www.disney.go.com/Disney World

Many human resource professional study the latest human resource practices by literally going to Disney World. The Disney Institute, which is a management training business set up by Disney, conducts a four-day seminar, cosponsored by the Society for Human Resource Management, for human resource professionals. The seminar, which is called "The Walt Disney Approach to Human Resource Management," features a fast-paced, multimedia mix of substantive lectures, discussions, presentations by Disney executives, and field trips to resort facilities. Topics covered in the seminar include the following: (1) employee relations, including issues such as equal employment opportunity, Americans with Disabilities Act, and other compliance issues; procedures for investigating sexual harassment complaints; administration of collective bargaining agreements; and Internet and E-mail usage policies; (2) management training, including issues such as mentoring, personal development plans and core training programs for managers, and the use of 360-degree feedback tools; (3) compensation and benefits, including issues such as benchmarking with industry leaders, use of published and customized survey data, bonus plans, and annual performance reviews.

Source: Adapted from Leon Rubis, "Show and Tell," *HR Magazine*, April 1998, pp. 110–17.

rectly related to the successful performance of the particular jobs for which the assessees are being evaluated. Only when these personality characteristics have been identified can exercises be selected for use in the assessment center. Research indicates that certain exercises are more relevant for measuring some personality traits than others. Exercises used in assessment centers include in-basket exercises, business games, group discussions, cases, interviews, and various paper-and-pencil tests. These exercises involve the assessees in situations that require decision making, leadership, written and oral communication, planning, and organizing. Assessors observe the assessees while they are involved in the various exercises and evaluate their performance based on the personality characteristics being assessed. Assessees are generally examined in groups of approximately six persons whose personality characteristics to be assessed are similar and who occupy similar positions in the organization.[8]

Selection of the assessment staff is another important element in an assessment center. Trained professionals such as industrial psychologists are frequently used as assessors. In addition, successful managers are often used as assessors in the belief that these people would best know the qualities required for success. Typically, several assessors are used in the evaluation process.

While the assessors observe the assessees in their performance of the various exercises, each assessor evaluates each assessee individually. The assessors then gather together and review each assessee in depth on each personality characteristic to be assessed. Each assessee is then ranked on a relative scale such as "more than acceptable," "acceptable," or "not acceptable."

The primary use of assessment centers has been as a predictor of success in some position for which the assessee is being considered. However, the method can also be used to identify special training that may be required by assessee.

Organizational Development (OD) Organizationwide, planned effort managed from the top, with the goal of increasing organizational performance through planned interventions and training experiences.

Organizational Development

Organizational development (OD) seeks to improve the performances of groups, departments, and the overall organization. Specifically, **organizational development** is an organizationwide, planned effort managed from the top, with the goal

T A B L E   1 0 – 4   **EVALUATION MATRIX**

What We Want to Know	What Might Be Measured	What to Look at (sources of data)
I. Are the trainees happy? If not, why? a. Concepts not relevant b. Format of the workshop c. Trainees not properly positioned	Trainee reaction during workshop Trainee reaction after workshop	Comments between trainees Comments to instructor Questions about exercises "Approach Behavior" to exercises "Approach Behavior" to project Questions about project, concepts
II. Do the materials teach the concepts? If not, why not? a. WS structure b. Lessons: • Presentation • Examples • Exercises	Trainee performance during workshop Trainee performance at end of workshop	Learning time Performance on exercises Presentations Action plan for project Use of tools on exercises Presentations
III. Are the concepts used? If not, why not? a. Concepts: • Not relevant • Too complex • Too sophisticated b. Inadequate tools c. Environment not supportive	Performance improvements projects* Problem-solving technique Ongoing management approach*	Discussion Documentation Results Discussion Documentation Results Discussion Meetings Documentation
IV. Does application of concepts positively affect the organization? If not, why not?	Problem-solving* Problem prediction and prevention* Performance measures*	Discussions Documentation Results Discussions Documentation Results Performance data

*Specific to a particular workshop.

Source: George S. Odiorne and Geary A. Rummler, *Training and Development: A Guide for Professionals* (Chicago: Commerce Clearing House, 1988), pp. 377–78.

of increasing organizational performance through planned interventions and training experiences. In particular, OD looks at the human side of organizations. It seeks to change attitudes, values, organizational structures, and managerial practices in an effort to improve organizational performance. The ultimate goal of OD is to structure the organizational environment so that managers and employees can use their developed skills and abilities to the fullest.

The initial phase of an OD effort is a recognition by management that organizational performance can and should be improved. Following this initial recognition, most OD efforts include the following phases: (1) diagnosis, (2) strategy planning, (3) education, and (4) evaluation.

Diagnosis involves gathering information from employees through the use of questionnaires or attitude surveys. Strategy planning is concerned with developing a

Web site: Training and
Development Resource
Center

www.tem.com/trdev

plan for organizational improvement based on these data. Strategy planning identifies problems in the organization and outlines steps to be taken to resolve the problems. Education consists of sharing the information obtained in the diagnosis with the employees who are affected by it and helping them realize the need for changed behavior. The education phase often involves the use of outside consultants working with individual employees or employee groups. This phase can also involve the use of the management development programs discussed earlier. Other techniques that might be used in the education phase are examined in the following section.

The evaluation phase is very similar to the diagnostic phase. Following diagnosis, strategy planning, and education, additional data are gathered through attitude surveys or questionnaires to determine the effects of the OD effort on the total organization. This information can then lead to additional planning and educational efforts.

Approaches to Management and Organizational Development

Behavior Modeling (Interaction Management) A method of training in which interaction problems faced by managers are identified, practiced, and transferred to specific job situations.

One approach used in management and organizational development is **behavior modeling,** or **interaction management.** Basically, behavior modeling involves identifying interaction problems faced by managers, such as gaining acceptance, overcoming resistance to change, motivating employees, or reducing tardiness. The sequence of learning activities in behavior modeling involves:

1. A filmed model or actual demonstration of the skills necessary to solve the problem being studied.
2. Practice in solving the problem through role playing for each trainee.
3. Reinforcement of the correct behaviors in solving the problem during the practice situation.
4. Planning by each trainee of how to transfer the skills back to the specific job situation.

Although behavior modeling is a relatively new technique, results have been encouraging.[9]

Adventure Learning (Experiential-Learning Programs) Programs that use many kinds of challenging outdoor activities to help participants achieve their goals.

Adventure learning, or **experiential-learning programs,** use many kinds of challenging outdoor activities, often involving physical risk, to help participants achieve their goals. The goals of adventure learning generally fall into two categories:

1. Group-focused objectives: These objectives include better communication, more creative problem-solving, more effective teamwork, and improved leadership. One activity often included in adventure learning is "The Wall," a 12- to 14-foot structure that teams must get over by working together. The wall is viewed as a symbol for any business challenge.
2. Personal growth objectives: These objectives include improved self-esteem, improved risk-taking skills, increased self-awareness, and better stress management. Rope activities are favorite methods for achieving personal growth objectives. One example of a rope activity is the "electric rope" game. A team has to get every member over a rope strung high up between two trees. Team members must try not to touch the rope, and they cannot use props. The electric rope is viewed as an analogy for a difficult business challenge the team faces at work.[10]

S U M M A R Y   O F   L E A R N I N G   O B J E C T I V E S

1. **Define management development.**
   Management development is concerned with developing the experience, attitudes, and skills necessary to become or remain an effective manager.

2. **Describe a management inventory.**

   A management inventory provides certain types of information about an organization's current management team. Information contained includes present position, length of service, retirement date, education, and past performance evaluations.

3. **Describe a management succession plan.**

   A management succession plan records potential successors for each manager within the organization.

4. **Define the in-basket technique.**

   The in-basket technique simulates a realistic situation by requiring trainees to answer one manager's mail and telephone calls.

5. **Explain programmed or computer-assisted instruction.**

   Programmed or computer-assisted instruction requires the trainee to read material on a particular subject and answer questions about the material. Correct answers allow the trainee to move on to more advanced or new material.

6. **Describe a business game.**

   Business games require a team of players to make decisions involving company operations in a setting of the company and its environment. They normally require the use of computer facilities.

7. **Define an assessment center.**

   An assessment center is a formal method aimed at evaluating an individual's potential as a manager and his or her developmental needs.

8. **Describe organizational development (OD).**

   Organizational development (OD) is an organizationwide, planned effort managed from the top, with the goal of increasing organizational performance through planned interventions and training experiences.

9. **Discuss behavior modeling.**

   Behavior modeling involves identifying interaction problems faced by managers and then attempting to solve the problems through the following sequence of learning activities: studying a filmed model or actual demonstration of the skills necessary to solve the problem, practicing problem solving through role playing, reinforcing the correct behaviors, and developing a plan for transferring the skills back to the specific job situation.

10. **Describe adventure learning.**

    Adventure learning uses many kinds of challenging outdoor activities, often involving physical risk, to help participants reach their goals.

REVIEW QUESTIONS

1. Define management development.
2. What is a management inventory? What is a succession plan?
3. Name three classifications for overall management development objectives, and give examples of each.
4. Describe the following on-the-job methods of management development:
   a. Understudy assignments
   b. Coaching
   c. Experience
   d. Job rotation
   e. Special projects
   f. Committee assignments
5. Describe the following methods of classroom training:
   a. Lectures
   b. Case studies
   c. Role playing

      d. In-basket technique
      e. Programmed instruction
      f. Business games
  6. What is an assessment center?
  7. What is organizational development (OD)?
  8. Outline the phases of organizational development.
  9. What is behavior modeling?
10. What is adventure learning?

DISCUSSION QUESTIONS

1. Outline a system for evaluating a management development program for supervisors.
2. "It is impossible to evaluate the effectiveness of a supervisory development program." Discuss.
3. "Management games are fun, but you don't really learn anything from them." Discuss.
4. Organizational development generally takes several years to produce any positive results. Describe some of the positive results that might accrue from such a program, thus making the waiting period worthwhile.

INCIDENT 10–1

The 40-Year Employee

John Brown, 62 years old, has been at the State Bank for 40 years. For the past 20 years, he has worked in the bank's investment department. During his first 15 years in the department, it was managed by Bill Adams. The department consisted of Bill, John, and two other employees. Bill made all decisions, while the others performed record-keeping functions.

Tom Smith took over the investment department after Bill Adams retired. Tom, 56, has worked for the State Bank for the past 28 years. Shortly after taking control of the department, Tom recognized that it needed to be modernized and staffed with people capable of giving better service to the bank's customers. As a result, he increased the department work force to 10 people. Of the 10 employees, only John and Tom are older than 33.

When Tom took over the department, John was able to be helpful since he knew all about how the department had been run in the past. Tom considered John to be a capable employee; after about a year, he promoted John to assistant vice president.

After he had headed the department for about a year and a half, Tom purchased a new computer package to handle the bond portfolio and its accounting. When the new system was implemented, John said he did not like the new system and preferred the old system. At that time, his attitude created no real problem, since there were still many other records to be kept. John continued to handle most of the daily record-keeping.

Over the next two years, further changes came about. As the other employees in the department became more experienced, they branched into new areas of investment work. The old ways of doing things were replaced by new, more sophisticated methods. John resisted these changes; he refused to accept or learn new methods and ideas. He slipped more and more into doing only simple but time-consuming busywork.

Presently a new computer system is being acquired for the investment section, and another department is being put under Tom's control. John has written Tom a letter stating he wants no part of the new computer system but would like to be the manager of the new department. In his letter, John said he was tired of being given routine tasks while the young people got all the exciting jobs. John contended that since he had been with the bank longer than anyone else, he should be given first shot at the newly created job.

Questions

1. Who has failed, John or the company?
2. Does the company owe something to a 40-year employee? If so, what?
3. What type of development program would you recommend for John?

INCIDENT 10–2

Consolidating Three Organizations

Sitting at his desk, Ray McGreevy considered the situation he faced. His small but prosperous real estate firm had tripled in size because of two simultaneous acquisitions. He now needed to develop a management team that could coordinate the three previously independent companies into one efficient firm. He knew this would be no easy task, because the two acquired companies had each been operated as independent entities.

In the seven years since Ray had started his real estate brokerage business, he had compiled an enviable record of growth and profits. His staff, originally consisting of himself and a secretary, had grown to more than 25 employees. His organization included himself as president, 2 vice presidents, 16 sales representatives, 4 secretaries, and 2 clerical workers. These employees were distributed equally between the two branches, each supervised by a vice president. The sales representatives reported to the vice president in their particular branch. The two branches covered a large geographic area that was divided into two regions.

About a year ago, Ray had decided to add a branch in a new area. After doing considerable research, he had decided it might be more feasible to acquire one of the smaller firms already operating in the area. A bank officer whom he had contacted approved his plans and promised to help in locating a company to buy and in financing the acquisition.

Several months went by, and Ray discussed possible mergers with two firms; however, satisfactory terms could not be reached. He was becoming slightly discouraged when the banker called him to set up a meeting with the owner of another real estate firm. This firm had been in business for approximately 30 years, and the owner had only recently decided to retire. The company, which was almost equal in size to Ray's, did not sell in his firm's geographic area. Therefore, it appeared to be a natural choice, and Ray was quite excited about prospects for acquiring it. The owner had agreed to accept payment over several years. Although the price was higher than Ray had originally intended to pay, the deal was too good to refuse.

Then, when the deal seemed ready to be closed, the owners of one of the other firms Ray had been interested in buying called and said they wished to renegotiate. Ray was able to make a favorable arrangement with them. After discussing his situation with the banker, he finally decided to purchase both firms. Although this plan far exceeded his original intentions, he knew opportunities such as these did not come along every day.

Now Ray pondered his next step. He had been so busy in the negotiations that he had not had time to develop a plan for managing his enlarged company. As an entrepreneur, he knew he needed to develop a professional team to manage the new business properly. He now had three more branches and about 45 additional employees.

There were so many questions to answer. Would it be better to operate the three branches as independent divisions? Should he retain the individual identities of the two new firms, or should he rename them after his original one? He needed answers to these and all his other questions.

Questions

1. Does organizational development hold the key to Ray's questions?

2. As a personnel consultant, what recommendations would you make to him?

EXERCISE

Training Methods

The On the Job example at the end of this chapter provides a brief description of many training methods used in management development. The class breaks into teams of two students each. Each team is assigned one of the training methods and is to prepare a 10-minute presentation on the uses, advantages, and disadvantages of the method.

NOTES AND ADDITIONAL READINGS

1. Ricky W. Griffen and William E. Cashin, "The Lecture and Discussion Method for Management Education: Pros and Cons," *Journal of Management Development* 8, no. 2 (1989), pp. 25–32.

2. For more information on the case study method, see Chimezie A. B. Osigweh, "Casing the Case Approach in Management Development," *Journal of Management Development* 8, no. 2 (1989), pp. 41–57.

3. A. J. Faria, "Business Gaming: Current Usage Levels," *Journal of Management Development* 8, no. 2 (1989), pp. 58–65.

4. For additional information, see Stephen A. Stumpf and Jane E. Dutton, "The Dynamics of Learning through Simulations: Let's Dance," *Journal of Management Development* 9, no. 2 (1990), pp. 7–15.

5. For additional information, see Albert Vicere, "Universities as Providers of Executive Education," *Journal of Management Development* 9, no. 4 (1990), pp. 23–31.

6. George S. Odiorne and Geary A. Rummler, *Training and Development: A Guide for Professionals* (Chicago: Commerce Clearing House, 1988), p. 375.

7. George Munchus III and Barbara McArthur, "Revisiting the Historical Use of the Assessment Centre in Management Selection and Development," *Journal of Management Development* 10, no. 1 (1991), pp. 5–13.

8. Ibid., p. 7.

9. Kenneth E. Hultman, "Behavior Modeling for Results," *Training and Development Journal*, December 1986, pp. 60–61.

10. Catherine M. Petrini, "Over the River and through the Woods," *Training and Development Journal*, May 1990, pp. 15–34.

Comparison of Training Methods*

Method	Definition	Strengths	Weaknesses
1. Lecture	A speech by the instructor, with very limited discussions.	Clear and direct methods of presentation. Good if there are more than 20 trainees. Materials can be provided to trainees in advance to help in their preparation. Trainer has control over time. Cost effective.	Since there is no discussion, it is easy to forget. Sometimes it is not effective. Requires a high level of speaking ability. Requires a high level of quick understanding by trainees.
2. Group discussion (conference)	A speech by the instructor, with a lot of participation (questions and comments) from the listeners. Sometimes an instructor is not necessary; however, a leader is needed.	Good if the participants are in small groups. Each participant has an opportunity to present own ideas. More ideas can be generated.	Sometimes discussions get away from the subjects. Some group leaders or instructors do not know how to guide discussions. Sometimes one strong individual can dominate others.
3. Role playing	Creating a realistic situation and having trainees assume parts of specific personalities in the situation. Their actions are based on the roles assigned to them. Emphasis is not on problem solving but on skill development.	Good if the situation is similar to the actual work situation. Trainees receive feedback that gives them confidence. Good for interpersonal skills. Teaches individuals how to act in real situations.	Trainees are not actors. Trainees sometimes are not serious. Some situations cannot be implemented in role playing. Uncontrolled role playing may not lead to any desirable results. If it is very similar to actual life, it may produce adverse reactions.
4. Sensitivity training (laboratory training)	Used for organizational development. Creating situations and examining the participants' reactions and behavior, then having feedback about behavior. Group members exchange thoughts and feelings in unstructured ways.	Helps individuals to find the reasons for their behavior (self-insight). Helps individuals to know the effects of their behavior on others. Creates more group interactions.	People may not like information about their behavior, especially if it is negative. May lead to conflict and anger within the group. May not be related or transferable to jobs.
5. Case study	A written narrative description of a real situation, issue, or incident that a manager faced in a particular organization. Trainees are required to propose a suitable solution or make an appropriate decision.	Cases can be very interesting. Much group discussion and interaction about many solutions, since there is no absolute solution. Develops trainees' abilities in effective communication and active participation. Develops trainees' ability to figure out various factors that influence their decision building.	A slow method of training. Often difficult to select the appropriate case for the specific training situation. Requires high level of skills by both trainees and trainer, as the discussion can become boring. Can create frustration on part of trainees, especially if they fail to arrive at a specific solution.

*Source: Sulaiman M. Al-Malik, unpublished paper, Georgia State University, Winter 1985.

Method	Definition	Strengths	Weaknesses
		Develops trainees' ability to make proper decisions in real-life situations (transfer of learning).	
6. Management games	Giving the trainees information about the organization and its environment, then dividing into teams. Each team is required to make an operational decision and then evaluate its decision.	Develops practical experience for the trainees. Helps in transferring knowledge and in applying administrative thoughts. Helps to evaluate and correct the trainees' behavior.	Often it is difficult to study the results of each team's decision. Some teams may not take it seriously. May be a slow process.
7. Simulation exercises	Same as management games, except a computer is used to input information and analyze the team decisions. Results of trainees' actions are evaluated and discussed.	Same as management games.	Same as management games. Costly. Difficult to simulate a very complex system.
8. Wilderness training	Several managers meet out of the workplace and live in cabins or tents for up to several days. They test their survival skills and learn about their own potentials (for creativity, cooperation, etc.).	People learn their limits and capabilities.	Very costly. May not be transferable.
9. In-basket training	Creates the same type of situations trainees face in daily work. Trainees observed on how they arrange the situations and their actions regarding them. Trainees evaluated on the basis of the number and quality of decisions. Used for management development and assessment centers.	Effective for corrective action or reinforcement. Widely used in assessment centers for measuring supervisory potential.	Tendency to be or become overly simplistic.
10. Incident process (problem-solving)	Simple variation of the case study method. The basic elements are given to the trainee, who then asks the instructor for the most sufficient information that will help him or her in making a decision. The instructor will give only the requested information.	Has immediate feedback from the instructor. Develops supervisory skills in fact seeking and decision making.	Requires high degree of instruction skills in forming answers.
11. Vestibule training	Setting up a training area very similar to the work area in equipment,	Fast way to train employees. Trainees can get the most from this method.	Very expensive.

(*continued*)

Method	Definition	Strengths	Weaknesses
	procedures, and environment, but separated from the actual one so trainees can learn without affecting the production schedule. Used for training typists, bank tellers, and the like.		
12. Apprenticeship training	Trainee works under guidance of skilled, licensed instructor and receives lower pay than licensed workers.	Develops special skills like mechanical, electronic, tailoring, etc. Extensive training.	Takes a long time.
13. Internship training	According to agreement, individuals in these programs earn while they learn, but at a lower rate than if they worked full time.	More chance for trainees to apply what they have learned. Trainees get exposure to both the organization and the job.	Takes a long time.
14. Projects	Similar to the group discussion method. Trainees analyze data and reach conclusions together.	Helps trainees to know more about the subject.	Requires instructor's time to ensure the group is going in the right direction.
15. Videotapes and movies	Recording and producing certain events or situations with clear descriptions in order to cover certain subjects. Can be shown many times, then reviewed and discussed to help trainees understand more fully.	Tapes can be played many times to ensure individual's understanding. Many events and discussions can be put on one tape. Because time length is known, presentation and follow-up can be scheduled.	Recording and producing has to be done by professionals to get good quality. Expensive.
16. Multiple management	Lower- and middle-level managers participate formally with top management in planning and administration.	Helps top management to identify top management candidates. Enhances employees' participation in the organization.	

Career Development

Learning Objectives

After studying this chapter, you should be able to:

1. Define career development and summarize its major objectives.
2. Name the three entities required to provide input for a successful career development program and briefly describe their respective responsibilities.
3. Describe the steps involved in implementing a career development program.
4. Define career pathing and career self-management.
5. List several myths employees hold related to career planning and advancement.
6. List several myths management holds related to career development.
7. Define a career plateau and a plateaued employee.
8. Describe the four principal career categories.
9. Distinguish between dual-career couples and dual-earner couples. Describe some possible ways organizations can accommodate dual-employed couples.
10. Define outplacement.
11. Explain what the glass ceiling is.

Not long ago, individuals joined an organization and often stayed with it for their entire working careers. Organizations frequently gave gold watches and length-of-service pins to reward loyal employees. However, the concept of organizational loyalty has faded in the decades following World War II. Starting in the mid-1960s, the average 20-year-old employee was expected to change jobs approximately six or seven times during his or her lifetime. According to current statistics from the U.S. Department of Labor, today's college graduates will, on average, have 8 to 10 jobs and as many as three careers in their lifetimes.[1]

Recent data from different sources reveal that although most employees remain happy in their work, they are growing increasingly concerned about their career prospects at their present companies.[2] Consequently, instead of thinking in terms of remaining with one organization, many employees now expect to pursue different careers. Corporate restructuring and the often resulting downsizing are causing many employees to change their careers even when they do not desire a change.[3] Thus, increased employee mobility and related environmental factors have made career development increasingly important for today's organizations. **Career development** is an ongoing, formalized effort by an organization that focuses on developing and enriching the organization's human resources in light of both the employees' and the organization's needs.

Career Development An ongoing, formalized effort by an organization that focuses on developing and enriching the organization's human resources in light of both the employees' and the organization's needs.

Why Is Career Development Necessary?

From the organization's viewpoint, career development can reduce costs due to employee turnover. According to a recent survey by the Society for Human Resources Management, dissatisfaction with potential career development was cited by 85 percent of respondents as the largest threat to employee retention.[4] If a company assists employees in developing career plans, these plans are likely to be closely tied to the organization; therefore, employees are less likely to quit. Taking an interest in employees' careers can also improve morale, boost productivity, and help the organization become more efficient.[5] The fact that an organization shows interest in an employee's career development has a positive effect on that employee. Under these circumstances, employees believe the company regards them as part of an overall plan and not just as numbers. An emphasis on career development can also have a positive effect on the ways employees view their jobs and their employers. HRM in Action 11.1 discusses how improved career development at Ciba Additives has fostered a "we attitude" among employees.

From the organization's viewpoint, career development has three major objectives:

* To meet the immediate and future human resource needs of the organization on a timely basis.
* To better inform the organization and the individual about potential career paths within the organization.
* To utilize existing human resource programs to the fullest by integrating the activities that select, assign, develop, and manage individual careers with the organization's plans.[6]

Career Planning Process by which an individual formulates career goals and develops a plan for reaching those goals.

Career planning is the process by which an individual formulates career goals and develops a plan for reaching those goals. Thus, career development and ca-

HRM IN ACTION

We Are Responsible for Our Own Career Development

11.1

www.cibasc.com

Ciba Additives, a division of Ciba U.S.A., located in Tarrytown, New York, manufactures and sells specialty chemicals. In the late 1980s, the company's president began moving away from a top-down, control style of management toward creating a work environment that was horizontal and cross-functional. After reviewing the best HR practices of a number of other companies, management determined that in addition to technical innovation and services, it wanted Ciba Additives to be recognized as a caring organization that respects and trusts its employees and provides a continuous learning environment.

As HR functions moved down the line, employees became more responsible for their own career development. They had to determine what they could do to make their jobs more enjoyable, professionally rewarding, and valued and also how they could increase their base compensation.

Ciba Additives introduced an employee development process to assist employees in reaching their goals. The company offered in-house programs, external symposia, workshops, and, in some instances, retraining to acknowledge employee loyalty and dedication. Cross-functional quality action teams and quality improvement teams were established to enhance this process. Employees were able to come together to solve problems about products, technology, facilities operations, customer service, and human resource issues. As a result of this joint problem-solving, employee cooperation, trust, mutual respect, and personal fulfillment increased.

Source: Stanley R. Kase, "Ciba Creates an HR Strategy for the Next Century," *Personnel Journal,* October 1995, pp. 109–12.

reer planning should reinforce each other. Career development looks at individual careers from the viewpoint of the organization, whereas career planning looks at careers through the eyes of individual employees.

Realistic career planning forces individuals to look at the available opportunities in relation to their abilities. For example, a person might strongly desire to be a history teacher until discovering that two history teachers are available for every job.

With a career plan, a person is much more likely to experience satisfaction while making progress along the career path. A good career path identifies certain milestones along the way. When a person consciously recognizes and reaches these milestones, he or she is much more likely to experience feelings of achievement. Furthermore, these feelings increase the individual's personal satisfaction and motivation.

Who Is Responsible for Career Development?

What are the responsibilities of both the organization and the individual with regard to career development? Which has the primary responsibility? The answer is that successful career development requires actions from three sources: the organization, the employee, and the employee's immediate manager.

Organization's Responsibilities

As defined earlier, career development is an ongoing, formalized effort by an organization that focuses on developing and enriching the organization's human resources in light of both the employee's and the organization's needs. The organization is the entity that has primary responsibility for instigating and ensuring that career development takes place. Specifically, the organization's responsibilities are to develop and communicate career options within the organization to the employee. The organization should carefully advise an employee concerning possible career paths to achieve that employee's career goals. Human resource personnel are generally responsible for ensuring that this information is kept current as new jobs are created and old ones are phased out. Working closely with both employees and their managers, human resource specialists should see that accurate information is conveyed and that interrelationships among different career paths are understood. Thus, rather than bearing the primary responsibility for preparing individual career plans, the organization should promote the conditions and create the environment that will facilitate the development of individual career plans by the employees. HRM in Action 11.2 describes a company wide training program used by Nissan Motors.

Employee's Responsibilities

The primary responsibility for preparing individual career plans rests with the individual employees. Career planning is not something one person can do for another; it has to come from the individual. Only the individual knows what she or he really wants out of a career, and certainly these desires vary appreciably from person to person.

Career planning requires a conscious effort on the part of the employee; it is hard work, and it does not happen automatically. Although an individual may be convinced that developing a sound career plan would be in his or her best interest, finding the time to develop such a plan is often another matter. The organization can help by providing trained specialists to encourage and guide the employee. This can best be accomplished by allotting a few hours of company time each quarter to this type of planning.

While the individual is ultimately responsible for preparing his or her individ-

HRM IN ACTION

Assessing Career Development Plans

11.2

www.nissan-na.com

At Nissan Motors, personal evaluation is institutionalized in a companywide training program that helps employees assess their career development plans. In this program employees also learn about different opportunities within the organization in case they feel they aren't a good fit in their present positions or if they have already reached the top of their present area.

T. J. Fjelseth, corporate manager of training and performance development, says the training has helped improve employee retention because of the heightened awareness of mobility options and management support. Even though some employees choose to leave the company shortly after their training because they do not see themselves as a good fit for their areas, Fjelseth does not see this as a negative: "If a person decides to leave, we still see that as a win–win situation because it gives the person opportunities to move on to something that's a better match, and we can find someone who has a stronger match."

Source: Louisa Wah, "Catalyst for Alignment," *Management Review*, October 1998, p. 50.

ual career plan, experience has shown that when people do not receive some encouragement and direction, little progress is made. HRM in Action 11.3 describes how Sears Credit has designed a career development process that stresses individual responsibility.

Manager's Responsibilities

It has been said that "the critical battleground in career development is inside the mind of the person charged with supervisory responsibility."[7] Although not expected to be a professional counselor, the manager can and should play a key role in facilitating the development of a subordinate's career. First and foremost, the manager should serve as a catalyst and sounding board. The manager should show an employee how to go about the process and then help the employee evaluate the conclusions.

Table 11–1 lists several roles a manager might perform to assist subordinates in developing their careers. Unfortunately, many managers do not perceive career counseling as part of their managerial duties. They are not opposed to this role; rather, they have never considered it as part of their job. To help overcome this and related problems, many organizations have designed training programs to help their managers develop the necessary skills in this area.

Figure 11–1 illustrates the career development roles of the organization at Corning, Inc., a $2.1 billion company that specializes in glass and ceramics, telecommunications, health and science technology, and consumer products. As the figure shows, successful career development results from a joint effort by the organization, the individual, and the immediate manager; the organization provides the resources and structure, the individual does the planning, and the immediate manager provides the guidance and encouragement.

Implementing Career Development

Successful implementation of a career development program involves four basic steps at the individual level: (1) an assessment by the individual of his or her abilities, interests, and career goals; (2) an assessment by the organization of the individual's abilities and potentials; (3) communication of career options and opportunities within the organization; and (4) career counseling to set realistic goals and plans for their accomplishment.[8]

HRM IN ACTION

Sears Credit Implements a Career Development Program

11.3

www.sears.com

Sears Credit, located in Hoffman Estates, Illinois, is responsible for all credit transactions in the retail stores and other field units of Sears Merchandise Group. In 1990, the firm employed about 13,000 people at 50 field locations. By 1994, consolidation had reduced the number of locations to 20 and shrunk the work force to 10,000. Although the firm closed several units, some of those remaining grew tremendously, from an average of 350 associates to 1,000 associates per operating center.

To respond to the major cultural, staffing, and structural changes at Sears Credit, senior management worked with human resources and training professionals to establish the company's overriding goals. Subsequently they determined that to bring about a major cultural change, Sears Credit needed a comprehensive, organizationwide career development process that would promote individual growth.

Sears Credit's career development process stressed individual responsibility and, since this was a relatively new concept for all associates, training sessions were held to help reframe their thinking and give them the tools to use in their career planning. Position descriptions were made available to them via E-mail, and a data bank of associates' desired career goals to be used for organizational planning and staffing decisions was created. One of the most important components of the career development system was a new broadbanding compensation system that rewarded developmental moves previously considered lateral and not entitled to a promotional increase.

Even though Sears Credit continues to experience changes, the company has learned that a comprehensive career development process is a critical contributor to organizational success. Most associates are now taking responsibility for their own career management. In fact, in a survey conducted by management, 93 percent of the associates reported that they have specific career goals and a plan to reach those goals. Sears Credit's career development program has also received national recognition from the American Society for Training and Development.

Source: Peg O'Herron and Peggy Simonsen, "Career Development Gets a Charge at Sears Credit," *Personnel Journal,* May 1995, pp. 103–6.

Individual Assessment

Many people never stop to analyze their abilities, interests, and career goals. It isn't that most people don't want to analyze these factors; rather, they simply never take the time. While this is not something an organization can do for the individual, the organization can provide the impetus and structure. A variety of self-assessment materials are available commercially, and some organizations have developed tailor-made forms and training programs for the use of their employees. Another option is the use of some form of psychological testing.

An individual's self-assessment should not necessarily be limited by current resources and abilities; career plans normally require that the individual acquire additional training and skills. However, this assessment should be based on reality. For the individual, this involves identifying personal strengths—not only the individual's developed abilities but also the financial resources available.

Assessment by the Organization

Organizations have several potential sources of information that can be used for assessing employees. Traditionally, the most frequently used source has been the performance appraisal process. The assessment center, discussed in Chapter 10,

TABLE 11-1

POTENTIAL CAREER DEVELOPMENT ROLES OF MANAGERS

Communicator
Holds formal and informal discussion with employees.
Listens to and understands an employee's real concerns.
Clearly and effectively interacts with an employee.
Establishes an environment for open interaction.
Structures uninterrupted time to meet with employees.

Counselor
Helps employee identify career-related skills, interests, and values.
Helps employee identify a variety of career options.
Helps employee evaluate appropriateness of various options.
Helps employee design/plan strategy to achieve an agreed-on career goal.

Appraiser
Identifies critical job elements.
Negotiates with employee a set of goals and objectives to evaluate performance.
Assesses employee performance related to goals and objectives.
Communicates performance evaluation and assessment to employee.
Designs a development plan around future job goals and objectives.
Reinforces effective job performance.
Reviews an established development plan on an ongoing basis.

Coach
Teaches specific job-related or technical skills.
Reinforces effective performance.
Suggests specific behaviors for improvement.
Clarifies and communicates goals and objectives of work group and organization.

Mentor
Arranges for employees to participate in a high-visibility activity either inside or outside the
    organization.
Serves as a role model in employee's career development by demonstrating successful
    career behaviors.
Supports employee by communicating employee's effectiveness to others in and out of
    organization.

Advisor
Communicates the informal and formal realities of progression in the organization.
Suggests appropriate training activities that could benefit employee.
Suggests appropriate strategies for career advancement.

Broker
Assists in bringing employees together who might mutually help each other in their careers.
Assists in linking employees with appropriate educational or employment opportunities.
Helps employee identify obstacles to changing present situation.
Helps employee identify resources enabling a career development change.

Referral agent
Identifies employees with problems (e.g., career, personal, health).
Identifies resources appropriate to an employee experiencing a problem.
Bridges and supports employee with referral agents.
Follows up on effectiveness of suggested referrals.

Advocate
Works with employee in designing a plan for redress of a specific issue at higher levels of
    management.
Works with employee in planning alternative strategies if a redress by management is not
    successful.
Represents employee's concern to higher-level management for redress of specific issues.

Source: Z. B. Leibowitz and N. K. Schlossberg, "Training Managers for Their Role in a Career Development System," *Training & Development Journal,* July 1981, p. 74. Copyright © 1981 by the American Society for Training and Development. Reprinted with permission. All rights reserved.

FIGURE 11–1 **CAREER PLANNING ROLES AT CORNING, INC.**

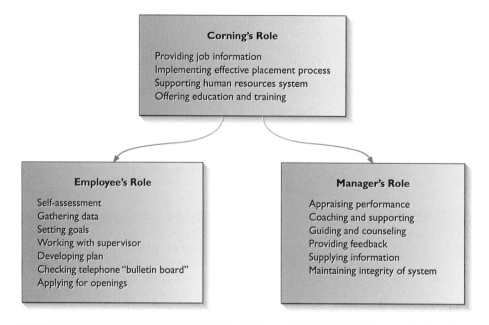

Source: Zandy B. Leibowitz, Barbara H. Feldman, and Sherry H. Mosley, "Career Development Works Overtime at Corning, Inc.," *Personnel*, April 1990, pp. 38–46. Copyright © 1990 by the American Management Association, New York, New York. All rights reserved. Reprinted by permission of the publisher.

can also be an excellent source of information. Other potential sources include personnel records reflecting information such as education and previous work experience. It is usually a good idea for an organization not to depend on any one source of information but to use as many as are readily available. Such an approach provides a natural system of checks and balances.

The organization's assessment of an individual employee should normally be conducted jointly by human resource personnel and the individual's immediate manager, who serves as a mentor.

Communicating Career Options

To set realistic career goals, an individual must know the options and opportunities that are available. The organization can do several things to facilitate such awareness. Posting and advertising job vacancies is one activity that helps employees get a feel for their options. Clearly identifying possible paths of advancement within the organization is also helpful. This can be done as part of the performance appraisal process. Another good idea is to share human resource planning forecasts with employees.

Career Pathing

Career Pathing A sequence of developmental activities involving informal and formal education, training, and job experiences that help make an individual capable of holding a more advanced job in the future.

Career pathing is a technique that addresses the specifics of progressing from one job to another in the organization. It can be defined as a sequence of developmental activities involving informal and formal education, training, and job experiences that help make an individual capable of holding more advanced jobs.[9] Career paths exist on an informal basis in almost all organizations. However, career paths are much more useful when formally defined and documented. Such formalization results in specific descriptions of sequential work experiences, as well as how the different sequences relate to one another. Table 11–2 outlines the basic steps in career pathing.

TABLE 11-2	**BASIC STEPS OF CAREER PATHING**

1. *Determine or reconfirm the abilities and end behaviors of the target job.* Because jobs tend to change over time, it is important to determine or confirm requirements and review them periodically.

2. *Secure employee background data and review them for accuracy and completeness.* Because people's interests and career objectives tend to shift, these also have to be confirmed. Also, it is often necessary to update an individual's records concerning skills, experience, etc.

3. *Undertake a needs analysis comparison that jointly views the individual and the targeted job.* Determine if the individual and the targeted job tend to match. Surprisingly, many organizations neglect to query individuals when questions arise concerning their backgrounds, potential abilities, and interests.

4. *Reconcile employee career desires, developmental needs, and targeted job requirements with those of organizational career management.* Individuals formalize their career objectives or modify them as circumstances warrant.

5. *Develop individual training work and educational needs using a time-activity orientation.* Identify the individual actions (work, education, and training experiences) necessary for the individual to progress to the targeted job.

6. *Blueprint career path activities.* This is the process of creating a time-oriented blueprint or chart to guide the individual.

Source: Adapted from E. H. Burack and N. J. Mathys, *Career Management in Organizations: A Practical Human Resource Planning Approach* (Lake Forest, IL.: Brace-Park Press, 1979), pp. 79–80.

Career pathing is most useful when used as part of the overall career-planning process. Figure 11–2 summarizes the major variables that affect the career-planning process and shows how career pathing fits into the process. Figure 11–3 illustrates a career progression plan that offers four career paths for office staff (employees enter the progression at the bottom of the chart and progress upward).

Career Self-Management

Career Self-Management
The ability to keep up with the changes that occur within the organization and industry and to prepare for the future.

Career self-management is closely related to the concept of career pathing. **Career self-management** is the ability to keep pace with the speed at which change occurs within the organization and the industry and to prepare for the future.[10] A relatively new concept, career self-management emphasizes the need of individual employees to keep learning because jobs that are held today may evolve into something different tomorrow, or may simply disappear entirely. Career self-management also involves identifying and obtaining new skills and competencies that allow the employee to move to a new position. The payoff of career self-management is more highly skilled and flexible employees and the retention of these employees. Career self-management requires commitment to the idea of employee self-development on the part of management and the providing of self-development programs and experiences for employees. HRM in Action 11.4 discusses how one firm has developed an innovative approach for fostering career self-management.

Career Counseling

Career counseling is the activity that integrates the different steps in the career-planning process. Career counseling may be performed by an employee's immediate manager, a human resource specialist, or a combination of the two. In most cases, it is preferable to have the counseling conducted by the immediate manager

FIGURE 11-2   MAJOR VARIABLES AFFECTING CAREER PLANNING

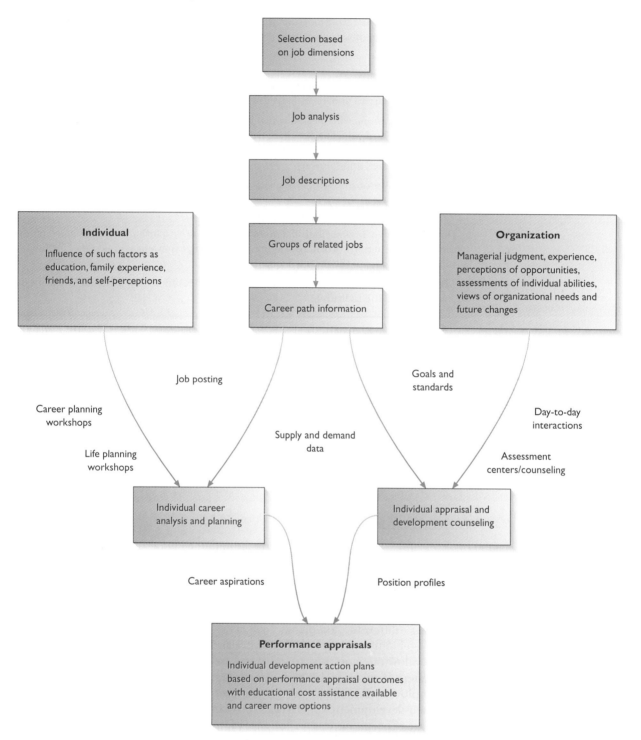

Source: Kenneth B. McRae. "Career-Management Planning: A Boon to Managers and Employees," *Personnel*, May 1985, p. 59. Copyright © 1985 by the American Management Association, New York, New York. All rights reserved. Reprinted by permission of publisher.

FIGURE 11–3   A CAREER PROGRESSION PLAN OFFERING FOUR CAREER PATHS

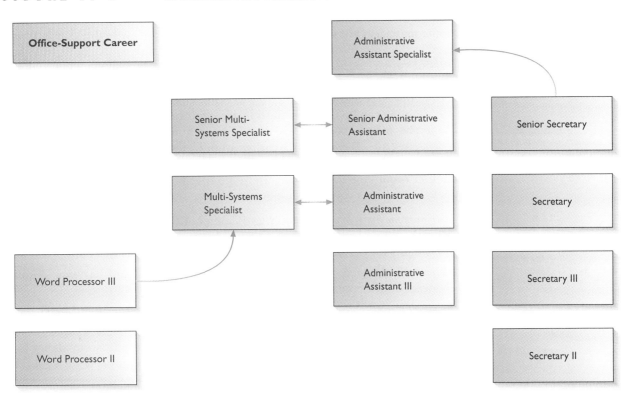

Source: Wendy Eigen, "Transform Office Jobs into Careers," *Personnel Journal,* October 1991, p. 104.

HRM IN ACTION

**Fostering Career
Self-Development**

11.4

www.raychem.com

Raychem, of Menlo Park, California, which enjoyed 1996 sales of $1.67 billion and a net income of $148 million, launched a career development center in 1994. The CEO at that time, Bob Saldich, made learning and self-development a visible part of the culture; employees were taught to view themselves as self-employed and encouraged to explore many career options.

Under its new CEO, Richard Kashnow, Raychem is building upon this culture of employee self-development by making employee development a key competency for Raychem managers. A recently initiated program, called HR Review, rates managers on their ability to develop their employees. An important function of the Raychem Career Development Center is to help employees develop a list of competencies needed for their current job or that they will need in the future. By providing resources on industry skill standards and looking at other successful companies, Raychem Career Development Center helps employees evaluate their skill level. Employees can then outline their own development plan. Individual development plans may include taking advantage of Raychem's tuition reimbursement program, participating in formal training programs at Raychem University, requesting developmental assignments, or seeking mentors to role model on the job.

According to HR Manager Suzanne Edises, "We want to provide development opportunities for our employees and we are seeking out the most efficient and effective ways to accomplish this."

Source: Jeanne C. Meister, "The Quest for Lifetime Employability," *Journal of Business Strategy,* May/June 1998, pp. 25–28.

with appropriate input from human resource personnel. The immediate manager generally has the advantage of practical experience, knows the company, and is in a position to make a realistic appraisal of organizational opportunities.

Some managers are reluctant to attempt counseling because they haven't been trained in the area. However, it is not necessary to be a trained psychologist to be a successful career counselor.[11] In fact, behavioral research and actual experience suggest that the characteristics that make people likable and effective are basically the same qualities that contribute to successful counseling.[12] Of course, the right type of training can be very beneficial to accomplished career counselors.

Generally, managers who are skilled in basic human relations are successful as career counselors. Developing a caring attitude toward employees and their careers is of prime importance. Being receptive to employee concerns and problems is another requirement. Following are some specific suggestions for helping managers become better career counselors.

1. *Recognize the limits of career counseling.* Remember that the manager and the organization serve as catalysts in the career development process. The primary responsibility for developing a career plan lies with the individual employee.

2. *Respect confidentiality.* Career counseling is very personal and has basic requirements of ethics, confidentiality, and privacy.

3. *Establish a relationship.* Be honest, open, and sincere with the subordinate. Try to be empathetic and see things from the subordinate's point of view.

4. *Listen effectively.* Learn to be a sincere listener. A natural human tendency is to want to do most of the talking. It often takes a conscious effort to be a good listener.

5. *Consider alternatives.* An important goal in career counseling is to help subordinates realize that a number of choices are usually available. Help subordinates to expand their thinking and not necessarily be limited by past experience.

6. *Seek and share information.* Be sure the employee and the organization have completed their respective assessments of the employee's abilities, interests, and desires. Make sure the organization's assessment has been clearly communicated to the employee and that the employee is aware of potential job openings within the organization.

7. *Assist with goal definition and planning.* Remember that the employee must make the final decisions. Managers should serve as "sounding boards" and help ensure that the individual's plans are valid.[13]

Reviewing Career Progress

Individual careers rarely go exactly according to plan. The environment changes, personal desires change, and other things happen. However, if the individual periodically reviews both the career plan and the situation, he or she can make adjustments so that career development is not impaired. On the other hand, a career plan that is not kept current rapidly becomes useless. Complacency is the greatest danger once a career plan has been developed. The plan must be updated as the situation and the individual change.

Career-Related Myths

Employees and managers hold many myths related to career development and advancement. Frequently, such myths are misleading and can inhibit career development and growth. The following sections explore these myths and provide evidence disproving them.

Myths Held by Employees[14]

Myth 1: There Is Always Room for One More Person at the Top: This myth contradicts the fact that the structures of the overwhelming majority of today's organizations have fewer positions available as one progresses up the organization. Adherence to this myth fosters unrealistic aspirations and generates self-perpetuating frustrations. There is nothing wrong with wanting to become president of the organization; however, an individual must also be aware that the odds of attaining such a position are slim. For example, General Motors Corporation has several hundred thousand employees and only one president. The major lesson to be learned from myth 1 is to pick career paths that are realistic and attainable.

Myth 2: The Key to Success Is Being in the Right Place at the Right Time: Like all the career-related myths, this one has just enough truth to make it believable. One can always find a highly successful person who attributes all of his or her success to being in the right place at the right time. People who adhere to this myth are rejecting the basic philosophy of planning: that a person, through careful design, can affect rather than merely accept the future. Adherence to myth 2 is dangerous because it can lead to complacency and a defeatist attitude.

Myth 3: Good Subordinates Make Good Superiors: This myth is based on the belief that those employees who are the best performers in their current jobs should be the ones who are promoted. This is not to imply that good performance should not be rewarded, for it should. However, when an individual is being promoted, those making the decision should look carefully at the requirements of the new job in addition to the individual's present job performance. How many times has a star engineer or salesperson been promoted into a managerial role, only to fail miserably? Similarly, outstanding athletes are frequently made head coaches, and everybody seems surprised when the former star fails as a head coach. Playing a sport and coaching require different talents and abilities. Because someone excels at one job does not mean she or he will excel at all jobs.

Myth 4: Career Development and Planning Are Functions of Human Resource Personnel: The ultimate responsibility for career development and planning belongs to the individual, not to human resource personnel or the individual's manager. Human resource specialists can assist the individual and answer certain questions, but they cannot develop a career plan for him or her. Only the individual can make career-related decisions.

Myth 5: All Good Things Come to Those Who Work Long, Hard Hours: People guided by this myth often spend 10 to 12 hours a day trying to impress their managers and move ahead rapidly in the organization. However, the results of these extra hours on the job often have little or no relationship to what the manager considers important, to the person's effectiveness on the job, or (most important in this context) to the individual's long-range career growth. Unfortunately, many managers reinforce this myth by designing activities "to keep everyone busy."

Myth 6: Rapid Advancement along a Career Path Is Largely a Function of the Kind of Manager One Has: A manager can affect a subordinate's rate of advancement. However, those who adhere to this myth often accept a defensive role and ignore the importance of their own actions. Belief in this myth provides a ready-made excuse for failure. It is easy and convenient to blame failures on one's manager.

Myth 7: The Way to Get Ahead Is to Determine Your Weaknesses and Then Work Hard to Correct Them: Successful salespeople do not emphasize the weak points of their products; rather, they emphasize the strong points. The same should be true in career development and planning. Individuals who achieve their career objectives do

so by stressing those things they do uncommonly well. The secret is to first capital-
ize on one's strengths and then try to improve deficiencies in other areas.

Myth 8: Always Do Your Best, Regardless of the Task: This myth stems from the puritan
work ethic. The problem is that believers ignore the fact that different tasks have
different priorities. Because there is only a limited amount of time, a person
should spend that time according to priorities. Those tasks and jobs that rank high
in importance in achieving one's career goals should receive the individual's best
effort. Those tasks that do not rank high should be done, but not necessarily with
one's best effort. The idea is to give something less than one's best effort to unim-
portant tasks in order to have time to give one's best effort to the important ones.

Myth 9: It Is Wise to Keep Home Life and Work Life Separated: An individual cannot
make wise career decisions without the full knowledge and support of his or her
spouse. Working wives and husbands should share their inner feelings concerning
their jobs so that their spouses will understand the basic factors that weigh in any
career decisions.

   A healthy person usually has interests other than a job. Career strategy should
be designed to recognize and support, not contradict, these other interests. Career
objectives should be a subset of one's life objectives. Too often, however, career objectives conflict with, rather than support, life objectives.

Myth 10: The Grass Is Always Greener on the Other Side of the Fence: Regardless of the
career path the individual follows, another one always seems a little more attractive. However, utopia does not exist. More than likely, the job John Doe holds involves many of the same problems every working person might face. As the individual assumes more and more personal responsibilities, the price of taking that
"attractive" job becomes higher in terms of possibly having to relocate, develop a
new social life, and learn new duties. This is not to say that job and related changes
should not be made; however, one should avoid making such changes hastily.

Myths Held by Managers[15]

Myth 1: Career Development Will Raise Expectations: Many managers fear that an emphasis on career development will raise employee expectations to unrealistically
high levels. Career development should do just the opposite: It should bring employees' aspirations into the open and match their skills, interests, and goals with
opportunities that are realistically available.

Myth 2: We Will Be Overwhelmed with Requests: This myth is based on the fear that
employees will deluge their managers for information about jobs in other parts of
the organization and that employees will expect the organization to provide them
with a multitude of career opportunities. While this fear is very realistic in the
minds of many managers, it is basically unfounded.

Myth 3: Managers Will Not Be Able to Cope: Management often becomes concerned
that introducing career development and planning will place managers in a counseling role for which they are ill prepared. While coaching and counseling should
be an important part of any manager's job, the key to career development and
planning is to place the responsibility primarily on the employee.

Myth 4: We Do Not Have the Necessary Systems in Place: This myth is based on the belief that before the organization can introduce career development, it must first
put in place a whole series of other human resource planning mechanisms, such
as job posting and succession planning. In reality, many organizations have implemented successful career development programs with few formal mechanisms be-

yond the basic requirement of providing employees with effective career-planning tools.

Dealing with Career Plateaus

Career Plateau The point in an individual's career where the likelihood of an additional promotion is very low.

Learners Individuals in an organization who have a high potential for advancement but are currently performing below standard.

Stars Individuals in an organization who are presently doing outstanding work and have a high potential for continued advancement.

Solid Citizens Individuals in an organization whose present performance is satisfactory but whose chance for future advancement is small.

Deadwood Individuals in an organization whose present performance has fallen to an unsatisfactory level and who have little potential for advancement.

A **career plateau** is defined as "the point in a career where the likelihood of additional hierarchical promotion is very low."[16] Career plateauing takes place when an employee reaches a position from which she or he is not likely to be promoted further.[17] Virtually all people reach a plateau in their careers; however, some individuals reach their plateaus earlier than others. Plateaued employees are those who "reach their promotional ceiling long before they retire."[18]

Certain factors in today's work environment indicate plateauing is becoming more prevalent.[19] The fact that employers are now depending more on older employees may well cause plateauing problems. Also, employees are generally educated and thus enter an organization at a higher position. These situations ultimately mean that fewer promotion possibilities exist.

Because it is inherently true that fewer positions are available as one moves up the hierarchical ladder, plateauing does not necessarily indicate failure. However, as this section will show, the case of a plateauee may need to be handled differently in some situations than that of an employee still on the rise in the organization.

Table 11–3 presents a model for classifying careers. The four principal career categories are:

- **Learners.** Individuals with high potential for advancement who are performing below standard (e.g., a new trainee).
- **Stars.** Individuals presently doing outstanding work and having a high potential for continued advancement; these people are on fast-track career paths.
- **Solid citizens.** Individuals whose present performance is satisfactory but whose chance for future advancement is small. These people make up the bulk of the employees in most organizations.
- **Deadwood.** Individuals whose present performance has fallen to an unsatisfactory level: they have little potential for advancement.[20]

Naturally, organizations would like to have all stars and solid citizens. The challenge, however, is to transform the learners into stars or solid citizens and keep the current stars and solid citizens from slipping into the deadwood category. Furthermore, there is a tendency to overlook solid citizens. The learners, stars, and deadwood usually get most of the attention in terms of development programs and stimulating assignments. Neglect of the solid citizens may result in their slipping into the deadwood category.

TABLE 11–3   **CLASSIFYING MANAGERIAL CAREERS**

Current Performance	Likelihood of Future Promotion	
	Low	High
High	Solid citizens (effective plateauees)	Stars
Low	Deadwood (ineffective plateauees)	Learners (comers)

Source: Adapted from T. P. Ference, J. A. Stoner, and E. K. Warren, "Managing the Career Plateau." *Academy of Management Review,* October 1977, p. 603.

Three actions can aid in managing the plateauing process: (1) prevent plateauees from becoming ineffective (prevent a problem from occurring); (2) integrate relevant career-related information systems (improve monitoring so that emerging problems can be detected and treated early); and (3) manage ineffective plateauees and frustrated employees more effectively (cure the problem once it has arisen).[21] The first action basically involves helping plateauees adjust to the solid-citizen category and realize they have not necessarily failed. Available avenues for personal development and growth should be pointed out. The second suggestion can largely be implemented through a thorough performance appraisal system. Such a system should encourage open communication between the manager and the person being appraised. The following section discusses how to manage ineffective plateauees.

Rehabilitating Ineffective Plateauees

Rehabilitating ineffective plateauees is difficult but certainly possible. The first question the manager might ask is "Why should we try and help ineffective plateauees; don't they often have an overall negative impact on the organization?" Certainly deadwood can have a negative impact, but there are also several good reasons to salvage these employees:

- *Job knowledge.* Plateaued employees have usually been in the job for quite some time and have amassed considerable job knowledge.
- *Organizational knowledge.* Plateaued employees not only know their jobs but also know the organization.
- *Loyalty.* Plateaued employees are usually not job-hoppers but have often demonstrated above-average loyalty to the organization.
- *Concern for the well-being of plateauees.* If the organization were to terminate all plateaued employees, this could have a disastrous impact on other employees. Also, the number of plateaued employees may be large.[22]

Given that an organization's management team wants to rehabilitate plateaued employees, what can be done? At least five possibilities exist:

1. *Provide alternate means of recognition.* If the chances for the employee to receive recognition through a future promotion are slim, look for alternative methods of recognition. Some possibilities include assigning the employee to a task force or giving other special assignments, participation in brainstorming sessions, representation of the organization to others, and training of new employees.
2. *Develop new ways to make their current jobs more satisfying.* The more employees can be turned on by their current jobs, the lower the likelihood that they will remain ineffective. Some possibilities here include relating employees' performance to total organizational goals and creating competition in the job.
3. *Effect revitalization through reassignment.* The idea here is to implement systematic job switching to positions at the same level that require many similar, though not exactly the same, skills and experiences as the present job.
4. *Utilize reality-based self-development programs.* Instead of assigning plateauees to developmental programs designed to help them move into future jobs (which a majority of development programs do), assign them to development programs that can help them perform better in their present jobs.
5. *Change managerial attitudes toward plateaued employees.* It is not unusual for managers and supervisors to give up on and neglect plateaued employees. Such actions are quickly picked up by the affected employees and only compound the problem.[23]

Because plateaued employees often include a significant number of employees who are worth rehabilitating, it would pay for most organizations to address this issue seriously.

The Impact of Dual-Employed Couples

Employment by both spouses has become commonplace in the decades following World War II.[24] In 1997, only 17 percent of households conformed to the traditional model of a wage-earning dad, a stay-at-home mom, and one or more children.[25] In 1996, both spouses worked in 60 percent of married households, representing 45 percent of the U.S. labor force.[26] Both economic and social pressures have encouraged this trend.

Dual-employed couples can usually be classified as either dual-career couples or dual-earner couples. With dual-career couples, both members are highly committed to their careers and view work as essential to their psychological sense of self and as integral to their personal identities.[27] They view their employment as part of a career path involving progressively more responsibility, power, and financial remuneration. With dual-earner couples, one or both of the members defines his or her employment as relating to rewards such as money for paying bills, an opportunity to keep busy, or an additional resource to help out. Dual-earner couples do not both see their employment as an integral part of their self-definition. As of 1997, dual-career couples represented approximately 20 percent of all dual-employed couples.

According to a recent survey, the biggest challenge for dual-employed couples is a lack of time followed by the difficulties in balancing personal and professional life.[28] The biggest advantage for dual-employed couples is increased income, followed by psychological benefits as a distant second.

Dual-career-couple situations can complicate the career development process for both individuals. A career opportunity that requires a geographical move for one member creates an obvious problem for the couple and their respective organizations. Other potential problems of dual-career couples include the need for child care, balancing time schedules, and emotional stresses. Engaging in the career-planning process can certainly help dual-career couples address potential problems before they become real.

Many organizations have responded to the needs of dual-career couples by instigating family-friendly policies and programs. Proactive corporate programs include child and elder care, flexible work scheduling, job sharing, part-time work, telecommuting, parental leave, and personal time.

Outplacement

Outplacement Benefit provided by an employer to help an employee leave the organization and get a job someplace else.

Outplacement refers to "a benefit provided by an employer to help an employee terminate and get a job someplace else."[29] Outplacement is a way of terminating employees that can benefit both the employees and the organization. The organization gains by terminating the employees before they become deadwood; employees gain by finding new jobs and at the same time preserving their dignity. In addition, an outplacement program can have a very positive effect on employee morale.

Skill assessment, establishment of new career objectives, résumé preparation, interview training, and generation of job interviews are services generally offered through an outplacement program. Other services might include training for those who notify terminated employees, office support, spouse involvement, and individual psychological counseling.

Most company outplacement programs involve the use of outplacement consultants or an outplacement firm. The normal procedure is for the outplacement consultant to be briefed by the manager before the employee is terminated. During this session, the outplacement consultant should obtain a clear understanding from the company of why the termination was necessary. After the manager notifies the employee of his or her termination, the outplacement consultant provides immediate support to the employee.

Breaking the Glass Ceiling

The term *glass ceiling* refers to invisible, yet real or perceived, barriers found in many organizational structures that appear to stymie the executive advancement opportunities of women and minorities.[30]

A 1990 study conducted by Korn/Ferry and the UCLA Graduate School of Management helped illustrate the realities of the glass ceiling.[31] The Korn/Ferry UCLA study reported that women and minorities held less than 5 percent of senior management positions. Furthermore, this represented only a 2 percent increase since 1979, when women and minorities held less than 3 percent of senior management positions. A mid 1990s study by Catalyst, a women's advocacy group headquartered in New York, found similar results.[32]

The Glass Ceiling Commission was created as part of the Civil Rights Act of 1991. The mandate of the Commission was to focus greater public attention on the importance of eliminating barriers and to promote work force diversity.[33] The commission, which was staffed by the U.S. Department of Labor, was asked to specifically look at the compensation systems and reward structures currently used in the workplace, and at how business fills management and decision-making positions, and trains and develops employees for advancement.

According to the commission's initial report, the three most common practices that contribute to the creation of a glass ceiling are (1) word-of-mouth recruiting (or using executive search firms without stating an interest in a diverse array of candidates), (2) inadequate access to developmental opportunities for women and minorities, and (3) a lack of responsibility among senior management for equal employment opportunity efforts.[34] Subsequently the commission formulated the following suggestions for toppling job-advancement barriers:

- Demonstrate commitment. Top management should communicate its dedication to diversity and enact policies that promote it.
- Hold line managers accountable for progress by including diversity in all strategic business plans. Performance appraisals, compensation incentives, and other evaluation measures should reflect this priority.
- Use affirmative action as a tool to ensure that all qualified individuals compete based on ability and merit.
- Expand your pool of candidates. Look for prospects from noncustomary sources who may have nontraditional backgrounds and experiences.
- Educate all employees about the strengths and challenges of gender, racial, ethnic, and cultural differences.
- Initiate family-friendly programs that help men and women balance their work and family responsibilities.[35]

Because many factors that contribute to the glass ceiling stem from the common tendency "to hire in one's own image," glass ceilings will be eliminated only when all employees are evaluated, hired, and promoted on the basis of merit. If followed, the previously discussed suggestions from the Glass Ceiling Commission should go a long way toward creating such a culture. HRM in Action 11.5 provides several examples of strategies being used by some companies to help break the glass ceiling.

Career Development Online

Today many companies are developing comprehensive, online career development centers. These online career development centers provide access to a wide variety of services to help employees manage their careers and, in some instances, even find jobs outside their present company. Online capabilities can provide many types of career-related information on demand. For example, employees can look up the competencies and skills required for jobs they aspire to have. Some of the online career planning resources being offered include:

HRM IN ACTION

Strategies for Breaking the Glass Ceiling

11.5

www.corning.com
www.tenneco.com
www.aa.com
www.dupont.com

The CEO and top executives of Corning attended a gender training program. A three-year follow-up program directs managers to incorporate what they learned into daily working life. One executive organizes special lunches with female managers and puts gender-bias "episodes" on every meeting's agenda. Corning also sponsors quality improvement teams that focus specifically on issues related to Blacks and women, hold mandatory workshops to reinforce its policies against racial bias and gender discrimination, and encourage better working relationships among its diverse employee sectors.

TennecoInc. has tied a part of an executive's bonus to his or her progress in promoting women and minorities, which has resulted in a 25 percent rise in the numbers hired. Tenneco also created eight advisory councils composed entirely of women. Networking seminars were encouraged.

American Airlines issued a directive that requires all officers to submit detailed, cross-functional development plans for all high-potential women in middle-management and above.

DuPont Co. has a rotation process that moves men and women through at least two or three functions before they reach top positions.

Source: Allison Eyring and Bette Ann Stead, "Shattering the Glass Ceiling: Some Successful Corporate Practices," *Journal of Business Ethics,* February 1998, pp. 245–51.

- Information about employment trends and job opportunities.
- Self-assessment tools, such as personality tests and interest indicators, that employees can use to determine which types of jobs they might best pursue.
- Links to online employment resources such as job listings and career development information.
- Individual online job counseling, including advice on preparing for interviews.[36]

In addition to company-sponsored online services, many resources are available on the Internet to help individuals with career development. These resources include job search guides, résumé preparation aids, job listings, career-related articles, and other similar services. There is little doubt that career-development resources online will continue to expand in the future.

SUMMARY OF LEARNING OBJECTIVES

1. **Define career development and summarize its major objectives.**

   Career development is an ongoing, formalized effort by an organization that focuses on developing and enriching the organization's human resources in light of both the employees' and the organization's needs. From the organization's viewpoint, career development has three major objectives: (1) to meet the immediate and future human resource needs of the organization on a timely basis, (2) to better inform the organization and the individual about potential career paths within the organization, and (3) to utilize existing human resource programs to the fullest by integrating the activities that select, assign, develop, and manage individual careers with the organization's plans.

2. **Name the three entities required to provide input for a successful career development program and briefly describe their respective responsibilities.**

   Successful career development results from a joint effort by the organization, the employee, and the immediate manager. The organization provides the resources and structure, the employee does the planning, and the immediate manager provides the guidance and encouragement.

3. **Describe the steps involved in implementing a career development program.**
   The implementation of a career development program involves four basic steps: (1) an assessment by the individual of his or her abilities, interests, and career goals; (2) an assessment by the organization of the individual's abilities and potential; (3) communication of career options and opportunities within the organization; and (4) career counseling to set realistic goals and plans for their accomplishment.

4. **Define career pathing and career self-management.**
   Career pathing is a technique that addresses the specifics of progressing from one job to another in the organization. Career self-management is the ability to keep pace with the speed at which change occurs within the organization and the industry and to prepare for the future.

5. **List several myths employees hold related to career planning and advancement.**
   Employees often hold many myths related to career planning and advancement: (1) there is always room for one more person at the top; (2) the key to success is being in the right place at the right time; (3) good subordinates make good superiors; (4) career development and planning are functions of human resource; (5) all good things come to those who work long, hard hours; (6) rapid advancement along a career path is largely a function of the kind of manager one has; (7) the way to get ahead is to determine your weaknesses and then work hard to correct them; (8) always do your best, regardless of the task; (9) it is wise to keep home life and work life separated; and (10) the grass is always greener on the other side of the fence.

6. **List several myths management holds related to career development.**
   Management personnel often hold certain myths related to career development: (1) career development will raise expectations to unrealistically high levels; (2) management will be overwhelmed with requests; (3) managers will not be able to cope; and (4) management does not have the necessary systems in place.

7. **Define a career plateau and a plateaued employee.**
   A career plateau is the point in a career where the likelihood of additional hierarchical promotion is very low. A plateaued employee is an employee who reaches his or her promotional ceiling long before retirement.

8. **Describe the four principal career categories.**
   The four principal career categories are learners, stars, solid citizens, and deadwood. Learners are individuals with a high potential for advancement who are performing below standard. Stars are individuals presently doing outstanding work, with a high potential for continued advancement. Solid citizens are individuals whose present performance is satisfactory but whose chance for future advancement is small. Deadwood refers to individuals whose present performance has fallen to an unsatisfactory level and who have little potential for advancement.

9. **Distinguish between dual-career couples and dual-earner couples. Describe some possible ways organizations can accommodate dual-employed couples.**
   With dual-career couples, both members are highly committed to their careers and view work as essential to their psychological sense of self and as integral to their personal identities. They view their employment as part of a career path involving progressively more responsibility, power, and financial remuneration. With dual-earner couples, one or both of the members defines his or her employment as relating to rewards such as money for paying bills, an opportunity to keep busy, or an additional resource to help out. Dual-earner couples do not both see their employment as an integral part of their self-definition. Many organizations have responded to the needs of dual-employed couples by updating their human resource policies to accommodate them. Some possibilities include provision of child and elder care, flexible work scheduling, job sharing, part-time work, telecommuting, parental leave, and personal time.

10. **Define outplacement.**

    Outplacement refers to a benefit provided by an employer to help an employee terminate employment with the organization and get a job someplace else.

11. **Explain what the glass ceiling is.**

    The term glass ceiling refers to invisible, yet real or projected barriers found in many organizational structures that appear to stymie the executive advancement opportunities of women and minorities.

REVIEW QUESTIONS

1. Define career development and career planning.
2. What are the three major objectives of career development from the organization's viewpoint?
3. What is the role of the individual employee in career development?
4. What are the four basic steps in implementing a career development program?
5. What are career pathing and career self-management?
6. Give some specific suggestions for helping managers become better career counselors.
7. How often should an individual review and revise his or her career plan?
8. Identify several myths employees often hold relating to career development and advancement.
9. Identify several myths managers often hold relating to career development.
10. Define the following categories: learners, stars, solid citizens, and deadwood.
11. Name and briefly describe several methods an organization might use to rehabilitate inefficient plateauees.
12. Distinguish between dual-career couples and dual-earner couples and what are some of the challenges these groups face?
13. What is outplacement, and how does it usually work?
14. What is the glass ceiling and what are the three most common practices that contribute to the glass ceiling?
15. Name several types of online career planning resources currently available.

DISCUSSION QUESTIONS

1. Do you think career development can adversely affect organizational performance in that the process sometimes convinces the involved parties to change jobs?
2. Is the concept of career development realistic in today's rapidly changing environment?
3. Discuss how career-related myths can inhibit career planning and growth.
4. Is it better to tell a person that he or she has reached a plateau in the organization or to allow the person to maintain hope of eventual promotion?
5. What advice would you offer today's employees regarding the problems faced by dual-employed couples?

INCIDENT 11–1

The Unhappy Telephone Line Installer

John James had been an installer-repairer for the telephone company for almost six years. Since the work kept him outdoors most of the day, he liked the job, the pay was good, and his coworkers were congenial. John had gone to work on this job right after high school graduation and had never considered doing anything else. Through the years, others in the same job occasionally had been promoted into supervisory positions, taken advantage of company-paid educational benefits, or had received recognition for outstanding service to the company.

John was close friends with Ross Bartlett, his partner on the line. Ross, who had been in his job about two years, was a good worker. About six months ago, Ross began to express dissatisfaction with the routine, monotonous work, saying there had to be some better way to make a living.

Last week, John learned the company would pay Ross's way to take college courses in business administration. That same day, John really began to feel some concern about himself and his status with the telephone company. He began having restless, sleepless nights as he thought back over the past years: what he had done with his life, where he was now in his career, and where he was going. His thoughts became so muddled that he realized he was going to need some help.

John had never set any personal goals for himself other than to live reasonably comfortably from day to day and month to month. He had come from a poor family and had received little encouragement or help from his parents to develop ambitions when he was young. The one thing his mother and father had insisted on was that someone in the family was going to be a high school graduate; luckily, John was that person. He never had any desire to go to college because graduation from high school had proven to be extremely difficult for him. John could not think of spending four more years in school when he needed and wanted to be out making money for himself and the family.

Now, with people around him moving on in their careers and John's career at a standstill, he felt he was at a dead end. He realized suddenly that he needed to do something, but he was not sure just what.

Questions

1. What advice might you give John?
2. Would a career plan help a person like John?
3. Is John's situation atypical of that of most employees?

INCIDENT 11-2

Hire Me, Hire My Husband!*

Pete Gettings, director of human resources for XYZ Company's research and development laboratories, was relating a success from his State University recruiting trip to Derek Hills, XYZ's manager of computer operations.

"Derek," Gettings said excitedly, "you know how you've had me looking for engineers who could add technical strength to your operation? Well, I've found one—a senior at State University and a straight-A student, with lots of ambition, interested in computers for what they can do in applications, and anxious to work in industry. I'm bringing her in for an interview—I'm sure you'll want to hire her, and I'm positive we can."

"But," Gettings continued, "that's the good news. The bad news is that she's married and she and her husband want to work for the same company. Her husband is a marketing major and a jock. He played four years of basketball for State but is not nearly good enough to consider a pro career. I met him; he's got lots of personality and a C-grade average. I don't see any particular talent in him, and I think our marketing people will turn him down flat. But if we want her, we've got to find him a job!"

Sally Finch and her husband, Mike, were brought in for interviews with exactly the results Pete Gettings had predicted. Everybody was impressed with Sally, for

*Source: W. Gale Cutler, "Hire Me, Hire My Husband!" Research-Technology Management 38, no. 4 (July–August 1995), pp. 57–58.

she had prepared well for the interview and was able to point out some unexploited applications of computers at XYZ. Her suggestions about product performance simulation were particularly thought provoking and impressive.

Her husband, on the other hand, did very poorly in his interview. Mike could discuss his basketball prowess, but little else. His earring and ponytail hairstyle did not fit the conservative atmosphere of XYZ either.

The interviews resulted in a very attractive offer to Sally and a rejection for Mike. Sally's response was a blunt retort that she and Mike would continue to look for opportunities to work for the same company. XYZ wanted to employ Sally so badly that it made a diligent search of local employment possibilities for her husband, thinking this might be a good alternative to employing both of them at XYZ. A small telemarketing firm finally exhibited some interest in employing Mike, and because of the excellent offer that XYZ had made to Sally, the pair decided to accept both offers.

Sally subsequently proved to be a valuable asset to XYZ's R&D computer operations, and her work resulted in some excellent product development progress for the company. Derek was pleased and continued to pay for her additional training.

Sally received two promotions during her first two years at XYZ. Occasionally Derek asked about her husband, and Sally's only response was that he was doing OK and they were considering buying a home. This was good news because XYZ felt that Sally was definitely an employee they wanted to keep.

As time went on, Derek saw Mike several times at departmental social functions and noted that he had matured and become a very self-assured individual. In conversations with him, Derek observed that Mike seemed to have all the characteristics of a successful young businessman. Derek, in fact, wondered to himself if XYZ had made a mistake in not hiring him.

Derek was surprised and ill prepared one morning when Sally walked into his office and told him she was resigning.

"What's the problem?" Derek asked.

"My husband has done very well in the telemarketing business and has been offered a promotion and transfer to the West Coast. His company has asked him to open and manage a new branch operation there. I'm certain I'll be able to find employment in our new location, and we think this is the chance of a lifetime for Mike. I'm sorry to leave XYZ, but I really see no other choice. I'm willing to stay a month or so to help train a replacement if you can find one quickly. Of course, if XYZ could come up with a job for Mike equivalent to the one he's been offered on the Coast, we would stay here."

Questions

1. Should XYZ find (or "create") a job for Mike to retain Sally, a valued and well-trained employee?

2. Should XYZ management have anticipated a possible retention problem due to different career paths when it placed Sally and Mike in jobs with separate companies?

3. Do situations such as the one presented here make companies cautious about offering positions to members of dual-career families?

EXERCISE 11-1

How Do You Rate as a Career Counselor?*

This quiz helps managers to examine their knowledge of the career counseling function and to discover those areas in which some skill building may be necessary.

---

*Source: Adapted from P. R. Jones, B. Kaye, and H. R. Taylor, "You Want Me to Do What?" *Training and Development Journal,* July 1981, p. 62. Copyright 1981, *Training & Development Journal,* American Society for Training and Development. Reprinted with permission. All rights reserved.

Rate your knowledge, skill, and confidence as a managerial career counselor by scoring yourself on a scale of 0 (low) to 10 (high) on each of the following statements:

_____ 1. I am aware of how career orientations and life stages can influence a person's perspective and contribute to career planning problems.

_____ 2. I understand my own career choices and changes and feel good enough about what I have done to be able to provide guidance to others.

_____ 3. I am aware of my own biases about dual-career paths and feel that I can avoid these biases in coaching others to make a decision on which way to go with their careers.

_____ 4. I am aware of how my own values influence my point of view, and I recognize the importance of helping others to define their values and beliefs so they are congruent with career goals.

_____ 5. I am aware of the pitfalls of not knowing what is going on within my organization. As a result, I try to stay informed about my organization so I can help others.

_____ 6. I know the norms existing within my own department as well as those within other departments and parts of the organization, so I can help others deal with them effectively.

_____ 7. I understand the organizational reward system (nonmonetary) well enough to help others make informed decisions about career goals, paths, and plans.

_____ 8. I have access to a variety of techniques I can use to help others articulate their skills, set goals, and develop action plans to realize their career decisions.

_____ 9. I am informed on the competencies required for career success in this organization in both the managerial and technical areas, so I can advise others on the particular skills they need to build on and how to go about developing that expertise.

_____ 10. I feel confident enough about my own skills as a career counselor that I can effectively help my people with their problems and plans and make midcourse corrections when necessary.

Scoring

Add up your score and rate yourself against the following scale:

0–30	It might be a good idea if you found *yourself* a career counselor.
31–60	Some of your people are receiving help from you. . . . However, do you know how many and which ones are not?
61–80	You're a counselor! You may not be ready for the big league yet, but you are providing help for your people.
81–100	Others have a lot to learn from you. You understand the importance of career counseling, and you know how to provide it.

EXERCISE 11–2

Becoming an Effective Career Planner

Look over the nine potential career-planning roles of managers listed in Table 11–1. Rank-order them in terms of which roles you think would best fit you (1 being the role you would fit best, 9 being the role you would fit least). After you have completed this ranking, complete the quiz presented in Exercise 11–1. How does your score on this quiz correlate with how you ranked the counselor role (i.e., if you scored high on this quiz, did you rank the role of the counselor relatively high, and vice versa)? Make a list of some things you might do to become a better counselor. Be prepared to share your list with the class.

NOTES AND ADDITIONAL READINGS

1. William J. Morin, "You Are Absolutely Positively on Your Own," *Fortune,* December 9, 1996, p. 222.
2. Peter James and Valerie Wark, "Replacing the Ladders," *People Management,* May 31, 1995, pp. 28–31; and Sharon Voros, "Managing Your Career: The New Realities," *Communication World,* February 1997, pp. 28–30.
3. "Today's Mercurial Career Path," *Management Review,* November 1994, pp. 40–43; and Sami M. Abbasi and Kenneth W. Hollman, "The Myth and Realities of Downsizing," *Records Management Quarterly,* April 1998, pp. 31–37.
4. Kenneth Hein, "Training Employees to Stay," *Incentive,* February 1998, p. 7.
5. Zandy B. Leibowitz, Barbara H. Feldman, and Sherry H. Mosley, "Career Development Works Overtime at Corning, Inc.," *Personnel,* April 1990, p. 38.
6. B. C. Winterscheid, "A Career Development System Coordinates Training Efforts," *Personnel Administrator,* August 1980, pp. 28–32.
7. A. B. Randolph, "Managerial Career Coaching," *Training and Development Journal,* July 1981, pp. 54–55.
8. T. H. Stone, *Understanding Personnel Management* (Hinsdale, Ill.: Dryden Press, 1981), p. 324.
9. E. H. Burack and N. J. Mathys, *Career Management in Organizations: A Practical Human Resource Planning Approach* (Lake Forest, Ill.: Brace-Park Press, 1979), p. 78.
10. Jeanne C. Meister, "The Quest for Lifetime Employability," *Journal of Business Strategy,* May/June 1998, pp. 25–28.
11. N. T. Meckel, "The Manager as Career Counselor," *Training and Development Journal,* July 1981, pp. 65–69.
12. R. R. Carkhuff, *Helping and Human Relations: A Primer for Lay and Professional Helpers,* vol. I & II (New York: Holt, Rinehart & Winston, 1969).
13. These suggestions are adapted from Meckel, "The Manager," pp. 67–69.
14. The myths are adapted from E. Staats, "Career Planning and Development: Which Way Is Up?" *Public Administration Review,* January–February 1977, pp. 73–76; and A. H. Soverwine, "A Mythology of Career Growth," *Management Review,* June 1977, pp. 56–60.
15. The myths in this section are drawn from Barbara Moses, "Giving Employees a Future," *Training and Development Journal,* December 1987, pp. 25–28.
16. T. P. Ference, J. A. F. Stoner, and E. K. Warren, "Managing the Career Plateau," *Management Review,* October 1977, p. 602.
17. Steven H. Applebaum and Dvorah Firestone, "Revisiting Career Plateauing: Same Old Problems—Avant Garde Solutions," *Journal of Managerial Psychology* 9, no. 5 (1994), pp. 12–21.
18. Beverly Kaye, "Are Plateaued Performers Productive?" *Personnel Journal,* August 1989, p. 57; Judith M. Bardwick, *The Plateauing Trap* (New York: American Management Association, 1986), pp. 1–17.
19. Lawson K. Savery, "Managing Plateaued Employees," *Management Decision,* May 1990, p. 46.
20. Ference, Stoner, and Warren, "Managing," pp. 603–4.
21. Ibid., p. 607.
22. Richard C. Payne, "Mid-Career Block," *Personnel Journal,* April 1984, p. 42.
23. Ibid., pp. 44–48.
24. Catherine R. Smith, "Trends and Directions in Dual Career Family Research," *Women in Management Review* 7, no. 1 (1992), pp. 23–28.

25. Nancy Ten Kate, "Two Careers, One Marriage," *American Demographics,* April 1998, p. 28.
26. Ibid.
27. Nancy Carter, "Solve the Dual-Career Challenge," *Workforce (Global Workforce Supplement),* October 1997, pp. 21–22.
28. Nancy Ten Kate, "Two Careers, One Marriage," p. 28.
29. T. M. Camden, "Using Outplacement as a Career Development Tool," *Personnel Administration,* January 1982, p. 35.
30. Cari M. Dominguez, "A Crack In The Glass Ceiling," *HR Magazine,* December 1990, pp. 65–66. It should be noted that some authors interpret the glass ceiling as applying only to women as opposed to women and minorities.
31. "The Glass Ceiling," *HR Magazine,* October 1991, pp. 91–92.
32. "Still Hitting the Glass Ceiling," *Business Week,* October 28, 1996, p. 202.
33. Robert Zachariasiewicz, "Breaking the Glass Ceiling," *Credit World,* May/June 1993, pp. 21–23.
34. "The Glass Ceiling," pp. 91–92.
35. "Dismantling the Glass Ceiling," *HR Focus,* May 1996, p. 12.
36. Jim Warner, "Creating a Virtual Career Development Center," *HR Focus,* October 1997, pp. 11–12.

Performance Appraisal Systems

Learning Objectives

After studying this chapter, you should be able to:

1. Define performance appraisal.
2. Define performance.
3. Explain management by objectives.
4. Describe the work standards approach to performance appraisal.
5. Describe essay appraisal.
6. Explain critical-incident appraisal.
7. Describe the graphic rating scale.
8. Describe the checklist method of performance appraisal.
9. Explain the forced-choice method of performance appraisal.
10. Define leniency, central tendency, recency, and the halo effect.

Performance appraisal systems require a coordinated effort between the human resource department and the managers of the organization who are responsible for conducting performance appraisals. Generally, the responsibilities of the human resource department are to:

1. Design the formal performance appraisal system and select the methods and forms to be used for appraising employees.

2. Train managers in conducting performance appraisals.

3. Maintain a reporting system to ensure that appraisals are conducted on a timely basis.

4. Maintain performance appraisal records for individual employees.

The responsibilities of managers in performance appraisals are to:

1. Evaluate the performance of employees.

2. Complete the forms used in appraising employees and return them to the human resource department.

3. Review appraisals with employees.

This chapter describes the performance appraisal process in detail.

Performance Appraisal: Definition and Uses

Performance Appraisal
Process of determining and communicating to an employee how he or she is performing on the job and, ideally, establishing a plan of improvement.

Web site: Archer North's Performance Appraisal

www.performance-appraisal.com

Performance appraisal is the process of determining and communicating to an employee how he or she is performing on the job and, ideally, establishing a plan of improvement. When properly conducted, performance appraisals not only let employees know how well they are performing but also influence their future level of effort and task direction. Effort should be enhanced if the employee is properly reinforced. The task perception of the employee should be clarified through the establishment of a plan for improvement.

One of the most common uses of performance appraisals is for making administrative decisions relating to promotions, firings, layoffs, and merit pay increases. For example, the present job performance of an employee is often the most significant consideration for determining whether to promote the person. While successful performance in the present job does not necessarily mean an employee will be an effective performer in a higher-level job, performance appraisals do provide some predictive information.

Performance appraisal information can also provide needed input for determining both individual and organizational training and development needs. For example, this information can be used to identify an individual employee's strengths and weaknesses. These data can then be used to help determine the organization's overall training and development needs. For an individual employee, a completed performance appraisal should include a plan outlining specific training and development needs.

Another important use of performance appraisals is to encourage performance improvement. In this regard, performance appraisals are used as a means of communicating to employees how they are doing and suggesting needed changes in behavior, attitude, skills, or knowledge. This type of feedback clarifies for employees the job expectations held by the manager. Often this feedback must be followed by coaching and training by the manager to guide an employee's work efforts. The development of a performance improvement plan is discussed in more depth later in this chapter.

Finally, two other important uses of information generated through performance appraisals are (1) input to the validation of selection procedures and (2) input to human resource planning. Both of these topics were described in detail in earlier chapters.

A concern in organizations is how often to conduct performance appraisals. There seems to be no real consensus on how frequently performance appraisals should be done, but in general the answer is as often as necessary to let employees know what kind of job they are doing and, if performance is not satisfactory, the measures that must be taken for improvement. For many employees, this cannot be accomplished through one annual performance appraisal. Therefore, it is recommended that for most employees, informal performance appraisals be conducted two or three times a year in addition to an annual formal performance appraisal.

Understanding Performance

Performance Degree of accomplishment of the tasks that make up an employee's job.

Performance refers to the degree of accomplishment of the tasks that make up an employee's job. It reflects how well an employee is fulfilling the requirements of a job. Often confused with *effort*, which refers to energy expended, performance is measured in terms of results. For example, a student may exert a great deal of effort in preparing for an examination and still make a poor grade. In such a case the effort expended was high, yet the performance was low.

Determinants of Performance

Job performance is the net effect of an employee's effort as modified by abilities and role (or task) perceptions. Thus, performance in a given situation can be

Web site: Performance
Measurement Resources

www.zigonnert.com

viewed as resulting from the interrelationships among effort, abilities, and role perceptions.

Effort, which results from being motivated, refers to the amount of energy (physical and/or mental) an individual uses in performing a task. *Abilities* are personal characteristics used in performing a job. Abilities usually do not fluctuate widely over short periods of time. *Role (task) perceptions* refer to the direction(s) in which individuals believe they should channel their efforts on their jobs. The activities and behaviors people believe are necessary in the performance of their jobs define their role perceptions.

To attain an acceptable level of performance, a minimum level of proficiency must exist in each of the performance components. Similarly, the level of proficiency in any one performance component can place an upper boundary on performance. If employees put forth tremendous effort and have excellent abilities but lack a clear understanding of their roles, performance will probably not be good in the eyes of their managers. Much work will be produced, but it will be misdirected. Likewise, an employee who puts forth a high degree of effort and understands the job but lacks ability probably will rate low on performance. A final possibility is the employee who has good ability and understanding of the role but is lazy and expends little effort. This employee's performance will likely be low. Of course, an employee can compensate up to a point for a weakness in one area by being above average in one or both of the other areas.

Environmental Factors as Performance Obstacles

Other factors beyond the control of the employee can also stifle performance. Although such obstacles are sometimes used merely as excuses, they are often very real and should be recognized.

Some of the more common potential performance obstacles include a lack of or conflicting demands on the employee's time, inadequate work facilities and equipment, restrictive policies that affect the job, lack of cooperation from others, type of supervision, temperature, lighting, noise, machine or equipment pacing, shifts, and even luck.

Environmental factors should be viewed not as direct determinants of individual performance but as modifying the effects of effort, ability, and direction. For example, poor ventilation or worn-out equipment may well affect the effort an individual expends. Unclear policies or poor supervision can also produce misdirected effort. Similarly, a lack of training can result in underutilized abilities. One of management's greatest responsibilities is to provide employees with adequate working conditions and a supportive environment to eliminate or minimize performance obstacles.

Selection of a Performance Appraisal Method

Whatever method of performance appraisal an organization uses, it must be job related. Therefore, prior to selecting a performance appraisal method, an organization must conduct job analyses and develop job descriptions.

Performance Appraisal Methods

This section will discuss each of the following performance appraisal methods:

1. Goal setting, or management by objectives (MBO).
2. Multi-rater assessment (or 360-degree feedback).
3. Work standards approach.

4. Essay appraisal.

5. Critical-incident appraisal.

6. Graphic rating scale.

7. Checklist.

8. Behaviorally anchored rating scale (BARS).

9. Forced-choice rating.

10. Ranking methods.

One study, conducted for the American Management Association (AMA), of 588 organizations belonging to AMA's human resources, finance, marketing, and information systems divisions explored the frequency of use of the various appraisal methods. The method most frequently mentioned was goal setting (used by 85.9 percent). This was followed by written essay statements (81.5 percent), description of critical incidents (79.4 percent), graphic rating scales (64.8 percent), weighted checklists (56.4 percent), and behaviorally anchored rating scales (35 percent). The least used were paired comparisons (16.3 percent), forced choice (22.8 percent), and forced distribution (26.4 percent).[1] Obviously, most organizations use more than one method.

Goal Setting, or Management by Objectives (MBO)

Management by Objectives (MBO) Consists of establishing clear and precisely defined statements of objectives for the work to be done by an employee; establishing an action plan indicating how these objectives are to be achieved, allowing the employee to implement the action plan, measuring objective achievement, taking corrective action when necessary, and establishing new objectives for the future.

The goal-setting approach to performance appraisal, or **management by objectives (MBO)** as it is more frequently called, is more commonly used with professional and managerial employees. Other names for MBO include management by results, performance management, results management, and work planning and review program.

The MBO process typically consists of the following steps:

1. Establishing clear and precisely defined statements of objectives for the work to be done by an employee.

2. Developing an action plan indicating how these objectives are to be achieved.

3. Allowing the employee to implement the action plan.

4. Measuring objective achievement.

5. Taking corrective action when necessary.

6. Establishing new objectives for the future.

For an MBO system to be successful, several requirements must be met. First, objectives should be quantifiable and measurable; objectives whose attainment cannot be measured or at least verified should be avoided where possible. Objectives should also be challenging yet achievable, and they should be expressed in writing and in clear, concise, unambiguous language.

Table 12–1 presents examples of how some poorly stated objectives might be better stated. Table 12–2 shows some typical areas in which a supervisor might set objectives.

MBO also requires that employees participate in the objective-setting process. Active participation by the employee is also essential in developing the action plan. Managers who set an employee's objectives without input and then ask the employee, "You agree to these, don't you?" are unlikely to get high levels of employee commitment.

A final requirement for the successful use of MBO is that the objectives and action plan must serve as a basis for regular discussions between the manager and the employee concerning the employee's performance. These regular discussions provide an opportunity for the manager and employee to discuss progress and modify objectives when necessary.

TABLE 12–1   **EXAMPLES OF HOW TO IMPROVE WORK OBJECTIVES**

Poor: To maximize production.

Better: To increase production by 10 percent within the next three months.

Poor: To reduce absenteeism.

Better: To average no more than three absent days per employee per year.

Poor: To waste less raw material.

Better: To waste no more than 2 percent of raw material.

Poor: To improve the quality of production.

Better: To produce no more than 2 rejects per 100 units of production.

Multi-Rater Assessment (or 360-Degree Feedback)

One currently popular method of performance appraisal is called *multi-rater assessment* or *360-degree feedback*. With this method, managers, peers, customers, suppliers, or colleagues are asked to complete questionnaires on the employee being assessed. The person assessed also completes a questionnaire. The questionnaires are generally lengthy. Typical questions are: "Are you crisp, clear, and articulate? Abrasive? Spreading yourself too thin?" The human resources department provides the results to the employee, who in turn gets to see how his or her opinion differs from those of the group doing the assessment. HRM in Action 12.1 describes 360-degree feedback in more detail.

Work Standards

Work Standards Approach
Method of performance
appraisal that involves
setting a standard or an

The **work standards approach** to performance appraisal is most frequently used for production employees and is basically a form of goal setting for these employees. It involves setting a standard or an expected level of output and then comparing each employee's performance to the standard. Generally, work standards

TABLE 12–2   **TYPICAL AREAS OF SUPERVISORY OBJECTIVES**

1. Production or output:
   Usually expressed as number of units per time period.
   Example: Our objective is to average 20 units per hour over the next year.

2. Quality:
   Usually expressed as number of rejects, number of customer complaints, amount of scrap.
   Example: Our objective is to produce fewer than 10 rejects per week for the next six months.

3. Cost:
   Usually expressed as dollars per unit produced or dollars per unit of service offered.
   Example: Our objective is for the cost of each widget produced to average less than $5 over the next three months.

4. Personnel:
   Usually expressed in terms of turnover, absenteeism, tardiness.
   Example: Our objective is to average fewer than three days of absenteeism per employee per year.

5. Safety:
   Usually expressed in terms of days lost due to injury.
   Example: Our objective is to reduce the number of days lost due to injury this year by 10 percent.

HRM IN ACTION

360-Degree Feedback

12.1

A comprehensive way to evaluate employee feedback is through 360-degree feedback. It is used by some of the most successful companies in America, including UPS, AT&T, Amoco, General Mills, and Procter & Gamble. Traditionally, companies evaluate employee performance by relying almost exclusively on supervisor ratings that generally follow two types: measuring personality characteristics and technical abilities or appraisal by objectives. The first type of evaluation is usually in the form of a questionnaire with the evaluator ultimately making a subjective judgment. The second type of evaluation places emphasis on the achievement of recognized goals rather than personal characteristics.

With 360-degree feedback, a person's job performance is evaluated by his or her immediate supervisor as well as other individuals who have either direct or indirect contact with the person's work. The person also conducts a self-assessment of his or her performance. Coworkers also evaluate the person. Additionally, subordinates, customers, clients (internal as well as external), and anyone else who has contact with the person make an evaluation. Thus, a full circle (360 degrees) of evaluations is made by those people above, below, inside, outside, and anywhere in between. These evaluations are typically made by having all of the above mentioned individuals complete a lengthy, anonymous questionnaire.

Source: Adapted from Marc Marchese, "Industry: The Poser of the 360-Degree Feedback," *Pennsylvania CPA Journal*, December 1995, pp. 19, 47.

expected level of output and then comparing each employee's level to the standard.

should reflect the average output of a typical employee. Work standards attempt to define a fair day's output. Several methods can be used to set work standards. Some of the more common ones are summarized in Table 12–3.

An advantage of the work standards approach is that the performance review is based on highly objective factors. Of course, to be effective, the affected employees must view the standards as being fair. The most serious criticism of work standards is a lack of comparability of standards for different job categories.

Essay Appraisal

Essay Appraisal Method of performance appraisal in which the rater prepares a written statement describing an individual's strengths, weaknesses, and past performance.

The essay appraisal method requires that the evaluation describe an employee's performance in written narrative form. Instructions are often provided as to the topics to be covered. A typical essay appraisal question might be "Describe, in your own words, this employee's performance, including quantity and quality of work, job knowledge, and ability to get along with other employees. What are the employee's strengths and weaknesses?" The primary problem with essay appraisals is that their length and content can vary considerably, depending on the rater. For instance, one rater may write a lengthy statement describing an employee's potential and little about past performance; another rater may concentrate on an employee's past performance. Thus, essay appraisals are difficult to compare. The writing skill of the appraiser can also affect the appraisal. An effective writer can make an average employee look better than the actual performance warrants.

Critical-Incident Appraisal

Critical-Incident Appraisal Method of performance appraisal in which the rater keeps a written record of incidents that illustrate both positive and negative behaviors of the employee. The rater then uses these incidents as a basis for evaluating the employee's performance.

The critical-incident appraisal method requires the evaluator to keep a written record of incidents as they occur. The incidents recorded should involve job behaviors that illustrate both satisfactory and unsatisfactory performance of the employee being rated. As they are recorded over time, the incidents provide a basis for evaluating performance and providing feedback to the employee.

TABLE 12-3   **FREQUENTLY USED METHODS FOR SETTING WORK STANDARDS**

Method	Areas of Applicability
Average production of work groups	When tasks performed by all employees are the same or approximately the same.
Performance of specially selected employees	When tasks performed by all employees are basically the same and it would be cumbersome and time-consuming to use the group average.
Time study	Jobs involving repetitive tasks.
Work sampling	Noncyclical types of work where many different tasks are performed and there is no set pattern or cycle.
Expert opinion	When none of the more direct methods (described above) apply.

The main drawback to this approach is that the rater is required to jot down incidents regularly, which can be burdensome and time-consuming. Also, the definition of a critical incident is unclear and may be interpreted differently by different people. This method may also lead to friction between the manager and employees when the employees believe the manager is keeping a "book" on them.

Graphic Rating Scale

Graphic Rating Scale Method of performance appraisal that requires the rater to indicate on a scale where the employee rates on factors such as quantity of work, dependability, job knowledge, and cooperativeness.

With the **graphic rating scale** method, the rater assesses an employee on factors such as quantity of work, dependability, job knowledge, attendance, accuracy of work, and cooperativeness. Graphic rating scales include both numerical ranges and written descriptions. Table 12–4 gives an example of some items that might be included on a graphic rating scale that uses written descriptions.

The graphic rating scale method is subject to some serious weaknesses. One potential weakness is that evaluators are unlikely to interpret written descriptions in the same manner due to differences in background, experience, and personality. Another potential problem relates to the choice of rating categories. It is possible to choose categories that have little relationship to job performance or to omit categories that have a significant influence on job performance.

Checklist

Checklist Method of performance appraisal in which the rater answers with a yes or no a series of questions about the behavior of the employee being rated.

In the **checklist** method, the rater makes yes-or-no responses to a series of questions concerning the employee's behavior. Table 12–5 lists some typical questions. The checklist can also have varying weights assigned to each question.

Normally the scoring key for the checklist method is kept by the human resource department; the evaluator is generally not aware of the weights associated with each question. But because raters can see the positive or negative connotation of each question, bias can be introduced. Additional drawbacks to the checklist method are that it is time-consuming to assemble the questions for each job category, a separate listing of questions must be developed for each job category, and the checklist questions can have different meanings for different raters.

Behaviorally Anchored Rating Scale (BARS)

The **behaviorally anchored rating scale (BARS)** method of performance appraisal is designed to assess behaviors required to successfully perform a job. The focus of

T A B L E 1 2 – 4	**SAMPLE ITEMS ON A GRAPHIC RATING SCALE EVALUATION FORM**

Quantity of work—the amount of work an employee does in a workday.

(　)	(　)	(　)	(　)	(　)
Does not meet minimum requirements.	Does just enough to get by.	Volume of work is satisfactory.	Very industrious, does more than is required.	Has a superior work production record.

Dependability—the ability to do required jobs well with a minimum of supervision

(　)	(　)	(　)	(　)	(　)
Requires close supervision; is unreliable.	Sometimes requires prompting.	Usually completes necessary tasks with reasonable promptness.	Requires little supervision; is reliable.	Requires absolute minimum of supervision.

Job knowledge—information an employee should have on work duties for satisfactory job performance

(　)	(　)	(　)	(　)	(　)
Is poorly informed about work duties.	Lacks knowledge of some phases of job.	Is moderately informed; can answer most questions about the job.	Understands all phases of job.	Has complete mastery of all phases of job.

Attendance—faithfulness in coming to work daily and conforming to work hours

(　)	(　)	(　)	(　)	(　)
Is often absent without good excuse, or frequently reports for work late, or both.	Is lax in attendance, or reporting for work on time, or both.	Is usually present and on time.	Is very prompt, regular in attendance.	Is always regular and prompt; volunteers for overtime when needed.

Accuracy—the correctness of work duties performed

(　)	(　)	(　)	(　)	(　)
Makes frequent errors.	Careless, often makes errors.	Usually accurate, makes only average number of mistakes.	Requires little supervision; is exact and precise most of the time.	Requires absolute minimum of supervision; is almost always accurate.

Behaviorally Anchored Rating Scale (BARS) Method of performance appraisal that determines an employee's level of performance based on whether or not certain specifically described job behaviors are present.

BARS and, to some extent, the graphic rating scale and checklist methods is not on performance outcomes but on functional behaviors demonstrated on the job. The assumption is that these functional behaviors will result in effective job performance.

Most BARSs use the term *job dimension* to mean those broad categories of duties and responsibilities that make up a job. Each job is likely to have several job dimensions, and separate scales must be developed for each. Table 12–6 illustrates a BARS written for the job dimension found in many managerial jobs of planning, organizing, and scheduling project assignments and due dates. Scale values appear on the left side of the table and define specific categories of performance. Anchors, which appear on the right side, are specific written statements of actual behaviors that, when exhibited on the job, indicate the level of performance on the

TABLE 12-5

SAMPLE CHECKLIST QUESTIONS

	Yes	No
1. Does the employee lose his or her temper in public?	_____	_____
2. Does the employee play favorites?	_____	_____
3. Does the employee praise employees in public when they have done a good job?	_____	_____
4. Does the employee volunteer to do special jobs?	_____	_____

scale opposite that particular anchor. As the anchor statements appear beside each scale value, they are said to "anchor" each scale value along the scale.

Rating performance using a BARS requires the rater to read the list of anchors on each scale to find the group of anchors that best describe the employee's job behavior during the period being reviewed. The scale value opposite the group of anchors is then checked. This process is followed for all the identified dimensions of the job. A total evaluation is obtained by combining the scale values checked for all job dimensions.

BARSs are normally developed through a series of meetings attended by both managers and job incumbents. Three steps are usually followed:

1. Managers and job incumbents identify the relevant job dimensions for the job.

TABLE 12-6

EXAMPLE OF A BEHAVIORALLY ANCHORED RATING SCALE

Scale Values	Anchors
7[ ] Excellent	Develops a comprehensive project plan, documents it well, obtains required approval, and distributes the plan to all concerned.
6[ ] Very good	Plans, communicates, and observes milestones; states week by week where the project stands relative to plans. Maintains up-to-date charts of project accomplishments and backlogs and uses these to optimize any schedule modifications required. Experiences occasional minor operational problems but communicates effectively.
5[ ] Good	Lays out all the parts of a job and schedules each part; seeks to beat schedule and will allow for slack. Satisfies customers' time constraints; time and cost overruns occur infrequently.
4[ ] Average	Makes a list of due dates and revises them as the project progresses, usually adding unforeseen events; instigates frequent customer complaints. May have a sound plan, but does not keep track of milestones; does not report slippages in schedule or other problems as they occur.
3[ ] Below average	Plans are poorly defined, unrealistic time schedules are common. Cannot plan more than a day or two ahead, has no concept of a realistic project due date.
2[ ] Very poor	Has no plan or schedule of work segments to be performed. Does little or no planning for project assignments.
1[ ] Unacceptable	Seldom, if ever, completes project, because of lack of planning, and does not seem to care. Fails consistently due to lack of planning and does not inquire about how to improve.

Source: C. E. Schneier and R. W. Beatty, "Developing Behaviorally Anchored Rating Scales (BARS)," *Personnel Administrator,* August 1979, p. 60.

2. Managers and job incumbents write behavioral anchors for each job dimension. As many anchors as possible should be written for each dimension.

3. Managers and job incumbents reach a consensus concerning the scale values to be used and the grouping of anchor statements for each scale value.

The use of a BARS can result in several advantages. First, BARSs are developed through the active participation of both managers and job incumbents. This increases the likelihood that the method will be accepted. Second, the anchors are developed from the observations and experiences of employees who actually perform the job. Finally, BARSs can be used to provide specific feedback concerning an employee's job performance.

One major drawback to the use of BARSs is that they take considerable time and commitment to develop. Furthermore, separate forms must be developed for different jobs.

Forced-Choice Rating

Forced-Choice Rating
Method of performance appraisal that requires the rater to rank a set of statements describing how an employee carries out the duties and responsibilities of the job.

Many variations of the forced-choice rating method exist. The most common practice requires the evaluator to rank a set of statements describing how an employee carries out the duties and responsibilities of the job. Table 12–7 illustrates a group of forced-choice statements. The statements are normally weighted, and the weights generally are not known to the rater. After the rater ranks all of the forced-choice statements, the human resource department applies the weights and computes a score.

This method attempts to eliminate evaluator bias by forcing the rater to rank statements that are seemingly indistinguishable or unrelated. However, the forced-choice method has been reported to irritate raters, who feel they are not being trusted. Furthermore, the results of the forced-choice appraisal can be difficult to communicate to employees.

Ranking Methods

Ranking Methods Methods of performance appraisal in which the performance of an employee is ranked relative to the performance of others.

When it becomes necessary to compare the performance of two or more employees, ranking methods can be used. Three of the more commonly used ranking methods are alternation, paired comparison, and forced distribution.

Alternation Ranking

The alternation ranking method lists the names of the employees to be rated on the left side of a sheet of paper. The rater chooses the most valuable employee on the list, crosses that name off the left-hand list, and puts it at the top of the column

---

TABLE 12-7   SAMPLE SET OF FORCED-CHOICE STATEMENTS

Instructions: Rank the following statements according to how they describe the manner in which this employee carries out duties and responsibilities. Rank 1 should be given to the most descriptive, and Rank 5 to the least descriptive. No ties are allowed.

Rank	Description
_____	Is easy to get acquainted with.
_____	Places great emphasis on people.
_____	Refuses to accept criticism.
_____	Thinks generally in terms of money.
_____	Makes decisions quickly.

on the right-hand side of the paper. The appraiser then selects and crosses off the name of the least valuable employee from the left-hand column and moves it to the bottom of the right-hand column. The rater repeats this process for all of the names on the left-hand side of the paper. The resulting list of names in the right-hand column gives a ranking of the employees from most to least valuable.

Paired Comparison Ranking

Paired comparison ranking is best illustrated with an example. Suppose a rater is to evaluate six employees. The names of these individuals are listed on the left side of a sheet of paper. The evaluator then compares the first employee with the second employee on a chosen performance criterion, such as quantity of work. If he or she believes the first employee has produced more work than the second employee, a check mark is placed by the first employee's name. The rater then compares the first employee to the third, fourth, fifth, and sixth employee on the same performance criterion, placing a check mark by the name of the employee who produced the most work in each paired comparison. The process is repeated until each employee has been compared to every other employee on all of the chosen performance criteria. The employee with the most check marks is considered to be the best performer. Likewise, the employee with the fewest check marks is the lowest performer. One major problem with the paired comparison method is that it becomes unwieldy when comparing more than five or six employees.

Forced Distribution

The forced-distribution method requires the rater to compare the performance of employees and place a certain percentage of employees at various performance levels. It assumes the performance level in a group of employees will be distributed according to a bell-shaped, or "normal," curve. Figure 12–1 illustrates how the forced-distribution method works. The rater is required to rate 60 percent of the employees as meeting expectations, 20 percent as exceeding expectations, and 20 percent as not meeting expectations.

One problem with the forced-distribution method is that in small groups of employees, a bell-shaped distribution of performance may not be applicable. Even where the distribution may approximate a normal curve, it is probably not a perfect curve. This means some employees probably will not be rated accurately. Also, ranking methods differ dramatically from the other methods in that one employee's performance evaluation is a function of the performance of other employees in the job. Furthermore, the Civil Service Reform Act does not permit the use of ranking methods for federal employees.

F I G U R E   1 2 – 1   **FORCED-DISTRIBUTION CURVE**

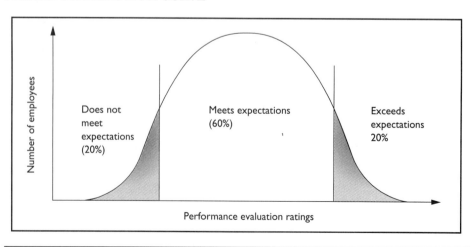

Potential Errors in Performance Appraisals

Leniency Occurs in performance appraisals when a manager's ratings are grouped at the positive end instead of being spread throughout the performance scale.

Central Tendency Tendency of a manager to rate most employees' performance near the middle of the performance scale.

Recency Tendency of a manager to evaluate employees on work performed most recently, usually one or two months prior to evaluation.

Halo Effect Occurs when a rater allows a single prominent characteristic of an employee to influence his or her judgment on each separate item in the performance appraisal.

Several common errors have been identified in performance appraisals. **Leniency** is the grouping of ratings at the positive end instead of spreading them throughout the performance scale. **Central tendency** occurs when appraisal statistics indicate that most employees are appraised as being near the middle of the performance scale. **Recency** occurs when evaluations are based on work performed most recently—generally work performed one to two months prior to evaluation. Leniency, central tendency, and recency errors make it difficult, if not impossible, to separate the good performers from the poor performers. In addition, these errors make it difficult to compare ratings from different raters. For example, it is possible for a good performer who is evaluated by a manager committing central tendency errors to receive a lower rating than a poor performer who is rated by a manager committing leniency errors.

Another common error in performance appraisals is the **halo effect**.[2] This occurs when a rater allows a single prominent characteristic of an employee to influence his or her judgment on each separate item in the performance appraisal. This often results in the employee receiving approximately the same rating on every item.

Personal preferences, prejudices, and biases can also cause errors in performance appraisals. Managers with biases or prejudices tend to look for employee behaviors that conform to their biases. Appearance, social status, dress, race, and sex have influenced many performance appraisals. Managers have also allowed first impressions to influence later judgments of an employee. First impressions are only a sample of behavior; however, people tend to retain these impressions even when faced with contradictory evidence.

Overcoming Errors in Performance Appraisals

As the preceding discussion indicates, the potential for errors in performance appraisals is great. One approach to overcoming these errors is to make refinements in the design of appraisal methods. For example, one could argue that the forced-distribution method of performance appraisal attempts to overcome the errors of leniency and central tendency. In addition, behaviorally anchored rating scales are designed to reduce halo, leniency, and central tendency errors, because managers have specific examples of performance against which to evaluate an employee. Unfortunately, because refined instruments frequently do not overcome all the obstacles, it does not appear likely that refining appraisal instruments will totally overcome errors in performance appraisals.

A more promising approach to overcoming errors in performance appraisals is to improve the skills of raters. Suggestions on the specific training that should be given to evaluators are often vague, but they normally emphasize that evaluators should be trained to observe behavior more accurately and judge it more fairly.

More research is needed before a definitive set of topics for rater training can be established. However, at a minimum, raters should receive training in the performance appraisal method(s) used by the company, the importance of the rater's role in the total appraisal process, the use of performance appraisal information, and the communication skills necessary to provide feedback to the employee.

Providing Feedback through the Appraisal Interview

After one of the previously discussed methods for developing an employee's performance appraisal has been used, the results must be communicated to the employee. Unless this interview is properly conducted, it can and frequently does result in an unpleasant experience for both manager and employee.

To prepare for the interview, the manager should answer the following questions:

1. What results should the interview achieve?
2. What good contributions is the employee making?
3. Is the employee working up to his or her potential?
4. Is the employee clear about the manager's performance expectations?
5. What training does the employee need to improve?
6. What strengths does the employee have that can be built on or improved?[3]

In addition, several basic guidelines need to be remembered in conducting the interview:

1. The manager must know the employee's job description.
2. The evaluation must be based on the employee's performance and not on his or her personality.
3. The manager must be positive and build on the employee's strengths.
4. The manager must be candid and specific.
5. The manager must listen to the employee as well as presenting her or his own views.
6. The manager must elicit employee feedback on how to improve performance.[4]

Some of the more important factors influencing the success or failure of appraisal interviews are the following:

1. The more employees are allowed to participate in the appraisal process, the more satisfied they will be with the appraisal interview and with the manager, and the more likely performance improvement objectives are to be accepted and met.
2. The more a manager uses positive motivational techniques (e.g., recognizing and praising good performance), the more satisfied the employee is likely to be with the appraisal interview and with the manager.
3. The mutual setting by the manager and the employee of specific performance improvement objectives results in more improvement in performance than does a general discussion or criticism.
4. Discussing and solving problems that may be hampering the employee's current job performance improve the employee's performance.
5. The more thought and preparation both the manager and the employee devote before the appraisal interview, the greater the benefits of the interview.
6. The more the employee perceives that performance appraisal results are tied to organizational rewards, the more beneficial the interview will be.

Many of the variables that have been identified and associated with positive outcomes from performance appraisal interviews are behaviors and skills that can be taught to managers responsible for conducting the interviews. The human resource department should play a key role in the development and implementation of these training programs.

Developing Performance Improvement Plans

Earlier in this chapter, we stated that a completed performance appraisal should include a performance improvement plan. This important step is often ignored. However, managers must recognize that an employee's development is a continuous cycle of setting performance goals, providing training necessary to achieve the goals, assessing performance as to the accomplishment of the goals, and then setting new, higher goals. A performance improvement plan consists of the following components:

1. **Where are we now?** This question is answered in the performance appraisal process.

2. **Where do we want to be?** This requires the evaluator and the person being evaluated to mutually agree on the areas that can and should be improved.

3. **How does the employee get from where he or she is now to where he or she wants to be?** This component is critical to the performance improvement plan. Specific steps to be taken must be agreed on. The steps may include training the employee will need to improve his or her performance and should also include how the evaluator will help the employee achieve the performance goals.

Performance Appraisal and the Law

Title VII of the Civil Rights Act permits the use of a bona fide performance appraisal system. Performance appraisal systems generally are not considered to be bona fide when their application results in adverse effects on minorities, women, or older employees.

A number of court cases have ruled that performance appraisal systems used by organizations were discriminatory and not job-related. In one case involving layoffs, *Brito et al.* v. *Zia Company,*[5] Spanish-surnamed workers were reinstated with back pay because the company had used a performance appraisal system of unknown validity in an uncontrolled and unstandardized manner. In *Mistretta* v. *Sandia Corporation,* performance appraisals were used as the main basis of layoff decisions affecting a disproportionate number of older employees.[6] The judge awarded the plaintiffs double damages plus all court costs.

In *Chamberlain* v. *Bissel, Inc.,* an evaluator expressed dissatisfaction with an employee's performance but did not inform the employee that his job was in jeopardy. On being terminated, the employee sued the company claiming he had never been warned that he might be dismissed. The Michigan state court ruled the company had been negligent in not informing the employee that he might be fired and awarded the employee $61,354 in damages.[7]

HRM IN ACTION

Performance Evaluation of the Poor Performer

12.2

A recent arbitration case illustrates some considerations in performance evaluation of the poor performer. An employee was moved to a different job after 21 years of service without any significant performance problems. The employee was in the new job for two years, during which period she had three different supervisors. Although the supervisors had expressed concerns about her performance and developed plans of action to provide her training, performance evaluations, and feedback, they neglected to follow through with these plans. In addition, the employee did not get along well with her assigned trainers, which hampered the instruction she received in the new job.

The employee was put on a 30-day probation that called for her termination if she did not improve her job performance. When she failed to meet her supervisor's expectations during this period, she was discharged. She filed a grievance protesting her discharge. The arbitrator did not award any back pay to the employee but directed management to reinstate her for a 12-week probationary period. He directed management to make sure that the employee received proper training and close performance monitoring during the 12-week probationary period.

Source: Adapted from William E. Lissy, "Labor Law for Supervisors: Incompetence," *Supervision,* July 1996, pp. 17–18.

In *Price Waterhouse* v. *Hopkins*,[8] the plaintiff, Ann Hopkins, charged she was denied a partnership at Price Waterhouse because of sexual stereotyping. Although Hopkins had generated more new business and logged more billable hours than any other candidate for partner, she was denied partnership consideration because the partners concluded she lacked the proper interpersonal skills. The court ruled that interpersonal skills was a legitimate performance evaluation measure, but it found that some of the evaluations of Hopkins were sexual stereotyping. For example, one member of the firm advised Hopkins to walk, talk, and dress in a more feminine fashion. In its decision, the Supreme Court found that Price Waterhouse had violated Title VII of the Civil Rights Act and stated that evaluating employees by assuming or insisting that they match a stereotype was illegal.[9] HRM in Action 12.2 describes the consequences of not following through on performance appraisals.

Many suggestions have been offered for making performance appraisal systems more legally acceptable. Some of these include (1) deriving the content of the appraisal system from job analyses; (2) emphasizing work behaviors rather than personal traits; (3) ensuring that the results of appraisals are communicated to employees; (4) ensuring that employees are allowed to give feedback during the appraisal interview; (5) training managers in how to conduct proper evaluations; (6) ensuring that appraisals are written, documented, and retained; and (7) ensuring that personnel decisions are consistent with the performance appraisals.[10]

SUMMARY OF LEARNING OBJECTIVES

1. **Define performance appraisal.**
   Performance appraisal involves determining and communicating to an employee how he or she is performing the job and, ideally, establishing a plan of improvement.

2. **Define performance.**
   Performance refers to the degree of accomplishment of the tasks that make up an employee's job.

3. **Explain management by objectives.**
   Management by objectives (MBO) consists of establishing clear and precisely defined statements of objectives for the work to be done by an employee, developing an action plan indicating how these objectives are to be achieved, allowing the employee to implement this action plan, measuring objective achievement, taking corrective action when necessary, and establishing new objectives for the future. MBO also requires that employees participate in the objective-setting process.

4. **Describe the work standards approach to performance appraisal.**
   The work standards approach involves setting a standard or expected level of output and then comparing each employee's performance to the standard.

5. **Describe essay appraisal.**
   The essay appraisal method requires that the rater describe an employee's performance in narrative form.

6. **Explain critical-incident appraisal.**
   This method requires the rater to keep a written record of incidents as they occur. Incidents should involve job behaviors that illustrate both satisfactory and unsatisfactory performances of the employee being rated.

7. **Describe the graphic rating scale.**
   With this method, the rater assesses an employee on factors such as quantity of work completed, dependability, job knowledge, attendance, accuracy of work, and cooperativeness.

8. **Describe the checklist method of performance appraisal.**

   In this method, the rater makes yes-or-no responses to a series of questions concerning the employee's behavior.

9. **Explain the forced-choice method of performance appraisal.**

   In this method, the rater is required to rank a set of statements describing how an employee carries out the duties and responsibilities of the job.

10. **Define leniency, central tendency, recency, and the halo effect.**

    Leniency refers to grouping ratings at the positive end of a curve instead of spreading them throughout the performance scale. Central tendency occurs when appraisal statistics indicate that most employees are appraised as being near the middle of the performance scale. Recency occurs when evaluations are based only on work performed most recently. The halo effect occurs when a rater allows a single prominent characteristic of an employee to influence his or her judgment on each separate item in the performance appraisal.

REVIEW QUESTIONS

1. Define performance appraisal.
2. What is performance? What factors influence an employee's level of performance?
3. Give at least three uses of performance appraisal information.
4. Describe the following methods used in performance appraisal:
   a. Management by objectives.
   b. Work standards.
   c. Essay.
   d. Critical-incident.
   e. Graphic rating scale.
   f. Checklist.
   g. Behaviorally anchored rating scale (BARS).
   h. Forced-choice rating.
   i. Ranking methods.
5. Define the following types of performance appraisal errors:
   a. Leniency.
   b. Central tendency.
   c. Recency.
   d. Halo effect.
6. Outline some conditions associated with the success or failure of appraisal interviews.
7. Describe some conditions that might make a performance appraisal system illegal.
8. Outline some recommendations for ensuring a legally acceptable performance appraisal system.

DISCUSSION QUESTIONS

1. How often do you think performance appraisals should be conducted?
2. What do you think about discussing salary raises and promotions during the performance appraisal interview?
3. What performance appraisal method do you believe would best apply to the evaluation of a college professor?
4. Was your last exam a performance appraisal? Use your last exam to discuss both the reasons for using performance appraisals and the limitations of such appraisals.

INCIDENT 12–1

The College Admissions Office

Bob Luck was hired to replace Alice Carter as administrative assistant in the admissions office of Claymore Community College. Before leaving, Alice had given a month's notice to the director of admissions, hoping this would allow ample time to locate and train her replacement. Alice's responsibilities included preparing and mailing transcripts at the request of students, mailing information requested by people interested in attending the college, answering the telephone, assisting students or potential enrollees who came to the office, and general supervision of clerical personnel and student assistants.

After interviewing and testing many people for the position, the director hired Bob, mainly because his credentials were good and he made a favorable impression. Alice spent many hours during the next 10 days training Bob. He appeared to be quite bright and seemed to quickly pick up the procedures involved in operating a college admissions office. When Alice left, everyone thought Bob would do an outstanding job.

However, little time had elapsed before people realized that Bob had not caught on to his job responsibilities. Bob seemed to have personal problems that were severe enough to stand in the way of his work. He asked questions about subjects that Alice had covered explicitly; he should have been able to answer these himself if he had comprehended her instructions.

Bob appeared to constantly have other things on his mind. He seemed to be preoccupied with such problems as his recent divorce, which he blamed entirely on his ex-wife, and the distress of his eight-year-old daughter, who missed her father terribly. His thoughts also dwelled on his search for peace of mind and some reasons for all that had happened to him. The director of admissions was aware of Bob's preoccupation with his personal life and his failure to learn the office procedures rapidly.

Questions

1. What would you do at this point if you were the director of admissions?
2. Describe how you might effectively use a performance appraisal in this situation.

INCIDENT 12–2

The Lackadaisical Plant Manager

Plant manager Paul Dorn wondered why his boss, Leonard Hech, had sent for him. He thought Leonard had been tough on him lately, and he was slightly uneasy at being asked to come to Leonard's office at a time when such meetings were unusual. "Close the door and sit down, Paul," invited Leonard. "I've been wanting to talk to you." After preliminary conversation, Leonard said that because Paul's latest project had been finished, he would receive the raise he had been promised on its completion.

Leonard went on to say that it was time for Paul's performance appraisal and they might as well do that now. Leonard explained that the performance appraisal was based on four criteria: (1) amount of high-quality merchandise manufactured and shipped on time, (2) quality of relationships with plant employees and peers, (3) progress in maintaining employee safety and health, and (4) reaction to demands of top management. The first criterion had a weight of 40 percent, and the rest had a weight of 20 percent each.

On the first item, Paul received an excellent rating. Shipments were at an all-time high, quality was good, and few shipments had arrived late. On the second item, Paul was also rated excellent. Leonard said plant employees and peers related well to Paul, labor relations were excellent, and there had been no major grievances since Paul had become plant manager.

However, on attention to matters of employee safety and health, the evaluation was below average. Leonard stated that no matter how much he prodded Paul about improving housekeeping in the plant, Paul never seemed to produce results. He also rated Paul below average on meeting demands from top management. He explained that Paul always answered yes to any request and then disregarded it, going about his business as if nothing had happened.

Seemingly surprised at the comments, Paul agreed that perhaps Leonard was right and that he should do a better job on these matters. Smiling as he left, he thanked Leonard for the raise and the frank appraisal.

As weeks went by, Leonard noticed little change in Paul. He reviewed the situation with an associate. "It's frustrating. In this time of rapid growth, we must make constant changes in work methods. Paul agrees but can't seem to make people break their habits and adopt more efficient ones. I find myself riding him very hard these days, but he just calmly takes it. He's well liked by everyone. But somehow he's got to care about safety and housekeeping in the plant. And when higher management makes demands he can't meet, he's got to say, 'I can't do that and do all the other things you want, too.' Now he has dozens of unfinished jobs because he refuses to say no."

As he talked, Leonard remembered something Paul had told him in confidence once. "I take Valium for a physical condition I have. When I don't take it, I get symptoms similar to a heart attack. But I only take half as much as the doctor prescribed." Now, Leonard thought, I'm really in a spot. If the Valium is what is making him so lackadaisical, I can't endanger his health by asking him to quit taking it. And I certainly can't fire him. Yet, as things stand, he really can't implement all the changes necessary to fulfill the goals we have set for the next two years.

Questions

1. What would you do if you were in Leonard's place?
2. What could have been done differently during the performance appraisal session?

EXERCISE

Developing a Performance Appraisal System

A large public utility has been having difficulty with its performance evaluation system. All operating employees and clerical employees are evaluated semiannually by their supervisors. The form the organization has been using appears in Exhibit 12–A; it has been in use for 10 years. The form is scored as follows: excellent = 5, above average = 4, average = 3, below average = 2, and poor = 1. The scores for each facet are entered in the right-hand column and totaled for an overall evaluation score.

In the procedure used, each supervisor rates each employee on July 30 and January 30. The supervisor discusses the rating with the employee and then sends the rating to the human resource department. Each rating is placed in the employee's personnel file. If promotions come up, the cumulative ratings are considered at that time. The ratings are also supposed to be used as a check when raises are given.

The system was designed by Joanna Kyle, the human resource manager who retired two years ago. Her replacement was Eugene Meyer. Meyer graduated 15 years ago with a degree in business from the University of Texas. Since then, he's had a variety of work experience, mostly in utilities. For about five of those years, he worked in human resources.

Meyer has been reviewing the evaluation system. Employees have a mixture of indifferent and negative feelings about it. An informal survey has shown that about

EXHIBIT 12-A   **A PERFORMANCE EVALUATION FORM**

Performance Evaluation

Supervisors: When you are asked to do so by the human resource department, please complete this form on each of your employees. The supervisor who is responsible for 75 percent or more of an employee's work should complete this form on the employee. Please evaluate each facet of the employee separately.

Facet			Rating			Score
Quality of work	Excellent	Above average	Average	Below average	Poor	
Quantity of work	Poor	Below average	Average	Above average	Excellent	
Dependability at work	Excellent	Above average	Average	Below average	Poor	
Initiative at work	Poor	Below average	Average	Above average	Excellent	
Cooperativeness	Excellent	Above average	Average	Below average	Poor	
Getting along with coworkers	Poor	Below average	Average	Above average	Excellent	

Total _____

Supervisor's signature _____

Employee name   _____

Employee number   _____

60 percent of the supervisors fill the forms out, give about three minutes to each form, and send them to the human resource department without discussing them with the employees. Another 30 percent do a little better. They spend more time completing the forms but communicate about them only briefly and superficially with their employees. Only about 10 percent of the supervisors seriously try to do what was intended.

Meyer also found out that the forms were rarely used for promotion or pay raise decisions. Because of this, most supervisors may have felt the evaluation program was a useless ritual. Where he had been previously employed, Meyer had seen performance appraisal as a much more useful experience, which included giving positive feedback to employees, improving future employee performance, developing employee capabilities, and providing data for promotion and compensation.

Meyer has not had much experience with the design of a performance appraisal system. He believes he should seek advice on the topic.

Write a report summarizing your evaluation of the strengths and weaknesses of the present appraisal system. Recommend some specific improvements or data-gathering exercises to develop a better system.

NOTES AND ADDITIONAL READINGS

1. Mary Zippo and Marc Miller, "Performance Appraisal: Current Practices and Techniques," *Personnel*, May–June 1984, p. 58.
2. For a more in-depth discussion of the halo effect, see R. Jacobs and S. W. J. Kozlowski, "A Closer Look at Halo Error in Performance Ratings," *Academy of Management Journal*, March 1985, pp. 201–12.

3. Peter M. Tafti, "Face to Face," *Training and Development Journal,* November 1990, p. 69.
4. Ibid., pp. 69–70.
5. 478 F. 2d 1200 (1973).
6. H. B. Winstanley, "Legal and Ethical Issues in Performance Appraisals," *Harvard Business Review,* November–December 1980, p. 188.
7. David C. Martin, "Performance Appraisal, 2: Improving the Rater's Effectiveness," *Personnel,* August 1986, pp. 28–33.
8. 57 USLW 4469 (1989).
9. Ginger C. Reed, "Employers' New Burden of Proof in Discrimination Cases," *Employment Relations Today,* Summer 1989, p. 112.
10. Roberta V. Bomberg, "Performance Appraisal, 1: Risks and Rewards," *Personnel,* August 1986, pp. 20–26.

Training Is Our Competitive Advantage: Arthur Andersen and Andersen Consulting

Arthur Andersen Worldwide Organization is the world's third largest accounting and consulting organization, with 1992 revenues of $5.6 billion. In 1989, the company was restructured into two business units, Arthur Andersen (which provides corporate specialty services and audit business, and tax advisory services) and Andersen Consulting (which aids clients in the application of the integration of information-based technologies for competitive advantage, strategic planning, and change management). The two business units share many support services, including training. Together they invest approximately 5.5 percent of their combined annual revenues, which amount to more than $300 million, in the development and training of their employees. This amount is significantly higher than the U.S. corporate average.

Lawrence Weinbach, managing partner and chief executive of the firm, says, "Education gives us our competitive edge. Anybody can hire smart people. It's what you do with them that makes the difference. In a professional service organization, all you have to sell are your people's abilities, so we invest in that." Andersen clearly hires its share of smart people. It aggressively recruits bright college graduates in such fields as accounting, computer science, engineering, and communications. However, unlike in many organizations, the company does not expect these recent graduates to be "up and running" on the job immediately. They are trained extensively in the culture and methods of what many employees call "The Firm" (not to be confused with any recent movies or novels by that title).

How did this emphasis on training as a competitive advantage begin at Arthur Andersen? Over 80 years ago, the company founder, Arthur Andersen, decided that the accountants he hired for audit and tax season work would do a higher-quality job if he not only made them year-round employees but provided them with training as well. Recently Steven M. Hronec commented, "as a partner, I expect training to be very responsive to our changing marketplace. Our clients' needs are changing and I expect training to be able to be done very quickly, very focused, and in a way that responds to these changes."

The Andersen Training Function

Unlike most U.S. companies, Andersen provides the most intensive training for new employees at the start of the career ladder. Virtually all new staff recruits, from countries across the globe, receive three weeks of professional education. The primary training site in the United States is the Center for Professional Education in St. Charles, Illinois. In addition, Andersen has training sites in the Netherlands and Spain.

For the most part, all employees receive the same initial training. Andersen has developed standard methodologies and approaches to problem solving that allow Andersen personnel from any country to work together to develop unique, effective solutions designed to fit individual business challenges. Herbert W. Desch, managing partner of the Professional Education Division (PED) and the organization's chief training officer, notes, "Individual brilliance is not as important as the ability to share different ideas and a variety of potential solutions through a worldwide team approach. As a global organization, we believe that clients ought to be able to get the same level of quality service from any of our offices. When you train for a worldwide culture and teach consistent methodologies for approaching complex tasks, you have a better chance of providing consistent quality while reaching solutions tailored to an individual client's needs." The global perspective is very much a part of the Andersen training process. Alan Malby, a manager with Andersen Consulting's London office, believes the cultural mix of trainees at the St. Charles facility leads to an international team spirit "which is particularly of benefit as projects get larger and people from other offices are drafted to complete projects."

Each person, new or experienced, in the Andersen organization of 48,000 professionals receives an average of 138 hours of training each year. Roughly one-third of the training takes place at the St. Charles center, a 151-acre campus where new recruits participate in rigorous training sessions, working up to 12 hours per day. The St. Charles training center also offers hundreds of special "schools" or courses that provide continual professional development for the company's experienced personnel. Most courses are taught by people from line operations. "In our culture it's an honor to teach," says Desch. Training sessions include topics in basic auditing, tax law, and state-of-the-art client/server technology specifically designed for the Andersen Consulting professionals.

The Andersen Professional Education Division (PED) handles training design and development, provides training support, and does curriculum planning. It uses several technologies to deliver training, including videoconferencing, digital interactive (DVI), CD-ROM, and desktop computers. Desch estimates that the division is one of the largest employers of instructional designers and technologists in the United States. To shorten the time between the recognition of new training needs and design and delivery of the actual training, PED has begun to use teams (called "group technology cells," similar to those used in manufacturing) made up of subject matter experts, educational experts, and graphic artists to bring new training programs to the staff quickly.

Training Responsiveness to Client Needs

The speed of training in new technologies and tax law changes provides Andersen with professionals who are up to date. A current example of this process is the aggressive training now under way in the area of client/server networks (networks of desktop computers are used by about 70 percent of Andersen Consulting's new business). Desch says, "Anticipating a market shift, we rolled out our first client/server training in just five months. Andersen Consulting has more than 3,000 professionals, and we'll have an additional 6,000 professionals, proficient in these applications, by 1993." Desch predicted that the company would have as many as 24,000 consulting professionals skilled in client/server solutions by the end of 1994.

More training, however, does not always mean better performance; therefore, Andersen's training staff monitors progress toward training objectives. Evaluation reports go to the partners. Every unit in the company that uses training must account for it, and all training is evaluated at least at the level of participants' reactions to the material and process. One recent program on state and local tax law was evaluated fully to determine effects on revenue and quantity of work. The evaluation showed that tax professionals who took the training had more billable hours than those who did not take the course.

Individual Career Development

From the perspective of Andersen's people, the training function provides many elements of what is needed for successful career development. As one recent recruit states, "To succeed, you need the desire and the opportunity. At Andersen Consulting, the opportunities for success match my ambitions. The winning attitude, the well-defined career opportunities, and the practical training I've found here push my potential to the limit. I believe in succeeding on my own merit. . . . I also think it's smart to have help."

During an individual's first five years as a consultant, he or she receives nearly 800 hours of formal training, an investment in human resources worth approximately $32,000. At the individual level, the emphasis is on providing both formal classroom training along with carefully chosen on-the-job experiences. Early job assignments cross business and technical areas, allowing new staff to discover interests and abilities. Training is used to support staff as they move up in levels of responsibility and broaden their skills. Opportunities for growth are constantly made available as people move from staff consultant to senior consultant, to manager, and, potentially, to associate partner and partner.

The Andersen Worldwide Organization considers itself an established team that takes great pride in the skills and abilities of its members. Part of the culture reinforced by training and work teams is the ability to pull from many resources to complete a job effectively. One junior staff member notes that "working with and as a team is extremely important here. If you challenge yourself as an individual and pull together as a team, you can get any job accomplished," This sense of team membership is extended through the use of a counselor (or mentor) program for new employees. An executive-level member of the organization is immediately assigned to each new hire. This "counselor" serves as a sounding board throughout the individual's career, offering advice on how best to achieve goals, providing performance feedback, and just listening.

The Andersen companies clearly believe the skills of their people are the lifeblood of their organization. Here training is not just a first-year proposition. The firm has developed lifelong training tailored to the individual's interests and to the needs of his or her clients. Although the emphasis may change from basic skills to advanced technical training, the goal remains to achieve superior performance.

Critical Thinking Questions

1. In what ways has Arthur Andersen & Company used the training function to meet its competitive challenges? Why is training so important to the success of this organization?

2. As a new recruit to either side of the Andersen businesses, what would your expectations be regarding career development opportunities? How might this play a role in the success of Andersen's recruiting programs?

3. Evaluate the counselor (or mentor) program concept that Andersen uses with new entry-level employees. What benefits may be associated with such a program?

4. The case states that during initial training sessions, workdays may be as long as 12 hours. In many of the large accounting/consulting firms, long workdays are the norm. What does this communicate about corporate culture in these firms? What personal characteristics might fit such a culture? What costs and benefits may be associated with this practice?

5. Andersen executives believe that assuring culturally diverse groups of trainees in their programs leads to more effective international business efforts. In what ways can this practice enhance Andersen's international operations?

6. Why is the practice of evaluating and justifying training programs important to the credibility of and management support for the Andersen professional development programs?

Compensating Employees

4

The Organizational Reward System

Learning Objectives

After studying this chapter, you should be able to:

1. Define organizational rewards.
2. Distinguish between intrinsic and extrinsic rewards.
3. List several desirable preconditions for implementing a pay-for-performance program.
4. Define job satisfaction and list its five major components.
5. Summarize the satisfaction-performance relationship.
6. Define compensation, pay, incentives, and benefits.
7. List several pieces of government legislation that have had a significant impact on organizational compensation.
8. Explain the equity theory of motivation.
9. Discuss internal, external, individual, and organizational equity.

f Few things evoke as much emotion as the organization's reward system. Employees often interpret the design and use of the organizational reward system as a reflection of management attitudes, intentions, and the entire organizational climate. Because of this, the organizational reward system is one of the most effective motivation tools managers have at their disposal. The responsibility for coordinating and administering the system usually resides with the human resource manager.

Defining the System

Organizational Reward System Organizational system concerned with the selection of the types of rewards to be used by the organization.

Organizational Rewards Rewards that result from employment with the organization; includes all types of rewards, both intrinsic and extrinsic.

Intrinsic Rewards Rewards

The organizational reward system consists of the types of rewards to be offered and their distribution. Organizational rewards include all types of rewards, both intrinsic and extrinsic, that are received as a result of employment by the organization. Intrinsic rewards are internal to the individual and are normally derived from involvement in certain activities or tasks. Job satisfaction and feelings of accomplishment are examples of intrinsic rewards. Most extrinsic rewards are directly controlled and distributed by the organization and are more tangible than intrinsic rewards. Pay and hospitalization benefits are examples of extrinsic rewards. Table 13–1 provides examples of both types of rewards.

Though intrinsic and extrinsic rewards differ, they are also closely related. Often the provision of an extrinsic reward provides the recipient with intrinsic rewards. For example, an employee who receives an extrinsic reward in the form of a pay raise may also experience feelings of accomplishment (an intrinsic reward) by interpreting the pay raise as a sign of a job well done.

T A B L E   1 3 - 1   **INTRINSIC VERSUS EXTRINSIC REWARDS**

Intrinsic Rewards	Extrinsic Rewards
Achievement	Formal recognition
Feelings of accomplishment	Fringe benefits
Informal recognition	Incentive payments
Job satisfaction	Pay
Personal growth	Promotion
Status	Social relationships
	Work environment

internal to the individual and normally derived from involvement in certain activities or tasks.

Extrinsic Rewards   Rewards that are controlled and distributed directly by the organization and are of a tangible nature.

Selection of Rewards

Selection of the rewards to be offered is critical if the reward system is to function effectively. As a first step, management must recognize what employees perceive as meaningful rewards. Pay is usually the first, and sometimes only, reward most people think about. There is little doubt that pay is a very significant reward. However, rewards should be viewed in the larger perspective as anything valued by employees and may include things such as office location, the allocation of certain pieces of equipment, the assignment of preferred work tasks, and informal recognition.

If an organization is going to distribute rewards—and all do—why should it not get the maximum in return? Such a return can be realized only if the desires of employees are known. Organizations should learn what employees perceive as meaningful rewards, which is not necessarily what management perceives. Traditionally, managers have assumed they are fully capable of deciding just what rewards employees need and want. Unfortunately, this is often not true. These differences in perception surfaced in a mid 1990s study that asked 1,000 employees to rank 10 possible rewards.[1] The employees' supervisors were also asked to rank how they thought their employees would rank the 10 choices. The employees ranked "interesting work" highest, while their supervisors ranked "good wages" as their employees' highest preference.

Another closely related, and often false, assumption is exemplified by the fact that most organizations offer the same mix of rewards to all employees. Studies have shown that many variables, such as age, sex, marital status, number of dependents, and years of service, can influence employee preferences for certain rewards.[2] For example, older employees are usually much more concerned with pension benefits than are younger employees.

Another dimension to be considered when selecting the types of rewards to offer is the intrinsic benefits that might accrue as a result of the rewards. All too often, managers and employees alike consider only the tangible benefits associated with a reward.[3]

In addition to the internal factors just mentioned are external factors that place limitations on an organization's reward system. These factors include such things as the organization's size, environmental conditions, the stage in the product life cycle, and the labor market. Since these external factors are usually beyond the control of the organization, this chapter will concentrate primarily on internal factors.

Relating Rewards to Performance

The free enterprise system is based on the premise that rewards should depend on performance. This performance-reward relationship is desirable not only at the organizational or corporate level but also at the individual level. The underlying theory is that employees will be motivated when they believe such motivation will lead to desired rewards. Unfortunately, many formal rewards provided by organizations cannot be connected to performance. Rewards in this category, including paid vacations, insurance plans, and paid holidays, are almost always determined by organizational membership and seniority rather than by performance.

Other rewards, such as promotion, can and should be related to performance. However, opportunities for promotion may occur only rarely. When available, the higher positions may also be filled on the basis of seniority or by someone outside the organization.

The primary organizational variable used to reward employees and reinforce performance is pay. Even though many U.S. companies have some type of pay-for-performance program, most do a poor job of relating the two.[4] Surveys repeatedly show that neither top management nor rank-and-file employees have much confidence that a positive relationship exists between performance and pay.[5] There is also evidence that paying for performance is becoming more prevalent in England and Europe.[6]

If relating rewards to performance is desirable, why is the practice not more widespread? One answer is that it is not easy to do; it is much easier to give everybody the same thing, as evidenced by the ever-popular across-the-board pay increase. Relating rewards to performance requires that performance be accurately measured, and this is often not easily accomplished (Chapter 12 discussed performance appraisal). It also requires discipline to actually relate rewards to performance. Another reason is that many union contracts require that certain rewards be based on totally objective variables, such as seniority. While no one successful formula for implementing a pay-for-performance program has yet been developed, a number of desirable preconditions have been identified and generally accepted:

1. *Trust in management.* If employees are skeptical of management, it is difficult to make a pay-for-performance program work.
2. *Absence of performance constraints.* Since pay-for-performance programs are usually based on an employee's ability and effort, the jobs must be structured so that an employee's performance is not hampered by factors beyond his or her control.
3. *Trained supervisors and managers.* The supervisors and managers must be trained in setting and measuring performance standards.
4. *Good measurement systems.* Performance should be based on criteria that are job specific and focus on results achieved.
5. *Ability to pay.* The merit portion of the salary increase budget must be large enough to get the attention of employees.
6. *Clear distinction among cost of living, seniority, and merit.* In the absence of strong evidence to the contrary, employees will naturally assume a pay increase is a cost-of-living or seniority increase.
7. *Well-communicated total pay policy.* Employees must have a clear understanding of how merit pay fits into the total pay picture.
8. *Flexible reward schedule.* It is easier to establish a credible pay-for-performance plan if all employees do not receive pay adjustments on the same date.[7]

HRM in Action 13.1 describes how Lincoln Electric Company has successfully related pay to performance. HRM in Action 13.2 discusses how U.S. West Communications overcame union opposition and implemented a pay-for-performance program in parts of its organization.

Job Satisfaction and Rewards

Job Satisfaction An employee's general attitude toward the job.

Job satisfaction is an employee's general attitude toward the job. The organizational reward system often has a significant impact on the level of employee job

HRM IN ACTION

Linking Pay to Performance at Lincoln Electric

13.1

www.lincolnelectric.com

Lincoln Electric Company celebrated its 100th anniversary in 1995. The Cleveland, Ohio-based manufacturer of arc welders has 2,000 blue-collar employees at its four U.S. plants. The employees do not belong to a union, have never gone out on strike, and deferred 614 weeks of vacation in 1994 to meet worldwide demand. Recent figures show that Lincoln's employees are two-and-a-half to three times more productive than employees of other, similar manufacturing companies.

The key to Lincoln's success is that the company bases pay on performance and sets virtually no limit on what employees can earn. Employees have not experienced a layoff since 1948 and have received an annual bonus for the past 61 years. When business is good, factory employees can receive a bonus equal to half of their yearly income. For example, in December 1993, the board of directors awarded an average bonus of $20,500 per employee. In 1996, the average annual pay on the factory floor was $55,000, and more than 25 floor workers made over $100,000.

Source: Anita Leinert, "A Dinosaur of a Different Color," *Management Review,* February 1995, pp. 24–29, and Richard M. Hodgetts, "Discussing Incentive Compensation with Donald Hastings of Lincoln Electric," *Compensation & Benefits Review,* September/October 1997, pp. 60–66.

satisfaction. In addition to their direct impact, the manner in which the extrinsic rewards are dispersed can affect the intrinsic rewards (and satisfaction) of the recipients. For example, if everyone receives an across-the-board pay increase of 5 percent, it is hard to derive any feeling of accomplishment from the reward. However, if pay raises are related directly to performance, an employee who receives a healthy pay increase will more than likely also experience feelings of accomplishment and satisfaction.

The five major components of job satisfaction are

- Attitude toward the work group.
- General working conditions.
- Attitude toward the company.

HRM IN ACTION

Overcoming Opposition to Pay for Performance

13.2

www.uswest.com

After a nasty two-week strike, Solomon Trujillo, U.S. West Communications Group president and chief executive, finally got his employees to accept a partial tying of pay to performance. The union adamantly opposed this idea even though it would mean extra money for many employees. Trujillo had good reason to fight for his plan: he had seen revenues per employee jump 47 percent after a similar system was implemented for sales representatives three years ago.

Tying pay to performance was quite a breakthrough for a Bell company. While wages for most employees will rise at the normal low-single digit rate, customer service technicians who opt to participate in the new plan can increase their salaries by an average of 20 percent if they meet their performance goals.

When Trujillo took over, U.S. West was in the worst shape of all the Baby Bells. Trujillo believes he can turn U.S. West around by installing performance-based incentives. Explains Trujillo, "I want to create an opportunity for people who move quickly to make more money. I want to be a gazelle, not a Godzilla."

Source: Christopher Palmeri, "A Gazelle, Not a Godzilla," *Forbes,* September 21, 1998, pp. 64–66.

- Monetary benefits.
- Attitude toward management.[8]

Other components include the employee's state of mind about the work itself and life in general. An employee's attitude toward the job may be positive or negative. Health, age, level of aspiration, social status, and political and social activities can all influence job satisfaction.

Job satisfaction is not synonymous with **organizational morale,** which is the possession of a feeling of being accepted by and belonging to a group of employees through adherence to common goals, confidence in the desirability of those goals, and the desire to progress toward the goals. Morale is the by-product of a group, while job satisfaction is more an individual state of mind. However, the two concepts are interrelated in that job satisfaction can contribute to morale and morale can contribute to job satisfaction.

Organizational Morale An employee's feeling of being accepted by and belonging to a group of employees through common goals, confidence in the desirability of those goals, and the desire to progress toward the goals.

The Satisfaction-Performance Controversy

For many years, managers generally have believed that a satisfied employee is necessarily a good employee. In other words, if management could keep all employees happy, good performance would automatically follow. Charles Greene has suggested that many managers subscribe to this belief because it represents "the path of least resistance."[9] Greene's thesis is that if a performance problem exists, increasing an employee's happiness is far more pleasant than discussing with the employee his or her failure to meet standards. Before discussing the satisfaction-performance controversy, we should point out that there are subtle but real differences between being satisfied and being happy. Although happiness eventually results from satisfaction, the latter goes much deeper and is far less tenuous than happiness.

The following incident illustrates two propositions concerning the satisfaction-performance relationship:

> As Ben walked by, smiling on the way to his office, Ben's boss remarked to a friend, "Ben really enjoys his job, and that's why he's the best damn worker I ever had. And that's reason enough for me to keep Ben happy." The friend replied, "No, you're wrong! Ben likes his job because he does it so well. If you want to make Ben happy, you ought to do whatever you can to help him further improve his performance."[10]

The first proposition is the traditional view that satisfaction causes performance. The second is that satisfaction is the effect rather than the cause of performance. In this position, performance leads to rewards that result in a certain level of satisfaction. Thus, rewards constitute a necessary intervening variable in the relationship. Another position considers both satisfaction and performance to be functions of rewards. It postulates that satisfaction results from rewards, but current performance also affects subsequent performance if rewards are based on current performance.

Research evidence generally rejects the more popular view that satisfaction leads to performance. However, it does provide moderate support for the view that performance leads to satisfaction. The evidence also strongly indicates that (1) rewards constitute a more direct cause of satisfaction than does performance and (2) rewards based on current performance enhance subsequent performance.[11]

While the assumption that job satisfaction and job performance are related has much intuitive appeal, reviews of the studies in this area do not support a strong relationship. Reporting on a comprehensive review of over 100 published studies involving job satisfaction and job performance, the authors stated that "the best estimate of the true population correlation between satisfaction and performance is relatively low."[12] One relationship that has been clearly established is that job satisfaction does have a positive impact on turnover, absenteeism, tardiness, accidents, grievances, and strikes.[13] Studies have also reported that experience, gender, and performance can have a moderating effect on these relationships.[14] In addition, organizations prefer satisfied employees simply because such employees make the work environment more pleasant. Thus, even though a satisfied employee is not necessarily a high performer, there are numerous reasons for cultivating employee satisfaction.

Other Factors Affecting Job Satisfaction

As mentioned earlier, a wide range of both internal and external factors affect an employee's level of satisfaction. A recent study of 3,351 U.S. employees found that workplace support was the most important factor affecting job satisfaction among the respondents.[15] Workplace support in this context refers to policies and actions, such as flexible schedules and providing child care, that make employees feel supported by the organization. The second most important factor was job quality as measured by autonomy, meaningfulness, opportunities for learning and advancement, and job security. By contrast, actual pay and access to benefits were found to have a relatively insignificant effect on employee satisfaction. The left portion of Figure 13–1 summarizes these and other factors that determine an employee's level of satisfaction or dissatisfaction. The total impact of these factors causes employees to be either generally satisfied or dissatisfied with their jobs. As indicated by the right side of Figure 13–1, employees who are satisfied with their jobs tend to be committed to the organization; these employees are likely to be very loyal and dependable. Employees who are dissatisfied with their jobs tend to behave in ways that can be detrimental to the organization; these employees are likely to experience higher rates of turnover, absenteeism, tardiness, and more accidents, strikes, and grievances.

Job satisfaction and motivation are not synonymous. Motivation is a drive to perform, whereas job satisfaction reflects the employee's attitude toward or happiness with the job situation. As Figure 13–1 suggests, a satisfied or "happy" employee is not necessarily a motivated or productive employee. The organizational reward system can influence both job satisfaction and employee motivation. The reward system affects job satisfaction by making the employee more or less comfortable as a result of the rewards received. The reward system influences motivation primarily through the perceived value of the rewards and their contingency on performance.

F I G U R E   1 3 – 1   **DETERMINANTS OF EMPLOYEE SATISFACTION AND DISSATISFACTION**

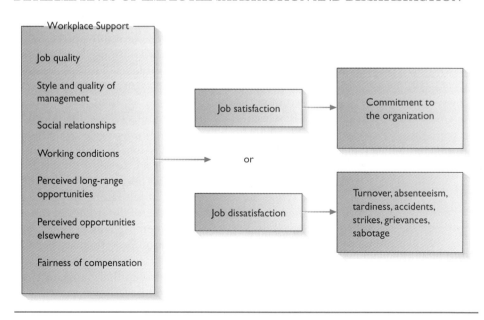

Employee Compensation

Compensation All the extrinsic rewards that employees receive in exchange for their work: composed of the base wage or salary, any incentives or bonuses, and any benefits.

Compensation and pay are not synonymous terms. **Compensation** refers to all the extrinsic rewards employees receive in exchange for their work. **Pay** refers only to the actual dollars employees receive in exchange for their work. Usually compensation is composed of the **base wage or salary,** any incentives or bonuses, and any benefits. The base wage or salary is the hourly, weekly, or monthly pay employees receive for their work. **Incentives** are rewards offered in addition to the base wage or salary and are usually directly related to performance. **Benefits** are rewards employees receive as a result of their employment and position with the organization. Paid vacations, health insurance, and retirement plans are examples of benefits. Table 13–2 presents some examples of the different types of compensation. The next three chapters cover base wages or salaries, incentives, and benefits, respectively.

Pay Refers only to the actual dollars employees receive in exchange for their work.

Base Wage or Salary
Hourly, weekly, or monthly pay that employees receive for their work.

Incentives Rewards offered in addition to the base wage or salary and usually directly related to performance.

Benefits Rewards employees receive as a result of their employment and position with the organization.

Compensation Policies

Certain policies must be formulated before a successful compensation system can be developed and implemented. Naturally, these policies are strongly influenced by the organization's objectives and its environment. Policies must deal with the following issues:

1. Minimum and maximum levels of pay (taking into consideration the worth of the job to the organization, the organization's ability to pay, government regulations, union influences, and market pressures).
2. General relationships among levels of pay (e.g., between senior management and operating management, operative employees, and supervisors).
3. The division of the total compensation dollar (i.e., what portion goes into base pay, into incentive programs, and into benefits).[16]

In addition to these issues, organizations must make decisions concerning how much money will go into pay increases for the next year, who will recommend them, and how raises will generally be determined. Another important decision concerns whether pay information will be kept secret or made public.

Pay Secrecy

Many organizations have a policy of not disclosing pay-related information. This includes information about the pay system as well as individual pay received. The justification for pay secrecy is usually to avoid any discontent that might result from employees' knowing what everybody else is being paid. Further justification is that many employees, especially high achievers, feel very strongly that their pay is nobody else's business.[17]

On the other hand, pay secrecy makes it difficult for employees to determine whether pay is related to performance. Also, pay secrecy does not eliminate pay comparisons; it may cause employees to overestimate the pay of their peers and

TABLE 13–2	COMPONENTS OF EMPLOYEE COMPENSATION		
	Base Wage or Salary	**Incentives**	**Benefits**
	Hourly wage	Bonuses	Paid vacation
	Weekly, monthly, or annual salary	Commissions	Health insurance
	Overtime pay	Profit sharing	Life insurance
		Piece rate plans	Retirement pension

underestimate the pay of their supervisors.[18] Both situations can unnecessarily create feelings of dissatisfaction. Also, when managers refuse to disclose pay, employees naturally become suspicious and often conclude that the managers are hiding something. Prior to when the National Labor Relations Board (NLRB) ruled that it was illegal, some companies actually forbade employees to discuss and/or disclose their pay. In 1992, the NLRB ruled that forbidding employees to discuss their pay constitutes a violation of the National Labor Relations Act (the National Labor Relations Act is discussed in Chapter 17).[19]

A good compromise on the issue of pay secrecy is to disclose the pay ranges for various job levels within the organization. This approach clearly communicates the general ranges of pay for different jobs, but it does not disclose exactly what any particular employee is making.

Government and Union Influence

Government legislation and union contracts can have a significant impact on organizational compensation. Both of these factors are discussed in the following sections.

Fair Labor Standards Act (FLSA)

The FLSA, commonly called the Wage and Hour Act, was passed in 1938 and has been amended several times. Its primary requirements are that individuals employed in interstate commerce or in organizations producing goods for interstate commerce must be paid a certain minimum wage and be paid time-and-a-half for hours over 40 worked in one week. (Table 13–3 shows how the minimum wage has changed over the years.) Section 218 of the FLSA permits states, localities, and collective bargaining agreements to set a higher standard than the federal minimum. In addition, the FLSA places restrictions on the employment of individuals between ages 14 and 18. The most complex parts of the law deal with possible exemptions. Amendments to the law have reduced the number of exemptions, but careful study is necessary to determine an organization's obligations.

Discussions of compensation systems often use the terms *exempt* and *nonexempt personnel*. Nonexempt employees are covered by the FLSA; they must be paid overtime and are subject to a minimum wage. Exempt employees are not covered by the FLSA and include executive, administrative, and professional employees.

Davis-Bacon Act

Passed by Congress on March 3, 1931, the Davis-Bacon Act requires that contractors and subcontractors on federal construction contracts in excess of $2,000 pay the prevailing wage rates for the locality of the project. This prevailing wage rate,

T A B L E   1 3 – 3   **HISTORY OF MINIMUM WAGE RATES**

Date	Rate per Hour	Date	Rate per Hour
October 24, 1938	$0.25	January 1, 1975	$2.10
October 24, 1939	0.30	January 1, 1976	2.30
October 24, 1945	0.40	January 1, 1978	2.65
January 25, 1950	0.75	January 1, 1979	2.90
March 1, 1956	1.00	January 1, 1980	3.10
September 3, 1961	1.15	January 1, 1981	3.35
September 3, 1963	1.25	April 1, 1990	3.80
February 1, 1967	1.40	April 1, 1991	4.25
February 1, 1968	1.60	October 1, 1996	4.75
May 1, 1974	2.00	September 1, 1997	5.15

which is determined by the secretary of labor, has normally been the same as the prevailing union rate for the area. Overtime of time-and-a-half must be paid for more than 40 hours per week.

Walsh-Healey Public Contracts Act

The Walsh-Healey Public Contracts Act, passed by Congress on June 30, 1936, requires that organizations manufacturing or furnishing materials, supplies, articles, or equipment in excess of $10,000 to the federal government pay at least the minimum wage for the industry as determined by the secretary of labor. Originally the Walsh-Healey Act called for overtime pay for anything over eight hours in a single day. However, the Defense Authorization Act of 1986 changed the requirement to overtime for hours worked over 40 in a week.

Federal Wage Garnishment Law

Garnishment   A legal procedure by which an employer is empowered to withhold wages for payment of an employee's debt to a creditor.

Garnishment is a legal procedure by which an employer is empowered to withhold wages for payment of an employee's debt to a creditor. The Federal Wage Garnishment Law, which became effective on July 1, 1970, limits the amount of an employee's disposable earnings that can be garnished in any one week and protects the employee from discharge because of garnishment. However, the law did not substantially alter state laws on this subject. For instance, if the state law prohibits or provides for more limited garnishment than the federal law, the state law is applied. Thus, a human resource manager must be familiar with state laws applicable to garnishment.

Equal Pay Act

The Equal Pay Act was introduced and discussed in Chapter 3. Signed into law on June 10, 1963, the Equal Pay Act was an amendment to the Fair Labor Standards Act, eliminating pay differentials based solely on sex. The law makes it illegal to pay different wages to men and women for jobs that require equal skill, effort, and responsibility and are performed under similar conditions. This law does not prohibit the payment of wage differentials based on seniority systems, merit systems that measure earnings by quantity and quality of production, or systems based on any factor other than sex.

Union Contracts

If an organization is unionized, the wage structure is usually largely determined through the collective bargaining process. Because wages are a primary concern of unions, current union contracts must be considered in formulating compensation policies. Union contracts can even affect nonunionized organizations. For example, the wage rates and increases paid to union employees often influence the wages paid to employees in nonunion organizations.

Impact of Comparable Worth

Comparable worth theory, introduced in Chapter 4, holds that while the true worth of jobs to the employer may be similar, some jobs (especially those held by women) are often paid a lower rate than other jobs (often held by men). A major problem associated with comparable worth theory is determining the worth of the jobs in question. How should job worth be established? U.S. courts have generally rejected cases based on comparable worth claims.[20] Although comparable worth has generally floundered in court, it has flourished at the collective bargaining table and in the political arena.[21]

The Importance of Fair Pay

As discussed earlier in this chapter employee motivation is closely related to the types of rewards offered and their method of disbursement. While there is considerable debate over the motivational aspect of pay, little doubt exists that inadequate pay can have a very negative impact on an organization. Figure 13–2 presents a simple model that summarizes the reactions of employees when they are dissatisfied with their pay. According to this model, pay dissatisfaction can influence employees' feelings about their jobs in two ways: (1) It can increase the desire for more money, and (2) it can lower the attractiveness of the job. An employee who desires more money is likely to engage in actions that can increase pay. These actions might include joining a union, looking for another job, performing better, filing a grievance, or going on strike. With the exception of performing better, all of the consequences are generally classified as being undesirable by management. Better performance results only in those cases where pay is perceived as being directly related to performance. On the other hand, when the job decreases in attractiveness, the employee is more likely to be absent or tardy, quit, or become dissatisfied with the job itself. Thus, while its importance may vary somewhat from situation to situation, pay satisfaction can and usually does have a significant impact on employee performance.

FIGURE 13–2   MODEL OF THE CONSEQUENCES OF PAY DISSATISFACTION

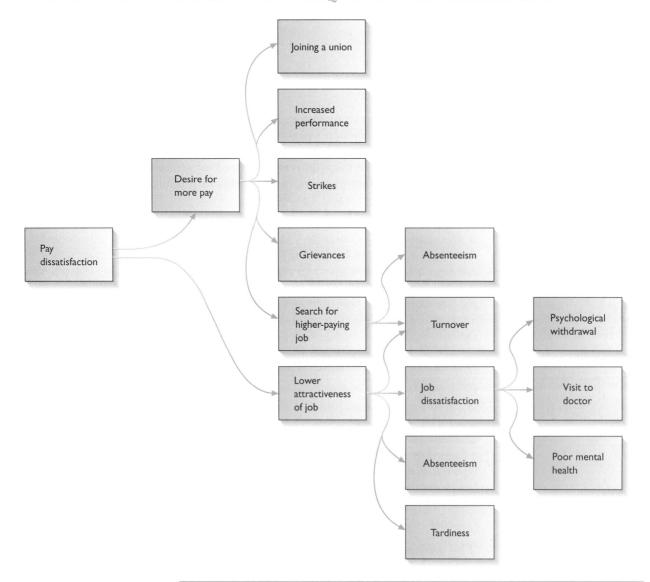

Source: Adapted from Edward E. Lawler III, *Pay and Organizational Effectiveness: A Psychological View* (New York: McGraw-Hill, 1971), p. 233.

Pay Equity

The equity theory of motivation basically holds that employees have a strong need to maintain a balance between what they perceive as their inputs to their jobs and what they receive from their jobs in the form of rewards. In this theory, employees who perceive inequities will take action to eliminate or reduce them. For example, if an employee believes he or she is underpaid, that employee will likely reduce expended effort by working more slowly, taking off early, or being absent. Similarly, if an employee believes she or he is being overpaid, that employee is likely to work harder or for longer hours.

Pay equity concerns whether employees believe they are being fairly paid. There are several dimensions of equity to consider in looking at pay equity. Internal equity concerns what an employee is being paid for doing a given job compared to what other employees in the same organization are being paid to do their jobs. External equity deals with what employees in other organizations are being paid for performing similar jobs. Individual equity addresses the issue of rewarding individual contributions and is very closely related to the pay-for-performance question. Organizational equity concerns how profits are divided up within the organization. In other words, do the employees believe the organization's profits are fairly distributed? It is important to recognize that employee interpretations of pay equity are based on their perceptions. Because employee feelings about pay equity are based on perceptions, organizations should do whatever they can to make these perceptions as accurate as possible. Also, it is not unusual for an employee to feel good about one or more of the equity dimensions and feel bad about the others. For example, an employee may feel good about his or her pay in comparison to what friends working in other organizations are making. She or he may also believe the company profits are fairly distributed within the company. However, this same person may be very unhappy about his or her pay relative to several other people in the same organization. HRM in Action 13.3 discusses pay inequities between women and men in today's work environment.

Internal Equity Addresses what an employee is being paid for doing a job compared to what other employees in the same organization are being paid to do their jobs.

External Equity Addresses what employees in an organization are being paid compared to employees in other organizations performing similar jobs.

Individual Equity Addresses the rewarding of individual contributions; is very closely related to the pay-for-performance question.

HRM IN ACTION

Gender Pay Inequities

13.3

While the pay gap between women and men has narrowed over the last 25 years, it is still substantial. The good news is that while the gap closed only 1 percentage point from 1970, when women earned 59 percent as much as men, to 1980, when they earned 60 percent as much, it closed by 8 points from 1980 to 1989.

Studies conducted in 1991 noted that women in full-time management jobs made only 61% of the salaries made by men in similar jobs. In 1992, the gap continued to close. Based on median weekly earnings, women working full-time earned 75 cents for every dollar earned by men full-time; by 1994, the figure had grown to 77 cents. Unfortunately from 1994 to 1998 the figure dropped back down to 75 cents.

Pay inequity is most prevalent for employees aged 16 to 24 years old. In that age group, women earn more than 90 percent of what men earn. However, the gap widens to roughly 75 percent of those at the height of their careers, in the 25 to 54-year-old group.

Sources: Diane Crispell, "Women's Earnings Gap Is Closing—Slowly," *American Demographics,* February 1991, p. 14; Steven E. Rhoads, "Pay Equity Won't Go Away," *Across the Board,* July–August 1993, pp. 37–41; and Teresa Brady, "How Equal Is Equal Pay? *Management Review,* March 1998, pp. 59–61.

FIGURE 13–3   MODEL OF THE DETERMINANTS OF PAY SATISFACTION

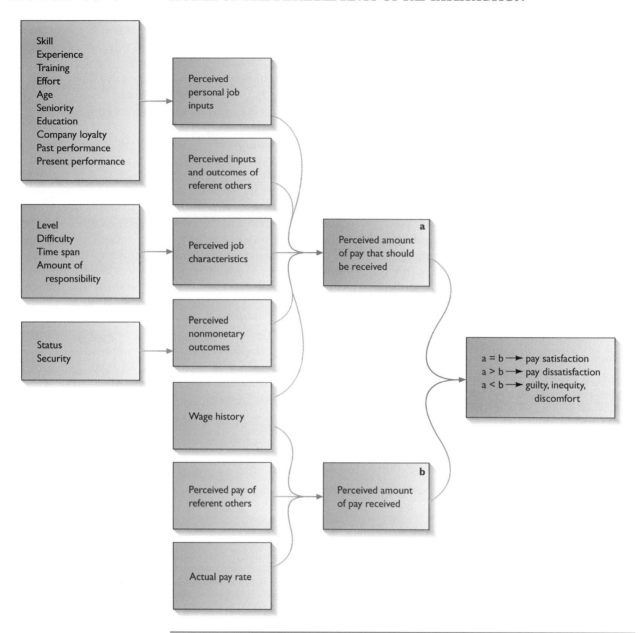

Source: Edward E. Lawler III, *Pay and Organizational Effectiveness: A Psychological View* (New York: McGraw-Hill, 1971), p. 215.

Organizational Equity
Addresses how profits are divided up within the organization.

Pay Satisfaction Model

Figure 13–3 presents a model of the determinants of pay satisfaction. The model is based on the idea that employees will be satisfied with their pay when their perception of what their pay is and of what they think it should be are in agreement. This happens when employees feel good about the internal and external equity of their pay.

Naturally, present pay is a primary factor influencing an employee's perception of equity. However, the person's wage history and perception of what others are getting also have an influence. For example, employees who have historically received high pay tend to lower their perception of present pay. Similarly, the higher the pay of friends and peers, the lower one's individual pay appears to be. These factors account for the fact that two people may view the same level of pay in a very different manner.

The model also shows that an employee's perception of what pay should be depends on several other factors, including job inputs, the perceived inputs and outcomes of friends and peers, and nonmonetary outcomes. Job inputs include all the experience, skills, and abilities an employee brings to the job in addition to the effort the employee puts into it. The perceived inputs and outcomes refer to the individual's perception of what friends and peers put into their jobs and what kind of pay they get in return. The nonmonetary outcomes received refer to the fact that certain nonmonetary rewards can sometimes substitute for pay, at least up to a point.

The model also makes allowances for employees who believe their pay *exceeds* what they think it should be. Research has shown that in such cases, people often experience feelings of guilt, inequity, and discomfort.[22]

The Role of the Human Resource Manager in the Reward System

The role of the human resource manager in the overall organizational reward system is to assist in its design and administer the system. Administering the system inherently carries the responsibility of ensuring that the system is fair to all employees. This places the burden of minimizing reward inequities and employees' perceptions of reward inequities squarely on the human resource manager. Many tools and techniques are available to assist human resource managers in this endeavor, and many of these are discussed in the following three chapters.

SUMMARY OF LEARNING OBJECTIVES

1. **Define organizational rewards.**
   Organizational rewards include all types of rewards, both intrinsic and extrinsic, that are received as a result of employment by the organization.

2. **Distinguish between intrinsic and extrinsic rewards.**
   Intrinsic rewards are rewards internal to the employee and are normally derived from involvement in certain activities or tasks. Extrinsic rewards are directly controlled and distributed by the organization and are more tangible than intrinsic rewards.

3. **List several desirable preconditions for implementing a pay-for-performance program.**
   Several preconditions have been identified for implementing a successful pay-for-performance program. These include (1) trust in management; (2) absence of performance constraints; (3) trained supervisors and managers; (4) good measurement systems; (5) ability to pay; (6) a clear distinction among cost of living, seniority, and merit; (7) a well-communicated total pay policy; and (8) a flexible reward schedule.

4. **Define job satisfaction and list its five major components.**
   Job satisfaction is an employee's general attitude toward the job. The five major components of job satisfaction are (1) attitude toward the work group, (2) general working conditions, (3) attitude toward the company, (4) monetary benefits, and (5) attitude toward supervision.

5. **Summarize the satisfaction-performance relationship.**
   Research evidence generally rejects the popular view that satisfaction leads to performance. The evidence does, however, provide moderate support for the view that performance leads to satisfaction. The evidence also provides strong indications that rewards constitute a more direct cause of satisfaction than does performance, and rewards based on current performance lead to subsequent

performance. In general, the best estimate of the correlation between satisfaction and performance is relatively low.

6. **Define compensation, pay, incentives, and benefits.**

   Compensation refers to all the extrinsic rewards employees receive in exchange for their work. Pay includes only the actual dollars employees receive in exchange for their work. Incentives are rewards offered in addition to the base wage or salary and are directly related to performance. Benefits are rewards employees receive as a result of their employment and position with an organization.

7. **List several pieces of government legislation that have had a significant impact on organizational compensation.**

   Numerous pieces of government legislation have affected organizational compensation. Some of the most significant include the Fair Labor Standards Act (FLSA), the Davis-Bacon Act, the Walsh-Healey Public Contracts Act, the Federal Wage Garnishment Law, and the Equal Pay Act.

8. **Explain the equity theory of motivation.**

   The equity theory of motivation holds that employees have a strong need to maintain a balance between what they perceive as their inputs to their jobs and what they receive from their jobs in the form of rewards. In this theory, employees who perceive inequities will take action to eliminate or reduce the inequities.

9. **Discuss internal, external, individual, and organizational equity.**

   Internal equity concerns what an employee is being paid for doing a given job compared to what other employees in the same organization are being paid to do their jobs. External equity deals with what employees in other organizations are being paid for performing similar jobs. Individual equity addresses the rewarding of individual contributions and is very closely related to the pay-for-performance question. Organizational equity concerns how profits are divided up within the organization.

REVIEW QUESTIONS

1. What are organizational rewards?
2. Explain the differences between intrinsic and extrinsic rewards.
3. What variables have been found to influence employee preferences for certain rewards?
4. Discuss two reasons organizations do a poor job of relating rewards to performance.
5. List eight preconditions that have been found to be desirable for establishing a successful pay-for-performance program.
6. What is job satisfaction? What are its major components?
7. Discuss the satisfaction-performance controversy.
8. Define compensation and distinguish it from pay.
9. What is the primary organizational variable that can be used to reward individuals and reinforce performance?
10. Describe some of the consequences of pay dissatisfaction.
11. What are the two general factors relating to the question of fair pay?
12. Describe the pay satisfaction model. How does it determine pay satisfaction?

DISCUSSION QUESTIONS

1. XYZ Company has just decided to take all of its 200 employees to Las Vegas for an expense-paid, three-day weekend to show its appreciation for their high level of performance this past year. What is your reaction to this idea?
2. Comment on the following statement: "Employees are not capable of deciding what rewards they should receive."

3. Recently a manager was overheard making the following comment: "Most employees are never satisfied with their pay anyway, so why should we even try? I think we should pay as little as possible and just accept the fact that the employees won't like it." If you were this manager's superior, what would you say.

4. Do you think a very loyal employee is necessarily a good employee? Why or why not?

INCIDENT 13-1

An Informative Coffee Break

On Monday morning, April 28, George Smith was given the news that effective May 1 he would receive a raise of 8 percent. This raise came two months before his scheduled performance appraisal. His manager, Loretta Weeks, informed him that the basis for the raise was his performance over the past several months and his potential worth to the company. He was told this was a very considerable increase.

On Tuesday, a group of George's coworkers were having their normal coffee break. The conversation turned to salary increases. One member of the group had received a performance review in April, but no indication of an impending salary adjustment had been given. George made a comment concerning the amount of any such increase, specifically questioning the range of increase percentages. Another coworker responded that she was surprised to have received an across-the-board 7 percent increase the previous Friday. A third individual had received a similar salary increase. Definitely astounded, George pressed for information, only to learn that several people had received increases of "around" 6 to 8 percent. George excused himself and left the group.

That evening, George wrestled with his conscience concerning the discussion that day. His first impression of his raise was that it had been given based on performance. His second impression was decidedly sour. Several questions were bothering him:

1. Why did his boss present the raise as a merit increase?

2. Was job performance really a basis for salary increases in his department?

3. Did his boss hide the truth regarding the raise?

4. Could he trust his boss in the future?

5. On what basis would further increases be issued?

Questions

1. What effect do you think this new information will have on the effort put forth by George Smith?

2. What can Loretta Weeks do to regain George Smith's confidence?

3. Has the concept of pay secrecy backfired on Loretta Weeks in this case? If so, how?

INCIDENT 13-2

Does Money Motivate?

About four months ago, Greg Holcomb was promoted to supervisor of the claims department for a large eastern insurance company. It is now time for all supervisors to make their annual salary increase recommendations. Greg doesn't feel comfortable in making these recommendations, since he has been in his job only a short time. To further complicate the situation, the former supervisor has left the company and is unavailable for consultation.

There are no formal company restrictions on the kinds of raises that can be given, but Greg's boss has said the total amount of money available to Greg for raises would be 8 percent of Greg's total payroll for the past year. In other words, if the sum total of the salaries for all of Greg's employees was $100,000 Greg would have $8,000 to allocate for raises. Greg is free to distribute the raises just about any way he wants, within reason.

Summarized below is the best information on his employees that Greg can find from the files of the former supervisor of the claims department. This information is supplemented by feelings Greg has developed during his short time as supervisor.

Sam Jones.   Sam has been with Greg's department for only five months. In fact, he was hired just before Greg was promoted into the supervisor's job. Sam is single and seems to be a carefree bachelor. His job performance so far has been above average, but Greg has received some negative comments about Sam from his coworkers. Present salary: $26,000.

Sue Davis.   Sue has been on the job for three years. Her previous performance appraisals have indicated superior performance. However, Greg does not believe the previous evaluations are accurate. He thinks Sue's performance is average at best. Sue appears to be well liked by all of her coworkers. Just last year she became widowed and is presently the sole supporter of her five-year-old child. Present salary: $28,000.

Evelyn Boyd.   Evelyn has been on the job for four years. Her previous performance appraisals were all average. In addition, she has received below-average increases for the past two years. However, Evelyn recently approached Greg and told him she feels she was discriminated against in the past due to both her age and her sex. Greg believes Evelyn's work so far has been satisfactory but not superior. Most employees do not seem to sympathize with Evelyn's accusations of sex and age discrimination. Present salary $24,000.

Jane Simond.   As far as Greg can tell, Jane is one of his best employees. Her previous performance appraisals also indicate she is a superior performer. In addition, Greg knows Jane badly needs a substantial salary increase due to some personal problems. In addition, all of Greg's employees are aware of Jane's problems. She appears to be well respected by her coworkers. Present salary: $25,000.

Ralph Dubose.   Ralph has been performing his present job for eight years. The job is very technical, and he would be difficult to replace. However, as far as Greg can discern, Ralph is not a good employee. He is irritable and hard to work with. In spite of this, Ralph has received above-average pay increases for the past two years. Present salary: $30,000.

Questions

1. What size raise would you give each of these employees?
2. What criteria did you use in determining the size of the raises?
3. What do you think would be the feelings of the other people in the group if they found out what raises you recommend?
4. Do you think the employees would eventually find out what raises others received? Would it matter?

E X E R C I S E

Relating Rewards to Performance

Think of the most recent job you held. This job could have been a summer, part-time, or full-time job. Which of the two situations described below better characterizes this job?

A. Rewards (monetary and nonmonetary) were tied directly to one's level of performance; management did attempt to discriminate between the high and low performers and did reward accordingly.

B. Everyone within very broad, general categories received basically the same rewards; one's level of performance did not substantially affect the rewards received.

Depending on which situation you selected, what effect do you think it had on your level of motivation? If you selected situation A, explain basically how the system worked. If you selected situation B, what specific recommendations would you make to improve the performance-reward relationship? Be prepared to discuss your answers with the class.

NOTES AND ADDITIONAL READINGS

1. Kenneth A. Kovach, "Employee Motivation: Addressing a Crucial Factor in Your Organization's Performance," *Employment Relations Today,* Summer 1995, pp. 93–107.

2. J. Brad Chapman and Robert Ottemann, "Employee Preference for Various Compensation Fringe Benefit Options," *Personnel Administrator,* November 1975, p. 34.

3. Many of the basic motivation theories (e.g., Herzberg's dual-factor theory and Maslow's need theory) are based on the assumption that intrinsic rewards greatly influence one's level of motivation.

4. Frederick S. Hills, Robert M. Madigan, K. Dow Scott, and Steven E. Markham, "Tracking the Merit of Merit Pay," *Personnel Administrator,* March 1987, p. 50.

5. E. James Brennan, "The Myth and the Reality of Pay for Performance," *Personnel Journal,* March 1985, p. 73; Thomas J. Bergmann, Harvey Gardersen, D. Wallace Weil, and B. R. Baliga, "Rewards Tied to Long-Term Success," *HR Magazine,* May 1990, p. 67.

6. "Paying for Performance: A Survey of Merit Pay," *Industrial Relations Review,* October 1994, pp. 554–57, and William Franklin and Andrew Guntert, "Making the Fat Cats Earn Their Cream," *Accountancy,* July 1998, pp. 38–39.

7. Hills, Madigan, Scott, and Markham, "Tracking the Merit," pp. 56–57.

8. Phillip B. Applewhite, *Organizational Behavior* (Englewood Cliffs, N.J.: Prentice Hall 1965), p. 22.

9. Charles N. Greene, "The Satisfaction-Performance Controversy," *Business Horizons,* October 1972, p. 31.

10. Ibid., p. 32.

11. Ibid., p. 40.

12. Michelle T. Iaffaldano and Paul M. Muchinsky, "Job Satisfaction and Job Performance: A Meta-Analysis," *Psychological Bulletin* 97, no. 2 (1985), pp. 251–73.

13. Donald P. Schwab and Larry I. Cummings, "Theories of Performance and Satisfaction: A Review," *Industrial Relations,* October 1970, pp. 408–29. For a summary of the related research, see E. A. Locke, "The Nature and Causes of Job Satisfaction," in *Handbook of Industrial and Organizational Psychology,* ed. M. D. Dunnette (Skokie, Ill.: Rand McNally, 1976), p. 1343.

14. Frederick A. Russ and Kevin M. McNeilly, "Links among Satisfaction, Commitment, and Turnover Intentions: The Moderating Effect of Experience, Gender, and Performance," *Journal of Business Research,* September 1995, pp. 57–65.

15. Michael Hickins, "Give A Little, Get a Lot," *Management Review,* October 1998, p. 6.

16. Richard I. Henderson, *Compensation Management: Rewarding Performance,* 3d ed. (Reston, Va.: Reston Publishing, 1979), pp. 264–65.

17. P. Thompson and J. Pronsky, "Secrecy or Disclosure in Management Compensation," *Business Horizons,* June 1975, pp. 67–74.

18. E. E. Lawler III, "Manager's Perceptions of Their Superiors' Pay and Their Supervisors' Pay," *Personnel Psychology,* Winter 1965, p. 413; E. E. Lawler III, "Should Managers' Compensation Be Kept under Wraps?" *Personnel,* January–February 1965, p. 17.

19. Betty Southard Murphy, Wayne E. Barlow, and D. Diane Hatch, "Rule Against Discussion of Salaries Violates NLRA," *Personnel Journal,* December 1992, pp. 22.

20. Betty Southard Murphy, Wayne E. Barlow, and D. Diane Hatch, "Comparable Worth Claims Rejected," *Personnel Journal,* January 1990, pp. 14–18.

21. Ibid., p. 18, and Laura Pincis and Bill Shaw, "Comparable Worth: An Economic and Ethical Analysis," *Journal of Business Ethics,* April 1, 1998, pp. 455–70.

22. E. E. Lawler III, *Pay and Organizational Effectiveness: A Psychological View* (New York: McGraw-Hill, 1971), pp. 244–47.

Base Wage and Salary Systems

14

Learning Objectives

After studying this chapter, you should be able to:

1. Define base wages and salaries and state the objective of any base wage and salary system.
2. Define job evaluation.
3. Name and briefly discuss the four basic conventional methods of job evaluation.
4. Explain the concepts of key jobs and compensable factors.
5. Differentiate between subfactors and degrees.
6. Explain the purpose of wage and salary surveys.
7. Discuss wage and salary curves.
8. Define pay grades and pay ranges.
9. Explain the concepts of skill-based pay, competency-based pay, and broadbanding.

Base Wages and Salaries
Hourly, weekly, and monthly pay that employees receive for their work.

Base wages and salaries are the hourly, weekly, or monthly pay that employees receive in exchange for their work. In most situations, base wages or salaries make up the largest portion of an employee's total compensation. In light of the facts that many organizations do not pay incentives and many employees discount or take for granted the value of benefits, base wages and salaries are often the focus of the compensation system in the eyes of employees.

Base wages and salaries form the foundation for most employees' perceptions of the fairness, or equity, of the pay system. As discussed in the previous chapter, if employees do not perceive they are being fairly paid, many possible negative effects (tardiness, absenteeism, turnover, strikes, etc.) may result. In addition, the base wage and salary system often reflects the atmosphere of the entire organization. If the base wage and salary system is perceived as being fair and equitable, the organization is usually viewed in the same light. Of course, the reverse is also true. It is therefore critical that an organization develop and maintain a sound base wage and salary system.

Web site: JobSmart's
Salary Info

www.jobsmart.org/tools/
salary

Objective of the Base Wage and Salary System

The primary objective of any base wage and salary system is to establish a structure for the equitable compensation of employees, depending on their jobs and their level of performance in their jobs. While this objective is straightforward, successfully attaining it is not easy. Figure 14–1 represents some of the basic policy questions that need to be addressed as a first step in establishing a base wage and salary system.

Most base wage and salary systems establish pay ranges for certain jobs based on

FIGURE 14-1   **SPECIFIC POLICY ISSUES IN DEVELOPING AND IMPLEMENTING A BASE WAGE AND SALARY STRUCTURE**

1. What is the lowest rate of pay that can be offered for a job that will entice the quality of employees the organization desires to have as its members?

2. What is the rate of pay that must be offered to employees to ensure that they remain with the organization?

3. Does the organization desire to recognize seniority and meritorious performance through the base pay schedule?

4. Is it wise or necessary to offer more than one rate of pay to employees performing either identical or similar work?

5. What is considered to be a sufficient difference in base rates of pay among jobs requiring varying levels of knowledge and skills and of responsibilities and duties?

6. Does the organization wish to recognize dangerous and distressing working conditions within the base pay schedule?

7. Should there be a difference in base pay progression opportunities among jobs of varying worth?

8. Do employees have a significant opportunity to higher-level jobs? If so, what should be the relationship between promotion to a higher job and changes in base pay?

9. Will policies and regulations permit employees to earn rates of pay higher than established maximums and lower than established minimums? What would be the reasons for allowing such deviations?

10. How will the pay structure accommodate across-the-board, cost-of-living, or other adjustments not related to employee tenure, performance, or responsibility and duty changes?

Source: R. I. Henderson, *Compensation Management: Rewarding Performance,* 3rd ed. (Reston, Va.: Reston Publishing, 1979), pp. 264–65. Reprinted with permission of Reston Publishing Co., a Prentice Hall Co., 11480 Sunset Hills Road, Reston, VA 22090.

the relative worth of the job to the organization. An employee's pay performance on the same job should then determine where that employee's pay falls within the job's range. The key to a sound base wage and salary system is the establishment of different pay ranges for the various jobs within the organization. A pay range for a given job establishes a range of permissible pay, with a minimum and a maximum. Establishing pay ranges involves two basic phases: (1) determining the relative worth of the different jobs to the organization (ensuring internal equity) and (2) pricing the different jobs (ensuring external equity). Job evaluation is the primary method used to determine the relative worth of jobs to the organization. Wage surveys represent one of the most commonly used methods for pricing jobs. Conventional job evaluations and wage surveys, as well as some new approaches to both, are discussed in the following sections.

Conventional Job Evaluation

Job Evaluation Systematic determination of the value of each job in relation to other jobs in the organization.

Job evaluation is a systematic determination of the value of each job in relation to other jobs in the organization. This process is used for designing a pay structure, not for appraising the performance of employees holding the jobs. The general idea of job evaluation is to enumerate the requirements of a job and the job's contribution to the organization and then classify it according to its importance. For instance, a design engineer's job would involve more complex requirements and a potentially greater contribution to an organization than that of an assembler of the designed product. Although both jobs are important, a determination must be made concerning the relative worth of each. While the overriding purpose of job evaluation is to establish the relative worth of jobs, it can serve several other purposes. Figure 14–2 lists potential uses of job evaluations.

The first step in a job evaluation program is to gather information on the jobs being evaluated. Normally, information is obtained from current job descriptions. If current job descriptions do not exist, it is usually necessary to analyze the jobs and create up-to-date descriptions.

The job evaluation process then identifies the factor or factors to be used in determining the worth of different jobs to the organization. Some frequently used factors are knowledge, responsibility, and working conditions.

The job evaluation process also involves developing and implementing a plan that uses the chosen factors for evaluating the relative worth of the different jobs to the organization. Such a plan should consistently place jobs requiring more of the factors at a higher level in the job hierarchy than jobs requiring fewer of the factors. Most conventional job evaluation plans are variations or combinations of four basic methods: job ranking, job classification, point, and factor comparison.

Job Ranking Method

Job Ranking Method Job evaluation method that ranks jobs in order of their difficulty from simplest to most complex.

Job ranking is the simplest, oldest, and least often used job evaluation technique. In the **job ranking method,** the evaluator ranks jobs from the simplest to the most difficult. Often the evaluator prepares cards with basic information about the jobs and then arranges the cards in the order of importance of the positions. The job ranking method produces only an ordering of jobs and does not indicate the relative degree of difference among them. For example, a job with a ranking of four is not necessarily twice as difficult as a job with a ranking of two.

Job Classification Method

Job Classification Method Job evaluation method that determines the relative worth of a job by comparing it to a predetermined scale of classes or grades of jobs.

A second type of job evaluation plan is the **job classification method,** or *job grading.* Certain classes or grades of jobs are defined on the basis of differences in duties, responsibilities, skills, working conditions, and other job-related factors. The relative worth of a particular job is then determined by comparing its description with the description of each class and assigning the job to the appropriate class. This method has the advantage of simplicity, but is not always precise because it evaluates the job as a whole. The number of required classes or grades depends on the

---

F I G U R E   1 4 – 2   **POTENTIAL USES OF JOB EVALUATIONS**

- To provide a basis for a simpler, more rational wage structure.
- To provide an agreed-on means of classifying new or changed jobs.
- To provide a means of comparing jobs and pay rates with those of other organizations.
- To provide a base for employee performance measurements.
- To reduce pay grievances by reducing their scope and providing an agreed-on means of resolving disputes.
- To provide incentives for employees to strive for higher-level jobs.
- To provide information for wage negotiations.
- To provide data on job relationships for use in internal and external selection, human resource planning, career management, and other personnel functions.

range of skills, responsibilities, duties, and other requirements among the jobs being evaluated. Normally, 5 to 15 classes will suffice. Since 1949, the U.S. government has used the job classification method to evaluate all civil service jobs.

Point Method

Point Method Job evaluation method in which a quantitative point scale is used to evaluate jobs on a factor-by-factor basis.

Surveys have shown that the point method has historically been the most widely used job evaluation plan in the United States. It has the advantages of being relatively simple to use and reasonably objective. When the **point method** is used, a quantitative point scale is developed for the jobs being evaluated. One scale usually cannot be used to evaluate all types of jobs. For example, different scales are normally required for clerical and production jobs. Another scale is usually required to evaluate management and professional jobs. Usually the human resource department decides which jobs are to be included in a specific evaluation scale.

Selection of Key Jobs

After deciding which jobs are to be evaluated on each specific scale, key (benchmark) jobs are selected. Key jobs represent jobs that are common throughout the industry or in the general locale under study. The content of key jobs should be commonly understood. If there is any confusion about the description of a job or what its pay should be, it should probably not be selected as a key job. The general idea is to select a limited number (20 percent is a good guideline) of key jobs that are representative of the entire pay structure and the major kinds of work being evaluated.[1] The selection of key jobs should adequately represent the span of responsibilities, duties, and work requirements of the jobs being evaluated. Because key jobs usually represent only a small number of all jobs being evaluated, they may supply only a limited amount of data. However, the commonality and widespread acceptance of key jobs provide a basis for sound understanding and agreement. The goal here is to select enough key jobs to represent each major internal variable in the pay structure for all the jobs being evaluated. A full and detailed job description is necessary for each key job.

Selecting Compensable Factors

Compensable Factors Characteristics of jobs that are deemed important by the organization to the extent that it is willing to pay for them.

Compensable factors are those factors or characteristics of jobs that are deemed important by the organization to the extent that it is willing to pay for them. The degree to which a specific job possesses these compensable factors determines its relative worth.

Early approaches to job evaluation proposed a set of universal factors. The belief was that a given set of factors—usually skill, responsibility, and working conditions—should apply to all jobs. This theory has gradually been replaced by one postulating that each organization must tailor its compensable factors to fit its own special requirements. Thus, complete adoption of any set of universal factors is not recommended.[2] For example, the compensable factors selected for evaluating production jobs might include skill, effort, and working conditions, whereas the compensable factors selected for evaluating managerial and professional jobs might be knowledge, responsibility, and decision-making requirements. Compensable factors selected for unionized jobs must be acceptable to both management and the union.

Job Subfactor Detailed breakdown of a single compensable factor of a job.

Degree Statements Written statements used as a part of the point method of job evaluation to further break down job subfactors.

In the point method, **job subfactors** are used to describe compensable factors in more detail. For instance, the compensable factor of responsibility might include subfactors for determining organizational policy, responsibility for the work of others, responsibility for the development and maintenance of customer goodwill, or responsibility for organizational assets. **Degree statements,** or *profile statements* as they are sometimes called, describe the specific requirements of each subfactor. Degree statements are in the form of written phrases. Table 14–1 presents possible degrees and subfactors for the compensable factor of responsibility. Breaking compensable factors into subfactors and degrees allows for a more precise definition of the job and facilitates the evaluation process.

TABLE 14-1	**POSSIBLE SUBFACTORS AND DEGREES FOR THE COMPENSABLE FACTORS OF RESPONSIBILITY, WITH SAMPLE JOBS**			
Subfactors	**First Degree (Junior Customer Service Representative)**	**Second Degree (Customer Service Representative)**	**Third Degree (Senior Customer Service Representative)**	**Fourth Degree (Sales/Service Manager)**
Determining organizational policy	May make suggestions to superior as to changes, most often minor, in organizational policy.	Often suggests changes in procedures applying mostly to affairs within departments.	May determine minor policies of organization with close control of supervisors; may interpret organizational policy to subordinates.	Determines organizational policy for large group of employees; incorrect execution would result in considerable loss.
Work of others; managerial ability required	Responsible only for own work, including individual work or work of "flow" nature.	Small amount of supervision; performs mechanical operations and may control some work.	Supervises many employees or a department, organizing and coordinating with other supervisors.	Responsible for coordination of groups of departments.
Development and maintenance of goodwill with customers and public	Has very little contact with customers or public.	Only contact with customers and public is checked through communications or occasional telephone calls.	Tact needed to avoid possible loss of goodwill through close contact with customers via letters or personal interviews.	Considerable contact with customers, other organizations, and public; tact and diplomacy needed.
Organization cash expenditures; judgment needed in expenditures of organization funds	Cash expenditures of not more than $100 monthly.	Cash expenditures of $101 to $300 monthly.	Cash expenditures of $301 to $1,000 monthly.	Cash expenditures of $1,001 to $5,000 monthly.

Source: Adapted from J. L. Otis and R. H. Leukart, *Job Evaluation*, 2nd ed. (Englewood Cliffs, N.J.: Prentice Hall, 1959), pp. 110–11.

Assigning Weights to Factors

Weights are assigned to each of the factors, subfactors, and degrees to reflect their relative importance. Naturally, the weight assigned varies from job to job. For example, skill might be the most important factor used in evaluating a machinist's job, while responsibility might be more critical to a supervisor's job.

While some systematic and helpful approaches exist for assigning weights, there is no one best method. Regardless of the technique used, both past experience and judgment play major roles in assigning weights. Generally, weights are assigned on the basis of a maximum number of points for any job; this number is often decided arbitrarily. Points are then assigned to the compensable factors, subfactors, and degrees on the basis of their relative importance. Table 14–2 presents a possible point breakdown that totals 1,000 points. In this example, the compensable factor of responsibility was deemed to be the most important factor and was awarded 360 points. The factor of responsibility was divided into four subfactors: responsibility for organizational policy, responsibility for the work of others, responsibility for goodwill and public relations, and responsibility for organizational cash expenditures. Each subfactor was further divided into four degrees. Note that the sum of the points for the highest degree for each of the subfactors totals the maximum number of points for the factor. In Table 14–2, 80 points for company policy plus 160 points for the work of others plus 80 points for goodwill and public relations plus 40 points for company cash equals 360 total points.

TABLE 14–2   **SAMPLE POINT VALUES**

Compensable Factor	Maximum Points	Subfactors	Assigned Points per Degree			
			First	Second	Third	Fourth
Skill	260	Job knowledge	35	70	105	140
		Experience	20	40	60	80
		Initiative	10	20	30	40
Effort	240	Physical	20	40	60	80
		Mental	40	80	120	160
Responsibility	360	For company policy	20	40	60	80
		For work of others	40	80	120	160
		For goodwill with customers and public	20	40	60	80
		For company cash	10	20	30	40
Job conditions	140	Working conditions	20	40	60	80
		Hazards	15	30	45	60
Total possible points	1,000					

Assigning Points to Specific Jobs

After the point scale has been agreed on, point values are derived for key jobs using the following steps:

1. Examine the job descriptions.
2. Determine the degree statement that best describes each subfactor for each compensable factor.
3. Add the total number of points.

The point totals should present the same general relationships that the actual pay scales show for the key jobs. That is, a rank ordering of the key jobs according to point totals should be approximately equivalent to a rank ordering of key jobs according to pay. This serves as a check on the appropriateness of the points that have been assigned to the degrees, subfactors, and factors. Nonkey jobs can then be evaluated in the same manner by determining the appropriate points for each factor from the scale and then totaling the points. Table 14–3 illustrates possible point totals for several banking jobs.

One drawback of the point method is the amount of time required to develop the point scale. However, once a scale has been properly formulated for the key jobs, it does not take long to evaluate the remaining jobs. Also, efforts should always be made to keep the system simple and easily understood by employees. HRM in Action 14.1 discusses how Bayer Corporation redesigned its point method system to reflect new values of the company.

Factor Comparison Method

Factor Comparison Method Job evaluation technique that uses a monetary scale for evaluating jobs on a factor-by-factor basis.

Eugene Benge originated the factor comparison method of job evaluation in 1926 to overcome the inadequacies that he perceived in the point method.[3] The **factor comparison method** is similar to the point method except that it involves a monetary scale instead of a point scale. As with the point method, key jobs are selected. It is absolutely essential that the rates of pay of key jobs be viewed as reasonable and fair to all those making evaluations. Compensable factors are then identified, just as with the point method.

POSSIBLE POINT TOTALS FOR KEY BANKING JOBS

Job	Points
Head teller	980
Loan teller	900
Teller	870
Secretary	750
Vault custodian	650
Courier	500

Unlike the point method, however, the factor comparison method does not break down the compensable factors into subfactors and degrees. Another difference between the two techniques involves the ranking of the compensable factors. In the factor comparison method, each compensable factor is ranked according to its importance in each key job. This is done by assigning a rank to every key job on one factor at a time rather than ranking one job at a time on all factors. For example, Table 14–4 gives a factor-by-factor ranking of key jobs within a bank. Notice how each key job is ranked for each compensable factor. Many proponents of the factor comparison method suggest that to validate the rankings, they should be done once or twice at later dates without reference to the previous rankings.

After each key job has been ranked on a factor-by-factor basis, the next step is to

---

HRM   IN   ACTION

Company Values and Job Evaluation at Bayer Corporation

14.1

www.bayer.com

Bayer Corporation, headquarters in Pittsburgh, Pennsylvania, is the largest subsidiary of the Bayer Group AG, based in Leverbusen, Germany. Currently Bayer Corporation has approximately 24,000 employees in the United States. In 1992, Bayer Corporation merged three businesses into one. Following the merger, senior management began developing a new set of corporate values focusing on customer loyalty, quality, and productivity. Senior management set out to send a clear message to employees: the key to a successful career at Bayer is to embrace the company's new values. Bayer's leaders knew that one way to get employees focused on the new values was to reflect them in the processes used to assess each job.

Prior to the merger, two of the three companies used a point-based job evaluation system. The third company used a much less formal method for evaluating its job. Realizing that a consistent job evaluation process was needed, a task force of senior managers was appointed to study the problem and come up with a recommendation. After evaluating several options, the task force recommended that the point system previously used by two of the three companies be redesigned so that more of the future values were reflected in the factors used to evaluate the jobs. The following factors were selected to be used: improvement opportunity, contribution, capability, expertise and complexity, leadership and integration, and relationship-building skills. The major differences between the new factors and the old is that the new factors place more emphasis on expected behaviors and outcomes instead of inputs and credentials. Bayer's top management believes that not only do they now have a single, consistent method for evaluating jobs but that the system clearly communicates and supports the company's new values.

Source: Jennifer J. Laabs, "Rating Jobs against New Values," *Workforce,* May 1997, pp. 38–49.

TABLE 14–4   **FACTOR-BY-FACTOR RANKING OF KEY BANKING JOBS**

	Compensable Factor				
Job	Mental Requirements	Skill	Physical	Responsibility	Working Conditions
Head teller	1	4	6	1	6
Loan teller	2	1	4	2	3
Teller	3	2	3	3	2
Secretary	4	3	5	5	5
Vault custodian	5	5	2	4	4
Courier	6	6	1	6	1

allocate the wage or salary for each job according to the ranking of the factors. It is important to remember that one of the selection criteria of a key job is that its pay rate must be viewed as reasonable and fair by the evaluators. Some proponents of the factor comparison method say that the pay should be allocated without reference to the factor rankings; others believe the evaluators should refer to the factor rankings when apportioning the pay. Regardless, the money allocation and the factor rankings must ultimately be consistent. If discrepancies occur that cannot be resolved, the job in question should be eliminated from the list of key jobs. Table 14–5 presents a sample pay allocation for the key jobs in Table 14–4. Notice how the figures for each column in Table 14–5 are consistent with the rankings for each column in Table 14–4.

As the final step in the factor comparison method, a monetary scale is prepared for each compensable factor. Each scale not only shows the rank order of the jobs but also establishes their relative differences in pay. Table 14–6 illustrates a monetary scale for the compensable factor of responsibility for banking jobs.

Other jobs are evaluated by studying their respective job descriptions and locating each job on the monetary scale for each compensable factor. The total worth of a given job is then determined by adding the dollar amounts assigned to each compensable factor.

Comparison of Job Evaluation Methods

The point and factor comparison methods are commonly referred to as *quantitative* plans because a number or dollar value is ultimately assigned to each job being

TABLE 14–5   **SAMPLE ALLOCATION PAY FOR KEY BANKING JOBS**

	Compensable Factor				
Job	Mental Requirements	Skill	Physical	Responsibility	Working Conditions
Head teller	$190.00	$59.00	$23.00	$113.00	$18.00
Loan teller	152.00	69.00	50.00	90.00	29.00
Teller	145.00	68.00	59.00	77.00	32.00
Secretary	138.00	66.00	27.00	45.00	23.00
Vault custodian	97.00	32.00	90.00	54.00	24.00
Courier	70.00	24.00	107.00	12.00	41.00

MONETARY SCALE FOR RESPONSIBILITY REQUIREMENTS IN BANKING JOBS

Monetary Value/Week	Key Job	Monetary Value/Week	Key Job
$ 9.00			
12.00	Courier	$ 63.00	
18.00		67.00	
22.50		72.00	
		77.00	Teller
31.50		81.00	
36.00		85.50	
40.50		90.00	Loan teller
45.00	Secretary	94.50	
49.50		99.00	
54.00	Vault custodian	103.50	
58.50		108.00	
		113.00	Head teller

evaluated. Numbers or dollars are assigned on the basis of the degree to which the job contains the predetermined compensable factors. The job classification and ranking methods, called *qualitative* or *nonquantitative techniques,* compare whole jobs. The point system and the job classification system have a common feature in that they evaluate jobs against a predetermined scale or class, whereas the factor comparison and job ranking methods evaluate jobs only in comparison to the other positions in the organization. Table 14–7 summarizes the advantages and disadvantages of each job evaluation method. HRM in Action 14.2 discusses the results of a British survey relating to the use of job evaluation.

Pricing the Job

The factor comparison method of evaluation is the only conventional technique that relates the worth of jobs to a monetary scale; even then, the results are derived primarily from the wage scale the organization currently uses. In general, job evaluation cannot be used to set the wage rate; however, it provides the basis for this determination. To ensure that external factors such as labor market conditions, prevailing wage rates, and living costs are recognized in the wage scale, information about these factors must be gathered.

Wage and Salary Surveys

Wage and Salary Survey
Survey of selected organizations within a geographical area or industry designed to provide a comparison of reliable information on policies, practices, and methods of payment.

Wage and salary surveys are used to collect comparative information on the policies, practices, and methods of wage payment from selected organizations in a given geographic location or particular type of industry. In addition to providing knowledge of the market and ensuring external equity, wage surveys can correct employee misconceptions about certain jobs. They can also have a positive impact on employee motivation.[4]

Wage or salary survey information can be obtained in two basic ways: (1) conducting your own survey or (2) purchasing or accessing a wage/salary survey undertaken by another party.

Conducting a Wage/Salary Survey

To design a wage survey, the jobs, organizations, and area to be studied must be determined, as must the method for gathering data. If the wage survey is done in

TABLE 14-7	ADVANTAGES AND DISADVANTAGES OF DIFFERENT JOB EVALUATION METHODS	
	Major Advantages	**Major Disadvantages**
Job ranking method	1. It is fast and easy to complete. 2. Because it can usually be done in hours, it is relatively inexpensive. 3. It is easy to explain.	1. It is limited to smaller organizations where employees are very familiar with various jobs. 2. This method assumes equal intervals between the rankings, and this is usually not true. 3. The method is highly subjective.
Job classification method	1. Because it has been used by federal, state, and local governments for years, it is readily accepted by employees. 2. It is readily adaptable to very large organizations with many offices that are geographically dispersed. 3. Because the classifications are broad and not specific, the system can last for years without substantial change.	1. The classification descriptions are so broad that they do not relate to specific jobs; this causes employees to question the grades of their respective jobs. 2. Because of the broad and general classifications, job evaluators may abuse the system.
Point method	1. It is detailed and specific—jobs are evaluated on a component basis and compared against a predetermined scale. 2. Employees generally accept this method because of its mathematical nature. 3. The system is easy to keep current as jobs change. 4. Because of its quantitative nature, it is easy to assign monetary values to jobs.	1. It is relatively time-consuming and costly to develop. 2. It requires significant interaction and decision making by the different parties involved in conducting the job evaluations.
Factor comparison method	1. It is relatively detailed and specific—jobs are evaluated on a component basis and compared against other jobs. 2. It is usually easier to develop than the point method. 3. It is tied to external market wage rates.	1. It is relatively difficult to explain to employees. 2. It is not easily adapted to changes in the jobs being evaluated.

conjunction with either the point or factor comparison method or job evaluation, the key jobs selected are normally the ones that are surveyed. A good rule of thumb is that a minimum of 30 percent of the jobs in an organization should be surveyed to make a fair evaluation of the organization's pay system.[5] When using the classification or ranking method, the organization should apply the same guidelines followed for selecting jobs with the point and factor comparison methods in choosing the jobs to be surveyed.

A geographic area, an industry type, or a combination of the two may be surveyed. The size of the geographic area, the cost-of-living index for the area, and similar factors must be considered when defining the scope of the survey. The organizations to be surveyed are normally competitors or companies that employ similar types of employees. When they are willing to cooperate, it is often desirable to survey the most important and most respected organizations in the area.

Web site: Salary Survey Data

www.wageweb.com

The three traditional methods of surveying wage data are personal interviews, telephone interviews, and mailed questionnaires. The most reliable and most expensive method is the personal interview. Mailed questionnaires are probably used

---

HRM IN ACTION

Uses of Job Evaluation in Britain

14.2

A recent survey of 316 British organizations suggests that job evaluation is widely used among the responding organizations. Of those organizations responding, 55 percent use some type of formal job evaluation system. Of those not currently using some type of formal job evaluation system, 22 percent intend to introduce one in the future. Most of the criticisms leveled against the conventional forms of job evaluation center around their flexibility in coping with professional and managerial employees, teamworking, and flatter organizational structures.

Among the responding organizations that do use a formal job evaluation system, the following statistics were reported:

- 29 percent use a point system.
- 21 percent use a job classification system.
- 11 percent use a factor comparison system.
- 68 percent use some type of proprietary job evaluation system.
- 66 percent are reasonably satisfied with the system they use.
- 21 percent expressed some dissatisfaction with their current system.
- 43 percent plan to make changes to their system in the future.

A more recent survey, reported in 1997, found that the proportion of organizations in the United Kingdom with formal job evaluation programs had increased significantly over the previous five years.

Source: Michael Armstrong, "Measuring Work: The Vital Statistics," *People Management,* September 21, 1995, pp. 34–35, and "Growth in Job Evaluation Schemes," *IRS Employment Review,* January 1997, p. ET7.

---

most frequently. However, mailed questionnaires should be used only to survey jobs that have a uniform meaning throughout the industry. If there is any doubt concerning the definition of a job, the responses to a mailed questionnaire may be unreliable. Another potential problem with mailed questionnaires is that they can be answered by someone who is not thoroughly familiar with the wage structure. The telephone method, which is quick but often yields incomplete information, may be used to clarify responses to mailed questionnaires.

The Internet represents the latest technology for conducting wage/salary surveys. The benefits of using the Internet are that it is inexpensive and quick. The major disadvantage of using the Internet is that all companies are not Internet-active and therefore are not reachable on the Internet. Figure 14–3 lists some topics that might be covered in a wage/salary survey.

Purchasing or Accessing Wage/Salary Surveys

Wage survey data can be purchased or accessed from a variety of sources. Since the early 1950s, consulting firms such as William Mercer, Watson Wyatt, and Coopers & Lybrand have sold compensation surveys; however, these surveys are usually relatively expensive.[6]

The Bureau of Labor Statistics of the U.S. Department of Labor, state and local governments, trade associations, and chambers of commerce are all potential sources for relatively inexpensive wage/salary surveys. Also a number of wage/salary surveys and other survey information are available on the Internet. Surveys available on the Internet fall into two broad categories: (1) surveys conducted by the federal government, and (2) surveys conducted by private research organizations, professional associations, employees' associations, and consulting firms.[7] Figure 14–4 lists a sample of some different web sites for obtaining wage/salary survey data.

FIGURE 14-3   **POSSIBLE TOPICS IN A WAGE SURVEY**

Length of workday	Vacation practices
Normal workweek duration	Holiday practices
Starting wage rates	Cost-of-living clauses
Base wage rates	Where paid
Pay ranges	How often paid
Incentive plans	Policy on wage garnishment
Shift differentials	Description of union contract
Overtime pay	

Pitfalls and Guidelines

Wage and salary surveys can be quite helpful if conducted and interpreted properly. If not done properly, they can yield very distorted and inaccurate information and are often the subject of much criticism centering on the following points.

- Too many surveys are being conducted.
- The quality of the resultant data is often questionable.
- Survey data are often difficult to interpret and use.
- Survey data can have a negative impact on merit pay plans.
- The use of such data can help fuel inflation.[8]

Figure 14–5 summarizes specific problems often associated with wage and salary surveys. Regardless of the type of survey used, the following guidelines should be followed to avoid problems:

1. *Assess the participating companies for comparability.* Not only should factors such as size and type of business be considered; intangibles, such as prestige, security, growth opportunity, and location, are also important.
2. *Compare more than base wage or salary.* The total compensation package, including incentives and benefits, should be considered. For example, a company might provide few benefits but compensate for this with high base wages and salaries.
3. *Consider variations in job descriptions.* The most widely acknowledged shortcoming of wage and salary surveys is that it is difficult to find jobs that are directly comparable. Usually more information than a brief job description is needed to properly match jobs in a survey.
4. *Correlate survey data with adjustment periods.* How recently wages and salaries were adjusted before the survey affects the accuracy of the data. Some companies may have just made adjustments, while others may not.[9]

FIGURE 14-4   **SAMPLE OF WEB SITES FOR WAGE/SALARY SURVEY DATA**

The U.S. Department of Labor	*http://www.dol.gov*
The U.S. Department of Labor, Bureau of Labor Statistics Home Page	*http://www.bls.gov*
The American Compensation Association	*http://www.acaonline.org*
The AFL-CIO Executive Pay Watch	*http://www.aflcio.paywatch.org*
Job Search Guide offering Links to more than 150 salary surveys	*http://jobsmart.org/tools/salary/index.html*

Source: Fay Hansen, "Guide to Salary Survey Data on the Web," *Compensation & Benefits Review,* March/April 1998, pp. 16–20.

FIGURE 14–5   **PROBLEMS ENCOUNTERED WHEN USING SALARY SURVEY DATA**

Job categories too broad or imprecise.

Industry categories too broad or imprecise.

Unadjusted for major benefits.

Salary categories too broad or imprecise.

Company type/size difficult to relate to own.

Out-of-date or undated data.

Samples of firms unrepresentative.

Samples of firms too small.

Survey based on unemployed and/or job seekers.

Survey too broad or imprecise in other ways.

Source: Adapted from "Executive Remuneration and Benefits Survey Report," John Courtis and Partners, 1980; as reported in Joan C. O'Brien and Robert A. Zawacki, "Salary Surveys: Are They Worth the Effort?" *Personnel,* October 1985, p. 73.

Comparable worth theory, which was discussed in Chapters 4 and 13, holds that every job should be compensated on the basis of its value to the employer and society. In this theory, factors such as availability of qualified employees and wage rates paid by other employers should be disregarded. Under the comparable worth theory, wage surveys would have no value. However, as discussed in Chapter 4, the Ninth Circuit Court of Appeals has ruled that the value of a particular job to an employer is only one of many factors that should influence the rate of compensation for that job.

Wage and Salary Curves

Wage and Salary Curves Graphical depiction of the relationship between the relative worth of jobs and their wage rates.

Wage and salary curves graphically show the relationship between the relative worth of jobs and their wage or salary rates. In addition, these curves can be used to indicate pay classes and ranges for the jobs. Regardless of the job evaluation method used, a wage curve plots the jobs in ascending order of difficulty along the abscissa (x-axis) and the wage rate along the ordinate (y-axis). If the point method is used for evaluation, the point totals are plotted against their corresponding wage rates, as shown in Figure 14–6, to produce a general trend.

To ensure that the final wage structure is consistent with both the job evaluations and the wage survey data, it is sometimes desirable to construct one wage curve based on present wages and one based on the survey data and compare the two. Any discrepancies can be quickly detected and corrected. Points of the graph that do not follow the general trend indicate that the wage rate for that job is too low or too high or that the job has been inaccurately evaluated. Underpaid jobs are sometimes called *green-circle* jobs; when wages are overly high, the positions are known as *red-circle* jobs. These discrepancies can be remedied by granting above- or below-average pay increases for the jobs in question.

Pay Grades and Ranges

Pay Grades Classes or grades of jobs that for pay purposes are grouped on the basis of their worth to an organization.

Pay Range Range of permissible pay, with a

To simplify the administration of a wage structure, jobs of similar worth are often grouped into classes, or **pay grades,** for pay purposes. If the point method is used for evaluating jobs, classes are normally defined within a certain point spread. Similarly, a money spread can be used for defining grades if the factor comparison method is used. Table 14–8 illustrates how grades might be defined for the jobs shown in Figure 14–6.

Usually, at the same time pay grades are established, **pay ranges** are determined for each grade. When this is done, each pay grade is assigned a range of permissible pay, with a minimum and a maximum. The maximum of a pay grade's range places

FIGURE 14–6   **WAGE CURVE USING THE POINT METHOD**

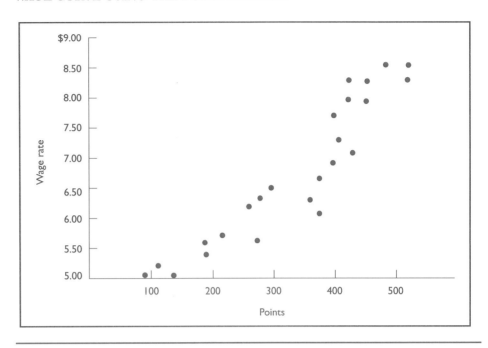

minimum and a maximum, that is assigned to a given pay grade.

a ceiling on the rate that can be paid to any employee whose job is classified in that grade. Similarly, the minimum of the pay grade's range places a floor on the rate that can be paid. Two general approaches for establishing pay grades and ranges are to have a relatively large number of grades with identical rates of pay for all jobs within each grade and to have a small number of grades with a relatively wide dollar range for each grade. Most pay structures fall somewhere between these extremes.

Ranges within grades are set up so that distinctions can be made among employees within grades. Ideally, the placement of employees within pay grades should be based on performance or merit. In practice, however, the distinction is often based solely on seniority. Figure 14–7 illustrates how pay ranges might be structured for the jobs in Figure 14–6.

On reaching the top of the range for a given grade, an employee can increase his or her pay only by moving to a higher grade. As shown in Figure 14–7, it is not unusual for the ranges of adjacent pay grades to overlap. Under such circumstances, it is possible for an outstanding performer in a lower grade to earn a higher salary than a below-average performer in a higher grade.

Base Wage/Salary Structure

Figure 14–8 illustrates how the various segments of the compensation process fit together to establish the base wage or salary structure for an organization.

TABLE 14–8   **ESTABLISHING WAGE GRADES**

Grade	Point Range	Grade	Point Range
1	0–150	4	351–450
2	151–250	5	451–550
3	251–350		

FIGURE 14-7   **ESTABLISHMENT OF PAY GRADES WITH RANGES**

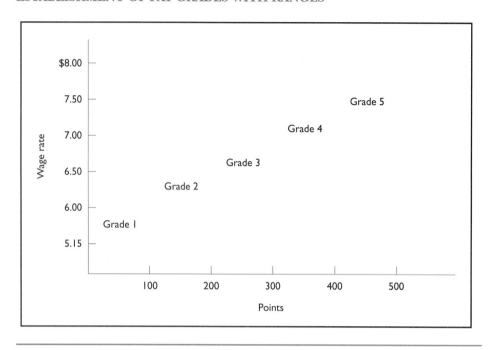

Compensation prices are shown on all sides of the figure to emphasize the fact that each step in the process is influenced by the organization's current compensation policies. Ideally, an organization's compensation system should produce a base wage/salary structure that is both internally and externally equitable. The job evaluation process should ensure internal equity, while wage surveys should ensure external equity. The performance appraisal process, discussed in Chapter 12, is then used to position an individual employee within the established range.

New Approaches to the Base Wage/Salary Structure

Several new perspectives and approaches to determining the base pay system have evolved over the last several years. This section describes three of the most popular of these approaches.

Skill-Based Pay[10]

As described previously in this chapter, conventional base pay systems compensate employees based on the work required to do a specific job as determined by job evaluations. Mike Guthman, a partner with Hewitt Associates (a compensation/benefits consulting firm), describes conventional base pay systems in the following manner: "In the past, everything revolved around jobs. We grouped tasks, called it a job, evaluated it, put it in a salary grade and the job was unchanging. People would do that job, progress and move on to another one, but the job would stay where it was."[11]

Many people believe narrowly defined job descriptions and pay scales that worked well in yesterday's industrial workplace do not work any longer. The emphasis today is on shifting toward how well individuals perform as opposed to how well their jobs are defined. Downsizing and the reduction of middle management

FIGURE 14–8   DEVELOPING THE BASE WAGE SALARY STRUCTURE

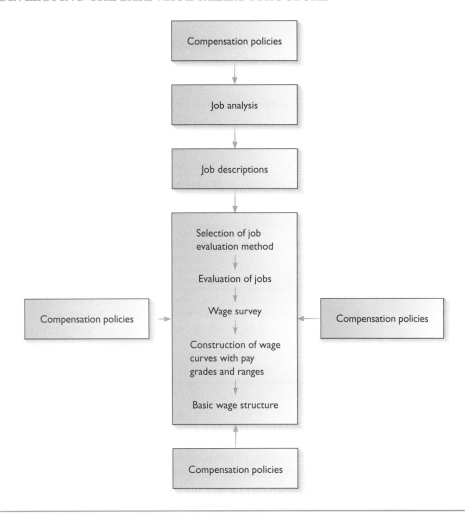

Skill-Based Pay Systems
Systems that compensate employees for the skills they bring to the job.

have resulted in fewer promotional opportunities for employees. To retain good employees, jobs must allow room for growth and employees must be motivated by things other than job titles. Skill-based pay (also known as *knowledge-based pay*) is one rapidly growing approach for achieving this. Skill-based pay systems compensate employees for the skills they bring to the job. Specifically, these pay systems pay employees for their range of knowledge, the number of business-related skills mastered, the level of those skills or knowledge, or some combination of level and range.

Under a typical skill-based system, companies hire employees at below-market rates. As employees gain skills and knowledge, their levels of base pay increase. In general, employees are expected to learn between 5 and 10 skills over a two- to five-year period. Of course, the number of skill levels and the time required vary from organization to organization. In a conventional job-based pay system, employees must wait for a job opening before they can be promoted. Under a skill-based pay system, employees are eligible for a pay increase when they have learned a new skill and demonstrated they can progress another step. Table 14–9 lists the potential benefits of a skill-based system.

The attractive list of potential benefits listed in Table 14–9 must be weighed against several potential concerns. Increased labor costs, topped-out employees, false expectations, and union agreements are some of the more frequently mentioned potential concerns. Direct labor and training costs do often rise. However,

T A B L E   1 4 – 9   **POTENTIAL BENEFITS OF A SKILL-BASED PAY SYSTEM**

Fits work force values

Increases staffing flexibility

Builds leaner staffing requirements

Encourages flatter organizational structure

Inspires higher quality and quantity productivity levels

Broadens incentives to increase knowledge and skills

Reinforces group participation

Deepens commitment when promotions are unavailable

Decreases overall labor costs

Improves understanding of operation

Greater productivity

Favorable quality outcomes

Scrap reduction

Source: Earl Ingram II, "The Advantages of Knowledge-Based Pay," *Personnel Journal,* April 1990, p. 138, and Brian Murray and Barry Gerhart, "An Empirical Analysis of a Skill-Based Pay Program and Plant Performance," *Academy of Management Journal,* February 1998, pp. 68–78.

they are usually offset by a reduced labor force and therefore lower total labor costs. Topped-out employees are those who have nowhere else to go. The issue of topped-out employees is not new to managers and arises in most organizations regardless of the pay system used. One option is to expose topped-out employees to broader jobs in other departments. The problems of false expectations occur when there are no vacancies in the job areas for which employees have been newly trained. The key is to be realistic about the current or near-term future needs of the organization. Unrealistic expectations can even lead to increased turnover as employees become disillusioned. It is generally recognized that skill-based pay systems do not work well in unionized organizations whose pay systems are based largely on seniority.

The American Compensation Association reports that skill-based pay is one of the fastest-growing concepts in the United States.[12] The percentage of Fortune 1000 companies using some form of skill-based pay increased from 40 percent in 1987 to 60 percent in 1993.[13] In a mid-1990s study of 97 skill-based pay plans, three-quarters or more of the respondents reported that the plans increased employee productivity, motivation, flexibility to adapt to changing production needs, and work team effectiveness.[14] The same respondents also reported enhanced recruitment and retention while reducing labor costs. HRM in Action 14.3 describes a skill-based pay system implemented by the city of Englewood, Colorado.

Most skill-based pay systems have focused on nonexempt employees working in manufacturing environments. This is primarily because it is relatively easy to identify and measure the skill sets needed by direct-labor employees. However, currently a movement is under way to extend the skills-based pay approach to professionals and managers. The result of this movement is called *competency-based pay.*

Competency-Based Pay

A *competency* is defined as "a trait or a characteristic that's required by a job holder to perform that job well."[15] A similar definition is "demonstrable characteristics of the person, including knowledge, skills, and behaviors, that enable performance."[16]

HRM IN ACTION

A Skill-Based Pay System in City Government

14.3

In 1990 the city of Englewood, Colorado, developed a skill-based pay system called "Creating Opportunities to Excel." To develop the plan, the administrative service staff of Englewood first developed a strategy outline that included (1) updating all job descriptions; (2) updating and verifying each job position's current salary; (3) defining the base job requirements, identifying the necessary skills, and assigning percentages to their importance; and (4) formulating career development plans.

Three steps were followed in implementing the strategy outline. The first step developed a new payline by determining the skill base for jobs and then assigning monetary values to each skill category. The second step established an individualized career development program for employees. The third step gave employees a choice as to whether or not they would participate in the plan.

Monica Lopez, human resource administrator for the city, says the program has improved communication between employees and management. Other benefits outlined by Lopez include higher individual satisfaction, better-defined personal and professional goals, increased employee empowerment, and cost effectiveness.

Source: Bill Leonard, "Creating Opportunities to Excel," *HR Magazine,* February 1995, pp. 47–51.

An employer interested in a competency-based pay system in a sales organization, for example, would examine the most successful salespeople in the organization and learn what it is that those people do well.[17] The identified elements might be managing accounts, conducting competitive research, or making good technical presentations. Once the elements for predicting sales success have been identified, they are categorized as competencies. All salespeople will then be compensated based on how well they demonstrated these identified competencies.

Figure 14–9 outlines the key design choices that must be made when developing a competency-based pay system. The process involves choosing between opposing design dimensions in the eight key areas shown. Competency-based pay is intuitively compelling in that it makes sense to put money behind those things the organization values.[18] A major problem with competency-based pay is that it can be

FIGURE 14–9   **DESIGNING COMPETENCY-BASED PAY**

Competency-based pay plans consist of eight key dimensions. Each of these dimensions offers two basic—and polar opposite—design choices. The choices in the left hand columns are most similar to traditional pay systems, while those in the right are more novel.

Narrow ← →	Generic
Existing ← →	Novel
Bottom-up ← →	Top-down
Complex, precise ← →	Elegant, nimble
Observable ← →	Abstract
Enduring value ← →	Temporary value
Permanent annuity ← →	One-time bonus
Marketplace value ← →	Strategic value

Source: Gerald E. Ledford, Jr., "Paying for the Skills, Knowledge and Competencies of Knowledge Work," *Compensation & Benefits Review,* July–August 1995, p. 58.

**Competency-Based
Pay at ACS**

14.4

www.acs.org/

The American Chemical Society (ACS) is the world's largest scientific society. It is a nonprofit educational and scientific organization with more than 150,000 chemical scientists and engineers as members. ACS is also one of the largest publishers of scientific information in the world and is highly regarded by professionals in industry, academia, and government.

Top management made a commitment to continuous improvement in the design, development, and delivery of leading-edge products and services to the society's membership. After identifying what skills and competencies its employees would need to implement this new commitment, the HR team concluded that ACS should make some adjustments in its compensation program. Initial assessment revealed that the current compensation program was sending the wrong message to employees. The HR team concluded that the compensation program should: (1) emphasize results and the value of contributions and de-emphasize the job hierarchy as the basis for reward and recognition programs; (2) emphasize adding value and de-emphasize the importance of job tenure as a value attribute; and (3) emphasize career development built on the acquisition and application of knowledge and skills, and de-emphasize equating career development with upward movement.

ACS has subsequently implemented a competency-based compensation system which the company believes will reinforce the competencies necessary to create a win/win situation for the society and its employees.

Source: Henry Jahja and Brian H. Kleiner, "Competency-Based Pay in the Manufacturing and Service Sectors," *Industrial Management,* September/October 1997, pp. 24–27.

---

difficult to measure when a competency has been mastered and is being demonstrated.[19] Currently, competency-based pay systems are not widely used, but their use is growing. HRM in Action 14.4 describes why the American Chemical Society implemented a competency-based pay system.

Broadbanding

Broadbanding A base-pay technique that reduces many different salary categories to several broad salary bands.

Broadbanding is "a base-pay technique that reduces many different salary categories to several broad salary bands."[20] Put another way, broadbanding is "the elimination of all but a few—3 to 10—comprehensive salary and job classifications.[21] In essence, broadbanding results in the clustering of jobs into wide categories or groups of jobs. The bands usually have minimum and maximum dollar amounts that overlap and an average width of 130 percent of the minimum.[22] For example, Band 1 may cover technicians from $33,000 to $74,000 and Band 2 may cover $60,000 to $140,000. Under broadbanding, a company with a conventional compensation system might have 30 salary ranges, each with a different job title. Under a banded system, these 30 ranges might be reduced to six bands with wider salary ranges and no job titles.

Major advantages of broadbanding are that managers have more autonomy in setting pay rates and it becomes easier to move employees around in the organization because broadbanding eliminates unnecessary distinctions among jobs.[23] This second advantage is especially important in today's organizations, which are flatter and have reduced promotional opportunities. Under conventional systems, employees are reluctant to take a lateral move or a downgrade even if doing so would be the best thing for their careers and for the company. Broadbanding can help overcome this reluctance. In addition, broadbanding can help improve communication teamwork by eliminating many of the frequent barriers to communication

---

HRM IN ACTION

Broadbanding at SNET

14.5

www.snet.com

Southern New England Telecommunications Corporation (SNET), based in New Haven, Connecticut, developed a broadbanding plan in 1996 and introduced it in 1997. The impetus for implementing broadbanding was to get away from the long-standing system of separate pay structures in favor of having one plan throughout the company.

"With the number of pay grades we had, people were constantly focused on the job the next step up," says Amy Moquet, VP of performance, rewards, and benefits at SNET. "We wanted people to focus less on what was going on internally and more on external customers. And we wanted people to be less hierarchical in their thinking, so we needed a flatter organization."

As a result of broadbanding, SNET reduced over 50 separate pay grades to just three overlapping bands. "Broadbanding gave us a common base of all our jobs throughout the company; it facilitated movement within the company and took attention off the minute differences between jobs," Moquet says. "It linked performance management, the compensation structure, and technical competencies—all leading toward career-development discussions."

As a part of implementing broadbanding, SNET revamped its performance-evaluation forms and process to focus more on goals, competencies, and technical skills.

Source: Matthew Budman, "How It Works: Practice at Three Companies," *Across The Board,* June 1998, pp. 26–27.

---

and development, namely, level, title, and status.[24] HRM in Action 14.5 discusses a broadbanded pay system implemented by Southern New England Telecommunications Corporation.

SUMMARY OF LEARNING OBJECTIVES

1. **Define base wages and salaries and state the objective of any base wage and salary system.**
   Base wages and salaries are the hourly, weekly, or monthly pay that employees receive in exchange for their work. The primary objective of any base wage and salary system is to establish a structure for the equitable payment of employees based on their jobs and their levels of job performance.

2. **Define job evaluation.**
   Job evaluation is a systematic determination of the value of each job in relation to other jobs in the organization.

3. **Name and briefly discuss the four basic conventional methods of job evaluation.**
   Most conventional job evaluation plans are variations or combinations of four basic methods: job classification, job ranking, point, and factor comparison. The job classification method defines certain classes or grades of jobs on the basis of differences in duties, responsibilities, skills, working conditions, and other job-related factors. In the job ranking method, the evaluator ranks whole jobs from the simplest to the most difficult. The point method develops a quantitative point scale for the jobs being evaluated. Jobs are broken down into certain recognizable factors, and the sum total value of these factors is compared against the scale to determine the job's worth. The factor comparison method is similar to the point method except that it involves a monetary scale instead of a point scale.

4. **Explain the concepts of key jobs and compensable factors.**

    Key jobs represent jobs that are common throughout the industry or in the general locale under study. The idea is to select a limited number of jobs that will represent the spectrum of jobs being evaluated with regard to responsibilities, duties, and work requirements. Once the key jobs have been evaluated, other jobs can be compared to them. Compensable factors are those characteristics of jobs that are deemed important by the organization to the extent that it is willing to pay for them. The degree to which a specific job possesses compensable factors determines its relative worth.

5. **Differentiate between subfactors and degrees.**

    Subfactors are used to describe compensable factors in more detail. Degrees are profile statements used to describe the specific requirements of each subfactor.

6. **Explain the purpose of wage and salary surveys.**

    Wage and salary surveys are used to collect comparative information on the policies, practices, and methods of wage payment from selected organizations in a given geographic location or particular type of industry.

7. **Discuss wage and salary curves.**

    Wage and salary curves graphically show the relationship between the relative worth of jobs and their wage or salary rates. A wage curve plots the jobs in ascending levels of difficulty along the abscissa (*x*-axis) and the wage rate along the ordinate (*y*-axis).

8. **Define pay grades and pay ranges.**

    A pay grade is a grouping of jobs of similar worth for pay purposes. A pay range is an assigned range of permissible pay, with a minimum and a maximum for each pay grade.

9. **Explain the concepts of skill-based pay, competency-based pay, and broadbanding.**

    Skill-based (or knowledge-based) pay systems compensate employees for the skills they bring to the job. Specifically, these pay systems pay employees for their range of knowledge, the number of business-related skills mastered, the level of those skills or knowledge, or some combination of level and range.

    A competency is a trait or a characteristic that a job holder needs to perform the job well. An employer interested in a competency-based pay system would examine the most successful employees in the organization and learn what those people do well. Once the elements have been identified, they are categorized as competencies, and all employees would then be compensated based on how well they demonstrated these identified competencies.

    Broadbanding reduces many different salary categories into several broad salary bands. In essence, broadbanding results in the clustering of jobs into wide categories or groups of jobs.

REVIEW QUESTIONS

1. Define base wages and salaries.
2. What is the primary objective of any base wage and salary system?
3. Define job evaluation.
4. List the four basic conventional methods of job evaluation.
5. What are compensable factors? Subfactors? Degrees?
6. Describe wage surveys and how they might be conducted.
7. What are the two basic ways of obtaining wage or salary survey information?
8. What is the purpose of wage curves?
9. What are pay grades and ranges?
10. Distinguish between conventional base pay systems and skill-based pay systems.

11. What are the differences between skill-based pay systems and competency-based pay systems?
12. What is broadbanding?

DISCUSSION QUESTIONS

1. Suppose your organization's recently completed wage survey showed that the pay rates of several jobs were either less or more than they should be. How might you bring these jobs into line?
2. The basic theory behind wage and salary administration is to pay people commensurately for their contributions. What should an organization do if an employee's contributions are not in line with those of others in the same type of job? For example, suppose the company accountant's contributions are deemed to be far in excess of what is usual for someone earning an accountant's pay.
3. How do you think that the Internet might impact the entire area of job evaluation?
4. Discuss some potential advantages and disadvantages of a skill-based system.

INCIDENT 14–1

Fair Pay for Pecan Workers

Cloverdale Pecan Company is one of the country's largest processors of pecans. Located in a medium-size southern town, it employs approximately 1,350 people. Although Cloverdale owns a few pecan orchards, the great majority of the nuts it processes are bought on the open market. The processing involves grading the nuts for both size and quality, and shelling, packaging, and shipping them to customers. Most buyers are candy manufacturers.

Cloverdale, which was started 19 years ago by the family of company president Jackson Massie, has been continually expanding since its inception. As do most growing companies, Cloverdale has always paid whatever was necessary to fill a vacancy without having a formal wage and salary system. Jackson Massie suspected that some wage inequities had developed over the years. His speculation was supported by complaints about such inequities from several good, long-term employees. Therefore, Massie hired a group of respected consultants to do a complete wage and salary study of all the nonexempt jobs in the company.

The study, which took five months to complete, confirmed Massie's suspicion. Wages of several jobs were found to vary from the norm. Furthermore, the situation was complicated by several factors. First, many of the employees earning too much were being paid according to union wage scales. Cloverdale is not unionized, but most of its competitors are. Second, many of those in underpaid jobs were being paid at rates equal to those for similar positions in other companies in Cloverdale's geographic area. Third, because of a tight labor market, many new employees had been hired at the top of the range for their respective grades. The study also revealed that the nature of many jobs had changed so much that they needed to be completely reclassified.

Questions

1. What should Cloverdale do to correct the existing wage inequities?
2. How could the company have prevented these problems?
3. If it is recommended that some jobs be placed in a lower pay grade, how might Cloverdale implement those adjustments?

INCIDENT 14-2

A Dead-End Street?

Early in December, Roger Tomlin was called in for his annual salary review. Roger was a staff engineer for Zee Engineering Company, which he had been with for just over 10 years. In the past, Roger had usually received what he considered to be a fair pay raise. During this salary review his manager, Ben Jackson, informed Roger that he was recommending a 10 percent raise. Ben went on to extol the fine job Roger had done in the past year and to explain that Roger should be especially proud of the above-average pay raise he would be getting. Upon reflection, Roger was rather proud; in 10 years, he had been promoted twice and his annual salary had gone from $32,000 to $69,000.

Things were moving along just fine for Roger until he discovered a few weeks later that a new engineer right out of college had just been hired by Zee at a starting salary of $47,000. It really upset Roger to think that a new, unproven engineer would be starting at a salary that high.

Roger's first move was to talk to several of his colleagues. Most were aware of the situation and didn't like it either. Lucy Johnson, who had been an engineer with Zee for over 12 years, asked Roger if he realized he was probably making less money, in actual dollars, than when he started at Zee. This really floored Roger. Roger realized inflation had eaten into everyone's paycheck, but he had never even considered the possibility that he had not kept up with inflation. That evening, on the way home from work, Roger stopped by the local library and looked up the consumer price index (CPI) for the past 10 years. According to Roger's figures, if his pay had kept up exactly with inflation, he would be making $69,500!

After a very restless night, the first thing Roger did upon arriving at work the next day was go straight to human resource manager Joe Dixon's office. After presenting his case about the new employee and about how inflation had eroded his pay, Roger sat back and waited for Joe's reply.

Joe started out by explaining that he understood just how Roger felt. At the same time, however, Roger had to consider the situation from the company's standpoint. The current supply and demand situation dictated that Zee had to pay $47,000 to get new engineers who were any good at all. Roger explained he could understand that, but he couldn't understand why the company couldn't pay him and other senior engineers more money. Joe again sympathized with Roger, but then went on to explain that it was a supply and demand situation. The fact was that senior engineers just didn't demand that much more pay than engineers just starting!

Questions

1. Do you think Roger is being fairly paid?
2. If you were Joe, how would you have responded to Roger?
3. Do you think a wage survey might help in this situation?
4. Should Joe establish pay grades for engineers?

EXERCISE 14-1

Ranking Jobs

Based on the seven job descriptions for the air transportation industry given in Exhibit 14–A, evaluate the relative worth of these jobs using the job ranking method.

EXHIBIT 14-A   **AIR TRANSPORTATION INDUSTRY JOB DESCRIPTIONS**

AIRPLANE-DISPATCH CLERK (air transportation) flight-operations-dispatch clerk. Compiles flight information to expedite movement of aircraft between and through airports. Compiles aircraft dispatch data, such as scheduled arrival and departure times at checkpoints and scheduled stops, amount of fuel needed for flight, and maximum allowable gross takeoff and landing weight. Submits data to DISPATCHER (air transportation) for approval and flight authorization. Receives messages on progress of flights. Posts flight schedules and weather information on bulletin board. Compiles such information as flight plans, ramp delays, and weather reports, using teletype, computer-printout terminal, and two-way radio, to anticipate off-schedule arrivals or departures, and notifies flight operations of schedule changes. Prepares message concerning flights for transmittal by radio, telegraph, or telegraphic typewriter to other stations on routes. May operate telegraphic typewriter or two-way radio to send messages. May issue maps to pilot. May duplicate weather maps and telegraph or radio messages (DUPLICATING-MACHINE OPERATOR [clerical] II). May record flight and weather information on tape recorder for playback to passengers in waiting areas. May verify presence of or locate scheduled flight crews, and post changes in flight crew schedule on bulletin board.

CARGO AGENT (air transportation) air-freight agent; customer service agent. Routes inbound and outbound air-freight shipments to their destinations: Takes telephone orders from customers and arranges for pickup of freight and delivery to loading platform. Assembles cargo according to destination. Weighs items and determines cost, using rate book. Itemizes charges, prepares freight bills, accepts payments, and issues refunds. Prepares manifest to accompany shipments. Notifies shippers of delays in departure of shipment. Unloads inbound freight, notifies consignees on arrival of shipments, and arranges for delivery to consignees. May force conditioned air into interior of plane for passenger comfort prior to departure, using mobile aircraft air-conditioning unit.

COMMUNICATION CENTER OPERATOR (air transportation). Operates airport authority communication systems and monitors electronic equipment alarms: Operates public address system to page passengers or visitors. Operates telephone switchboard to receive or place calls to and from terminal. Operates two-way internal radio system to communicate with departments. Operates terminal courtesy telephone system to communicate with passengers or visitors. Observes electronic monitoring panel to detect serious malfunction of elevators, escalators, shuttle train, fire alarms, emergency doors, or heating, air-conditioning, and ventilating system.

GATE AGENT (air transportation). Assists passengers and checks flight tickets at entrance gate or station when boarding or disembarking airplane of commercial airline: Examines passenger tickets to ensure that passengers have correct flight or seat, or directs passengers to correct boarding area, using passenger manifest, seating chart, and flight schedules. Verifies names on passenger manifest or separates portions of passenger's ticket and stamps or marks ticket or issues boarding pass to authorize passenger to board airplane. Directs passengers to air-terminal facilities. Opens gate or allows passengers to board airplane. Assists elderly, disabled, or young passengers to board or depart from airplane, such as moving passengers in wheelchairs. May announce flight information, using public address system. May post flight information on flight board.

RESERVATIONS AGENT (air transportation) telephone-sales agent. Makes and confirms reservations for passengers on scheduled airline flights: Arranges reservations and routing for passengers at request of TICKET AGENT (any industry) or customer, using timetables, airline manuals, reference guides, and tariff book. Types requested flight number on keyboard of online computer reservation system and scans screen to determine space availability. Telephones customer or TICKET AGENT (any industry) to advise of changes in flight plan or to cancel or confirm reservation. May maintain advance or current inventory of available passenger space on flights. May advise load control personnel and other stations of changes in passenger itinerary to control space and ensure utilization of seating capacity on flights.

(Continues)

EXHIBIT 14-A **(Continued)**

SUPERVISOR, TICKET SALES (air transportation) load ticket-sales agent; senior passenger agent; senior ticket-sales agent. Supervises and coordinates activities of personnel engaged in selling tickets for scheduled airline flights in airline ticket office or terminal: Instructs and trains agents. Adjusts disputes between customers and agents. Prepares reports, such as volume of ticket sales and cash received. Maintains records on data, such as weight and location of passengers, cargo, and mail, to ensure compliance with load specifications. Suggests travel itineraries for customers. May reserve space for passengers (RESERVATIONS AGENT [air transportation]) and sell tickets for scheduled flights (TICKET AGENT [any industry]). Performs other duties as described under SUPERVISOR (clerical).

TICKETING AGENT (air transportation) teleticketing agent; ticket agent. Compiles and records information to assemble airline tickets for transmittal or mailing to passengers: Reads coded data on booking cards to ascertain destination, carrier, flight number, type of accommodation, and stopovers en route. Selects ticket blank, invoice, and customer account card (if applicable) and compiles, computes, and records identification and fare data, using tariff manuals, rate tables, flight schedules, and pen or ticket imprinter. Separates and files copies of completed tickets. Clips completed tickets and invoices to booking cards and routes to other workers for teletype transmittal or mails tickets to customers. Computes total daily fares, using adding machine, to compile daily revenue reports.

Source: These job descriptions are taken from U.S. Department of Labor, Employment and Training Administration, *Dictionary of Occupational Titles,* 4th ed., rev. (Washington, D.C.: U.S. Government Printing Office), 1991.

You may find it helpful to prepare a 3″ × 5″ card on each job and then arrange the cards accordingly. Once you have completed your rankings, go to the library and find any pertinent wage survey data relating to these jobs (a good source of wage survey data is published by the U.S. Department of Labor). After you have gathered sufficient wage survey data, determine whether or not the data support your rankings. Be prepared to discuss your findings with the class.

EXERCISE 14-2

Wage/Salary Survey

Visit each of the five Web sites listed in Figure 14–4 and look for any information that you might find useful if conducting a wage/salary survey for human resource employees.

Questions

1. Did you find useful information? If so, what and where?

2. Did you find some of the Web sites to be easier to maneuver around in than others? If so, which ones were easier?

3. Did any of the data surprise you as to the "going rate" for the different H.R. positions?

NOTES AND ADDITIONAL READINGS

1. Roger J. Plachy, "Compensation Management: Cases and Applications," *Compensation and Benefits Review,* July 1989, p. 26.

2. Richard I. Henderson, *Compensation Management: Rewarding Performance* (Reston, Va.: Reston Publishing, 1976), p. 123.

3. Richard I. Henderson, *Compensation Management: Rewarding Performance,* 4th ed. (Reston, Va.: Reston Publishing, 1985), p. 293.

4. Joan C. O'Brien and Robert A. Zawacki, "Salary Surveys: Are They Worth the Effort?" *Personnel,* October 1985, p. 72.

5. Margaret Dyekman, "Take the Mystery out of Salary Survey," *Personnel Journal,* June 1990, p. 104.

6. Jerry Useem, "State-of-the-Art Compensation," *Inc.,* October 1998, p. 118.

7. Fay Hansen, "Guide to Salary Survey Data on the Web," *Compensation & Benefits Review,* March/April 1998, pp. 16–20.

8. O'Brien and Zawacki, "Salary Surveys," p. 71.

9. Michael A. Conway, "Salary Surveys: Avoid the Pitfalls," *Personnel Journal,* June 1985, pp. 62–65.

10. Much of this section is based on Shari Cauldron, "Master the Compensation Maze," *Personnel Journal,* June 1993, p. 64B.

11. Ibid.

12. Ibid.

13. Gerald E. Ledford, Jr. "Paying for the Skills, Knowledge, and Competencies of Knowledge Work," *Compensation & Benefits Review,* July–August 1995, pp. 55–58.

14. Ibid.

15. Ibid.

16. Ibid., and Henry Jahja and Brian H. Kleiner, "Competency-Based Pay in Manufacturing and Service Sectors," *Industrial Management,* September/October 1997, pp. 24–27.

17. Gerald E. Ledford, Jr., "Paying for the Skills," pp. 55–58.

18. Darrell J. Cira and Ellen R. Benjamin, "Competency-Based Pay: A Concept in Evolution," *Compensation & Benefits Review,* September/October 1998, pp. 21–28.

19. Kathryn Tyler, "Compensation Strategies Can Foster Lateral Moves and Growing in Places," *HR Magazine,* April 1998, pp. 64–71.

20. Bill Leonard, "New Ways to Pay Employees," *HR Magazine,* February 1994, pp. 61–62.

21. Tyler, "Compensation Strategies," pp. 21–28.

22. Ibid.

23. Cauldron, "Master the Compensation Maze," p. 648.

24. Gary L. Bergel, "Choosing the Right Pay Delivery System to Fit Banding," *Compensation,* July–August 1994, pp. 34–38.

Incentive Pay Systems

Learning Objectives

After studying this chapter, you should be able to:

1. Describe the two basic requirements of an effective incentive plan.
2. List and briefly discuss at least three types of individual incentives.
3. Distinguish between a bonus and a merit pay increase.
4. Discuss the role bonuses play in managerial compensation.
5. Differentiate between nonqualified stock options and incentive stock options (ISOs).
6. Differentiate among the following different types of stock option related plans: stock for stock swaps, stock appreciation rights, phantom stock plans, restricted stock plans, premium-priced options, and performance-vesting options.
7. Describe how group incentives work.
8. Explain what a gain-sharing plan is.
9. Discuss Scanlon-type plans.
10. Explain how an employee stock ownership plan (ESOP) works.
11. Identify what distinguishes variable pay plans from most other incentive pay plans.

Incentive Pay Plans Pay plans designed to relate pay directly to performance or productivity; often used in conjunction with a base wage and salary system.

Incentive pay plans attempt to relate pay to performance to reward above-average performance rapidly and directly. Although good performance can be rewarded through the base wage or salary structure either by raising an individual's pay within the range of the job or by promoting the individual into a higher pay grade, these rewards are often subject to delays and other restrictions. Therefore, such rewards are often not viewed by the recipients as being directly related to performance. Incentive pay plans attempt to strengthen the performance-reward relationship and thus motivate the affected employees. The idea is to have employees think of themselves as business partners by sharing the financial risks and rewards of doing business. Another advantage to incentive pay is that it is not permanent and must be earned each year. Most incentive pay programs tie pay directly to profitability, thus allowing companies to grow and shrink payroll expenses in response to the success of the business.

Because of minimum wage laws and labor market competition, most incentive plans include a guaranteed hourly wage or salary. The guaranteed wage or salary is normally determined from the base wage or salary structure. Thus, incentive plans usually function in addition to, not in place of, the base wage/salary structure discussed in Chapter 14.

Incentive systems can be categorized on more than one basis. Probably the most popular basis is whether the plan is applied on an individual, group, or organizational level. In addition, plans are sometimes classified according to whether they apply to nonmanagerial employees or to professional and managerial employees. This chapter classifies incentives as individual, group, or organizational and, where appropriate, distinguishes between nonmanagerial and managerial employees within these categories. Some plans apply to nonmanagerial and managerial employees alike.

A 1996 survey by Hewitt Associates reported that 61 percent of the responding companies have some form of performance-related rewards that must be earned each year.[1] This figure was up from 57 percent in 1991 and 44 percent in 1989.

Requirements of Incentive Plans

There are two basic requirements for an effective incentive plan. The first concerns the procedures and methods used to appraise employee performance. If incentives are to be based on performance, employees must believe their performance and the performance of others are accurately and fairly evaluated. Naturally, performance is easier to measure in some situations than in others. For example, the performance of a commissioned salesperson is usually easy to measure, whereas the performance of a middle manager is often more difficult to evaluate. A key issue in performance measurement is the degree of trust in management. If the employees distrust management, it is almost impossible to establish a sound performance appraisal system. (Performance appraisal was discussed at length in Chapter 12.)

The second requirement is that the incentives (rewards) must be based on performance. This may seem like an obvious requirement, yet it is often violated. Employees must believe there is a relationship between what they do and what they get. Individual-based incentive plans require that employees perceive a direct relationship between their own performances and their subsequent rewards. Group-based plans require employees to perceive a relationship between the group's performance and the subsequent rewards of the group's members. Furthermore, the group members must believe their individual performances have an impact on the group's overall performance. Organization-based plans have the same basic requirements group plans do. Employees must perceive a relationship between the organization's performance and their individual rewards; in addition, employees must believe their individual performances affect the performance of the organization.

Individual Incentives

While there are many types of individual incentive plans, all are tied in some measure to the performance of the individual. At nonmanagerial levels in an organization, individual incentives are usually based on the performance of the individual as opposed to those of the group or organization. However, at managerial levels, individual incentives are often based on the performance of the manager's work unit.

The primary advantage of the individual incentive system is that the employees can readily see the relationship between what they do and what they get. With group- and organization-based plans, this relationship is often not so clear. Because of this advantage, individual incentives can also cause problems. Competition among employees can reach the point of producing negative results. For example, salespeople may not share their ideas with one another for fear that their peers will win a prize that is being offered to the top salesperson.

Piece Rate Plans

As early as 1833, many cotton mills in England used individual piece rate incentives.[2] Piece rate plans are the simplest and most common type of incentive plan. Under such a plan, the employer pays an employee a certain amount for every unit he or she produces. In other words, an employee's wage is figured by multiplying the number of units produced by the rate of pay for each unit. The rate of pay for each unit is usually based on what a fair wage should be for an average employee. For example, if a fair wage for an average machine operator is determined to be $90 per day and it is also determined that the average machine operator should be able to produce 30 units per day, the unit rate of pay would be $3 per unit.

Differential Piece Rate Plan
Piece rate plan devised by Frederick W. Taylor that pays one rate for all acceptable units produced up to some standard and then a higher rate for all pieces produced if the output exceeds the standard.

Several variations of the straight piece rate plan have been developed. In 1895, Frederick W. Taylor proposed his **differential piece rate plan.** Under Taylor's plan, one rate is paid for all acceptable units produced up to some standard, or predetermined amount, and then a higher rate for all units produced if the output exceeds the standard. Thus, if the standard were 30 units per day, an employee producing 30 or fewer units might receive $2.50 per unit. However, if the employee produced 31 units, he or she might receive $3 for all 31 units produced for a total of $93. Other plans pay a higher rate only for those units produced above the standard.

Plans Based on Time Saved

Standard hour plans are similar to piece rate plans except that a standard time is set in terms of the time it should take to complete a particular job. Incentive plans based on time saved give an employee a bonus for reaching a given level of production or output in less than the standard time. For example, suppose a body shop repairperson is assigned to do a task for which the standard time is two hours (this is precisely how insurance companies compute the cost of repairing damaged autos). If the repairperson completes the task in $1\frac{1}{2}$ hours, she or he is paid for two hours. If the task takes $2\frac{1}{2}$ hours, the repairperson is paid for that amount of time. Should the repairperson consistently take longer than the standard time, either the standard will need to be adjusted or the productivity of the repairperson should be examined.

Plans Based on Commissions

Commission Plan
Incentive plan that rewards employees, at least in part, based on their sales volume.

The previously discussed incentive plans are primarily applicable to production-type jobs. However, some incentive plans apply to other types of jobs. One of the most prevalent types is based on commission. Many salespeople work under some type of **commission plan.** Although a variety of such plans exist, they all reward employees, at least in part, based on sales volume. Some salespeople work on a straight commission basis: their pay is entirely determined by their volume of sales. Others work on a combination of salary plus commission. Under this type of plan, a salesperson is paid a guaranteed base salary plus a commission on sales. Under a third type of commission plan, salespeople are paid a monthly draw that is later subtracted from their commissions. The purpose of the draw is to provide salespeople with enough money on a monthly basis to cover their basic expenses. The difference between a draw plan and the guaranteed salary plus commission plan is that the draw is really an advance against future commissions and must be repaid. The draw plan is especially useful for salespeople whose sales tend to fluctuate dramatically from month to month or season to season.

A commission plan has the advantage of relating rewards directly to performance. Salespeople on a straight commission know that if they do not produce, they will not be paid. A major disadvantage of commission plans is that things beyond the control of an employee can adversely affect sales. For example, a product might be displaced almost overnight by a technological breakthrough. Other environmental factors, such as the national economy, the weather, and consumer preferences, can also affect an employee's sales.

Individual Bonuses

Bonus Reward that is offered on a one-time basis for high performance.

A **bonus** is a reward offered on a one-time basis for high performance. It should not be confused with a merit increase. A **merit pay increase** is a reward that is based on performance but is also perpetuated year after year. A bonus may be in cash or in some other form. For example, many sales organizations periodically

Merit Pay Increase   Reward based on performance but also perpetuated year after year.

offer prizes, such as trips, for their top salespeople. A positive aspect of bonuses is that they must be earned each year and the organization is not obligated over the long run. One potential problem with bonuses is that they can become an extension of salary. This occurs when awarding the bonus becomes practically guaranteed because the bonus is not tied to profits or some other measure of performance. In such circumstances, the recipients begin to expect the bonus. They do not view it as resulting from their individual performances or from the profits of the organization. Serious dissatisfaction can result if the expected bonus is not granted because of a decline in profits or any other legitimate reason.

Suggestion Systems

Suggestion Systems
Systems that usually offer cash incentives for employee suggestions that result in either increased profits or reduced costs.

The Employee Involvement Association (EIA), formerly the National Association of Suggestion Systems (NASS), is a Chicago-based, not-for-profit group that represents companies regarding employee involvement programs, including suggestion programs. The EIA has approximately 6,000 member companies that have some type of formal suggestion system in place.[3] The EIA also estimates that its member companies save $6,224 for each idea implemented. American Airlines estimates that in six years its suggestion system, called "IdeAAs in Action," saved the company nearly $250 million and that employee participation grew from 6 to 20 percent over this same time period.[4] Most **suggestion systems** offer cash incentives for employee suggestions that positively affect the organization. Examples include suggestions resulting in increased profits, reduced costs, or improved customer relations. In addition to the obvious organizational benefits, suggestion plans can provide a means for making employees feel more a part of the organization and for improving communications between management and employees. The key to having a successful suggestion system is to clearly communicate exactly how the system works. Employees must believe that each and every suggestion will be fairly evaluated. Modern suggestion systems generally involve specific procedures for submitting ideas and utilize committees to review and evaluate suggestions. HRM in Action 15.1 describes the results some companies have had with suggestion systems.

HRM IN ACTION

Profits from Suggestion Systems

15.1

www.eia.com
www.bell-atl.com

According to the Employment Involvement Associates (EIA), the average savings for companies with formal suggestion programs is $33,500 per 100 employees. Some companies have saved much more. Haworth, Inc., of Holland, Michigan, implemented its IDEAS suggestion system in 1991. IDEAS allows employees to implement ideas on their own after informing their supervisor, or to work with people in other departments to implement an idea that concerns their job. According to Haworth, the program has saved as much as $8 million in a single year.

Bell Atlantic's Champion program has generated $54 million for the company over the past several years, through products proposed and created by employees. Even though Bell Atlantic's proposal process is long and arduous, an employee's reward can be significant. If a proposed product goes to market, the employee responsible for the idea can receive an initial financial reward *and* a share of its profits.

Source: Robert Carey, "Employee Ideas Get Unboxed," *Incentive* (Performance Supplement), June 1995, p. 4.

Incentives for Managerial Personnel

Incentives for managerial personnel generally take the form of annual bonuses, long-term performance planning, or some type of stock option. These are discussed in the following sections.

Annual Bonus

By far the most common type of incentive for managerial employees is the annual cash bonus. Although cash bonuses have always been popular among managers, they have become even more popular as a result of the 1986 Tax Reform Act. A 1998 survey of over 1,200 companies by Watson Wyatt Data Services reported that approximately 79 percent of the companies had a bonus plan or other form of variable pay program in which their executives were eligible.[5] A similar 1996 survey of 1,445 companies conducted by the Conference Board reported that almost 89 percent awarded bonuses to their top executives.[6] Most plans provide a year-end bonus based on that year's performance, usually measured in terms of profits but sometimes measured by other means. Even though managerial bonuses are usually based on organizational or group performance, they are considered individual incentives because of the key roles managers play in the success of an organization. Typically, a bonus is paid in cash as a lump sum soon after the end of the performance year. It is not unusual for executives to defer receiving some portion of a cash bonus until a later date for income tax purposes.

As Table 15–1 shows, the popularity of bonus plans grew substantially from 1970 to 1996. Bonuses often make up a substantial portion of total compensation. In its 1998 survey, Watson Wyatt Data Services found that bonuses comprised 34.2 percent of total salary received by managers (see Table 15–2).[7] Another interesting finding of this survey was that the percentage was even greater for higher-level managers (see Table 15–3).

Long-Term Performance Plans

Performance Share Plan (Unit Plan) Incentive plan that awards top executives a set number of performance units at the beginning of the performance period; actual

In recent years, some companies have adopted managerial incentive plans based on the attainment of certain long-term corporate financial performance goals as opposed to the more common annual bonus plans. Generally known as **performance share plans** or **unit plans,** these plans usually award top executives a set number of performance units at the beginning of a performance period. The actual value of the units is then determined by the company's performance over the performance period, usually from three to five years. Table 15–4 indicates the prevalence of performance share plans for executives in 1996.

T A B L E   1 5 – 1 **BONUS PLANS: 1970 COMPARED TO 1985 AND 1996**

Type of Business	Number of Companies Surveyed			Percentage Having Bonus Plans		
	May 1970	May 1985	May 1996	May 1970	May 1985	May 1996
Manufacturing	419	475	646	65%	92%	94%
Retail trade	90	68	115	40	81	97
Commercial banking	248	171	101	19	81	96
Insurance	174	132	72	18	67	100
Energy and utilities	106	97	102	6	36	100

Sources: H. Fox, *Top Executive Compensation* 1981 ed. (New York: Conference Board, 1980), p. 4; H. Fox and C. Peck, *Top Executive Compensation* 1986 ed. (New York Conference Board, 1985), p. 2; C. Peck, H. M. Silvert, and K. Worrell, *Top Executive Compensation* 1996 ed. (New York: Conference Board, 1997), p. 20.

TABLE 15-2   BONUSES AS A PERCENTAGE OF SALARIES

Industry Category	Number of Executives	Percentage Paying Bonuses	Average Bonus (as a percentage of salary)
Durable goods manufacturing	2719	70.2%	31.2%
Non–durable goods manufacturing	1525	67.9	34.0
Utilities and energy	753	69.5	30.7
Retail and wholesale trade	795	76.6	34.7
Services	1828	74.5	39.2
Banking and finance	328	64.9	27.9
Insurance	832	82.5	43.2
Health care	774	37.1	24.8
Nonprofits	663	10.0	14.5
All industry categories combined	10,271	65.5	34.2

Source: The ECS Survey of Top Management Compensation, Summary Report, 1998/1999 (Rochelle Park, N.J.: Watson Wyatt Data Services, 1998), p. 80.

Stock Options for Managerial Personnel

value of the units is then determined by the company's performance over the performance period.

Qualified Stock Options
Stock options approved by the Internal Revenue Service for favorable tax treatment.

Stock option plans are generally designed to give managers an option to buy company stock at a predetermined, fixed price. If the price of the stock goes up, the individual exercises the option to buy the stock at the fixed price and realizes a profit. If the price of the stock goes down, the stock option is said to be "underwater," and the manager does not purchase the stock. The idea behind such plans is to provide an incentive for managers to work hard and increase company profits, thus increasing the price of the stock.

Before the passage of the Tax Reform Act of 1976, two major forms of stock options were available: qualified and nonqualified. **Qualified stock options** were those approved by the Internal Revenue Service (IRS) for favorable tax treatment. A qualified option was not taxed until the option was exercised and, in the

TABLE 15-3   EXECUTIVES ELIGIBLE FOR AND RECEIVING BONUS AND/OR OTHER CASH COMPENSATION PAYMENTS

Position	Number of Executives	Average Paid (as a % of salary)	
		All Eligible Executives*	Executives Actually Receiving Awards**
Chief executive officer	572	49.5%	62.3%
Chief operating officer	261	41.7	55.6
Top subsidiary executive	171	46.4	54.5
Top group executive	311	42.5	49.8
Top division executive	300	37.6	45.2
Executive vice president	227	31.2	40.3
Administrative vice president	182	31.4	35.9

* Includes all eligible executives, including those who did not receive an award.

** Includes only executives both eligible for and receiving awards.

Source: The ECS Survey of Top Management Compensation, Summary Report, 1998/1999 (Rochelle Park, N. J.: Watson Wyatt Data Services, 1998), p. 80.

PREVALENCE OF LONG-TERM PERFORMANCE PLANS

Industry Category	Total Companies	1996 With Long-Term Performance Plans	
		Number	Percent
Telecommunications	18	13	72%
Financial services/investment	28	15	54
Utilities	82	38	46
Manufacturing	646	290	45
Construction	26	11	42
Diversified service	176	71	40
Energy	20	8	40
Commercial banking	101	39	39
Insurance	72	28	39
Retail trade	115	44	38
Wholesale trade	80	30	38
Transportation	42	15	36
Communication	39	11	28

Source: C. Peck, H. M. Silvert, and K. Worrell, *Top Executive Compensation* 1996 ed. (New York: Conference Board, 1997), p. 22.

interim, was treated as a capital asset. Income realized from the eventual sale of the stock was usually taxed as a long-term capital gain. To qualify for a tax advantage, the stock option plan and the recipient had to adhere to certain conditions prescribed by the IRS. These conditions centered primarily around the length of time the executive was required to hold the option before purchasing and selling the stock and the basis for establishing the price the executive paid for it. **Nonqualified options** are similar to qualified options, except that they are subject to a less favorable tax rate. They are not subject to the same restrictions.

As a result of the Tax Reform Act of 1976, no new qualified stock options were created after May 20, 1976 (with a few exceptions). In addition, the act ordered that all qualified options in existence prior to the passage of the act had to be exercised before May 21, 1981. It also affected nonqualified options by increasing the period over which one had to hold an exercised stock option to enjoy long-term capital gains tax rates. However, with the adoption of the Economic Recovery Tax Act of 1981, the qualified stock option was resurrected under the new name of **incentive stock option (ISO).** Under an ISO, a manager does not have to pay any tax until he or she sells the stock. The major drawback to ISOs is that the company granting such options does not get tax reductions, which it does with nonqualified options. Because of tax ramifications, ISOs tend to be preferred by the recipients, while nonqualified options tend to be favored by the granting organizations.

Table 15–5 presents the results of a survey of all types of stock options (nonqualified and ISOs) offered in 1986 and 1996. As Table 15–5 indicates, there was generally continued growth in the use of stock option plans in that 10-year period.

Stock options often represent the largest portion of an executive's total compensation. For example, of the $230.7 million Travelers Group chairman Sanford Weill received in 1997, only $7.5 million was base salary. The rest came primarily from stock options accumulated over several years. Table 15–6 shows the salary bonuses and long-term incomes for the top 10 of the country's top-paid executives in 1997. Most of the long-term compensation reflected in Table 15–6 is in the form of stock options.

Nonqualified Stock Options Similar to qualified options, except that they are subject to a less favorable tax rate and are not subject to the same restrictions.

Incentive Stock Option (ISO) Form of qualified stock option plan in which the manager does not have to pay any tax until the stock is sold.

TABLE 15-5   **PREVALENCE OF STOCK OPTIONS, MAY 1986 AND MAY 1996**

Industry Category	May 1986		May 1996	
	Total Companies	Percentage with Stock Option Plan	Total Companies	Percentage with Stock Option Plan
Energy	26	—	20	100%
Manufacturing	427	82%	646	95
Communications	34	—	39	95
Trade	140	73	195	95
Commercial banking	81	61	101	94
Insurance: stock	61	45	52	69
Diversified services	81	100	176	97
Utilities	106	24	82	72

Source: C. Peck, H. M. Silvert, and K. Worrell, *Top Executive Compensation* 1996 ed. (New York: Conference Board, 1997), p. 23.

Stock-for-Stock Swap
Allows options to be exercised with shares of previously purchased company stock in lieu of cash; postpones the taxation of any gain on stock already owned.

Stock Appreciation Rights (SARs) Type of nonqualified stock option in which an executive has the right to relinquish a stock

Stock-for-Stock Swaps: A substantial proportion of companies with stock option plans provide for **stock-for-stock swaps.** This procedure allows options to be exercised with shares of previously purchased company stock in lieu of cash. The advantage is that this arrangement postpones the taxation of any gain on stock already owned.

In something of a turn of events, some companies are now requiring that top executives and directors own a certain amount of company stock. A survey of 350 companies by Towers Perrin found that 16 percent of the companies had adopted or were preparing "guidelines" specifying how much stock executives must own.[8] An increasing number of companies are paying directors in stock and also requiring them to purchase a certain amount of stock.[9]

Stock Appreciation Rights (SARs): **Stock appreciation rights (SARs)** are often used with stock option plans. Under an SAR, an executive has the right to relinquish a stock option and receive from the company an amount equal to the appreciation

TABLE 15-6   **THE TOP-PAID CHIEF EXECUTIVES, 1997**

	1997 Salary and Bonus (thousands of dollars)	Long-Term Compensation	Total Pay
1. Sanford Weill, Travelers Group	$ 7,453	$223,272	$230,725
2. Roberto Goizueta, Coca-Cola	4,052	107,781	111,832
3. Richard Scrushy, HealthSouth	13,399	93,391	106,790
4. Ray Irani, Occidental Petroleum	3,849	97,657	101,505
5. Eugene Isenberg, Nabors Industries	1,675	82,872	84,547
6. Joseph Costello, Cadence Design Systems	584	66,258	66,842
7. Andrew Grove, Intel	3,255	48,958	52,214
8. Charles McCall, HBO & Co.	1,725	49,684	51,409
9. Philip Purcell, Morgan Stanley Dean Witter	11,274	39,533	50,807
10. Robert Shapiro, Monsanto	1,834	47,491	49,326

Source: Adapted from *Business Week*, April 20, 1998, p. 64.

option and receive from the company an amount equal to the appreciation in the stock price from the date the option was granted. Under an SAR, the option holder does not have to put up any money, as would be required in a normal stock option plan.

Phantom Stock Plan Special type of stock option plan that protects the holder if the value of the stock being held decreases; does not require the option holder to put up any money.

Restricted Stock Plan Plan under which a company gives shares of stock to participating managers, subject to certain restrictions; the major restriction of most plans is that shares are subject to forfeiture until "earned out" over a stipulated period of continued employment.

Premium-Priced Options Stock options with an exercise price significantly above stock's current market price.

The Status of Executive Pay

Performance-Vesting Options Stock options priced at market price but only exercisable if stock price reaches or exceeds price goal within defined period.

in the stock price from the date the option was granted. The gain is taxed as ordinary income at the time it is received. The advantage of SARs is that the receiver does not have to put up any money to exercise the option, as he or she would with a normal stock option plan. Holders of SARs may have as long as 10 years to exercise their rights.

Phantom Stock Plans: **Phantom stock plans** can work in several ways. In one form, the company awards stock as a part of its normal bonus plan. The receiver then defers this "phantom" stock until retirement. At retirement, the holder receives the accumulated shares of stock or the equivalent value. The second form of phantom stock is very similar to SARs. The receiver is credited with phantom stock. After a stipulated period of time, usually three to five years, the receiver is paid, in cash or equivalent shares, an amount equal to the appreciation in the stock. The major advantage of phantom stock plans is that the receiver does not have to put up any money at any point in the process. Also, if the value of the stock decreases, the holder does not lose any money.

Restricted Stock Plans: Under a **restricted stock plan,** a company gives shares of stock, subject to certain restrictions, to participating managers. The major restriction of most plans is that the shares are subject to forfeiture until they are "earned out" over a stipulated period of continued employment. As with SARs and phantom stock plans, the receivers do not put up or risk any of their own money. An advantage from the organization's viewpoint is that restricted stock plans provide an incentive for executives to remain with the organization. For example, in addition to $4.1 million in salary, Coca-Cola chairman Roberto Goizueta received 1 million shares of restricted stock worth $81 million in 1991.[10] To cash the stock in, Goizueta had to stick around until 1996.

Premium-Priced and Performance-Vesting Options: **Premium-priced options** are similar to standard stock options except that the exercise price of the option is set significantly above the current market price of the stock (versus the usual practice of setting it at or near the current market price). The holder realizes a gain only when the market value exceeds the exercise price.

Performance-vesting options, also called price-vesting options, are priced at the market price but only exercisable if the stock price reaches or exceeds a price goal within a defined period. If the stock price does not reach the price goal within the stipulated time frame, the option is forfeited. HRM in Action 15.2 discusses some well known companies that have implemented premium-priced or performance-vesting option plans.

According to Pearl Meyer, an executive pay consultant in New York, in 1997 the typical U.S. CEO pay package was 20 percent salary, 27 percent short-term (annual) incentives, 16 percent long-term incentives, and 36 percent stock-based pay (mostly options, which could not be exercised for at least three years).[11]

As indicated in Table 15–6, it is not uncommon for CEOs to be awarded bonuses and stock options that reach eight digits. In 1997, the *median* CEO total compensation was more than $3 million.[12] This represented an increase of 30 percent from 1996. The median total compensation for CEOs of the Forbes 200 Best Small Companies rose 21 percent in 1998 to $500,000, up from $415,000 in 1997.[13] A recent study by compensation consultants Towers Perrin found that CEOs in the United States as a group now earn 185 times as much as their employees' average pay.[14] This is up from a ratio of 142 to 1 in 1992.

The main idea behind most stock option plans was to link pay to performance. However, when there is a sustained bull market, tying executive reward to price may be fundamentally flawed.[15] The problem is that when most stocks are going up, stock prices often provide an inaccurate measure of a company's actual strength. HRM in Action 15.3 provides examples of how poor performance can result in huge rewards.

HRM IN ACTION

**Implementing
Premium-Priced or
Performance-Vesting
Options**

15.2

www.monsanto.com
www.cdgate.com
www.citicorp.com

Premium-priced options are used by Monsanto, Transamerica, Ecolab, and Colgate-Palmolive. At Colgate-Palmolive, CEO Reuben Mark received a megagrant of 2.6 million premium-priced options in lieu of annual standard options for seven years. To collect, the stock price must hit a lofty price. Once the stock does hit the target price, Mark can keep only the gain above that price. In 1998, Monsanto installed an aggressive premium-priced option plan covering CEO Robert Shapiro and 31 other executives. For Shapiro and his executives to make any money on the options, the stock price must increase from $50.22 on the day of the grant to $75.33 by the year 2003. Because Shapiro and the other executives have to pay for their option, they must raise the share price even higher before they can start cashing in.

Citicorp and DuPont both have installed performance-vesting options. Under Citicorp's 1998 plan, CEO John Reed received 300,000 options at a price of $121 per share. Over 50 other Citicorp executives are also participating in the program. As with standard options, Reed and the others gain the entire appreciation over the $121 per share price; however, they can only exercise their options when and if the stock price reaches $200 per share within five years.

Source: Shawn Tully, "Raising the Bar," *Fortune,* June 8, 1998, pp. 272–78.

HRM IN ACTION

Pay for Performance?

15.3

www.att.com
www.heinz.com
www.apple.com

During former AT&T CEO Robert Allen's nine-year tenure, the telecom giant lost market share, made disastrous strategical errors, like the acquisition and subsequent divestiture of NCR, and trailed its competitors in stock performance. In 1995, when AT&T announced a major restructuring and 40,000 layoffs, Allen received 858,000 stock options in addition to his $5.8 million salary and other compensation.

Anthony O'Reilly, the chief executive of H. J. Heinz, revived the food giant in the 1980s and provided sizzling returns to shareholders. During this time period, O'Reilly was well compensated, thanks mostly to stock options. In 1990, desperate to keep its to-date superstar, the Heinz board granted O'Reilly a staggering 4 million shares of stock in options. Since 1990, Heinz return to shareholders has been less than the S&P 500 and the S&P food index. In spite of the less than desirable returns, O'Reilly pocketed a whopping $61.5 million when he exercised his options in 1996.

Apple Computer's former chief executive, Gilbert Amelio, was lured to the company as a turnaround expert in February 1996. Part of the package to attract Amelio was a grant of 1 million stock options—exercisable at the then current price of $26.25 per share. Amelio never did turn the company around and was ousted in July 1997. A month after his firing, Apple's stock price rose above the exercise price, making his option worth something.

Source: Shaifali Puri, "Pay for Underperformance," *Fortune,* December 8, 1997, pp. 52–56.

Because of the huge dollars often involved and because of examples like those in HRM in Action 15.3, many employees and stockholders have become angry with what many executives are being paid. Institutional investors are also sending out signals that they want more linkage between pay and performance.[16] While the reaction has not been universal, there is a trend toward the special types of equity grants (such as premium-priced and performance-vested options) that do relate executive rewards to actual company performance.

Group Incentives

Group Incentives
Incentives based on group rather than individual performance.

Because jobs can be interdependent, it is sometimes difficult to isolate and evaluate individual performance. In these instances, it is often wise to establish incentives based on group or team performance. For example, an assembly-line operator must work at the speed of the line. Thus, everyone working on the line is dependent on everyone else. With **group incentives,** all group members receive incentive pay based on the performance of the entire group. Depending on the specific situation, the group may be as large as the entire organizational work force or as small as three or four members of a work team. Many group incentive plans are based on such factors as profits or reduction in costs of operations.

Group incentive plans are designed to encourage employees to exert peer pressure on group members to perform. For instance, if a group member is not performing well and thus is lowering the production of the entire group, the group will usually pressure the individual to improve, especially if a group incentive plan is in operation. A disadvantage of group incentives is that the members of the group may not perceive a direct relationship between their individual performances and that of the group. Size and cohesiveness of the group are two factors that affect this relationship. Usually smaller groups are more cohesive because more employees are likely to perceive a relationship between their performances and that of the group. Another potential disadvantage is that different groups can become overly competitive with one another to the detriment of the entire organization.

Self-Directed Work Teams: The philosophy behind any type of work team is that teams can contribute to improved performance by identifying and solving work-related problems. The basic idea is to motivate employees by having them participate in decisions that affect them and their work. Self-directed work teams are teams of employees that accomplish tasks within their area of responsibility without direct supervision. Each team makes its own job assignments, plans its own work, performs equipment maintenance, keeps records, obtains supplies, and makes selection decisions of new members into the work unit.

Although self-directed work teams are well-established in Europe and especially in Scandinavia, they are relatively new in the U.S.[17] However, recent surveys predict that as many as 40 percent of U.S. employees will be participating in self-directed teams by the year 2000.[18] Most companies that use self-directed work teams usually incorporate some type of group incentive pay based on the performance of the respective work teams. HRM in Action 15.4 describes how Saturn has implemented such a system.

Organizationwide Incentives
Incentives that reward all members of the organization based on the performance of the entire organization.

Organizationwide incentives reward members based on the performance of the entire organization. With such plans, the size of the reward usually depends on the salary of the individual. Most organizationwide incentive plans are based on establishing cooperative relationships among all levels of employees. One of the first and most successful organizationwide incentive plans was the Lincoln Electric plan, developed by James F. Lincoln.[19] In addition to providing many other benefits, this plan calls for a year-end bonus fund for employees based on the profits of the company. Thus, the plan encourages employees to unite with management to reduce costs and increase production so that the bonus fund will grow.

Some of the most common organizationwide incentive plans include gain-

HRM IN ACTION

Self-Directed Work Teams at Saturn

15.4

www.saturn.com

Since its inception, Saturn Corporation has billed itself as "a different kind of company." One way that has differentiated Saturn from most other companies is that it has a compensation system that motivates self-managed work teams to take risks and reap rewards for meeting quality and productivity goals.

At Saturn, total compensation is made up of base pay, risk pay, and reward pay. The base pay is lower than the market rate and that's the risk part. Team members have to make up that difference; however, they can go well beyond the market rate by earning more pay as a reward. The risk and reward system uses a combination of performance measures, including output, quality, training, and teamwork in its incentive formula.

One key to Saturn's compensation system is that it's shared by all employees; everybody is on the same program. Because results are reported on a quarterly basis, employees have the opportunity to see real results on a short-term basis and to improve where needed. In good years, when demand for Saturn cars has been high, reward pay has reached as high as $10,000 per employee per year.

Sources: Stephanie Overman, "Saturn Teams Working and Profiting," *HR Magazine,* March 1995, pp. 72–74, and Kenan S. Abosh, "Variable Pay: Do We Have the Basics in Place?" *Compensation & Benefits Review,* July/August 1998, pp. 12–22.

sharing plans, Scanlon-type plans, and employee stock ownership plans (ESOPs). These three types of plans are discussed in the following sections.

Gain-Sharing or Profit-Sharing Plans

Gain Sharing Programs also known as *profit sharing, performance sharing,* or *productivity incentives;* generally refer to incentive plans that involve employees in a common effort to achieve the company's productivity objectives. Based on the concept that the resulting incremental economic gains are shared among employees and the company.

Different companies know **gain sharing** by different names, such as *profit sharing, performance sharing,* or *productivity incentives.* These programs generally refer to incentive plans that involve employees in a common effort to improve organizational performance and then reward employees immediately when their performance improves.[20] Gain sharing is based on the concept that employees and the company share the resulting incremental economic gains. While many variants of gain sharing exist, they are all based on the same principles. First, the company must be able to measure its output; then, when employees reduce labor costs by increasing productivity, they share in the savings. For example, if it is determined that 25 percent of net production costs should be attributable to labor costs, any improvement below this target would be put into a bonus pool to be shared with employees. The division of these gains or profits, which are given in addition to normal wages and salaries, is usually based on an employee's base salary or job level. However, many variations are possible, including plans that give all employees the same amount, plans based on seniority, and plans based on individual performance. One survey of 223 companies using some type of gain sharing reported that 95 of the responding companies had custom-designed plans.[21]

Studies have shown that the average gain-sharing system raises productivity 25 percent and that quality also increases.[22] The U.S. General Accounting Office reports that firms with gain-sharing programs experience lower turnover and absenteeism, fewer grievances, and improved labor-management relations. One potential drawback to gain-sharing/profit-sharing plans is that the average employee may not perceive a direct relationship between individual output and the performance of the entire organization. However, it is not unusual for executives and top managers to have a significant amount of their total compensation based on the profits of the company. HRM in Action 15.5 discusses how Whirlpool successfully introduced a gain-sharing program.

HRM IN ACTION

Gain Sharing at Whirlpool

15.5

www.whirlpool.com

Benton Harbor, Michigan-based Whirlpool Corporation implemented a gain-sharing program that slashed $36.4 million in costs the first two years it was in place. In 1992 alone, two of the company's plants cut $800,000 in utility costs. Quality has also benefited; in 1995, 98 percent fewer quality problems occurred than in 1990.

Whirlpool's program is designed to provide employees with incentives to treat their work as though they were owners of the company. Whirlpool places all monies from cost savings, business improvements, and productivity gains into a fund for each specific facility, from which employees receive a quarterly cash payout for their efforts. In some facilities, this has resulted in more than $2,500 a year per employee. Because hourly and salaried employees share equally in any gains, the program has helped reduce the culture gap between the two groups. Even though the company maintains a philosophy that gain sharing should never replace wages, the program has alleviated pressure for base wage increases.

Source: Samuel Greengard, "Leveraging a Low-Wage Work Force," *Personnel Journal,* June 1995, p. 100.

Scanlon-Type Plans

Scanlon Plan
Organizationwide incentive plan that provides employees with a bonus based on tangible savings in labor costs.

The **Scanlon plan** was developed by Joseph Scanlon in 1927 and introduced at the LaPointe Machine Tool Company in Hudson, Massachusetts.[23] The Scanlon plan provides employees with a bonus based on tangible savings in labor costs and is designed to encourage employees to suggest changes that might increase productivity. Companies establish departmental committees composed of management and employee representatives to discuss and evaluate proposed labor-saving techniques. Usually the bonus paid is determined by comparing actual productivity to a predetermined productivity norm. Companies measure actual productivity by comparing the actual payroll to the sales value of production for the time period being measured. They place any difference between actual productivity and the norm in a bonus fund. The employees and the company share the bonus fund. Most Scanlon plans pay 75 percent of the bonus fund to employees and 25 percent to the company. Under the Scanlon plan, any cost savings are paid to all employees, not just to the employees who made the suggestions. Some companies have found that it is beneficial to review and modify their Scanlon plans periodically to take into account any changes that have occurred.[24]

Employee Stock Ownership Plans (ESOPs)

Employee Stock Ownership Plan (ESOP) Form of stock option plan in which the organization provides for purchase of its stock by employees at a set price for a set time period based on the employee's length of service and salary and the profits of the organization.

An **employee stock ownership plan (ESOP)** is a plan for providing employee ownership of company stock. ESOPs are generally executed in the form of a stock bonus plan or a leveraged plan. With either plan, an ESOP is established when the company sets up a trust, called an *employee stock ownership trust (ESOT)*, to acquire a specified number of shares of its own stock for the benefit of participating employees. With a stock bonus plan, the company annually gives stock to the ESOT or gives cash to the ESOT for buying stock. With a leveraged plan, the trust borrows a sum of money to purchase a specified number of shares of the company's stock. Generally, the company guarantees the loan. Then the company annually pays into the trust an agreed-on sum necessary to amortize and pay the interest on the loan. Under either plan, as the stock is received by the trust, it is credited to an account established for each employee. Allocations are usually based on relative pay, length of service, or some combination of the two. When the employee retires or leaves the company, the stock is either given to the employee or purchased by the trust under a buy-back arrangement.

The popularity of ESOPs grew rather dramatically from the mid-1970s to the late 1980s. For example, in 1988, over 9,000 companies had enrolled nearly 10 million employees in ESOPs. This was up from fewer than 500,000 covered employees in 1975.[25] Growth of ESOPs from the late 1980s through the mid 1990s almost ceased.[26] However, according to the National Center for Employee Ownership, the number of ESOPs is on the rise again.[27] As of mid-1997, about 10,000 companies had ESOPs in place with a net increase of 600 for the previous year.[28]

The amount contributed to ESOP plans is limited to 15 percent of the total payroll of covered employees or up to 25 percent for plans that combine stock bonus and other annuity plans. The contribution of employees is limited to the lesser of $30,000 or 25 percent of their annual compensation. One appealing feature of ESOPs is that they have specific tax advantages for both the organization and the employees. For example, the organization can use pretax dollars to pay back the loan used to purchase the stock. The dividends a company pays on stock held by its ESOP are treated like interest and are also deductible. An advantage that has recently emerged is using an ESOP to rebuff an unfriendly takeover. The more stock an ESOP holds, the better equipped the company is to fend off an unwanted tender offer. Employees benefit by being able to defer any capital gains until the stock is actually distributed. ESOPs can also give employees some voice in running the company. Table 15–7 summarizes the primary benefits of ESOPs for the organization, the employee, and the stockholders.

One underlying assumption of an ESOP is that having a piece of the action causes employees to take more interest in the success of the company. Several studies have shown that companies combining an ESOP with employee participation in decision making enjoy sharply higher sales and earnings growth.[29] Recent surveys have reported that most companies' financial figures and other performance measures improve following the implementation of an ESOP.[30] On the other hand, ESOPs can have a limited effect as incentives. This is especially true when each employee owns only a minuscule amount of stock. Also, it is possible that the price of the stock will go down rather than up. Thus, some employees view a stock option plan as more of a benefit than an incentive.

Table 15–8 summarizes the most frequently used incentive plans for nonmanagerial and managerial employees.

Variable Pay

Variable pay is an approach to compensation that attempts to reward employees by linking a percentage of their pay to certain performance accomplishments. Like

TABLE 15–7	**MAJOR BENEFITS OF EMPLOYEE STOCK OWNERSHIP PLANS**	
To Organization	**To Employees**	**To Stockholders**
Allows use of pretax dollars to finance debt.	Favorable tax treatment of lump-sum distribution, deferment of tax until distribution, and gift and estate tax exemptions.	Provides ready market to sell stock.
Increases cash flow.		Establishes definite worth of shares for estate purposes.
Provides a ready buyer for stock.	Allows employees to share in the success of the company.	Maintains voting control of company.
Provides protection against unwanted tender offers.	Provides a source of capital gains income for employees.	Protects the company from having to come up with large sums of money to settle an estate.
Protects the company from estate problems.	Can allow employees some voice in running the company.	
Can result in substantial tax savings.		Can result in preferential consideration for a government-guaranteed loan.
Can motivate employees by giving them a piece of the action.		

T A B L E   1 5 – 8   **SUMMARY OF MOST COMMONLY USED INCENTIVE PLANS**

Personnel	Type of Plan		
	Individual	**Group**	**Organizational**

Nonmanagers	Piece rate plans
	Plans based on time saved
	Commission plans
	Bonuses based on individual
	  performance
	Suggestion systems
		Bonuses based on group
		  performance
			Lincoln Electric plan
			Gain-sharing/profit-sharing
			  plans
			Scanlon-type plans
			Employee stock ownership
			  plans (ESOPs)

Managers	Bonuses based on organizational
	  performance (annual and
	  long-term)
	Stock option plans
	  Stock appreciation rights (SARs)
	  Phantom stock plans
	  Restricted stock plans
	Suggestion systems
		Bonuses based on group
		  performance
			Lincoln Electric plan
			Gain-sharing/profit-sharing
			  plans
			Scanlon-type plans
			Employee stock ownership
			  plans (ESOPs)

many types of incentive pay programs, most variable pay programs do not affect an employee's base salary, but they do make a percentage of potential total pay dependent on performance. One difference between variable pay programs and most of the previously described incentive programs is that most variable pay programs make *all* employees' pay variable as opposed to the pay of certain groups, such as senior executives or salespeople. A second difference is that many variable pay programs utilize individual, group, and organizational performance measures or some combination of these to determine an individual's incentive pay. For example, Chicago-based Ameritech Corporation uses a variable pay program for all 68,000 of its employees. Most Ameritech employees have 60 percent of their potential incentive pay based on group achievement and 40 percent based on individual achievement.[31] American Express has a variable pay plan that bases individual incentive pay 50 percent on company performance, 25 percent on performance of an individual's business unit, and 25 percent on individual achievement.

The real benefit of variable pay programs is that compensation for all levels of employees is tied to some type of performance measures and employees perceive this direct relationship between pay and performance.

Making Incentive Plans Work

Incentive plans have existed in one form or another for a long time. New plans are periodically developed, often as a result of changes in tax laws. As several examples in this chapter demonstrated, incentive compensation can make up a significant portion of an individual's total compensation. This is especially true with executives. If an incentive plan is to function as intended and generate higher performance among employees, it must be clearly communicated to employees and must be viewed as being fair. It also follows that the more employees understand an incentive plan, the more confidence and trust they will develop in the organization.

SUMMARY OF LEARNING OBJECTIVES

1. Describe the two basic requirements of an effective incentive plan.
  For an incentive plan to be effective, employees must believe their perfor-

mances and the performances of others are accurately and fairly evaluated and that the incentives (rewards) are based on performance.

2. **List and briefly discuss at least three types of individual incentives.**
   The differential piece rate plan pays employees one rate for all acceptable units produced up to some standard and then a higher rate for all pieces produced if the output exceeds the standard. Incentive plans based on time saved give an employee a bonus for reaching a given level of production or output in less than the standard time. Under the commission plan, employees are rewarded, based partly on their sales volume.

3. **Distinguish between a bonus and a merit pay increase.**
   A bonus is a reward offered on a one-time basis for high performance. A merit pay increase is a reward also based on performance, but perpetuated year after year.

4. **Discuss the role bonuses play in managerial compensation.**
   Bonuses are by far the most common type of incentive pay used for managers. The 1986 Tax Reform Act made bonuses even more popular. A 1991 survey reported that bonuses made up over 28 percent of total salaries.

5. **Differentiate between nonqualified stock options and incentive stock options (ISOs).**
   Stock option plans generally give managers an option to buy company stock at a predetermined, fixed price within a set period of time. Nonqualified stock options do not qualify for favorable tax treatment. Incentive stock options (ISOs) have certain tax advantages. Under an ISO, a recipient does not have to pay any tax until he or she sells the stock.

6. **Differentiate among the following different types of stock option related plans: stock-for-stock swap, stock appreciation rights, phantom stock plans, restricted stock plans, premium-priced options, and performance-vesting options.**
   Stock-for-stock swaps allow options to be exercised with shares of previously purchased company stock in lieu of cash. Stock appreciation rights (SARs) are often used with stock option plans. Under an SAR, an executive has the right to relinquish a stock option and receive from the company an amount equal to the appreciation in the stock price from the date the option was granted. In one form of phantom stock, the company awards stock as a part of its normal bonus plan. The receiver then defers this phantom stock until retirement when he or she then receives the accumulated shares of stock or its equivalent value. With another form of phantom stock, the receiver is credited with phantom stock and often after a stipulated period of time (usually three to five years) he or she is paid, in cash or equivalent shares, an amount equal to the appreciation in the stock. Under a restricted stock plan, a company gives shares of stock, subject to certain restrictions. Premium-priced options are similar to standard options except that the exercise price of the stock is set substantially above the current market price of the stock. Performance-vesting options, also called price-vesting options, are priced at the market price but only exercisable if the stock price reaches or exceeds a price goal within a specified time period.

7. **Describe how group incentives work.**
   Under a group incentive plan, all members of a specified group receive incentive pay based on the performance of the entire group. Many group incentive plans are based on factors such as profits or reduction in costs of operations.

8. **Explain what a gain-sharing plan is.**
   Gain sharing is also known as profit sharing, performance sharing, or productivity incentives. Gain-sharing plans generally refer to incentive plans that involve employees in a common effort to achieve the company's productivity objective. Gain sharing is based on the concept that the resulting incremental economic gains are shared among employees and the company.

9. **Discuss Scanlon-type plans.**

Scanlon-type plans provide employees with a bonus based on tangible savings in labor costs and are designed to encourage employees to suggest changes to increase productivity. Under a Scanlon-type plan, any cost savings are paid to all employees, not just to employees who made the suggestions.

10. **Explain how an employee stock ownership plan (ESOP) works.**

An employee stock ownership plan (ESOP) provides for employee ownership of company stock. ESOPs are generally executed in the form of a stock bonus plan or a leveraged plan. With either plan, an ESOP is established when the company sets up a trust, called an employee stock ownership trust (ESOT), to acquire a specified number of shares of its own stock for the benefit of participating employees. With a stock bonus plan, the company annually gives stock to the ESOT or gives cash to the ESOT for buying stock. With a leveraged plan, the trust borrows a sum of money to purchase a specified number of shares of the company's stock.

11. **Identify what distinguishes variable pay plans from most other incentive pay plans.**

Variable pay is an approach to compensation that attempts to reward employees by linking a percentage of their pay to certain performance accomplishments. One difference between variable pay programs and most other incentive programs is that most variable pay programs make all employees' pay variable as opposed to that of certain groups, such as senior executives or salespeople. In addition, many variable pay programs utilize individual, group, and organizational performance measures or some combination of these to determine an individual's incentive pay.

REVIEW QUESTIONS

1. What are two essential requirements of an effective incentive plan?
2. Outline the advantages and disadvantages of individual incentive plans.
3. What is a piece rate plan?
4. What is an incentive plan based on time saved?
5. Describe an incentive plan based on commission.
6. What is a suggestion plan?
7. What is a long-term performance plan?
8. Define a stock option plan.
9. Define each of the following stock option related plans: stock for stock swaps, stock appreciation rights, phantom stock plans, restricted stock plans, premium-priced options, and performance-vesting options.
10. Name the advantages and disadvantages of a group incentive plan.
11. What are self-managed work teams?
12. Describe the most common types of organizationwide incentive plans.
13. What are the benefits of an ESOP to employees? To the organization? To stockholders?
14. What are the major factors that differentiate variable pay plans from most other types of incentive pay plans?

DISCUSSION QUESTIONS

1. It has been said that incentive plans work only for a relatively short time. Do you agree or disagree? Why?
2. If you were able to choose the type of incentive pay system your company offered, would you choose an individual, a group, or an organizationwide incentive plan? Why?

3. If you were president of Ford Motor Company and could design and implement any type of incentive plan, what general type would you recommend for top management? For middle management? For supervisory management? For production employees?

4. What do you think about the way executive compensation has escalated in recent years? Do you think it is usually justifiable? Why or why not?

INCIDENT 15–1

Rewarding Good Performance at a Bank

The performance of a bank branch manager is often difficult to measure. Evaluation can include such variables as loan quality, deposit growth, employee turnover, complaint levels, or audit results. However, many other factors that influence performance, such as the rate structure, changes in the market area served by the branch, and loan policy as set by senior management, are beyond the branch manager's control. The appraisal system presently used by First Trust Bank is based on points. Points are factored in for a manager's potential productivity and for the actual quality and quantity of work. In this system, the vast majority of raises are between 4 and 10 percent of base salary.

Sales growth is a major responsibility of a branch manager. Although many salespeople are paid a salary plus bonuses and commissions, no commissions are paid on business brought in by a branch manager. Therefore, one problem for the bank has been adequately rewarding those branch managers who excel at sales.

In May 1999, First Trust Bank opened a new branch on Northside Parkway, located in a high-income area. Three competing banks had been in the neighborhood for some 15 years. Jim Bryan, who had grown up in the Northside Parkway area, was selected as branch manager. In addition to Jim, the branch was staffed with five qualified people. Senior executives of the bank had disagreed about the feasibility of opening this branch. However, it was Jim's responsibility to get the bank a share of the market, which at that time consisted of approximately $28 million in deposits.

After one year of operation, this branch had the fastest growth of any ever opened by First Trust Bank. In 12 months, deposits grew to $6 million, commercial loans to $1 million, and installment loans to $0.5 million. As measured by Federal Reserve reports, the new branch captured 50 percent of the market growth in deposits over the 12 months. The customer service provided was extremely good, and branch goals for profit were reached ahead of schedule. Aware of the success, Jim looked forward to his next raise.

The raise amounted to 10 percent of his salary. His boss said he would like to have given Jim more, but the system wouldn't allow it.

Questions

1. Should Jim have been satisfied with his raise since this was the maximum raise the system allowed?

2. Do you think the bank currently offers adequate sales incentives to its branch managers? If not, what would you recommend?

INCIDENT 15–2

Part-Time Pool Personnel

Crystal Clear Pool Company builds and maintains swimming pools in a large midwestern city. Crystal Clear handles pool maintenance through a contractual arrangement with the owners of the pools. Although individualized maintenance plans are available at a premium, the basic contract calls for Crystal Clear to vacuum the pools and adjust their chemical balance once a week. For 80 percent of the maintenance customers, the standard contract covers the months of May through September. The remaining 20 percent, who have either indoor or covered pools, require service year-round.

Because of the seasonal nature of the work, Crystal Clear hires many students during the summer. The maintenance staff is divided into three-person crews, each assigned to service six pools per day. In the summer, one permanent employee and two student employees comprise a team, with the permanent employee responsible for training the students. All maintenance crews are paid on a straight hourly basis.

The present system has been in force for several years, but it has resulted in at least two problems that seem to be getting more serious each year. The first is that the students hired for the summer demand to be paid the same wage rates that apply to the permanent employees. The reason is that the college students can get other summer jobs at these rates and are simply not willing to work for less. Naturally, the permanent employees resent the idea of being paid the same wages as the students. The second major problem involves the assignment of the pools, which vary in size and geographic location. The employees claim this is unfair because of the travel time required and differences in pool size. Some pools take three to four times as long to clean as others. Thus, some teams must work harder than others to service the six assigned pools.

Questions

1. What suggestions do you have for Crystal Clear to help remedy their compensation problems?

2. Can you think of any way to implement an incentive program at Crystal Clear? (Do not ignore the scheduling problems that might be created by such a program.)

3. In general, how do you think the problem of having to pay student employees the same rate as permanent employees could be resolved?

EXERCISE

Implementing Incentives

Assume you have been hired as a consultant to a medium-size sales organization to help it structure an incentive system for its three basic categories of employees. The first category is the sales force composed of 20 salespeople all working on a straight commission. The second category is composed of seven support employees (two secretaries and five packer/shippers). All seven work on a straight hourly wage rate. The third category is made up of the two owner/managers.

The owner/managers like the straight commission system the salespeople are on, but they suspect that many of the salespeople tend to slack off once they have attained an acceptable level of sales for any given month. The seven support employees appear to be steady workers, but management believes their performance could be enhanced with the right incentive program. The owner/managers are satisfied with their current salaries but would like to look for some tax shelter for any additional profits.

Your job is to design an incentive plan that will include parts that will be attractive to each of the three categories of employees. Be prepared to present your plan to the class.

NOTES AND ADDITIONAL READINGS

1. Donna Brown Hagarty, "New Ways to Pay," *Management Review,* June 1994, pp. 34–36, and Valerie Frazier, "Variable Compensation Plans Yield Low Return," *Workforce,* April 1997, pp. 21–25.
2. Skip Berry, "Ideas That Pay Off," *Nation's Business,* April 1991, p. 34.
3. Melissa Master, "Save Your Old Shoeboxes," *Across the Board,* February 1998, p. 62.
4. Michael A. Verespej, "Suggestion Systems Gain Lustre," *Industry Week,* November 16, 1992, pp. 11–18.
5. *The ECS Survey of Top Management Compensation, Summary Report 1998/99,* (Rochelle Park, N.J.: Watson Wyatt Data Services, 1998), p. 74.
6. C. Peck, H. M. Silvert, and K. Worrell, *Top Executive Compensation* (New York: Conference Board, 1996), p. 20.
7. *The ECS Survey of Top Management Compensation, Summary Report 1998/99,* p. 80.
8. Jennifer Reese, "Buy Stock—or Die," *Fortune,* August 23, 1995, pp. 14–16.
9. Michael A. Verespej, "Rubber Stamps: Going out of Style," *Industry Week,* October 19, 1998, pp. 11–12.
10. *Business Week,* May 4, 1992, p. 143.
11. Thoman A. Stewart, "CEO Pay: Mom Wouldn't Approve," *Fortune,* March 31, 1997, pp. 119–20.
12. Bethany McLean, "Where's the Loot Coming From?" *Fortune,* September 7, 1998, pp. 128–30.
13. Thomas G. Condon and Brian Zajac, "Feeling Your Pain," *Forbes,* November 2, 1998, pp. 280–92.
14. Ann Fisher, "Readers On CEO Pay: Many Are Angry, a Few Think the Big Guy Is Worth It," *Fortune,* June 8, 1998, p. 296.
15. John A. Byrne, "How Executive Greed Costs Shareholders $675 Million," *Business Week,* August 10, 1998, p. 29.
16. "The Problems with Executive Pay," *Journal of Business Strategy,* March/April 1998, pp. 16–20.
17. Renee Beckham, "Self-Directed Work Teams: The Wave of the Future?" *Hospital Material Management Quarterly,* August 1998, pp. 48–60.
18. G. L. Stewart and C. C. Manz, "Leadership for Self-Managing Work Team: A Typology and Integrative Model," *Human Relations* 48 (1995), pp. 747–69.
19. C. W. Brennan, *Wage Administration,* rev. ed. (Homewood, Ill.: Richard D. Irwin, 1963), pp. 228–89.
20. Kevin M. Paulsen, "Lessons Learned from Gainsharing," *HR Magazine,* April 1991, p. 70.
21. Carla O'Dell and Jerry McAdams, *People, Performance, and Pay* (Houston: The American Productivity Center, 1987), p. 34.
22. Prescott Behn, "An Answer to the Japanese Challenge," *HR Magazine,* August 1990, p. 76.
23. Brennan, *Wage Administration,* p. 299.
24. J. Ramquist, "Labor-Management Cooperation—the Scanlon Plan at Work," *Sloan Management Review,* Spring 1982, pp. 49–55.
25. Christopher Farrell and John Hoerr, "ESOPs: Are They Good for You?" *Business Week,* May 15, 1989, p. 118; John Hoerr and James R. Norman, "ESOPs: Revolution or Ripoff?" *Business Week,* March 20, 1989.
26. Steve Kaufman, "ESOP's Appeal on the Increase," *Nation's Business,* June 1997, pp. 43–44.
27. Ibid.
28. Ibid.
29. Christopher Farrell, Tim Smart, and Keith Hammonds, "Suddenly, Blue Chips Are Red-Hot for ESOPs," *Business Week,* March 20, 1989.

30. Peter Weaver, "An ESOP Can Improve a Firm's Performance," *Nation's Business,* September 1996, p. 63.

31. Shari Caudron, "Master the Compensation Maze," *Personnel Journal,* June 1993, p. 64C.

Employee Benefits

Learning Objectives

After studying this chapter, you should be able to:

1. Define employee benefits.
2. Describe how employee benefits have grown over the last several years.
3. Summarize those benefits that are legally required.
4. Differentiate between a defined-benefit pension plan and a defined-contribution pension plan.
5. Discuss the attractiveness of a cash-balance plan to employees.
6. What is a 401(k) plan and how does it differ from a 403(b) plan?
7. Explain the purposes of the Employee Retirement Income Security Act (ERISA) and the Retirement Equity Act.
8. Distinguish between an IRA, a Roth IRA, and a Keogh plan.
9. Describe a health maintenance organization (HMO) and a preferred provider organization (PPO).
10. Explain the concept of a floating holiday.
11. Discuss two reasons employees are often unaware of the benefits their organizations offer.
12. Explain the concept of a flexible-benefit plan.

Employee Benefits (Fringe Benefits) Rewards that employees receive for being members of the organization and for their positions in the organization; usually not related to employee performance.

Employee benefits, sometimes called **fringe benefits,** are those rewards that employees receive for being members of the organization and for their positions in the organization. Unlike wages, salaries, and incentives, benefits are usually not related to employee performance. Figures compiled by the U.S. Chamber of Commerce show that payments by organizations for employee benefits in 1996 averaged $14,086 per year per employee.[1] This figure includes social security, pensions, holidays, and vacations. The 1996 figure is down $573 from 1995 and represents the third year in a row that the figure has dropped. These same sources indicated that benefit payments varied widely among the reporting companies, ranging from under 18 percent of total payroll to over 65 percent of total payroll. The average of $14,086 represents approximately 41.3 percent of total compensation received by the average employee.

The term *fringe benefits* was coined over 40 years ago by the War Labor Board. Reasoning that employer-provided benefits such as paid vacations, holidays, and pensions were "on the fringe of wages," the agency exempted them from pay controls.[2] It has been argued that this action, more than any single event, led to the dramatic expansion of employee benefits that has since occurred. However, because of the significance of benefits to total compensation, many employers have dropped the word *fringe* for fear that it has a minimizing effect.

What Are Employee Benefits?

Table 16–1 lists potential employee benefits. In general, these can be grouped into five major categories, which are not all mutually exclusive: (1) legally required, (2) retirement related, (3) insurance related, (4) payment for time not worked, and (5) other. Table 16–2 categorizes many of the most common employee benefits. Table 16–3 shows how total benefit expenditures are allocated among the major categories. Most benefits apply to all employees of the organization; however, some are reserved solely for executives. Certain benefits, such as health insurance, are often extended to include spouses. An increasing number of organizations are extending benefits coverage to include unmarried heterosexual and homosexual partners of unmarried employees. According to a recent survey by Towers Perrin, the New York–based consulting firm, 23 percent of the respondents currently offer or are considering, offering benefits to employees' domestic partners, the partners' children, or both.[3] Another survey by Buck Consultants, a subsidiary of the Mellon Bank Corporation, found that while less than 10 percent of the responding employers offered some form of domestic partner benefits, nearly 30 percent were considering offering the benefits in the future.[4] HRM in Action 16.1 discusses why IBM began offering some benefits to domestic partners. It also lists numerous organizations that offer some benefits to domestic partners.

TABLE 16–1   **POTENTIAL EMPLOYEE BENEFITS**

Accidental death, dismemberment insurance	Health maintenance organization fees	Professional activities
Birthdays (vacation)	Holidays (extra)	Psychiatric services
Bonus eligibility	Home health care	Recreation facilities
Business and professional memberships	Hospital-surgical-medical insurance	Resort facilities
Cash profit sharing	Incentive growth fund	Retirement gratuity
Club memberships	Interest-free loans	Sabbatical leaves
Commissions	Layoff pay	Salary
Company medical assistance	Legal, estate-planning, and other professional assistance	Salary continuation
Company-provided automobile	Loans of company equipment	Savings plan
Company-provided housing	Long-term disability benefit	Scholarships for dependents
Company-provided or subsidized travel	Matching educational donations	Severance pay
Day care centers	Nurseries	Shorter or flexible work week
Deferred bonus	Nursing-home care	Sickness and accident insurance
Deferred compensation plan	Opportunity for travel	Social security
Deferred profit sharing	Outside medical services	Social service sabbaticals
Dental and eye care insurance	Paid attendance at business, professional, and other outside meetings	Split-dollar life insurance
Discount on company products	Parking facilities	State disability plans
Education costs	Pension	Stock appreciation rights
Educational activities (time off)	Personal accident insurance	Stock bonus plan
Employment contract	Personal counseling	Stock option plans (qualified, non-qualified, tandem)
Executive dining room	Personal credit cards	Stock purchase plan
Free checking account	Personal expense accounts	Survivors' benefits
Free or subsidized lunches	Physical examinations	Tax assistance
Group automobile insurance	Political activities (time off)	Training programs
Group homeowners' insurance	Price discount plan	Vacations
Group life insurance	Private office	Wages
		Weekly indemnity insurance

Source: D. J. Thomsen, "Introducing Cafeteria Compensation in Your Company," *Personnel Journal,* March 1977, p. 125. Reprinted with permission of *Personnel Journal,* Costa Mesa, CA. All rights reserved.

EXAMPLES OF COMMON BENEFITS, BY MAJOR CATEGORY

Legally Required	Retirement Related	Insurance Related	Payment for Time Not Worked	Other
Social security	Pension fund	Medical insurance	Vacation	Company discounts
Unemployment compensation	Annuity plan	Accident insurance	Holidays	Meals furnished by company
Workers' compensation	Early retirement	Life insurance	Sick leave	Moving expenses
State disability insurance	Disability retirement	Disability insurance	Military leave	Severance pay
	Retirement gratuity	Dental insurance	Election day	Tuition refunds
		Survivor benefits	Birthdays	Credit union
			Funerals	Company car
			Paid rest periods	Legal services
			Lunch periods	Financial counseling
			Wash-up time	Recreation facilities
			Travel time	

Growth in Employee Benefits

Prior to the passage of the Social Security Act in 1935, employee benefits were not widespread. Not only did the act mandate certain benefits, but its implementation greatly increased the general public's awareness of employee benefits. By this time, unions had grown in strength and had begun to demand more benefits in their contracts. Thus, the 1930s are generally viewed as the birth years for employee benefits.

As productivity continued to increase throughout and after World War II, more and more employee benefits came into existence, although the categories used differ slightly from those described earlier. Figure 16–1 shows how employee benefits grew from 1956 to 1996. 1996 represented the third year in a row that per-employee expenditures on benefits declined. Most of the decline is attributable to lower medical costs, which will be discussed later in this chapter. The following sections describe many of the more popular benefits offered by today's organizations.

Legally Required Benefits

As mentioned earlier, the law mandates certain benefits. This section discusses three benefits that fall in this category: social security, unemployment, and workers' compensation benefits.

BENEFITS EXPENDITURES, BY MAJOR CATEGORIES

Legally required benefits (employer's share only)	21.30%
Retirement related	15.25
Insurance related	24.21
Payment for time not worked	33.66
Other	5.56
Total	99.98%

Source: Based on figures from U.S. Chamber of Commerce Survey Research Center, *Employee Benefits* (Washington, D.C.: Chamber of Commerce of the United States, 1997), p. 13.

**Domestic Partner
Benefits**

16.1

www.ibm.com

Effective January 1, 1997, IBM extended health care coverage to the partners of gay and lesbian employees. The policy covers all of IBM's 110,000 employees throughout the U.S. At the time, this made IBM the largest U.S. company to offer benefits to this group. According to company officials, the policy covers only same-sex couples because opposite-sex domestic partners have the option of getting legally married. IBM officials said they implemented the policy because a rapidly growing number of other high-tech companies had and IBM didn't want to risk losing top talent. "It was a business decision," said Jill Kanin-Lovers, IBM's vice president of human resources. "We want to be in a position to attract and retain a broad spectrum of employees."

Microsoft, Apple Computer, Xerox, Hewlett-Packard, and Lotus Development Corp. are some of the other high-tech companies to offer domestic partner benefits. Some other organizations that recognize domestic partner benefits include:

The Village Voice, New York
American Psychological Association, Washington, D.C.
Greenpeace International, Washington, D.C.
Planned Parenthood, New York
Albert Einstein College of Medicine, New York
American Civil Liberties Union, New York
City of San Francisco, California
Berkeley Unified School District, California
City of Laguna Beach, California
City of Santa Cruz, California
City of East Lansing, Michigan
Montefiore Medical Center, New York
American Friends Services Committee, Pennsylvania
National Organization for Women, Washington, D.C.
Lambda Legal Defense & Education Fund, New York
Human Rights Campaign Fund, Washington, D.C.
Gardener's Supply Co., Vermont
City of Berkeley, California
City of West Hollywood, California
City of Seattle, Washington
Santa Cruz Metropolitan Transit District, California

Source: Jennifer J. Laabs, "Unmarried—with Benefits," *Personnel Journal,* December 1991, pp. 62–70, and "IBM Becomes Largest Employer to Offer Domestic Partner Benefits," *Business & Health,* October 1996, p. 16.

Social Security

Social Security Federally administered insurance system designed to provide funds upon retirement or disability or both and to provide hospital and medical reimbursement to people who have reached retirement age.

Social security is a federally administered insurance system. Under current federal laws, both employer and employee must pay into the system, and a certain percentage of the employee's salary is paid up to a maximum limit. Table 16–4 shows how social security costs have changed over the past several years.

With few exceptions, social security is mandatory for employees and employers. The most noteworthy exceptions are state and local government employees. For these employees to become exempt, a majority must vote to do so, and another retirement system must be substituted. Self-employed persons are required to contribute to social security at a rate higher than that paid by a typical employee, but lower than the combined percentage paid by both employer and employee. The

F I G U R E   1 6 – 1   **TOTAL EMPLOYEE BENEFITS AS A PERCENTAGE OF PAYROLL, 1956–1996**

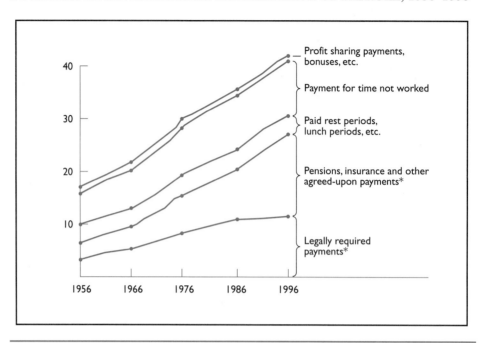

*Employer's share only.

Source: U.S. Chamber of Commerce Survey Research Center, *Employee Benefits* (Washington, D.C.: Chamber of Commerce of the United States, 1997), p. 41.

payments distributed under social security can be grouped into three major categories: retirement benefits, disability benefits, and health insurance.

Retirement Benefits under Social Security

To be eligible for periodic payments through social security, a person must have reached retirement age, actually be retired, and be fully insured under the system. The full periodic allotment to which the retiree is entitled may begin at age 65 for persons born before 1938. The age requirement increases slightly for persons born during 1938 or later (up to a maximum of age 67 for those born during 1960 or later). Those who retire as early as age 62 receive lesser amounts. A person is considered fully retired when he or she is earning from gainful employment less than a prescribed amount of money. (Money earned from gainful employment does not include income from investments, pensions, or other retirement programs). In 1998, this was $15,500 for people age 65 through 69 and $9,600 for people 62 to 64. However, these amounts change almost every year. Persons 70 and older are eligible for full retirement benefits regardless of their level of earned income. People aged 62–69 who earn more than the maximum amount allowed can still receive benefits but they are reduced depending on the age bracket.

The size of the retirement benefit varies according to the individual's average earnings under covered employment. However, there are maximum and minimum limits to what eligible individuals and their dependents can receive. Table 16–5 lists dependents who may be eligible for retirement benefits if an eligible employee dies.

Disability Benefits

Pensions may be granted under social security to eligible employees who have a disability that is expected to last at least 12 months or to result in death. To be eligible, a person must have worked in a job covered by social security for at least 5 out of 10 years before becoming disabled. These pensions are calculated with basically the same methods used for calculating retirement benefits.

TABLE 16-4

CHANGES IN SOCIAL SECURITY COSTS, 1978–99

Year	Percentage Paid by Employee	Maximum Taxable Pay	Maximum Tax
1978	6.05%	$17,700	$1,071
1979	6.13	22,900	1,404
1980	6.13	25,900	1,588
1981	6.65	29,700	1,975
1982	6.70	32,400	2,171
1983	6.70	35,700	2,392
1984	7.00	37,800	2,646
1985	7.05	39,600	2,792
1986	7.15	42,000	3,003
1987	7.15	43,800	3,132
1988	7.51	45,000	3,380
1989	7.51	48,000	3,605
1990	7.65	51,300	3,924
1991	7.65	53,200	4,070
1992	7.65	55,500	4,246
1993	7.65	57,600	4,406
1994	7.65	60,600	4,636*
1995	7.65	61,200	4,682*
1996	7.65	62,700	4,797*
1997	7.65	65,400	5,003*
1998	7.65	68,400	5,233*
1999	7.65	72,600	5,554*

*As of 1994, 1.45% (of the total 7.65%) going to Medicare was not limited by a maximum taxable pay. In prior years, this portion had been limited to an amount somewhat higher than the maximum taxable pay for the remaining 6.20%.

TABLE 16-5

DEPENDENTS ELIGIBLE FOR RETIREMENT BENEFITS IN THE EVENT OF DEATH OF A COVERED EMPLOYEE

1. Widow or widower at age 65, or age 60 if reduced benefits are chosen.

2. Widow or widower at any age, if caring for a child of the deceased. The child must be entitled to social security and be either disabled or under 18.

3. Disabled widow or widower 50 to 59 (at age 60 becomes eligible in above-mentioned widow or widower category).

4. Unmarried children under 18, or within two months following their 19th birthday for full-time students in high school, and those 18 or over who became disabled before reaching 22.

5. Dependent parents 62 or older.

6. Divorced wife if she is not married and is (1) caring for a child who is under 18 or disabled and who is entitled to social security benefits or (2) age 62 and was married to the deceased for 10 years.

Health Insurance

Health insurance under social security, commonly known as Medicare, provides partial hospital and medical reimbursement for persons over 65. Hospital insurance, which is known as Part A, is financed through the regular social security funds. Most hospital expenses and certain outpatient, posthospital, and home nursing expenses are covered by Part A of Medicare. The medical insurance, known as Part B, helps a participant pay for a number of different medical procedures and supplies that are completely separate from hospital care. For example, normal outpatient visits and checkups would fall under Part B. Participation in the medical insurance program (Part B) of Medicare is voluntary and requires the payment of a monthly fee by those wishing to receive coverage. This fee was $43.80 per month in 1998.

Problems Facing Social Security

Almost everyone is aware of the financial crisis faced by social security, which stems from major demographic changes that have taken place since the system was established. The basic problem is that fewer and fewer people are and will be working to support more and more retirees as the "baby boom" generation reaches retirement age.

Under the Social Security Board of Trustees' best estimates in late 1998, Social Security payments will exceed income by the year 2013.[5] By the year 2032, Social Security assets will be depleted. To resolve this imbalance, Congress must cut Social Security benefits, increase revenue to the program, or enact some combination of these options.[6] Many experts believe that the long-term solution to the Social Security problem is for individuals to supplement Social Security by some other type of retirement plan (other types of retirement plans are discussed later in this chapter).

Unemployment Compensation

Unemployment Compensation Form of insurance designed to provide funds to employees who have lost their jobs and are seeking other jobs.

Unemployment compensation is designed to provide funds to employees who have lost their jobs through no fault of their own and are seeking other jobs. Title IX of the Social Security Act of 1935 requires employers to pay taxes for unemployment compensation. However, the law was written in such a manner as to encourage individual states to establish their own unemployment systems. If a state established its own unemployment compensation system according to prescribed federal standards, the proceeds of the unemployment taxes paid by an employer go to the state. By 1937, all states and the District of Columbia had adopted acceptable unemployment compensation plans.

To receive unemployment compensation, an individual must submit an application through the state employment office and must meet three eligibility requirements: The individual must (1) have been covered by social security for a minimum number of weeks, (2) have been laid off (in some states, discharged employees may qualify), and (3) be willing to accept any suitable employment offered through the state's unemployment compensation commission. Many disputes have arisen regarding "suitable employment."

Generally, unemployment compensation is limited to a maximum of 26 weeks. Extended benefits can continue up to an additional 13 weeks during times of high unemployment. The amount received, which varies from state to state, is calculated on the basis of the individual's wages or salary received in the previous period of employment. The upper limit paid by most states is generally quite low. For example, in 1996 the range was from a $15 weekly minimum in Hawaii to a maximum weekly benefit of $400 in Connecticut.[7]

Unemployment compensation is usually funded through taxes paid by employers; however, in some states, employees also pay a portion of the tax. The Federal Unemployment Tax Act (FUTA) requires all profit-making employers to pay a tax on the first $7,000 of wages paid to each employee. The rate paid varies from employer to employer based on the number of unemployed people an organization has drawing from the state's unemployment fund. Thus, the system is designed to encourage organizations to maintain stable employment. Since the passage of the Tax Reform Act of 1986, unemployment compensation has been fully taxable.

Workers' Compensation

Workers' Compensation
Form of insurance that protects employees from loss of income and extra expenses associated with job-related injuries or illness.

Workers' compensation is meant to protect employees from loss of income and to cover extra expenses associated with job-related injuries or illness. Table 16–6 summarizes the types of injuries and illnesses most frequently covered by workers' compensation laws. Since 1955, several states have allowed workers' compensation payments for job-related cases of anxiety, depression, and certain mental disorders. Although some form of workers' compensation is available in all 50 states, specific requirements, payments, and procedures vary among states. However, certain features are common to virtually all programs:

1. The laws generally provide for replacement of lost income, medical expense payments, rehabilitation of some sort, death benefits to survivors, and lump-sum disability payments.

2. The employee does not have to sue the employer to get compensation; in fact, covered employers are exempt from such lawsuits.

3. The compensation is normally paid through an insurance program financed through premiums paid by employers.

4. Workers' compensation insurance premiums are based on the accident and illness record of the organization. Having a large number of paid claims results in higher premiums.

5. An element of coinsurance exists in the workers' compensation coverage. Coinsurance is insurance under which the beneficiary of the coverage absorbs part of the loss. In automobile collision coverage, for example, there is often coinsurance in the amount of $100 deductible for each accident. In workers' compensation coverage, there is coinsurance in that the workers' loss is usually not fully covered by the insurance program. For example, most states provide for a maximum payment of only two-thirds of wages lost due to the accident or illness.

6. Medical expenses, on the other hand, are usually covered in full under workers' compensation laws.

7. It is a no-fault system; all job-related injuries and illnesses are covered regardless of where the fault for the disability is placed.[8]

TABLE 16–6   **JOB-CONNECTED INJURIES USUALLY COVERED BY WORKERS' COMPENSATION**

Accidents in which the employee does not lose time from work

Accidents in which the employee loses time from work

Temporary partial disability

Permanent partial or total disability

Death

Occupational diseases

Noncrippling physical impairments, such as deafness

Impairments suffered at employer-sanctioned events, such as social events or during travel related to organization business

Injuries or disabilities attributable to an employer's gross negligence

---

Source: Russell L. Greenman and Eric J. Schmertz, *Personnel Administration and the Law,* 2nd ed. (Washington, D.C.: Bureau of National Affairs, 1979), pp. 190–91. Copyright © 1979 by The Bureau of National Affairs, Inc. Reprinted with permission.

Workers' compensation coverage is compulsory in all but a few states. In these states, it is elective for the employer. When it is elective, any employers who reject the coverage also give up certain legal protections.

Benefits paid are generally provided for four types of disability: (1) permanent partial disability, (2) permanent total disability, (3) temporary partial disability, and (4) temporary total disability. Before any workers' compensation claim is recognized, the disability must be shown to be work-related. This usually involves an evaluation of the claimant by an occupational physician. One major criticism of workers' compensation involves the extent of coverage provided by different states. The amounts paid, ease of collecting, and the likelihood of collecting all vary significantly from state to state.

After a decade of yearly double-digit increases in the cost of workers' compensation, in the early 1990s at least 35 states began to make changes in their workers' compensation laws.[9] These changes included tighter eligibility standards, benefit cuts, improved workplace safety, and campaigns against fraud. Recent data indicate that these changes are paying off. The rates of increases in the cost of workers' compensation have slowed considerably, and in 1993 the cost actually declined.[10] From 1993 through 1996, the cost of workers' compensation insurance continued to decrease.[11]

Retirement-Related Benefits

In addition to the benefits required by law under social security, many organizations provide additional retirement benefits. These benefits are in the form of private pension and retirement plans.

Pension Plans

Private Pension Plans Employee benefit that provides a source of income to people who have retired; funded either entirely by the organization or jointly by the organization and employee during employment.

Pension and retirement plans, which provide a source of income to people who have retired, represent money paid for past services. **Private pension plans** can be funded entirely by the organization or jointly by the organization and the employee during the time of employment. Plans requiring employee contributions are called contributory plans; those that do not are called noncontributory plans. Funded pension plans are financed by money that has been set aside previously for that specific purpose. Nonfunded plans make payments to recipients out of current contributions to the fund. One popular form of pension plan is the **defined-benefit plan.** Under a defined-benefit plan, the employer pledges to provide a benefit determined by a definite formula at the employee's retirement date. The other major type of retirement plan is the **defined-contribution plan,** which calls for a fixed or known annual contribution instead of a known benefit.

Defined-Benefit Plan Pension plan under which an employer pledges to provide a benefit determined by a definite formula at the employee's retirement date.

Defined-Contribution Plan Pension plan that calls for a fixed or known annual contribution instead of a known benefit.

The 1996 survey reported by the U.S. Chamber of Commerce found that approximately 87 percent of the participants had pension plans.[12] This can be compared with the fact that less than one sixth of the work force was covered by private pension plans prior to 1948.

Pension Rights

An inherent promise of security in some form exists in every pension plan. However, if the pension benefits are too low or the plan is seriously underfunded, this promise of security is breached, and employees who have spent most of their working lives with companies that have pension plans do not receive an adequate pension—or any, in some cases.

Vesting   Right of employees to receive money paid into a pension or retirement fund on their behalf by their employer if they leave the organization prior to retirement.

Another problem involves the vested rights of employees. **Vesting** refers to the rights of employees to receive the dollars paid into a pension or retirement fund by their employer if they leave the organization prior to retirement. For example, a vested employee can receive the funds invested by the employer at some later date. If not vested, the employee cannot receive the funds paid by the employer. A frequent approach is *deferred full vesting*, in which an employee, on meeting certain age and service requirements, enjoys full vested rights. A similar approach, called *deferred graded vesting*, gradually gives the employee an increasing percentage of benefits until the age and service requirements for full vesting are met.

Vesting requirements historically have caused problems for both employees and employers. In many old plans, the employee who was terminated or quit before retirement age did not receive any pension benefits regardless of the number of years worked under the pension plan or how close retirement was. Even under plans that did provide vesting rights, the requirements were strict in terms of length of service. Requirements for vesting are often made stringent by employers in an effort to keep employees from leaving the organization, at least until their rights have become fully vested. On the other hand, employers have experienced the problem of employees quitting after being vested in the pension plan to draw out the funds credited to them. To counteract this, employers have incorporated provisions in their pension plans stating that funds other than those contributed by the employee will not be distributed until the employee reaches a certain age, even if he or she has left the organization.

Defined-Benefit Plans

Defined-benefit plans have a specified formula for calculating benefits. Although there are numerous such formulas, the most popular approach has been the *final-average-pay plan*, in which the retirement benefit is based on average earnings in the years, generally two or five, immediately preceding retirement. The actual benefit sum is then computed as a function of the person's calculated average earnings and years of service. In another common approach, the *flat-benefit plan*, all participants who meet the eligibility requirements receive a fixed benefit regardless of their earnings.

Plans affecting salaried employees usually use the final-average-pay plan. Plans limited to hourly paid employees have traditionally used the flat-benefit plan. Where hourly and salaried employers are both affected, a final-average pay formula may be modified to provide a minimum dollar benefit for participants in the lower pay classifications. Many final-average-pay plans are now calculated with an offset, or deduction, for the employee's social security benefits. In these cases, the amount of social security a person receives is taken into account when determining how much she or he will receive from the pension plan. The 1996 U.S. Chamber of Commerce survey reported that 39 percent of the respondents made payments into defined-benefit plans.[13]

Cash-Balance Plans: The *cash-balance plan* is a hybrid of the traditional defined-benefit plan. The major difference is that *cash-balance plans* allow employees to take their cash-balance pension money with them in the form of a lump sum when they leave the organization. Another advantage of cash-balance plans is that participants can track the growth of their retirement funds in current dollars through regular statements. Participants in traditional defined-benefit plans are apprised only of what they should get at retirement. Thus, cash-balance plans are easier for the average employee to comprehend than are traditional defined-benefit plans. One drawback to cash-balance plans is that relatively junior employees can build up sizable cash balances and, once vested, leave the organization and take the cash with them. Traditional defined-benefit plans do not offer such ease of portability and therefore encourage employees not to leave.

Defined-Contribution Plans

With defined-contribution plans, every employee has a separate pension account to which the employee and the employer contribute. If only the employer contributes, it is a *noncontributing plan*. When both the employee and the employer contribute, it is a *contributing plan*. With a defined-contribution plan, the contributed money is invested and projections are made as to expected retirement income. However, the organization is *not* bound by these projections and hence unfunded liability problems do not occur. The benefits paid are a function of the rules of the plan and the actual value of the plan. Because the organization does not have a potential liability problem and because they are very portable, defined contribution plans have become increasingly popular.

401(k) Plan Allows employees to defer a portion of their pay into the plan, making contributions tax deductible (up to a limit).

The most popular type of defined-contribution plan is the **401(k) plan.** These plans were named after section 401(k) of the Internal Revenue Code, which became effective in 1980. The advantage of a 401(k) plan is that contributions are tax deductible up to a limit. Usually a 401(k) plan is set up to allow employees to defer a portion of their pay into the plan. Often employers will match employee contributions to some extent. The 1986 Tax Reform Act limited tax-exempt contributions under a 401(k) plan. In 1999, the limit was $10,000 per year per employee (this figure often changes from year to year). The 1996 Chamber of Commerce survey reported that 57 percent of the respondents made payments into 401(k) plans.[14] HRM in Action 16.2 describes how one company has successfully implemented a cash-balance plan paired with a 401(k) plan.

The **403(b)**, or Tax Deferred Annuity (TDA), plans are very similar to 401(k) plans except that they may only be used in not-for-profit organizations. These organizations are usually religious, charitable, and educational but also include other entities such as social clubs organized and operated for pleasure, recreation, and other non-profitable purposes.[15] As of January 1, 1997, the not-for-profit organization could also use 401(k) plans for the first time. Because the differences between the two type plans are subtle, most not-for-profit plan sponsors have chosen to stay with the familiar TDA plans rather than make changes.[16]

ERISA and Related Acts

Employee Retirement Income Security Act (ERISA) Federal law passed in 1974 designed to give employees increased security for their retirement and pension plans and to ensure the fair treatment of employees under pension plans.

In an effort to ensure the fair treatment of employees under pension plans, Congress passed the **Employee Retirement Income Security Act (ERISA)** in 1974. This law was designed to ensure the solvency of pension plans by restricting the types of investments that could be made with the plan's funds and providing general guidelines for fund management. ERISA also requires that employees have vested rights in their accrued benefits after certain minimum requirements have been met. Table 16–7 summarizes the major provisions of ERISA.

Since its inception, ERISA has been criticized as being overly costly. In fact, it

---

HRM IN ACTION

Cash-Balance Plan Paired with a 401(k) Plan

16.2

www.countrymark.com

In 1991, Indianapolis-based Countrymark merged with another farm co-op, Indiana Farm Bureau Cooperative Association (IFBCA). Countrymark recently switched from a traditional defined-benefit plan to a cash-balance plan paired with a 401(k) plan. IFBCA had offered a cash-balance pension plan since 1988. Benefits manager Joseph Worley believes the $80 million cash-balance plan offers Countrymark's 1,300 salaried and nonunion hourly employees "visibility, rewards, flexibility and accessibility."

Every month Countrymark assigns pay credits ranging from 3 percent of the employee's salary (for employees who have worked for the company less than five years) to 9 percent (for 30-year-plus veterans). Each cash-balance account also collects monthly interest credits based on the one-year Treasury bill rate.

Under the 401(k) plan that is paired with the cash-balance plan, participants can kick in as much as 15 percent of their pay and Countrymark will match half of the first 6 percent of that amount. There is also a profit-sharing kicker. If Countrymark does well, the notes from the company go up to two-thirds of the first 6 percent. Approximately 90 percent of Countrymark's eligible employees participate in the 401(k) option.

Source: Julie Rohrer, "Cash and Carry," *Institutional Investor,* April 1995, pp. 139–40.

TABLE 16–7   **MAJOR PROVISIONS OF ERISA**

Subject	Provisions
Eligibility	Prohibited plans from establishing eligibility requirements of more than one year of service, or an age greater than 25, whichever is later.
Vesting*	Established new minimum standards; employer has three choices: *a.* 100 percent vesting after 10 years of service. *b.* 25 percent after 5 years of service, grading up to 100 percent after 15 years. *c.* 50 percent vesting when age and service (if the employee has at least 5 years of service) equal 45, grading up to 100 percent vesting 5 years later.
Funding	Required the employer to fund annually the full cost for current benefit accruals and amortize past-service benefit liabilities over 30 years for new plans and 40 years for existing plans.
Plan termination insurance	Established a government insurance fund to insure vested insurance pension benefits up to the lesser of $750 a month or 100 percent of the employee's average wages during highest-paid five years of employment; the employer pays an annual premium of $1 per participant and is liable for any insurance benefits paid up to 30 percent of the company's net worth.
Fiduciary responsibility	Established the "prudent man" rule as the basic standard of fiduciary responsibility; prohibits various transactions between fiduciaries and parties-in-interest; prohibits investment of more than 10 percent of pension plan assets in the employer's securities.
Portability	Permitted an employee leaving a company to make a tax-free transfer of the assets behind his vested pension benefits (if the employer agrees) or of his vested profit-sharing or savings plan funds to an individual retirement account.
Individual retirement accounts (IRAs)	Provided a vehicle for transfers as noted above and permits employees of private or public employers that do not have qualified retirement plans to deduct 15 percent of compensation, up to $1,500, each year for contributions to a personal retirement fund. Earnings on the fund are not taxable until distributed.
Reporting and disclosure	Required the employer to provide employees with a comprehensive booklet describing plan provisions and to report annually to the Secretary of Labor on various operating and financial details of the plan.
Lump-sum distributions	Changed the tax rules to provide capital gains treatment on pre-1974 amounts and to tax post-1973 amounts as ordinary income, but as the employee's only income and spread over 10 years.
Limits on contributions and benefits	Limited benefits payable from defined-benefit pension plans to the lesser of $75,000 a year or 100 percent of average annual cash compensation during the employee's three highest paid years of service.
	Limited annual additions to employee profit-sharing accounts to the lesser of $25,000 or 25 percent of the employees' compensation that year.

*These requirements were changed by subsequent legislation.

Source: Adapted from D. G. Carlson, "Responding to the Pension Reform Law," *Harvard Business Review,* November–December 1974, p. 134.

has been reported that several companies dropped their pension plans rather than comply with ERISA.[17] Another major complaint has been that it causes an unwieldy amount of paperwork.

Retirement Equity Act Act passed in 1984 that liberalized eligibility requirements, vesting provisions, maternity/paternity leaves, and spouse survivor benefits of retirement plans.

In 1984, Congress passed the **Retirement Equity Act.** The overall impact of this act was to liberalize the eligibility requirements, vesting provisions, maternity/paternity leaves, and spouse survivor benefits of retirement plans. Table 16–8 summarizes the major provisions of the Retirement Equity Act.

The Tax Reform Act of 1986 provided for employees to become vested sooner than under ERISA and other legislation. The provisions of the Tax Reform Act of 1986 were generally applicable for plan years beginning after December 31, 1988. For plans beginning after this date, the general vesting provisions must follow one of two schedules:

TABLE 16–8

MAJOR PROVISIONS OF THE RETIREMENT EQUITY ACT

- Employees must be allowed to participate in a plan that qualifies for special tax treatment no later than age 21 with one year of service (previously, it was age 25 with one year of service).
- Vesting credit must be awarded for years of service beginning at age 18 (previously, service before age 22 could be ignored in most plans).
- For both vesting and participation purposes, as many as 501 hours of service must be awarded to any employee on maternity or paternity leave.
- An election to waive spouse survivor benefits must be made in writing by both the participant and spouse and witnessed by a plan representative or notary public.

Source: Stephen P. Kurash and Gene F. Fasoldt, "An Outline of Changes Required by the New Retirement Equity Act," *Personnel Journal,* November 1984, pp. 80–84.

- Cliff vesting, under which no vesting is provided during the first five years of service and the participant becomes vested after five years of service.
- Graded vesting, under which the participant becomes 20 percent vested after three years of service with an additional 20 percent vesting per year until the participant is 100 percent vested after seven years of service.

Mandatory Retirement

An amendment to the Age Discrimination in Employment Act (ADEA) that took effect on January 1, 1987, forbade mandatory retirement at any age for companies employing 20 or more people in the private sector (there are certain exceptions, as covered in Chapter 2) and for federal employees. Prior to the effective date of this amendment, January 1, 1979, employers could choose any age for mandatory retirement.

Early Retirement

Amended Age Discrimination in Employment Act (ADEA) Forbids mandatory retirement at any age for all companies employing 20 or more people in the private sector and in the federal government.

As an alternative to mandatory retirement, some organizations offer incentives to encourage early retirement. This method of reducing the work force is often viewed as a humanitarian way to reduce the payroll and reward long-tenured employees. The types of incentives offered vary, but often include a lump-sum payment plus the extension of other benefits, such as medical insurance. Another popular incentive is to credit the employee with additional years of service that can be used under a defined-benefit plan.

Most pension plans have special allowances for voluntary early retirement. Usually an employee's pension is reduced by a stated amount for every month that he or she retires before age 65. Popular early retirement ages are 55, 60, and 62. Most plans require that an individual have worked a minimum number of years with the organization to be eligible for early retirement. Early retirement has grown in popularity, partly because of the pension benefits available. Presently, the earliest an employee can receive social security retirement benefits at a reduced rate is at age 62.

Employees Not Covered by Pension Plans

Individual Retirement Accounts (IRA) Individual pension plan for employees not covered by private pension plans.

In 1981, legislation was enacted to allow employees to set up individual plans called individual retirement accounts (IRAs). Although the basic purpose of IRAs was to provide an option for employees not covered by private pension plans, anyone who has an earned income can invest in an IRA. With an IRA, an individual could originally make tax-exempt contributions to a maximum of $2,000 per year. In conjunction with a spouse-homemaker, a married person could contribute up to $2,250 per year. The 1986 Tax Reform Act drastically decreased the tax advantages of an IRA. From its effective date until January 1, 1998, IRA contributions (up to $2,000 single, $2,250 married) were totally deductible only if the individual's income was less than $25,000 (single) or $40,000 (married filing jointly) and the employee was covered by a company pension plan. Employees not covered by a company pension plan could deduct their entire contribution up to $2,000 single, $2,250 married, regardless of income. Interest earned on IRA accounts was still tax deferrable. The Tax Relief Act of 1997 (TRA 97), which went into effect January 1, 1998, raised the income limits for the deductibility of contributions to an IRA. Under the TRA 97, the maximum IRA deduction starts phasing out for single taxpayers at $30,000 and is zero by $40,000. For married couples, the range is $50,000 to $60,000. By the year 2005 the range for a single taxpayer will be increased to $50,000–$60,000, with the range for married couples eventually reaching $80,000–$100,000 in the year 2007. Another major change brought about by TRA 97 is that for a married couple filing a joint return, a spouse who is not an active participant in a qualified pension plan can now make a $2,000 deductible contribution to an IRA. The deduction is phased out if the combined income is between $150,000 and $160,000.

The **Roth IRA,** which was also created by the Taxpayer Relief Act of 1997, allows for nondeductible contributions of up to $2,000 annually ($4,000, married filing jointly), less the total amounts contributed to any other IRAs. All earnings in a Roth IRA then accumulate tax-deferred, and qualified distributions are made free of federal income tax and penalties. In order for withdrawals from a Roth IRA to be qualified as tax free, the withdrawals must be made: after the attainment of age $59\frac{1}{2}$, or due to death or disability, or for first-time home buyer expenses up to a lifetime limit of $10,000. Contributions to Roth IRAs are phased out from $95,000 through $110,000 of income for single taxpayers and $150,000 to $160,000 for joint filers. The Roth IRA is especially attractive for young employees because of the long-term growth potential of the investment. Although it can be complicated, it is possible in many circumstances to convert a traditional IRA to a Roth IRA.

A plan similar to IRAs, called a Keogh plan, has been set up for self-employed persons. Under a **Keogh plan,** self-employed persons can currently make tax-exempt annual contributions of up to $30,000 or 25 percent of net self-employment income, whichever is less.

Roth IRA Retirement plan that allows individuals to make nondeductible contributions and tax-free withdrawals with certain restrictions.

Keogh Plan Retirement plan allowing self-employed persons to make tax-exempt annual contributions of up to $30,000 or 25 percent of net self-employment income, whichever is less.

Preretirement Planning

A benefit that has recently evolved is preretirement planning. The purpose of such a planning program is to help employees prepare for retirement, both financially and psychologically. At the most basic level, preretirement planning provides employees with information about the financial benefits they will receive upon retirement. The subjects include social security, pensions, employee stock ownership, and health and life insurance coverage. Other programs go beyond financial planning and cover such topics as housing, relocation, health, nutrition, sleep, exercise, part-time work, second careers, community service, recreation, and continuing education.

The rapid pace of change in today's world, accentuated by changing federal laws and uncertainty concerning social security, have enhanced the need for some type of preretirement planning. This need is not expected to diminish in the near future.

Insurance-Related Benefits

Insurance programs of various types represent an important part of any benefit package. For example, the U.S. Chamber of Commerce reported that of 802 companies surveyed in 1996, 97 percent provided some form of medical insurance.[18] At the same time, however, many employees of small companies (which are not included in the U.S. Chamber of Commerce survey) are not covered by company-sponsored health insurance. Company-sponsored medical insurance programs are designed so that the employer pays either the entire premium or a portion of it, with the employee responsible for the balance. The entire issue of health insurance has been vigorously debated by the U.S. Congress over the last several years. Although no major legislative changes related to health insurance have been enacted, the debate is continuing.

Health Insurance

In addition to normal hospitalization and outpatient doctor bills, some plans now cover prescription drugs and dental, eye, and mental health care. Many health care plans incorporate a deductible, which requires the employee to pay a certain amount of medical expenses each year (usually $50 to $200 per person) before the insurance becomes effective. The health insurance plan then pays the bulk of the remaining expenses. Some plans pay the entire cost of health insurance for both the employees and dependents, some plans require the employee to pay part of the cost for dependents only, and some plans require the employee to pay part of the cost for both.

Over the years, two distinct health insurance plans have evolved: the base plan and the major medical expense plan. *Base plans* cover expenses for specified services within certain limits established for each kind of service. *Major medical plans* define a broad range of covered expenses, including all services that may be required for successful treatment. When used alone, a major medical plan is referred to as a *comprehensive plan*. Many organizations supplement a base plan with a major medical expense plan. The reason for combining the two is usually to reduce the deductible amount for certain types of treatment. The precise coverage, size of the deductible, and other specifics vary considerably among plans.

Managed Care

Due to rapidly escalating health care costs, many organizations have turned to various forms of managed care. The idea behind *managed care* programs is for the provider of the heath care, usually an insurance company, to organize and manage the program in a manner that will control costs. Managed care can be provided in a variety of forms. The health maintenance organization (HMO) and the preferred provider organization (PPO) are two of the most popular types of managed care programs.

Health Maintenance Organizations (HMOs): The Health Maintenance Organization Act of 1973 ushered in the concept of one-stop, prepaid medical services as an alternative to traditional insurance programs. Under this arrangement, organizations contract with an approved health maintenance organization (HMO) to provide all of the basic medical services the organization's employees need for a fixed price. HMOs can be structured in many different ways. Some HMOs own their facilities and pay doctors to work for them; others contract with a physician group to care for its patients; and still others contract either with individual doctors or with networks of independent physicians practicing in their own offices. Advantages of HMOs include emphasis on prevention of health problems and costs that are usually lower than those of traditional coverage. One major disadvantage, from the employee's viewpoint, is that employees must use physicians employed or approved by the HMO, and these may or may not be the doctors of their choice. A second disadvantage from the employee's viewpoint is that, in many instances, the HMO must preapprove certain procedures and treatments. Because of these disadvantages and the resulting general employee discontent, the picture of HMOs is not as bright as in the past.

HMO enrollments have slowed considerably. 1997 was the third consecutive year of declining profits and the first year of actual industrywide loss.[19] As of April 1998, 83.7 million Americans were members of 789 HMOs nationwide.[20]

Preferred Provider Organizations (PPOs): Preferred provider organizations (PPOs) are another alternative that emerged during the 1980s. A PPO is formed by con-

Health Maintenance Organization (HMO)
Health service organization that contracts with companies to provide certain basic medical services around the clock, seven days a week, for a fixed cost.

Preferred Provider Organizations (PPO)
Formed by contracting with

a group of doctors and hospitals to provide services at a discount or otherwise attractive price. Such providers are designated as "preferred" providers of care.

tracting with a group of doctors and hospitals to provide services at a discounted or otherwise attractive price. In exchange, these providers are designated as "preferred" providers of care. The major difference between an HMO and a PPO is that under a PPO, employees have much more freedom to choose their own doctors. PPOs do not restrict the provision of care to their own providers. They do, however, offer incentives, such as higher reimbursement levels, when care is received from a PPO member.

Dental Insuranc

Dental insurance has been one of the fastest-growing types of employee benefits in recent years. Surveys conducted by the Conference Board show that the number of companies providing dental plans grew from 8 percent in 1973 to 19 percent in 1975 and 41 percent in 1981.[21] In the 1996 Chamber of Commerce survey, 51 percent of the respondent companies provided dental insurance.[22] Some major medical expense plans include dental treatment, but most dental insurance is provided as a separate plan. The majority of dental plans specify a deductible and require the employee to pay a portion of the cost of services.

Life Insurance

Life insurance is a benefit commonly available from organizations. When provided for all employees, it is called *group life insurance.* Costs of this type of insurance, based on the characteristics of the entire group covered, are typically the same per dollar of insurance for all employees. Generally, the employer provides a minimum coverage, usually $10,000 to $20,000. Employees often have the option to purchase more insurance at their own expense. A physical examination is usually not required for coverage. Presently, employers can provide up to a maximum of $50,000 worth of life insurance for an employee without the cost of the policy being considered as income to the individual. The 1996 Chamber of Commerce survey reported that 84 percent of those companies surveyed provided at least some payment for life insurance.[23]

Accident and Disability Insurance

Disability Insurance Designed to protect employees who experience long-term or permanent disability.

In addition to health, dental, and life insurance, many organizations provide some form of accident or disability insurance, or both. Most accident insurance is designed to provide funds for a limited period of time, usually up to 16 weeks. The amount of benefit is often some percentage of the accident victim's weekly salary. **Disability insurance** is designed to protect the employee who experiences a long-term or permanent disability. Normally, a one- to six-month waiting period is required following the disability before the employee becomes eligible for benefits. As with accident insurance, disability insurance benefits are usually calculated as a percentage of salary.

Payment for Time Not Worked

It is now standard practice for organizations to pay employees for certain times when they do not work. Rest periods, lunch breaks, and wash-up times represent times not worked that are almost always taken for granted as part of the job. Recognized holidays, vacations, and days missed because of sickness, jury duty, and funerals represent other compensated times that are not worked.

Paid Holidays and Paid Vacations

Christmas Day, New Year's Day, Thanksgiving Day, Independence Day, Labor Day, and Memorial Day are currently provided as paid holidays by most companies.

Floating Holiday Holiday
that is observed at the
discretion of the employee
or the employer.

One relatively new concept is the **floating holiday,** which is observed at the discretion of the employee or the employer. The number of paid holidays provided by most companies appears to have stabilized at an average of 9 to 10 per year.

Typically, an employee must meet a certain length-of-service requirement before becoming eligible for a paid vacation. Also, the time allowed for paid vacations generally depends on the employee's length of service. Unlike holiday policies that usually affect everyone in the same manner, vacation policies may differ among categories of employees. Most organizations allow employees to take vacation by the day or week but not in units of less than a day.

Other Benefits

In addition to the previously discussed major benefits, organizations may offer a wide range of additional benefits, including food services, exercise facilities, health and first-aid services, financial and legal advice, counseling services, educational and recreational programs, day care services, adoption assistance, and purchase discounts. Employee assistance programs, a type of general service related to employee well-being, are discussed in Chapter 20.

The extent and attractiveness of these benefits vary considerably among organizations. For example, purchase discounts would be especially attractive to employees of a retail store or an airline.

The Benefit Package

Unfortunately, many benefit packages are thrown together piecemeal and are poorly balanced. There are many reasons for this. The major problem is that companies often add or delete new benefits without examining their impact on the total package. Also, they frequently add or delete benefits for the wrong reasons, such as a whim of a top executive, union pressures, or a fad. The key to any successful benefit package is to plan the package and integrate all of the different components. Such an approach ensures that any new benefit additions or deletions will fit in with the other benefits currently offered.

Many small companies have found they can lower the cost and keep benefits relatively high by working through their professional associations. In these cases, the professional or industry association offers different benefit options to its members. The association often can offer relatively attractive pricing because of the ability to group its members together.

Communicating the Benefit Package

Although most organizations provide some form of benefits to their employees, the average employee often has little idea of what he or she is receiving. An early 1990s survey of 600 human resource managers found that over 77 percent believed employees generally did not understand the benefit programs provided by their respective companies.[24] Why are employees often unaware of their benefits? One explanation is that organizations do not make much of an effort to communicate their employee benefits.

Another possible explanation is that descriptive material on benefits, when available, is often not easily understood by employees. One provision of the Employee Retirement Income Security Act of 1974 (ERISA) requires an employer to communicate at specified intervals certain types of benefit information in a manner employees can understand. Several methods can be used to evaluate the readability of written documents. Generally, in these methods the number of words per sentence and the percentage of difficult polysyllabic words in the passage are counted in a readability index related to a school-grade reading level.[25] The basic goal is to match the readability index of the benefit description to the educational level of the organization's employees.

The method used to communicate the benefit package is as important as the readability of the document. One successful method of communication is a personalized statement sent periodically to each employee. The employee earnings and benefits letter shown in Figure 16–2 is an example of such a statement. For organizations that use a computerized payroll system, some benefit information can easily be printed on each employee's check stub. The latest method for communicating benefits is to use intranet technology. Having access restricted to qualified users, the intranet, without any additional operating cost, can provide benefit information around-the-clock, seven days a week.[26] With the intranet, employees can log on at work or from any location and instantly access company information regarding most employee benefits, such as medical and dental plans. With this technology employees can even revise benefit forms and update their records. Other methods for communicating benefit information include posters and visual presentations, such as videos, slide shows, and flip charts. Meetings and conferences can also be used to explain an organization's benefits. HRM in Action 16.3 describes how LG&E Energy Corporation is using the intranet to communicate its benefits to employees.

Employee Preferences among Benefits

If an organization expects to get the maximum return from its benefit package in terms of such factors as motivation, satisfaction, low turnover, and good relations with unions, the benefits should be those most preferred by its employees. Ironically, however, organizations traditionally have done little to ensure that this is the case. Historically, they have offered uniform benefit packages selected by the human resource department and top management. Only on rare occasions or when demanded by a union contract are employees consulted concerning their benefit preferences.

Organizations that provide benefits without input from their employees assume management always knows what is best for the employees and that all employees need and desire the same benefits. Not too long ago, a "typical" employee was a middle-aged male who worked full time, supported 2.5 children, and had a wife who stayed home.[27] With the increasing diversity of today's work force, "there really is no such thing as a typical employee."[28] Given that the work force is far from homogeneous, it is not surprising that studies have shown that factors such as sex, age, marital status, number of dependents, years of service, and job title appear to influence benefit preferences.[29]

Flexible-Benefit Plans

write in def

Flexible-Benefit Plan (Cafeteria Plan)   Benefit plan that allows employees to select from a wide range of options how their direct compensation and benefits will be distributed.

401 K
IRA
Employee Benefits

Because of the differences in employee preferences, some companies began to offer flexible benefit plans in the mid-1970s. Under a **flexible-benefit plan,** individual employees have some choice as to specific benefits each will actually receive; usually employees select from among several options how they want their direct compensation and benefits to be distributed. The idea is to allow employees to select benefits most appropriate to their individual needs and lifestyles. For example, a middle-aged employee with several children in school might choose to take a set of benefits that differs from those chosen by a young, single employee.

Flexible plans are also called **cafeteria plans** because they provide a "menu," or choice of benefits, from which employees select. The selection possibilities within a flexible-benefit plan may vary considerably from plan to plan. Some plans limit

FIGURE 16-2   **SAMPLE EMPLOYEE EARNINGS AND BENEFITS LETTER**

Company Name
Address
Date

Employee's Name
Address

Dear

    Enclosed are your W-2 forms showing the amount of taxable income that you received from _____ during the year ____. Listed below in Section A are your gross wages and a cost breakdown of various benefit programs that you enjoy. In addition to the money you received as wages, the company paid benefits for you that are not included in your W-2 statement. These are benefits that are sometimes overlooked. In an easy-to-read form, here's what _____ paid to you for the year ____.

Section A—Paid to you in your W-2 earnings:

Cost-of-living allowance _____
Shift premium _____
Service award(s) _____
Vacation pay _____
Holiday pay _____
Funeral pay _____
Jury duty pay _____
Military pay _____
Accident & sickness benefits _____
Regular earnings _____
Overtime earnings _____
Allowances _____
    Gross wages _____

Section B—Paid for you and not included on your W-2 earnings:

Company contributed to pension plan _____
Company cost of your health insurance payments _____
Company cost of your dental insurance _____
Company cost of your life & accidental death insurance _____
Company cost for social security tax on your wages _____
Company cost of the premium for your workers' compensation _____
Company cost for the tax on your wages for unemployment compensation _____
Company cost for the tuition refund _____
Company cost for safety glasses _____
Company cost for exercise facilities _____
Company cost for financial planning services _____
    Total cost of benefits not included in W-2 earnings _____
      Total _____ paid for your services for the year ____ _____

    You have earned the amount on the bottom line, but we want to give you a clearer idea of the total cost of your services to the company, and the protection and benefits that are being purchased for you and your family.
        Sincerely,

        Manager of Human Resources

Source: Adapted from J. C. Claypool and J. P. Cargemi, "The Annual Employee Earnings and Benefits Letter," *Personnel Journal,* July 1980, p. 564.

HRM IN ACTION

Communicating Benefits through the Intranet

16.3

www.lgeenergy.com

LG&E Energy Corporation began constructing an intranet in 1996. The intranet was designed to serve a wide range of corporate communications interests with a major one being benefits communication. The LG&E Energy home page includes links to eight major business functions, as well as links to many other pages, including the company phone directory and recent news reports about the company and industry. Users can access the benefits home page directly or by linking through the Administration and Human Resources home pages. Once users get into the benefits home page they can access all kinds of information about their 401(k) plan, their medical and dental insurance, and even assistance in balancing the demands of work and family life.

According to George Seitz, LG&E's manager of information technology planning. "The intranet has the effect of extending the hours of the benefits department to 24-hours-a-day, seven-days-a-week, without any additional operating cost. Employees can sign on during the evening and weekends and retrieve a great deal of information about benefits and services even when the department is closed." Seitz also believes that the intranet has other major benefits: "Using the intranet to keep employee records current not only eliminates a once-tedious and time-consuming administrative job, but it also allows employees to control the accuracy and timeliness of their own records. The intranet allows people to manage a great deal of information that was once managed by other staff departments such as information systems and human resources."

While LG&E Energy hasn't performed a cost-benefit analysis of its intranet, usage data show that the system has become an important and often-used part of the organization's total management information system.

Source: Frank E. Kuzmits, "Communicating Benefits: A Double-Click Away," *Compensation & Benefits Review,* September/October 1998, pp. 60–64.

---

the choices to only a few types of coverage, such as life insurance and health insurance. Others allow employees to choose from a wide range of options.

The number of companies offering flexible plans is not huge, but it has been growing steadily since 1980. TRW Systems and Energy Group, Education Testing Service, American Can, Northern States Power, and North American Van Lines (a subsidiary of PepsiCo) were some of the first companies to offer flexible benefits.

Why Are Flexible Plans Attractive?

Flexible plans may be of interest to organizations for several reasons:

1. Employee benefits are a very significant component of overall compensation.

2. Flexible benefits can allow employers to limit their contributions without alienating employees, since options give employees some control over the distribution of benefits.

3. Lifestyles have changed in the past several years, causing employees to reevaluate the need for certain traditional benefits. For example, in a family where both spouses work and receive family medical insurance, one coverage is sufficient.

4. Benefits can be useful in recruiting and retaining employees. However, when a mandatory benefit package is largely unresponsive to a prospective employee's needs or to the retention of present employees, the organization is wasting money.

5. The high cost of benefits is causing organizations to try to communicate effectively the real cost to the employee. By making specific benefit choices, the employee becomes highly familiar with the costs associated with each benefit.

6. There can be positive tax ramifications for employees. Also, because certain benefits are taxable and others are not, different benefit mixes can be attractive to different employees (the tax ramifications of flexible plans are discussed shortly).

7. A flexible plan can have a positive impact on employee attitudes and behavior.

8. It can lower overall health care costs.[30]

Problems with Flexible Plans

Flexible plans are not without their difficulties. The major problems are as follows:

1. A flexible plan requires more effort to administer.

2. Unions often oppose flexible plans because they are required to give up control over the program details or face losing some of their previously negotiated benefit improvements.

3. Employees may not choose those benefits that are in their own best interests.

4. Tax laws limit the amount of individual flexibility in certain situations.[31]

Tax Implications of Flexible Plans

Flexible plans can have certain tax advantages by allowing employees to purchase benefits on a pretax basis.[32] Contributions made under a flexible plan are generally not subject to social security tax (FICA).

Flexible-benefit plans that offer employees choices between taxable and nontaxable benefits are subject to special rules under the Internal Revenue Code's Section 125, enacted in 1978. Plans that offer choices only among nontaxable benefits are not subject to Section 125. The Deficit Reduction Act (DEFRA) of 1984

HRM IN ACTION

Flexible-Benefit Program at ICL

16.4

www.icl.com

ICL is a large information technology company based in the United Kingdom. "Unless you have been self-employed, you probably don't appreciate the value of company benefits," says Catherine Turner, employment director at ICL, explaining the reasoning behind ICL's recent introduction of a flexible benefits program. "Our original objective was twofold. We wanted to find a medium for communicating to individuals what the benefits were, and we wanted to give people the opportunity to choose what they want."

The program was launched in 1997 after various focus groups had helped identify what benefits should be included. The ICL programs allow employees to opt for a higher level of salary with a lower benefits package or a lower level of salary with a higher benefits package. The program includes pension plans, life insurance, medical insurance, the buying and selling of holiday time, dental insurance, a critical illness plan, and child care vouchers. For all entitlement calculations, the company works on the basis of the salary an employee would have received had the flex programs not changed the proportion of overall income spent on benefits.

The pilot group was given two months or so to make their selection and then asked to sign up. "The most popular option," says Turner, "was to increase the accrual rate in pensions. Not many people traded up on holidays. In fact more employees sold holidays than bought them—the problem most people have is finding time to take holidays." The company rolled out flexible benefits to all its U.K. employees in April. Of the original pilot group, well over 90 percent signed up for the flex program.

Source: "Flex Means More in Terms of Value rather than More Per Se," *Management Today,* July 1998, p. 68.

clarified many of the tax questions that had clouded flexible benefits since the inception of Section 125. The following list summarizes many of the requirements resulting from Section 125 and/or DEFRA:

- An employer cannot require an employee to complete more than three years of service before becoming eligible under the plan.

- Flexible plans must offer a choice between only taxable and statutory nontaxable benefits. Taxable benefits allowed include cash, group term life insurance in excess of $50,000 and group term life insurance for dependents. Statutory nontaxable benefits include group term life insurance, group legal services, accident and health benefits, dependent care assistance, and certain types of deferred compensation. Vacation days are also treated as nontaxable benefits.

- If more than 25 percent of the total nontaxable benefits in the plan are provided for key employees, as defined by Section 416(i)(1) of the Internal Revenue Code, the key employees will be taxed on the value of those benefits.

- Employee benefits elections must be irrevocable and made at the beginning of the period of coverage.

- No change in coverage is allowed except in the case of a change in family status.

- No cash-out or carryover of individual balances is allowed if the selected benefits are not fully used. In other words, any monies left in an account at the end of the year must be forfeited.

Although the present laws do place certain restrictions, there is still considerable opportunity for establishing effective flexible plans, and the potential gains from flexible plans are large enough to merit consideration. After a brief hiatus as a result of the federal health reform initiatives in 1993–1994, flexible benefit packages are reemerging as a vehicle of choices for broad-based employee benefit and total compensation planning.[33] HRM in Action 16.4 describes how one U.K. company has implemented a flexible-benefit program.

SUMMARY OF LEARNING OBJECTIVES

1. **Define employee benefits.**
   Employee benefits, sometimes called fringe benefits, are those rewards that organizations provide to employees for being members of the organization. In general, benefits can be grouped into five major categories: (1) legally required, (2) retirement related, (3) insurance related, (4) payment for time not worked, and (5) other.

2. **Describe how employee benefits have grown over the last several years.**
   Employee benefits have grown steadily over the past several years. Specifically, they grew from approximately 15 percent of total compensation in 1951 to approximately 39 percent of total compensation in 1994.

3. **Summarize those benefits that are legally required.**
   The three primary benefits mandated by law are social security, unemployment compensation, and workers' compensation benefits. Social security is a federally administered insurance system. Under current federal laws, both employer and employee must pay into the system, and a certain percentage of the employee's salary is paid up to a maximum limit. The payment distributed under social security can be grouped into three major categories: retirement benefits, disability benefits, and health insurance. Unemployment compensation is designed to provide funds to employees who have lost their jobs through no fault of their own and are seeking other jobs. Unemployment compensation is usually funded through taxes paid by employers; however, in some states employees also pay a portion of the tax. Workers' compensation is meant to protect employees from loss of income and extra expenses

associated with job-related injuries or illnesses. Workers' compensation coverage varies significantly among different states.

4. **Differentiate between a defined-benefit pension plan and a defined-contribution pension plan.**

   Under a defined-benefit pension plan, the employer pledges to provide a benefit determined by a definite formula at the employee's retirement date. A defined-contribution pension plan calls for a fixed or known annual contribution instead of a known benefit.

5. **Discuss the attractiveness of a cash-balance plan to employees.**

   Cash-balance plans are attractive to employees because they allow employees to take their cash-balance pension money with them in the form of a lump sum when they leave the organization. Cash-balance plans also allow participants to track the growth of their retirement funds in current dollars through regular statements.

6. **What is a 401(k) plan and how does it differ from a 403(b) plan?**

   A 401(k) plan is a defined-contribution pension plan named after section 401(k) of the Internal Revenue Code. A 401(k) plan allows employees to make tax deductible contributions up to certain limits ($10,000 per year in 1999). Often employers will match the employee contributions to some extent. The 403(b) or Tax Deferred Annuity (TDA) plans are very similar to 401(k) plans except that they may only be used in not-for-profit organizations.

7. **Explain the purposes of the Employee Retirement Income Security Act (ERISA) and the Retirement Equity Act.**

   ERISA was passed by Congress in 1974 in an effort to ensure the fair treatment of employees under pension plans. The law was designed to ensure the solvency of pension plans by restricting the types of investments that can be made with the plan's funds and providing general guidelines for fund managers. The overall impact of the Retirement Equity Act, which was passed in 1984, was to liberalize the eligibility requirements, vesting provisions, maternity/paternity leaves, and spouse survivor benefits of retirement plans.

8. **Distinguish between an IRA, a Roth IRA, and a Keogh plan.**

   An IRA is a type of individual pension plan that can be used to make tax deductible contributions up to a limit of $2,000 per year per person. When withdrawals are subsequently made from an IRA they are taxable as ordinary income. With a Roth IRA non-tax-deductible contributions of up to $2,000 per year per person can be made. When withdrawals are subsequently made, they are tax-free. A Keogh is a type of pension plan similar to a traditional IRA except that it is designed for use by self-employed persons.

9. **Describe a health maintenance organization (HMO) and a preferred provider organization (PPO).**

   HMOs provide certain basic medical services for an organization's employees for a fixed price. Advantages of HMOs include an emphasis on prevention of health problems and generally lower costs. A major drawback is that employees must use physicians employed or approved by the HMO. PPOs are similar to HMOs in many ways. A PPO is formed by contracting with a group of doctors and hospitals to provide services at a discounted or otherwise attractive price. Under a PPO, employees are free to go to any doctor or facility on an approved list.

10. **Explain the concept of a floating holiday.**

    A floating holiday is a holiday observed at the discretion of the employee or the employer.

11. **Discuss two reasons employees are often unaware of the benefits their organizations offer.**

    One reason is that organizations often make little effort to communicate their employee benefits. A second reason is that descriptive material, when provided, is often not easily understood by employees.

12. Explain the concept of a flexible-benefit plan.

Under a flexible-benefit plan, individual employees have some choice as to the specific benefits they will actually receive; usually employees select from among several options how they want their direct compensation and benefits to be distributed. Flexible plans are also known as cafeteria plans or benefits.

REVIEW QUESTIONS

1. What is social security? Describe the three major categories of social security.
2. Briefly explain how unemployment compensation works.
3. What types of injuries and illnesses are covered by workers' compensation?
4. Describe the differences between defined-benefit pension plans and defined-contribution pension plans.
5. What is the most popular type of defined-contribution plan? How does it work?
6. What is a cash-balance plan?
7. State the overriding purpose of the Employee Retirement Income Security Act (ERISA).
8. What are three pension alternatives for individuals not covered by private pension plans?
9. Discuss some of the insurance programs offered to employees by organizations.
10. What is a health maintenance organization (HMO)? A preferred provider organization (PPO)?
11. Why are many employees unaware of some of the benefits provided by their organizations?
12. What is the flexible approach to benefits? List the advantages and disadvantages of flexible plans.

DISCUSSION QUESTIONS

1. If an average production employee were given the option to have an additional $100 per month in salary or the equivalent of $200 per month in voluntary benefits, which do you think the employee would choose? Why? What are the implications of your answer for management?
2. Develop and discuss at least two arguments in support of social security. Compare and contrast your arguments.
3. If your employer offered you an option to join an HMO, would you be interested? Why or why not?
4. Many people believe employers use pension vesting requirements solely for the purpose of retaining employees. If this is completely or even partially true, do you think such behavior is ethical? Why or why not?

INCIDENT 16-1

Who Is Eligible for Retirement Benefits?

Preston Jones, 51, had been an hourly worker in a machine shop of Armon Company for 21 years and four months. On a Christmas holiday, he suffered a severe heart attack and was hospitalized for three weeks. At his release, his doctor said he was to rest at home for a couple of months. After his recuperation period, his doctor, along with Armon Company's physicians, was to decide whether or not Preston should be retired for disability reasons. They never got the opportunity to make this decision; in February, Preston died of a second heart attack. He left a wife, four sons, two daughters, and two daughters-in-law. Mrs. Jones still had four children at home.

As a part of Preston's estate, his wife received the normal group insurance payments, the balance of his savings plan account, and the other benefits due her. However, she did not receive a pension from Armon as a survivor of an eligible employee.

When Mrs. Jones and the company representatives had discussed the settlement, she had inquired about her husband's pension and about her right to receive it. The human resource department had stated that since contributions to this fund were made only by the company, no survivor's benefits were provided.

Questions

1. What do you think Mrs. Jones should do at this point?
2. What does the Employment Retirement Income Security Act of 1974 have to say about this issue?

INCIDENT 16–2

Benefits for Professionals

LJT, Architects, a small architectural firm organized as a sole proprietorship, serves clients in the New York metropolitan area. Anticipating a good year, Len Elmore, the principal, hopes for a gross of between $300,000 and $400,000.

In an architectural practice, revenue is produced by providing a variety of services that range from creating a design and generating the construction documents used by a contractor in executing the project to visiting the site periodically to verify that construction is progressing according to specifications. Architects are also responsible for coordinating their work with that of the engineers and other consultants associated with projects.

Many small architectural firms such as LJT, Architects, have no permanent employees. They hire workers for a particular project with the understanding that they might remain after a particular phase of the project is completed but they might also be laid off. Employees are usually needed for the functions of design, development, and production of construction documents, which include approximately 50 to 70 percent of the services provided under a standard architectural agreement.

Firms acquire the personnel needed for these projects in several ways. They hire personnel on a full-time permanent or temporary basis or on a part-time basis to moonlight (i.e., as a second job). An employee might also be borrowed from another firm whose contracted work has been completed with no new work foreseen immediately. Len believes that hiring full-time temporary or permanent employees gives him more control over the production aspect of his practice.

At this time, Len does not follow any formal personnel policies. He prefers to "work things out" as issues and problems arise. When hiring, he will agree verbally to certain broad terms of employment, compensation, and benefits common to local professional offices, such as two weeks' vacation per year. He usually insists on a two-week to one-month probationary period during which the salary paid is slightly less than normal. A spot check of some of his colleagues leads him to believe his salary rates are comparable with those of similar employers. Because the nature of the employment tends to be temporary, Len suggests a contract arrangement with his employees, in which no taxes are withheld and no government-required benefits are provided.

Len's plans for expansion include adding employees until his staff numbers 10. For him, this is the best staff size to provide high-quality professional services.

However, the employment situation is easing for workers in architectural firms; more newspaper ads seek applicants, and fewer callers contact Len for jobs. Those coming for interviews ask more than "When do I start?" Many ask about vacations, sick leave, paid holidays, medical insurance, and profit-sharing plans. Others want to know about the possibilities of advancement with LJT, Architects, and about such long-range benefits as pensions and education leave.

In view of the situation, Len has decided to look into providing his employees with a benefit package. At the same time, however, he fears his practice may be too small to begin providing these benefits, which may prove to be extremely expensive. He has set aside money from his own earnings to provide these extras for himself and has difficulty understanding why his employees cannot do the same.

Questions

1. What recommendations would you make to Len?
2. How much do you think your recommendations would cost?

EXERCISE

Taking a Raise

Assume you are currently employed as a human resource specialist for a medium-size company. You have been in your job for a little over two years, and your current salary is $42,000 per year. Two months ago, your company announced it was going to implement a flexible-benefit plan in conjunction with this year's salary raises. Your annual salary review was held last week, and you were informed that your raise would be equivalent to $3,000. For your salary level, the following options are available:

1. Take the entire raise as a monthly salary increase.
2. Take as much of the $3,000 as you desire in the form of vacation at the equivalent of $200 per day.
3. Have as much as you desire of the $3,000 put into a tax-sheltered retirement plan.
4. Purchase additional term life insurance at the cost of $250 per $100,000 of face value.
5. Purchase dental insurance at the cost of $20 per month for yourself and $10 per month for each dependent.

The company currently provides full health insurance at no cost to employees. How would you elect to take your raise? Be prepared to share your answer with the class.

NOTES AND ADDITIONAL READINGS

1. U.S. Chamber Survey Research Center, *Employee Benefits* (Washington, D.C.: Chamber of Commerce of the United States, 1997), pp. 9, 12.
2. R. M. McCaffery, "Employee Benefits: Beyond the Fringe?" *Personnel Administrator*, May 1981, p. 26.
3. Elaine McShulskis, "Increased Interest in Domestic Partner Benefits," *HR Magazine*, February 1997, pp. 28–29.
4. Bill Leonard, "Many Employers Considering Domestic Partner Benefits," *HR Magazine*, October 1998, pp. 30–31.
5. Martha Priddy Patterson, "Social Security Reform: Start with the Facts," *Compensation & Benefits Review*, September/October 1998, pp. 42, 44.
6. Janice M. Gregory, "Social Security Reform: The Facts from the Employer's

Viewpoint," *Compensation & Benefits Review,* September/October 1998, pp. 56–59.

7. Arthur L. Rouselle Jr., "Reducing Unemployment Compensation Insurance Taxes," *Management Accounting,* May 1996, p. 16.

8. S. Ledvinka, *Federal Regulations of Personnel and Human Resource Management* (Boston: Kent Publishing, 1981), p. 144.

9. *CFO,* June 1995, p. 52.

10. Ibid.

11. Bill Leonard, "Study Finds Workers' Comp Costs Have Decreased Sharply," *HR Magazine,* February 1998, p. 10; and Elaine McShulskis, "Workers' Comp Costs Drop," *HR Magazine,* March 1998, p. 28.

12. U.S. Chamber Survey Research Center, *Employee Benefits,* p. 32.

13. Ibid.

14. Ibid.

15. Herb Smith, "401(k) vs. 403(b): New Choices for Not-for-Profit Companies," *Fund Raising Management,* October 1998, p. 36.

16. Ibid.

17. P. S. Greenlaw and W. D. Biggs, *Modern Personnel Management* (Philadelphia: W. B. Saunders, 1979), p. 513.

18. U.S. Chamber Survey Research Center, *Employee Benefits,* p. 32.

19. "The Lowdown on HMOs," *Business & Health,* October 1998, p. 12.

20. Ibid.

21. *Profile of Employee Benefits* (New York: Conference Board, 1981), p. 6.

22. U.S. Chamber Survey Research Center, *Employee Benefits,* p. 34.

23. Ibid.

24. Jennifer J. Laabs, "Use Creativity to Educate Your Benefits Audience," *Personnel Journal,* February 1992, p. 64.

25. R. L. Kager, "Do Employees Understand Your Benefits Program?" *Personnel Administrator,* October 1975, pp. 29–31.

26. Frank E. Kuzmits, "Communicating Benefits: A Double-Click Away," *Compensation & Benefits Review,* September/October 1998, pp. 60–64.

27. John A. Haslinger, "Flexible Compensation: Getting a Return on Benefit Dollars," *Personnel Administrator,* June 1985, p. 39.

28. Laabs, "Use Creativity," p. 59.

29. Carolyn A. Baker, "Flex Your Benefits," *Personnel Journal,* May 1988, p. 54.

30. R. B. Cockrum, "Has the Time Come for Employee Cafeteria Plans?" *Personnel Administrator,* July 1982, p. 67; "Flex Contained Health Costs for Most Employers," *Employee Benefit Plan Review,* May 1994, pp. 20–22.

31. Adapted from J. H. Shea, "Cautions about Cafeteria-Style Benefit Plans," *Personnel Journal,* January 1981, pp. 37–38.

32. Richard Gisonny and Steven Fein, "Better Benefits Emerge from Tax-wise Choices," *HR Magazine,* February 1991, p. 37.

33. Randall K. Abbott, "Flexible Compensation: Past, Present, and Future," *Compensation & Benefits Management,* Summer 1997, pp. 18–24.

Budget Rent-A-Car and International Compensation

In Budget Rent-A-Car's corporate offices in Lisle, Illinois, Jack McEnery, corporate vice president of training and compensation, and Sylvia McGeachie, vice president of human resources for Europe, the Middle East, and Africa, were discussing the implementation of the new incentive plan. The plans appeared to be developing smoothly, and both were pleased by the progress they had made in resolving various administrative issues. It was, however, clear from the discussion that neither previous practice nor theory was available to guide their actions. Most organizations have only recently begun to cope with the ambiguous issues being discussed by McEnery and McGeachie.

Suddenly, McGeachie became quiet and thoughtful and then said, "You know, Jack, France mandated compulsory profit sharing in 1967 for companies operating within France. This is going to affect our incentive plan. Are we going to factor in this required compensation before the incentives are determined? We certainly don't want to pay for both. That would mean, in effect, a double bonus for managers."

In France, the law of 1967 enacted mandatory, private profit sharing. Any employer with more than 100 employees must establish a profit-sharing plan within a prescribed framework. The total employees' share in profits is determined at the end of each year. The minimum requirement is that the profit-sharing formula apply to the excess, if any, of the after-tax profit minus 5 percent of invested capital. Allocation is made on the basis of salary. Typically, the profit sharing is distributed in the form of company shares, with a restriction that employees cannot cash these shares for five years.

Budget's incentive plan was designed to support a global strategy that would reward salaried employees for achieving corporate goals. If 70 percent of the corporate goals regarding profitability are reached, there is a payout to all exempt employees. The amount is based both on profit and on the salary grade of the exempt employee. No base pay is at risk; however, considerable additional compensation may be possible when profit goals are achieved. For example, a manager may receive 25 percent of his or her salary immediately and 25 percent after three years. A vice president may receive 40 percent of his or her salary via an immediate payout and an equivalent amount in three years. Twenty percent of the payout relates to the level of total corporate profitability, another 20 percent relates to regional profitability, and 60 percent depends on the achievement of local goals (in this case, France).

Budget's intention was to align pay practices with business strategy and also compensate employees internationally in a fair, comparable manner. The philosophy was that of "think globally, but act locally." Since France had mandated profit sharing, however, several issues occurred to McEnery and McGeachie as they discussed the incentive plan.

Budget's History

Budget was founded in 1958 by Morris Mirkin and Jules Lederer in a Los Angeles storefront. They began renting Chevys at $4 a day and $0.4 a mile. In the mid 1960s, Budget began international operations when it opened operations in Canada and Puerto Rico. Expansion into Great Britain occurred a few years later.

By 1993, Budget Rent-a-Car was the third largest company in the car rental industry. There were approximately 3,200 locations worldwide (about half owned by licensees). Sales in 1992 were $2.4 billion, with half of the sales accounted for by licensees. There were 160,000 vehicles available for rent worldwide.

Issues in Compensation

As their discussion continued, McEnery asked McGeachie, "Do you think that with the mandated profit-sharing process in France we can create a sufficiently motivating environment with Budget's incentive plan? I think it is important that we avoid underpayment, since that will be frustrating and may be perceived as unfair by employees. On the other hand, overpayment is both inappropriate for Budget and possibly demotivating. Why, after all, if you already get a high reward for moderate effort make an extraordinary effort?"

"I agree," McGeachie responded, "but I think that if we ensure that the rewards are high enough beyond the legal requirements, motivation will be strong. We must try to ensure in France that approximately the same level of pay related to profit is at risk as in other countries. It is my perception after working a great deal with the French that although historically the government has had a socialistic orientation, there would be few differences among the French managers in how they would react to incentives as compared with other Europeans. French managers have become cosmopolitan in understanding the trends of business across Europe, and incentive compensation is a very important issue right now. We must discuss the issue with our people in France, but I think in this area, at least, we will see similar reactions and motivation."

After some consideration, McEnery suggested, "So we have to consider the factors that might interfere with the level of the reward." "That's right," said McGeachie, "and one critical issue to consider is the income tax rate of the French. Although the income tax also funds health care coverage and pensions, it is very high. There is a rapidly sliding scale based on income, with no deductions allowed except for dependents. For instance, the income tax rate is 50 percent at the American equivalent of approximately $52,000. The same incentive amount will equate to less reward in France as compared with the United States because of taxes."

"Let me play devil's advocate," said McEnery, "and suggest that while pay is a concern of the company and employees, the income tax rate is the concern of the citizen and the government of a country." (Some compensation specialists believe that the analysis should be pretax; otherwise, every time a government changes the tax structure, the compensation structure of organizations would need revision.)

The discussion was continued later with the marketing manager in France, Bertrand Guidard. Guidard stated, "Employee reactions to incentives will depend, in France, on the level of the employee. Higher-level employees are very concerned about profitability in France since they recognize this relates to the future of Budget in France as well as to their bonus. The incentive plan is very motivating for managers, although I don't believe that lower-level employees are motivated by the idea of possible incentives. We need an incentive plan, although it has to be possible to reach."

Conclusions

In international compensation, two forces must be considered simultaneously. First, there must be a global vision that allows an organization to formulate a business strategy that crosses national borders. Many argue that a single marketplace has been created by the competitiveness of global operations. Particularly in a service organization, the ability to attract and retain customers is critical. The emphasis on quality in service has become a monumental concern. Poor service may send more customers to your global competition than price or quality.

The second consideration is the impact of local conditions. Culture, and even operations of an international organization, will vary across borders. Therefore, an international compensation decision involves the reinforcement of global strategy but also must recognize and reward differences in cultural approaches. Communication about both basic compensation philosophy and the way goals are set, measured, and rewarded is critical.

The management of human resources may be the key to global success. Compensation strategies therefore need to reinforce the concept of service delivery. The incentive plan described for Budget was designed to maintain the motivation and satisfaction of management employees, as well as to ensure the company's competitive ability to attract and retain the best employees.

Critical Thinking Questions

1. What do you think Budget should do about the incentive plan in France?

2. Do you think that compensation decisions should be made pretax or posttax? Defend your position.

3. What should "think globally, act locally" mean when implementing an incentive plan such as Budget's?

4. Put yourself in the position of a manager at Budget. How would you reconcile the issue of government-mandated profit sharing versus additional incentives designed by Budget? Would compensation be likely to affect your behavior or other managers' behavior in different ways?

Sources: "The Quality Imperative—What It Takes to Win in the Global Economy," *Business Week,* October 25, 1991 (whole issue); D. J. Carey and P. D. Howes, "Developing a Global Pay Program," *Journal of International Compensation and Benefits* 1, no. 1 (1992), pp. 30–34; F. K. Hahn, "Shaping Compensation Packages in Global Companies," *Journal of Compensation and Benefits,* November–December, 1991, pp. 11–16; J. S. Hyman and R. G. Kantor, "The Globalization of Compensation," *Journal of International Compensation and Benefits* 1, no. 1 (1992), pp. 25–29; M. J. Marquardt and D. W. Engel, *Global Human Resource Development* (Englewood Cliffs, N.J.: Prentice Hall, 1993).

Understanding Unions

The Legal Environment and Structure of Labor Unions

Learning Objectives

After studying this chapter, you should be able to:

1. Describe the conspiracy doctrine.
2. Define injunction.
3. Explain a yellow-dog contract.
4. Define the Railway Labor Act.
5. Describe the Norris–La Guardia Act.
6. Define the Wagner Act.
7. Explain the Taft-Hartley Act.
8. Describe right-to-work laws.
9. Explain the Landrum-Griffin Act.
10. Describe the AFL–CIO.
11. Define amalgamation and absorption.

P**rior to the Industrial Revolution in the 19th century, an individual was usually born into a level in society with a predestined standard of living. Custom and tradition kept a person's position relatively stable. After the Industrial Revolution, people were able to contract for employment by offering their skills and services for a wage. However, once people had been hired, they and their work output became the property of the employer.**

Before long employees resorted to joint action to gain some influence over the terms and conditions of their employment. Initially, the public and the courts frowned on these attempts. For the most part, the relationships between employees and management were unilateral: Employees asking for higher wages approached their employers with a "take it or we'll strike" attitude, and employers usually refused or ignored their requests. Generally, the result was a test of economic strength to determine whose wage decisions would prevail. In most instances, employers prevailed. HRM in Action 17.1 illustrates some of the consequences of early strikes.

As time passed, society became more aware of the plight of employees. Legislation was enacted that was much more favorable toward employees and unions. This chapter explores how the legal environment surrounding union-management relations has evolved. It also describes the organizational structure of unions and current issues facing unions.

HRM IN ACTION

Strike at Colorado Fuel and Iron Company (CFI)

17.1

Colorado Fuel and Iron Company (CFI) owned about 300,000 acres of mineral-rich land in Southern Colorado. This geographical insulation enabled CFI to impose rather primitive conditions over its 30,000 workers. Most of the workers lived in company-owned camps located 10 to 30 miles from any big towns. Within the camps, 151 persons contracted typhoid in 1912 and 1913 because of unsanitary conditions. Wages were paid in a currency valid only in company stores.

These conditions sparked union-organizing activity. The United Mine Workers (UMW) demanded an eight-hour day, enforcement of safety regulations, removal of armed guards, and abolition of company currency. The company refused to negotiate on these issues.

Thus, in September 1913, up to 10,000 workers at Colorado Fuel and Iron Company went on strike. After the strike began, tension rose quickly. CFI hired a large number of guards from outside the state, armed them, and paid their salaries.

Violence erupted almost immediately. First, a company detective and a union organizer were killed. A few days later, CFI troops broke up a strikers' mass meeting and killed three workers. Vengeful miners then killed four company men. Governor Ammons called out the National Guard to protect all property and those people who were still working.

On April 20, 1914, a major battle erupted between the strikers and the National Guardsmen. A fire that resulted led to the deaths of two women and 11 children. Several battles occurred over the next several days, and finally, on April 28, 1914, several regiments of federal troops were called in to end the war.

Source: Graham Adams, Jr., *Age of Industrial Violence, 1910–1915* (New York: Columbia University Press, 1966), pp. 146–75.

The Legal Environment of Labor-Management Relations

The first unions in America appeared between 1790 and 1820. These were local organizations of skilled craftspeople, such as shoemakers in Philadelphia, printers in New York, tailors in Baltimore, and other similar groups.

The demands of these unions were similar to those unions of today. Unions wanted job security, higher wages, and shorter working hours. When management did not agree to these demands, these early unions resorted to strikes, or "turn-outs," as they were then called. A *strike* is the collective refusal of employees to work.

To offset the pressure of these unions, employers formed associations and took legal action against the unions. In the **Philadelphia Cordwainers (shoemakers) case of 1806,** the jury ruled that groups of employees banded together to raise their wages constituted a conspiracy in restraint of trade. This decision established the **conspiracy doctrine,** which stated that a union could be punished if either the means used or the ends sought were deemed illegal by the courts.

Philadelphia Cordwainers (shoemakers) case of 1806
Case in which the jury ruled that groups of employees banded together to raise their wages constituted a conspiracy in restraint of trade.

Conspiracy Doctrine
Notion that courts can punish a union if they deem

Over the next 35 years, unions ran up against the conspiracy doctrine on numerous occasions. Some courts continued to rule that labor unions were illegal per se. Others ruled that the means unions used (e.g., strikes) to achieve their demands were illegal or that the ends sought (e.g., closed shops) were illegal. A *closed shop* prohibits an employer from hiring anyone other than a union member.

In 1842, in the landmark Massachusetts case *Commonwealth* v. *Hunt,* the Supreme Court of Massachusetts rejected the doctrine that the actions of labor

that the means used or the ends sought by the union are illegal.

Commonwealth* v. *Hunt
Landmark court decision in 1842 that declared unions were not illegal per se.

Injunction   Court order to stop an action that could result in irreparable damage to property when the situation is such that no other adequate remedy is available to protect the interests of the injunction-seeking party.

unions were illegal per se. The court noted that the power of a labor union could be used not only for illegal purposes but also for legal purposes. This decision, of course, left open the door for legal actions questioning the means used and ends sought by labor unions. Thus, even after 1842, the legal environment for unions remained vague and uncertain. Some courts held that a closed shop was a lawful objective; thus, strikes to obtain a closed shop were legal. Other courts reached an opposite conclusion. During this time, the legality of union activities depended to a large extent on the court jurisdiction in which the case occurred.

By the 1880s, most courts had moved away from the use of the conspiracy doctrine, and the injunction became a favorite technique used by the courts to control union activities. An **injunction** is a court order to stop an action that could result in irreparable damage to property when the situation is such that no other adequate remedy is available to protect the interests of the injunction-seeking party. During this time, the normal procedure used in seeking an injunction in a labor dispute was as follows:

1. The complainant (usually the employer) went to court, filed a complaint stating the nature of the property threat, and requested relief.
2. The judge normally issued a temporary restraining order halting the threatened action until a case could be heard.
3. Shortly thereafter, a preliminary hearing was held so the judge could decide whether to issue a temporary injunction.
4. Finally, after a trial, a decision was made as to whether a permanent injunction should be issued.

Injunctions had three effects. First, failure of the union to abide by the temporary restraining order or the temporary injunction meant rising contempt-of-court charges. Second, compliance meant a waiting period of many months before the matter came to trial. Often this waiting period was enough to destroy the effectiveness of the union. Third, the courts placed a broad interpretation on the term *property*. Historically, courts had issued injunctions to prevent damage to property where an award of money damages would be an inadequate remedy. However, during this time, the courts held that an employer's property included the right to operate the business and make a profit. Thus, the expectation of making a profit became a property right. Any strike, even a peaceful one, could be alleged to be injurious to the expectation of making a profit and could be stopped by an injunction.

Injunctions were generally granted by the courts upon request and were frequently used to control union activities until the 1930s. The attitude of the courts over this time seems to have been that management had the right to do business without the interference of unions.

Yellow-Dog Contract   Term coined by unions to describe an agreement between an employee and an employer stipulating that, as a condition of employment, the worker would not join a labor union. Yellow-dog contracts were made illegal by the Norris–La Guardia Act of 1932.

Hitchman Coal & Coke Co.* v. *Mitchell   Supreme Court case of 1917 that upheld the legality of yellow-dog contracts.

Another device used by employers to control unions during this time was the **yellow-dog contract.** The name was coined by the labor unions to describe an agreement between an employee and an employer that, as a condition of employment, the employee would not join a labor union. These contracts could be oral, written, or both.

In 1917, the Supreme Court upheld the legality of yellow-dog contracts in *Hitchman Coal & Coke Co.* v. *Mitchell.* This case involved the management of Hitchman Coal & Coke Company, whose employees had been unionized in 1903, and the United Mine Workers (UMW) in West Virginia. In 1906, the union called a strike against the company. However, management defeated the union and resumed operations as a nonunionized company. To ensure that it remained nonunionized, management required all of its employees, as a condition of employment, to sign an agreement saying that they would not join a union as long as they were employed by Hitchman.

Later the United Mine Workers sent an organizer back into West Virginia. The organizer secretly contacted and signed up the employees of Hitchman Coal. When enough employees signed up, a strike was called and the mine was closed.

However, Hitchman management brought a suit against the union, alleging that the organizer had deliberately induced the employees to break their agreements with the company. The Supreme Court ruled in favor of management and thus upheld the enforceability of the yellow-dog contract. Yellow-dog contracts were used until they were declared illegal by the Norris–La Guardia Act of 1932 (discussed later in this chapter).

Sherman Anti-Trust Act (1890)

The Sherman Anti-Trust Act was signed into law in 1890. The law made trusts and conspiracies that restrain interstate commerce illegal and forbade persons from monopolizing or attempting to monopolize interstate trade or commerce. Furthermore, any person who believed he or she had been injured by violations of the act was given the right to sue for triple the amount of damages sustained and the costs of the suit, including a reasonable attorney's fee.

Danbury Hatters Case
Landmark case of 1908 in which the Supreme Court decided that the Sherman Anti-Trust Act applied to all unions.

Generally, it is agreed that the primary intent of Congress in passing the Sherman Anti-Trust Act was to protect the public from the abuses of corporate monopolies. However, in 1908, in the landmark **Danbury Hatters case,** the Supreme Court decided that the Sherman Anti-Trust Act applied to all unions. In this case, the United Hatters Union, while attempting to unionize Loewe & Company of Danbury, Connecticut, called a strike and initiated a national boycott against the company's products. The boycott was successful, and Loewe filed a suit against the union alleging violation of the Sherman Anti-Trust Act. The Court further held that the individual members of the union were jointly liable for the money damages awarded.

Clayton Act (1914)

Labor unions rejoiced at the passage of the Clayton Act in 1914. In fact, Samuel Gompers, one of the leading spokespersons of the early labor movement, called the Clayton Act the "Industrial Magna Carta."[1] Sections 6 and 20 were of particular importance to labor:

> *Section 6: The labor of a human being is not a commodity or article of commerce. Nothing contained in the antitrust laws shall be construed to forbid the existence and operating of labor . . . organizations . . . or to forbid or restrain individual members of such organizations from lawfully carrying out the legitimate objects thereof; nor shall such organizations, or the members thereof be held or construed to be illegal combinations or conspiracies in restraint of trade under the antitrust laws.*
>
> *Section 20: No restraining order or injunction shall be granted by any court of the United States . . . in any case between an employer and employees, or between persons employed and persons seeking employment, unless necessary to prevent irreparable injury to property, or to a property right, of the party making the application, for which injury there is no adequate remedy at law.*

Duplex Printing Co. v. Deering
Case in which the Supreme Court ruled that unions were not exempt from the control of the Sherman Anti-Trust Act.

However, the joy of the unions was short-lived. The Supreme Court, in the 1921 case *Duplex Printing Co.* v. *Deering,*[2] basically gutted the intent of the Clayton Act because of the vague wording of the law. At the time, Duplex was the only nonunionized company manufacturing printing presses. The union attempted to organize the company, requesting that customers not purchase Duplex presses, that a trucking company not transport Duplex presses, and that repair shops not repair Duplex presses. The company asked for an injunction against the union but was denied by both the U.S. district and circuit courts on the basis of Section 20 of the Clayton Act. However, in a split decision, the Supreme Court overruled the lower courts. In this decision, the Court ruled that Section 6 of the Clayton Act did not exempt unions from the control of the Sherman Act. Furthermore, the

Court's decision meant that the issuance of injunctions was largely unchanged by the Clayton Act.

Railway Labor Act (1926)

Railway Labor Act An act enacted in 1926 that set up the administrative machinery for handling labor relations within the railroad industry; was the first important piece of prolabor legislation.

Legislation and its interpretations by the courts were largely antiunion prior to the passage of the **Railway Labor Act** in 1926. This act, which set up the administrative machinery for handling labor relations within the railroad industry, was the first important piece of prolabor legislation in the United States. The act was extended to airlines in 1936.[3]

One provision established the National Mediation Board to administer the act. Another provision eliminated yellow-dog contracts for railroad employees. The act also established mechanisms for mediation and arbitration of disputes between employers and unions within the industry. However, the original act applied only to railroad employees and not to those employed in other industries.

Norris–La Guardia Act (1932)

Norris–La Guardia Act of 1932 Prolabor act that eliminated the use of yellow-dog contracts and severely restricted the use of injunctions.

The **Norris–La Guardia Act of 1932** was particularly important to labor unions because it made yellow-dog contracts unenforceable and severely restricted the use of injunctions. The law prohibited federal courts from issuing injunctions to keep unions from striking, paying strike benefits, picketing (unless the picketing involved fraud or violence), and peacefully assembling.

Other parts of the law further restricted the issuance of injunctions. For example, the law required the employer to show that the regular police force was either unwilling or unable to protect the employer's property before an injunction could be issued. Temporary restraining orders could not be issued for more than five days.

The Norris–La Guardia Act also gave employees the right to organize and bargain with employers on the terms and conditions of employment. However, its major weakness was that it established no administrative procedures to ensure implementation of the rights. Employees could gain bargaining rights only if their employer voluntarily agreed to recognize the union or if the employees struck and forced recognition. In other words, the law gave employees the right to organize but did not require management to bargain with their union.

National Labor Relations (Wagner) Act (1935)

National Labor Relations Act (Wagner Act) Prolabor act of 1935 that gave workers the right to organize, obligated the management of organizations to bargain in good faith with unions, defined illegal management practices relating to unions, and created the National Labor Relations Board (NLRB) to administer the act.

The **National Labor Relations Act,** commonly known as the **Wagner Act** (named after its principal sponsor, Senator Robert Wagner Sr., of New York) was passed in 1935. The bill signaled a change in the federal government's role in labor-management relations. As a result of this law, government took a much more active role.

The Wagner Act gave employees the right to organize unions, bargain collectively with employers, and engage in other concerted actions for the purpose of mutual protection. Of course, the Norris–La Guardia Act had already granted these rights. However, the Wagner Act went further in that it required employers to recognize unions chosen by employees and to bargain with such unions in good faith. Furthermore, the act prohibited employers from engaging in uncertain unfair labor practices, including

1. Interference with, restraint of, or coercion of employees in exercising their rights under the act.

2. Domination of, interference with, or financial contributions to a union.

3. Discrimination in regard to hiring, firing, or any term or condition of employment to encourage or discourage membership in a union.

4. Discharge of or discrimination against an employee for filing charges or giving testimony under the act.

5. Refusal to bargain in good faith with the legal representative of the employees.

"Take it or leave it" that GE Presented

In addition, the act established a three-member National Labor Relations Board (NLRB) to administer the Wagner Act (the NLRB is discussed later in this chapter). The act also established procedures for use in union elections and directed the NLRB to conduct such elections and investigate unfair practices.

Labor-Management Relations (Taft-Hartley) Act (1947)

After the passage of the Wagner Act, union membership grew from approximately 6 percent of the total work force to approximately 23 percent in 1947. Accompanying this growth was an increase in union militancy. Strikes became much more frequent and widespread. In 1946, a record 4.6 million employees participated in strikes. A nationwide steel strike, an auto strike, two coal strikes, and a railroad strike negatively influenced scores of other industries, causing shortages and layoffs.

It was against this background of events that the **Labor-Management Relations Act** was passed in 1947. Known as the **Taft-Hartley Act,** it was an amendment and extension of the Wagner Act. The Taft-Hartley Act marked another change in the legislative posture toward union-management relations. The act basically placed government in the role of referee to ensure that both unions and management dealt fairly with each other.

Under the Taft-Hartley Act, employees have the right to organize a union, bargain collectively with an employer, and engage in other concerted activities for the purpose of collective bargaining. The act also spelled out unfair labor practices by employers and prohibited managers from forming or joining a labor union. Most provisions of the act are identical to those of the Wagner Act, but one unfair practice was changed significantly. Under the Wagner Act, employers were prohibited from discriminating in regard to hiring, firing, or any term or condition of employment to encourage or discourage membership in a union. However, the Wagner Act permitted closed and preferential shop agreements. With a closed shop, only union members can be hired, and the preferential shop requires that union members be given preference in filling job vacancies. The Taft-Hartley Act made closed and preferential shops illegal. However, the act permitted agreements in the construction industry, which required union membership within seven days of employment. The act also permitted in the construction industry a practice referred to as a *union hiring hall,* under which unions referred people to employers with existing job openings.

Unlike the Wagner Act, the Taft-Hartley Act also established a number of unfair union practices. In general, unions were forbidden to

1. Coerce employees who do not want to join.

2. Force employers to pressure employees to join a union.

3. Refuse to bargain in good faith with an employer.

4. Force an employer to pay for services not performed (featherbedding).

5. Engage in certain types of secondary boycotts (taking action against an employer that is not directly engaged in a dispute with a union).

6. Charge excessive initiation fees when union membership is required because of a union shop agreement. A *union shop agreement* requires employees to join the union and remain members as a condition of employment.

The Taft-Hartley Act also contained an important provision, the so-called free-speech clause. This clause stated that management has the right to express its opinion about unions or unionism to its employees, provided they carry no threat of reprisal or force.

Labor-Management Relations Act (Taft-Hartley Act) Legislation enacted in 1947 that placed the federal government in a watchdog position to ensure that union-management relations are conducted fairly by both parties.

Secondary Boycott Issue involving other employers (secondary employers) in the relationship between a union and an employer (the primary employer).

The Taft-Hartley Act also prohibited secondary boycotts. The concept of secondary boycott is a complex issue, but basically concerns involving other employers (secondary employers) in the relationship between a union and an employer (the primary employer). For example, if a union attempts to persuade a large customer of a primary employer to stop doing business with the primary employer until the primary employer agrees to the union's demands, this is a secondary boycott, which is illegal. However, distinguishing between a primary and secondary employer is very complex and has been the subject of many unfair labor practice charges that have been ruled on by the NLRB.

National Labor Relations Board

National Labor Relations Board (NLRB) Five-member panel created by the National Labor Relations Act and appointed by the president of the United States with the advice and consent of the Senate and with the authority to administer the Wagner Act.

Office of the General Counsel Separate and independent office created by the Taft-Hartley Act to investigate unfair labor practice charges and present those charges with merit to the NLRB.

The Taft-Hartley Act also expanded the size of the National Labor Relations Board (NLRB) and created the Office of the General Counsel. Presently, the board is a five-member panel appointed by the president of the United States with the advice and consent of the Senate. Each member serves for a five-year term. One of the five is appointed as board chairperson by the president, with Senate confirmation. The general counsel, a separate office independent from the board, is appointed by the president and approved by the Senate for a four-year term.

The relationship between the five-member board and the general counsel is similar to the relationship between the judge (or jury) and the prosecutor. In unfair labor practice cases, the board sits as the judge and general counsel acts as the prosecutor. Anyone can file an unfair labor practice complaint with the general counsel. Frequently, people refer to filing an unfair labor practice charge with the board, but it is actually filed with the general counsel. After the charge is filed, the general counsel investigates it and decides the merit of the charge. If the general counsel decides the act has been violated, a complaint is issued. The case is then tried before the board, which decides whether a violation has occurred.

The division of authority between the board and the general counsel applies only to unfair labor practice charges. Union election procedures are handled solely by the board. The role of the board in union election campaigns is described in greater depth in Chapter 18.

Much of the work of the board and the Office of the General Counsel is carried out in regional offices established by the board. Each regional office is headed by a regional director appointed by the board. The regional director serves as the local representative of the general counsel in processing unfair labor practice charges and as the local representative of the board in administering union election procedures.

Right-to-Work Laws

Section 14(b) of the Taft-Hartley Act is one of the most controversial sections of the law. It states:

> *Nothing in this act shall be construed as authorizing the execution or application of agreements requiring membership in a labor organization as a condition of employment in any state or territory in which such execution or application is prohibited by state or territory law.*

Right-to-Work Laws Legislation enacted by individual states under the authority of Section 14(b) of the Taft-Hartley Act that can forbid various types of union security arrangements, including compulsory union membership.

Thus, section 14(b) leaves to the states and territories the right to pass laws prohibiting union shops and other arrangements for compulsory union membership. Laws passed by individual states prohibiting compulsory union membership are called right-to-work laws, and states that have passed such legislation are right-to-work states. Presently there are 21 right-to-work states: Alabama, Arizona, Arkansas, Florida, Georgia, Idaho, Iowa, Kansas, Louisiana, Mississippi, Nebraska, Nevada, North Carolina, North Dakota, South Carolina, South Dakota, Tennessee, Texas, Utah, Virginia, and Wyoming. In these states, employees in unionized organizations are represented by the union but are not required to belong to the union or pay union dues. Unions argue that employees who choose not to belong or pay union dues get a free ride.

The Taft-Hartley Act also created an independent agency known as the Federal Mediation and Conciliation Service within the federal government. This agency assists parties in labor disputes to settle such disputes through conciliation and mediation. Finally, the act also established procedures that can be used by the president of the United States for resolving labor disputes that imperil the national health and safety.

Labor-Management Reporting and Disclosure (Landrum-Griffin) Act (1959)

Labor-Management Reporting and Disclosure Act (LMRDA) (Landrum-Griffin Act)   Legislation enacted in 1959 regulating labor unions and requiring disclosure of certain union finance information to the government.

Even after the passage of the Taft-Hartley Act, complaints continued concerning corruption and heavyhanded activity by certain unions. Thus, Congress created the Senate Select Committee on Improper Activities in the Labor or Management Field, better known as the McClellan Committee. Between 1957 and 1959, the McClellan Committee held hearings on union activities. HRM in Action 17.2 summarizes the findings of the McClellan Committee. As a result of these hearings, in 1959 Congress passed the **Labor-Management Reporting and Disclosure Act (LMRDA),** usually called the **Landrum-Griffin Act.** This act, which was also an amendment to and extension of the Wagner Act, was aimed primarily at regulating internal union affairs and protecting the rights of individual union members.

The main provisions of the act are as follows:

1. Union members are guaranteed the right to vote in union elections.
2. Union members are guaranteed the right to oppose their incumbent leadership both in union meetings and by nominating opposition candidates.
3. A majority affirmative vote of members by a secret ballot is required before union dues can be increased.
4. Reports covering most financial aspects of the union must be filed with the U.S. Department of Labor.

HRM IN ACTION

Findings of the McClellan Committee

17.2

In its hearings, the McClellan Committee uncovered the following facts about a few unions:

1. Rank-and-file members have no voice in some unions' affairs, notably in financial matters, and frequently are denied secret ballots.
2. Some international unions have abused their right to place local unions under trusteeship by imposing the trusteeship merely to plunder the local union's treasury or boost the ambitions of candidates for high office.
3. Certain managements have bribed union officials to get sweetheart contracts or other favored treatment.
4. There is frequent misuse of union funds through lack of adequate inspection and auditing procedures.
5. Some unions resort to acts of violence to keep their members in line.
6. Some employers and their agents follow improper practices to influence employees in exercising the rights guaranteed them by the NLRA.
7. Organizational picketing is sometimes misused to extort money from employers or to influence employees in their selection of representation.
8. There are cases of infiltration of unions at high levels by criminals.
9. A "no-man's land" sometimes exists, in which employers and unions cannot resort either to the NLRB or to state agencies for relief.

Source: Benjamin J. Taylor and Fred Witney, *Labor Relations Law* (Englewood Cliffs, N.J.: Prentice Hall, 1971), p. 474.

5. Officers and employees of unions are required to report any financial dealings with employees that might potentially influence the union member's interests.

6. Each union is required to have a constitution and bylaws filed with the U.S. Department of Labor.

7. Rigid formal requirements are established for conducting both national and local union elections.

8. Union members are allowed to bring suit against union officials for improper management of the union's funds and for conflict-of-interest situations.

9. Trusteeships that allow national or international unions to take over the management of a local union can be established only under provisions specified in the constitution and bylaws of the union and only to combat corruption or financial misconduct.

Civil Service Reform Act (1978)

Executive Orders Orders issued by the president of the United States for managing and operating federal government agencies.

Prior to 1978, labor-management relations within the federal government were administered through **executive orders.** These orders are issued by the president of the United States and relate to the management and operation of federal government agencies. Executive Order 10988, issued by President Kennedy, gave federal employees the right to join unions and required good-faith bargaining by both unions and federal agency management. Executive Order 11491, issued by President Nixon, defined more precisely the rights of federal employees in regard to unionization by establishing unfair labor practices for both unions and federal agency management. It also established procedures to safeguard these rights.

Civil Service Reform Act Legislation enacted in 1978 regulating labor-management relations for federal government employees.

In 1978, the **Civil Service Reform Act** was passed. Basically, it enacted into law the measures that had previously been adopted under Executive Orders 10988 and 11491. The act gave federal employees the right to organize and establish procedures for handling labor-management relations within the federal government. The main provisions of the act are as follows:

Federal Labor Relations Authority (FLRA) Three-member panel created by the Civil Service Reform Act whose purpose is to administer the act.

1. Established the **Federal Labor Relations Authority (FLRA)** to administer the act. The FLRA is composed of three members, not more than two of whom may be members of the same political party. Members of the authority are appointed by the president, with approval of the Senate, for a term of five years.

2. Created the Office of the General Counsel within the FLRA to investigate and prosecute unfair labor practices. The general counsel is appointed by the president, with approval of the Senate, for a term of five years.

Federal Services Impasses Panel (FSIP) Entity within the FLRA whose function is to provide assistance in resolving negotiation impasses within the federal sector.

3. Created the **Federal Services Impasses Panel (FSIP)** within the FLRA to provide assistance in resolving negotiation impasses between federal agencies and unions. The panel is composed of a chairperson and at least six other members who are appointed by the president for a term of five years.

4. Established unfair labor practices for the management of federal agencies and unions.

5. Established the general areas that are subject to collective bargaining.

6. Required binding arbitration for all grievances that have not been resolved in earlier stages of the grievance procedure.

7. Prohibited strikes in the federal sector.

Union Structures

As the previously described legislation was passed and court actions taken, organizational units were developed within the union movement to deal with problems and take advantage of opportunities. Four basic types of such units exist:

- Federations of local, national, and international unions (e.g., **AFL–CIO**).
- National or international unions.
- City and state federations.
- Local unions.

Some important dates relating to the development of the different union organizational units are shown in Table 17–1.

AFL–CIO 1955

Structurally speaking, the **American Federation of Labor–Congress of Industrial Organizations (AFL–CIO)** is the largest organizational unit within the union movement. Its primary goal is to promote the interests of unions and workers. The AFL–CIO resulted from the 1955 merger of the American Federation of Labor and the Congress of Industrial Organizations.

Formed in 1886, the AFL was composed primarily of **craft unions,** which had only skilled workers as members. Most such unions had members from several related trades (e.g., the Bricklayers, Masons, and Plasterers International Union). The CIO, formed in 1938, was developed to organize **industrial unions,** which have as members both skilled and unskilled workers in a particular industry or group of industries. The United Automobile Workers is an example of an industrial union.

Technically speaking, the AFL–CIO is not itself a union but is merely an organization composed of affiliated national and international unions, affiliated state and local bodies, local unions affiliated directly with the AFL–CIO, and eight trade and industrial departments. The AFL–CIO is merely a loose, voluntary federation of unions.

The basic policies of the AFL–CIO are set and its executive council elected at a national convention held every two years. The executive council—the president, secretary-treasurer, and 33 vice presidents—carries out the policies established at the convention. Each affiliated national and international union sends delegates to the convention. The number of delegates a particular union sends is determined by the size of its membership.

To deal with specific concerns, the AFL–CIO president appoints and supervises standing committees that work with staff departments to provide services to the union membership. The general board meets at the call of the president or the executive council and acts on matters referred to it by the executive council.

Not all national and international unions belong to the AFL–CIO. Presently, for example, the United Automobile Workers and the United Mine Workers do not belong. However, a majority of unions are affiliated with the AFL–CIO.

Web site: AFL-CIO

www.aflcio.org

American Federation of Labor–Congress of Industrial Organizations (AFL–CIO) Combination of national, international, and local unions joined together to promote the interests of unions and workers. The AFL–CIO was formed in 1955 by the amalgamation of the American Federation of Labor (AFL) and the Congress of Industrial Organizations (CIO).

Craft Unions Unions having only skilled workers as members. Most craft unions have members from several related trades (e.g., Bricklayers, Masons, and Plasterers International Union).

Industrial Unions Unions having as members both skilled and unskilled workers in a particular industry or group of industries.

T A B L E   1 7 – 1   **IMPORTANT DATES IN THE LABOR MOVEMENT**

Year	Event
1792	First local unions: Philadelphia Shoemaker's Union
1833	First city federation: New York, Philadelphia, Baltimore
1850	First national union: International Typographical Union
1869	First attempt to form a federation of unions: Knights of Labor
1886	Formation of American Federation of Labor (AFL)
1938	Formation of Congress of Industrial Organizations (CIO)
1955	AFL–CIO merger

National and International Unions

The organizational structure of most national and international unions is similar to that of the AFL–CIO. Unions are called international because they often have members in both the United States and Canada. In general, both national and international unions operate under a constitution and have a national convention with each local union represented in proportion to its membership. Unusually the convention elects an executive council, which normally consists of a president, a secretary-treasurer, and several vice presidents. Normally, the president appoints and manages a staff for handling matters such as organizing activities, research, and legal problems.

The field organization of a national or an international union usually has several regional or district offices headed by a regional director. Under the regional director are field representatives who are responsible for conducting union organizing campaigns and assisting local unions in collective bargaining and handling grievances.

City and State Federations

City federations receive their charters from the AFL–CIO and are composed of local unions within a specified area. Local unions send delegates to city federation meetings, which are generally held on a biweekly or monthly basis.

The primary function of city federations is to coordinate and focus the political efforts of local unions. During elections, city federations usually endorse a slate of candidates. Most city federations maintain an informal lobby at the city hall and present labor issues to legislative committees. City federations do not always focus their efforts only on labor issues. Other issues and activities frequently addressed by city federations include school board policies, community fund-raising drives, and public transportation problems.

State federations are also chartered by the AFL–CIO and are composed of local unions and city federations. The main goal of state federations is to influence political action favorable to unions. Efforts are made to persuade union members to vote for union-endorsed candidates. During state legislative sessions, the state federation actively lobbies for passage of bills endorsed by labor unions.

Local Unions

Most local unions operate under the constitution of their national or international union. However, a number are independent in that they operate without a national affiliation. Furthermore, a local union can be affiliated directly with the AFL–CIO without being connected with a national or international union.

As a rule, the membership of a local union elects officers, who carry out the union activities. In a typical local union, the members elect a president, vice president, and secretary-treasurer and usually form several committees. For example, a bargaining committee is usually appointed to negotiate the contract for the union, and a grievance committee is usually appointed to handle grievances for the membership. The latter committee is generally composed of a chief steward and several departmental stewards. The stewards recruit new employees into the union, listen to employee complaints, handle grievances, and observe management's administration of the union contract. Generally, most local union officials work at a regular job but have some leeway in using working time to conduct union business. In large locals, most officials are full-time, paid employees of the union. The local usually depends heavily on the field representative of its national or international union for assistance in handling contract negotiations, strikes, and arbitration hearings.

In those industries where membership is scattered among several employers, local unions often have a business agent who is a full-time, paid employee of the local union. This agent manages internal union activities, negotiates contracts, meets with company officials to resolve contract interpretation issues, handles grievances, and serves as an active participant in arbitration hearings.

Current and Future Developments in the Labor Movement

Web site: Find Law

www.findlaw.com

Between 1935 (the year the National Labor Relations Act was passed) and the end of World War II, union membership quadrupled (see Figure 17–1). During the post–World War II era through 1970, union membership continued to grow. Between 1970 and 1980, union membership grew by slightly more than 1 million members, but as a percentage of the total work force it dropped significantly. In addition, union membership dropped in the 1980s by approximately 5 million workers, and it has continued to drop as a percentage of the total work force. In contrast, union membership for government employees has grown during the 1980s. Unions also hold a much higher percentage of the government work force. It is expected that unions will take several initiatives to maintain and increase membership.

Web site: Internet
Law Library

www.law.house.gov

Historically, labor unions have gained their strength from blue-collar production workers. However, the work force has grown and will continue to grow principally in the service sector of the economy. Less than 10 percent of the service sector is currently organized. Unions have been successful in organizing narrow segments of the service sector, such as teachers, pilots, and musicians. However, it is expected that a major emphasis of future organizing campaigns will be directed toward convincing unorganized white-collar employees that their personal and professional needs can be satisfied through union representation.

By the late 1990s, investments in private pension plans are expected to reach approximately $3 trillion. Labor unions are likely to attempt to influence how these monies are invested. Specifically, unions will probably request that the funds not be invested in stock of antiunion companies or companies that engage in antiunion practices.

Amalgamation Union
merger that involves two or

Another likely development is the continued increase in union mergers. Union mergers take two basic forms. An **amalgamation** involves two or more unions, normally of roughly equal size, forming a new union. An **absorption** involves the

---

FIGURE 17–18   **UNION MEMBERSHIP HISTORY AS A PERCENTAGE OF THE U.S. WORK FORCE, 1921–1998**

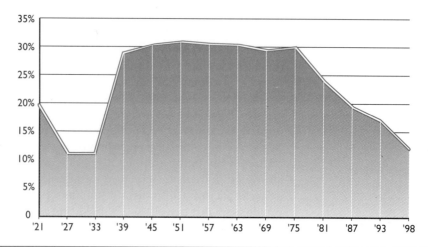

Source: U.S. Department of Labor

more unions, usually of approximately the same size, forming a new union.

Absorption   Union merger that involves the merger of one union into a considerably larger one.

merging of one union into a considerably larger one. Roughly 50 of the AFL–CIO affiliates have under 50,000 members, and another 30 have under 100,000 members. Larger unions can, of course, bring much more pressure on management, not only in negotiating collective bargaining agreements but also in union organizing campaigns.

SUMMARY OF LEARNING OBJECTIVES

1. **Describe the conspiracy doctrine.**
   The conspiracy doctrine established that a union could be punished if either the means used or ends sought by the union were deemed illegal by the courts.

2. **Define injunction.**
   An injunction is a court order to stop an action that can result in irreparable damage to property when the situation is such that no adequate remedy is available to protect the interests of the injunction-seeking party.

3. **Explain a yellow-dog contract.**
   A yellow-dog contract (a term coined by labor unions) is an agreement between a worker and an employer stipulating, as a condition of employment, that the worker will not join a labor union. Yellow-dog contracts are now illegal.

4. **Define the Railway Labor Act.**
   This act set up the administrative machinery for handling labor relations within the railroad and airline industries.

5. **Describe the Norris–La Guardia Act.**
   This act made yellow-dog contracts unenforceable and severely limited the use of injunctions. It also gave employees the right to organize and bargain with employers on the terms and conditions of employment.

6. **Define the Wagner Act.**
   This act gave employees the right to organize unions, bargain collectively with employers, and engage in other concerted actions for the purpose of mutual protection.

7. **Explain the Taft-Hartley Act.**
   This act basically placed government in the role of referee to ensure that both unions and management deal fairly with each other.

8. **Describe right-to-work laws.**
   Right-to-work laws were passed by individual states and prohibit compulsory union membership.

9. **Explain the Landrum-Griffin Act.**
   This act aimed primarily to regulate internal union affairs and protect the rights of individual union members.

10. **Describe the AFL–CIO.**
    The AFL–CIO is a voluntary federation of unions whose primary goal is to promote the interests of unions and workers.

11. **Define amalgamation and absorption.**
    An amalgamation involves two or more unions, normally of roughly equal size, forming a new union. An absorption involves the merging of one union into a considerably larger one.

REVIEW QUESTIONS

1. Explain the ruling in the Philadelphia Cordwainers case of 1806.
2. What was the decision in the *Commonwealth* v. *Hunt* case of 1842?

3. What is an injunction? How were injunctions used against labor unions?
4. What is a yellow-dog contract?
5. List the major benefits gained by unions with the passage of the Norris–La Guardia Act of 1932.
6. What unfair employer practices were specified by the Wagner Act of 1935?
7. What unfair union practices were specified by the Taft-Hartley Act of 1947?
8. Outline the main areas covered by the Landrum-Griffin Act of 1959.
9. Outline the main areas covered by the Civil Service Reform Act of 1978.
10. Briefly describe the four basic types of union organizational units.
11. What trends have occurred in labor union membership from 1935 to the present?

DISCUSSION QUESTIONS

1. Why did legislation take a prounion turn in the 1930s?
2. Discuss your feelings about the following statement: "Management should always fight hard to keep unions out of their organization."
3. Do you think white-collar employees should join unions? Why or why not?
4. Do you believe college professors and nurses are good candidates for unionization? Why or why not?

INCIDENT 17–1

Unions and Management

IAM Local 709 voted to end a strike against the Marietta plant of Lockheed-Georgia Company. The contract that was agreed on contained a wage increase of about 13 percent and improved retirement, insurance, and other benefits. The company also agreed to pay employees for the seven days over the Christmas and the two days over the Thanksgiving holidays that were missed during the strike.

For the Marietta workers, the main issue was their right to "bump" workers with less seniority from projects during times when there are not enough jobs to go around. Lockheed officials claimed the bumping procedure, whereby an employee having at least one day's seniority over another could take the junior's job, would hurt production so badly that it could force the company to abandon projects. Lockheed's initial proposal had been that an employee without at least three months' seniority over the junior employee would not be allowed to bump. After the union rejected this proposal, the company proposed to change the seniority requirement to at least one month. At that point, negotiations broke down.

The last Lockheed offer, which was accepted, was that the seniority system remain the same for all current Lockheed employees. However, anyone hired after Lockheed's offer was accepted would have to have at least one month's seniority to be able to bump another worker.

Questions

1. Why do you think unions insisted on seniority as the criterion in the preceding example?
2. Do you think seniority should be used in any process within a company? Why or why not?

INCIDENT 17–2

Voluntary Resignations during a Strike*

In July 1985, the Supreme Court ruled in a 5–4 decision that unions cannot fine employees who resign their union membership during a strike and return to work in violation of union rules.

The case involved a seven-month strike by the Pattern Makers' League against clothing companies in Illinois and Wisconsin. The union had a rule prohibiting resignations during a strike and enforced it by fining 10 employees the approximate amount they earned after they returned to work during the strike.

The Court, upholding the view of the National Labor Relations Board, said that imposing fines and other restrictions on employees who quit the union during a strike "impairs the policy of voluntary unionism."

Questions

1. Do you think unions should be able to restrict resignations during a strike? Why or why not?

2. Do you think this decision has had any effect on union membership?

EXERCISE

Need for Unions

The class breaks into teams of four to five students. Each team should prepare to debate on the following statements:

1. Unions served a useful purpose in the past but have outlived their usefulness.

2. Unions are needed today as much as they have been in the past. Without unions, wages and working conditions of the average employee would deteriorate.

After the debate, the instructor will list on the board some points made by each team, and the class will discuss the issues involved.

NOTES AND ADDITIONAL READINGS

1. Samuel Gompers, "The Charter of Industrial Freedom," *American Federationist*, November 1914, pp. 971–72.
2. 254 U.S. 445 (1921).
3. See Dennis A. Arouca and Henry H. Pettit, Jr., "Transportation Labor Regulation: Is the Railway Labor Act or the National Labor Relations Act the Better Strategy Vehicle?" *Labor Law Journal*, March 1985, pp. 145–72.

---

*Adapted from Stephen Wermiel, "Justices Rule Unions Can't Fine Members Who Quit, Resume Work during a Strike," *The Wall Street Journal,* June 28, 1985, p. 5.

Union Organizing Campaigns and Collective Bargaining

Learning Objectives

After studying this chapter, you should be able to:

1. Define collective bargaining.
2. Explain the captive-audience doctrine.
3. Define bargaining unit.
4. Explain certification, recognition, and contract bars.
5. Describe good-faith bargaining.
6. Discuss boulwarism.
7. Explain medication.
8. Define checkoff.
9. Explain seniority.
10. Define lockout and strike.

Collective Bargaining
Process that involves the negotiation, drafting, administration, and interpretation of a written agreement between an employer and a union for a specific period of time.

Collective bargaining is a process that involves the negotiation, drafting, administration, and interpretation of a written agreement between an employer and a union for a specific period of time. The end result of collective bargaining is a contract that sets forth the joint understandings of the parties as to wages, hours, and other terms and conditions of employment. Contracts cover a variety of time periods, the most common being three years.

The basic components of the collective bargaining process are

1. Negotiation of relevant issues in good faith by both management and the union.

2. Incorporation of the parties' understandings into a written contract.

3. Administration of the daily working relationships according to the terms and conditions of employment specified in the contract.

4. Resolution of disputes in the interpretation of the terms of the contract through established procedures.

Normally the human resource department serves as management's primary representative in all aspects of the collective bargaining process.

Union Membership Decision

Before the collective bargaining process begins, the employees of an organization must decide whether they want to be represented by a union. Thus, an important prerequisite to understanding the collective bargaining process is knowledge of what attracts employees to unions.

Reasons for Joining

A variety of factors influence an employee's desire to join a union. Employees who are dissatisfied with their wages, job security, benefits, the treatment they receive from management, and their chances for promotion are more likely to vote for union representation. Another important factor in determining employees' interest in union membership is their perception of the ability of the union to change the situation. If employees do not believe unionization will change the economic and working conditions that dissatisfy them, they are unlikely to vote for unionization.

While wages, benefits, working conditions, and job security are the main issues contributing to the decision to join a union, other factors include employees' desires for:

1. Better communication with management.
2. Higher quality of management and supervision.
3. Increased democracy in the workplace.
4. Opportunity to belong to a group where they can share experiences and comradeship.

The Opposition View

Understanding why employees oppose unionization is as important as knowing why they favor it. The major reasons for not joining a union are satisfactory wages, benefits, working conditions, and job security. Some employees also have a negative image of labor unions, believing unions have too much political influence, require members to go along with decisions made by the union, and have leaders who promote their own self-interests. Other reasons include the belief that unions abuse their power by calling strikes, causing high prices, and misusing union dues and pension funds.

Some employees identify with management and view unions as adversaries. However, dissatisfaction with wages, benefits, and working conditions can quickly break down this negative attitude toward unions.

Many organizations have avoided unionization. In most cases, the managements of those organizations have provided satisfactory wages, benefits, working conditions, and job security for their employees. Other management practices that decrease the likelihood of unionization include creating a procedure for handling employee complaints, eliminating arbitrary and heavyhanded management and supervisory practices, establishing a meaningful system of two-way communication between management and employees, eliminating threats to employees' job security, and making employees feel like they are part of the organization.

Web site: United States National Labor Relations Board

www.nlrb.gov

Union Organizing Campaign

Most often, union organizing campaigns begin when one or more employees request that the union begin an organizing campaign. In some instances, national and international unions contact employees in organizations that have been targeted for organizing campaigns. Generally, however, unions will not attempt to organize a facility unless there is a strong body of support among the employees. Typically, the union begins a campaign to interest employees in joining it. After the union generates sufficient interest, employees sign authorization cards indicating they would like to have an election to vote for or against representation by a union. If 30 percent of the employees sign these authorization cards, the National Labor Relations Board (NLRB) may be requested to come in and supervise an election. In practice, it is unlikely the NLRB will be petitioned unless over 50 percent sign authorization cards.

Several restrictions have been placed on where and when support for the unions can be solicited.[1] Generally, employees in favor of the union can orally solicit support from other employees in work and nonwork areas, but only on nonwork time. In addition, if management allows employees to engage in casual conversation while they are working, the employees can discuss union matters if production is not hindered. Union literature can be distributed only on nonworking time, and management can limit the distribution of literature to nonwork areas.

The NLRB rarely approves exceptions to the general rules for oral solicitation and distribution of union literature. However, some exceptions have been granted. For example, department stores can establish rules prohibiting oral solicitation on the sales floor, provided employees are generally prohibited from casual conversations on the sales floor because customers are waiting for service.

The rights to orally solicit union support and distribute union literature on company property apply only to employees. Generally management can prohibit union organizers from entering company property for these purposes.[2] One exception in this area is that if management allows other solicitors to enter company property, they cannot exclude union organizers.

Captive-Audience Doctrine
Management's right to speak against a union to employees on company time and to require employees to attend the meeting.

Under the so-called **captive-audience doctrine,** management has the right to speak against the union on company time to employees and require employees to attend the meeting.[3] On the other hand, the union does not have the right to reply on company time. The primary exception to the captive-audience doctrine is that management is prohibited from giving a speech on company time to a mass employee audience in the 24 hours immediately before an election. However, the 24-hour rule applies only to a speech before a large group. Managers are permitted to talk against the union to employees individually or in small groups during the last 24 hours.

Determining the Bargaining Unit

When the union obtains signed authorization cards from at least 30 percent of the employees, either the union or the employer can petition the National Labor Relations Board to conduct a representation election. In the event the union has signed authorization cards from more than 50 percent of the employees, the union can make a direct request to the employer to become the bargaining agent of the employees. When this happens, the employer normally refuses, and the union then petitions the NLRB for an election.

After a petition is filed, a representative of the NLRB (called an *examiner*) verifies that the authorization requirement has been fulfilled and then makes a determination as to the appropriate bargaining unit. A **bargaining unit** (or *election unit*) is defined as a group of employees in a plant, firm, or industry that is recognized by the employer, agreed on by the involved parties, or designated by the NLRB or its regional director as appropriate for the purposes of collective bargaining.

Bargaining Unit Group of employees in a plant, firm, or industry that is recognized by the employer, agreed on by the parties to a case, or designated by the NLRB as appropriate for the purposes of collective bargaining.

Although the NLRB is ultimately responsible for establishing an appropriate bargaining unit, the parties usually have a great deal of influence on this decision. Most elections are known as **consent elections,** in which the parties have agreed on the appropriate bargaining unit. When this is not the case, the NLRB must make the bargaining unit decision guided by a concept called **community of interest.**

Consent Elections Union elections in which the parties have agreed on the appropriate bargaining unit.

Community of Interest Concept by which the NLRB makes a bargaining unit decision based on areas of employee commonality.

Informational Picketing Patrolling at or near an employer's facility by individuals carrying signs to publicize the fact that the union is requesting an election to become the bargaining agent for the employees of the organization.

Gissel Bargaining Orders Situations in which the NLRB orders management to bargain with the union; named after a landmark Supreme Court decision, *NLRB* v. *Gissel Packing Company.*

12-Month Rule Provides that no election can be held in any bargaining unit within which a valid election has been held within the preceding 12-month period.

Community-of-interest factors include elements such as similar wages, hours, and working conditions; the employees' physical proximity to one another; common supervision; the amount of interchange of personnel within the proposed unit; and the degree of integration of the employer's production process of operation.

Election Campaigns

During the election campaign, certain activities, called *unfair labor practices,* are illegal. These include (1) physical interference, threats, or violent behavior by the employer toward union organizers; (2) employer interference with employees involved in the organizing drive; (3) discipline or discharge of employees for prounion activities; and (4) threatening or coercing of employees by union organizers. After filing for an election with the NLRB, a union can picket an employer only if the employer is not presently unionized, the petition has been filed with the NLRB within the past 30 days, and a representation election has not been conducted during the preceding 12 months. Picketing of this type is called **informational picketing.** Individuals patrol at or near the place of employment carrying signs to publicize the fact that the union is requesting an election to become the bargaining agent for the employees.

During the election campaign, management usually initiates a campaign against a union, emphasizing the costs of unionization and the loss of individual freedom that can result from collective representation. Management can legally state its opinion about the possible ramifications of unionization if its statements are based on fact and are not threatening. Management can also explain to employees the positive aspects of their current situation. However, promises to provide or withhold benefits in the future in the event of unionization or nonunionization are prohibited. An employer can conduct polls to verify union strength prior to an election, but in general it may not question employees individually about their preferences or otherwise threaten or intimidate them.

During the election campaign, unions emphasize their ability to help employees satisfy their needs and improve their working conditions. The ability of the union to sell these concepts to employees is a critical factor in the union's success in an election campaign. Employees must believe the union cares about their problems, can help resolve them, and can assist in improving their wages, benefits, and working conditions. Unions are legally prohibited from coercing or threatening individual employees if they do not join the union.[4]

The actual impact of an election campaign is unclear. However, the campaign tactics of both management and the union are monitored by the NLRB. If the practices of either party are found to be unfair, the election results may be invalidated and a new election conducted. Furthermore, charges of unfair labor practices against management, if serious enough, can result in the NLRB ordering management to bargain with the union. Such situations are called **Gissel bargaining orders.** Gissel bargaining orders are named after a landmark Supreme Court decision, *NLRB* v. *Gissel Packing Company,*[5] which held that bargaining orders by the NLRB are an appropriate remedy for certain types of employer misconduct. Gissel bargaining orders are rarely issued by the NLRB.

Election, Certification, and Decertification

If management and the union agree to conduct the election as a consent election, balloting often occurs within a short period of time. However, if management does not agree to a consent election, a long delay may occur. Delays in balloting often increase the likelihood that management will win the election. As a result, management frequently refuses to agree to a consent election.

In union elections, the time when an election can be held is an important issue. The so-called **12-month rule** provides that no election can be held in any

Certification Bar
Condition occurring when
the NLRB will not permit
another election in the
bargaining unit within 12
months of a union's
certification.

Recognition Bar   Condition
occurring when the NLRB
prohibits an election for up
to 12 months after an
employer voluntarily
recognizes a union.

Contract Bar Doctrine
Doctrine under which the
NLRB will not permit an
election in the bargaining
unit covered by a contract
until the contract expires,
up to a maximum of three
years.

Web site: Federal Labor
Relations Authority

www.flra.gov

Good-Faith Bargaining
Sincere intention of both
parties to negotiate
differences and reach a
mutually acceptable
agreement.

Boulwarism   Named after a
General Electric vice
president; occurs when
management makes its best
offer at the outset of
bargaining and firmly
adheres to the offer
throughout the bargain
sessions. The NLRB has
ruled that this is not good-
faith bargaining and is
therefore illegal.

bargaining unit within which a valid election has been held within the preceding 12-month period. Also, the NLRB will not permit another election in the bargaining unit within 12 months of a union's certification. This is called a **certification bar.** The NLRB also prohibits an election for up to 12 months after an employer voluntarily recognizes a union. This is called a **recognition bar.** Finally, after a contract is agreed on by both parties, the NLRB does not normally permit an election in the bargaining unit covered by a contract until the contract expires, up to a maximum of three years. This is known as the **contract bar doctrine.**

When the exact date for the election is finally established, the NLRB conducts a secret-ballot election. If the union receives a majority of the ballots cast, it becomes certified as the exclusive bargaining representative of all employees in the unit. Exclusive bargaining representative means the union represents all employees (both union members and nonmembers) in the bargaining unit in negotiating their wages, hours, and terms and conditions of employment. It is important to note that the union does not have to receive a positive vote from a majority of employees in the bargaining unit. It has to receive only a majority of the votes cast.

After a union has been certified, it remains by law the exclusive bargaining representative for all employees until the employees within the unit desire otherwise. In the event the employees want to oust the union, they can file a petition with the NLRB for a decertification election. If 30 percent of the employees support the petition to decertify and a valid election to oust the union has not been held within the preceding year, a decertification election is conducted. If a majority of the voting employees vote to decertify the union, it no longer legally represents them. Figure 18–1 summarizes the steps involved in an organizing campaign.

Good-Faith Bargaining

After a union is certified, the employer is required by law to bargain in good faith with the union. Of course, bargaining between an employer and the union also takes place before the expiration of an existing contract. The National Labor Relations Act stipulates the legal requirement of **good-faith bargaining** for private enterprise organizations, whereas the Civil Service Reform Act of 1978 makes the same requirement of federal agencies. Unfortunately, good faith—or the lack of it—is not explicitly defined in either of these laws. Over the years, however, decisions of the NLRB, the Federal Labor Relations Authority (FLRA), and the courts have interpreted good-faith bargaining to be the sincere intention of both parties to negotiate differences and to reach an agreement acceptable to both. Good-faith bargaining does not require the parties to agree; it merely obligates them to make a good-faith attempt to reach an agreement. Thus, the existence of good faith is generally determined by examining the total atmosphere in the collective bargaining process. The essential requirement is that a bona fide attempt be made to reach an agreement.

Several bargaining situations have been taken to the NLRB to determine the presence or lack of good-faith bargaining. A key case involved General Electric Company's use of **boulwarism,** which was named after a General Electric vice president, Lemuel Boulware, and means that management makes its best offer at the outset of bargaining and firmly adheres to the offer throughout the bargaining sessions. The NLRB has ruled that boulwarism is not good-faith bargaining.[6] In its decision, the NLRB held that boulwarism was illegal because the company not only adhered to a rigid position at the bargaining table but, in this case, had also mounted a publicity campaign to convince its employees that the company's offer was best. The company belittled the union in its literature. Since the employer simply ignored the union and went directly to the employees with its proposal, it violated its duty to bargain in good faith with the employees' exclusive bargaining representative (i.e., the union).

FIGURE 18-1   STEPS INVOLVED IN A UNION ORGANIZING CAMPAIGN

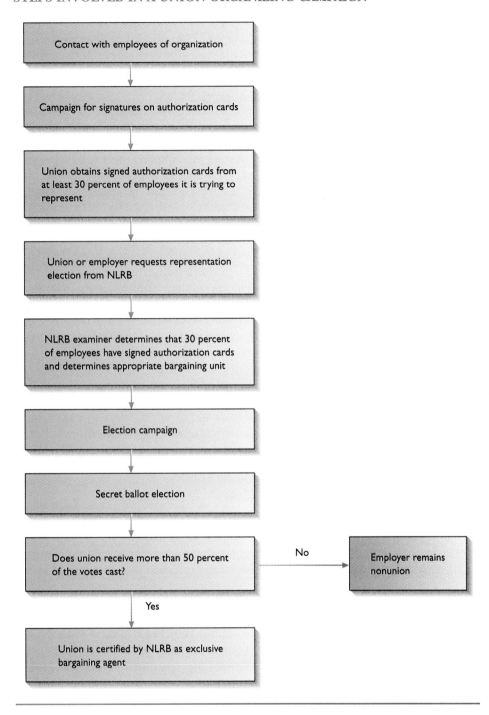

Web site: Labor link

www.laborlink.org

Participants in Negotiations

A number of parties may be either directly or indirectly involved in the collective bargaining process. The primary participants are, of course, the employer and union representatives. However, several third parties can play a significant role.

Employer's Role

Participation of the employer in collective bargaining may take one of several forms. The single-company agreement is most common. Under this approach, representatives of a single company meet with representatives of the union and negotiate a contract. Of course, it is possible for one company to have several unions representing different groups of employees. In this situation, representatives of the company would negotiate a different contract with each union. Furthermore, it is possible for one company and one union to negotiate different contracts for each of the company's facilities or plant locations.

In some industries, multiemployer agreements are common. Generally, individual employers in these industries are small and are in a weak position relative to the union. Employers then often pool together in an employer association. A single agreement is negotiated by the association for all involved employers. Multiemployer agreements may be on a local level (e.g., the construction industry within a city), a regional level (e.g., coal and mining), or at the national level (railroad industry). When multiemployer bargaining occurs on a regional or national basis, it is often referred to as *industrywide bargaining*.

In large organizations such as General Motors, master agreements on wage and benefit issues are negotiated between corporate officials and officials of the national or international union. However, in addition to the master agreement, local supplements are negotiated at the plant level. Local supplements deal with issues that are unique to each plant.

Union's Role

Union participation in negotiations can take several forms. In single-company agreements, the size of the company determines the nature of the union participation. For smaller companies, the local union normally works closely with a field representative of the international or national union in negotiations. In these instances, the international representative gives advice and counsel to the local union and frequently serves as the principal negotiator for the union.

In large companies with multiple plants, negotiations are conducted by the top officials of the national or international union. For example, the president of the United Automobile Workers (UAW) is normally a chief negotiator in negotiations with Ford, General Motors, and Chrysler. Local union officials and a field representative of the national or international union negotiate local supplements to the master agreement for large companies.

In those industries with multiemployer agreements, union participation is usually directed by the president of the national or international union. However, in these types of negotiations, representatives of the local unions to be covered by the multiemployer agreement normally serve on the union's negotiating committee. It is also possible for several unions to bargain jointly with a single employer. This type of negotiation is called **coordinated bargaining.**

Coordinated Bargaining A form of bargaining in which several unions bargain jointly with a single employer.

Role of Third Parties

Several third parties can and frequently do become involved in the collective bargaining process. Typically the services of third parties are not required unless one or both parties feels the other party is not bargaining in good faith, or the parties reach an impasse in negotiations.

National Labor Relations Board (NLRB)

The National Labor Relations Act (discussed in Chapter 17) requires both unions and management to bargain in good faith. Refusal to bargain by either party can be overridden by an order of the National Labor Relations Board (NLRB). Furthermore, if the board's order has been properly issued, the U.S. Court of Appeals is required to order enforcement under the threat of contempt-of-court penalties.

Besides refusing to bargain, other kinds of behavior can be held to be unfair labor practices. Some of these were described earlier in this chapter. The NLRB has the authority to determine whether a particular behavior is unfair. If either party believes an unfair labor practice has occurred during negotiations, a charge can be filed with the NLRB. An NLRB representative then investigates the charge and determines whether it is warranted. If so, the parties are given the opportunity to reach an informal settlement before the NLRB takes further action. If an informal settlement cannot be reached, the NLRB issues a formal complaint against the accused party, and a formal hearing is then conducted by an NLRB trial examiner. Upon completion of the hearing, the examiner makes recommendations to the NLRB. Either party may appeal the recommendations of the examiner to the board. If the board decides the party named in the complaint has engaged or is engaging in an unfair labor practice, it can order the party to cease from such practice and can take appropriate corrective action. Either party can appeal decisions of the NLRB to the U.S. Circuit Court of Appeals and even the U.S. Supreme Court.

Federal Labor Relations Authority (FLRA)

The Federal Labor Relations Authority (FLRA) was given its authority by the Civil Service Reform Act of 1978 and serves as the counterpart to the NLRB for federal sector employees, unions, and agencies. Under procedures similar to those of the NLRB, the FLRA investigates unfair labor practice charges, conducts hearings on unfair labor practices, and can issue orders to cease from any such practices.

Federal Services Impasses Panel (FSIP)

If the parties in the federal sector reach an impasse in negotiations, either party may request the Federal Services Impasses Panel (FSIP) to consider the matter. The FSIP, an entity within the FLRA, has the authority to recommend solutions to resolve an impasse and take whatever action is necessary to resolve the dispute, as long as the actions are not inconsistent with the Civil Service Reform Act of 1978. In addition, the parties may agree to adopt a procedure for binding arbitration of a negotiation impasse, but only if the procedure is approved by the FSIP. The FSIP is considered to be the legal alternative to a strike in the federal sector.

Federal Mediation and Conciliation Service (FMCS)

Federal Mediation and Conciliation Service (FMCS) Independent agency within the federal government that provides mediators to assist in resolving contract negotiation impasses.

Created by the National Labor Relations Act, the **Federal Mediation and Conciliation Service (FMCS)** exists as an independent agency within the executive branch of the federal government. The jurisdiction of the FMCS encompasses employees of private enterprise organizations engaged in interstate commerce, federal government employees, and employees in private, nonprofit hospitals and other allied medical facilities.

One of the responsibilities of the FMCS is to provide mediators to assist in resolving negotiation impasses. **Mediation** (or *conciliation,* as it is often called) is a process whereby both parties invite a neutral third party (called a *mediator*) to help resolve contract impasses. Mediators help the parties find common ground for continuing negotiations, develop factual data on issues over which the parties disagree, and set up joint study committees involving members of both parties to examine more difficult issues. In negotiations where the parties have become angry and/or antagonistic toward each other, the mediator often separates them and serves as a buffer, carrying proposals and counterproposals between the parties.

Mediators cannot impose decisions on the parties. Various state agencies and private individuals, such as lawyers, professors, and arbitrators, also provide mediation services.

Arbitrators

Mediation Process whereby both parties invite a neutral third party (called a mediator) to help resolve contract impasses. The mediator, unlike an arbitrator, has no authority to impose a solution on the parties.

Arbitration Process whereby the parties agree to settle a dispute through the use of an independent third party (called an arbitrator). Arbitration is binding on both parties.

Conventional Interest Arbitration Form of arbitration in which the arbitrator listens to arguments from both parties and makes a binding decision, which can be identical to the position of either party or different from the positions of both parties.

Final-Offer Interest Arbitration Form of arbitration in which the arbitrator is restricted to selecting the final offer of one of the parties.

Although arbitration is most frequently used in the resolution of grievances during a contract period, it can be used to resolve impasses during collective bargaining. Arbitration of contract terms is called *interest arbitration* or *contract arbitration*. Interest arbitration is rarely used in the private sector but is common in the public sector. Such arbitration can take one of two forms: conventional and final-offer. Under conventional interest arbitration, the arbitrator listens to arguments from both parties and makes a binding decision, which can be identical to the position of either party or different from the positions of both parties. In final-offer interest arbitration, the arbitrator is restricted to selecting the final offer of one of the parties. Furthermore, interest arbitration can be either voluntary or mandatory. Both the Federal Mediation and Conciliation Service and the American Arbitration Association (AAA) provide lists of certified arbitrators.

Collective Bargaining Agreements

The collective bargaining agreement (or union contract) results from the bargaining process and governs the relations between employer and employees for a specific period of time. The contract specifies in writing the mutual agreements reached by the parties during the negotiations. Under the Taft-Hartley Act, collective bargaining agreements are legally enforceable contracts. Suits charging violation of a contract between an employer and a union may be brought in any district court of the United States having jurisdiction over the parties.

As discussed earlier in this chapter, the National Labor Relations Act obligates employers and unions to bargain in good faith on wages, hours, and other terms and conditions of employment. These are called mandatory subjects of negotiation. However, as would be expected, controversy has developed over the subjects covered by the phrase "other terms and conditions of employment." Unions attempt to expand the mandatory area by giving a broad interpretation to the phrase. Employers, on the other hand, naturally resist this expansion. Numerous NLRB and court decisions have been rendered concerning this issue. For example, the Supreme Court ruled in one decision that all management decisions representing a departure from prior practice that significantly impair (1) job tenure, (2) employment security, and (3) reasonably anticipated work opportunities must be negotiated as mandatory subjects.[7] The number of mandatory bargaining items has definitely expanded over the years.

An issue on which the parties are not required to bargain is called a *nonmandatory*, or *permissive, issue*. During contract negotiations, the parties (if both agree) may bargain about permissive issues, but neither party is legally required to do so. Furthermore, it is an illegal labor practice for one party to insist on bargaining about a permissive issue.[8]

The difficulties of establishing a group of mandatory and permissive issues for all organizations are great. Subjects in one industry or organization that are appropriately handled through collective bargaining may be inappropriate in another industry or organization. Ultimately, however, the courts and the NLRB decide whether an issue is mandatory or permissive.

In addition to mandatory and permissive issues, there is a small group of prohibited issues that cannot be included in a collective bargaining agreement. The leading examples are the closed shop and a hot-cargo clause. A *closed shop* requires employers to hire only people who are union members. A *hot-cargo clause* results when an employer agrees with a union not to handle or use the goods or services of another employer.

For the federal sector, the Civil Service Reform Act of 1978 makes it mandatory to bargain over "conditions of employment." The act defines conditions of employment as personnel policies, practices, and matters affecting working conditions. Table 18–1 summarizes the prohibited and permitted issues for federal government employees. HRM in Action 18.1 explains the relationship between collective bargaining and the Family and Medical Leave Act of 1993.

Specific Issues in Collective Bargaining Agreements

While each contract is different, most contracts include five issues: (1) management rights, (2) union security, (3) wages and benefits, (4) individual security (seniority) rights, and (5) dispute resolution.

Management Rights

The question of how many of their prerogatives can be retained in the union-employer relationship is of great concern to most employers. The primary purpose of the management rights clause is to retain for management the right to direct all business activities. Items that are normally regarded as an integral part of management rights include the rights to direct the work force, determine the size of the work force (including the number and class of employees to be hired or laid off), set working hours, and assign work. Generally, in the management rights clause,

---

TABLE 18–1   **PROHIBITED AND PERMITTED COLLECTIVE BARGAINING ISSUES IN THE FEDERAL SECTOR**

Prohibited Issues

Negotiation of wage rates

Mission, budget, or organization of the agency

Number of employees

Internal security practices of the agency

Hiring, assigning, directing, laying off, and retaining employees in the agency; suspending, removing, reducing grade or pay; or taking other disciplinary action against employees

Assigning work, making determinations with respect to contracting work, and determining the personnel by which agency operations shall be conducted

Filling vacant positions from properly ranked and certified candidates

Taking whatever actions may be necessary to carry out the agency mission during emergencies

Permitted Issues

Numbers, types, and grades of employees or positions assigned to any organizational subdivision, work project, or tour of duty

Technology, means, and methods of performing work

Procedures used by the agency management to exercise its authority in carrying out duties that cannot be negotiated

Arrangements for employees adversely affected by the exercise of management's authority in carrying out duties that cannot be negotiated

HRM IN ACTION

Collective Bargaining and the Family and Medical Leave Act

18.1

The Family and Medical Leave Act of 1993 (FMLA), which was described in detail in Chapter 3, permits qualified employees to take prolonged, unpaid leave for family- and health-related reasons without fear of losing their jobs. However, the FMLA does not reduce the employment benefits that have been bargained for by union members in a collective bargaining agreement. The FMLA sets a minimum, and unions may still bargain for benefits in excess of those required by the law. Union members also benefit from the FMLA because collective bargaining agreements that do not meet FMLA standards can be voided. Union members can seek redress under both the FMLA and the collective bargaining process.

the union insists on a sentence specifying that management will not discriminate against the union.

Union Security

Union security clauses deal with the status of employee membership in the union and attempt to ensure that the union has continuous strength. Nearly all contracts provide some type of union security clause. Union security is provided in several forms. A **union shop** requires that all employees in the bargaining unit join the union and retain membership as a condition of employment. A modified union shop requires all employees hired after the effective date of the agreement to acquire and retain union membership as a condition of employment. The inclusion of a "grandfather" clause enables employees who are not members of the union as of the effective date of the contract to remain nonmembers. Under an **agency shop** provision, employees are not required to actually join the union, but they are required to pay a representation fee as a condition of employment. A provision for **maintenance of membership** does not require that an employee join the union, but employees who do join are required to remain members for a stipulated period of time as a condition of employment.[9]

As discussed in the previous chapter, the Taft-Hartley Act permits states to pass legislation that guarantees the right to work regardless of union membership. States that have passed this legislation are known as right-to-work states. The Taft-Hartley Act also prohibits two additional forms of union security: the closed shop and the preferential shop. In a closed shop, only union members can be hired, whereas the preferential shop requires that union members be given preference in filling job vacancies. However, in certain industries, such as construction, exceptions to the act's provisions are permitted.

In addition to providing a means for maintaining union membership, union security provisions often include checkoff procedures. A **checkoff** is an arrangement made with the company under which it agrees to withhold union dues, initiation fees, and assessments from the employees' paychecks and submit this money to the union. Individual union members must sign cards authorizing the withholding before such arrangements can be made.

Wages and Employee Benefits

Traditionally, increased wages have been the primary economic goal of unions. Most contracts contain a provision for general wage increases during the life of the contract. **Cost-of-living adjustments (COLA)** are common in many industries. COLA clauses tie wage increases to rises in the Bureau of Labor Statistics consumer price index (CPI). Most COLA clauses call for hourly increases in wages for

Union Shop   Provision in a contract that requires all employees in a bargaining unit to join the union and retain membership as a condition of employment; most right-to-work laws outlaw the union shop.

Agency Shop   Contract provision that does not require employees to join the union but requires them to pay the equivalent of union dues as a condition of employment.

Maintenance of Membership   Contract provision that does not require an employee to join the union but does require employees who do join to remain members for a stipulated time period.

Checkoff   Arrangement between an employer and a union under which the employer agrees to withhold union dues, initiation fees, and assessments from the employees' paychecks and submit this money to the union.

Cost-of-Living Adjustments (COLA) Contract provision that ties wage increases to rises in the Bureau of Labor Statistics consumer price index.

each specified rise in the CPI. Adjustments can be made on a quarterly, semiannual, or annual basis. A recent trend has been an attempt by the management of many organizations to eliminate or restrict the use of COLA clauses.

Other wage issues specified in contracts include overtime pay and rates of pay for work on Saturdays, Sundays, holidays, and the sixth or seventh consecutive day of work. Other employee compensation items normally contained in contracts include supplementary pay for shift differentials, reporting and call-in or call-back pay, temporary-transfer pay, hazardous-duty pay, and job-related expenses. Each of these terms is defined in Table 18–2.

The benefits normally covered in union contracts include holidays, vacations, insurance, and pensions. Pay is usually required in union contracts for all recognized holidays. Eligibility for holiday pay is of one or two types: a length-of-service requirement or a work requirement. Normally, an employee must have worked a minimum of four weeks with the employer before being eligible for holiday pay. Furthermore, an employee generally must work the day before and the day after a holiday to receive holiday pay.

Most union contracts provide vacation provisions. Vacation entitlement is usually tied directly to the employee's length of service. One trend in contracts has been an increase in the amount of vacation time per year and a reduction in the amount of service required for receiving increased vacations.

Most union contracts contain clauses providing health, accident, and life insurance benefits. Many union contracts also contain major medical insurance, accidental death and dismemberment benefits, dental insurance, and coverage for miscellaneous medical expenses such as prescription drugs.

Individual Security (Seniority) Rights

Seniority An employee's relative length of service with an employer.

Seniority refers to an employee's relative length of service with an employer. Seniority may be measured on the basis of the employee's length of service in a job classification or a department or on the individual's length of service with one plant or with the company as a whole.

Job security for employees is a basic concern for unions. The seniority system is the method most commonly used to achieve job security. In general, union contract provisions specify that seniority is to be used within the bargaining unit for

TABLE 18–2

DEFINITIONS OF TYPICAL SUPPLEMENTARY PAY ITEMS

Item	Definition
Shift differential pay	Bonus paid for working less desirable hours of work
Reporting pay	Pay given to employees who report for work as scheduled but find on arrival that no work is available
Call-in or call-back pay	Pay earned when employees are called in or back to work at some time other than their regularly scheduled hours
Temporary-transfer pay	Pay given when employees are temporarily transferred to another job (if the transfer is to a lower-paying job, normally the employee continues to receive the old rate of pay; if to a higher-paying job, the employee is usually paid the higher rate)
Hazardous-duty pay	Pay given for performing jobs that, from a safety or health point of view, are considered to be riskier than usual
Job-related expenses	Covers travel expenses, work clothes, or tools required for the job

transfers to higher-level jobs, layoffs, recalls from layoffs, and choice of work shifts and vacation periods.

Seniority systems are designed to benefit employees with greater length of service. Thus, women and minorities, generally the most recently hired employees, can be adversely affected by a seniority system. Section 703(a) of the 1964 Civil Rights Act prohibits discrimination on the basis of race, color, religion, sex, or national origin. However, Section 703(h) exempts bona fide seniority systems from the mandate of Section 703(a). Section 703(h) suggests that bona fide seniority may have a disproportionate impact on a certain class of people and still be deemed valid. However, such a system may not be the result of an intent to discriminate against a class of individuals.[10] In the *Stotts* case discussed in Chapter 3, the Supreme Court ruled that a judge could not impose an affirmative action plan that required white employees to be laid off when the otherwise applicable system would have required the layoff of African American employees with less seniority. It is important to note that this decision did not ban affirmative action programs. It did indicate, however, that seniority systems may limit the application of certain affirmative action measures.[11]

Dispute Resolution

Inevitably, disputes arise during the life of a contract. Most contracts contain specific clauses describing how disputes are to be resolved.

A "no-strike" clause pledges the union to cooperate in preventing work stoppages. No-strike pledges can be either unconditional or conditional. Unconditional pledges ban any interference with production during the life of the contract. Conditional pledges permit strikes under certain circumstances. The no-strike ban most commonly is lifted after exhaustion of the grievance procedure or after an arbitration award has been violated. In return for a no-strike pledge, the union normally asks for a promise on the part of the company not to engage in lockouts during the term of the contract. A **lockout** is a refusal of the employer to let employees work.

Lockout   Refusal of an employer to let its employees work.

The grievance procedure provision is the most common method for resolving disputes arising during the term of the contract. The final step in the dispute resolution procedure is usually arbitration. Both grievance procedures and arbitration are discussed in Chapter 19.

Impasses in Collective Bargaining

At the end of the contract period, if a new agreement has not been reached, employees can continue working under the terms of the old contract until a new agreement is reached or a strike is called. Union officials will not recommend that the employees continue working unless significant progress is being made in contract negotiations.

If no progress is being made and the contract expires, a strike is frequently called. A **strike** occurs when employees collectively refuse to work. Strikes are not permitted for most public employees. To strike, the union must first hold a vote among its members. Unless the vote is heavily in favor of a strike, one will not be called. When a strike does occur, union members picket the employer. In picketing, individual members patrol at or near the place of employment to publicize the existence of a strike, discourage employees from working, and discourage the public from dealing with the employer. Frequently members of other unions will refuse to cross the picket line of a striking union. For example, unionized truck drivers often refuse to deliver goods to an employer involved in a strike. HRM in Action 18.2 describes a strike at General Motors.

Strike   Collective refusal of employees to work.

The purpose of a strike is to bring economic hardship to the employer, forcing the employer to agree to union demands. The success of a strike is determined by

HRM IN ACTION

Strike at General Motors

18.2

www.gm.com

In 1994, General Motors found that good pay isn't enough when its well-paid workers struck the Buick City plant in Flint, Michigan. Workers at Buick City were earning as much as $1,200 per week, with overtime—and that was the problem. Compulsory overtime pushed the workweek up to as much as 60 hours, leading to exhaustion, injuries, increases in illness and absenteeism, and a dangerous decline in morale.

The strike ended rather quickly. General Motors agreed to hire approximately 500 new employees. Many of them were former employees who had been laid off when General Motors was experiencing difficult times. General Motors also agreed to institute an ergonomics program and set up a physical rehabilitation center. General Motors also withdrew a letter notifying the United Auto Workers that it intended to outsource the loading of finished cars onto rail cars.

Source: "How Burnout Led to Rebellion: How to Protect Your Operation," *Supervisory Management,* March 1995, p. 3.

how severely the union is able to interrupt the organization's operations. Employers often attempt to continue operations by using supervisory and management personnel, people not in a striking bargaining unit, people within the bargaining unit who refuse to go on strike, or people hired to replace striking employees. Attempts to continue operations through these methods can increase the difficulty of reaching an agreement and often result in violence.

When the president of the United States believes a strike may jeopardize the national health and safety, the emergency dispute provisions of the Taft-Hartley Act can be used. Under these provisions, the president is authorized to appoint a special board of inquiry, which makes a preliminary investigation of the impasse prior to issuing an injunction to halt the strike. If the impasse is not resolved during this preliminary investigation, the president can issue an injunction prohibiting the strike action for 80 days. This is called a *cooling-off period.* The parties then have 60 days to resolve the impasse, after which the NLRB is required to poll the employees to see whether they will accept the employer's last offer. If the employees do not agree to accept the employer's last offer, the injunction is dissolved and the president can refer the impasse to Congress and recommend a course of action.

Trends in Collective Bargaining

Technological change and increased use of automation, changing government regulations, rising foreign competition, the decline in the percentage of blue-collar employees, and high rates of unemployment are just some of the variables that influence the collective bargaining process.[12] These and other variables can change rapidly, making virtually useless a contract provision negotiated two years earlier.

One form of collective bargaining that has evolved to cope with these rapidly changing variables involves the establishment of joint-labor-management committees that meet regularly over the contract period to explore issues of common concern. The essential characteristics of this new form of collective bargaining are as follows:

1. Meetings are held frequently during the life of the contract and are independent of its expiration.

2. Discussions examine external events and potential problem areas rather than internal complaints about current practices.

3. Outside experts such as legal, economic, actuarial, medical, and industry specialists play a major role in making the final decision on some issues.

4. Participants in the meetings are encouraged to take a problem-solving rather than an adversarial approach.

Another likely trend in collective bargaining within U.S. companies is productivity bargaining. Under productivity bargaining, unions and management develop a contract whereby the union agrees to exchange old work procedures and methods for new and more effective ones in return for gains in pay and working conditions. Productivity bargaining involves not only reaching an agreement but also creating an atmosphere of ongoing cooperation in which the changes called for in the agreement can be implemented.

A final trend involves what has been called "take-back bargaining." This form of bargaining involves asking unions to make concessions on wages and benefits. It has occurred in industries especially hard hit by foreign competition.

SUMMARY OF LEARNING OBJECTIVES

1. **Define collective bargaining.**
   Collective bargaining involves the negotiation, drafting, administration, and interpretation of a written agreement between an employer and a union for a specific period of time.

2. **Explain the captive-audience doctrine.**
   Under this doctrine, management has the right to speak to employees against the union on company time and require employees to attend the meeting. The union does not have the right to reply on company time. However, management is prohibited from giving a speech on company time to a mass-employee audience in the 24 hours immediately before a union election.

3. **Define bargaining unit.**
   A bargaining unit is a group of employees in a plant, firm, or industry that is recognized by the employer, agreed on by the parties to a case, or designated by the NLRB or its regional director as appropriate for the purposes of collective bargaining.

4. **Explain certification, recognition, and contract bars.**
   Under a certification bar, the NLRB will not permit another election within 12 months of a union's certification. Under a recognition bar, the NLRB will not permit an election for up to 12 months after an employer voluntarily recognizes a union. Under a contract bar, the NLRB does not normally permit an election on the bargaining unit covered by a contract until the contract expires, up to a maximum of three years.

5. **Describe good-faith bargaining.**
   Good-faith bargaining is the sincere intention of both parties to negotiate differences and reach an agreement acceptable to both.

6. **Discuss boulwarism.**
   Boulwarism is a form of collective bargaining under which management makes its best offer at the outset of bargaining and adheres to its position throughout the bargaining sessions. Boulwarism is in violation of an employer's obligation to negotiate in good faith and is illegal.

7. **Explain mediation.**
   Mediation is a process whereby both parties invite a neutral third party to help resolve contract impasses.

8. **Define checkoff.**
   Checkoff is an arrangement a union makes with a company under which the

company agrees to withhold union dues, initiation fees, and assessments from the employees' paychecks and submit this money to the union.

9. Explain seniority.
Seniority refers to an employee's relative length of service with an employer.

10. Define lockout and strike.
A lockout is a refusal of the employer to let employees work. A strike occurs when employees collectively refuse to work.

REVIEW QUESTIONS

1. What is collective bargaining?
2. Describe some of the reasons employees join unions.
3. What is a bargaining unit?
4. Define some unfair labor practices that can occur during a union election campaign.
5. Define good-faith bargaining.
6. What is a multiemployer agreement?
7. Describe the roles of the following third parties in the collective bargaining process:
   a. NLRB
   b. FLRA
   c. FSIP
   d. FMCS
   e. Mediators
   f. Arbitrators
8. Define the following union security clauses:
   a. Union shop
   b. Agency shop
   c. Maintenance of membership
   d. Closed shop
   e. Preferential shop
9. What is the purpose of COLA clauses in a union contract?
10. Define seniority.
11. What is a strike?

DISCUSSION QUESTIONS

1. "Seniority provisions in a contract discriminate against women and minorities." What is your opinion of this statement?
2. "Right-to-work laws should be rescinded." Discuss.
3. Identify several management rights that you believe should not be subject to collective bargaining.
4. Why do you think collective bargaining is increasing among white-collar employees?

INCIDENT 18–1

Florida National Guard and NAGE

The Florida National Guard employs full-time civilian technicians to assist in training the guard and to help repair and maintain the guard's equipment and supplies. As a condition of their employment, these technicians are required to maintain membership in the guard. The technicians are represented by the National Association of Government Employees (NAGE).

During negotiations between NAGE and the Florida National Guard, the technicians submitted through their unions a proposal whereby the technicians could opt to wear either their military uniform or agreed-on civilian attire while performing their technician duties. The parties were unable to reach an agreement on this issue. Consequently, NAGE asked the Federal Services Impasses Panel (FSIP) to resolve the matter. FSIP directed the parties to adopt the proposal as part of their collective bargaining agreement. The guard refused.

NAGE then filed an unfair labor practice charge with the Federal Labor Relations Authority (FLRA). The FLRA concluded that wearing the uniform was not within the guard's duty to bargain and dismissed the charge.

Questions

1. Do you feel that the National Guard should bargain over this issue?

2. If you had been advising the National Guard, would you have recommended that it bargain over this issue? Why or why not?

INCIDENT 18–2

Retiree Benefits

Federal courts have ruled that two companies cannot require retirees and their dependents covered by collective bargaining agreements to pay part of their health care costs. One company is trying to make its retirees pay monthly premiums and deductibles, while the second company is trying to impose copayments and deductibles on its retirees. In the case of the first company, a federal judge reinstated the benefits to retirees since the benefits were intended to outlast the life of the labor contract. In the case of the second company, a U.S. district court ordered the company to reinstate the benefits of the retirees pending the outcome of a jury trial.

Questions

1. Should a company be allowed to make changes to the health benefits of retired employees who are covered by a collective bargaining agreement? Why or why not?

2. Why do you think the court system was involved in the resolution of this disagreement?

EXERCISE

Contract Negotiations*

You will be put on a team of three to four students. Each team will be required to negotiate a contract for a company or a union.

The company's wage scale, $8.40 per hour, compares favorably with most firms in its area but is about 8 percent below those firms that employ workers of equivalent skill. Wages have not increased in proportion to cost-of-living increases over the past three years.

---

*Adapted from James A. Vaughan and Samuel D. Deep, "Exercise Negotiations," *Program of Exercises for Management and Organizational Behavior* (Beverly Hills, Calif.: Glencoe Press, 1975), pp. 137–52.

At the last bargaining session, the company and union took the following positions:

1. *Hospital and medical plan*
   Past contract: Company paid one-fourth of cost, employee paid remaining three-fourths.
   Union: Demanded that company pay full cost.
   Company: Refused to pay more than one-fourth.

	Proportion of company payment				
Company	1/4	2/4	3/4	4/4	Union
	0	20,000	40,000	60,000	

Increase in total dollar value per year

2. *Wages*
   Past contract: $8.40 per hour.
   Union: Demanded an increase of 60 cents per hour.
   Company: Refused outright.

	Cents increase per hour							
Company	0	10	20	30	40	50	60	Union
	0	31,200	62,400	93,600	124,800	156,000	187,200	

Total dollar value per year

3. *Sliding pay scale to conform to cost of living*
   Past contract: Pay scale is fixed through the term of the contract.
   Union: Demanded pay increases in proportion to increases to the cost of living.
   Company: Rejected outright.

	No	Yes	Union
Company	0	120,000	

Total dollar value per year

4. *Vacation pay*
   Past contract: Two weeks' paid vacation for all employees with one year of service.
   Union: Wants three weeks' paid vacation for employees with 10 years of service.
   Company: Rejected.

	2 weeks/ 1 year	3 weeks/ 20 years	3 weeks/ 15 years	3 weeks/ 10 years	Union
Company					
	0	10,000	20,000	30,000	

Total dollar value per year

Each week on strike (10 minutes of negotiations in the exercise) costs the company $40,000 in lost profits and the employees $40,000 in lost wages.

1. Negotiate the above contract issues with another team (as assigned by your instructor).

2. At the end of negotiations, your instructor will summarize the beginning, ending, and costs for each negotiation.

NOTES AND ADDITIONAL READINGS

1. See *Norris K. W. Printing Co.,* 231 NLRB NO. 156, 97 LRRM 1080 (1977); and *United Parcel Service, Inc.,* 234 LLRB No. 11, 97 LRRM 1212 (1978).
2. See *NLRB* v. *Babcock & Wilcox, Co.,* 351 U.S. 105, 38 LRRM 2001 (1956).
3. See *Peerless Plywood Co.,* 107 NLRB No. 106, 33 LRRM 1151 (1953).
4. For discussion of organizing tactics by unions, see Kenneth Gilberg and Nancy Abrams, "Countering Unions' New Organizing Techniques," *Personnel,* June 1987, pp. 12–16.

5. *NLRB* v. *Gissel Packing Company,* 395 U.S. 575 (1969).

6. *General Electric Company,* 150 NLRB 192(1964).

7. *Fiberboard Paper Products Corp.* v. *NLRB,* 379 U.S. 203 (1984).

8. *NLRB* v. *Wooster Division of Borg-Warner Corp.,* 356 U.S. 342 (1958).

9. See, for instance, Edward Brantley and Mel E. Schnake, "Exceptions to Compulsory Union Membership," *Personnel Journal,* June 1988, pp. 114–22.

10. Theresa Johnson, "The Future of Affirmative Action: An Analysis of the Stotts Case," *Labor Law Journal,* October 1985, p. 783.

11. Ibid, p. 788.

12. See, for instance, Gary N. Chaison and Mark S. Plovnick, "Is There a New Collective Bargaining?" *California Management Review,* Summer 1986, pp. 54–61.

Employee
Relations

Learning Objectives

After studying this chapter, you should be able to:

1. Define organizational discipline.
2. Explain the hot-stove rule.
3. Describe progressive discipline.
4. Explain employment at will.
5. Define grievance procedures.
6. Define just cause.
7. Explain due process.
8. Describe the duty of fair representation.
9. Define grievance arbitration.

employee relations deals with the administration of discipline and grievance-handling procedures. When a manager must take action against an employee for violating an organizational work rule or for poor performance, he or she uses the organization's disciplinary procedure to resolve the problem. When an employee has a complaint against the organization or its management, she or he normally uses the grievance procedure to resolve the problem. Some organizations have very formal discipline and grievance procedures, others are less formal, and some organizations have no set procedures at all. This chapter describes typical discipline and grievance-handling procedures.

Discipline Defined

Discipline Action taken against an employee who has violated an organizational rule or whose performance has deteriorated to the point where corrective action is needed.

Organizational **discipline** is action taken against an employee who has violated an organizational rule or whose performance has deteriorated to the point where corrective action is needed. Sixty years ago, a manager who objected to an employee's performance or behavior could simply say, "You're fired!" and that was it. Justification often played little, if any, part in the decision. At that time, managers had the final authority to administer discipline at will.

In applying organizational discipline, the primary question should be, "Why are employees disciplined?" Too many managers, when faced with a discipline problem in their organization, immediately think of what and how much: What should the penalty be? How severely should the employee be punished? The ultimate form of discipline is discharge, or organizational capital punishment as it is

sometimes called. Organizations should use discharge in the case of repeated offenses or when the act committed is such that discharge is believed to be the only
reasonable alternative.

Rather than an end in itself, discipline should be viewed as a learning opportunity
for the employee and as a tool to improve productivity and human relations.

Causes of Disciplinary Actions

Generally disciplinary actions are taken against employees for two types of conduct:

1. Poor job performance or conduct that negatively affects an employee's job performance. Absenteeism, insubordination, and negligence are examples of behaviors that can lead to discipline.
2. Actions that indicate poor citizenship. Examples include fighting on the job or
theft of company property.

Table 19–1 lists the reasons that often lead to disciplinary actions against or the
discharge of employees.

The Discipline Process

The first step in the disciplinary process is the establishment of performance requirements and work rules. Performance requirements are normally established
through the performance appraisal process, discussed in Chapter 12. Work rules
should be relevant to successful performance of the job. Because implementation
of work rules partially depends on the employee's willingness to accept them, periodic review of their applicability is essential. In addition, it is often desirable to solicit employee input either directly or indirectly when establishing work rules.
Work rules are more easily enforced when employees perceive them as being fair
and relevant to the job.

TABLE 19–1 **REASONS FOR DISCIPLINE OR DISCHARGE OF EMPLOYEES**

Absenteeism	Theft
Tardiness	Disloyalty to employer (includes competing with employer, conflict of interest)
Loafing	Moonlighting
Absence from work	Negligence
Leaving place of work (includes early quitting)	Damage to or loss of machinery or materials
Sleeping on job	Unsatisfactory performance
Assault and fighting among employees	Refusal to accept job assignment
Horseplay	Refusal to work overtime
Insubordination	Participation in prohibited strike
Sexual harassment	Misconduct during strike
Racial slur	Slowdown
Threat to or assault of management representative	Possession or use of drugs
Abusive language to supervisor	Possession or use of intoxicants
Profane or abusive language	Distribution of drugs
Falsifying company records (including time records, production records)	Obscene or immoral conduct
	Attachment or garnishment of wages
Falsifying employment application	Gambling
Dishonesty	Abusing customers

Source: Adapted from F. Elkouri and E. Elkouri, *How Arbitration Works,* 4th ed. (Washington, D.C.: Bureau of National Affairs, 1985), pp. 691–707.

The second step in the process is to communicate the performance requirements and work rules to employees. This is normally handled through orientation and performance appraisal. Work rules are communicated in a variety of ways. Generally, an individual who is hired receives a manual that describes the work rules and policies of the organization. The human resource department or the new employee's supervisor explains these work rules and policies to the new employee during orientation. Furthermore, new employees may be required to sign a document indicating they have received and read the manual. In unionized organizations, work rules and the corresponding disciplinary actions for infractions are frequently part of the labor contract. Bulletin boards, company newsletters, and memos are also commonly used to communicate work rules. In any case, management bears the responsibility for clearly communicating all work rules to employees.

The final step in the disciplinary process is the application of corrective action (discipline) when necessary. Corrective action is needed when an employee's work performance is below expectations or when violations of work rules have occurred.

Prediscipline Recommendations

Before an employee is disciplined, management can take several steps to ensure that the action will be constructive and will not likely be rescinded by higher levels of management. Adequate records are of utmost importance in discipline cases. Written records often have a significant influence on decisions to overturn or uphold a disciplinary action. Past rule infractions and overall performance should be recorded.

Another key responsibility of management is the investigation. Things that appear obvious on the surface are sometimes completely discredited after investigation. Accusations against an employee must be supported by facts. Many decisions to discipline employees have been overturned due to an improper or less than thorough investigation. Undue haste in taking disciplinary action, taking the action when the manager is angry, and improper and incomplete investigations frequently cause disciplinary actions to be rescinded. An employee's work record should also be considered a part of the investigation. Good performance and long tenure with the organization are considerations that should influence the severity of a disciplinary action. Naturally, the investigation must take place before any discipline is administered. A manager should not discipline an employee and then look for evidence to support the decision.

A typical first step in the investigation of the facts is for management to discuss the situation with the employee. Providing the employee with an opportunity to present his or her side of the situation is essential if a disciplinary system is to be viewed positively by employees.

Employees represented by a union are allowed to have a union representative present during any disciplinary interview. This right is protected by the National Labor Relations Board (NLRB).[1] The most significant NLRB policy in this area was supported by a Supreme Court decision in 1975. In *NLRB* v. *Weingarten*,[2] an employee was investigated for allegedly underpaying for food purchased from the employer. The employee requested and was denied union representation at an interview held after the employee was charged with the underpayments. The union filed unfair labor practice charges against the company with the NLRB. The NLRB ruled that the employee had a right to refuse to submit to an interview without union representation but also ruled that this right was available only if the employee requested union representation and applied only when disciplinary actions might reasonably be expected as a result of the interview. However, in a later case, the NLRB ruled that an employee does not have the right to union representation when management meets with the employee simply to inform him or her of discipline that has been previously determined.[3]

Thus, as the law presently stands, management must be prepared to allow the

NLRB v. *Weingarten*
Supreme Court decision in 1975 holding that an employee has the right to refuse to submit to a disciplinary interview without union representation.

presence of a union representative in any investigatory meeting. This means management must not only deal with the employee and the problem but also must do so in the presence of a union representative, who normally acts in the role of an employee advocate.

Besides being involved in the investigation, the union should be kept informed on matters of discipline. Some organizations give unions advance notice of their intention to discipline an employee. Also, copies of warnings are sometimes sent to the union.

Administering Discipline

Hot-Stove Rule Set of guidelines used in administering discipline that calls for quick, consistent, and impersonal action preceded by a warning.

Administering discipline should be analogous to the burn received when touching a hot stove. Often referred to as the **hot-stove rule,** this approach emphasizes that discipline should be directed against the act rather than the person. Other key points of the hot-stove rule are immediacy, advance warning, and consistency. Figure 19–1 outlines the hot-stove rule.

Immediacy refers to the length of time between the misconduct and the discipline. For discipline to be most effective, it must be taken as soon as possible but without involving an emotional, irrational decision. Notation of rules infractions in an employee's record does not constitute advance warning and is not sufficient to support disciplinary action. An employee must be advised of the infraction for it to be considered a warning. Noting that the employee was warned about the infraction and having the employee sign a form acknowledging the warning are both good practices. Failure to warn an employee of the consequences of repeated violations of a rule is one reason often cited for overturning a disciplinary action.

A key element in discipline is consistency. Inconsistency lowers morale, diminishes respect for management, and leads to grievances. Striving for consistency does not mean that past infractions, length of service, work record, and other mitigating factors should not be considered when applying discipline. However, an employee should believe that any other employee under essentially the same circumstances would receive the same penalty. Similarly, management should take steps to ensure that personalities are not a factor when applying discipline. The

---

FIGURE 19–1   **HOT-STOVE RULE FOR APPLYING DISCIPLINE**

1. The hot stove burns immediately. Disciplinary policies should be administered quickly. There should be no question of cause and effect.
2. The hot stove gives a warning and so should discipline.
3. The hot stove consistently burns everyone who touches it. Discipline should be consistent.
4. The hot stove burns everyone in the same manner regardless of who they are. Discipline must be impartial. People are disciplined for what they have done and not because of who they are.

employee should understand that the disciplinary action is a consequence of what was done and not caused by his or her personality. A manager should avoid arguing with the employee and should administer the discipline in a straightforward, calm manner. Administering discipline without anger or apology and then resuming a pleasant relationship aids in reducing the negative effects of discipline. A manager should also administer discipline in private. The only exception would be in the case of gross insubordination or flagrant and serious rule violations, where a public reprimand would help the manager regain control of the situation. Even in this type of situation, the objective should be to gain control and not to embarrass the employee.

Lower-level managers should be very reluctant to impose disciplinary suspensions and discharges. Usually discipline of this degree is reserved for higher levels of management. Even a lower-level manager who does not have the power to administer disciplinary suspensions or discharges, however, is nearly always the one who must recommend the action to higher management. Since discipline of this nature is more likely to be reviewed, more costly to the organization, and more likely to be reflected in overall morale and productivity, it is very important for lower-level managers to know when it should be recommended. Observing the hot-stove rule is essential for administering suspensions and discharges.

Corrective (Progressive) Discipline The normal sequence of actions taken by management in disciplining an employee; oral warning, written warning, suspension, and finally discharge.

Management is expected to use **corrective** or **progressive discipline** whenever possible. Progressive or corrective discipline means the normal sequence of actions taken by management in disciplining an employee would be oral warning, written warning, suspension, and discharge. Some offenses, however, may justify discharge, such as stealing, striking a coworker or member of management, and gross insubordination. Management must be able to show, generally through the preponderance of evidence, that the offense was committed. Attention to the points covered regarding prediscipline recommendations is especially important in supporting a decision to discharge an employee.

As in any lesser discipline, but even more essential in suspension and discharge, the employee has the right to a careful and impartial investigation. This involves allowing the employee to state his or her side of the case, gather evidence to support that side, and, usually, question the accuser. In the case of very serious offenses, the employee may be suspended pending a full investigation.

The suggestions outlined in the preceding paragraphs are designed to assist managers in applying discipline in a positive manner and with minimal application of the harsher forms of discipline. In the disciplinary procedure, observance of these suggestions should reduce the chance of a grievance or, if a grievance is filed, the chance of having the disciplinary action overruled. Table 19–2 provides a checklist of rules to observe when applying discipline.

Legal Restrictions

Alexander v. Gardner-Denver Supreme Court decision in 1974 that ruled that using the final and binding grievance procedure in an organization does not preclude an aggrieved employee from seeking redress through court action.

The Civil Rights Act of 1964 and the Age Discrimination in Employment Act of 1967 as amended in 1978 changed an employer's authority in making decisions and taking actions involving employment conditions. Specifically, Title VII of the Civil Rights Act prohibits the use of race, color, religion, sex, or national origin as the basis of any employment condition. The Age Discrimination in Employment Act makes similar prohibitions involving persons over 40 years of age. Discipline is, of course, a condition of employment and is subject to these laws. Under these laws, employees have the right to appeal to the Equal Employment Opportunity Commission (EEOC) and to the courts any disciplinary action they consider discriminatory.

The landmark case guaranteeing employees this right was decided in 1974 by the Supreme Court in **Alexander v. Gardner-Denver.** In that case, the Supreme Court ruled that using the grievance procedure in an organization did not preclude the aggrieved employee from seeking redress through court action.[4] Basically, the

TABLE 19-2	CONSIDERATIONS IN DISCIPLINING OR DISCHARGING EMPLOYEES

1. Avoid hasty decisions.

2. Document all actions and enter the evidence in the personnel file.

3. Thoroughly and fully investigate the circumstances and facts of the alleged offense.
   a. Notify the employee of the nature of the offense.
   b. Obtain the employee's version of the circumstances, reasons for the actions, and the names of any witnesses.
   c. If suspension is required until the investigation is completed, inform the employee:
      (1) To return 24 to 72 hours later to receive the decision.
      (2) That there will be reinstatement with pay if the decision is in the employee's favor.
      (3) Of the discipline to be imposed if it is not in the employee's favor.
   d. Interview all witnesses to the alleged misconduct. Obtain signed statements, if necessary.
   e. Check all alternative possible causes (e.g., broken machinery).
   f. Decide whether the employee committed the alleged offense.

4. Determine the appropriate discipline. Consider:
   a. Personnel record: length of service, past performance, past disciplinary record. Has corrective discipline ever been applied?
   b. Nature of the offense.
   c. Past disciplinary action for other employees in similar situations.
   d. Existing rules and disciplinary policies.
   e. Provisions in the labor contract, if one exists.

5. Advise the employee of the nature of the offense, the results of the investigation, the discipline to be imposed, and the rationale behind the discipline.

Court decided that the Civil Rights Act guaranteed individuals the right to pursue remedies of illegal discrimination regardless of prior rejections in another forum.

Discipline and Unions

Web site: Labor link

www.laborlink.org

Unions have greatly affected management's authority to administer discipline. Central to the goals of unionism is the desire to protect employees from arbitrary and unfair treatment. The philosophy of unions has been that employees are economically dependent on the employer and, as a result, are helpless against the whims of management. Therefore, disciplinary policy is viewed as being an integral part of the collective bargaining process. Union contracts contain provisions specifying how management can deal with employees accused of rule violations or misconduct. Table 19–3 gives some sample rules for discipline from a typical union contract.

While management usually reserves the right to make reasonable rules for employee performance and conduct, the union can question management's application and the reasonableness of these rules through the grievance procedure. Furthermore, when management establishes new work rules, they must usually notify the union before the rules can be implemented.

Discipline in Nonunionized Organizations

Until recently, management decisions on discipline or discharge in nonunionized organizations have been relatively free of judicial review. Courts intervened only in those cases violating legislation concerning equal employment opportunity.

T A B L E   1 9 – 3   **DISCIPLINE RULES IN TYPICAL LABOR CONTRACTS**

Offense	Discipline
Minor	
Absence without notification as per existing absentee and lateness policy	First offense—written warning
	Second offense—one-day suspension
Horseplay	Third offense—two-day suspension
Major	
Possession of, drinking, smoking, or being under the influence of, intoxicants or narcotics on company property	First offense—written warning that may result in suspension of up to three days without pay
Sleeping on the job	Second offense treated as an intolerable offense
Gambling on company property	
Intolerable	
Stealing company or personal property	First offense—subject to discharge
Fighting on company property	

Source: Adapted from the labor agreement between Babcock and Wilcox Company and the Laborers International Union of North America.

Employment at Will   Term used to describe the situation in which an employer hires employees to work for an indefinite period of time and the employees do not have a contract limiting the circumstances under which they can be discharged. Under these conditions, the employer can terminate the employee at any time for any reason or for no reason at all.

Generally, the concept of employment at will has applied. **Employment at will** means that when an employer in the private sector hires employees to work for an indefinite period of time and the employees do not have a contract limiting the circumstances under which they can be discharged, the employer can terminate the employees at any time for any reason or for no reason at all.

The situation has been gradually changing as the courts have begun to hear discharge cases involving allegations of capricious or unfair treatment in nonunionized organizations. In some cases, the courts have ruled in favor of the discharged employees when the employee had not been guaranteed due process under company procedures. Basically, the courts seem to be moving toward requiring nonunionized organizations to use a wrongful discharge standard, which is somewhere between the employment-at-will and just-cause positions.

In light of these developments, many organizations have established appeal procedures for disciplinary actions taken by management. The most common type of nonunion appeal procedure is an open-door policy that allows employees to bring appeals to successively higher levels of management. An open-door policy gives an employee the right to appeal a disciplinary action taken against him or her to the manager's superior.

The Grievance Procedure

Grievance Procedures   Systematic means of resolving disagreements over the collective bargaining agreement and providing assurance that the terms and conditions agreed to in negotiations are properly implemented.

Nonunionized as well as unionized organizations have grievance procedures. The main emphasis in this section is on grievance procedures in unionized organizations. In this context, **grievance procedures** are a systematic means of resolving disagreements over the collective bargaining agreement and providing assurance that the terms and conditions agreed to in negotiations are properly implemented. Grievance procedures outline the steps to be taken by employees in appealing any management action they believe violates the union contract. Grievance procedures are used not only to appeal disciplinary actions but also to resolve matters concerning contract interpretation.

In general, the grievance process is initiated by an employee who has a complaint regarding some action perceived to be inconsistent with the terms of the union contract. While it is highly unlikely that the organization would initiate a grievance, it can do so. Initially, the grievant (aggrieved employee) contacts the union representative (usually called a *union steward*), and they discuss the events causing the grievance. The grievant and the union steward then meet with the grievant's supervisor. If a mutually agreeable settlement cannot be reached at this meeting, the grievance is then put into writing. Generally, in the next step, the union steward discusses the grievance with the department manager or another appropriate management representative. Management then presents a reaction, usually in writing. If the grievance is not resolved at this point, the next step usually involves the human resource or labor relations manager and higher officials of the union, such as the business agent or international representative. After fully investigating and discussing the grievance, the human resource department usually issues the final company decision. In the event the grievance is still unresolved, the party initiating the grievance can request arbitration. Grievance arbitration (discussed later in this chapter) is a process whereby the employer and union agree to settle a dispute through an independent third party. Because of the expense to both the union and management, every attempt should be made to resolve grievances in the stages before arbitration. Figure 19–2 illustrates the steps normally involved in a grievance procedure. Table 19–4 outlines the grievance procedure in an actual union contract.

Just Cause

Just Cause Requires that management initially bear the burden of proof of wrongdoing in discipline cases and that the severity of the punishment must coincide with the seriousness of the offense.

All union contracts recognize the right of management to discipline or discharge employees for just cause. In fact, in most discipline or discharge cases, the basic issue is whether or not management acted with just cause. In general, **just cause** concerns the burden and degree of proof of wrongdoing and the severity of punishment.

It is generally agreed that the burden of proof in matters of discipline and discharge lies with the company. However, once the case has been established by the company, the burden of proof shifts to the union to disprove or discredit the company's contention.

Once an organization proves that an employee was guilty of wrongdoing, the second area of concern in determining just cause relates to the severity of the punishment. Just cause results when the severity of the punishment coincides with the seriousness of the wrongdoing. The following general guidelines are frequently used by arbitrators for determining just cause as it relates to the severity of punishment:

1. Consider the past performance of the employee.
2. Consider previous disciplinary actions taken against other employees in similar situations.
3. Consider unusual circumstances surrounding the alleged offense.

Due Process

Due Process Right of an employee to be dealt with fairly and justly during the investigation of an alleged offense and the administration of any subsequent disciplinary action.

Due process refers to the employee's right to be dealt with fairly and justly during the investigation of an alleged offense and the administration of discipline. Due process typically guarantees that the employee will be notified of the allegations and have them explained, that an impartial investigation will be held prior to the imposition of discipline, and that the employee can present his or her version of the incident. As discussed earlier, unionized employees have the right to union representation in the disciplinary review if they request it and if disciplinary actions might reasonably be expected to result.

A breach of due process during the grievance procedure can result in either a modification or a complete reversal of a disciplinary action. Procedural requirements are often spelled out in the grievance procedures of the contract. Failure to follow such provisions may constitute a breach of due process. In general, to

F I G U R E   1 9 – 2   **GENERAL PROCESS FOLLOWED IN A UNION GRIEVANCE PROCEDURE**

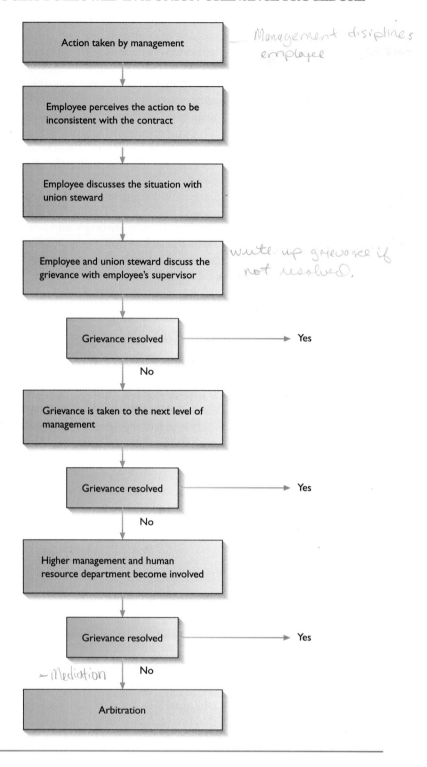

Action taken by management — *Management disciplines employee*

Employee perceives the action to be inconsistent with the contract

Employee discusses the situation with union steward

Employee and union steward discuss the grievance with employee's supervisor — *write up grievance if not resolved.*

Grievance resolved → Yes

No

Grievance is taken to the next level of management

Grievance resolved → Yes

No

Higher management and human resource department become involved

Grievance resolved → Yes

~ Mediation   No

Arbitration

TABLE 19–4	TYPICAL UNION GRIEVANCE PROCEDURE

Purpose

(53) The procedure under this article is available to the union for the presentation and settlement of grievances arising under the interpretation or application of the terms of this agreement as they relate to wages, hours of work, and working conditions and all other conditions of employment, including discharge cases.

Foreman and superintendent's step

(54) *a.* An employee or group of employees, having a question, dispute, or alleged grievance arising under the terms of this agreement, shall present the matter verbally to his or her supervisor in person or in company with his or her departmental steward. The supervisor and the steward shall use their best efforts to resolve the matter.

b. If deemed necessary by the supervisor or the departmental steward, the departmental head and a grievance committee may be requested to participate in reaching a satisfactory settlement.

c. If the grievance cannot be settled satisfactorily in the foregoing step within three working days, it may be reduced to writing on forms provided by the company. The grievance shall be signed by the aggrieved employee or employees, and the departmental steward. The departmental supervisor shall have two working days thereafter to submit a decision in writing. The grievance shall be considered abandoned or settled if it is not appealed to the next step within five working days.

Industrial relations manager's step

(55) If the disposition in the foregoing step has not satisfactorily settled the grievance, it may be appealed to the industrial relations manager's step, not later than five working days from the time of receiving the foreman's disposition. The industrial relations manager shall review and investigate the grievance, conferring with a member of the grievance committee and such other persons essential to resolving the issue. The company's disposition shall be given to the union within three working days following such conference. The grievance shall be considered abandoned or settled if it is not appealed to the next step within 10 working days.

General manager's step

(56) If the industrial relations manager's disposition has not satisfactorily settled the employee grievance, it may then be appealed by the union grievance committee to the general manager (or designated representative) within 10 working days, in a further effort to adjust the grievance. An international union staff representative shall participate in all general manager appeal step meetings. Any grievance not appealed within the time limit shall be automatically closed on the basis of the previous decision and shall not be subject to further appeal. The general manager shall issue the company's final disposition of the grievance within five working days after the appeal meeting is held. Any grievance not appealed to arbitration in writing as hereinafter provided within 21 working days after the issuance of the general manager's decision shall automatically be closed on the basis of such decision and shall not be subject to further appeal.

Arbitration

(57) If a grievance shall not be satisfactorily disposed of under the preceding steps, it may be submitted to arbitration upon proper notification by the union. Notice of appeal of a grievance by the union to arbitration shall be given in writing to the company not later than 21 working days following the date of the written decision of the general manager. This time limit may be extended by mutual agreement.

Source: Agreement between Powermatic Houdaille, Inc., and United Steelworkers of America. Used with permission.

ensure that an employee is afforded due process, all contract terms should be followed, adequate warning should be given prior to the discipline, explicit statements should be made to the employee and the union about taking possible disciplinary action if the employee's actions do not change, and a full and fair investigation should be conducted immediately after the offense.

Duty of Fair Representation

Duty of Fair Representation
Under the National Labor Relations Act of 1935, the statutory duty of a union to fairly represent all employees in the bargaining unit, whether or not they are union members.

Under the National Labor Relations Act of 1935, the union has a statutory duty to fairly represent all employees in the bargaining unit, whether or not they are union members. This duty has been termed **duty of fair representation.**

The rationale underlying the duty of fair representation is that the union is the exclusive representative of all employees in the bargaining unit. The extent of the union's duty to fairly represent its members and other employees was defined in a landmark case, *Vaca* v. *Sipes,* in 1967.[6] In this case, an employee who had a history of high blood pressure returned to work after six months of sick leave. Although his personal physician and another doctor had certified his fitness to resume work, the company doctor concluded that his blood pressure was too high to permit his reinstatement, and as a result he was permanently discharged. The employee filed a grievance, and the union took the grievance through the steps leading up to arbitration. The employee was then sent to a new doctor at the union's expense. When this examination did not support the employee's contention that he could safely return to work, the union decided not to take the grievance to arbitration, even though the employee demanded it. The employee sued the officers and representatives of the union for breach of their duty of fair representation. The case ultimately went to the Supreme Court, which held that (1) an individual does not have the absolute right to have a grievance taken to arbitration; (2) a union must make decisions as to the merits of particular grievances in good faith and nonarbitrarily; and (3) if a union decides in good faith and in a nonarbitrary manner that a grievance is not meritorious, a breach of fair representation does not exist, even if it is proved that the grievance was, in fact, meritorious.

Vaca v. *Sipes* Supreme Court decision in 1967 that held that a union is not obligated to take all grievances to arbitration but has the authority to decide whether or not the grievance has merit. If such a decision is made fairly and nonarbitrarily, the union has not breached its duty of fair representation.

An exception to this court ruling is included in a provision of the Taft-Hartley Act, which states that an individual employee may present a grievance to the employer without the aid of the union. However, this is contingent on the fact that any resulting adjustments must be consistent with the terms of the contract and must be conveyed to the union. This has been interpreted as meaning that the employer is under no obligation to consider such grievances. However, if a grievance is presented to the employer by the union, the employer is obligated to consider it and to resolve it through arbitration (if this is provided for in the contract) when the grievance has not been resolved in the earlier stages of the grievance process.

In addition, individuals cannot take the case into their own hands if they think it is not being effectively handled. Courts have held that the employee must thoroughly exhaust the grievance procedure before taking individual action, and such action is then contingent on proof of a breach of the duty of fair representation.

Bowen v. *United States Postal Service* (1983) Supreme Court decision that established that an employee may be entitled to recover damages from both the union and the employer in cases where the employer has violated the labor agreement and the union has breached its duty of fair representation.

A 1983 Supreme Court decision, ***Bowen* v. *United States Postal Service*,**[7] established that an employee may be entitled to recover damages from both the union and the employer in cases where the employer has violated the labor agreement and the union has breached its duty of fair representation. HRM in Action 19.1 details a case in which the union was ruled to have violated its duty of fair representation.

Time Delays

Perhaps the greatest criticism of the grievance procedure is that a great deal of time may be necessary to resolve a grievance that goes through the entire process. Often the internal stages of appeal may take several months to complete. If the

Fair Representation: United Glass and Ceramic Workers of North America

19.1

Earl Carpenter was employed by the predecessor of West Virginia Flat Glass in August 1977 to work on the production line. In June 1978, he injured his back and was unable to work for several months. While he was out, the company halted production and sold the plant. When the plant reopened in October 1979, Carpenter attempted to return to work. After another injury, he claimed he was unable to do the heavy renovation work that was then available at the plant. His doctor, Dr. Martin, gave him a "light duty" slip, but the company had no light work available. Carpenter then obtained a "no duty" slip.

West Virginia Flat Glass asked Dr. Wilson, the company doctor, to examine Carpenter. Dr. Wilson did not explicitly state whether Carpenter could or could not work. He reported on November 13, 1979, that Carpenter had a 5 percent permanent partial disability and that maximum improvement had been achieved. Based on these findings and Carpenter's claim that he was unable to perform heavy labor without pain, the company discharged him on November 19, 1979.

The local union filed a timely grievance, taking the position that Carpenter was able to work and that his position was supported by his treating physician, Dr. Martin. The company took the position, based on Dr. Wilson's report, that Carpenter was unable to work and therefore was properly discharged. The local union processed the grievance through the first three stages of the grievance process without success.

At the fourth stage, under the terms of the collective bargaining agreement, the international union became involved. A representative from the international union met with company officials in April 1980, and the parties agreed to obtain a third opinion as to whether Carpenter could work from a doctor chosen by Dr. Martin and Dr. Wilson. The parties agreed to be bound by that opinion. The agreement also provided that Carpenter should relinquish his claim for back pay. Carpenter approved the agreement.

Carpenter was examined by the third doctor, Dr. Mills, who reported on April 25, 1980, that Carpenter had a 5 percent permanent partial disability and that maximum improvement had been reached. He did not state specifically whether he thought Carpenter was able to work in the plant. The company interpreted the report to be consistent with Dr. Wilson's diagnosis of November 1979, the union agreed, and the company affirmed the discharge on May 7, 1980.

On September 29, 1980, Carpenter filed suit under §301 of the National Labor Relations Act, 29 U.S.C. §185(b), against the company for wrongful discharge and against the local union for breaching its duty to represent him fairly in the grievance process. In July 1981, he amended his complaint to include the international union. He subsequently settled his claims against the local union and his employer.

Carpenter's principal complaint against the international union was its failure to contact Dr. Mills about his April 1980 report, which failed to answer the parties' inquiry about whether Carpenter could work. The international union contended that it was justified in not pursuing the matter because Dr. Mills' report was consistent with Dr. Wilson's report.

(Continues)

19.1
(Continued)

In his testimony at the trial. Dr. Mills acknowledged that although he had been asked to determine Carpenter's ability to work, he had not reported on this question. Neither the company nor the international union called this omission to his attention. He testified that in his opinion at the time of his examination, Carpenter was physically able to work.

The plant manager testified that if Dr. Mills' report had stated that Carpenter could return to work, he would have abided by this decision and reemployed Carpenter.

The Circuit Court of Appeals ruled that the international union did not fairly represent Earl Carpenter.

Source: Adapted from *Carpenter* v. *West Virginia Flat Glass,* 119LRRM 2846.

case goes to arbitration, the parties usually request a list of potential arbitrators from an arbitration service. The parties must contact the arbitrator and must agree on an acceptable date for the hearing—one that coincides with the schedules of the union representatives, the company representatives, and the arbitrator. Furthermore, after the hearing has taken place, the parties may desire to submit briefs, which can take several additional weeks. When the hearing is closed upon receipt of all briefs, the arbitrator normally renders a decision within 30 to 60 days. Thus, many months and sometimes a year or more may elapse before a final decision is reached. An argument could be made that this time delay in itself denies the grievant due process.

Grievance Arbitration

Grievance Arbitration
Arbitration that attempts to settle unresolved disputes arising during the term of the collective bargaining agreement that involve questions of its interpretation or application.

Grievance arbitration is the process whereby the involved parties voluntarily agree to settle a dispute through the use of an independent third party. In the United States, arbitration evolves from the voluntary agreement by two parties to submit their unresolved disputes to a privately selected neutral third party (an arbitrator). Both parties agree in advance to abide by the arbitrator's decision. The arbitrator, who functions in a quasi-judicial role, must work within the framework that the parties have negotiated in their collective bargaining agreement. Arbitrators have no legal power to subpoena witnesses or records and are not required to conform to legal rules of hearing procedures, other than that of giving all parties the opportunity to present evidence. HRM in Action 19.2 describes a discipline situation that was overturned by an arbitrator.

Grievance arbitration attempts to settle unresolved disputes arising during the term of the collective bargaining agreement that involve questions of its interpretation or application. Provision for grievance arbitration generally is not mandated by law. However, most labor contracts provide an arbitration clause as the final step in the grievance process. This is considered to be the *quid pro quo* (even exchange) for the union's agreement to a no-strike clause.

Web site: Federal Mediation & Conciliation Services

www.fmcs.gov

An arbitrator may serve on either a temporary (ad hoc) or permanent basis. In ad hoc arbitration, the parties select an arbitrator to hear a single case. Permanent arbitrators settle all grievance disputes arising between the parties for a period of time.

Web site: American Arbitration Association

www.adr.org

Arbitrators charge for their services. Normally arbitrators' charges are paid on a 50–50 basis by the company and the union. Both the Federal Mediation and Conciliation Service (FMCS) and the American Arbitration Association (AAA) provide lists of qualified arbitrators to the parties upon request. FMCS's services are available to both the private and public sector. AAA is a private, nonprofit organization that also provides lists of arbitrators to both the private and public sectors.

HRM IN ACTION

Discharge at American Motors

19.2

http://americanmotors.com

The grievant had been employed as a shipping and receiving clerk at American Motors for 10 years. On November 30, the grievant asked a purchasing clerk to look up the purchasing information (part number, location, and price) on several parts, including a jeep door. The grievant testified that his intention was to buy the door for a sheriff friend who was going to fix a DUI ticket for him. The grievant obtained the door and stored it on a shelf near his workplace until he completed his shift. At quitting time, the grievant left his workplace, carrying the door, and proceeded to the parking lot.

The grievant was seen putting the door in his van by a member of management. Later that evening, another employee contacted the grievant and informed him that a member of management had seen him carrying the door to his van. On December 1, the grievant brought in a check to cover the price of the door. The company refused to accept the check and fired the employee for misappropriation of company property.

Union witnesses testified to many instances where employees removed parts from the company without the prior knowledge or approval of management and paid for them at a later date. Much evidence was also presented that procedures for removing and paying for parts were haphazardly observed and not in writing.

The arbitrator overruled the discharge because of management's failure to establish, communicate, and properly administer a procedure for removing parts.

Source: Labor arbitration award by Lloyd L. Byars. Case involved the American Motors Corporation and the United Automobile Workers.

Enterprise Wheel Supreme Court ruling in 1960 holding that as long as an arbitrator's decision involves the interpretation of a contract, the courts should not overrule the arbitrator merely because their interpretation of the contract was different from that of the arbitrator.

Generally, court reviews of arbitration awards have been extremely narrow in scope. The attitude of the U.S. Supreme Court was expressed in the **Enterprise Wheel** case: "It is the arbitrator's interpretation which was bargained for, and so far as the arbitrator's decision concerns interpretation of the contract, the courts have no business overruling him because their interpretation of the contract is different from his."[8] In spite of this opinion, courts have overturned some arbitration awards in discharge cases. However, the tendency, for the most part, has been to defer to the arbitrator's decision.

SUMMARY OF LEARNING OBJECTIVES

1. **Define organizational discipline.**

   Organizational discipline is action taken against an employee when the employee has violated an organizational rule or when the employee's performance has deteriorated to the point where corrective action is needed.

2. **Explain the hot-stove rule.**

   The hot-stove rule emphasizes that discipline should be directed against the act rather than the person. Key points of the hot-stove rule are immediacy, advance warning, and consistency.

3. **Describe progressive discipline.**

   Progressive discipline means that the normal sequence of actions taken by management in disciplining an employee would be oral warning, written warning, suspension, and discharge.

4. **Explain employment at will.**

   Employment at will means that when an employer in the private sector hires employees to work for an indefinite period of time and the employees do not have a contract limiting the circumstances under which they can be discharged, the employer can terminate the employees at any time for any reason or for no reason at all.

5. **Define grievance procedures.**
   Grievance procedures are a systematic means of resolving disagreements over the collective bargaining agreement and providing assurance that the terms and conditions agreed to in negotiations are properly implemented.

6. **Define just cause.**
   Just cause concerns the burden and degree of proof of wrongdoing and the severity of punishment.

7. **Explain due process.**
   Due process refers to the employee's right to be dealt with fairly and justly during the investigation of an alleged offense and the administration of discipline.

8. **Describe the duty of fair representation.**
   The duty of fair representation refers to the union's statutory duty to fairly represent all employees in the bargaining unit, whether or not they are union members.

9. **Define grievance arbitration.**
   Under grievance arbitration, the involved parties voluntarily agree to settle a dispute through the use of an independent third party. Grievance arbitration attempts to settle unresolved disputes arising during the term of the collective bargaining agreement that involve questions of its interpretation or application.

REVIEW QUESTIONS

1. Define organizational discipline.
2. What are the three types of conduct that normally result in the disciplining of an employee?
3. Outline the steps in the disciplinary process.
4. What was the significance of the decision in the *NLRB* v. *Weingarten* case?
5. List the key points of the hot-stove rule.
6. What was the significance of the decision in the *Alexander* v. *Gardner-Denver* case?
7. What are grievance procedures?
8. Define just cause, due process, and duty of fair representation.
9. What is arbitration?

DISCUSSION QUESTIONS

1. "Unions make it almost impossible to discipline employees." Do you agree or disagree? Discuss.
2. Two employees violate the same work rule. One is above average in performance and has been with your company for eight years. The other employee is an average performer who has been with your company for a little over a year. Should these employees receive the same discipline? Why or why not?
3. Under the doctrine of fair representation, unions are required to represent both members and nonmembers in the bargaining unit. Do you think unions should be required to represent nonmembers? Explain.
4. If you were starting your own company, what type of grievance procedure would you establish for your employees?

INCIDENT 19-1

Tardy Tom

On September 30, 1995, a large, national automobile-leasing firm in Columbus, Ohio, hired Tom Holland as a mechanic. Tom, the only mechanic employed by the firm in Columbus, was to do routine preventive maintenance on the cars. When he first began his job, he was scheduled to punch in on the time clock at 7 A.M. On October 30, 1995, Tom's supervisor, Russ Brown, called him to his office and said, "Tom, I've noticed during October that you've been late for work seven times. What can I do to help you get here on time?"

Tom replied, "It would be awfully nice if I could start work at 8 A.M. instead of 7 A.M."

Russ then stated, "Tom, I'm very pleased with your overall work performance, so it's OK with me if your workday begins at 8 A.M."

During the month of November 1995, Tom was late eight times. Another conversation occurred similar to the one at the end of October. As a result of it, Tom's starting time was changed to 9 A.M.

On January 11, 1996, Russ Brown posted the following notice on the bulletin board:

Any employee late for work more than two times in any one particular pay period is subject to termination.

On January 20, 1996, Russ called Tom into his office and gave him a letter that read, "During this pay period, you have been late for work more than two times. If this behavior continues, you are subject to termination." Tom signed the letter to acknowledge that he had received it.

During February 1996, Tom was late eight times and between March 1 and March 11, five times. On March 11, 1996, Russ notified Tom that he had been fired for his tardiness.

On March 12, 1996, Tom came in with his union representative and demanded that he get his job back. Tom alleged that there was another employee in the company who had been late as many times as he had, or more. Tom further charged that Russ was punching the time clock for this employee because Russ was having an affair with her. The union representative stated that three other people in the company had agreed to testify, under oath, to these facts. The union representative then said, "Russ, rules are for everyone. You can't let one person break a rule and penalize someone else for breaking the same rule. Therefore, Tom should have his job back."

Questions

1. What is your position regarding this case?
2. What would you do if you were an arbitrator in this dispute?

INCIDENT 19-2

Keys to the Drug Cabinet

John Brown, a 22-year-old African-American, had been employed for only two-and-a-half weeks as a licensed practical nurse in a local hospital's alcohol and drug treatment center. John worked the 11 P.M. to 7 A.M. shift. His responsibilities included having charge of the keys to the drug cabinet.

One morning at 1 A.M., he became ill. He requested and received permission from the night supervisor, Margaret Handley, to go home. A short time later, the supervisor realized that John had failed to leave the keys when he signed out. She immediately tried to reach him by telephoning his home.

More than a dozen attempts to call John proved futile; each time Margaret got a busy signal. Finally, at 3 A.M., a man answered but refused to call John to the phone, saying John was too ill to talk. She became frantic and decided to call the police to retrieve the keys.

The police arrived at John's home at 6:30 A.M. They found him preparing to leave to return the keys to the hospital. The police took the keys and returned them.

Later that day, John reported to work on his assigned shift, apologized for not returning the keys, and questioned the necessity of calling the police.

Two days later, the unit director, Marcus Webb, informed John that he had been terminated. The reason cited for the discharge was that he had failed to leave the drug cabinet keys before leaving the hospital and that the keys had been in his possession from 1 A.M. to 7 A.M. the following day. John learned that Margaret Handley had been verbally reprimanded for her handling of the case.

John filed an appeal regarding his dismissal with the human resource director of the hospital. However, the unit director's recommendation was upheld.

Following this decision, John immediately filed charges with the EEOC that he had been discriminated against because of his race. Both the night supervisor and the unit director were white. He requested full reinstatement with back pay. He also requested that his personnel file be purged of any damaging records that alluded to the incident.

Questions

1. What would your decision be if you were asked to decide this case?
2. Should a supervisor and a lower-level employee be disciplined equally? Explain.

EXERCISE

Mock Arbitration

Following is a situation in which you are to conduct a mock arbitration. The class will be divided into teams, five to six students per team. Each team will then be assigned to represent either the union or the company. Your team must decide on the witnesses you want at the hearing. Your opposing team must be given the names and job titles of your witnesses. During class time, two teams will conduct the mock arbitration.

Situation

Background

General Telephone Company of the Southeast (Georgia), hereinafter referred to as the company, provides local telephone service within certain areas of the state of Georgia. Its employees, as defined by Article I and Appendix A of the Agreement, are represented by the Communication Workers of America, hereinafter referred to as the union. The parties are operating under an agreement that became effective June 27, 1996.

The grievant, Cassandra Horne, was hired by the company as a service representative on June 4, 1990. On August 30, 1997, she was promoted to installer-repairer and was responsible for installing and repairing residential and single-line business for customers. The grievant's record is free of any disciplinary entries, and she is considered by her supervisor, Fred Carter, to be a satisfactory employee.

On May 19, 1998, the grievant suffered an on-the-job injury to her knee while attempting to disconnect a trailer from a company van. At some time after the injury, the grievant went on disability for approximately eight weeks. She then returned to work with a statement from the company physician, allowing her to perform her normal work. After approximately three weeks, the grievant was still experiencing pain in her knee and was diagnosed by a different physician as having a tear in the cartilage below her kneecap. She went back on disability and had surgery performed on October 19, 1998, to repair cartilage and ligament damage to her knee.

During the grievant's absence, her disability benefits expired, and she agreed to take a six-month leave of absence beginning November 10, 1998. When the grievant's leave expired on May 11, 1999, she was terminated from her employment with the company.

The company argued that the company physician had stated the grievant could not perform installer-repairer work and that no other jobs were open that could be performed by the grievant. The union argued that the grievant had been cleared by her personal physician and that she felt she could do the work of installer-repairer. A grievance was filed at Step I on May 12, 1999, and was denied by the division personnel manager, Jerry L. Leynes. The grievance was submitted to arbitration and is now properly before the arbitrator for decision and award.

The company states that the issue before the arbitrator is as follows: Did the company violate the contract by separating the grievant from her position as an installer-repairer; and if so, what should be the remedy? The union states that the issue before the arbitrator is as follows: Is the discharge of the grievant for just or proper cause; and if not, what should the remedy be?

Pertinent provisions of the agreement

Article 1, Recognition: The company recognizes the union as the whole and exclusive collective bargaining agency with respect to rates of pay, hours of employment, and other conditions of employment for all employees within the exchanges coming under the operating jurisdiction of the above-named company. All supervisory and professional employees and those performing confidential labor relations duties are excluded from the bargaining unit.

Article 4, Work Jurisdiction:

1. The company recognizes the right of its employees to perform its work and will make every reasonable effort to plan its work to accomplish this end.
2. The company agrees that in its employment of contract labor to assist in the carrying out of its programs of construction, installation, removal, maintenance, and/or repair of telephone plant, it will not lay off or reduce to part-time status, nor continue on layoff or part-time status, any regular employee performing the same work as that which is being performed by contract labor.

Article 11, Absences from Duty:

1. Leave of absence, without pay, not to exceed six (6) months will be granted by the company for good and compelling reason upon receipt of written request for such leave. Each such request will be approved or disapproved dependent on the merit of the request. Such leaves may be extended for an additional period of not to exceed three (3) months.
    1.1 Working for another employer during leave shall constitute grounds for termination of employment.
    1.2 Applying for unemployment compensation during leave may constitute grounds for termination of employment, except this shall not be applicable where the employee has requested reinstatement in accordance with the provisions of this article and no work is available.
    1.3 A leave of absence shall not carry a guarantee of reemployment, but the

employee concerned, desiring to return from leave, shall be given opportunity for reemployment before any new employees are hired, provided the returning employee is qualified to perform the work.

Article 12, Paid Absences:

4. In cases of physical disability resulting from compensable accidental injury while on the job, the company will pay the difference, if any, between the amount paid to the employee under workers' compensation and the employee's basic rate in accordance with the schedule set forth below. No waiting period will be required.

    4.1 Up to five (5) years' accredited service, full pay not to exceed thirteen (13) weeks.

Article 23, Discharges, Suspensions, and Demotions:

1. Requirements and limitations

    1.1 Any discharge, suspension, or demotion shall be only for proper cause and by proper action.

    1.2 Any employee who is discharged, suspended, or demoted shall, at the time of discharge, suspension, or demotion, be given a written statement setting forth the complete reasons for such action.

NOTES AND ADDITIONAL READINGS

1. See Chapter 17 for a description of the NLRB.
2. *NLRB* v. *Weingarten,* 202 NLRB 446 (1975).
3. *Baton Rouge Water Works,* 246 NLRB 161 (1980).
4. *Alexander* v. *Gardner-Denver,* 415 U.S. 36, 7 FEP 81 (1974).
5. Marvin J. Levin, "The Erosion of the Employment-at-Will Doctrine: Recent Developments," *Labor Law Journal* (February 1994), pp. 79–89.
6. *Vaca* v. *Sipes,* 386 U.S. 171, 87 Sup. CT, 903, 17 L. Ed 2d 843 (1967).
7. *Bowen* v. *United States Postal Service,* 81 U.S. (1983).
8. *United Steelworkers of America* v. *Enterprise Wheel and Car Corporation,* 46 LRRM 2423 S. CT. (1960).

Employee Safety and Health

Learning Objectives

After studying this chapter, you should be able to:

1. State the purpose of the Occupational Safety and Health Act (OSHA) and discuss its major provisions.
2. List the three major causes of accidents in the workplace.
3. Define frequency rate and severity rate.
4. Offer several suggestions for promoting safety in the workplace.
5. Discuss the Hazard Communication rule.
6. Differentiate between stress and burnout.
7. Name several work-related consequences of alcohol and drug abuse.
8. Offer several guidelines for implementing a drug-testing program.
9. Discuss the legal requirements for terminating an employee with acquired immunodeficiency syndrome (AIDS).
10. Explain the three basic types of employee assistance programs (EAPs).
11. List several specific things an organization can do to help reduce violence in its workplace.

Employee safety and health are important concerns in today's organizations. The National Safety Council estimates that 5,100 deaths and 3.8 million disabling injuries resulted from occupational accidents in 1997;[1] the associated total work accident cost was estimated to be over $127.7 billion.[2]

As early as 1970, new cases of occupational diseases were estimated to exceed 300,000 each year.[3] As these figures indicate, the costs associated with workplace injuries or illnesses are high. Other indirect costs include employers' costs for health insurance and workers' compensation (both discussed in Chapter 16). Recent figures show that the average U.S. employee must produce $980 worth of goods and services just to offset the cost of work-related injuries.[4] These costs vividly illustrate an incentive for organizations to reduce work-related injuries and illnesses and to improve overall employee health.

While health costs have escalated dramatically in recent decades, occupational injuries and illnesses have been around for a long time. For example, 35,000 occupational deaths occurred in 1936.[5] In spite of the known injuries and associated costs, for years many organizations did very little to reduce the problem. Because of this, a bipartisan U.S. Congress passed the Occupational Safety and Health Act in 1970.

Occupational Safety and Health Act

Occupational Safety and Health Act Federal law enacted in 1971 to ensure safe and healthful working conditions for every working person.

General-Duty Clause Clause in the Occupational Safety and Health Act covering those situations not addressed by specific standards; in essence, it requires employers to comply with the intent of the act.

The **Occupational Safety and Health Act** became effective on April 28, 1971. The act established federal regulations relating to employee safety and health. OSHA applies to all businesses with one or more employees. (There are certain exceptions, such as self-employed persons.) Its stated purpose is "to assure so far as possible every working man and woman in the nation safe and healthful working conditions and to preserve our human resources."[6] The act contains a **general duty clause** to cover those situations not addressed by specific standards. This clause states that each employer "shall furnish . . . a place of employment which is free from recognized hazards that are causing or likely to cause death or serious physical harm to . . . employees." In essence, the general-duty clause requires employers to comply with the intent of the act.

The Occupational Safety and Health Administration (OSHA) of the U.S. Department of Labor enforces the act and is authorized to

1. Encourage employers and employees to reduce workplace hazards and to implement new or improve existing safety and health programs.
2. Provide for research in occupational safety and health and develop innovative ways to deal with occupational safety and health problems.
3. Establish "separate but dependent responsibilities and rights" for employers and employees for the achievement of better safety and health conditions.
4. Maintain a reporting and record-keeping system to monitor job related injuries and illnesses.
5. Establish training programs to increase the number and competence of occupational safety and health personnel.
6. Develop mandatory job safety and health standards and enforce them effectively.
7. Provide for the development, analysis, evaluation, and approval of state occupational safety and health programs.[7]

Since 1970 when OSHA was established, occupational fatality rates have been cut in half and the number of cases of occupational injuries per 100 full-time workers dropped 35 percent from 1973 to 1996.[8] While OSHA cannot claim all the credit for these impressive reductions, it has certainly had a major impact.

OSHA Standards

OSHA establishes legally enforceable standards relating to employee health and safety. Usually the human resource department is responsible for being familiar with these standards and ensuring that the organization complies with them.

Currently OSHA publishes six volumes of standards (see Table 20–1) covering four major categories: general industry, maritime, construction, and agriculture. The *Federal Register,* available in many public and college libraries, also regularly publishes all OSHA standards and amendments. Annual subscriptions can be purchased from the Superintendent of Documents, U.S. Government Printing Office, Washington, D.C. 20402. OSHA also offers a subscription service through the Superintendent of Documents. In addition to providing all standards, interpretations, and regulations, the OSHA subscription service periodically sends out notices of changes and additions.

Federal Register Periodical found in many public and college libraries that regularly publishes all OSHA standards and amendments.

Establishment of Standards

OSHA can initiate standards on its own or on petitions from other parties, including the U.S. Secretary of Health and Human Services (HHS), the National

T A B L E   2 0 – 1   **STANDARD MANUALS PUBLISHED BY OSHA**

Volume	Title
I	*General Industry Standards and Interpretations* (includes agriculture)
II	*Maritime Standards and Interpretations*
III	*Construction Standards and Interpretations*
IV	*Other Regulations and Procedures*
V	*Field Operations Manual*
VI	*OSHA Technical Manual*

Marshall v. *Barlow's, Inc.*
1978 Supreme Court decision that ruled that employers are not required to admit OSHA inspectors onto their premises without a search warrant; also ruled that probable cause needed to obtain the search warrant is much less than that required in a criminal matter.

Institute for Occupational Safety and Health (NIOSH), state and local governments, and nationally recognized standards producing organizations, employers, labor organizations, or any other interested party. NIOSH, which was established by the act as an agency under HHS, conducts research on various safety and health problems. NIOSH recommends most of the standards adopted by OSHA.

Workplace Inspections

OSHA compliance officers (inspectors) are authorized under the act to conduct workplace inspections. Originally employers were not given advance notice of inspections and could not refuse to admit OSHA inspectors. However a 1978 Supreme Court decision, *Marshall* v. *Barlow's, Inc.*,[9] ruled that employers are not required to admit OSHA inspectors onto their premises without a search warrant. At the same time, however, the court ruled that the probable cause needed to obtain a search warrant would be much less than what would be required in a criminal matter. HRM in Action 20.1 summarizes the *Marshall* v. *Barlow's, Inc.,* case.

Inspection Priorities

Because OSHA does not have the resources to inspect all workplaces covered by the act, a system of inspection priorities has been established:

Those situations involving imminent danger.

Investigation of fatalities and catastrophes resulting in the hospitalization of five or more employees.

HRM IN ACTION

Marshall* v. *Barlow's, Inc. Barlow's, Inc., is an electrical and plumbing installation business in Pocatello, Idaho. In September 1975, an OSHA inspector asked Mr. Barlow if he could search the business for safety violations. When Mr. Barlow asked the inspector whether complaints had been filed against the business, the inspector said no, that Barlow's had turned up as part of a routine selection procedure. Mr. Barlow refused to allow the inspection.

20.1

www.osha.gov

Three months later, Secretary of Labor Ray Marshall petitioned the U.S. district court for the state of Idaho to issue an order forcing Barlow to admit the inspector. Barlow again refused and sought an injunction to prevent what he considered to be a warrantless search. On December 30, 1976, a three-judge court ruled in Barlow's favor, and Marshall appealed. On May 23, 1978, the U.S. Supreme Court ruled that OSHA's searches of work areas for safety hazards and violations were unconstitutional without a warrant.

Source: "Marshall v. Barlow's, Inc.," Supreme Court Reporter 98A (St. Paul, Minn.: West Publishing, 1980), pp. 1816–34.

Employee complaints of alleged violations of standards or of unsafe or un-healthful working conditions.

Programs of inspection aimed at specific high-hazard industries, occupations, or health substances.

Reinspection of organizations previously cited for alleged serious violations.

Inspection Procedures

Upon the OSHA inspector's arrival, the representatives of the employer should first ask to see the inspector's OSHA credentials. Normally the inspector then conducts a preliminary meeting with the top management of the organization. The manager of the human resource department is usually present at this meeting. At this time, the inspector explains the purpose of the visit, the scope of the inspection, and the standards that apply. The inspector then usually requests an employer representative (often someone from the human resource department), an employee representative, and a union representative (where applicable) to join in an inspection tour of the facility. The inspector then proceeds with the inspection tour, which may cover part or all of the facilities. Afterward the inspector meets again with the employer or the employer representatives. During this meeting, the inspector discusses what has been found and indicates all apparent violations for which a citation may be issued or recommended.

Citations

In some cases, the inspector has the authority to issue citations at the work site immediately following the closing conference. This occurs only in cases where immediate protection is necessary. Normally citations are issued by the OSHA area director and sent by certified mail. Once the citation is received, the employer is required to post a copy of the citation at or near the place where the violation occurred for three days or until the violation is corrected, whichever period is longer.

Penalties

Table 20–2 summarizes the five major types of violations that may be cited and the respective penalties that may be proposed. Under certain conditions some of the proposed penalties can be adjusted downward. Additional penalties may be imposed for such things as falsifying records and assaulting an inspector.

Record-Keeping/Reporting Requirements

Employers of 11 or more persons must maintain records of occupational injuries and illnesses as they occur. This includes all occupational illnesses, regardless of severity, and all occupational injuries resulting in death, one or more lost workdays, restriction of work or motion, loss of consciousness, transfer to another job, or medical treatment other than first aid.

OSHA Form 200 (Log and Summary of Occupational Injuries and Illnesses) Form for recording all occupational injuries and illnesses. Each occurrence must be recorded on this form within six working days from the time the employer learns of the accident or illness.

Many OSHA standards have special record-keeping and reporting requirements, but all employers covered by the act must maintain two forms. **OSHA Form 200 (Log and Summary of Occupational Injuries and Illnesses)** requires that each occupational injury and illness be recorded within six working days from the time the employer learns of the accident or illness. **OSHA Form 101 (Supplementary Record of Occupational Injuries and Illnesses)** requires much more detail about each injury or illness. It must also be completed within six working days from the time the employer learns of the work-related injury or illness. Both Form 200 and Form 101 are maintained on a calendar-year basis. These forms must be retained for five years by the organization and must be available for inspection.

T A B L E   2 0 - 2   **TYPES OF OSHA VIOLATIONS**

Violation	Definition	Proposed Penalty
Other than serious	Violation that has a direct relationship to job safety and health but probably would not cause death or serious physical harm.	Up to $7,000 for each violation (discretionary).
Serious	Violation where there is substantial probability that death or serious physical harm could result and that the employer knew or should have known of the hazard.	Up to $7,000 for each violation (mandatory).
Willful	Violation that the employer intentionally and knowingly commits. The employer either knows that what he or she is doing constitutes a violation or is aware that a hazardous condition exists and has made no reasonable effort to eliminate it.	Up to $70,000 for each willful violation with a minimum mandatory penalty of $5,000 for each violation. A violation resulting in death of an employee is punishable by a court-imposed fine or by up to six months' imprisonment, or both; a fine of up to $250,000 for an individual or $500,000 for a corporation may be imposed for a criminal conviction.
Repeated	Violation of any standard, regulation, rule, or order where, on reinspection, another violation of the same section is found.	Up to $70,000 for each such violation.
Failure to correct prior violation	Failure to correct previous violation cited by OSHA.	Civil penalty of up to $7,000 for each day the violation continues beyond the prescribed abatement date.

Source: All about OSHA (Washington, D.C.: U.S. Department of Labor, 1995), pp. 26–27.

OSHA Form 101 (Supplementary Record of Occupational Injuries and Illnesses)   Form that requires much more detail about each injury or illness. Form 101 must be completed within six working days from the time the employer learns of an occupational injury or illness.

The Causes of Accidents

Accidents are caused by a combination of circumstances and events, usually resulting from unsafe work acts, an unsafe work environment, or both.

Personal Acts

It has been estimated that unsafe personal acts cause as much as 80 percent of organizational accidents.[10] Unsafe personal acts include such things as taking unnecessary risks, horseplay, failing to wear protective equipment, using improper tools and equipment, and taking unsafe shortcuts.

It is difficult to determine why employees commit unsafe personal acts. Fatigue, haste, boredom, stress, poor eyesight, and daydreaming are all potential reasons. However, these reasons do not totally explain why employees intentionally neglect to wear prescribed equipment or do not follow procedures. Most employees think of accidents as always happening to someone else. Such an attitude can easily lead to carelessness or a lack of respect for what can happen. It is also true that some people get a kick out of taking chances and showing off.

Research studies have also shown that employees with positive attitudes have fewer accidents than employees with negative attitudes.[11] This is not surprising when one considers that negative attitudes are likely to be related to employee carelessness.

Physical Environment

Accidents can and do happen in all types of environments, such as offices, parking lots, and factories. Certain work conditions, however, seem to result in more accidents. Table 20–3 lists commonly encountered unsafe work conditions.

Accident Proneness

A third reason often given for accidents is that certain people are accident prone. Some employees, due to their physical and mental makeup, are more susceptible to accidents. This condition may result from inborn traits, but it often develops as a result of an individual's environment. However, this tendency should not be used to justify an accident. Given the right set of circumstances, anyone can have an accident. For example, an employee who was up all night with a sick child might very well be accident prone the next day.

How to Measure Safety

Frequency Rate Ratio that indicates the frequency with which disabling injuries occur.

Disabling Injuries Work-related injuries that cause an employee to miss one or more days of work.

Severity Rate Ratio that indicates the length of time injured employees are out of work.

Accident frequency and accident severity are the two most widely accepted methods for measuring an organization's safety record. A **frequency rate** is used to indicate how often disabling injuries occur. **Disabling injuries** cause an employee to miss one or more days of work following an accident. Disabling injuries are also known as *lost-time injuries*. A **severity rate** indicates how severe the accidents were by calculating the length of time injured employees were out of work. Only disabling injuries are used in determining frequency and severity rates. Figure 20–1 gives the formulas for calculating an organization's frequency and severity rates.

Neither the frequency rate nor the severity rate mean much until they are compared with similar figures for other departments or divisions within the organization, for the previous year, or for other organizations. It is through these comparisons that an organization's safety record can be objectively evaluated.

TABLE 20–3	UNSAFE CONDITIONS IN THE WORK ENVIRONMENT

Unguarded or improperly guarded machines (such as an unguarded belt)

Poor housekeeping (such as congested aisles, dirty or wet floors, loose carpeting, and improper stacking of materials)

Defective equipment and tools

Poor lighting

Poor or improper ventilation

Improper dress (such as wearing clothes with loose and floppy sleeves when working on a machine that has rotating parts)

Sharp edges

F I G U R E   2 0 – 1   **FORMULAS FOR COMPUTING ACCIDENT FREQUENCY RATE AND SEVERITY RATE**

$$\text{Frequency rate} = \frac{\text{Number of disabling injuries} \times 1 \text{ million}}{\text{Total number of labor-hours worked each year}}$$

$$\text{Severity rate} = \frac{\text{Days lost* due to injury} \times 1 \text{ million}}{\text{Total number of labor-hours worked each year}}$$

*The American National Standards Institute has developed tables for determining the number of lost days for different types of accidents. To illustrate, an accident resulting in death or permanent total disability is charged with 6,000 days (approximately 25 working years).

Organizational Safety Programs

The heart of any organizational safety program is accident prevention. It is obviously much better to prevent accidents than to react to them. A major objective of any safety program is to get the employees to "think safety." Therefore, most programs are designed to keep safety and accident prevention on employees' minds. Many different approaches are used to make employees more aware of safety. However, four basic elements are present in most successful safety programs. First, it must have the genuine (rather than casual) support of top and middle management. If upper management takes an unenthusiastic approach to safety, employees are quick to pick up on this. Second, it must be clearly established that safety is a responsibility of operating managers. All operating managers should consider safety to be an integral part of their job. Third, a positive attitude toward safety must exist and be maintained. The employees must believe the safety program is worthwhile and produces results. Finally, one person or department should be in charge of the safety program and responsible for its operation. Often the human resource manager or a member of the human resource staff has primary responsibility for the safety program.

Promoting Safety

Many things can be done to promote safety. Suggestions include the following:

1. Make the work interesting. Uninteresting work often leads to boredom, fatigue, and stress, all of which can cause accidents. Often simple changes can be made to make the work more meaningful. Attempts to make the job more interesting are usually successful if they add responsibility, challenge, and other, similar factors that increase employees' satisfaction with the job.

2. Establish a safety committee composed of operative employees and representatives of management. The safety committee provides a means of getting employees directly involved in the operation of the safety program. A rotating membership is desirable. The size should usually range from 5 to 12 members. Normal duties for the safety committee include inspecting, observing work practices, investigating accidents, and making recommendations. Committee meetings should be held at least once a month on company time, and attendance should be mandatory.

3. Feature employee safety contests. Give prizes to the work group or employee having the best safety record for a given time period. Contests can also be held to test safety knowledge. Prizes can be awarded periodically to employees who submit good accident prevention ideas.

4. Publicize safety statistics. Monthly accident reports should be posted. Ideas as to how accidents can be avoided should be solicited.

5. Use bulletin boards throughout the organization. Pictures, sketches, and cartoons

can be effective if properly presented. One thing to remember when using bulletin boards is to change them frequently.

6. Encourage employees, including supervisors and managers, to have high expectations for safety. Recognize positive safety actions, and acknowledge those who contribute to safety improvements.

7. Periodically hold safety training programs and meetings. Have employees periodically attend and participate in these meetings as role players or instructors. The next section discusses how to establish a safety training program for the first time.

Establishing a Safety Training Program

There are several basic steps that should be followed when initially establishing a safety training program:[12]

1. Assess the training needs by examining accident and injury records and talking to department heads about their perceived needs. Regardless of severity, try and find out where problems are located, what the potential causes might be, and what has been done in the past to correct them.

2. Gauge the level of employees' safety skills. Use written tests, employee interviews, and general observations to determine the level of employee knowledge about their job.

3. Design a program to solve the problem. Outside resources such as consultants, equipment vendors, and even OSHA can be helpful. For best results, use a variety of teaching methods and involve employees as much as possible.

4. Get line managers on board. Once top management has embraced a safety philosophy, inform line managers about safety problems throughout the organization. Emphasize that they can help set the proper tone through example and instruction.

5. Evaluate the program's effectiveness. Try and answer two basic questions: Did the program change employees' behavior? Did the program impact business results in a positive manner?

6. Fine-tune the safety process. Periodically review the training program and make adjustments to incorporate new safety standards and to account for business and industry changes.

HRM in Action 20.2 describes an incentive program used by one company to improve safety.

Employee Health

Until recently, safety and accident prevention received far more attention than did employee health. However, this has changed. Statistics show that occupational diseases may cost industry as much or more than occupational accidents.[13] Furthermore, while the total number of nonfatal job-related injuries and illnesses in the United States has dropped in certain recent years, the total number of illnesses has risen over the same periods.[14] In addition, there are many diseases and health-related problems that are not necessarily job-related but may affect job performance. Many organizations now not only attempt to remove health hazards from the workplace but also have investigated programs to improve health.

Occupational Health Hazards

"A coal miner in West Virginia can't breathe. A pesticide plant worker in Texas can't walk. A hospital anesthesiologist in Chicago suffers a miscarriage."[15] These

---

HRM IN ACTION

Incentives for Safety

20.2

A leading Oregon-based paper company implemented an incentive-based program to improve its safety record. Under the program, employees earn Safety Stamps by working accident-free on an individual, departmental, and plantwide basis. If an individual goes one month without an accident, he or she receives five Safety Stamps. If a department goes one month without an accident, each employee in the department receives four Safety Stamps. If the entire plant goes one month without an accident, every employee in the plant receives three Safety Stamps. The Safety Stamps are redeemable for merchandise from the C.A. Short Company catalog.

The company also issues Safety Stamps for Milestone Awards. If the entire plant works safely for 250,000 hours, each employee gets two Safety Stamps; for 750,000 safe work hours, each employee gets four Safety Stamps; and for 1,000,000 safe work hours, each employee gets five Safety Stamps. Since the company implemented this program, its accident rate has been reduced by 43 percent, lost-time accidents have gone down 67 percent, and workers' compensation costs have gone down 67 percent.

Source: "Job Safety First," *Incentive* (People Performance Supplement), October 1997, pp. 24–26.

---

people, along with hundreds of other employees, are victims of occupational diseases. An occupational illness can be defined as any abnormal condition or disorder (other than that resulting from an occupational injury) caused by exposure to environmental factors associated with employment. Approximately 439,000 new cases of occupational illnesses were reported among U.S. employees in private industry during 1996.[16] The U.S. Department of Labor uses seven major categories to classify occupational illnesses: (1) occupational skin diseases or disorders, (2) dust diseases of the lungs, (3) respiratory conditions due to toxic agents, (4) poisoning (systemic effects of toxic materials), (5) disorders due to physical agents (other than toxic materials), (6) disorders associated with repeated trauma, and (7) all other occupational illnesses. In 1996, the overall incidence rate of occupational illnesses was 52 per 10,000 full-time employees in private industry.[17] Of the total number of occupational illnesses, disorders with repeated trauma were the most common, followed by skin diseases and disorders.

Toxic Substance Control Act Federal law passed in 1976 requiring the pretesting for safety of new chemicals marketed.

Increased awareness of occupational disease was one factor that contributed to the passage of the Occupational Safety and Health Act. In addition, the Toxic Substance Control Act of 1976 requires the pretesting of certain new chemicals marketed each year. A 1980 rule issued by OSHA requires organizations to measure for safety, and record employee exposure to, certain potentially harmful substances. These medical records must be made available to employees, their designated representatives, and OSHA. Furthermore, these records must be maintained for 30 years, even if the employee leaves the job. Additional rules have been issued related to specific hazards.

Cancer and the Workplace

For years, society has been aware of certain occupational diseases, such as black lung disease. However, only in recent years has the potential extent of occupational diseases been realized. Table 20–4 lists 10 major substances that have been linked to occupational diseases. Note that 7 of the 10 may produce some form of cancer. One government study estimated that between 20 and 38 percent of all cancer in this country is occupationally related.[18] In October 1977, OSHA issued a policy aimed at regulating carcinogens (substances that have been identified as causing cancer) in the workplace.

TABLE 20-4   **TEN SUSPECTED HAZARDS IN THE WORKPLACE**

Potential Dangers	Disease That May Result
Arsenic	Lung cancer, lymphoma
Asbestos	White lung disease (asbestosis), cancer of lungs and lining of lungs, cancer of other organs
Benzene	Leukemia, aplastic anemia
Bichloromethylether (BCME)	Lung cancer
Coal dust	Black lung disease
Coke oven emissions	Cancer of lungs and kidneys
Cotton dust	Brown lung disease (byssinosis), chronic bronchitis, emphysema
Lead	Kidney disease, anemia, central nervous system damage, sterility, birth defects
Radiation	Cancer of thyroid, lungs, and bone; leukemia; reproductive effects (spontaneous abortion, genetic damage)
Vinyl chloride	Cancer of liver and brain

Source: "Is Your Job Dangerous to Your Health?" *U.S. News & World Report,* February 5, 1979, p. 42. Copyright, February 5, 1979, *U.S. News & World Report.*

Hazard Communications

Because of the threats posed by chemicals in the workplace, OSHA issued its hazard communication rule in the early 1980s. This rule is also known as the *right-to-know rule.* The basic purpose of the rule is to ensure that employers and employees know what chemical hazards exist in their workplace and how to protect themselves against those hazards. The goal of the rule is to reduce the incidence of illness and injuries caused by chemicals.

The **Hazard Communication Standard** establishes uniform requirements to ensure that the hazards of all chemicals imported into, produced, or used in the workplace are evaluated and that the results of these evaluations are transmitted to affected employers and exposed employees. OSHA has developed a variety of materials to help employers and employees implement effective hazard communication programs. According to an Environmental Protection Agency report released in April 1998, only a small percentage of chemicals currently being produced or imported into the U.S. are being fully tested for health and ecological effects.[19]

Hazard Communication Standard   Standard issued by OSHA in the early 1980s that established uniform requirements to ensure that the hazards of all chemicals imported into, produced, or used in the workplace are evaluated and that the results of these evaluations are transmitted to affected employers and exposed employees.

Stress   Mental and physical condition that results from a perceived threat of danger (physical or emotional) and the pressure to remove it.

Stress in the Workplace

Stress is the mental and physical condition that results from a perceived threat of danger (physical or emotional) and the pressure to remove it.[20] The potential for stress exists when an environmental situation presents a demand threatening to exceed a person's capabilities and resources for meeting it.[21] Stress manifests itself among employees in several ways, including increased absenteeism, job turnover, lower productivity, and mistakes on the job. In addition, excessive stress can result in both physical and emotional problems. Some common stress-related disorders include tension and migraine headaches; coronary heart disease; high blood pressure; muscle tightness in the chest, neck, and lower back; gastritis, indigestion; ulcers; diarrhea; constipation; bronchial asthma; rheumatoid arthritis; and some menstrual and sexual dysfunctions.[22] From a psychological perspective, inordinate or prolonged stress can adversely affect personal factors such as concentration, memory, sleep, appetite, motivation, mood, and the ability to relate to others.[23]

Table 20–5 lists some of the more common sources and suggested causes of job-related stress.

In 1997, work-related stress accounted for 12 percent of all unscheduled absences.[24] The cost for employers is currently estimated to be between $200 billion and $300 billion annually as assessed by absenteeism, employee turnover, direct medical costs, workers' compensation, and other legal costs.[25] In an effort to combat this, many organizations conduct training programs designed to help reduce employee stress. Most of these programs attempt to teach employees self-help techniques for individually reducing their own stress.

Burnout Occurs when work is no longer meaningful to a person; can result from stress or a variety of other work-related or personal factors.

Burnout

Burnout occurs when work is no longer meaningful to a person. Burnout can result from stress or a variety of other work-related or personal factors. Figure 20–2

T A B L E   2 0 – 5   COMMON SOURCES OF SUGGESTED CAUSES OF JOB-RELATED STRESS

Sources	Suggested Causes
Threat of job loss	Cutbacks due to recessionary period or other factors beyond the control of the employee.
Job mismatch	Job demands skills or abilities that the employee does not possess (job incompetence). Job does not provide opportunity for the employee to fully utilize skills or abilities (underutilization).
Conflicting expectations	Formal organization's concept of expected behavior contradicts the employee's concept of expected behavior. Informal group's concept of expected behavior contradicts the employee's concept.
Role ambiguity	Employee is uncertain or unclear about how to perform on the job. Employee is uncertain or unclear about what is expected in the job. Employee is unclear or uncertain about the relationship between job performance and expected consequences (rewards, penalties, etc.).
Role overload	Employee is incompetent at job. Employee is asked to do more than time permits (time pressure).
Fear/responsibility	Employee is afraid of performing poorly or failing. Employee feels pressure for high achievement. Employee has responsibility for other people.
Working conditions	Job environment is unpleasant; for example, there is inadequate lighting or improper regulation of temperature and noise. Requirements of the job may unnecessarily produce pacing problems, social isolation, and so forth. Machine design and maintenance procedures create pressure. Job involves long or erratic work hours.
Working relationships	Individual employees have problems relating to and/or working with superiors, peers, and/or subordinates. Employees have problems working in groups.
Alienation	There is limited social interaction. Employees do not participate in decision making.

Source: Adapted from Charles R. Stoner and Fred L. Fry, "Developing a Corporate Policy for Managing Stress," *Personnel,* May–June 1983, p. 70. Reprinted by permission of publisher, from *Personnel,* May–June. Copyright 1983 by American Management Association, New York. All rights reserved.

FIGURE 20-2   THE PATH TO PROFESSIONAL BURNOUT

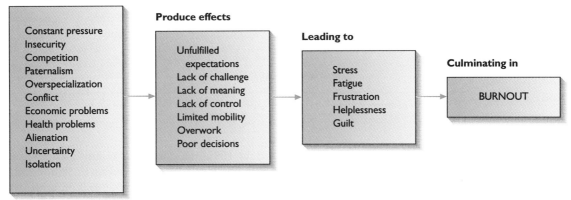

Working conditions

Constant pressure
Insecurity
Competition
Paternalism
Overspecialization
Conflict
Economic problems
Health problems
Alienation
Uncertainty
Isolation

Produce effects

Unfulfilled
  expectations
Lack of challenge
Lack of meaning
Lack of control
Limited mobility
Overwork
Poor decisions

Leading to

Stress
Fatigue
Frustration
Helplessness
Guilt

Culminating in

BURNOUT

Source: Donald P. Rogers, "Helping Employees Cope with Burnout," *Business,* October–December 1984, pp. 3–7. Copyright © 1984 by the College of Business Administration, Georgia State University, Atlanta. Reprinted by permission.

illustrates the sequence of events that often leads to professional burnout. As burnout has become more recognized, certain related myths have surfaced.[26]

Myth 1: Burnout is just a new-fangled notion that gives lazy people an excuse not to work.   Although burnout is a relatively recent term, the behavior has been around for centuries. History is full of examples of people, such as writers, artists, and scientists, who gradually or suddenly stopped producing.

Myth 2: As long as people really enjoy their work they can work as long and hard as they want and never experience burnout.   Any work that inherently includes significant and continuing frustration, conflict, and pressure can lead to burnout.

Myth 3: Individuals know when they are burning out and, when they do, all they need to do is take off for a few days or weeks and then they'll be as good as new.   Unfortunately, most people do not realize that burnout is occurring until it reaches its later stages.

Myth 4: Individuals who are physically and psychologically strong are unlikely to experience burnout.   Physically and psychologically strong individuals may indeed be able to work harder than less strong people. However, without proper stress skills, an inordinate amount of work can still cause serious damage.

Myth 5: Job burnout is always job-related.   Burnout usually results from a combination of work, family, social, and personal factors.

From the organization's viewpoint, the first step in reducing burnout is to identify those jobs with the highest potential for burnout. Certain jobs are more likely to lead to burnout than others (Table 20–6 lists 10 jobs whose occupants are highly susceptible to burnout). Once those jobs have been identified, several actions are possible. Some of the possibilities include redesigning the jobs, clarifying expectations, changing work schedules, improving physical working conditions, and training the jobholders. HRM in Action 20.3 describes how some companies are offering employees workplace sabbaticals to help reduce job-related stress.

Alcoholism and Drug Abuse

The National Clearinghouse for Alcohol and Drug Information estimated for 1998 that 12.8 million people in the United States used illicit drugs, 32 million people were alcohol binge drinkers, and 11 million were heavy drinkers.[27] The

T A B L E   2 0 – 6   **TEN JOBS LIKELY TO PRODUCE BURNOUT**

Air traffic controller	Psychologist
Garment industry buyer	Social worker
Insurance executive	Stock trader
Lawyer	Teacher
Nurse and doctor	Truck driver

Source: Julie Batten, "10 Jobs That Cause Burnout," *Careers*, December 1985, p. 43.

clearinghouse also estimated that, in 1995, the cost of drug and alcohol abuse to the U.S. economy was $165.5 billion.[28] The U.S. Department of Labor estimates that drug use in the workplace costs employers between $75 billion and $100 billion in lost time, accidents, health care, and workers' compensation costs.[29] Compared to most employees, substance abusers:

* Are late 3 times more often.
* Request time off 2.2 times more often.
* Have 2.5 times as many absences of eight days or more.
* Use 3 times the normal level of sick benefits.
* Are 5 times more likely to file a workers' compensation claim.
* Are involved in accidents 3.6 times more often.[30]

In addition, substance abuse results in reduced productivity, reduced work quality, damage to property and equipment, theft, lower morale, safety violations, and poor decision making.

Alcoholism

For years, people viewed alcoholics as people lacking self-control and morals. Today alcoholism is recognized as a disease with no single cause. Alcoholism does not strike any particular group; it can strike employees from the janitor to the chief executive officer.

The National Council on Alcoholism estimates that the economic loss to the employer of an alcoholic employee amounts to 25 percent of the employee's

---

HRM IN ACTION

Reducing Stress with Sabbaticals

20.3

Companies in Silicon Valley have been offering workplace sabbaticals since the early 1970s. The idea behind these sabbaticals is to give necessary relief from the turbulent grind of corporate high tech—to let employees recharge their batteries.

Today the computer industry is not alone in using sabbaticals to combat stress and burnout. Major law firms, consulting practices, and other high-stress industries offer sabbaticals to counter job stress and employee burnout. Even McDonald's offers sabbaticals for key employees. Other well-known companies offering some form of sabbatical include AT&T, Wells Fargo, Xerox, and Time Inc.

The requirements to qualify for a sabbatical vary significantly from company to company, but most require a minimum amount of service (usually several years). The length and compensation for the sabbatical also vary significantly among companies, but the leave time must always be taken all at once.

Source: Christopher J. Bachler, "Workers Take Leave of Job Stress," *Personnel Journal*, January 1995, pp. 38–48.

wages.[31] Compared to nonalcoholic employees, alcoholics incur twice the rate of absenteeism caused by illness. Alcoholics are also two to three times more likely to be involved in a work-related accident.[32] Some people estimate that as many as 50 percent of all problem employees in industry are actually alcoholics.[33]

In spite of the well-documented costs associated with alcoholism, organizations have only recently undertaken widespread efforts to reduce employee alcoholism. A 1973 survey reported that only 400 major U.S. companies had any type of program designed to help overcome employee alcoholism.[34] Similar surveys subsequently reported that the number had grown to over 5,000 by 1982, over 9,000 by 1987, over 10,000 by 1991, and over 20,000 by 1998.[35]

Many organizations have established in-house alcoholic treatment programs. Most of the available information indicates that in-house alcoholic treatment programs achieve a high rate of success, based on both recovery rates and cost-effectiveness measures.[36] For example, the New York City Police Department reports a 75 percent recovery rate; Du Pont, 66 percent; Consolidated Edison, 60 percent; Illinois Bell, 57 percent; Eastman Kodak, 75 percent; General Motors, 80 percent; and Inland Steel, 82 percent.[37] Programs for combating alcoholism are normally administered as part of an employee assistance program (EAP). EAPs are discussed at length later in this chapter.

Other Drugs

The use of drugs other than alcohol is a relatively new phenomenon. Other drug usage usually falls into one of three categories: marijuana abuse, prescription drug abuse, and hard-drug abuse. According to the National Clearinghouse for Alcohol and Drug Information, 71 percent of all drug users are currently employed.[38] Although most employees who use drugs are young, they are not all blue-collar employees. Employees on drugs are often much more difficult to detect than are drinking employees; alcohol can usually be smelled, whereas drugs cannot. Also, it is relatively easy to pop a pill at lunch or on a break undetected.

Drug Testing

As a result of the increased use of drugs in the workplace, more and more companies have begun to use some form of drug testing for both job applicants and existing employees. For example, the percentage of Fortune 500 companies routinely testing job applicants and/or existing employees for drug use grew from 5 percent in 1983, to 33 percent in 1987, to 95 percent in 1998.[39] While many, if not most, large companies do utilize drug testing, the practice is far less prevalent in small businesses. Certain legal risks are involved in drug testing, and therefore extreme caution should be exercised. An employer can be exposed to substantial liability for defamation for making a false accusation of drug or alcohol use (juries have made awards as high as $450,000 for such defamation).[40] The following guidelines are suggested for implementing a drug-testing program:

- Establish a routine, uniform, organizationwide policy for substance abuse and adhere to it in a consistent and nondisciplinary manner.
- Assume employees are drug-free until proven otherwise.
- Make negative test scores a bona fide occupational qualification whenever possible.
- Include testing in uniform preemployment agreements and have them signed by new employees. For existing employees, establish drug tests as a prerequisite to recalls, promotions, and transfers.
- Train supervisors to detect and refer problem employees for testing.
- Use a high-quality type of urinalysis, not just the cheapest method.
- Use monitored laboratories that employ blind testing to ensure the integrity of the testing procedures. Blind testing requires that those performing the tests do not know the identity of those being tested.

- Use appropriate supervision and custody arrangements to ensure that the samples tested are valid.
- Require tested employees to list all legal over-the-counter drugs they are taking at the time of testing.
- Develop and maintain profiles of well-employee urinalysis results that can later be used for comparative purposes.
- Keep all results confidential.[41]

One criticism of drug-testing programs in general is that they tend to focus on off-duty conduct. Many employees view this as an invasion of privacy, which has led to morale problems and numerous lawsuits. However, a survey conducted by *Industry Week* in 1992 found that the number of employees who view drug testing as an invasion of privacy decreased substantially from 1988 to 1992.[42] To avoid the potential problems associated with traditional drug testing, a new form of testing, called *performance* or *impairment testing,* has emerged.[43] Instead of testing for byproducts that may or may not cause impairment, performance testing measures physical variables such as coordination and response time to certain tasks. For example, a test might consist of watching a CRT screen and manipulating a joystick or keyboard. The person's score can then be compared to a standard or to a previous score. Commercial performance tests are relatively new in most areas of the country. HRM in Action 20.4 describes a performance test currently used by several companies.

AIDS

As defined by the U.S. Centers for Disease Control (CDC), AIDS is "a reliably diagnosed disease that is at least moderately indicative of an underlying cellular im-

---

HRM IN ACTION

Performance Testing

20.4

www.godurango.com/
purgatory.html

Some employers have turned to testing an employee's ability to perform a safety-sensitive job. These job performance exams are usually computer-based and check an employee's visual acuity, coordination, and reaction time. Performance Factors of Golden, Colorado, markets Factor 1000 which measures responses while the test subject tries to keep a diamond-shaped cursor aligned with the center of a computer screen. The cursor moves randomly and quickly, so the subject's responses must be fast and accurate. Each subject establishes his or her own baseline score and must match that score to pass the test. The test takes only 30 seconds to complete, and employees have eight chances to match or beat their baseline score.

Purgatory Resort, a large ski resort, in Durango, Colorado, began using Factor 1000 in June 1994 for all employees in safety-sensitive jobs such as ski lift operators, skiing instructors, and childcare personnel. Every employee in a safety-sensitive job must take the test when they report for work. Employees who can't match or beat their baseline scores are usually sent home for the day. Personnel who repeatedly fail the test must take drug tests.

The vast majority of Purgatory's employees have reacted positively to the test and many view it as a challenge to "beat the computer." Although it's too early to draw any final conclusions as to the test's impact on safety, one immediate positive effect was that the resort's premiums for both liability and workers' compensation insurance went down.

Source: Bill Leonard, "Performance Testing Can Add an Extra Margin of Safety," *HR Magazine,* February 1996, pp. 61–64.

munodeficiency in a person who has had no known underlying cause of cellular immunodeficiency nor any other cause of reduced resistance reported to be associated with that disease."[44] The CDC estimates that 1 in 6 U.S. organizations with more than 50 employees and 1 in 15 organizations with 15 to 49 employees have or have had an employee with HIV or AIDS.[45]

The Vocational Rehabilitation Act of 1973 and numerous state laws offer certain protection to employees infected with AIDS. Under these laws, AIDS-infected employees may file discrimination suits if employment opportunities are denied solely on the basis of their having AIDS. The **Vocational Rehabilitation Act** of 1973 prohibited discrimination against otherwise qualified handicapped individuals solely on the basis of their disability. It should be noted, however, that the Vocational Rehabilitation Act applies only to federal contractors who hold a contract of $2,500 or more, subcontractors to such an employer, recipients of federal financial aid, and federal agencies. Companies that do not meet the previously stated requirements of the Vocational Rehabilitation Act are subject only to applicable state and local statutes, which may vary considerably from state to state.

If an individual with AIDS is covered by the Vocational Rehabilitation Act, certain other issues must be addressed. These issues include determining if the individual meets the definition of a handicapped individual, if the handicapped individual is otherwise qualified to do the job, and if the employee's contagiousness poses a threat to others. If the infected employee does not meet the provision for being handicapped, is not otherwise qualified, or does pose a threat to others, he or she is not protected by the Vocational Rehabilitation Act.

However, the Vocational Rehabilitation Act does not prevent employers from terminating an employee who can no longer perform the duties of his or her job, provided the employer made reasonable accommodations. Reasonable accommodations are defined as those that do not pose undue financial or administrative burdens on the employer.

Since no cure or vaccine for AIDS presently exists, many organizations are turning to education as the most viable means of combating both the medical and social dilemmas posed by AIDS. In addition to developing formal policies for dealing with AIDS, companies are developing in-depth training programs to educate their work forces about AIDS. Table 20–7 summarizes many of the potential benefits of AIDS education in the workplace. HRM in Action 20.5 discusses an AIDS educational program used by First Union National Bank.

Vocational Rehabilitation Act   Legislation enacted in 1973 that prohibits discrimination against otherwise qualified handicapped individuals solely on the basis of their disability; applies only in certain situations involving federal contracts, recipients of federal assistance, or federal agencies.

TABLE 20–7	POTENTIAL BENEFITS OF AIDS EDUCATION IN THE WORKPLACE

- Prevent new infections among employees by helping everyone understand how HIV is and is not transmitted. This prevents suffering, loss of good employees, and further impact on the company's health insurance costs.

- Alert managers and supervisors to the legal issues raised by HIV infection in the workplace. The overwhelming majority of AIDS-related lawsuits related to the workplace involve discrimination and violation of confidentiality. Good training can prevent those problems.

- Prevent discrimination by fearful or misinformed employees who can virtually halt productivity. Through education, the same employees are equally capable of creating a humane, supportive (and therefore healthy) working environment.

- Prepare managers and supervisors to consider reasonable accommodation requests from people disabled by HIV infection.

- Raise morale. It is not unusual for companies to report positive effects on morale after employee HIV training.

Source: Nancy L. Breuer, "AIDS Issues Haven't Gone Away," *Personnel Journal,* January 1992, p. 48.

HRM IN ACTION

AIDS Training at First Union

20.5

www.firstunion.com

Until recently, Ches Gwinn, senior vice president for compensation and benefits at Charlotte, North Carolina–based First Union National Bank, did not think AIDS was a business problem. However, when Gwinn analyzed the numbers, he changed his mind. Looking at the national estimates of AIDS infections—1 in every 250 Americans—and applying that estimate to First Union's population of approximately 34,000 employees, Gwinn figured the bank had 300 to 350 cases of HIV infections. Using the American Medical Association's estimate of $120,000 for medical costs of an AIDS case from infection to death, Gwinn calculated that the bank could spend between $30 million and $40 million on AIDS over the next 10 years.

Based on the above calculations, Gwinn immediately implemented a pilot AIDS training program designed to train managers and supervisors about the transmission, prevention, and handling of AIDS cases. The response to the pilot training program was overwhelmingly positive. As a result, the bank plans to expose all of its approximately 3,000 managers and supervisors to the program.

Source: Nancy L. Breuer, "Emerging Trends for Managing AIDS in the Workplace," *Personnel Journal,* June 1995, pp. 126–27.

Employee Assistance Programs (EAPs)
Company-sponsored programs designed to help employees with personal problems such as alcohol and drug abuse, depression, anxiety, domestic trauma, financial problems, and other psychiatric/medical problems.

Employee Assistance Programs (EAPs)

Many large organizations and a growing number of smaller ones are attempting to help employees with personal problems. These problems include not only alcohol and drug abuse but depression, anxiety, domestic trauma, financial problems, and other psychiatric/medical problems. This help is not purely altruistic; it is largely based on cost savings. The help is generally offered in the form of **employee assistance programs (EAPs).**

Cost of Personal Problems

A primary result of personal problems brought to the workplace is reduced productivity. Absenteeism and tardiness also tend to increase. Increased costs of insurance programs, including sickness and accident benefits, are a direct result of personal problems brought to the workplace. Lower morale, more friction among employees, more friction between supervisors and employees, and more grievances also result from troubled employees. Permanent loss of trained employees due to disability, retirement, and death is also associated with troubled employees. Difficult to measure, but a very real cost associated with troubled employees, is the loss of business and a damaged public image.

Organization Involvement

Until recently, organizations attempted to avoid employees' problems that were not job-related. Although aware of the existence of these problems, most managers did not believe they should interfere with employees' personal lives. In the past, organizations tended to get rid of troubled employees. In recent years, however, cost considerations, unions, and government legislation altered this approach. The accepted viewpoint now is that employees' personal problems are private until they begin affecting their job performance. When and if that happens, personal problems become a matter of concern for the organization.

Studies have shown that absenteeism can be significantly reduced by employee assistance programs. It has also been found that EAPs help to reduce on-the-job accidents and grievances. Workers' compensation premiums, sickness and accident benefits, and trips to the infirmary also tend to decrease with an EAP. A 1995 survey found that approximately 82 percent of U.S. companies with 1,000 employees or more sponsor some type of EAP.[46]

475

Types of EAPs

Organizations may offer employee assistance to varying degrees. For example, some organizations may offer only an education program while others may provide a complete diagnosis and treatment program. The most common type of EAP employs a coordinator who evaluates the employee's problem only sufficiently to make a referral to the proper agency or clinic for diagnosis. Sometimes the coordinator serves only as a consultant to the organization and is not a full-time employee. This type of program is especially popular with smaller employers and branch operations of large employers. In a second type of program, the organization hires a qualified person to diagnose the employee's problem; then the employee is referred to the proper agency or clinic for treatment. Under a third type of program, diagnosis and treatment are provided in-house directly by the organization. Because of the complexities of maintaining a full-service facility and hiring appropriate professional staff, most companies do not find this approach to be cost-effective.

Features of a Successful EAP

For an EAP to succeed, it must first be accepted by the employees; they must not be afraid to use it. Experience has shown that certain elements are critical to the success of an EAP. Table 20–8 summarizes several of the most important characteristics of an EAP.

A U.S. Department of Labor study found that for every dollar an employer invests in an EAP, it saves from $5 to $16.[47] Because of the obvious benefits to both employees and employers, EAPs are expected to continue to grow in popularity.

Wellness Programs

In addition to EAPs, many companies have installed programs designed to prevent illness and enhance employee wellness. These programs are referred to as **wellness**

TABLE 20–8

TEN CRITICAL ELEMENTS OF AN EAP

Element	Significance
Management backing	Without this at the highest level, key ingredients and overall effect are seriously limited.
Labor support	The EAP cannot be meaningful if it is not backed by the employees' labor unit.
Confidentiality	Anonymity and trust are crucial if employees are to use an EAP.
Easy access	For maximum use and benefit.
Supervisor training	Crucial to employees needing understanding and support during receipt of assistance.
Union steward training	A critical variable is employees' contact with the union—the steward.
Insurance involvement	Occasionally, assistance alternatives are costly, and insurance support is a must.
Breadth of services component	Availability of assistance for a wide variety of problems (e.g., alcohol, family, personal, financial, grief, medical).
Professional leadership	A skilled professional with expertise in helping, who must have credibility in the eyes of the employee.
Follow-up and evaluation	To measure program effectiveness and overall improvement.

Source: Adapted from F. Dickman and W. G. Emener, "Employee Assistance Programs: Basic Concepts, Attributes, and an Evaluation," *Personnel Administrator,* August 1982, p. 56. Reprinted with permission from the *Personnel Administrator,* published by the Society for Human Resource Management, Alexandria, VA.

Wellness Programs
Company-implemented programs designed to prevent illness and enhance employee wellness.

programs and include such things as periodic medical exams, stop-smoking clinics, improved dietary practices, hypertension detection and control, weight control, exercise and fitness, stress management, accident-risk reduction, immunizations, and cardiopulmonary resuscitation training (CPR). Some of the documented results of wellness programs include fewer sick days, reduced coronary heart disease, and lower major medical costs. Many also believe employee productivity increases for employees participating in exercise and fitness programs. Numerous studies have reported a very attractive return on investment for most types of wellness programs.[48] Experts in the wellness field report that even small companies can offer wellness programs and that they do not have to be expensive.

In light of the continual rise in health care costs, it is predicted that company-sponsored wellness programs will grow rapidly in the future. HRM in Action 20.6 describes a new wellness program successfully implemented by Sara Lee Knit Products.

Violence in the Workplace

Violence in the workplace, once an exception to daily work life, has become much more commonplace. Reports show some form of violence has occurred in nearly one-third of all companies within the last five years.[49] Every year, approximately one million incidents result in some two million victims.[50] Even more alarming is the fact that an average of 15 people per week are murdered at their workplace.[51] According to the U.S. Department of Labor, homicide ranks third among work-related deaths in the United States and is the leading cause of death for women in the workplace.[52]

Given that violence is growing in the workplace, what can organizations do to protect their employees and physical resources? It is important that companies concentrate on avoiding or heading off violence rather than simply dealing with it after it occurs.[53] Most companies can do several things to avoid falling victim to violent incidents:

- *Hire carefully, but realistically.* Screen out potential employees whose histories show a propensity to violence. A full background check can be done in many states for $50 or less.

HRM IN ACTION

Wellness Program at Sara Lee Knit Products

20.6

www.saralee.com

Healthy employees do not just happen; they are created. One does not stumble on large groups of well-conditioned, energetic, fit workers accidentally. However, such groups do exist at workplaces that have made a commitment to health. These companies focus on preventive health and a corporate culture that encourages a healthy lifestyle at all levels. Sara Lee Knit Products is one company that believes in wellness programs. The Winston-Salem, North Carolina–based company encourages employee involvement in the design and continued evolution of its wellness program.

In addition to providing workout and weightlifting equipment and aerobics classes, the company has an incentive program whereby employees earn points for attending classes, going to HealthFit seminars, and recruiting coworkers into the program. The points may be cashed in for prizes on a quarterly basis or accrued to the end of the year. Because the company believes in a holistic approach to health, the wellness center also addresses employees' mental and emotional health needs.

Source: Gillian Flynn, "Companies Make Wellness Work," *Personnel Journal,* February 1995, pp. 63–66.

- *Draw up a plan and involve employees in it.* Develop a plan for preventing violence and for dealing with it if it does occur. Reporting requirements for both violence and threats of violence should be an integral part of the plan. The plan should also be shaped by employee participation.

- *As part of the plan, adopt a "zero tolerance" policy.* "Zero tolerance" does not necessarily mean dismissal; but rather, it means the perpetrator of the violence will face consequences of some kind. When discipline is called for, its purpose should be to teach, not to punish.

- *Enlist the aid of professionals—with an eye on the cost.* Go to external resources when necessary to get help if a problem or a potential problem reveals itself. A few hours with a psychologist or a legal professional can defuse a simmering situation. It might even be necessary to hire a security firm temporarily in some instances.

While all of the above measures should help a company avoid violence in the workplace, the best protection may lie in developing a corporate culture that makes violence all but unthinkable. Violence is much less likely to take place in an environment where employees feel appreciated and believe they are treated with respect.

SUMMARY OF LEARNING OBJECTIVES

1. **State the purpose of the Occupational Safety and Health Act and discuss its major provisions.**
   The stated purpose of the act is "to assure so far as possible every working man and woman in the nation safe and healthful working conditions." The act established the Occupational Safety and Health Administration (OSHA) to set up standards and to conduct workplace inspections. Many OSHA standards have special record-keeping and reporting requirements that companies must adhere to.

2. **List the three major causes of accidents in the workplace.**
   The three major causes of work-related accidents are unsafe personal acts, an unsafe physical environment, and accident proneness.

3. **Define frequency rate and severity rate.**
   A frequency rate indicates how often disabling injuries occur. A severity rate indicates how severe accidents were by calculating the average length of time injured employees were unable to work.

4. **Offer several suggestions for promoting safety in the workplace.**
   Many things can be done to promote safety in the workplace. Some suggestions include (1) make the work interesting; (2) establish a safety committee; (3) feature employee safety contests; (4) publicize safety statistics; (5) hold periodic safety meetings; and (6) post safety-related pictures, cartoons, and sketches on bulletin boards.

5. **Discuss the Hazard Communication rule.**
   The Hazard Communication rule, also known as the right-to-know rule, is intended to ensure that employers and employees know what chemical hazards exist in the workplace and how to protect themselves against these hazards. The rule requires that certain chemicals be evaluated for danger and that the results be communicated to affected employers and exposed employees.

6. **Differentiate between stress and burnout.**
   Stress is the mental and physical condition that results from a perceived threat of danger (physical or emotional) and the pressure to remove it. Burnout occurs when work is no longer meaningful to a person. Burnout can result from stress or from a variety of other work-related or personal factors.

7. **Name several work-related consequences of alcohol and drug abuse.**

   Possible work-related consequences of alcohol and drug abuse include absenteeism, tardiness, reduced productivity, poor decision making, equipment damage, safety violations, lower morale, and even outright theft to pay for drugs.

8. **Offer several guidelines for implementing a drug-testing program.**

   Suggested guidelines for implementing a drug-testing program include (1) establish a routine, uniform, organizationwide policy for substance abuse and adhere to it in a consistent manner; (2) assume employees are drug-free until proven otherwise; (3) make negative drug testing scores a bona fide occupational qualification whenever possible; (4) include drug testing as a part of a preemployment agreement; (5) train supervisors to detect and refer problem employees for testing; (6) use a high-quality type of test; (7) use monitored laboratories to process and interpret the test results; (8) use appropriate supervision and custody arrangements to ensure that the samples tested are valid; (9) require tested employees to list all legal drugs they are taking; (10) develop and maintain profiles of well-employee urinalysis results that can later be used for comparative purposes; and (11) keep all results confidential.

9. **Discuss the legal requirements for terminating an employee with acquired immunodeficiency syndrome (AIDS).**

   First, it must be determined if the employee is covered by the Vocational Rehabilitation Act of 1973. If the employee is not covered by this act, the company is subject only to applicable state and local statutes, which vary considerably from state to state. If the individual is covered by the Vocational Rehabilitation Act, it must be determined if he or she meets the provisions of a handicapped individual, is otherwise qualified, and whether his or her contagiousness poses a threat to others. If the infected employee does not meet the provisions for being handicapped, is not otherwise qualified, or poses a threat to others, she or he is not protected by the act. The act does not prevent employers from terminating employees who can no longer perform their job duties, provided the company made reasonable accommodations.

10. **Explain the three basic types of employee assistance programs (EAPs).**

    The most common type of EAP employs a coordinator who evaluates the employee's problem sufficiently to make a referral to the proper agency or clinic for diagnosis. In a second type, the organization hires a qualified person to diagnose the employee's problem and then refers the employee to a proper agency or clinic for treatment. Under a third type of EAP, diagnosis and treatment of the problem are provided directly by the organization.

11. **List several specific things an organization can do to help reduce violence in its workplace.**

    Most companies can do several things to avoid violent incidents. These include (1) hiring carefully, (2) drawing up a plan and involving employees in its development, (3) adopting a "zero tolerance" policy, and (4) enlisting the aid of professionals when necessary.

REVIEW QUESTIONS

1. What is the Occupational Safety and Health Administration (OSHA) authorized to do?
2. What is the general-duty clause as it relates to OSHA?
3. List the inspection priorities established by OSHA.
4. What is the usual inspection procedure followed by OSHA?
5. Name and discuss the three primary causes of accidents.
6. How do organizations measure their safety records?
7. What four basic elements are present in most successful safety programs?

8. What can be done to promote safety in organizations?

9. What does the Toxic Substance Control Act of 1976 require?

10. Distinguish between stress and burnout.

11. List several guidelines that should be followed when implementing a drug-testing program.

12. Define performance testing and describe how it differs from normal drug testing.

13. How does the Vocational Rehabilitation Act of 1973 affect the dismissal of employees with AIDS?

14. Describe the three general types of employee assistance programs (EAPs).

15. List four things an organization might do to avoid violent incidents in its workplace.

DISCUSSION QUESTIONS

1. Express your personal philosophy regarding the responsibilities of management, especially human resource managers, for the well-being of employees.

2. On July 1, 1985, the president, plant manager, and foreman of Film Recovery Systems, Inc., were sentenced to 25 years in the Illinois state prison and fined $10,000 each after being found guilty of murder in the 1983 death of an employee exposed to cyanide in a silver-recovery process.* The court found that the three executives were "totally knowledgeable of the hazards of cyanide" and failed to communicate those hazards to employees, who were mostly undocumented Polish and Mexican immigrants. What is your reaction to what are believed to be the first work-related homicide convictions in the United States?

3. Do you think an organization has any responsibility to help employees with health problems totally unrelated to their work environment?

INCIDENT 20-1

Safety Problems at Blakely

Several severe accidents have recently occurred in the 12-employee assembly department of Blakely Company, which has a total work force of 65 employees. The supervisor of this department, Joe Benson, is quite perturbed and, in response to questions by the general manager and owner of the company, claimed the employees do not listen to him. He has warned them about not taking safety precautions, he explained, but he can't police their every move. The general manager countered, "Accidents cost us money for repairs, lost time, medical expenses, human suffering, and what not. It's important that you stop it. Your department has a bad safety record—the worst in the company. You are going to have to correct it."

Joe believed he had taken the necessary precautions but was not getting satisfactory results. He also believed there were more possibilities of accidents occurring in his department than in any other department of the company. He decided to talk it over with the human resource manager, Fay Thomas. Fay suggested scheduling a 10-minute safety talk by a different employee each week. The first subject would be "using machine guards." Joe thought that "good housekeeping and safety" and "no smoking" would also be good subsequent subjects.

Fay suggested that Joe schedule part of his time to review his department periodically. Furthermore, she suggested that any unsafe act he discovered should

---

*See Betty S. Murphy, Wayne E. Barlow, and D. Diane Hatch, "Murder in the Workplace," *Personnel Journal*, October 1985, p. 27.

result in an immediate two-day suspension for the offender. "You have to get tough when it comes to safety. Your people are taking safety much too lightly. Of course, you start by making an announcement of what you are going to do. Put a notice to that effect on the bulletin board. Then enforce it to the letter."

Joe believed that simply talking personally to each of his employees and urging them to work safely might get better results. However, he was convinced that some type of incentive was needed. As a result, he devised a plan in which the employee with the fewest safety violations over the next three months would be given a day off with pay. Joe's plan was approved by his boss.

Questions

1. What is Joe's problem?
2. In your opinion, how did this problem develop? What were its main causes? Discuss.
3. What actions do you recommend Joe take? Why?

I N C I D E N T   2 0 – 2

To Fire or Not to Fire?*

David Butler is a former drug user who has spent time in jail. For the past three years he has been straight, as far as everyone knows. Currently David operates a forklift for Adams, Inc., a small construction company. Lately David has begun having seizures, or "flashbacks," as a result of his earlier use of the drug PCP. David has been carefully evaluated by EAP professionals and found to be clean of current drug use. The professionals say that flashbacks of this nature are quite common in ex-addicts. Mishandling of David's machine could be potentially dangerous to him and his coworkers. David has already had some flashbacks while at the controls, and in every case the seizure merely caused him to release the handle, which simply stopped the machine automatically. This is the only job David is qualified to do within the company.

Questions

1. Should David be allowed to continue on the job?
2. Are there any options other than leaving David alone or firing him?

E X E R C I S E

Filing OSHA Reports

Assume you are the director of human resources for your company and that one of your responsibilities is to handle all contact with OSHA. Three days ago, on Monday, two injuries occurred in the plant. In the first case, a machine operator got careless and smashed his thumb. The operator received first aid on the floor, went home early, and was back on the job the next morning. In the second case, an office worker slipped while going down some steps and broke her arm. She is expected to report back to work at the start of the next week.

1. What OSHA forms should be filed in each of these cases? When should the forms be filed?

---

*This case is adapted from an actual situation reported in *Management Review,* August 1991, p. 23.

2. Go to your library or a local OSHA office and get copies of the OSHA forms needed for each of the cases described above. Complete the forms. Make any reasonable assumptions about the accidents that you deem necessary.

NOTES AND ADDITIONAL READINGS

1. *Accident Facts* (Chicago: National Safety Council, 1998), p. 48.
2. Ibid.
3. *All about OSHA* (Washington, D.C.: U.S. Department of Labor, 1995), p. 1.
4. *Accident Facts,* p. 48.
5. David S. Thelan, Donna Ledgerwood, and Charles F. Walters, "Health and Safety in the Workplace: A New Challenge for Business Schools," *Personnel Administrator,* October 1985, p. 37.
6. *All about OSHA,* p. 2.
7. Ibid., p. 4.
8. Barbara Somervill, "OSHA Aims to Be User-Friendly," *Industrial Distribution,* March 1998, p. 87; Charles Kelly, "Another Perspective: Collaborating in Safety," *Electric Perspectives,* May/June 1998, p. 184.
9. *Marshall* v. *Barlow's, Inc.,* 76-1143 (1978).
10. G. R. Terry and L. W. Rue, *A Guide to Supervision* (Homewood, Ill.: Learning Systems, 1982), p. 131.
11. John D. Jordan and Rabbi D. Simons, "It's No Accident: What You Think Is What You Do," *Personnel Journal,* April 1984, pp. 16–20, and Russ Tarbell, "Gaining More Safety Success," *Professional Safety,* February 1997, p. 42.
12. "Developing A Safety Training Program," *HR Focus,* September 1996, p. 10.
13. Craig S. Weaver, "Understanding Occupational Disease," *Personnel Journal,* June 1989, pp. 86–94.
14. Mary Jane Fisher, "Repeated Trauma Spurs Rise in Worker Illnesses," *National Underwriter,* January 9, 1995, pp. 15, 17.
15. "Is Your Job Dangerous to Your Health?" *U.S. News & World Report,* February 5, 1979, p. 41.
16. *News: USDL-97-453* (Washington, D.C.: U.S. Department of Labor, Bureau of Labor Statistics, 1997), p. 3.
17. Ibid., pp. 1–3 (calculations by author based on these data).
18. M. C. Anderson, R. N. Isom, K. Williams, and L. J. Zimmerman, eds., *Proceedings of a Conference for Workers on Job-Related Cancer,* Houston, Texas, March 30, 1981, p. 29.
19. Glenn Hess, "EPA Developing Basic Principles for Chemical Testing Initiative," *Chemical Market Reporter,* July 6, 1998, pp. 1, 13.
20. Genevieva La Greca, "The Stress You Make," *Personnel Journal,* September 1985, p. 43.
21. J. E. McGarth, "Stress and Behavior in Organizations," in *Handbook of Industrial and Organizational Psychology,* ed. M. D. Dunnette (Skokie, Ill.: Rand McNally, 1976), p. 1352.
22. Michael E. Cavanagh, "What You Don't Know about Stress," *Personnel Journal,* July 1988, p. 55; "The Warning Signs of Stress," *Restaurant Business,* March 1, 1991, p. 140.
23. Cavanagh, "What You Don't," p. 55.
24. Lisa Schiff, "Downsizing Workplace Stress," *Business & Health,* November 1997, pp. 45–46.
25. Gail Dutton, "Cutting-Edge Stressbusters," *HR Focus,* September 1998, pp. 11–12.
26. These myths are adapted from Cavanagh, "What You Don't Know," pp. 56–57.
27. Leslie A. Bryan, Jr., "Drug Testing in the Workplace," *Professional Safety,* October 1998, pp. 28–32.

28. Ibid.
29. Jane Easter Bahls, "Drugs in the Workplace," *HR Magazine,* February 1998, pp. 80–87.
30. Rhonda Cooke, "Hotline for Help," *Credit Union Management,* March 1997, pp. 23–24.
31. Steven H. Appelbaum and Barbara T. Shapiro, "The ABCs of EAPs," *Personnel,* July 1989, p. 40.
32. Ibid.
33. Gopal C. Pati and John I. Adkins, Jr., "The Employer's Role in Alcoholism Assistance," *Personnel Journal,* July 1983, p. 69.
34. "Battling Employee Alcoholism," *Dun's Business Monthly,* June 1982, p. 48.
35. Ibid.; Leslie Stackel, "EAPs in the Work Place," *Employee Relations Today,* Autumn 1987, p. 289; and Roberta Reynes, "Programs That Aid Troubled Workers," *Nation's Business,* June 1998, pp. 73–74.
36. Pati and Adkins, "The Employer's Role," p. 69.
37. Ibid.
38. Bahls, "Drugs in the Workplace," pp. 80–87.
39. Ibid.; Ian A. Miners, Nick Nykadyn, and Diane Traband, "Put Drug Detection to the Test," *Personnel Journal,* August 1987, p. 96.
40. James R. Redeker and Jonathan A. Segel, "Profits Low? Your Employees May Be High!" *Personnel,* June 1989, p. 75.
41. These guidelines are adapted from Miners, Nykadyn, and Traband, "Put Drug Detection to the Test," p. 97.
42. Michael A. Verespej, "Drug Users—Not Testing—Anger Workers," *Industry Week,* February 17, 1992, pp. 33–34.
43. Redeker and Segel, "Profits Low," p. 77; Cory R. Fine, "Video Tests Are the New Frontier in Drug Testing," *Personnel Journal,* June 1992, p. 150.
44. David L. Wing, "AIDS: The Legal Debate," *Personnel Journal,* August 1986, p. 114.
45. "AIDS Presents New Challenges for Employers," *Employee Benefit Plan Review,* March 1998, p. 35.
46. Gary S. Cohen, Lawrence H. Gard, and William R. Hefferman, "Employee Assistance Programs: A Preventive, Cost-Effective Benefit," *Journal of Health Care Finance,* Spring 1998, pp. 45–53.
47. Roberta Reynes, "Programs That Aid Troubled Workers," *Nation's Business,* June 1998, pp. 73–74.
48. For example, see James S. Howard, "Employee Wellness: It's Good Business," *D&B Reports,* May–June 1987, pp. 34–37; Fred W. Schott and Sandra Wendel, "Wellness with a Track Record," *Personnel Journal,* April 1992, pp. 98–104; David Chenoweth, "Studies Indicate Fitness, Flexibility Training Help Reduce Risk of Injuries," *Occupational Health & Safety,* October 1993, pp. 24–26; Phaedra Brotherton, "Paybacks Are Healthy," *HR Magazine,* August 1998, pp. F2–F6.
49. Barry Brandman, "Fight Workplace Violence," *Transportation and Distribution,* September 1997, pp. 87–92.
50. Ibid.
51. Ibid.
52. Malcolm P. Coco Jr., "The New War Zone: The Workplace," *SAM Advanced Management Journal,* Winter 1998, pp. 15–20.
53. Much of this section is drawn from Michael Barrier, "The Enemy Within," *Nation's Business,* February 1995, pp. 18–21.

Labor Relations

The courts and legislative bodies in the United States over the past several decades have been giving employees tremendous protection. Rights of privacy, rights to sue for all kinds of reasons, and rights to a safe workplace are among just some of the legal protections employees now enjoy. Society has said that the individual worker is no longer going to be powerless in the face of the large corporation.

Business schools are now making business law and employee relations an important part of the curriculum. Both in the regular curriculum and in continuing education, business schools are training employers about their legal responsibilities to their employees. Many business people today are in the dark about ever-changing legislation designed to protect the American worker.

The reason for all this legislation is the belief that employers have occasionally gone too far in their treatment of employees. As one observer stated, "I feel most strongly that employers have to get with it in terms of being fair—treating the employees humanely, but firmly. Even children need certain guidelines or rules and regulations in order to learn how to live with their family and in order to live with society. Employees have to know what mommy and daddy expect and in this case mommy and daddy may be a corporate employer or a public employer. Mommy and daddy have to communicate and the kids have to communicate. The key to good employment relations is communication."

The issue of privacy in the workplace provokes the extremes. Employees wish the same type of total privacy that they have in their own homes. To an employer the workplace is their home, and the employer believes that it's privileged to know what is going on in the workplace.

That employer attitude makes some people uncomfortable, because the employee has very limited power. Privacy rights for employees certainly should be protected for those who make use of employee assistance programs (EAP), for example. If an individual is going to use an organization's EAP programs, privacy should be protected in the same way as a clinic or physician would protect their patients' privacy.

The trend toward employer involvement in the private lives of employees is likely to continue. As one observer said, "There's going to be more testing being done. I think employees are going to recognize that it's going to be done and more and more companies will be doing it. Somewhere employees and employers are going to have to meet in the middle, and communication is the key. I believe that if an employer communicates with employees why certain kinds of testing must be done, employees will respect that and voluntarily agree that that is an appropriate workplace rule."

Right now, a hot topic in discrimination is the Americans with Disabilities Act (ADA). This law requires employers to show with persuasive evidence that a handicapped or disabled person cannot do a job. Employers for many years had taken the easy way out by saying to a disabled applicant when they came through the door, "I'm sorry, I just can't use you." Under the ADA, they can no longer say that. They're going to have to say, "What can I do to help you perform the job." That's a new attitude that's going to require a new approach.

Laura Pincus of Depaul University said, "The ADA has increased the cost to the employer that, for example, has to hire a reader for a deaf person, or get the single desk that fits the wheelchair. We can't ignore that. That's a cost to the company. What you are getting in return is individuals who were previously unemployable. You're making them employable, giving them valuable positions, and in turn giving society a valuable individual who can now perform and is no longer on welfare or supported by society in some other way. So, when you look at the cost to society, the purpose of implementation is really to decrease costs across the board. In time, employers are going to recognize this as just a standard of work."

Employment law has become very complex, and, for many employers, extremely confusing. That's one of the major problems with employment law. This confusion leads some employers to retain employees whom they would rather fire. They are afraid of firing them because they aren't sure what the consequences would be. Employers often feel they aren't being given sufficient direction concerning acceptable behavior.

James Clark, of the law firm of Pedersen & Houpt, said, "I think most people assume that because the employer has historically had the upper hand over the employee it was up until recently the case that you could fire anyone you wanted for any reason and the assumption was that everyone was an employee at will or an employee at whim." Mike Metzger of Indiana University said that's not the case today: "It's getting harder to fire people because the legal protections of the employment environment in general are increasing. So employers have to do a better job of hiring." Bob Cramer of Career Concepts USA added, "I believe corporations in America today are following affirmative action guidelines more out of fear than actually trying to comply with them. They're afraid of the lawsuits where somebody says, 'Hey, I'm being discriminated against,' or, 'You don't have enough of this type of individual.' So they're doing anything and everything they can to bolster up their affirmative action area."

Depaul's Laura Pincus pointed out that proponents of affirmative action legislation place the blame for workplace imbalances in numbers of employees from different racial or ethnic classes directly on the employer. Affirmative action proponents argue that employers simply need to try harder to hire the underrepresented groups. But this "trying harder" can lead to serious questions. Matt McArther, of the law firm of Pope, Ballard, Shepard, & Fowle, related a story that demonstrates a difficulty with this approach: "I have a client who for years was faced with a notable lack of black employees. He tried to find them. He tried to encourage his personnel department to hire them. And they just never seemed to find any. Until he turned around and said, 'The next three people you hire will be black.' That worked. He got his black employees. But what if you're the white applicant who walked through the door beside those black employees? Wouldn't that have been reverse discrimination? Yes, I think it would. This is sort of tied up with the idea of quotas. Well, nobody is imposing a quota, but what they are doing is creating such a difficult standard for an employer to defend himself, that the only way they have of staying out of the soup is to establish a quota."

The new legal environment for employers is much more complex than it was just twenty or thirty years ago. Some of the complexities represent clear improvements in working conditions for employees. Other legislation and rules are burdensome and perhaps unnecessary. A good rule of thumb for all employers and managers is to be diligent about carefully documenting actions taken with employees. Whether disciplinary action or job changes, employers and managers should be sure that a written record of official interactions is kept on file. Joan Eagle, of the law firm of Schwartz & Freeman, said, "I always tell employers that if it's not in writing it doesn't exist. When litigation occurs or when someone files a discrimination charge with an agency the lawyers will ask you what documents you have to show the person was warned or disciplined before being terminated. Employers who don't have that kind of material are very susceptible to be found liable for discrimination charges and other kinds of charges."

Employees are protected by unions, although their power has diminished over the years. Management consultant Richard Laner said: "The power of the union has diminished. Therefore, they're shifting their focus primarily to the legislative body where instead of going in and having a union contract provide certain things, they are contributing money to legislators in state and federal governments to put into law what they can't get at the bargaining table."

The lessons to take away from this video are that, from an employee's perspective, legislation and unions are two ways to work for improvements in working conditions. From an employer's perspective, careful documentation of actions taken with employees can be important protection against time-consuming and costly litigation. For both employees and employers, communication is the key to effective labor relations.

Critical Thinking Questions

1. The Americans with Disabilities Act has made it mandatory that employers give equal consideration to disabled individuals for jobs. What effect does the ADA have on employers other than that?

2. What legal developments besides those mentioned in the video will have an effect on labor relations?

3. The power of labor unions has declined dramatically over the past several decades. What factors have precipitated this decline?

Glossary of Terms

absorption Union merger that involves the merging of one union into a considerably larger one.

acquired immunodeficiency syndrome (AIDS) A life-threatening disease that, although not communicable in most work settings, is causing many work-related debates that have yet to be legally resolved.

adventure learning (experiential-learning programs) Programs that use many kinds of challenging outdoor activities to help participants achieve their goals.

adverse impact Condition that occurs when the selection rate for minorities or women is less than 80 percent of the selection rate for the majority group in hiring, promotions, transfers, demotions, or any selection decision.

affirmative action plan Written document outlining specific goals and timetables for remedying past discriminatory actions.

Age Discrimination in Employment Act (ADEA) Prohibits discrimination against employees over 40 years of age by all companies employing 20 or more people in the private sector.

agency shop Contract provision that does not require employees to join the union but requires them to pay the equivalent of union dues as a condition of employment.

Alexander v. Gardner-Denver Supreme Court decision in 1974 that ruled that using the final and binding grievance procedure in an organization does not preclude an aggrieved employee from seeking redress through court action.

amalgamation Union merger that involves two or more unions, usually of approximately the same size, forming a new union.

American Federation of Labor–Congress of Industrial Organizations (AFL–CIO) Combination of national, international, and local unions joined together to promote the interests of unions and workers. The AFL–CIO was formed in 1955 by the amalgamation of the American Federation of Labor (AFL) and the Congress of Industrial Organizations (CIO).

Americans with Disabilities Act (ADA) Gives disabled persons sharply increased access to services and jobs.

applicant flow record Form completed voluntarily by a job applicant and used by an employer to obtain information that might be viewed as discriminatory.

apprenticeship training Giving instruction, both on and off the job, in the practical and theoretical aspects of the work required in a skilled occupation or trade.

aptitude tests Means of measuring a person's capacity or latent ability to learn and perform a job.

arbitration Process whereby the parties agree to settle a dispute through the use of an independent third party (called an arbitrator). Arbitration is binding on both parties.

assessment center Formal method used in training and/or selection and aimed at evaluating an individual's potential as a manager by exposing the individual to simulated problems that would be faced in a real-life managerial situation.

bargaining unit Group of employees in a plant, firm, or industry that is recognized by the employer, agreed on by the parties to a case, or designated by the NLRB as appropriate for the purposes of collective bargaining.

base wage or salary Hourly, weekly, or monthly pay that employees receive for their work.

behaviorally anchored rating scale (BARS) Method of performance appraisal that determines an employee's level of performance based on whether or not certain specifically described job behaviors are present.

behavior modeling (interaction management) Method of training in which interaction problems faced by managers are identified, practiced, and transferred to specific job situations.

benchmarking Thoroughly examining internal practice and procedures and measuring them against the ways other successful organizations operate.

benefits Rewards employees receive as a result of their employment and position with the organization.

board or **panel interview** Interview method in which two or more people conduct a single interview with one applicant.

bona fide occupational qualification (BFOQ) Permits employer to use religion, age, sex, or national origin as a factor in its employment practices when reasonably necessary to the normal operation of that particular business.

bonus Reward that is offered on a one-time basis for high performance.

bottom line concept When the overall selection process does not have an adverse impact, the government will usually not examine the individual components of that process for adverse impact or evidence of validity.

boulwarism Named after a General Electric vice president; occurs when management makes its best offer at the outset of bargaining and firmly adheres to the offer throughout the bargaining sessions. The NLRB has ruled that this is not good-faith bargaining and is therefore illegal.

Bowen v. United States Postal Service **(1983)** Supreme Court decision that established that an employee may be entitled to recover damages from both the union and the employer in cases where the employer has violated the labor agreement and the union has breached its duty of fair representation.

Broadbanding A base-pay technique that reduces many different salary categories to several broad salary bands.

burnout Occurs when work is no longer meaningful to a person; can result from stress or a variety of other work-related or personal factors.

business game Method of classroom training that simulates an organization and its environment and requires participants to make operating decisions based on the situation.

business necessity Condition that comes into play when an employer has a job criterion that is neutral but excludes members of one sex at a higher rate than members of the opposite sex. The focus in business necessity is on the validity of stated job qualifications and their relationship to the work performed.

cafeteria plans of benefits Plans that give employees the opportunity to choose, from among a wide range of alternatives, how their benefits will be distributed.

campus recruiting Recruitment activities of employers on college and university campuses.

captive-audience doctrine Management's right to speak against a union on company time to employees and to require employees to attend the meeting.

career development An ongoing formalized effort by an organization that focuses on developing and enriching the organization's human resources in light of both the employee's and the organization's needs.

career pathing Sequence of developmental activities involving informal and formal education, training, and job experiences that help make an individual capable of holding a more advanced job in the future.

career planning Process by which an individual formulates career goals and develops a plan for reaching those goals.

career plateau Point in an individual's career where the likelihood of an additional promotion is very low.

career self-management The ability to keep up with the changes that occur within the organization and industry and to prepare for the future.

case study Method of classroom training in which the student analyzes real or hypothetical situations and suggests not only what to do but also how to do it.

central tendency Tendency of a manager to rate all employees at or near the center of the performance scale.

certification bar Condition occurring when the NLRB will not permit another election in the bargaining unit within 12 months of a union's certification.

checklist Method of performance appraisal in which the rater answers with a yes or no a series of questions about the behavior of the individual being rated.

checkoff Arrangement between an employer and a union under which the employer agrees to withhold union dues, initiation fees, and assessments from the employees' pay checks and submit this money to the union.

Civil Rights Act (1991) Permits women, persons with disabilities, and persons who are religious minorities to have a jury trial and sue for punitive damages if they can prove intentional hiring and workplace discrimination. Also requires companies to provide evidence that the business practice that led to the discrimination was not discriminatory but was job-related for the position in question and consistent with business necessity.

Civil Service Reform Act Legislation enacted in 1978 regulating labor-management relations for federal government employees.

classroom training Most familiar training method; useful for quickly imparting information to large groups with little or no knowledge of the subject.

client/server networks Relatively new systems that use personal computers (PCs) linked together to process information in a very efficient manner.

coaching Method of management development conducted on the job, which involves experienced managers advising and guiding trainees in solving managerial problems.

collective bargaining Process that involves the negotiation, drafting, administration, and interpretation of a written agreement between an employer and a union for a specific period of time.

commission plan Incentive plan that rewards employees, at least in part, based on their sales volume.

commitment manpower planning (CMP) Systematic approach to human resource planning designed to get managers and their subordinates thinking about and involved in human resource planning.

Commonwealth v. Hunt Landmark court decision in 1842 that declared unions were not illegal per se.

communication Transfer of information that is meaningful to those involved.

community of interest Concept by which the NLRB makes a bargaining unit decision based on areas of worker commonality.

comparable worth theory Idea that every job has a worth to the employer and society that can be measured and assigned a value.

compensable factors Characteristics of jobs that are deemed important by the organization to the extent that it is willing to pay for them.

compensation All the extrinsic rewards that employees receive in exchange for their work; composed of the base wage or salary, any incentives or bonuses, and any benefits.

concentration Practice of having more minorities or women in a job category than would reasonably be expected when compared to their presence in the relevant labor market.

concurrent validity Validity established by identifying a criterion predictor, administering it to current employees, and correlating the test data with the current employees' performance.

consent elections Union elections in which the parties have agreed on the appropriate bargaining unit.

conspiracy doctrine Notion that courts can punish a union if they deem that the means used or the ends sought by the union are illegal.

construct validity Extent to which a selection criterion measures the degree to which job candidates have identifiable characteristics determined to be relevant to successful job performance.

content validity Extent to which the content of a selection procedure or instrument is representative of important aspects of job performance.

contract bar doctrine Doctrine under which the NLRB will not permit an election in the bargaining unit covered by a contract until the contract expires, up to a maximum of three years.

conventional interest arbitration Form of arbitration in which the arbitrator listens to arguments from both parties and makes a binding decision, which can be identical to the position of either party or different from the positions of both parties.

coordinated bargaining Form of bargaining in which several unions bargain jointly with a single employer.

corrective (progressive) discipline Normal sequence of actions taken by management in disciplining an employee: oral warning, written warning, suspension, and finally discharge.

cost-of-living adjustments (COLA) Contract provision that ties wage increases to rises in the Bureau of Labor Statistics consumer price index.

craft unions Unions having only skilled workers as members. Most craft unions have members from several related trades (e.g., Bricklayers, Masons, and Plasterers International Union).

criteria of job success Ways of specifying how successful performance of the job is to be measured.

criterion predictors Factors such as education, previous work experience, and scores on company-administered tests that are used to predict successful performance of a job.

critical-incident appraisal Method of performance appraisal in which the rater keeps a written record of incidents that illustrate both positive and negative behaviors of the employee; the rater then uses these incidents as a basis for evaluating the employee's performance.

cross training *See* Job rotation

Danbury Hatters case Landmark case of 1908 in which the Supreme Court decided that the Sherman Anti-Trust Act applied to all unions.

data Raw material from which information is developed: composed of facts that describe people, places, things, or events and that have not been interpreted.

deadwood Individuals in an organization whose present performance has fallen to an unsatisfactory level and who have little potential for advancement.

defined-benefit plan Pension plan under which an employer pledges to provide a benefit determined by a definite formula at the employee's retirement date.

defined-contribution plan Pension plan that calls for a fixed or known annual contribution instead of a known benefit.

degree statements Written statements used as a part of the point method of job evaluation to further break down job subfactors.

Delphi technique Judgmental method of forecasting that uses a panel of experts to make initially independent estimates of future demand. An intermediary then presents each expert's forecast and assumptions to the other members of the panel. Each expert is then allowed to revise his or her forecast as desired. This process continues until some consensus or composite emerges.

departmental and job orientation Specific orientation that describes topics unique to the new employee's specific department and job.

differential piece rate plan Piece rate plan devised by Frederick W. Taylor that pays one rate for all acceptable pieces produced up to some standard and then a higher rate for all pieces produced if the output exceeds the standard.

disability insurance Designed to protect employees who experience a long-term or permanent disability.

disabling injuries Work-related injuries that cause an employee to miss one or more days of work.

discipline Action taken against an employee who has violated an organizational rule or whose performance has deteriorated to the point where corrective action is needed.

disparate impact Unintentional discrimination involving employment practices that appear to be neutral but adversely affect a protected class of people.

disparate impact doctrine States that when the plaintiff shows that an employment practice disproportionately excludes groups protected by Title VII, the burden of proof shifts to the defendant to prove that the standard reasonably relates to job performance.

disparate treatment Intentional discrimination and treating one class of employees differently from other employees.

downsizing Laying off of large numbers of managerial and other employees.

due process Right of an employee to be dealt with fairly and justly during the investigation of an alleged offense and the administration of any subsequent disciplinary action.

Duplex Printing Co. v. Deering Case in which the Supreme Court ruled that unions were not exempt from the control of the Sherman Anti-Trust Act.

duties One or more tasks performed in carrying out a job responsibility.

duty of fair representation Under the National Labor Relations Act of 1935, the statutory duty of a union to fairly represent all employees in the bargaining unit, whether or not they are union members.

element Aggregation of two or more micromotions; usually thought of as a complete entity, such as picking up or transporting an object.

employee assistance programs (EAPs) Company-sponsored programs designed to help employees with personal problems such as alcohol and drug abuse, depression, anxiety, domestic trauma, financial problems, and other psychiatric/medical problems.

employee benefits (fringe benefits) Rewards that an organization provides to employees for being members of the organization; usually not related to employee performance.

employee leasing companies Provide permanent staffs at customer companies.

Employee Retirement Income Security Act (ERISA) Federal law passed in 1974, designed to give employees increased security for their retirement and pension plans and to ensure the fair treatment of employees under pension plans.

employee stock ownership plan (ESOP) Form of stock option plan in which an organization provides for purchase of its stock by employees at a set price for a set time period based on the employee's length of service and salary and the profits of the organization.

Employer Information Report (Standard Form 100) Form that all employers with 100 or more employees are required to file with the EEOC; requires a breakdown of the employer's work force in specified job categories by race, sex, and national origin.

employment at will Term used to describe the situation in which an employer hires employees to work for an indefinite period of time and the employees do not have a contract limiting the circumstances under which they can be discharged. Under these conditions, the employer can terminate the employee at any time for any reason or for no reason at all.)

employment parity Situation in which the proportion of minorities and women employed by an organization equals the proportion in the organization's relevant labor market.

empowerment Form of decentralization that involves giving subordinates substantial authority to make decisions.

Enterprise Wheel Supreme Court ruling in 1960 holding that as long as an arbitrator's decision involves the interpretation of a contract, the courts should not overrule the arbitrator merely because their interpretation of the contract was different from that of the arbitrator.

equal employment opportunity The right of all persons to work and to advance on the basis of merit, ability, and potential.

Equal Employment Opportunity Commission (EEOC) Federal agency created under the Civil Rights Act of 1964 to administer Title VII of the act and to ensure equal employment opportunity; its powers were expanded in 1979.

Equal Pay Act Prohibits sex-based discrimination in rates of pay paid to men and women working on the same or similar jobs.

ERISA *See* Employment Retirement Income Security Act

ESOP *See* Employee stock ownership plan

essay appraisal Method of performance appraisal in which the rater prepares a written statement describing an employee's strengths, weaknesses, and past performance.

executive orders Orders issued by the president of the United States for managing and operating federal government agencies.

external equity Addresses what employees in an organization are being paid compared to employees in other organizations performing similar jobs.

extrinsic rewards Rewards that are controlled and distributed directly by the organization and are of a tangible nature.

factor comparison method Job evaluation technique that uses a monetary scale for evaluating jobs on a factor-by-factor basis.

Family and Medical Leave Act (FMLA) 1993 act enabling qualified employees to take prolonged unpaid leave for family- and health-related reasons without fear of losing their jobs.

Federal Labor Relations Authority (FLRA) Three-member panel created by the Civil Service Reform Act whose purpose is to administer the act.

Federal Mediation and Conciliation Service (FMCS) Independent agency within the federal government that, as one of its responsibilities, provides mediators to assist in resolving contract negotiation impasses.

Federal Register Periodical found in many public and college libraries that regularly publishes all OSHA standards and amendments.

Federal Services Impasses Panel (FSIP) Entity within the FLRA whose function is to provide assistance in resolving negotiation impasses within the federal sector.

final-offer interest arbitration Form of arbitration in which the arbitrator is restricted to selecting the final offer of one of the parties.

flexible-benefit plan Same as cafeteria plan of benefits.

floating holiday Holiday that may be observed at the discretion of the employee or the employer.

forced-choice rating Method of performance appraisal that requires the rater to rank a set of statements describing how an employee carries out the duties and responsibilities of the job.

4/5ths or 80 percent rule Limit used to determine whether or not there are serious discrepancies in hiring decisions and other employment practices affecting women or minorities.

401(k) plan Most popular type of defined contribution plan, named after section 401(K) of the Internal Revenue Code. Allows employees to defer a portion of their pay into the plan, thus making contributions tax deductible (up to a limit).

frequency rate Ratio that indicates the frequency with which disabling injuries occur.

gain sharing Programs also known as *profit sharing, performance sharing,* or *productivity incentives;* generally refers to incentive plans that involve employees in a common effort to achieve the company's productivity objectives. Based on the concept that the resulting incremental economic gains are shared among employees and the company.

garnishment Legal procedure by which an employer is empowered to withhold wages for payment of an employee's debt to a creditor.

general-duty clause Clause in the Occupational Safety and Health Act covering those situations not addressed by specific standards; in essence, it requires employers to comply with the intent of the act.

Gissel bargaining orders Situations in which the NLRB orders management to bargain with the union; named after a landmark Supreme Court decision, *NLRB* v. *Gissel Packing Company.*

good-faith bargaining Sincere intention of both parties to negotiate differences and reach a mutually acceptable agreement.

graphic rating scale Method of performance appraisal that requires the rater to indicate on a scale where the employee rates on factors such as quantity of work, dependability, job knowledge, and cooperativeness.

graphology (handwriting analysis) Use of a trained analyst to examine a person's handwriting to assess the person's personality, emotional problems, and honesty.

grievance arbitration Arbitration that attempts to settle unresolved disputes arising during the term of the collective bargaining agreement that involve questions of its interpretation or application.

grievance procedures Systematic means of resolving disagreements over the collective bargaining agreement and providing assurance that the terms and conditions agreed to in negotiations are properly implemented.

group incentives Incentives based on group rather than individual performance.

group interview Interview method in which several applicants are questioned together.

halo effect Occurs when managers allow a single prominent characteristic of an employee to influence their judgment on separate items of a performance appraisal.

handicapped individual Person who has a physical or mental impairment that substantially limits one or more major life activities, has a record of such impairments, or is regarded as having such an impairment.

Hazard Communication Standard Standard issued by OSHA in the early 1980s that established uniform requirements to ensure that the hazards of all chemicals produced or used in, or imported into, the workplace are evaluated and that the results of these evaluations are transmitted to affected employers and exposed employees.

health maintenance organization (HMO) Health service organization that contracts with companies to provide certain basic medical services around the clock, seven days a week, for a fixed cost.

Hitchman Coal & Coke Co. v. Mitchell Supreme Court case of 1917 that upheld the legality of yellow-dog contracts.

hot-stove rule Set of guidelines used in administering discipline that calls for quick, consistent, and impersonal action preceded by a warning.

human resource functions Tasks and duties that human resource managers perform (e.g., determining the organization's human resource needs; recruiting, selecting, developing, counseling, and rewarding employees; acting as liaison with unions and government organizations; and handling other matters of employee well-being).

human resource generalist Person who devotes a majority of working time to human resources issues, but does not specialize in any specific area.

human resource management Activities designed to provide for and coordinate the human resources of an organization.

human resource planning (HRP) Process of determining the human resource needs of an organization and ensuring that the organization has the right number of qualified people in the right jobs at the right time.

human resource specialist Person specially trained in one or more areas of human resource management (e.g., labor relations specialist, wage and salary specialist).

Immigration Reform and Control Act 1986 act making it illegal for a person or other entity to hire, recruit, or refer for U.S. employment anyone known to be an unauthorized alien.

in-basket technique Method of classroom training in which the trainee is required to simulate the handling of a specific manager's mail and telephone calls and to react accordingly.

incentive pay plans Pay plans designed to relate pay directly to performance or productivity; often used in conjunction with a base wage/salary system.

incentive stock option (ISO) Form of qualified stock option plan in which the manager does not have to pay any tax until the stock is sold.

incentives Rewards offered in addition to the base wage or salary and usually directly related to performance.

incident method Form of case study in which students are initially given the general outline of a situation and receive additional information from the instructor only as they request it.

individual equity Addresses the rewarding of individual contributions; is very closely related to the pay-for-performance question.

individual retirement account (IRA) Individual pension plan for employees not covered by private pension plans.

industrial unions Unions having as members both skilled and unskilled workers in a particular industry or group of industries.

information Data that have been interpreted and that meet a need of one or more managers.

informational picketing Patrolling at or near an employer's facility by individuals carrying signs to publicize the fact that the union is requesting an election to become the bargaining agent for the employees of the organization.

injunction Court order to stop an action that could result in irreparable damage to property when the situation is such that no other adequate remedy is available to protect the interests of the injunction-seeking party.

input function Provides the capabilities needed to get human resource information into the HRIS.

interaction management *See* Behavior modeling

interest tests Tests designed to determine how a person's interests compare with the interests of successful people in a specific job.

internal equity Addresses what an employee is being paid for doing a job compared to what other employees in the same organization are being paid to do their jobs.

intrinsic rewards Rewards internal to the individual and normally derived from involvement in certain activities or tasks.

job Group of positions that are identical with respect to their major or significant tasks and responsibilities and sufficiently alike to justify their being covered by a single analysis. One or many persons may be employed in the same job.

job advertising Placement of help-wanted advertisements in daily newspapers, in trade and professional publications, or on radio and television.

job analysis Process of determining and reporting pertinent information relating to the nature of a specific job.

job bidding Requirement that employees bid for a job based on seniority, experience, or other specific qualifications. *See also* Job posting.

job classification method Job evaluation method that determines the relative worth of a job by comparing it to a predetermined scale of classes or grades of jobs.

job depth Freedom of jobholders to plan and organize their own work, work at their own pace, and move around and communicate.

job design Process of structuring work and designating the specific work activities of an individual or group of individuals to achieve certain organizational objectives.

job evaluation Systematic determination of the value of each job in relation to other jobs in the organization.

job knowledge tests Tests used to measure the job-related knowledge of an applicant.

job posting Method of making employees aware of job vacancies by posting a notice in central locations throughout an organization and giving a specified period to apply for the job.

job ranking method Job evaluation method that ranks jobs in order of their difficulty from simplest to most complex.

job rotation (cross training) Training that requires an individual to learn several different jobs in a work unit or department and perform each for a specified time period.

job satisfaction An employee's general attitude toward the job.

job scope Number and variety of tasks performed by the jobholder.

job specification Description of the qualifications that a person holding a job must possess to perform the job successfully.

job subfactor Detailed breakdown of a single compensable factor of a job.

just cause Requires that management initially bear the burden of proof of wrongdoing in discipline cases and that the severity of the punishment must coincide with the seriousness of the offense.

Keogh plan Retirement plan allowing self-employed persons to make tax-exempt annual contributions of up to $30,000 or 25 percent of net self-employment income, whichever is less.

Labor-Management Relations Act (Taft-Hartley Act) Legislation enacted in 1947 that placed the federal government in a watchdog position to ensure that union-management relations are conducted fairly by both parties.

Labor-Management Reporting and Disclosure Act (LMRDA) (Landrum-Griffin Act) Legislation enacted in 1959 regulating labor unions and requiring disclosure of certain union financial information to the government.

Landrum-Griffin Act of 1959 Labor-Management Reporting and Disclosure Act, regulating labor unions and requiring disclosure of union financial information to the government.

learners Individuals in an organization who have a high potential for advancement but who are currently performing below standard.

leniency Occurs in performance appraisals when a manager's ratings are grouped at the positive end instead of being spread throughout the performance scale.

lockout Refusal of an employer to let its employees work.

maintenance of membership Contract provision that does not require an employee to join the union but does require employees who do join to remain members for a stipulated time period.

management by objectives (MBO) Consists of establishing clear and precisely defined statements of objectives for the work to be done by an employee, establishing an action plan indicating how these objectives are to be achieved, allowing the employee to implement the action plan, measuring objective achievement, taking corrective action when necessary, and establishing new objectives for the future.

management development Process concerned with developing the experience, attitudes, and skills necessary to become or remain an effective manager.

management inventory Specialized, expanded form of skills inventory for an organization's current management team; in addition to basic types of information, it usually includes a brief assessment of past performance and potential for advancement.

management succession plan Chart or schedule that shows potential successors for each management position within an organization.

managerial estimates Judgmental method of forecasting that calls on managers to make estimates of future staffing needs.

Marshall v. *Barlow's, Inc.* 1978 Supreme Court decision that ruled that employers are not required to admit OSHA inspectors onto their premises without a search warrant; also ruled that probable cause needed to obtain the search warrant would be much less than that required in a criminal matter.

mediation Process whereby both parties invite a neutral third party (called a mediator) to help resolve contract impasses. The mediator, unlike an arbitrator, has no authority to impose a solution on the parties.

merit pay increase Reward based on performance but also perpetuated year after year.

microcomputer Very small computer, ranging in size from a "computer on a chip" to a typewriter-size unit.

micromotion Simplest unit of work; involves very elementary movements such as reaching, grasping, positioning, or releasing an object.

minicomputer Small (desk size) electronic, digital, stored-program, general-purpose computer.

motion study Involves determining the motions and movements necessary for performing a task or job and then designing the most efficient methods for putting those motions and movements together.

National Labor Relations Act (Wagner Act) Prolabor act of 1935 that gave workers the right to organize, obligated the management of organizations to bargain in good faith with unions, defined illegal management practices relating to unions, and created the National Labor Relations Board (NLRB) to administer the act.

National Labor Relations Board (NLRB) Five-member panel created by the National Labor Relations Act and appointed by the president of the United States with the advice and consent of the Senate and with the authority to administer the Wagner Act.

needs assessment Systematic analysis of the specific training management development activities required by an organization to achieve its objectives.

NLRB v. *Weingarten* Supreme Court decision in 1975 holding that an employee has the right to refuse to submit to a disciplinary interview without union representation.

nonqualified stock options Similar to qualified options, except that they are not subject to a less favorable tax rate and are not subject to the same restrictions.

Norris–La Guardia Act of 1932 Prolabor act that eliminated the use of yellow-dog contracts and severely restricted the use of injunctions.

occupation Grouping of jobs or job classes that involve similar skill, effort, and responsibility within a number of different organizations.

occupational parity Situation in which the proportion of minorities and women employed in various occupations within an organization is equal to their proportion in the organization's relevant labor market.

Occupational Safety and Health Act Federal law enacted in 1971 to ensure safe and healthful working conditions for every working person.

Office of Federal Contract Compliance Programs (OFCCP) Office within the U.S. Department of Labor that is responsible for ensuring equal employment opportunity by federal contractors and subcontractors.

Office of the General Counsel Separate and independent office created by the Taft-Hartley Act to investigate unfair labor practice charges and present those charges with merit to the NLRB.

Older Workers Benefit Protection Act Provides protection for employees over 40 years of age in regard to fringe benefits and gives employees time to consider an early retirement offer.

on-the-job training (OJT) Training showing the employee how to perform the job and allowing him or her to do it under the trainer's supervision.

operating manager Person who manages people directly involved with the production of an organization's products or services (e.g., a production manager in a manufacturing plant or a loan manager in a bank).

organizational development (OD) Organizationwide, planned effort managed from the top, with the goal of increasing organizational performance through planned interventions and training experiences.

organizational equity Addresses how profits are divided up within the organization.

organizational inducements Positive features and benefits offered by an organization to attract job applicants.

organizational morale An employee's feeling of being accepted by and belonging to a group of employees through common goals, confidence in the desirability of those goals, and the desire to progress toward the goals.

organizational objectives Statements of expected results that are designed to give the organization and its members direction and purpose.

organizational orientation General orientation that presents topics of relevance and interest to all employees.

organizational replacement chart Chart that shows both incumbents and potential replacements for given positions within an organization.

organizational reward system Organizational system concerned with the selection of the types of rewards to be used by the organization.

organizational rewards Rewards that result from employment with the organization; includes all types of rewards, both intrinsic and extrinsic.

organizational vitality index (OVI) Index that results from ratio, analysis; reflects the organization's human resource vitality as measured by the presence of promotable personnel and existing backups.

organizationwide incentives Incentives that reward all members of the organization, based on the performance of the entire organization.

orientation Introduction of new employees to the organization, work unit, and job.

orientation kit Packet of written information given to a new employee to supplement the verbal orientation program.

OSHA Form 101 (Supplementary Record of Occupational Injuries and Illnesses) Form that requires detailed information about each occupational injury or illness. Form 101 must be completed within six working days from the time the employer learns of an occupational injury or illness.

OSHA Form 200 (Log and Summary of Occupational Injuries and Illness) Form for recording all occupational injuries and illnesses. Each occurrence must be recorded on this form within six working days from the time the employer learns of the accident or illness.

outplacement Benefit provided by an employer to help an employee leave the organization and get a job someplace else.

outsourcing Subcontracting work to an outside company that specializes in that particular type of work.

panel interview See Board interview

parallel forms Method of showing a test's reliability; involves giving two separate but similar forms of the test at the same time.

pay Refers only to the actual dollars employees receive in exchange for their work.

pay grades Classes or grades of jobs that for pay purposes are grouped on the basis of their worth to an organization.

pay range Range of permissible pay, with a minimum and a maximum, that is assigned to a given pay grade.

performance appraisal Process of determining and communicating to an employee how he or she is performing on the job, and ideally, establishing a plan of improvement.

performance share plan (unit plan) Incentive plan that awards top executives a set number of performance units at the beginning of the performance period; actual value of the units is then determined by the company's performance over the performance period.

Performance-Vesting Options Stock options priced at market price but only exercisable if stock price reaches or exceeds price goal within defined period.

personality tests Tests that attempt to measure personality traits.

personnel requisition form Describes the reason for the need to hire a new person and the requirements of the job.

phantom stock plan Special type of stock option plan that protects the holder if the value of the stock being held decreases; does not require the option holder to put up any money.

Philadelphia Cordwainers **(shoemakers) case of 1806** Case in which the jury ruled that combinations of workers to raise their wages constituted a conspiracy in restraint of trade.

point method Job evaluation method in which a quantitative point scale is used to evaluate jobs on a factor-by-factor basis.

polygraph Machine that records fluctuations in a person's blood pressure, respiration, and perspiration on a moving roll of graph paper in response to questions asked of the person; commonly known as a *lie detector.*

position Collection of tasks and responsibilities constituting the total work assignment of a single employee. There are as many positions as there are employees in the organization.

predictive validity Validity that is established by identifying a criterion predictor such as a test, administering the test to all job applicants, hiring people without regard to their test scores, and at a later date correlating the test scores with the performance of these people on the job.

preferred provider organization (PPO) Formed by contracting with a group of doctors and hospitals to provide services at a discount or otherwise attractive price. Such providers are designated as "preferred" providers of care.

Pregnancy Discrimination Act Requires employers to treat pregnancy just like any other medical condition with regard to fringe benefits and leave policy.

Premium-Priced Options Stock options with an exercise price significantly above stock's current market price.

private pension plans Employee benefit that provides a source of income to people who have retired; funded either entirely by the organization or jointly by the organization and employee during employment.

proficiency tests Tests that measure how well a job applicant can do a sample of the work that is to be performed.

programmed instruction Method of classroom training in which material is presented in text form or on computer video displays; students are required to correctly answer questions about the subject presented, before progressing to more advanced material.

psychomotor tests Tests that measure a person's strength, dexterity, and coordination.

qualified stock options Stock options approved by the Internal Revenue Service for favorable tax treatment.

Railway Labor Act An act enacted in 1926 that set up the administrative machinery for handling labor relations within the railroad industry; was the first important piece of prolabor legislation.

ranking methods Methods of performance appraisal in which the performance of an individual is ranked relative to the performance of others.

ratio analysis Tool used in human resource planning to measure the organization's human resource vitality as indicated by the presence of promotable personnel and existing backups.

realistic job previews (RJP) Method of providing complete job information, both positive and negative, to the job applicant.

recency Tendency of a manager to evaluate employees on work performed most recently—one or two months prior to evaluation.

recognition bar Condition occurring when the NLRB prohibits an election for up to 12 months after an employer voluntarily recognizes a union.

recruitment Process of seeking and attracting a pool of people from which qualified candidates for job vacancies can be chosen.

Rehabilitation Act of 1973 Prohibits discrimination of handicapped individuals.

reengineering Fundamental rethinking and radical redesign of business processes to achieve dramatic improvements in cost, quality, service, and speed.

relevant labor market Generally refers to the geographical area in which a company recruits its employees.

reliability Refers to the reproducibility of results with a criterion predictor.

reports library Type of computer software program that stores the program and historical data necessary to generate reports that are periodically requested.

responsibilities Obligations to perform certain tasks and assume certain duties.

restricted stock plan Plan under which a company gives shares of stock to participating managers, subject to certain restrictions; major restriction of most plans is that shares are subject to forfeiture until "earned out" over a stipulated period of continued employment.

Retirement Equity Act Act passed in 1984 that liberalized eligibility requirements, vesting provisions, maternity/paternity leaves, and spouse survivor benefits of retirement plans.

reverse discrimination Condition under which there is alleged preferential treatment of one group (minority or women) over another group rather than equal opportunity.

rightsizing Continuous and proactive assessment of mission-critical work and its staffing requirements.

right-to-sue letter Statutory notice by the EEOC to the charging party if the EEOC does not decide to file a lawsuit on behalf of the charging party.

right-to-work laws Legislation enacted by individual states under the authority of Section 14(b) of the Taft-Hartley Act that can forbid various types of union security arrangements, including compulsory union membership.

Roth IRA Retirement plan that allows individuals to make nondeductible contributions and tax-free withdrawals with certain restrictions.

Scanlon plan Organizationwide incentive plan that provides employees with a bonus based on tangible savings in labor costs.

scenario analysis Using work-force environmental scanning data to develop alternative work-force scenarios.

secondary boycott Issue involving other employers (secondary employers) in the relationship between a union and an employer (the primary employer).

selection Process of choosing from those available the individuals who are most likely to perform successfully in a job.

seniority An employee's relative length of service with an employer.

severity rate Ratio that indicates the length of time injured employees are out of work.

sexual harassment Unwelcome sexual conduct that has the purpose or effect of unreasonably interfering with an individual's work performance or creating an intimidating, hostile, or offensive work environment.

skill-based pay systems Systems that compensate employees for the skills they bring to the job.

skills inventory Consolidated list of biographical and other information on all employees in the organization.

social security Federally administered insurance system designed to provide funds upon retirement or disability or both and to provide hospital and medical reimbursement to people who have reached retirement age.

solid citizens Individuals in an organization whose present performance is satisfactory but whose chance for future advancement is small.

split halves Method of showing a test's reliability; involves dividing the test into halves to determine whether performance is similar in both sections.

stars Individuals in an organization who are presently doing outstanding work and have a high potential for continued advancement.

stock appreciation rights (SARs) Type of nonqualified stock option in which an executive has the right to relinquish a stock option and receive from the company an amount equal to the appreciation in the stock price from the date the option was granted. Under an SAR, the option holder does not have to put up any money, as would be required in a normal stock option plan.

stock-for-stock swap Allows options to be exercised with shares of previously purchased company stock in lieu of cash; postpones the taxation of any gain on stock already owned.

stress Mental and physical condition that results from a perceived threat of danger (physical or emotional) and the pressure to remove it.

stress interview Interview method that puts the applicant under pressure, to determine whether he or she is highly emotional.

strike Collective refusal of employees to work.

structured interview Interview conducted using a predetermined outline.

subfactor Detailed breakdown of a single compensable factor of a job.

succession planning Technique that identifies specific people to fill future openings in key positions throughout the organization.

suggestion systems Systems that usually offer cash incentives for employee suggestions that result in either increased profits or reduced costs.

systemic discrimination Large differences in either occupational or employment parity.

Taft-Hartley Act of 1947 Labor-Management Relations Act, which placed the federal government in a watchdog position to ensure that union-management relations are conducted fairly by both parties.

task Consisting of one or more elements, one of the distinct activities that constitute logical and necessary steps in the performance of work by an employee. A task is performed whenever human effort, physical or mental, is exerted for a specific purpose.

temporary help People working for employment agencies who are subcontracted out to businesses at an hourly rate, for a period of time specified by the businesses.

test-retest One method of showing a test's reliability; involves testing a group and giving the same group the same test at a later time.

time study Analysis of a job or task to determine the elements of work required to perform it, the order in which these elements occur, and the times required to perform them effectively.

Title VII of the Civil Rights Act of 1964 Keystone federal legislation that covers disparate treatment and disparate impact discrimination; created the Equal Employment Opportunity Commission.

Toxic Substance Control Act Federal law passed in 1976 requiring the pretesting for safety of new chemicals marketed.

training Learning process that involves the acquisition of skills, concepts, rules, or attitudes to increase employee performance.

turnaround documents Simple reports that show the current data values of an HRIS and provide a place to indicate any changes.

12-month rule Provides that no election can be held in any bargaining unit within which a valid election has been held within the preceding 12-month period.

understudy assignments Method of on-the-job training in which one individual, designated as the heir to a job, learns the job from the present jobholder.

underutilization Practice of having fewer minorities or women in a particular job category than their corresponding numbers in the relevant labor market.

unemployment compensation Form of insurance designed to provide funds to employees who have lost their jobs and are seeking other jobs.

union shop Provision in a contract that requires all employees in a bargaining unit to join the union and retain membership as a condition of employment; most right-to-work laws outlaw the union shop.

unstructured interview Interview conducted without a predetermined checklist of questions.

user-friendly computer Computer that requires very little technical knowledge to use.

utilization evaluation Part of the affirmative action plan that analyzes minority group representation in all job categories, past and present hiring practices, and upgrades, promotions, and transfers.

Vaca* v. *Sipes Supreme Court decision in 1967 that held that a union is not obligated to take all grievances to arbitration but has the authority to decide whether or not the grievance has merit. If such a decision is made fairly and nonarbitrarily, the union has not breached its duty of fair representation.

validity Refers to how accurately a predictor actually predicts the criteria of job success.

vesting Right of employees to receive the money paid into a pension or retirement fund on their behalf by their employer if they leave the organization prior to retirement.

Vietnam-Era Veterans Readjustment Assistance Act Prohibits federal government contractors, and subcontractors with federal government contracts of $10,000 or more from discriminating in hiring and promoting Vietnam and disabled veterans.

Vocational Rehabilitation Act Legislation enacted in 1973 that prohibits discrimination against otherwise qualified handicapped individuals solely on the basis of their disability; applies only in certain situations involving federal contracts, recipients of federal assistance, or federal agencies.

wage and salary curves Graphical depiction of the relationship between the relative worth of jobs and their wage rates.

wage and salary survey Survey of selected organizations within a geographical area or industry designed to provide a comparison of reliable information on policies, practices, and methods of payment.

Wagner Act of 1935 National Labor Relations Act; prolabor act that gave workers the right to organize, obligated the management of organizations to bargain in good faith with unions, defined illegal management practices relating to unions, and created the National Labor Relations Board (NLRB) to administer the act.

weighted application form Assigns different weights or values to different questions on an application form.

wellness programs Company-implemented programs designed to prevent illness and enhance employee wellness.

work sampling Observation method based on taking statistical samples of job actions throughout the workday to determine the requirements and demands of the job.

work standards approach Method of performance appraisal that involves setting a standard or expected level of output and then comparing each employee's level to the standard.

workers' compensation Form of insurance that protects employees from loss of income and extra expenses associated with job-related injuries or illness.

yellow-dog contract Term coined by unions to describe an agreement between a worker and employer stipulating that, as a condition of employment, the worker would not join a labor union. Yellow-dog contracts were made illegal by the Norris–La Guardia Act of 1932.

Name Index

Subject Index